Footprint

Rajasthan & Gujarat Handbook

The travel guide

Robert & Roma Bradnock
Assisted by Anil Mulchandani

The King is coming,
Beat the drums and thali!
The Bhils are dancing.
The Bhands are dancing, too!

Hajari Bandh, a wandering jester from Chittaurgarh
(J and U Emigh – 'A Joker in the deck' from 'The
idea of Rajasthan')

Rajasthan & Gujarat Handbook
First edition
© Footprint Handbooks Ltd 2001

Published by Footprint Handbooks
6 Riverside Court
Lower Bristol Road
Bath BA2 3DZ. England
T +44 (0)1225 469141
F +44 (0)1225 469461
Email discover@footprintbooks.com
Web www.footprintbooks.com

ISBN 1 900949 92 X
CIP DATA: A catalogue record for this
book is available from the British Library

Distributed in the USA by
Publishers Group West

Credits

Series editors
Patrick Dawson and Rachel Fielding

Editorial
Editor: Stephanie Lambe
Maps: Sarah Sorensen

Production
Typesetting: Richard Ponsford and
Leona Bailey
Maps: Robert Lunn and Claire Benison
Colour maps: Kevin Feeney

Cover: Camilla Ford

Design
Mytton Williams

Photography
Front cover: gettyone Stone
Back cover: Impact Photo Library
Inside colour section: Bob Ascott, Eye
Ubiquitous, Ffotograff, gettyone Stone,
Images Colour Library, Impact Photo
Library, James Davis Travel Photography,
La Belle Aurore, Pictures Colour Library,
Robert Harding Picture Library.

Print
Manufactured in Italy by LEGOPRINT

Rajasthan & Gujarat

PUNJAB

PAKISTAN

HARYANA

UTTAR PRADESH

◆ *Gajner*

Bikaner ○

SHEKHAWATI DISTRICT

DELHI □

◆ *Sariska*

Bharatpur ○   ○ Agra

Jaisalmer ○

RAJASTHAN

Jaipur ○

Jodhpur ○

Pushkar ○   ○ Ajmer   *Ranthambhore* ◆

Kumbhalgarh ○

Mount Abu ○

Chittaurgarh ○

○ Bundi

○ Kota

Udaipur ○

Bhuj ○

Dasada ○

GUJARAT

● **Gandhinagar**

Ahmadabad ○

MADHYA PRADESH

Dwarka ○   Jamnagar ○

○ Vadodora

Porbandar ○

Junagadh ○   Bhavnagar ○

Palitana ○

Surat ○

Diu ○

Daman ○

MAHARASHTRA

N

0 km   100

0 miles   100

The Government of India state that "the external boundaries of India are neither correct nor authenticated"

Arabian Sea

MUMBAI □

JAMMU & KASHMIR

PAKISTAN   HIMACHAL PRADESH

PUNJAB   TIBET (CHINA)

DELHI □   HARYANA   NEPAL

RAJASTHAN   UTTAR PRADESH   ASSAM

BIHAR

GUJARAT   MADHYA PRADESH   WEST BENGAL

ORISSA   KOLKATA □

MAHARASHTRA   Bay of Bengal

MUMBAI □   ANDHRA PRADESH

GOA

Arabian Sea   KARNATAKA

CHENNAI □

KERALA   TAMIL NADU

SRI LANKA

Indian Ocean

Contents

Left: Words of the wise.

4

Right: Ripples in the Thar desert.

A foot in the door

Highlights

More than 700 years ago Marco Polo travelled the desert route through Rajasthan with caravans carrying the finest jewellery and precious stones in the world – gold, lapis lazuli and rubies. Camel caravans still bring wealth to their owners – and a dream of the magical, mysterious east. The Rajput princes have left their indelible mark on much of Rajasthan and Gujarat, visible in the palaces and forts scattered through cities, towns and villages. You can trace the evolution of the states' colourful history, sampling at first hand these buildings through which much of that history took shape. Alongside this is a rich cultural imprint. Jain and Hindu temples and Muslim mosques and tombs are scattered through a landscape where tribal traditions are still strong. All this is set in territory that ranges from the rugged, arid hills of the Aravallis to the tracts of desert or salt pans of western Rajasthan and Gujarat and the rich fertile lowlands of the southeast which harbour and protect majestic wildlife.

A living history Jaipur, a unique experiment in town planning, Jodhpur with its rugged Meherangarh Fort, or Udaipur, its shimmering Lake Palace overlooked by the massive walls of the Shiv Niwas – all owe their origins to the grandiose building plans of Rajput clans. The cities were also centres of stunning craftsmanship and high taste. But as ridgetop forts like Bundi, Chittaurgarh or Kumbhalgarh demonstrate, the Rajputs were also concerned with sheer power. In times of peace, summer palaces offered respite from the heat by seeking the cooling breezes drifting across artificially constructed lakes and provided opportunities for indulging in royal leisurely pursuits. Such extravagant building was not restricted to Rajasthan, for Gujarat too has its share of remarkable palaces such as those at Vadodara, Bhavnagar or Gondal. The Muslims, and ultimately the British, also left their architectural imprint, evident in some of the more exotically eclectic buildings of the later Maharajas. Look no further than the art deco of the Umaid Bhavan Palace in Jodhpur for proof.

From desert to savanna Riding on camelback west of Jaisalmer, India's Thar desert disappears into a series of horizonless mirages, an eerie and stark environment. Rajasthan's first British chronicler, James Tod, was constantly reminded that the regional names *Marusthali* and *Marwar* meant 'land of death'. From the salt pans of Gujarat to the sand deserts of Bikaner, this westernmost region of India bordering Pakistan has never offered much hope to agriculturalists but was rich in opportunities for traders. It is perhaps the emptiest landscape in the whole of India. But travel east and south and you get a quite different picture. The jagged ridges of the Aravalli hills rise over 1500 m, and to their east the much wetter terrain, still forested in places, has rich agricultural land in the lower valleys between the open dusty savanna. The yellowish brown landscape turns miraculously green once a year as the monsoon showers sweep across the country.

Tiger, tiger... Nothing can quite prepare you for the first glimpse of a tiger in the wild. Power and grace breathe through every silent footstep, and the forests of Ranthambhore offer perhaps one of the best sighting opportunities in the world. Project Tiger has given a measure of protection from hunting and loss of habitat, and today in the wildlife parks and sanctuaries of Rajasthan and Gujarat you can see not just tigers but deer, antelope, wild boar, the huge but relatively docile mugger crocodile or the even bigger fish eating gharial. Birds also abound. Many species of migratory birds fly in every winter. Wonderful and rare species such as the Siberian crane can be seen alongside the flash of a kingfisher, the stunning blue and green of the peacock, or the flocks of rose-ringed parakeets, while kites and vultures circle over the parched scrub and open forest in the constant search for prey or carrion.

Left: The city ghats on Udaipur's Lake Pichola offer a quiet spot for a bathe.
Below: Sari-clad women walk past Jaipur's Hawa Mahal - Palace of the Winds - where once queens and princesses would gaze down unseen from the balconied windows above.
Bottom left: Meherangarh Fort towers above the blue washed houses of Jodhpur.
Bottom right: Detail on one of Shatrunjaya's 800 Jain temples, Palitana.
Next page: How's my make up?

Right: Lighting up in the dawn, the 100-year old cenotaph Jaswant Tada.
Below: Typical murals decorate the interior walls of a haveli in Jaisalmer.

Above: Jaisalmer's Jain temples rise above the city's central fort area.
Right: The vividly decorated bedroom of a former Maharajah of Jodhpur in Meherangarh Fort.
Next page: This business is no laughing matter.

Power, wealth and sanctity

Tucked away in the folds of the arid hills and perched precariously on sharp ridges, the forts and palaces of Rajasthan seem to come straight out of another world, a world of conflict and struggle, but also of opulence and refined taste, of medieval chivalry and archaic codes of honour. Today many of the most exclusive forts and palaces have opened their doors to visitors, making it possible to enjoy a unique lifestyle. The reputation of the Lake Palace in Udaipur is world-wide. But how many have heard of such wonderfully romantic hotel palaces as Deogarh, Bambora's Karni Fort, Neemrana and Kuchaman? In Gujarat too, you have wonderful 'heritage' destinations to explore as at Balaram, Gondal, Bhavnagar and Poshina. As the princes have lost traditional power and income many have opened their former homes as hotels. They can be not just spectacularly beautiful but astonishing value.

The mirage of power

The merchant communities of the western desert margins turned their profits into some of the most beautifully decorated domestic architecture in India, the *havelis*. Often built in sandstone, these courtyard houses, scattered through the towns of Gujarat and Rajasthan, gave the merchants an opportunity for ostentatious displays of wealth and taste. In Shekhawati, the painted havelis form an open-air art gallery. Wander through the narrow streets of Jaisalmer or Bikaner and you will come across these magnificent homes, the sandstone carved into the most intricate of patterns. In the *pols*, or community districts, of Ahmadabad, such houses were built of wood, but were equally beautifully decorated, with wooden jali screens. The trade which sustained these houses may have gone, but the decorative treasures remain. Equally impressive are Gujarat's step wells, or *baolis*, some dating from as much as one thousand years ago. The seven storeyed Rani-ki-Vav stepwell of Patan, or the beautifully carved Adalaj Vav near Ahmadabad for example, are believed to date from the 11th century.

A wealth of taste

All India's religious communities have established at least a toe-hold in Rajasthan and Gujarat. Hinduism, the religion of most of the princely rulers and of the majority of their subjects, has left a profound imprint on the culture of the contemporary states. However, minority religions have also left their imprint. The Muslims not only conquered territory from the 13th century onwards, they also created some of the most beautiful monuments in India, from the tombs of Agra, Fatehpur Sikri, Ajmer and Ahmadabad to the great mosques of Gujarat. Although the Jains may be one of the smallest of India's minority communities, they too have made a vital mark. Their banking and business skills have taken them far afield, but their wealth has often gone into temple building – with astonishing results. Using marble as a favoured medium, their masons have carved some of the most intricately ornate sculpture in lavish profusion. The typically plain exterior of the 1000-year old Adinatha temple in Mount Abu or the towering pinnacles of the glistening white Ranakpur temple give little hint of their wonderfully carved interiors. Hardly a surface is left unadorned, yet the overall effect is stunningly clean and pure. Many of the Jain temples are also centres of pilgrimage, none more so than the Palitana complex of temples on Shatrunjaya Hill in Gujarat, when at key festivals like the Mahavir Jayanti streams of pilgrims climb the 3500 or so steps to the more than 800 temples that spread over the summit. The silence on the hilltop is only broken by the tinkling of bells and the pligrims' chanting.

A religious melting pot

Right: Tribal women gather at spring fair near Chotta Udepur.
Below: Dust at dusk – the great autumn camel fair at Pushkar.

Above: Bhils pipe in the Spring festival near Chotta Udepur.
Right: Auspicious gateway and street stalls greet guests to a festive gathering in Jaipur.
Next page: On the look out at Ranthambhore...

A riot of colour

Rajasthan and Gujarat are never more colourful than during the great festivals. **Festivals** The spring festival, Holi, is known as the festival of colours and although in some places it all gets a bit out of hand most continue to combine worship, trade and a lot of fun. Rajasthan's world famous Pushkar camel fair is equalled in scale by the donkey and camel fair at Vautha in Gujarat, both of them held in November. In mid-January Ahmadabad and other Gujarati towns drop everything to participate in the kite festival, celebrating Makar Sankranti, when the sun starts its journey back to the north. The skies fill with paper kites, fighting to cut each other down with their glass-encrusted strings. Some of the tribal festivals have a much more practical purpose. At Tarnetar, tribal women have the chance in August and September each year to choose a husband by walking round a field viewing eligible young men who wait on view under richly embroidered umbrellas. When a young woman stops and talks to one of the men it is the sign for marriage negotiations to begin in earnest.

Rajasthan once belonged almost exclusively to the tribal communities – Bhils, Minas, **Tribals** Garasias are the best known among many tribal groups – but gradually the Rajput clans colonized the land and incorporated the tribals into their social and economic system. Yet tribal identities remain important. Once hunters and gatherers, the Bhils for example put their skills to good use in military tactics, much appreciated by Rajput princes who gave them key roles in their defences. This is illustrated by the ceremonies in which the Maharana of Udaipur, the acknowledged head of all Rajpur clans, is crowned by the anointment of his forehead with the blood of a Bhil chieftain, symbolising the indissoluble bond between them. Today the Bhils are mainly farmers but they have retained their own religious rites, gods and festivals. If you are in southeastern Rajasthan in January or February you can see thousands of Bhils congregate for the Baneshwar fair at the confluence of the Mahi and Som rivers. Other tribals are renowned for their knowledge and care of wildlife. The Bishnois venerate the Black Buck, once threatened by hunting to extinction, and their intimate knowledge of the environment has been an inspiration to environmentalists across India.

Rajasthan and Gujarat's colourful reputation rests in part on the stunning clothing **Textiles** worn by men and women across the states. Turbans in red, blue or gold, brilliantly dyed saris, heavy tribal jewellery – all testify to the wealth of traditional weaving and dyeing. These skills now play a vital part in the rural economy. In some villages like Khaitoon near Kota hundreds of villagers produce fiine silk and cotton saris with embroidered *zari* borders. Hand-crafted block printing makes use of carefully cut hand-held wood blocks to print in several colours, traditionally using a range of vegetable dyes, and the intricacies of *ikat* weaving or the tie and dye *bandhani* represent the special skills of particular regions. Kachchh is famous for its embroidery and for its mirror work. Hundreds of villagers are hoping that a quick return to full production after January's devastating earthquake will enable them to restore their earnings and a degree of normality. The Calico Museum in Ahmadabad, if you are in that area, should not be missed. It has one of the most remarkable collections of textiles in the world.

Essentials

2

Essentials

Planning your trip

Where to go

Rajasthan and Gujarat offer an almost daunting range of possibilities for travellers. You could travel for weeks without seeing it all. Here we suggest some possible tours ranging from two to three week trips, to options for a much longer stay by combining some of the tours that we offer. Travel networks of road, rail and air are so interconnected that you can combine parts of the routes given below in a range of different ways. Travel agencies are listed through the book, who can make the necessary arrangements for a relatively small fee, saving you time and bother, but remember that air tickets can be difficult to get at short notice for some trips. Allow a little more time if you are planning to travel entirely by road and rail. However, if you use overnight trains for longer journeys you can cover almost as much ground in the same time as flying. Figures in brackets are number of nights we suggest you spend.

The golden triangle (14 days)

Most tourists take the route entering Rajasthan from the golden triangle of **Delhi** (3), **Agra** (2) and **Jaipur** (4), the last being the capital of Rajasthan. Day visits to Amber and Samode nearby should not be missed. The Keoladeo Ghana National Park of **Bharatpur** (2) has Rajasthan's finest bird sanctuary and historic attractions in Bharatpur town and Deeg. **Ranthambore** and **Sariska** national parks (3 at either) are off the Jaipur-Agra road and offer the opportunity for good game viewing as well as nearby architectural complexes like the forts of Ranthambore and Alwar respectively.

The desert triangle (16 days)

It is possible to add on the desert triangle of **Bikaner** (2)-**Jaisalmer** (3)-**Jodhpur** (3) from **Delhi** (3) and **Jaipur** (2) via the towns of **Shekhawati** (3), which are known for their painted *havelis* and converted forts and palaces. The desert destinations have wonderful examples of sandstone architecture besides providing a base to visit the dunes, wildlife sanctuaries and picturesque villages of the Thar desert.

The Mewar triangle (16 days)

The Mewar circuit can be accessed from **Delhi** (3) and **Jaipur** (2), calling on the way at **Ajmer** (1) and **Pushkar** (1), centres of pilgrimage for Muslims and Hindus respectively, or from **Jodhpur** (2), the largest city of the desert triangle. Mewar has the great forts of **Chittaurgarh** (1) and **Kumbhalgarh** (2), with the fine Jain temples of Ranakpur and Mount Abu, as well as the princely city of **Udaipur** (3). The lakes of Udaipur and the hill station of **Mount Abu** (3) offer a respite from the warm plains of Rajasthan.

Hadoti (add 10 days)

Southeastern Rajasthan has recently come into the limelight as a tourist zone. This region includes the medieval fort and monuments of **Bundi** (2), the historic city of **Kota** (2) on the banks of the river Chambal, the old forts and temples of Jhalawar district and the prehistoric and historic sites of **Baran** district (1). This circuit can be accessed by road or rail from Jaipur, visiting **Ranthambore National Park** (3) on the way, or by road from **Chittaurgarh** (2) via the historic temple complexes of Menal, Bijolia and Bardoli.

North Gujarat (add 5 days)

North Gujarat has many medieval monuments including the Jain temples of Kumbhariya and Taranga, the stepwell of Patan, the Sun temple of Modhera, the monumental *torana* gateways of Vadnagar and the historic temples of Shamlaji and Vijaynagar. These sites fall in the triangle of **Ahmadabad-Mount Abu-Udaipur**, and are often visited by those continuing from Rajasthan into Gujarat or catching a train or flight from Ahmadabad after visiting Mount Abu and Udaipur. There are heritage hotels in this region. Ahmadabad has a fascinating array of historic monuments and fine museums.

Essentials

Essentials

Saurashtra
(add 12 days)
The Kathiawad Peninsula has splendid tourist destinations. While there are flights from Mumbai to Diu and several towns in Saurashtra, the popular route is by road from Ahmadabad to **Bhavnagar** (2). This takes in the archaeological ruins of Lothal, and the Velavadhar National Park. You can then visit **Palitana**'s (2) sacred Shatrunjaya summit crowned by more than 800 Jain temples. West of Bhavnagar is **Junagadh** (2), with its variety of monuments from Mauryan to the colonial period, and neighbouring Mount Girnar, another temple-covered summit. South from Junagadh is the **Gir Lion National Park** (2), the shore temple of **Somnath** and the Union Territory of **Diu** (3) with its Portuguese past and quiet beaches. It is possible to travel from Junagadh to Mahatma Gandhi's birthplace, **Porbandar** (1), and follow the coast to the shore temple of Dwarka. Heritage hotels of Bhavnagar and Gondal offer a suitable base to tour the region.

Kachchh
(add 6 days)
When the area recovers from the damage of the January 2001 earthquake Kachchh will again have a wide range of sightseeing attractions. You can fly to Bhuj from Mumbai or drive from Ahmadabad through the villages along the Little Rann sanctuary, like **Dasada** (1), a princely town in Surendranagar district (1), or travel north from Saurashtra. With **Bhuj** (4) as the base it is possible to visit interesting **craft villages**, the beaches of Mandvi, the shore temples of Narayan Sarovar-Koteshwar and the Jain temples of Bhadreshwar.

South Gujarat
(add 11 days)
The southern Gujarat circuit begins at **Vadodara** (3), a couple of hours by road or rail from Ahmadabad, which is a city full of royal palaces. Around Vadodara are the great forts of Champaner-Pawagadh and Dabhoi, and the holy Narmada ghats of Chandod. South from Vadodara **Surat** (2) is known for its European architecture. With your own transport it is possible to escape to the hill station of **Saputara** (3) in the Dangs district. The coast road south from Surat makes it possible to visit the former Portuguese colony of **Daman** and enjoy a beach break (3).

Special interest travel

Wildlife
You can expect to see a good selection of desert wildlife even on a short tour of the parks, but the destinations also allow you to see some of the rich architectural heritage and interesting tribal villages of the two states. In three to four weeks you can cover a representative cross-section of both. Most national parks charge foreigners Rs 100 or more for entry. Camera fees, vehicle charges and guides (usually compulsory), can add greatly to the cost. At Ranthambore and Gir, you can expect to pay Rs 350 per head for each trip into the park in an open bus (Canter) but a jeep shared between two can cost as much as Rs 1,100.

Rajasthan route From **Delhi** (3), this begins with the triangle of **Bharatpur** (2), **Sariska** or **Ranthambore** (3), ending at **Jaipur** (2) (10 days). You can extend this from Jaipur to the desert triangle of **Bikaner** (2), **Gajner** (2) and **Jaisalmer** (3) which have desert national parks. Continue to **Jodhpur** (2) and **Sambhar** Salt Lake (2) which is one of the important wetland ecosystems in India (21 days).

Gujarat route To see lions, desert wild ass, blackbuck in addition to a large number of unusual birds you will need to travel to Gujarat. From **Delhi** (3), the route takes you on a circuit from **Ahmadabad** (4) to visit bird sanctuaries like Thol and Nalsarovar. Travel to **Velavadhar** National Park, on the way to **Bhavnagar** (3) which is close to the hill-top Jain temple complex in Palitana. From there go to **Gir Lion National Park** (2), and then north to **Dasada** (2) near the border of the Little Rann of Kachchh (13 days).

Gujarat also has India's first marine national park, offshore from the 200 km **Jamnagar** coastline, and Khijadiya Bird Sanctuary near Jamnagar city, but they can be hard to access (and permits for the marine park are difficult to get). Serious birders should find **Porbandar** and **Kachchh** district rewarding. There are many sanctuaries in the eastern hills of Gujarat from the Aravallis in the north to the Sahiyadris around Saputara but animal sightings are few and far between.

Those interested in visiting holy places for their architecture and atmosphere, could **Religious sites** begin at **Delhi** (3) and **Jaipur** (2) and visit **Ajmer** (2) with its Muslim mosques and tombs, and neighbouring **Pushkar** (2), one of the holiest Hindu pilgrimage spots. From there travel to **Jodhpur** (2) and visit the Jain temples of Osian. Then on to **Ranakpur** (1) to see exquisite Jain temples. **Udaipur** (3) is the ideal staging post for **Nathdwara's Shrinathji Temple**, one of the richest Hindu temples in India known for its devotional pichchwai paintings. Travel south from Udaipur into north Gujarat, which has splendid 11th-12th century temples at Modhera, Patan, Taranga *et cetera*, and continue to **Ahmadabad** (3) with its many mosques and temples. Saurashtra has sacred mountain summits like **Palitana** near Bhavnagar (2), and **Girnar** near Junagadh (3), with shore temples at Somnath and Dwarka. You can include **Diu** (3) to see interesting Portuguese period churches.

When to go

Late-October to early March is the most pleasant period to visit Rajasthan and Gujarat, *See also page 425* especially the desert districts of Jaisalmer, Jodhpur, Bikaner and Kachchh. The summer months of April to June get extremely hot while the southwest monsoon (July to September), in addition to being very humid, brings other hazards. Road surfaces are often damaged by heavy rain, most national parks are closed and some remote places become inaccessible.

Tours and tour operators

You may choose to try an inclusive package holiday or let a specialist operator quote for a tailor-made tour. Out of season these can be worth exploring. The lowest prices quoted in early 2001 from the UK vary from about US$550 for a week (flights, hotel and breakfast) in the low season, to over US$3,000 for three weeks during the peak season. Most will chalk out individual itineraries and cover the major sights with small groups.

Essentials

Ace, T01223-835055, ace@studytours.org Cultural study tours, expert led; **Adventures Abroad**, T0114-2473400 (USA & Canada, T800 665 3998, Australia T800 890 790), info@adventures-abroad.org Outward bound; **Asian Journeys**, T01604-234401, F234866, www.asianjourneys.com Fairs, festivals, culture, religion; **Andrew Brock** (Coromandel), T01572-821330, abrock@aol.com Special interest (crafts, textiles, botany etc); **Banyan Tours**, T01672-564090, www.india-traveldirect.com Tailored tours, local contact. **Cox & Kings** (Taj Group), T020-78735001, F6306038. Palaces, forts, tourist high spots; **Discovery Initiatives**, T020-79786341, www.discoveryinitiatives.com Wildlife safaris; **Dragoman**, T01728-86113, www.dragoman.co.uk Overland, adventure, camping; **Exodus Travels**, T020-87723822, sales@exodustravels.co.uk **Gateway to India**,

T0870-4423204, F4423205, www.gateway-to-india.com Tailor-made, off-the-beaten-track, local reps; *Greaves Tours*, T020-74879111, F74860722, sbriggs@greavesuk.com Railways, cities, heritage; *Indian Magic*, T020-84274848, sales@indiamagic.co.uk Homestays, small-scale, pulse of India; *Indo Asian Tours*, T0091-11-4691733, F4620533 (Delhi), www.indoasia-tours.com Professional tour operators. *Paradise Holidays*, T0091-11-6145116, F6145112 (Delhi), www. paradiseholidays.com Wide range of tours, experienced. *Pettitts*, T01892-515966, F521500, pettitts@centrenet. co.uk Unusual locations, activities, wildlife; *Royal Expeditions*, T0091-11-6238545, F6475954 (Delhi), www.royalexpeditions.com Tailor made tours, walking, wildlife, culture. *Spirit of India*, USA T888-3676147, inquire@spirit-of-india.com Focused, local experts; *Trans Indus*, T020-85662729, F8405327, www.transindus.co.uk Activities, wildlife. *Western & Oriental*, T020-73136611, F73136601, enquiries@westernoriental. com Upmarket, unique heritage hotels.

Essentials

Finding out more

There are Government of India Tourist offices in Delhi and the state capitals, as well as state tourist offices in the major cities of Rajasthan and Gujarat. They produce their own tourist literature, supply lists of hotels (and of paying guest accommodation in some cities of Rajasthan). The quality of material is improving though maps handed out are often inadequate. The Tourism Development Corporations run modest hotels and mid-way motels with restaurants which are adequate (though rarely efficiently run). They also offer tours of the city, neighbouring sights and overnight and regional packages and have a list of approved guides. The officers can put you in touch with car rental firms but their advice may not always be unbiased.

Don't take advice from unofficial 'Tourist Offices' at airports or railway stations. See also page for a list of useful websites

Language

Hindi, spoken as a mother tongue by over 400 million people, is India's official language. The use of English is also enshrined in the Constitution for a wide range of official purposes, notably communication between Hindi and non-Hindi speaking states. Most of the regional languages have their own scripts. In all there are 15 major and several hundred minor languages and dialects.

Some languages are listed on page 408

Disabled travellers

India is not geared up specially for making provisions for the physically handicapped or wheelchair bound traveller. Access to buildings, toilets (sometimes 'squat' type), pavements, kerbs and public transport can prove frustrating, but it is easy to find people to

Essentials

India tourist offices overseas

Australia *Level 1, 2 Picadilly, 210 Pitt St, Sydney, NSW 2000, T612-292644855, F92644860.*

Canada *60 Bloor St, West Suite No 1003, Toronto, Ontario, T416-9623787, F9626279.*

France *11-13 Bis Boulevard Hausmann, F75009, Paris T45233045, F45233345.*

Germany *Baserler St 48, 60329, Frankfurt AM-Main 1, T069-2429490, F24294977.*

Italy *Via Albricci 9, Milan 20122, T8053506, F72021681.*

Japan *Pearl Building, 9-18 Chome Ginza, Chuo Ku, Tokyo 104, T33-5715062, F5715235.*

The Netherlands *Rokin 9-15, 1012 Amsterdam, T020-6208791, F6383059.*

Singapore *20 Kramat Lane, 01-01A United House, Singapore 0922. T2353800, F2358677.*

Sweden *Sveavagen 9-11 1st Flr, S-III 57 Stockholm 11157, T468-101187, F210186.*

Switzerland *1-3 rue de Chantepoulet, 1201 Geneva, T41-227321813, F7315660.*

Thailand *3rd Flr, KFC Bldg, 62/5 Thaniya Rd, Bangkok 10500, T662-2352585, F2368411.*

UK *7 Cork St, London W1X 2AB, T020-74373677, F74941048.*

USA *3550 Wilshire Blvd, Room 204, Los Angeles, California 90010. T213-3808855, F3806111; Suite 1808, 1270 Avenue of Americas, New York, NY 10020, T212-5864901, F5823274.*

give a hand with lifting and carrying. Provided there is an able-bodied companion to scout around and arrange help, and so long as you are prepared to pay for at least mid-price hotels or guest houses, private car-hire and taxis, India should be perfectly rewarding, even if in a somewhat limited way.

Some travel companies specialize in exciting holidays, tailor-made for individuals depending on their level of disability. For those with access to the internet, a Global Access – Disabled Travel Network Site is www.geocities. com/Paris/1502 It is dedicated to providing travel information for 'disabled adventurers' and includes a number of reviews and tips from members of the public. You might also want to read *Nothing Ventured*, edited by Alison Walsh (Harper Collins), which gives personal accounts of worldwide journeys by disabled travellers, plus advice and listings.

Gay and lesbian travellers

Indian law forbids homosexual acts for men (but not women) and carries a maximum sentence of life imprisonment. Although it is common to see young males holding hands in public, it doesn't necessarily indicate a gay relationship and is usually an expression of friendship. Overt displays of affection between homosexuals and hetrosexuals give offence and should be avoided.

Student travellers

Full time students qualify for an ISIC (International Student Identity Card) which is issued by student travel and specialist agencies (eg *Usit*, *Campus*, *STA*) at home. A card allows certain travel benefits (eg reduced prices) and acts as proof of student status within India which may allow ticket concessions into a few sites. For details contact *STIC* in *Imperial Hotel*, Janpath, New Delhi, T3327582. Those intending to study in India may get a one year student visa (see below).

Travelling with children

Children of all ages are widely welcomed, being greeted with a warmth in their own right which is often then extended to those accompanying them. However, care should be taken when travelling to remote areas where health services are primitive since children can become more rapidly ill than adults. It is best to visit India in the cooler months since you need to protect children from the sun, heat, dehydration and mosquito bites. Cool showers or baths help and of course avoiding being out during the hottest part of the day. Diarrhoea and vomiting are the most common problems, so take the usual precautions, but more intensively. Breastfeeding is best and most convenient for babies. In the big cities you can get safe baby foods and formula milk. It doesn't harm a baby to eat an unvaried and limited diet of familiar food carried in packets for a few weeks if the local dishes are not acceptable, but it may be an idea to give vitamin and mineral supplements. Wet wipes, always useful, are sometimes difficult to find in India as are disposable nappies. The biggest hotels provide babysitting.

See also health, page 65

Essentials

Volunteering

It is best to arrange voluntary work well in advance with organisations in India (addresses are given in some towns); alternatively, contact an organisation abroad. In the UK: *International Voluntary Service*, 7 Upper Bow, Edinburgh EH1 2JN, T0131-2266722, F2266723, www.ivsgbn.demon.co.uk or *VSO*, 317 Putney Bridge Rd, London SW15 2PN. T0208-7807200, F7807300, www.vso.org.uk Alternatively, students may spend part of their 'year off' helping in a school through 'GAP', teach English or help with a conservation project through 'i to i' International Projects, 1 Cottage Rd, Headingly, Leeds, LS6 4DD, T0870-332332, www.i-to-i.com In the USA: *Council for International Programs*, 1101 Wilson Blvd Ste 1708, Arlington, VA 22209.

Women travellers

Although it is relatively safe for women to travel around India most people find it an advantage to travel with a companion. Even so, privacy is rarely respected and there can be a lot of hassle, pressure and intrusion on your personal space, as well as outright harassment. Backpackers setting out alone often meet like-minded travelling companions at budget hotels. If you are blonde, you are quite naturally likely to attract more attention. Some seasoned travellers find that dyeing their hair dark, helps. One way of dealing with people who hassle you on the street is to simply say "thank you", smile and walk away. If you show annoyance, it may result in more pestering or abusive language.

See also page 37

Before you travel

Getting in

Virtually all foreign nationals require a visa to enter India. Nationals of Bhutan and Nepal only require a suitable means of identification. The rules regarding visas change frequently and arrangements for application and collection also vary from town to town so it is essential to check details and costs with the relevant office. These remain closed on Indian national holidays. In London, applications are processed in an hour or two hours (0800-1200). Visitors from countries which do not have an Indian representation may apply to the resident British representative, or enquire at the *Air India* office. An application on the prescribed form should be accompanied by three passport photographs and your passport which should be valid for at least three months beyond the period of the visit.

Documents
For overseas embassies & consulates, see page 26

Essentials

 Indian embassies and consulates

Australia 3-5 Moonah Place, Yarralumla, Canberra T6273-3999; Level 2, 210 Pitt St, Sydney T9223-9500; Melbourne T93846-0141.

Austria Kärntner Ring 2, A-1015 Vienna, T01-5058666, F5059219.

Bangladesh Road 2 Dhanmodi RA, House 129, Dhaka-2, T503606, Chittagong T654021.

Belgium 217-Chaussée de Vleurgat, 1050 Brussels, T6409802, F6489638. Consulates: Ghent T09-263423, Antwerp T03-2341122.

Bhutan India House Estate, Thimpu, T09752-22162.

Canada 10 Springfield Rd, Ottawa, Ontario K1M 1C9, T613-7443751. Consulates: Toronto T416-9600751, Vancouver T604-6628811.

Denmark Vangehusvej 15, 2100 Copenhagen, T3118-2888, F3927-0218.

Finland Satamakatu 2 A8, 00160 Helsinki-16, T608927. France, 15 Rue Alfred Dehodencq, Paris, T40507070.

Germany Pohlstr 20, 10785 Berlin, T030-4853002, F4853003. Consulates: Bonn T0228-540132; Frankfurt T069-271040, Hamburg T040-338036, Munich T089-92562067, Stuttgart T0711-1530050.

Ireland 6 Lesson Park, Dublin 6, T01-4970843.

Israel, 4 Kaufmann St, Sharbat, Tel Aviv 68012, T0368-580585, F510143.

Italy Via XX Settembre 5, 00187 Rome, T06-4884642. Consulates: Milan T02-8690314, Genoa T010-54891.

Japan 2-11, Kudan Minami 2-Chome, Chiyoda-ku, Tokyo 102, T03-32622391. Consulate: Kobe T078-2418116.

Korea 37-3, Hannam-dong, Yongsan-Ku, Seoul, T7984257, F7969534. Malaysia, 19 Malacca St, Kuala Lumpur, T221766.

Maldives Mafabbu Aage 37, Orchid Magu, Male 20-02, T323015.

Nepal Lainchour, PO Box No 292, Kathmandu, T211300.

Netherlands Buitenrustweg 2, The Hague (2517KD), T070-3469771.

New Zealand 10th Flr, Princess Tower, 180 Molesworth St (PO Box 4045), Wellington, T4736390.

Pakistan G5 Diplomatic Enclave, Islamabad, T050-8144731, Karachi T021-814371.

Singapore India House, 31 Grange Rd, Singapore 0923, T7376777.

Spain Avda Pio XII 30-32, 28016 Madrid, T457-0209. Consulate: Barcelona T93-2120422.

Sri Lanka 36-38 Galle Rd, Colombo 3, T421605 Kandy, T446430.

Sweden Adolf Fredriks Kyrkogata 12, Box 1340, 11183 Stockholm, T08-107008, F248505.

Switzerland 17 Kirchenfeldstrasse 28 CH-3005, Berne, T031-3511110.

Thailand 46, Soi 23 (Prasarn Mitr) Sukhumvit 23, Bangkok 10110, T2580300. Also in Chiang Mai.

UK India House, Aldwych, London WC2B 4NA, T020-78368484 (0930-1300, 1400-1730; visas 0800-1200), www.Hcilondon.org Consulates: The Spencers, 19 Augusta St, Hockley, Birmingham, B18 6DS, T0121-2122782; 6th Flr, 134 Renfrew St, Glasgow 3 7ST, T0141-3310777, F331-0666.

USA 2107 Massachusetts Ave, Washington DC 20008, T202-9397000. Consulates: New Orleans T504-5828105, New York T212-8797800, San Francisco T415-6680662, Chicago T312-5950405.

Visas Visa fees vary according to nationality. In mid-2000 the following visa rules applied: **Transit** For passengers en route to another country (valid for 3-5 days). **Tourist** Six month visa, from the date of issue with multiple entry. Most visitors require this type. **Business** Up to one year from the date of issue. A letter from company giving the nature of business is required. **Five year** For those of Indian origin only, who have held Indian passports. **Student** Valid up to one year from the date of issue. Attach a letter of acceptance from Indian institution, and an AIDS test certificate. Allow up to three months for approval. **Visa extensions** Applications should be made to the Foreigners' Regional Registration Offices at New Delhi, Mumbai, Kolkata or Chennai, or an office of the Superintendent of Police in the District Headquarters. After 6 months, those with a tourist visa must leave India and apply for a new visa – the Nepal office is known to be difficult. Anyone staying in India for a period of longer than 180 days (6 months) must register at a convenient Foreigners' Registration Office.

Rajasthan and Gujarat states do not require permits. Some areas are politically sensitive. The border regions and tribal areas are subject to restrictions and special permits may be needed to visit them.

Restricted & protected areas

Essentials

No foreigner needs to register within the 180 day period of their tourist visa. All foreign visitors who stay in India for more than 180 days are required to register at the nearest Foreigners' Registration Office and get an **income tax clearance** exemption certificate from the Foreign Section of the Income Tax Department in Delhi, Mumbai, Kolkata or Chennai.

Registration

Foreigners should apply to the Indian representative in their country of origin for the latest information about **work** permits. Periodically some Indian states have introduced prohibition. Gujarat enforces prohibition but not Rajasthan. When applying for your visa you can ask for an **All India Liquor Permit**. You can also get the permit from any Government of India Tourist Office in Delhi or the state capitals.

Permits

What to take

Here are some items you might find particularly helpful in India: Loose-fitting, light cotton **clothes** are good for travelling almost anywhere at any time of year, being cool and comfortable with the added advantage of being quick drying. Pale colours may give some protection against mosquitoes. Sarongs are useful – they can be used as a skirt, scarf, towel etc. Women should dress modestly. Brief shorts and tight vest tops are best avoided, though on the beach 'modest' swim wear is fine. Locally bought, inexpensive and cool *kurta pyjama* for men, and *shalwar kameez* for women are excellent options on the plains but it can be cold in the desert and on the hills between December and February, where some heavier clothing is essential. Comfortable shoes, sandals or trainers are essential and difficult to replace. Take high-factor sun screen and a sun hat.

Travel light. Most essentials are available in the larger cities, items are cheap & laundry services are generally speedy

It is best to take a sufficient supply of personal **medicines** from home, including inhalers and anti-malarial drugs (Proguanil is not available from pharmacists). For protection against mosquitoes, take *Mosiguard* repellent, recommended by MASTA. Most **toiletries**, contact lens cleaners, tampons and barrier contraceptives are available in the larger cities. Contact lens wearers can be affected by the high level of pollution in some large cities so carry your specs as well (plus your prescription).

As for **photography**, given the dusty conditions, a UV filter is best left on the lens permanently and a polarising filter can often give you stronger colours, better contrast and a bluer sky. Although good quality films are available in all major cities and tourist centres, including increasingly APS film, it is best to take rolls from home and certainly any specialist camera batteries. In India, only buy films from a reputable shop since hawkers and roadside stalls may not be reliable and check the carton carefully as well as the expiry date.

Photocopies of essential **documents**, passport identification and visa pages, and spare photos are useful when applying for permits or in case of loss or theft.

Budget travellers Nets are rarely provided in cheap hotels so try to take an impregnated mosquito net. Earplugs come in handy especially during festivals when

Essentials

Money matters

It can be difficult to use torn or very worn currency notes. Check notes carefully when you are given them and refuse any that are damaged.

A good supply of small denomination notes always comes in handy for bus tickets, cheap meals and tipping.

Remember that if offered a large note the recipient will never have any change!

It can be worth carrying a few clean, new sterling or dollar notes for use where travellers' cheques and credit cards are not accepted.

loudspeakers playing Hindi film music tend to work overtime all the time. On overnight journeys, blocking out the perpetual light is effective with eye-shades (given away by some airlines). A good padlock to secure your budget room(secret combination number recommended). A cotton, sheet sleeping bag which can cover a pillow, makes all the difference when you can't be sure of clean linen. Toilet paper, soap, towel and the washbasin plug may all be missing so be prepared.

Money

Prices in the handbook are quoted in Rupees, although top hotels often quote rates in US$. Very few people are familiar with international currencies apart from currency touts on city street corners. You do best to think in Rupee terms.

Currency Indian currency is the Indian Rupee (Re/Rs). It is **not** possible to purchase these before you leave. If you want cash on arrival it is best to get it at the airport bank. Rupee notes are printed in denominations of Rs 500, 100, 50, 20, 10. The Rupee is divided into 100 paise. Coins are minted in denominations of Rs 5, 2, 1, and 50, 25, 20, 10 and 5 paise, though coins below 50 paise are rarely seen. Carry money, mostly as TCs, in a money belt worn under clothing. Have enough for daily requirements in an easily accessible place. The new Rs 500 note is difficult to change outside of the big cities, but it has also encouraged a wave of convincing forged copies. Always check the security features carefully and avoid changing with unlicensed dealers.

Travellers' Travellers' cheques (TCs) issued by Thomas Cook and American Express are accepted
cheques without difficulty in the major towns and tourist centres. Most banks, but not all, will accept US$ or £ sterling TCs, so it is a good idea to carry some of each. Other major currency TCs are also accepted in some larger cities. The introduction of the Euro in 2002 may not be universally adopted in Indian banking for some time, so do not rely on the new currency for the foreseeable future. TCs can be exchanged in banks, hotels, or a growing number of private dealers the latter often offering a faster service at a higher rate. They can be used directly for payment in the more expensive hotels and souvenir shops, as well as for purchasing airline tickets and foreign quota train tickets. Otherwise, ensure that you have enough cash to cover your needs. Your passport and visa must be shown. In banks, encashing any form of currency nearly always takes up to 30 minutes or longer, so it is worth taking larger denomination TCs and changing enough money to last for some days. If you are travelling to remote areas it can be worth buying Indian Rupee TCs from a major bank, as these are more widely accepted than foreign currency ones. If stolen, you must get a police report and be prepared to contact the issuing company with the numbers of the stolen checks, your receipt and a plausible story! For some, the wait for replacement checks can take weeks, so take great care of them!

Exchange rates

	Rs		Rs
Australian $	25	Japanese Yen	0.38
Dutch Guilders	18.85	New Zealand $	19.8
Euro	41.4	Swiss Francs	27
French Francs	6.3	UK £	67
German DM	21.2	US $	47

Credit cards

Major credit cards are increasingly acceptable in the main centres, though in smaller cities and towns it is still rare to be able to pay by credit card. Payment by credit card can sometimes be more expensive than payment by cash, whilst some credit card companies charge a premium on cash withdrawals *Visa* and *Mastercard* have a growing number of ATMs in major cities, but many ATMs only deal with local account holders. It is however straightforward to obtain a cash advance against a credit card. Railway Reservation centres in 17 major cities are now taking payment for train tickets by Visa card which can be very quick as the queue is very short, although they cannot generally be used for Tourist Quota tickets!

Changing money

Request some Rs 100 & 50 notes. Rs 500 (which can be mistaken for Rs 100) notes can reduce 'wallet bulge' but can be difficult to change. If you cash sterling, always make certain that you have been given Rupees at the sterling & not at the dollar rate

The *State Bank of India* and several others in major towns are authorized to deal in foreign exchange. Some give cash against *Visa/Master* cards (eg *Standard Chartered, Grindlays, Bank of Baroda* who print a list of their participating branches, *Andhra Bank*). *American Express* cardholders can use their cards to get either cash or TCs in the four major cities. They also have offices in Ahmadabad and Vadodara. The larger cities and tourist centres have **licensed money changers** with offices usually in the commercial sector. Changing money through unauthorized dealers is illegal. Liberalisation of the currency market introduced by the then prime minister, Narasimha Rao, in the mid-1990s effectively destroyed the currency black market overnight. Consequently, premiums on the street corner are very small and highly risky, especially with the influx of fake Rs 500 notes. Large **hotels** change money 24 hours a day for guests, but banks often give a substantially better rate of exchange than hotels.

It is best to get exchange on arrival at the airport bank or the Thomas Cook counter. Thomas Cook has a high reputation for excellent service and has branches across the country. Many international flights arrive during the night, and it is generally far easier and less time consuming to change money at the airport than in the city.

You should be given a foreign currency **encashment certificate** when you change money through a bank or authorized dealer, ask for one if it is not automatically given. It allows you to change Indian Rupees back to your own currency on departure, so ensure that you have a valid one at this time. It also enables you to use Rupees to pay hotel bills or buy air tickets for which payment in foreign exchange may be required although in practice, those using mid-range or cheaper hotels rarely have to produce them. The certificates are only valid for three months.

Transferring money to India

HSBC, Barclays and *Standard Chartered Grindlays* and others can make 'instant' transfers to their offices in India but charge a high fee (about US$30). *Standard Chartered Grindlays* issues US$ TCs. *Western Union* have a growing number of agents throughout the country. Sending a bank draft (up to US$1,000) by post (four to seven days by *Speedpost*) is the cheapest option.

Cost of living

The cost of living in India remains well below that in the West. The average wage is about Rs 10,000 per month (US$220) for government employees according to government statistics – manual workers, unskilled labourers (women are often paid less than men), farmers and others in rural areas earn considerably less.

Cost of travelling Most food, accommodation and public transport, especially rail and bus, are exceptionally cheap. There is a widening range of moderately priced but clean hotels and restaurants outside the big cities, making it possible to get a great deal for your money. Budget travellers sharing a room, eating in local restaurants, and using the cheapest means of travel can expect to spend around Rs 420-500 (about US$10-12) a day, though you can each get by on less in the south. Those looking for the comfort of the occasional night in a simple a/c room, and using reserved seats on trains and luxury buses, should budget for about US$25-30 a day. However, if you travel alone and are looking for reasonably comfortable a/c rooms, use taxis and second class a/c train berths, expect to spend US$70-75 a day. When shopping or hiring an unmetered vehicle, bargaining is expected, and essential.

Getting there

Air

India is accessible by air from virtually every continent. Most international flights arrive in Delhi or Mumbai from which you can fly to some cities in Rajasthan and Gujarat (*Air India*) permits ticketing through to Ahmadabad and allows customs formalities to be completed at the destination although the flight is routed through Delhi or Mumbai where you need to change planes. Some international carriers permit 'open-jaw' travel, arriving in, and departing from, different cities in India. Some (eg *Air India*, *British Airways*) have convenient non-stop flights from London taking only nine hours.

The cheapest fares from Europe tend to be with Central European, Central Asian or Middle Eastern airlines (see below). With such airlines it pays to confirm your return flight as early as possible. You can also get good discounts from Australasia, Southeast Asia and Japan. If you plan to visit two or more South Asian countries within three weeks, you may qualify for a 30% discount on your international tickets. Ask your National Tourist office. International air tickets can be bought in India though payment must be made in foreign exchange.

Stop-overs & Round-the-World tickets You can arrange several stop-overs in India on Round-the-World and long distance tickets. Round-the-World tickets allow you to fly in to one and out from another international airport. You may be able to arrange some internal flights using international

carriers eg *Air India*, www.airindia.com sometimes allows stop-overs within India for a small extra charge.

Companies dealing in volume and taking reduced commissions for ticket sales can offer better deals than the airlines themselves. The national press carry their advertisements. *Usit*, T0870-2401010, www.usitcampus.co.uk *Campus* is good for students and have offices in several university cities. *Trailfinders* of London, T020-79383939, worldwide agencies. *STA*, in London, T020-73616262, T0870-1606070, www.sta travel.co.uk has over 100 offices worldwide offering special deals for under-26s. *Travelbag*, T01420-80828, www.travelbag.adventures.co.uk quotes competitive fares. General Sales Agents (GSAs) for specific airlines can sometimes offer attractive deals: *Jet Airways*, 188 Hammersmith Rd, London W6 7DJ, T020-89701500, for *Gulf Air*, *Kuwait Airways* etc, and *Welcome Travels*, 58 Wells St, London W1P 3RA, T020-74363011, for *Air India*, offer good discounts.

Ticket agents

The best deals are offered from the UK (try www.cheapflights.com which also provides additional useful information). You can pick up attractive deals on *Air India* which flies direct to Delhi and Mumbai throughout the year. A few European airlines (eg *Lufthansa*, *KLM*) and several from the Middle East (eg *Emirates*, *Gulf Air*, *Kuwait Airways*, *Royal Jordanian*) offer good discounts to Mumbai and other Indian regional capitals from London, but fly via their hub cities, so adding to the journey time. *Virgin Atlantic* now offer three weekly London-Delhi-London service. Good deals can be offered by General Sales Agents (GSAs), see above. Consolidators in UK quote competitive fares: *Bridge the World*, T020-79110900, www.bridgetheworld.com *Flightbookers*, T0870-0107000 from the UK or T020-77572626 from abroad, www.ebookers.com *North South Travel*, T01245-608291 (profits to charity, good concessions).

From the UK, Continental Europe & the Middle East

Qantas, *Singapore Airlines*, *Thai Airways*, *Malaysian Airlines*, *Cathay Pacific* and *Air India* are the principal airlines connecting the continents. They fly to one of the Indian regional capitals. *STA* and *Flight Centres* offer discounted tickets from their branches in major cities in Australia and New Zealand. *Abercrombie & Kent*, *Adventure World*, *Peregrine*, and *Travel Corporation* of India, organize tours.

From Australasia via the Far East

From the east coast, it is best to fly direct to India from New York via London by *Air India* (18 hours). Discounted tickets on *British Airways*, *KLM*, *Lufthansa*, *Gulf Air* and *Kuwait Airways* are sold through agents although they will invariably fly via their country's capital cities. From the west coast, it is best to fly via Hong Kong, Singapore or Bangkok to Delhi, Kolkata or Mumbai using one of those countries' national carriers. *Hari World Travels*, www.hariworld.com and *STA*, www.sta-travel.co.uk have offices in New York, Toronto and Ontario. Student fares are also available from *Council Travel*, www.counciltravel.com with several offices in the USA and *Travel Cuts*, www.travel cuts.com in Canada.

From North America & Canada

International airlines vary in their arrangements and requirements for security, in particular the carrying of equipment like radios, tape-recorders, lap-top computers and batteries. It is advisable to ring the airline in advance to confirm what their current regulations are. Internal airlines often have different rules from the international carriers. You are strongly advised not to pack valuables in your luggage. Avoid repacking at the airport.

Airline security

Overland

Get your Indian visa in advance, before arriving at the border

Crossings between India and its neighbours are affected by the political relations between them. Several road border crossings are open periodically, but permission to cross cannot be guaranteed. The reopening of Iran to travellers of most nationalities has reinstated the Istanbul-Teheran-Quetta route. We highly recommend Footprint's Pakistan Handbook, which is invaluable for anyone contemplating the journey.

Touching down

Airport information

Duty free

Some airports have duty free shops though the range of goods is very limited

Tourists are allowed to bring in all personal effects 'which may reasonably be required' without charge. The official customs allowance includes 200 cigarettes or 50 cigars, 0.95 litres of alcohol, a camera with five rolls of film and a pair of binoculars. Valuable personal effects or professional equipment must be registered on a **Tourist Baggage Re-Export Form** (TBRE), including jewellery, special camera equipment and lenses, lap-top computers, sound and video recorders. These forms require the serial numbers of such equipment. It saves considerable frustration if you know the numbers in advance and are ready to show the serial numbers on the equipment. In addition to the forms, details of imported equipment may be entered into your passport. Save time by completing the formalities while waiting for your baggage. It is essential to keep these forms for showing to the customs when leaving India, otherwise considerable delays are very likely at the time of departure.

Currency regulations

There are no restrictions on the amount of foreign currency or TCs a tourist may bring into India. If you were carrying more than US$10,000 or its equivalent in cash or TCs you need to fill in a currency declaration form.

Prohibited items

The import of dangerous drugs, live plants, gold coins, gold and silver bullion and silver coins not in current use are either banned or subject to strict regulation. It is illegal to import firearms into India without special permission. Enquire at consular offices abroad for details.

Export restrictions

Export of gold jewellery purchased in India is allowed up to a value of Rs 2,000 and other jewellery (including settings with precious stones) up to a value of Rs 10,000. Export of antiquities and art objects over 100 years old is restricted. Ivory, skins of all animals, *toosh* wool, snake skin and articles made from them are banned, unless you get permission for export. For further information enquire at the Indian High Commission or consulate, or access the Government of India at www.indiagov.org or the customs at www.konark.ncst.ernet.in/customs/

Documentation

The formalities on arrival in India have been increasingly streamlined during the last five years and the facilities at the major international airports greatly improved. However, arrival can still be a slow process. Disembarkation cards, with an attached customs declaration, are handed out to passengers during the inward flight. The immigration form should be handed in at the immigration counter on arrival. The customs slip will be returned, for handing over to the customs on leaving the baggage collection hall. The immigration formalities at both Delhi and Mumbai can be very slow. You may well find that there are delays of over an hour in processing passengers passing through immigration who need help with filling forms.

Touching down

Electricity 220-240 volts AC. Some top hotels have transformers. There may be pronounced variations in the voltage, and power cuts are common. Socket sizes vary so you are advised to take a universal adaptor (available at most airports). Many hotels even in the higher categories don't have electric razor sockets. During power cuts, diesel generators are often used in the medium and higher category hotels to provide power for essential equipment but this may not always cover air-conditioning.

Hours of business Banks: 1030-1430, Monday-Friday; 1030-1230, Saturday. Top hotels sometimes have a 24-hour service. **Post offices**: Usually 1000-1700, Monday-Friday; Saturday mornings.

Government offices: 0930-1700, Monday-Friday; 0930-1300, Saturday (some open on alternate Saturday only). **Shops**: 0930-1800, Monday-Saturday. Bazars keep longer hours. There are regional variations.

IDD 91. A double ring repeated regularly means it is ringing. Equal tones with equal pauses means engaged.

Official time GMT +5½ hours through-out the year (USA, EST +10½ hours).

Weights and measures The metric system has come into universal use in the cities. In remote rural areas local measures are sometimes used.

Essentials

Departure tax Rs 500 is payable for all international departures other than those to neighbouring SAARC countries, when the tax is Rs 250 (not reciprocated by Sri Lanka). This must be paid in Rupees in India unless it is included in your international ticket; check when buying. Look for 'FT' in the tax column of your ticket 'Security Check' your baggage before checking-in at Departure.

Public transport to & from airport
See pages 79 & 357 for detailed information

Most major international airports have special **bus** services into the town centre from early morning to around midnight. **Pre-paid taxis** to the city are available at all major airports. Some airports have up to three categories, limousine, luxury and ordinary. The first two usually have prominent counters, so you may have to insist if you want to use the standard service. Insist on being taken to your chosen destination even if the driver claims the city is unsafe or the hotel has closed down.

Rules, customs and etiquette

Most travellers experience great warmth and hospitality in India. You may however, be surprised that with the warm welcome comes an open curiosity about personal matters. Total strangers on a train, for example, may ask for details about your job, income and family circumstances, or discuss politics and religion.

Conduct Respect for the foreign visitor should be reciprocated by a sensitivity towards local customs and culture. How you dress is mostly how people judge you. Clean, modest clothes and a smile go a long way. Scanty, tight clothing draws unwanted attention. Nudity is not permitted on beaches in India and although there are some places where this ban is ignored, it causes widespread offence. Displays of intimacy are not considered suitable in public.

You may at times be justifiably frustrated by delays, bureaucracy and inefficiency, but displays of anger and rudeness will not achieve anything positive, and may in fact make things worse. We suggest you remain patient and polite. The concept of time and punctuality is also rather vague so be prepared to be kept waiting.

Courtesy   It takes little effort to learn and use common gestures of courtesy but they are greatly appreciated by Indians. The *greeting* when meeting or parting, used universally among the Hindus across India, is the palms joined together as in prayer, sometimes accompanied with the word *namaste*. Muslims use the greeting *assalām aleikum*, with the response *waleikum assalām*, meaning 'peace be with you'; "please" is *mehrbani-se*; "thank you" is often expressed by a smile, or with the somewhat formal *dhannyabad*, *shukriya* (Urdu).

Hands & eating   Traditionally, Indians use the right hand for eating, cutlery being alien at the table except for serving spoons. In rural India, don't expect table knives and forks though you might find small spoons. Use your right hand for giving, receiving, eating or shaking hands as the left is considered to be unclean since it is associated with washing after using the toilet.

Women   Indian women in urban and rural areas differ in their social interactions with men. Certainly, to the westerner, Indian women may seem to remain in the background and appear shy when approached, often hiding their face and avoiding eye contact. Yet you will see them working in public, often in jobs traditionally associated with men in the West, in the fields, in construction sites or in the market place. Even from a distance, men should not photograph women without their consent.

Women do not, in general, shake hands with men since physical contact is not traditionally acceptable between acquaintances of the opposite sex. A westernized city woman, however, may feel free to shake hands with a foreign visitor. In traditional rural circles, it is still the custom for men to be offered food first, separately, so don't be surprised if you, as foreign guest (man or woman), are awarded this special status when invited to an Indian home, and never set eyes on your hostess.

Visiting religious sites   Visitors to all religious places should be dressed in clean, modest clothes; shorts and vests are inappropriate. Always remove shoes before entering (and all leather items in Jain temples). Take thick socks for protection when walking on sun-baked stone floors. Menstruating women are considered 'unclean' and should not enter places of worship.

Non-Hindus are sometimes excluded from the inner sanctum of **Hindu** temples and occasionally even from the temple itself. Look for signs or ask. In certain temples, and on special occasions, you may only enter if you wear unstitched clothing such as a *dhoti*.

In **Muslim** mosques, visitors should only have their face, hands and feet exposed; women should also cover their heads. Mosques may be closed to non-Muslims shortly before formal prayers.

Some temples have a register or a receipt book for **donations** which works like an obligatory entry fee. The money is normally used for the upkeep and services of the temple or monastery. In some pilgrimage centres, as at Pushkar, priests can become unpleasantly persistent. In general, if you wish to leave a donation, put money in the donation box. Some priests do not handle money. It is also not customary to shake hands with a priest or monk. **Alms** Sanyasis (holy men), and some pilgrims, depend on gifts of money.

Begging   Beggars are often found in busy street corners in large Indian cities, as well as at bus and train stations where they often target foreigners for special attention. Visitors usually find this very distressing, especially the sight of severely undernourished children or those displaying physical deformity. You may be particularly affected when some persist on making physical contact. You might find a firm "*Jaao*" (go away) works. In the larger cities, beggars are often exploited by syndicates which cream off most of their takings. Yet those seeking alms near religious sites are another matter, and you may see Indian worshippers giving freely to those less fortunate than themselves,

First impressions

On arrival at any of India's major cities the first impressions can take you aback. The exciting images of an ancient and richly diverse culture which draw many visitors to India can be completely overwhelmed by the immediate sensations which first greet you. You need to be prepared for:

Pollution *All the cities suffer from bad air pollution, particularly in the winter.*
Noise *Many people find India incredibly noisy, as radios, videos and loudspeakers seem to blare in unlikely places at all times of day and night.*
Smells *India has an almost baffling mixture of smells, from the richly pungent and unpleasant to the delicately subtle.*

Pressure *From stepping out of the airport or hotel everybody seems to clamour to sell you their services. Taxi and rickshaw drivers are always there when you don't want them, much less often when you do. There often seems to be no sense of personal space or privacy. Young women are often stared at and sometimes touched.*
Public hygiene – *or lack of it. It is common to see people urinating in public places (eg roadside), and defecating in the open countryside. These can all be daunting and make early adjustment to India difficult. Even on a short visit you need to give yourself time and space to adjust!*

Essentials

since this is tied up with gaining 'merit'. How you deal with begging is a matter of personal choice but it is perhaps better to give to a recognized charity than to make largely ineffectual handouts to individuals.

Young children sometimes offer to do 'jobs' such as call a taxi, carry shopping or pose for a photo. You may want to give a coin in exchange. However, it is not helpful to hand out sweets, 'school pens' and money indiscriminately to open-palmed children who tag on to any foreigner. Some prefer to give fruit, tea and biscuits to beggars.

Charitable giving A pledge to donate a part of one's holiday budget to a local charity would be an effective formula for 'giving'. Some visitors like to support self-help co-operatives, orphanages, refugee centres, disabled or disadvantaged groups, or international charities which work with local partners, by either making a donation or by buying their products. Some of these are listed under the appropriate towns. A few (which also welcome volunteers) are listed here: www//Indiacharitynet.com is useful. *Novartis*, T0044-616977200, novartis.foundations@group.novartis.com (sustainable development, leprosy). *Oxfam*, Sushil Bhawan, 210 Shahpur Jat, New Delhi 110049, T011-6491774; 274 Banbury Rd, Oxford OX2 7D2, UK, oxindia@giasdl01.vsnl.net.in (400 grassroots projects). *SOS Children's Villages*, A-7 Nizamuddin (W), New Delhi 110013, T011-4647835, www.pw2.netcom/sanjayd/sos.html (over 30 poor and orphaned children's projects in India eg opposite Pital Factory, Jhotwara Rd, Jaipur 302016, T0141-322393). *Urmul Trust*, Urmul Dairy, Ganganagar Rd, Bikaner, Rajasthan, T523093 (health care, education and rural crafts in Rajasthani villages).

Tipping A tip of Rs 10 to a bell-boy carrying luggage in a modest hotel (Rs 20 in a higher category) would be appropriate. In up-market restaurants, a 10% tip is acceptable when 'Service' is not already included, while in places serving very cheap meals, round off the bill with small change. Indians don't normally tip taxi drivers but a small extra amount over the fare is welcomed. Porters at airports and railway stations often have a fixed rate displayed but will usually press for more. Ask fellow passengers what the fair rate is (about Rs 20 per piece) – they will nearly always advise.

Photography   Many monuments now charge a camera fee ranging from Rs 20-50 for still cameras, and as much as Rs 500 for video cameras (more for professionals). Special permits are needed from the Archaeological Survey of India, New Delhi for using tripods and artificial lights. When photographing people, it is polite to first ask – they will usually respond warmly with smiles, although the 'moment' may have been lost as they line up, military style! Visitors often promise to send copies of the photos – don't unless you really mean to do so. Photography of airports, military installations, bridges and in tribal and 'sensitive border areas', is not permitted.

Safety

Personal security   In general the threats to personal security for travellers are remarkably small. In most areas it is possible to travel either individually or in groups without any risk of personal violence. However, care is necessary in some places, and basic common sense needs to be used with respect to looking after valuables.

Some parts of India are subject to political violence. The Vale of Kashmir and Jammu remains under tight military control. Even when the border area is relatively quiet, the army is massively deployed and on constant alert. Despite the promises of travel touts that Kashmir is completely safe, tourists who visit, do so at considerable risk. In the great majority of places visited by tourists, violent crime and personal attacks are extremely rare.

Theft   Theft is not uncommon. It is best to keep travellers' cheques, passports and valuables with you at all times since you can't regard hotel rooms as automatically safe; even hotel safes don't guarantee secure storage. Avoid leaving valuables near open windows even when you are in the room. Use your own padlock in a budget hotel when you go out. Pickpockets and other thieves operate in the big cities. Crowded areas are particularly high risk. Take special care of your belongings when getting on or off public transport.

Never accept food or drink from casual acquaintances. Travellers have reported being drugged & then robbed

Confidence tricksters   These are particularly common where people are on the move, notably around railway stations or places where budget tourists gather. A common plea is some sudden and desperate calamity; sometimes a letter will be produced in English to back up the claim. The demands are likely to increase sharply if sympathy is shown. See also page 57.

Security on trains   It can be difficult to keep an eye on your belongings when travelling. Nothing of value should be left close to open train windows. First class a/c compartments are self-contained and normally completely secure. Second class a/c compartments, which have much to recommend them especially in the summer, are larger, allowing more movement of passengers but are not so secure. Attendants may take little notice of what is going on, so luggage should be chained to a seat for security overnight. Locks and chains are easily available at main stations and bazaars. Some travellers prefer to reserve upper berths which offer some added protection against theft and also have the benefit of allowing daytime sleeping.

Police   If you have items stolen, they should be reported to the police as soon as possible. Keep a separate record of vital documents, including passport details and travellers' cheques numbers. Larger hotels will be able to assist in contacting and dealing with the police. Dealings with the police can be very difficult and in the worst regions such as Bihar even dangerous. The paperwork involved in reporting losses can be time consuming and irritating, and your own documentation (eg passport and visas) may be demanded. In some states the police themselves sometimes demand bribes, though

Some towns have introduced special Tourist Police to help the foreign traveller

tourists should not assume, however, that if procedures move slowly they are automatically being expected to offer a bribe. The traffic police, particularly in Delhi, are tightening up very hard on traffic offences. They have the right to make on-the-spot fines for speeding and illegal parking. If you face a demand for a fine, insist on a receipt. If you have to go to a

No smoking please

Several state governments (including Rajasthan) have passed a law banning smoking in all public buildings and transport but exempting "open spaces". To avoid fines, check for notices.

police station, try to take someone with you. If you face really serious problems, for example in connection with a driving accident, you should contact your consular office as quickly as possible. You should ensure you always have your International driving licence and motorbike or car documentation with you.

Drugs Certain areas have become associated with foreigners taking drugs. The government takes the misuse of drugs very seriously. Anyone charged with the illegal possession of drugs risks facing a fine of Rs 100,000 and a minimum 10 years imprisonment. Several foreigners have been imprisoned for drugs related offences in the last decade.

Women travelling alone There are some problems to watch out for and some simple precautions to take to avoid both personal harassment and giving offence. Modest dress is always advisable: loose-fitting non-see-through clothes, covering the shoulders, and skirts, dresses or shorts of a decent length. Many find the *shalwar-kameez*-scarf ideal. In mosques women should be covered from head to ankle. Unaccompanied women are most vulnerable in major cities, crowded bazars, beach resorts and tourist centres where men may follow them and touch them. "Eve teasing" is the euphemism for physical harassment; some buses have seats reserved for women. If you are harassed, it can be effective to make a scene. Be firm and clear if you don't wish to speak to someone. Many railway booking offices have separate women's ticket queues or ask women to go to the head of the general queue. It is best to be accompanied at night, especially when travelling by rickshaw or taxi in towns. Be prepared to raise an alarm if anything unpleasant threatens. Women have reported that they have been molested while being measured for clothing in tailors' shops, especially in North India. If possible, take a friend with you.

Advice It is better to seek advice on security from your own embassy than from travel agencies. Before you travel you can contact: **British Foreign & Commonwealth Office**, Travel Advice Unit, Consular Division, 1 Palace Street, London SW1E 5HE, UK, T020-72384503, F72384545, www.fco.gov.uk/travel **US State Department's Bureau of Consular Affairs**, Overseas Citizens Services, Room 4800, Department of State, Washington, DC 20520-4818, USA, T0202-6474225, F6473000, www.travel.state.gov/travel_warnings.html **Australian Department of Foreign Affairs,** Canberra, Australia, T06-62613305, www.dfat.gov.au/consular/advice.html Canadian official advice is on www.dfait-maeci.gc.ca/travelreport/menu_e.htm

Where to stay

India has an enormously wide range of accommodation. You can stay safely and very cheaply by western standards right across the country. In all the major cities there are also high quality hotels, offering a full range of personal and business facilities. In small centres even the best hotels are far more variable. In the peak season (October to April for most of India) bookings can be extremely heavy in popular destinations. It is

Essentials

Hotel categories

LL (US$250+) and **L** (US$150-250) These are exceptional hotels. They are in the metropolitan cities or in exclusive locations such as a commanding coastal promontory, a lake island or a scenic hilltop, with virtually nothing to fault them. They have high class business facilities, specialist restaurants and well-stocked bars, several pools, sports.

AL (US$100-150) and **A** (US$50-100) Most major towns have at least some in these categories which too reach high international standards but are less exclusive. Many quote an inflated 'dollar price' to foreigners.

B (US$25-50) Comfortable but not plush, choice of restaurants, pool, some have a gym. These are often aimed at the business client.

C (US$15-25) and **D** (Rs 400-750) In many small towns the best hotel is in the C category, but they are not necessarily the best value. Some charge higher prices for a flash reception area, usually central a/c, restaurant, satellite TV, foreign exchange and travel desk. **D** hotels often offer very good value though quality and cleanliness can vary widely. Most have some a/c rooms with bath, satellite TV, restaurants. **D** hotels may have some rooms in the **E** price range, so if you are looking for good but cheap accommodation, start here!

E (Rs 200-400) Simple room with fan (occasionally air-cooler or a/c), often shared toilet and shower. May not have a restaurant or provide bed linen, towel etc.

F (under Rs 200) Very basic, shared toilet (often 'squat'), bucket and tap, variable cleanliness and hygiene. **E** and **F** category hotels are often in busy parts of town. They may have some rooms for under Rs 100, and dormitory beds for under Rs 50. Some only have four or six beds.

sometimes possible to book in advance by phone, fax or e-mail either from abroad or in India itself. However, double check your reservation, and always try to arrive as early as possible in the day.

Hotels

Palaces & forts
Reserve these hotels in advance

To allow you to experience something different, several old Maharajas' palaces and forts have been privately converted into comfortable and unusual hotels. They retain the inherent character, ambience and interiors of the property but have modernized bathrooms and amenities (eg TV, fridge). Many of these are individual homes where former ruling families still reside. They treat guests as if they were part of a house party. Others are managed by well known chains while a few (eg Neemrana Fort on the Jaipur-Delhi road, and Balaram Palace on the Ahmadabad-Mt Abu road) are run by private entrepreneurs. Many merchants' *havelis* and mansions belonging to the *rawals* and *thakurs*, too, have been converted to atmospheric hotels with a lot of character.

Some of the converted palaces, forts and *havelis*, offer good facilities in charming buildings. However, occasionally, even in the most expensive of the conversions, while some rooms may have excellent views others have little or none. Some places, especially in more remote rural areas, remain very simple; facilities may be rudimentary (eg hot water may come in buckets), and despite efforts at their control, pests like rats are sometimes found. If you are carrying food, keep it stored in sealed containers.

The **Heritage Hotels Association**, 9 Sardar Patel Marg, C Scheme, Jaipur, T382214, can supply a list of member hotels which are particularly attractive. For **Historic Resort Hotels** (HRH) in former palaces, contact City Palace, Udaipur 313001, T0294-528016, F528006, www.hrhindia.com These are in Udaipur, Kumbhalgarh, Jodhpur, Jaisalmer,

Gajner, Bikaner, Kolayat and Jaipur. *WelcomHeritage*, C-7, J Block, Saket, T11-6868992, F11-6868994, welcomheritage@bigfoot.com has properties in Jodhpur, Bal Samand, Kota, Ranakpur, Mount Abu, Sardar Samand, Khimsar, Nagaur and Jaisalmer. The *Taj Group* too owns some former royal lodges, F022-2837272, www.tajhotels.com.

Some tour companies specialize in arranging unusual historic destinations: *North West Safaris*, 92 Kamdhenu Complex, Ahmadabad, T079-6302019, F6560962, ssibal@ad1.vsnl.net.in and *Curvet India*, Delhi T/F6840037.

Accommodation in the national parks and wildlife sanctuaries varies from comfortable royal hunting lodges in some (eg Sawai Madhopur Lodge, Ranthambore and Ramgarh Lodge facing Jamwa Ramgarh Lake) and 'Palaces' (eg Gajner, Sariska) to very spartan rooms often lacking hot water and electricity (eg Bagha ke Bagh, Ghanerao, Forestry Department Rest Houses). **Jungle lodges & camps**

Tent resorts and camps are popular in Rajasthan. Some are permanent or semi-permanent camps, self-contained with attached showers, which are situated in orchards or farms and charge about US$100 on full board for two. The Maharajah of Jodhpur Royal Camp imitates hunting tents used by them in the 1930s which are pitched inside forts like Nagaur or near their palace properties, and have showers and flush toilets. Temporary camps are set up for fairs and festivals by Rajasthan and Gujarat Tourism and private hoteliers, as at Pushkar. Hut camps near the Rann of Kachchh (eg Dasada) offer novel cottages that resemble local village houses with thatched roofs and mud walls but have modern bathrooms.

Guest houses in towns and cities usually provide very basic accommodation, generally with Indian squat toilets and running cold water with hot water brought in buckets, but there could be exceptions. Destinations in Rajasthan offer paying guest accommodation. These vary from rooms in a family home to small hotels. A list is available from the Tourist Reception Centres. Contact Ramesh Jangid, *Alternative Travels*, Nawalgarh, 333042, Rajasthan, if you want to experience rural life with home-stays in villages. **Guest houses**

The categories are not star ratings and individual facilities vary considerably. Modest hotels may not have their own restaurant but will often offer 'room service', bringing in food from outside. In Rajasthan and Gujarat many restaurants only serve vegetarian food. Some hotels operate a '24 hour check-out' system. Make sure that this means that you can stay 24 hours from the time of check-in. **Price categories** *The categories are based on prices of double rooms excluding taxes*

Expect to pay more in Delhi and Mumbai. Prices away from large cities tend to be lower for comparable hotels. The higher category palace hotels charge US$150 for a double room (some exceeding US$750), while family run *Heritage Hotels* may cost Rs1200-2200 per person, and include all meals.

Hotels in beach resorts and hill-stations, because of their location and special appeal, often deviate from the description of our different categories.

Large reductions are made by hotels in all categories out-of-season in many resorts. Always ask if any is available. You may also request the 10% agent's commission to be deducted from your bill if you book direct. Clarify whether the agreed figure includes all taxes. **Off-season rates**

In general most hotel rooms rated at Rs 1,200 or above are subject to an expenditure tax of 10%. Many states levy an additional luxury tax of between 10% and 25%, and some hotels add a service charge of 10%. Taxes are not necessarily payable on meals, so it is worth settling the meals bill separately from the room bill. Most hotels in the **Taxes**

C category and above accept payment by credit card. Check your final bill carefully. Visitors have complained of **incorrect bills**, even in the most expensive hotels. The problem particularly afflicts groups, when last-minute extras appear mysteriously on some guests' bills. Check the evening before departure, and keep all receipts.

Facilities You have to be prepared for difficulties which are uncommon in the West. It is best to inspect the room and check that all equipment (a/c, TV, water heater, flush) works before checking in at a modest hotel.

Power supply In some states power cuts are common, or hot water may be restricted to certain times of day. The largest hotels have their own generators but it is best to carry a good torch.

Air-conditioning (a/c) Usually, only category **B** and above have central a/c. Elsewhere a/c rooms are cooled by individual units and occasionally by large 'air-coolers' which can be noisy and unreliable. When they fail to operate tell the management as it is often possible to get a rapid repair done, or to transfer to a room where the unit is working. During power cuts generators may not be able to cope with providing air-conditioning. Fans are provided in all but the cheapest of hotels.

Heating Hotels in hill stations often supply wood fires in rooms. Usually there is plenty of ventilation, but ensure that there is always good air circulation, especially when charcoal fires are provided in a basket.

Toilets Apart from those in the **A** category and above, 'attached bath' does not necessarily refer to a bathroom with a bathtub. Most will provide a bathroom with a toilet, basin and a shower. In the lower priced hotels and outside large towns, a bucket and tap may replace the shower, and an Indian 'squat' toilet instead of a Western WC (squat toilets are very often the cleaner). Even mid-price hotels, which are clean and pleasant, don't always provide towels, soap and toilet paper.

Water supply In some regions water supply is rationed periodically. Keep a bucket filled to use for flushing the toilet during water cuts. Occasionally, tap water may be discoloured due to rusty tanks. During the cold weather and in hill stations, **hot water** will be available at certain times of the day, sometimes in buckets, but is usually very restricted in quantity. Electric water heaters may provide enough for a shower but not enough to fill a bath tub! For details on drinking water see page 54.

Laundry Can be arranged very cheaply (eg a shirt washed and pressed for Rs 15-20 in **C-D** category; Rs 50 in luxury hotels) and quickly in 12-24 hours. It is best not to risk delicate fibres, though luxury hotels can usually handle these and also dry-clean items.

Insects At some times of the year and in some places mosquitoes can be a real problem and not all hotels have mosquito-proof rooms or mosquito nets. If you have any doubts check before confirming your room booking. In cheap hotels you need to be prepared for a wider range of insect life, including flies, cockroaches, and ants. Poisonous insects are extremely rare in towns. Hotel managements are nearly always prepared with insecticide sprays. Many small hotels in mosquito-prone areas supply nets. Remember to shut windows and doors at dusk. Electrical mat and pellets are now widely available, as are mosquito coils which burn slowly. Dusk and early evening are the worst times for mosquitoes so trousers and long-sleeved shirts are advisable, especially out of doors. At night, fans can be very effective in keeping mosquitoes off. As well as insects, expect to find spiders larger and hairier than those you see at home; they are mostly harmless and more frightened of you than you are of them! Scorpion are found in rural areas, though you rarely come across them (but always check shoes/boots before putting them on). You are more likely to have a resident gecko (a harmless house lizard) in your room. They are your friends as they keep the number of mosquitoes down.

Service Where staff training is lacking, the person who brings up your cases may proceed to show you light switches, room facilities, TV tuning, and hang around waiting for a tip. Room boys may enter your room without knocking or without waiting for a response to a knock. Both for security and privacy, it is a good idea to lock your door when you are in the room. It is worth noting these failings in the comments book when leaving as the management may take action.

Noise Hotels close to temples can be very noisy, especially during festivals. Music blares from loudspeakers late at night and from very early in the morning, often making sleep impossible. Mosques call the faithful to prayers at dawn. Some find earplugs helpful.

Other types of accommodation

Railway stations often have 'Retiring Rooms' or 'Rest Rooms' which may be hired for periods of between one and 24 hours by anyone holding an onward train ticket. They are cheap and simple though some stations have a couple of a/c rooms, which are often heavily booked. They are convenient for short stops, though some can be very noisy. Some major airports (eg Delhi, Mumbai) have similar facilities. | **Railway & airport retiring rooms**

In many areas there are government guest houses, ranging from 'Dak Bungalows' to 'Circuit Houses', often in attractive locations. The latter are now reserved almost exclusively for travelling government officers, but Dak Bungalows may sometimes be available for overnight stays, particularly in remote areas. They are usually extremely basic, with a caretaker who can sometimes provide a simple meal, given sufficient notice. Travelling officials always take precedence, even over booked guests. | **Government rest houses** *Check the room rate in advance as foreigners are sometimes overcharged*

These, catering for Indian businessmen, are springing up fast in or on the outskirts of many small and medium sized towns. Most have some air-conditioned rooms and attached showers. They are variable in quality but it is increasingly possible to find excellent value accommodation even in remote areas. | **Indian style hotels**

The Department of Tourism runs 16 hostels, each with about 50 beds, usually organized into dormitory accommodation. The YHA also have a few sites all over India. Travellers may also stay in religious hostels (*dharamshalas*) for up to three days. These are primarily intended for pilgrims and are sometimes free of charge though voluntary offerings are always welcome. Usually only vegetarian food is permitted; smoking and alcohol are not. | **Hostels**

Mid-price hotels with large grounds are sometimes willing to allow camping. Regional tourist offices have details of new developments. For information on YMCA camping facilities contact: YMCA, The National General Secretary, National Council of YMCAs of India, PB No 14, Massey Hall, Jai Singh Rd, New Delhi 1. | **Camping**

Getting around

Air

India has a comprehensive network linking the major cities of the different states. In addition to *Indian Airlines* (the nationalized carrier) www.nic.in/indianairlines and its subsidiary *Alliance Air*, there are several private airlines such as *Jet Airways* www.jetairways.com and *Sahara*, www.saharaairline.com which provide supplementary flights on several routes as well as filling gaps in a particular area, as with *Jagson*. Three more private airlines are due to commence operations in the domestic sector during 2001 – *Crown Air*, *North Star Aviation* and *Royal Airways*. Ask your

Essentials

travel agent for details of their services. Competition from the efficiently run private sector has, in general, improved the quality of services provided by the nationalized airlines. The airports authorities too have made efforts to improve handling on the ground.

Although flying is expensive (see individual cities for prices), for covering vast distances or awkward links on a route it is an option worth considering (though delays and re-routing can be irritating). However, for short distances, and on some routes (eg Delhi-Agra-Delhi) it makes more sense to travel by train.

Air tickets All the major airlines are connected to the central reservation system and there are local travel agents who will book your tickets for a fee if you don't want to spend precious time waiting in a queue. Remember that tickets are in great demand in the peak season on some sectors particularly between Rajasthan and Delhi (eg Udaipur- Delhi) so it is essential to get them months ahead. Some travellers have found it easier to book their return flight via Mumbai instead of Delhi. If you are able to pre-plan your trip, it is even possible to ask if the internal flights can be booked at the time you buy your international air ticket at home through an agent (eg *Trailfinders*, SD Enterprises, London) or direct (eg *Jet Airways*).

Payment Foreign passport holders buying air tickets in India must pay the 'US dollar rate' (higher than published Rupee rates) and pay in foreign exchange (major credit cards, travellers' cheques accepted), or in rupees against an encashment certificate which will be endorsed accordingly. There is very little difference in prices quoted by competing airlines.

Special fares *Indian Airlines*, www.indian-airlines/nic.in and *Jet Airways*, www.jetairways.com offer special 7, 15 and 21 day unlimited travel, deals from around US$300-750 (some are limited to one sector) which represent good savings. Youth fares 25% discount is given on US$ fares for anyone between 12 and 30 years. Night savers 25% discount fares are being introduced on late night flights between some metropolitan cities.

Delays Be prepared for delays, especially in North India during the winter. Nearly all northern routes originate in New Delhi, where from early December through to February, smog has become an increasingly common morning hazard, sometimes delaying departures by several hours. These delays then affect the whole northern system for the rest of that day.

Air travel tips **Security** *Indian Airlines* don't permit batteries in cabin baggage, and once confiscated, you may never see your batteries again. You may need to identify your baggage after they have been checked in and just before they are loaded onto the plane. All baggage destined for the hold must be X-rayed by security before check-in, so do this first on arrival at the airport.

Telephone There is a free telephone service at major airports (occasionally through the tourist office counter) to contact any hotel of your choice.

Wait-lists If you don't have a confirmed booking and are 'wait-listed' it pays to arrive early at the airport and be persistent in enquiring about your position.

Road

Road travel is often the only choice for reaching many of the places of outstanding interest in which India is so rich. For the uninitiated, travel by road can also be a worrying experience because of the apparent absence of conventional traffic regulations and also in the mountains, especially during the rainy season when landslides are possible. Vehicles drive on the left – in theory. Routes around the major cities are usually crowded with lorry traffic (especially at night), and the main roads are often poor and slow. There are few motorway-style expressways but most main roads are single carriageway. Some district roads are quiet, and although they are not fast they can be a good way of seeing the country and village life if you have the time.

Other than the national highways the roads within Rajasthan are not as well maintained as in most of Gujarat and the distances are long, but the state has good accommodation and it is even possible to make a trip staying at heritage hotels, travelling less than three to four hours a day.

Buses now reach virtually every part of India, offering a cheap, if often uncomfortable means of visiting places off the rail network. Very few villages are now more than 2 or 3 km from a bus stop. Services are run by the State Corporation from the State Bus Stand (and private companies which often have offices nearby). The latter allow advance reservation and though tickets prices are a little higher, they have fewer stops and are a bit more comfortable. **Bus**

There are three categories: **A/c luxury coaches**: Though comfortable for sight-seeing trips, apart from the very best 'sleeper coaches', even these can be very uncomfortable for really long journeys. Often the air conditioning is very cold, so wrap up warm! Journeys over 10 hours can be extremely tiring so it is better to go by train if there is a choice.

Express buses: Run over long distances (frequently overnight), these are often called 'video coaches' and can be an appalling experience unless you appreciate loud film music blasting through the night. Ear plugs and eye masks may ease the pain. They rarely average more than 45 km per hour.

Local buses: These are often very crowded, quite bumpy and slow and usually poorly maintained. However, over short distances, they can be a very cheap, friendly and easy way of getting about. Even where signboards are not in English someone will usually give you directions. Many larger towns have minibus services which charge a little more than the buses and pick up and drop passengers on request. Again very crowded, and with restricted headroom, they are the fastest way of getting about many of the larger towns.

Bus travel tips Some towns have different bus stations for different destinations. Booking on major long-distance routes is now computerized. Book in advance where possible and avoid the back of the bus where it can be very bumpy. If your destination is only served by a local bus you may do better to take the Express bus and 'persuade' the driver, with a tip in advance, to stop where you want to get off. You will have to pay the full fare to the first stop beyond your destination but you will get there faster and more comfortably. When an unreserved bus pulls into a bus station, there is usually an unholy scramble for seats, whilst those arriving have to struggle to get off! In many areas there is an unwritten 'rule of reservation' using handkerchiefs or bags thrust through the windows to reserve seats. Some visitors may feel a more justified right to a seat having fought their way through the crowd, but it is generally best to do as the local people do and be prepared with a handkerchief or 'sarong'. As soon as it touches the seat, it is yours!

A car provides a chance to travel off the beaten track, and gives unrivalled opportunities for seeing something of India's great variety of villages and small towns. Until recently the most widely used hire car was the Hindustan Ambassador. However, it is often very unreliable, and although they still have their devotees, many find them uncomfortable for long journeys. For a similar price, Maruti cars and vans (Omni) are much more reliable and comfortable, and are now the preferred choice in many areas. Gypsy 4WDs and Jeeps are also available, especially in the national parks and the desert. Maruti Esteems are comfortable and have optional reliable a/c, so are **Car** recommended in the hot weather. A specialist operator can be very helpful in arranging itineraries and car hire in advance.

Car hire, with a driver, is generally cheaper than in the West. A car shared by three or four can be very good value. Two or three-day trips from main towns can also give excellent opportunities for sightseeing off the beaten track in reasonable comfort. Local drivers often know their way much better than drivers from other states, so where possible it is a good idea to get a local driver who speaks the state language, in addition to being able to communicate with you. Drivers may sleep in the car overnight, though hotels sometimes provide a bed for them. You are responsible for all their expenses, including their meals. A tip at the end of the tour of Rs 100 per day in addition to their daily allowance is perfectly acceptable. Check beforehand if fuel and inter-state taxes are included in the hire charge. Be sure to check carefully the mileage at the beginning and end of the trip.

Cars can be hired through private companies. International companies such as *Hertz*, *Europcar* and *Budget* operate in some major cities and offer reliable cars; their rates are generally higher than those of local firms, eg *Sai Service*, *Wheels*). The price of an imported car can be three times that of the Ambassador.

Car hire rates

Economy car with driver	Regular a/c Maruti 800 Ambassador	Premium a/c Maruti 800 Ambassador	Luxury a/c Maruti 1000 Contessa	Esteem Opel etc
8 hrs/80 km	Rs 800	Rs 1,000	Rs 1,400	Rs 1,800+
Extra km	Rs 4-7	Rs 9	Rs 13	Rs 18
Extra hour	Rs 40	Rs 50	Rs 70	Rs 100
Out of town				
Per km	Rs 7	Rs 9	Rs 13	Rs 18
Night halt	Rs 100	Rs 200	Rs 250	Rs 250

Importing a car Tourists may import their own vehicles into India with a Carnet de Passage (Triptyques) issued by any recognized automobile association or club affiliated to the Alliance Internationale de Tourisme in Geneva.

Self-drive Car hire is still in its infancy and many visitors may find the road conditions difficult and sometimes dangerous. If you drive yourself it is essential to take great care. Pedestrians, cattle and a wide range of other animals roam at will. This can be particularly dangerous when driving after dark especially as even other vehicles often carry no lights.

When booking emphasize the importance of good tyres & general roadworthiness **Car travel tips Fuel**: On main roads across India petrol stations are reasonably frequent, but some areas are poorly served. Some service stations only have diesel pumps though they may have small reserves of petrol. Always carry a spare can. Diesel is widely available and normally much cheaper than petrol. Petrol is rarely above 92 octane. **Insurance**: Drivers must have third party insurance. This may have to be with an Indian insurer, or with a foreign insurer who has a national guarantor. You must also be in possession of an 'International Driving Permit', issued by a recognised driving authority in your home country (eg the AA in the UK, apply at least six weeks before leaving). **Asking the way**: Can be very frustrating as you are likely to get widely conflicting advice each time you stop to ask. On the main roads, 'mile' posts periodically appear in English and can help. Elsewhere, it is best to ask directions often. **Accidents**: Often produce large and angry crowds very quickly. It is best to leave the scene of the

The hazards of road travel

On most routes it is impossible to average more than 50-60 kph in a car. Journeys are often very long, and can seem an endless succession of horn blowing, unexpected dangers and unforeseen delays. Villages are often congested – beware of the concealed spine-breaking speed bumps – and cattle, sheep and goats may wander at will across the road. Directions can also be difficult to find.

Drivers frequently don't know the way, maps are often hopelessly inaccurate and map reading is an almost entirely unknown skill. Training in driving is negligible and the test often a farce. You will note a characteristic side-saddle posture, one hand constantly on the horn, but there can be real dangers from poor judgement, irresponsible overtaking and a general philosophy of 'might is right'.

Essentials

accident and report it to the police as quickly as possible thereafter. **Provisions**: Ensure that you have adequate food and drink, and a basic tool set in the car.

The *Automobile Association* offers a range of services to members. In New Delhi, AA of Upper India, Lilaram Bldg, 14F Connaught Place. In Mumbai, Western India AA, Lalji Narainji Memorial Bldg, 76, Vir Nariman Rd.

'Yellow-top' taxis in cities and large towns are metered although tariffs change fre- **Taxi** quently. These changes are shown on a fare chart which should be read in conjunction with the meter reading. Increased night time rates apply in some cities, and there is a small charge for luggage, insist on the taxi meter being 'flagged' in your presence. If the driver refuses, the official advice is to call the police. This may not work, but it is worth trying. When a taxi doesn't have a meter, you will need to fix the fare before starting the journey. Ask at the hotel desk for a guide price.

Taxi tips At stations and airports it is often possible to share taxis to a central point. It is worth looking for fellow passengers who may be travelling in your direction and get a pre-paid taxi. At night, always have a clear idea of where you want to go and insist on being taken there. Taxi drivers may try to convince you that the hotel you have chosen 'closed three years ago', is 'completely full' or is an 'unsafe den'. You may have to say that you have an advance reservation. See individual city entries for more details.

Auto-rickshaws ('autos') are almost universally available in towns across India and are **Rickshaws** the cheapest convenient way of getting about. In addition to using them for short jour- *It is best to walk a* neys it is often possible to hire them by the hour, or for a half or full day's sight-seeing. *short distance away* In some areas younger drivers who speak some English and know their local area well, *from a hotel gate* may want to show you around. However, rickshaw drivers are often paid a commission *before picking up an* by hotels, restaurants and gift shops, so advice is not always impartial. Drivers some- *auto to avoid paying* times refuse to use a meter, quote a ridiculous price or attempt to stop short of your *an inflated rate* destination. If you have real problems it can help to threaten to go to the police.

Chhakras One of the most distinctive features of Gujarat's transport is the ubiquitous *chhakra* or *chhagra*. This hybrid motorbike cum autorickshaw has evolved out of its old Enfield engine and chassis to a completely new three wheeled vehicle. A diesel Kirloskar tubewell pump engine has replaced the petrol driven 'Enfield' while the old gear box has been retained, along with its chassis. However, Bullet motorcycle springs have been added, designed to allow the chhakra to take 500 kg of goods. Licensed only for the transport of freight, throughout Gujarat they have become one of the commonest means of passenger transport.

Cycle-rickshaws and horse-drawn tongas These are more common in the more rustic setting of a small town or the outskirts of a large one. You will need to fix a price by bargaining. The animal attached to a tonga usually looks too undernourished to have the strength to pull the driver, leave alone passengers.

Cycling

You are usually not far from a 'puncture wallah' who can make minor repairs cheaply

Cycling is an excellent way of seeing the quiet by-ways of India and is particularly enjoyable if you travel with a companion. It is easy to hire bikes in most small towns from about Rs 20 per day. Indian bikes are heavy and without gears, but on the flat they offer a good way of exploring comparatively short distances outside towns. In the more prosperous tourist resorts, mountain bikes are now becoming available, but at a higher hire charge. It is also quite possible to tour more extensively and you may then want to buy a cycle.

Buying a bicycle There are shops in every town and the local Raleighs are considered the best, with Atlas and BSA good alternatives; expect to pay around Rs 1,200-1,500 for a second-hand Indian bike but remember to bargain. At the end of your trip you can usually sell it quite easily at half that price. Imported bikes have the advantage of lighter weight and gears, but are more difficult to get repaired, and carry the much greater risk of being stolen or damaged. If you wish to take your own, it is quite easy if you dismantle it and pack it in its original shipping carton. Be sure to take all essential spares including a pump. All cyclists should take bungy cords (to strap down a back-pack) and good lights from home, although cycling at night is not recommended; take care not to leave your machine parked anywhere with your belongings though. Bike repair shops are universal and charges are nominal.

It is possible to cover 50 to 80 km a day quite comfortably – "the National Highways are manic but country roads, especially along the coast, can be idyllic, if rather dusty and bumpy". You can even put your bike on a boat for the backwater trip or on top of a bus. Should you wish to take your bike on the train, allow plenty of time for booking it in on the brake van at the Parcels office, and for filling in forms.

It is best to start a journey early in the morning, stop at mid-day and resume cycling in the late afternoon. Night-riding, though cooler, can be hazardous because of lack of lighting and poor road surfaces. Try to avoid the major highways as far as possible. Fortunately foreign cyclists are usually greeted with cheers, waves and smiles and truck drivers are sometimes happy to give lifts to cyclists (and their bikes). This is a good way of taking some of the hardship out of cycling round India.

Motorcycling Motorcycling across India is particularly attractive for bike enthusiasts. It is easy to buy new Indian-made motorcycles including the Enfield Bullet and several 100cc Japanese models, including Suzukis and Hondas made in collaboration with Indian firms. Buying new ensures greater reliability and fixed price – (Indian Rajdoots are less expensive but have a poor reputation for reliability). Buying second hand in Rupees takes more time but is quite possible; expect to get a 30-40% discount. You can get a broker to help with the paper-work involved (certificate of ownership, insurance etc) for a fee. They charge about Rs 5,000 for a 'No Objection Certificate' (NOC) which is essential for resell-ing; it is easier to have the bike in your name.

When selling, don't be in a hurry, and only negotiate with "ready cash" buyers. A black bike is easier to sell than a coloured one! Repairs are usually easy to arrange and quite cheap. Bring your own helmet and an International Driving Permit.

Peter and Friends Classic Adventures, an Indo-German company based in Goa at Casa Tres Amigos, Socol Vado 425, Assagao (4 km west on Anjuna road), T0832-273351, F276124, includes organized motorbike tours in Rajasthan, ranging from four days to three weeks. *Chandertal Tours & Himalayan Folkways*, based in the UK, includes Royal Enfield tours of Rajasthan. Contact 20 The Fridays, East Dean,

Eastbourne, East Sussex, BN20 0DH, UK, T00-911323422213, www.steali.co.uk/india
For good information on biking tours in Rajasthan, try www.aventuremoto.com,
asia_bike_tours@hotmail.com and motoraid@yahoo.com

Hitchhiking is uncommon in India, partly because public transport is so cheap. If you   **Hitchhiking**
try, you are likely to spend a very long time on the roadside. However, getting a lift on
motorbikes/scooters and on trucks in areas with little public transport can be worthwhile. It is not recommended for women on their own.

Train

Essentials

Trains can still be the cheapest and most comfortable means of travelling long dis-   *See map on page 479*
tances saving you hotel expenses on overnight journeys. It gives access to booking station Retiring Rooms, which can be useful from time to time. Above all, you have an
ideal opportunity to meet local travellers and catch a glimpse of life on the ground
although the dark glass fitted on a/c coaches does restrict vision.

There are over 170 air-conditioned 'high-speed' *Shatabdi* (or 'Century') for day travel,   **High-speed**
and *Rajdhani Express* ('Capital City') for overnight journeys. These cover large sections   **trains**
of the network but as they are in high demand you need to book them up to 60 days
ahead. Meals and drinks are usually included.

You can travel like a maharaja on the *New Palace on Wheels* which gives visitors an   **Royal trains**
opportunity to see some of the 'royal' cities in Rajasthan during the winter months for
around US$250 a day (see page 47). The diesel *Palace on Wheels* has been widely publi-
cized. Weekly departures (Wednesday) from Delhi, from October to mid-April. The itin-
erary includes Jaipur and Amber Fort, followed by overnight travel to Chittaurgarh,
Udaipur (*Lake Palace Hotel*), Jaisalmer, Jodhpur (*Umaid Bhawan Palace*) and Bharatpur
ending with visits to Fatehpur Sikri, Agra and Delhi. It is a well packaged but rather
compressed taster for some of the key sites. Travelling by night means that you don't
see much of the countryside.
  The *Royal Orient* is Gujarat's answer to the famous *Palace on Wheels*. It uses the
metre-gauge carriages no longer needed in Rajasthan, and runs an eight-night tour
from Delhi visiting Chittaurgarh, Udaipur, Junagadh, Somnath, Sasan Gir, Diu,
Palitana, Ahmadabad and Jaipur. There are guided visits on a/c coaches. Conversions
mean comfortable, well-fitted cabins with baths shared between two, attractive dining
saloons serving delicious Indian-western food, a bar and library – a regal experience
with polite, turbaned staff. Contact **The Royal Orient**, A/6 Emporia Building, Baba Kharak
Singh Marg, New Delhi, T3364724, F3734015, tcgl.del@rmt.sprintrpg.emvsnl.net.in
  The oldest working **steam** engine, *Fairy Queen* built in 1855, has been commissioned to run a weekend tour for 50 passengers, twice a month in the winter. It starts
in Delhi and visits Sariska Tiger Sanctuary (transfer by road from Alwar, and costs Rs
8,000). Contact in New Delhi: National Rail Museum, T6881816, F6880804,
www.icindia.com/fairy

A/c First Class, available only on main routes and cheaper than flying, is very comfort-   Classes
able (bedding provided). It will also be possible for tourists to reserve special coaches
(some a/c) which are normally allocated to senior railway officials only. **A/c Sleeper**,
two and three-tier, are clean and comfortable and good value. **A/c Executive Class**,
with wide reclining seats are available on many *Shatabdi* trains at double the price of
the ordinary **a/c Chair Car** which are equally comfortable. **Second Class** (non-a/c) two
and three-tier, provides exceptionally cheap travel but can be crowded and uncomfortable, and toilet facilities can be unpleasant. It is nearly always better to use the
Indian style toilets as they are better maintained.

Riding the rails

High class, comfortable, and by Indian standards quick new Express trains have brought many journeys within daytime reach. But while they offer an increasingly functional means of covering long distances in comfort, it is the overnight trips which still retain something of the early feel of Indian train travel. The bedding carefully prepared – and now available on a/c Second Class trains – the

early morning light illuminating another stretch of hazy Indian landscape, the spontaneous conversations with fellow travellers – these are still on offer, giving a value far beyond the still modest prices. Furthermore, India still has a complete guide to its rail timetables. The Trains at a Glance *available at stations (Rs 25) lists all important trains.*

Indrail passes These allow travel across the network without having to pay extra reservation fees and sleeper charges but you have to spend a high proportion of your time on the train to make it worthwhile (see boxes). However, the advantages of pre-arranged reservations and automatic access to 'Tourist Quotas' can tip the balance in their favour for some travellers.

Tourists (foreigners and Indians resident abroad) may buy these passes for periods ranging from seven to 90 days from the tourist sections of principal railway booking offices, and pay in foreign currency, major credit cards, travellers' cheques or rupees with encashment certificates. Rail-cum-air tickets are also to be made available.

Indrail passes can also conveniently be bought abroad from special agents. For most people contemplating a single long journey soon after arriving in India, the Half or One day Pass with a confirmed reservation is worth the peace of mind; 2 or 4 Day Passes are also sold. The **UK** agent is *SD Enterprises Ltd*, 103, Wembley Park Drive, Wembley, Middx HA9 8HG, England, T020-89033411, F89030392, dandpani@dircon.co.uk They make all necessary reservations and offer excellent advice. They can also book *Indian Airlines* and *Jet Airways* internal flights. Other **international agents** are: **Australia**: *Adventure World*, PO Box 480, North Sydney NSW 2060, T9587766, F9567707. **Canada**: *Hari World Travels*, 1 Financial Place, 1 Adelaide St East, Concou Level, Toronto, T0416-3662000, F3666020. **Denmark**: *Danish State Railways*, DSW Travel Agency Div, Reventlowsgade – 10, DK 1651 Kobenhaven V. **Finland**: *Intia-Keskus*, Yrjonkatu 8-10, 00120 Helsinki, Finland, T46856-266000, F100946. **France**: *Le Monde de L'Inde et de L'Asie*, 15 Rue Des Ecoles, Paris 75005. **Germany**: *Asra-Orient*, Kaiserstrasse 50, D-6000 Frankfurt/M, T069253098, F69232045, asra-orient@t-online-d **Hong Kong**: *Cheung Hung*, B1&2 Carnarvon Mansion, 12 Carnarvon Rd, Tisimshatsui, Kowloon, Hong Kong, T852-2369-5333, F2739-9899. **Israel**: *Teshet*, 32 Ben Yehuda St, Tel Aviv 63805, T6290972, F6295126. **Japan**: *Japan Travel Bureau*, Overseas Travel Div, 1-6-4 Marunouchi, Chiyoda-ku, Tokyo-100, T031-284739. **Malaysia**: *City East West Travels*, 23 Jalan Yapah Shak, 50300, Kuala Lumpur, T2930569, F2989214. **South Africa**: *MK Bobby Naidoo*, PO Box 2878, Durban, T3094710. **Thailand**: *SS Travel*, 10/12-13 Convent Rd, SS Building, Bangkok, T2367188, F2367186. **USA**: *Hari World Travels*, 25W 45th St, 1003, New York, NY 10036, T9573000, F9973320.

A White Pass allows first class a/c travel; a Green, a/c two-tier Sleepers and Chair Cars; and the Yellow, only second class travel. Passes up to four days' duration are only sold abroad.

Cost A/c first class costs about double the rate for two-tier shown below, and non a/c second class about half. Children (five to 12) travel at half the adult fare. The young (12-30)

Train touts

Many railway stations – and some bus stations and major tourist sites – are heavily populated with touts. Self-styled 'agents' will board trains before they enter the station and seek out tourists, often picking up their luggage and setting off with words such as "Madam!/Sir! Come with me madam/sir! You need top class hotel ..." They will even select porters to take your luggage without giving you any say. If you have succeeded in getting off the train or even in obtaining a trolley you will find hands eager to push it for you. For a

first time visitor such touts can be more than a nuisance. You need to keep calm and firm. Decide in advance where you want to stay. If you need a porter on trains, select one yourself and agree a price **before** the porter sets off with your baggage. If travelling with a companion one can stay guarding the luggage while the other gets hold of a taxi and negotiates the price to the hotel. It sounds complicated, and sometimes it feels it. The most important thing is to behave as if you know what you are doing!

and senior citizens (65+) are allowed a 30% discount on journeys over 500 km (just show passport).

Period	A/c 2-tier US$	Period	A/c 2-tier US$
½ day	26	21 days	198
1 day	43	30 days	248
7 days	135	60 days	400
15 days	185	90 days	530

Fares for individual journeys are based on distance covered and reflect both the class and the type of train. Higher rates apply on the Mail and Express trains and the air conditioned *Shatabdi* and *Rajdhani Expresses*.

Food and drink It is best to carry some though tea and snacks are sold on the platforms (through the windows). Carry plenty of small notes and coins on long journeys. Rs 50 and Rs 100 notes can be difficult to change when purchasing small food items. On long distance trains, the restaurant car is often near the upper class bogies (carriages).

Rail travel tips

Timetables Regional timetables are available cheaply from station bookstalls; the monthly 'Indian Bradshaw' is sold in principal stations, while the handy 'Trains at a Glance' (Rs 25) lists popular trains likely to be used by most foreign travellers. The latter is available from reservation offices in the larger cities (ask at the tourist counter first). For those planning extensive travel by train it is recommended that a copy is purchased at the earliest opportunity.

Delays Always allow plenty of time for booking and for making connections. Delays are common on all types of transport. The special *Shatabdi and Rajdhani Express* are generally quite reliable. Ordinary Express and Mail trains have priority over local services and occasionally surprise by being punctual, but generally the longer the journey time, the greater the delay. Delays on the rail network are cumulative, so arrivals and departures from mid-stations are often several hours behind schedule. Allow at least 2 hours for connections, more if the first part of the journey is long distance.

Tickets You can save a lot of time and effort by asking a travel agent to get yours for a small fee, usually around Rs 25-50. Non-Indrail Pass tickets can be bought over the counter. It is always best to book as far in advance as possible (usually up to 60 days). Avoid touts at the station offering tickets, hotels or money changing.

Ladies' queues Separate (much shorter) ticket queues may be available for women.

Quotas A large number of seats are technically reserved as 'quotas' for various groups of travellers (civil servants, military personnel, foreign tourists etc). In addition, many stations have their own quota for particular trains so that a train may be 'fully booked' when there are still some tickets available from the special quota of other stations. These are only sold on the day of departure so wait-listed passengers are often able to travel at the last minute. Ask the Superintendent on duty to try the 'Special' or 'VIP Quota'. The 'Tatkal' system realeases a small percentage of seats at 0800 on the day before a train departs; you pay an extra Rs 50 to get on an otherwise heavily booked train.

Reservations Ask for the separate Tourist Quota counter at main stations, and while queuing fill up the Reservation Form which requires the number, name, departure time of the train, and the passenger's name, age and sex; you can use one form for up to four passengers. If you don't have a reservation for a particular train but carry an Indrail Pass, you may get one by arriving about three hours early. Remember that Tourist Quota tickets must be paid for in foreign currency, so have an exchange certificate (and your passport) handy. It is possible to buy tickets for trains on most routes countrywide at many of the 520 computerised reservation centres across India.

Porters Carry prodigious amounts of luggage. Rates vary from station to station but are usually around Rs 5 per item of luggage (board on the station platform). They can be quite aggressive particularly on the main tourist routes: be firm but polite and remember that they will always leave the train when it pulls out of the station!

Getting a seat It is usually impossible to make seat reservations at small 'intermediate' stations as they don't have an allocation. You can sometimes use a porter to get you a seat in a 2nd class carriage. For about Rs 20 he will take the luggage and ensure that you get a seat!

Berths It is worth asking for upper berths, especially in second class three-tier sleepers, as they can also be used during the day time when the lower berths are used as seats, and which may only be used for lying down after 2100.

Overbooking Passengers with valid tickets but no berth reservations are sometimes permitted to travel overnight, causing great discomfort to travellers occupying lower berths. Wait-listed passengers should confirm the status of their ticket in advance by calling enquiries at the nearest computerised reservation office. At the station, check the reservation charts (usually on the relevant platform) and contact the Station Manager or Ticket Collector.

Bedding Travelling at night in the winter can be very cold in North India and in a/c coaches. Bedding is provided on second class a/c sleepers. On others it can be hired for Rs 20 from the Station Manager for first class.

Ladies' compartments A woman travelling alone, overnight, on an unreserved second class train can ask if there is one of these.

Security Keep valuables close to you, securely locked, and away from windows. For security, carry a good lock and chain to attach your luggage. There are usually metal loops under the lower berth for this purpose.

Left-luggage Bags left in station cloakrooms must be lockable. Don't leave any food in them. These are especially useful when there is time to sight-see before an evening train, although luggage can be left for up to 30 days.

Pre-paid taxis Many main stations have a pre-paid taxi (or auto-rickshaw) service which offers a reliable, fair-price service. Give your receipt to the driver upon reaching the destination.

Keeping in touch

Communications

Access is becoming increasingly available in major cities and tourist centres as cyber **Internet**
cafés mushroom and PCOs (Public Call Office) are beginning to offer the service, but in
small towns the machines can be woefully slow. Internet access is spreading wider to
reach remote areas, and is becoming faster year by year. As access improves, surfing
charges fall, ranging from Rs 100 per hour (US$2.50) in remote places and some hotels
to as little as Rs 25 (US$0.50) in big towns.

The post is frequently unreliable and delays are common. It is advisable to use a post **Post**
office where it is possible to hand over mail for franking across the counter, or a top
hotel post box. Valuable items should only be sent by **Registered Mail**. Government
Emporia or shops in the larger hotels will send purchases home if the items are difficult
to carry. **Airmail** service to Europe, Africa and Australia takes at least a week and a little
longer for the Americas. **Speed post** (which takes about four days to the UK) is available from major towns. Specialist shippers deal with larger items, normally approximately US$150 per cubic metre. **Courier services** (eg *DHL*) are available in the larger
towns. At some main post offices you can send small packages under 2 kg as Letter Post
(rather than parcel post) which is much cheaper at Rs 220. 'Book Post' (for printed paper)
is cheaper still, approximately Rs 170 for 5 kg. Book parcels must be sewn in cloth (best
over see-through plastic) with a small open 'window' slit for contents to be seen.

Parcels Check that the post office holds necessary customs declaration forms *The process can*
(two/three copies needed). Write 'No commercial value' if returning used clothes, *take up to 2 hrs!*
books etc. Air mail is expensive; sea mail slow but reasonable (10 kg, Rs 800). 'Packers'
outside post offices will do all necessary cloth covering, sealing etc for Rs 20-50; you
address the parcel, obtain stamps from a separate counter; stick stamps and one customs form to the parcel with glue available (the other form/s must be partially sewn
on). Post at the Parcels Counter and obtain a Registration slip. **Maximum dimen-
sions**: Height 1 m, width 0.8 m, circumference 1.8 m. **Cost**: Sea mail Rs 775 for first kilogram, Rs 70 each extra kilogram. Air mail also Rs 775 first kilogram, Rs 200 each subsequent kilogram.

Warning Many people complain that private shops offering a postal service actually
send cheap substitutes. It is usually too late to complain when the buyer finds out. It is
best to buy your item and then get it packed and posted yourself.

Poste restante facilities Widely available in even quite small towns at the GPO where
mail is held for one month. Ask for mail to be addressed to you with your surname in capitals and underlined. When asking for mail at Poste Restante check under surname as
well as Christian name. Any special issue foreign stamps are likely to be stolen from enve-
lopes in the Indian postal service and letters may be thrown away. Advise people who are
sending you mail to India to use only definitive stamps (without pictures).

International Direct Dialling is now widely available in privately run call 'booths', usu- **Telephone**
ally labelled on yellow boards with the letters 'PCO-STD-ISD'. You dial the call yourself, *International code:*
and the time and cost are displayed on a computer screen. They are by far the best *00 91. Phone codes for*
places from which to telephone abroad. Cheap rate (2100-0600) means long queues *towns are printed*
may form outside booths. Telephone calls from hotels are usually much more expen- *after the town name*
sive (check price before calling). One disadvantage of the tremendous pace of the

Essentials

 ## The email explosion

As the internet shrinks the world, travellers are increasingly using emails to keep in touch with home. Their free accounts are invariably with **hotmail.com**, **yahoo.com**, **email.com** or **backpackers.com**; usually the less common the provider, the quicker the access.

India has its own set of problems which can be frustrating: very few machines which may also be out-dated; untrained staff and poor technical support; the server may be unreliable; the system may be clogged with users, especially during day; there may be frequent power cuts ... There are exceptions, of course.

New offices are opening weekly and new towns are getting connected. To track down the most reliable and best value internet service, ask other travellers. The length of the queue can be a good indicator. On the web, you can get a list from **www.netcafeguide.com** Don't always head for the cheapest since they may also have the oldest and slowest

equipment. Rates vary, but in mid-1999, it cost around Rs 50 for 30 minutes.

Hot tips
■ Use the folder facility to save mail
■ Keep your in-box clear to reduce loading time
■ Avoid junk mail by not giving your address to on-line companies
■ Avoid downloading and using scanned pictures and documents
■ Save files and back up regularly

The system can be efficient and satisfying but it can also become an expensive habit with more than its fair share of frustrations. As one sending an email to us mused, "many a hard-up traveller will wax lyrical about 'getting away from it all' and escaping 'the pressure of western society'. They will then spend hours and several hundred rupees a week slaving over a computer keyboard in some hot and sticky back street office".

telecommunications revolution is the fact that millions of telephone numbers go out of date every year. Current telephone directories themselves are often out of date and some of the numbers given in the Handbook will have been changed even as we go to press. Directory enquiries, **197**, can be helpful but works only for the local area code. **Ringing tone**: Double ring, repeated regularly. **Engaged**: Equal length, on and off. Both are similar to UK ringing and engaged tones.

Fax services are available from many PCOs and larger hotels, who charge either by the minute or per page.

Media

Newspapers   International newspapers (mainly English language) are sold in the bookshops of top hotels in major cities, and occasionally by booksellers elsewhere. India has a large English language press. They all have extensive analysis of contemporary Indian and some international issues. The major papers now have internet sites which are excellent for keeping daily track on events, news and weather. The best known are: **The Hindu**, www.hinduonline.com/today/, **The Hindustan Times** www.hindustantimes.com, **The Independent**, **The Times of India** www.timesofindia.com/ and **The Statesman** www.thestatesman.org/ **The Economic Times** is possibly the best for independent reporting and world coverage. **The Telegraph**, published in Kolkata, www.telegraphindia.com/ has good foreign coverage. **The Indian Express**, www.expressindia.com/ has stood out as being consistently critical of the Congress Party and Government. **The Asian Age** is now published in the UK and India simultaneously and gives good coverage of Indian and international affairs. Of the fortnightly magazines, some of the most widely read are **Sunday**, **India Today** and **Frontline**, all

Best short-wave frequencies

BBC World service *Signal strength varies throughout the day, with lower frequencies better during the night. The nightly "South Asia Report" offers up to the minute reports covering the sub-continent. Try 15310, 17790 or 1413, 5975, 11955, 17630, 17705. More information on www.bbc.uk/ worldservice/sasia*

Voice of America *1400-1800 GMT; 1575, 6110, 7125, 9645, 9700, 9760, 15255, 15395 Mhz. www.voa.gov/sasia*

Deutsche Welle *0600-1800 GMT; 6075, 9545, 17845; other frequencies include 17560, 12000 and 21640.*

of which are current affairs journals on the model of Time or Newsweek. To check weather conditions, try www.wunderground.com

India's national radio and television network, *Doordarshan*, broadcasts in national and regional languages but things have moved on. The advent of satellite TV has hit even remote rural areas. The 'Dish' can help travellers keep in touch through Star TV from Hong Kong (accessing BBC World, CNN etc), VTV (music) and Sport, now available even in some modest hotels in the smallest of towns. The decision by the government to issue more licences to satellite broadcasters in 2001 will result in up to 50 available channels, from MTV to Maharishi Veda Vision!

Television & radio

Food and drink

You find just as much variety in dishes and presentation crossing India as you would on an equivalent journey across Europe. Combinations of spices give each region its distinctive flavour.

Food
See page 443 for further details

The larger hotels, open to non-residents, often offer **buffet** lunches with Indian, Western and sometimes Chinese dishes. These can be good value (Rs 250-300; but around Rs 450 in the top grades) and can provide a welcome, comfortable break in the cool. The health risks, however, of food kept warm for long periods in metal containers are considerable, especially if turnover at the buffet is slow. We have received several complaints of stomach trouble following a buffet meal, even in five star hotels.

It is essential to be very careful since food hygiene may be poor, flies abound and refrigeration in the hot weather may be inadequate and intermittent because of power cuts. It is best to eat only freshly prepared food by ordering from the menu (especially meat and fish dishes); avoid salads and cut fruit.

If you are unused to spicy food, go slow! Stick to Western or mild Chinese meals in good restaurants, and try the odd Indian dish to test your reaction. Those used to Indian spices may choose to be more adventurous. Popular local restaurants are obvious from the number of people eating in them. Try a traditional *thali*, which is a complete meal served on a large stainless steel plate (or very occasionally on a banana leaf). Several preparations, placed in small bowls, surround the central serving of wholewheat *chapati* and rice. A vegetarian *thali* would include *daal* (lentils), two or three curries (which can be quite hot), and crisp poppadums, although there are regional variations. A variety of pickles are offered – mango and lime are two of the most popular. These can be exceptionally hot, and are designed to be taken in minute quantities alongside the main dishes. Plain *dahi* (yoghurt), or *raita*, usually acts as a bland 'cooler'.

Rajasthani cuisine Rajasthani food varies regionally between the arid desert districts and the greener eastern areas. Typical dishes are *Daal-Bhatti-Choorma*, little breads full of clarified butter roasted over hot coals served with a dry, flaky sweet made of gram flour, and *Ker-Sangri* made with a desert fruit and beans.

Millets, lentils and beans are basic ingredients. *Sogra* (thick and rather heavy millet *chapatis*) and *makkai ka roti* (maize flour *chapatis*) are very popular, served with *ghee*. Game (wild boar, fowl) feature in local non-vegetarian dishes. *Sohita* (mutton cooked with millet), *sulla* (mutton *kebabs* which have been marinated in piquant vegetables and cooked over charcoal), *Khud kharghosh* (rabbit), *Ker kumidai saliria* (beans with cumin and chillies) are also favourites. *Mawa-ki-kachori* is a particularly rich dessert consisting of pastry stuffed with nuts and coconut and smothered in syrup. *Halwas* and *kheer* (made with thickened milk) are other favourite sweets.

Gujarati cuisine Whilst Gujarat has a long coastline and an almost endless supply of fish and shellfish, strict Jainism in the past and orthodox Hinduism today have encouraged the widespread adoption of a vegetarian diet. Gujaratis base their diet on rice, wholemeal *chapati*, a wide variety of beans and pulses which are rich in protein, and coconut and pickles. A *thali* would include all these, the meal ending with sweetened yoghurt. The dishes themselves are not heavily spiced, though somewhat sweeter than those of neighbouring Rajasthan. Kathiawadi food is less sweet, more spicy and stronger on ginger and garlic than in the rest of Gujarat. Popular dishes include: *kadhi*, a savoury yoghurt curry with chopped vegetables and a variety of spices; *undhyoo*, a combination of potatoes, sweet potatoes, aubergines (egg plants) and beans cooked in an earthenware pot; Surat *paunk* made with tender kernels of millet, sugar balls, savoury twists and garlic chutney. Eating freshly prepared vegetable snacks from street vendors is popular. A large variety of *ganthia* or *farsan* (light savoury snacks prepared from chickpea and wheat flour) is a speciality in the state. Desserts are very sweet. Surat specializes in *gharis* made with butter, dried fruits and thickened milk, and rich *halwa*. *Srikhand* is saffron-flavoured yoghurt with fruit and nuts. Unusual village theme restaurants around Ahmadabad like *Vishala* and *Rajwadu* offer traditional rural cuisine in simple but atmospheric surroundings.

Western food Many city restaurants offer some so-called European options such as toasted sandwiches, stuffed pancakes, apple pies, crumbles and cheese cakes. Italian favourites (pizzas, pastas) can be very different from what you are used to. Western confectionery, in general, is disappointing. Ice creams, on the other hand, can be exceptionally good. There are excellent Indian ones as well as international brands such as *Cadbury's* and *Walls*.

Fruit India has many delicious tropical fruits. Some are highly seasonal (eg mangoes, pineapples and lychees), while others (eg bananas, grapes, oranges) are available throughout the year. It is safe to eat the ones you can wash and peel.

Drink **Drinking water** Used to be regarded as one of India's biggest hazards. It is still true that water from the tap or a well should never be considered safe to drink since public water supplies are often polluted. Bottled water is now widely available although not all bottled water is mineral water, some is simply purified water from an urban supply. Buy from a shop or stall, check the seal carefully (some companies now add a second clear plastic seal around the bottle top) and avoid street hawkers; when disposing bottles puncture the neck which prevents misuse but allows recycling for storage. There is growing concern over the mountains of plastic bottles that are collecting and the waste of resources to produce them, so travellers are encouraged to use alternative methods of getting safe drinking water. You may wish to purify water yourselves (see

A cup of chai!

Not long ago, when you stopped at a road side tea stall nearly anywhere in India and asked for a cup of chai, the steaming hot sweet tea would be poured out into your very own, finely handthrown, beautifully shaped clay cup! Similarly, whenever a train drew into a railway station, almost any time of day or night, and you heard the familiar loud call of "chai garam, garam chai!" go past your window, you could have the tea served to you in your own porous clay cup.

True, it made the tea taste rather earthy but it added to the romance of travelling. Best of all, when you had done with it, you threw it away and it would shatter to bits on the road side (or down on the railway track) – returning 'earth to earth'. It was the

eco-friendly "disposable" cup of old – no question of an unwashed cup which someone else had drunk out of, hence unpolluted and 'clean'. And, of course, it was good business for the potter.

But, time moves on, and we have now advanced to tea stalls that prefer thick glass tumblers (which leave you anxious when you glance down at the murky rinsing water). A step ahead – those catering for the transient customer now offer the welcome hot chai in an understandably convenient, light, hygienic, easy-to-stack, thin plastic cup which one gets the world over, sadly lacking the biodegradability of the earthen pot. With the fast disappearing terracotta cup we will lose a tiny bit of the magic of travelling in India.

Essentials

'Health' below). A portable water filter is a good option, carrying the drinking water in a plastic bottle in an insulated carrier. Always carry enough drinking water with you when travelling. It is important to use pure water for cleaning teeth.

Hot drinks Tea and coffee are safe and widely available. Both are normally served sweet and with milk. If you wish, say 'no sugar' (*chini nahin*), 'no milk' (*dudh nahin*) when ordering. Alternatively, ask for a pot of tea, and milk and sugar to be brought separately. Freshly brewed coffee is a common drink in South India, but in the North, ordinary city restaurants will usually serve the instant variety. Even in aspiring smart cafés, *Espresso* or *Capuccino* may not turn out quite as one would expect in the West.

Soft drinks Bottled carbonated drinks such as 'Coke', 'Pepsi', 'Teem' and 'Gold Spot' are universally available but always check the seal when you buy from a street stall. There are now also several brands of fruit juice sold in cartons, including mango, pineapple and apple. Don't add ice cubes as the water source may be contaminated. Take care with fresh fruit juices or *lassis* as ice is often added (partly to reduce the amount of liquid given and thus increase profits!). Juice stalls often charge an extra rupee for drinks without ice.

Alcohol Indians rarely drink alcohol with a meal, water being on hand. In the past, wines and spirits were generally either imported and extremely expensive, or local and of poor quality. Now, the best Indian whisky, rum and brandy (IMFL or 'Indian Made Foreign Liquor') are widely accepted, as are good Champagneoise and other wines from Maharashtra. If you hanker after a bottle of imported wine, you will only find it in the top restaurants and have to pay Rs 800-1,000 at least. For the urban elite, cooling Indian beers are popular when eating out and so are widely available, though you may need to check the 'chill' value. The 'English Pub' has appeared in the major cities, where the foreign traveller too would feel comfortable. Seedy, all male drinking dens in the larger cities are perhaps best avoided. Head for the better hotel bar instead. In rural India, local rice, palm, cashew or date juice *toddy* and *arak* should be treated with great caution!

For liquor permits, see page 27

☞ Two masala dosai and a pot of tea!

A traveller reported that a hotel bar prohibition has had some unexpected results. One traveller to Ooty reported that the hotel bar had closed, apparently permanently. He found however that it was still possible to obtain alcoholic drinks from the restaurant. Having ordered and been served a beer, he was intrigued that when the bill came it was made out for "2 masala dosai". The price was, of course, correct for the beer!

Another traveller found that a well-known hotel in the heart of New Delhi also appeared to have been forced

to adapt its attitude to serving alcohol to the prevailing laws. Asked in the early evening for a double whisky the barman was very happy to comply until he was asked to serve it in the garden. On being told that he could only drink it in the bar the visitor expressed great disappointment, on which the barman relented, whispering that if the visitor really wanted to drink it outside he would serve it to him in a tea pot!

If you are thirsting for alcohol in a prohibitionist area perhaps you need to order two masala dosai and a pot of tea.

Because of increased rates of bar licences in Rajasthan, many hotels and restaurants have stopped serving alcohol and there are few bars outside the upmarket hotels. You can however buy alcoholic drinks from shops in a city and have them in your hotel room. In some heritage hotels, owners 'invite' guests to join them for drinks. Some others will serve beer even if it is not listed and bill you for soft drinks at the price of the beer consumed! Gujarat enforces strong prohibition, and drinking in restaurants and public places is illegal. Tourists can drink in `private' (eg closed hotel rooms) for which permits are available and liquor can be bought from wine shops in upmarket hotels.

Shopping

India excels in producing fine crafts at affordable prices through the tradition of passing down of ancestral skills. You can get handicrafts of different states from the government emporia in the major cities which guarantee quality at fixed prices (no bargaining), but many are poorly displayed, not helped by reluctant and unenthusiastic staff. Private upmarket shops and top hotel arcades offer better quality, choice and service but at a price. Vibrant and colourful local bazars (markets) are often a great experience but you must be prepared to bargain.

Bargaining can be fun and quite satisfying. It is best to get an idea of prices being asked by different stalls for items you are interested in, before taking the plunge. Some shopkeepers will happily quote twice the actual price to a foreigner showing interest, so you might well start by halving the asking price. On the other hand it would be inappropriate to do the same in an established shop with price-tags, though a plea for the "best price" or a "special discount" might reap results even here. Remain good humoured throughout. Walking away slowly might be the test to ascertain whether your custom is sought and you are called back!

The country is a vast market place but there are regional specializations. The larger cities give you the opportunity to see a good selection from all over India. If you are planning to travel widely, wait to find the best places to buy specific items. Export of certain items is controlled or banned (see page 32).

Rajasthan has had a tradition of carpet and dhurrie weaving using camel wool and cotton. Weaving of traditional woollen dhurries became associated with prisoners in Bikaner, Jaipur and Ahmadabad jails but today attractive dhurries in pastel colours are produced in small commercial units as a cottage industry. The pile carpets made near Jaipur based on floral and geometrical patterns are of medium quality with around 120 knots per square inch.

Carpets & dhurries
Flat woven cotton dhurries in subtle colours are good buys

Rajasthan is famed for cut and uncut gemstones (emeralds. sapphires, rubies and diamonds). *Kundan* work specializes in setting stones in gold; sometimes *meenakari* (enamelling) complements the setting on the reverse side of the pendant, locket or earring. Whether it is chunky tribal silver jewellery or precious gems set in gold, or semi-precious stones in silver, the visitor is drawn to the arcade shop window as much as the way-side stall. It is best to buy from a reputable shops (and if in Jaipur, get expensive purchases checked by the Gem Testing Laboratory). Make sure your knowledge is up to scratch if considering investing in gems or jewellery, and never be persuaded to buy for an unknown third-party.

Jewellery

Essentials

Miniature paintings on old paper (they are not real antiques) and new silk, sometimes using natural colours derived from minerals, rocks and vegetables, following old techniques are produced in varying degrees of quality. Sadly the industry is reaching mass production levels in Rajasthan's back alleys though fine examples can still be found in good crafts shops. Coveted contemporary Indian art is exhibited in modern galleries in the state capitals often at a fraction of London or New York prices.

Paintings

Ornamental pieces of perforated marble *jali* work are produced in both states. Artisans in Agra inspired by the Taj Mahal continue the tradition of inlaying tiny pieces of gem stones on fine white marble, to produce something for every pocket, from a small coaster to a large table top. Softer soap stone is cheaper.

Stoneware

Colourful Rajasthani printed cottons using vegetable dyes and tie-and-dye *bandhani* from Saurashtra and Kachchh are special textiles of the region. The unique double *ikat* produced in Patan by just two families are the most prized. *Sober* handspun *khadi* was inspired by Mahatma Gandhi while a variety of skilled embroidery is produced by tribal groups across the two states.

Textiles

Taxi and rickshaw drivers and tour guides sometimes insist on recommending certain shops where they expect a commission, but prices there are invariably inflated. Some shops offer to pack and post your purchases but small private shops can't always be trusted. Unless you have a specific recommendation from a person that you know, only make such arrangements in government emporia or a large store. Don't enter into any arrangement to help 'export' marble items, jewellery etc which a shopkeeper may propose by making tempting promises of passing on some of the profits to you. Several visitors have been cheated through misuse of their credit card accounts, and have been left with unwanted purchases. Make sure that credit cards are not run off more than once when making a purchase.

Pitfalls

Holidays and festivals

India has an extraordinary wealth of festivals with many celebrated nationwide, while others are specific to a particular state or community or even a particular temple. Many festivals fall on different dates each year depending on the Hindu lunar calendar so check with the tourist office.

The Hindu Calendar

For the Hindu calendar see page 402

Some major regional festivals are listed below. A few count as national holidays: **26 January**: *Republic Day*; **15 August**: *Independence Day*; **2 October**: *Mahatma Gandhi's Birthday*; **25 December**: *Christmas Day*.

January   *New Year's Day* (1 January) is accepted officially when following the Gregorian calendar but there are regional variations which fall on different dates, often coinciding with spring/harvest time in March and April.

Makar Sankranti or *Uttarayana*, marks the end of winter and the beginning of the spring harvest, to 'welcome the sun to the northern tropic'. Ahmadabad, Vadodara, Surat, Jaipur, Bhavnagar and Rajkot celebrate the occasion with special fervour. (14-15 January).

Modhera Dance Festival is held each January at the Sun Temple, Modhera. The West Zone Culture Centre, Gujarat's Culture Department and Gujarat Tourism organize the event jointly. Each evening, the temple plinth becomes the stage for classical dances while the illuminated sculpted façade acts as the backdrop. Leading dancers and groups of performing artistes are invited to participate. Tents are set up for those who want to spend the night at Modhera and during the day excursions to Patan and nearby places of interest are offered. (18-20 January 2002).

Camel Festival, at Bikaner, organized by Rajasthan Tourism, features camel polo, races, dancing camels and camel obedience competitions. The fire dances of the Siddh Naths are another attraction. (27-28 Jan 2002, 17-18 Jan 2003).

February   *Nagaur Fair* is one of the best known camel and cattle marts in Rajasthan. (19-22 February 2002, 8-11 February 2003).

Desert Festival at Jaisalmer is a jamboree of classical and folk performances, desert musicians, folk crafts, camel polo, 'Mr Desert' competition and desert sports. (25-27 February 2002, 14-16 February 2003).

Baneshwar Fair is one of Rajasthan's largest tribal fairs. *Vagad Festival* offers an insight into tribal culture of Dungarpur and Bhenswada districts. (25-27 February 2002; 14-16 February 2003).

Shekhawati Festival in February highlights rural dances, rural games, *havelis* and agriculture of the four districts of Shekhawati.

March   *Kachchh Mahotsav*, a Desert Festival at Bhuj, features the cuisine, music, dances and handicrafts of Kachchh. Each evening, the fair ground turns into a market for selling handicrafts of the region, with a stage for cultural performances. During the day, bus trips are organised to places of interest including temples, beaches, craft villages,

The Kite festival

The sky over Gujarat and Rajasthan are a splash of colour each year at Makar Sankranti (14-15 January). It is the time for kite flying and kite fights in which the idea is to bring down the opponents' kites by severing their kite strings. There are two methods of doing this – dheel, during which the strings are slackened rapidly, and ghaseti, which involves skilful manoeuvring to slice the opponent's kite string. The kites generally flown are the `Indian fighters' and the skill of the kite flyer, the strength of the string and the balance of the kite are key factors that decide the victory in these 'fights' (kites from Bareily made with boiled bamboo are highly rated for their ability to balance themselves in the breeze). The kites come in a variety of colours and are often quite decorative, some even taking the shape of eagles or film stars! After dark, larger and stronger kites are flown, their strings carrying lanterns lit by candles. The 'fight' itself is called a pench, the special kite string sharpened by using glass powder and rice paste is called manjah, the bamboo and wood reels are called phirkis. The days before Makar Sankranti are a flurry of activity, as work begins on making manjah and winding the string on phirkis. Kites in bright colours are turned out by thousands, and ephemeral markets are set up around town. Beside local artisans, kite and string makers from other parts of India come to sell their products. Gujarat Tourism organises a kite festival during this period inviting kite clubs and enthusiasts from around the world to exhibit their kites, while in Rajasthan, Umaid Bhawan Palace in Jodhpur arranges a desert kite festival.

Essentials

archaeological sites etc. A special desert village is created for the occasion offering local cuisine to package tourists. The festival coincides with **Sivaratri** when a large colourful fair is held at the Dhrang temple near Bhuj. (10-12 March 2002).

Sivaratri marks the night when Siva danced his celestial dance of destruction (*Tandava*) celebrated with feasting and fairs at Siva temples, but preceded by a night of devotional readings and hymn singing. Orthodox Saivites fast during the day and offer prayers every three hours. Devotees who remain awake through the night believe they will win the Puranic promise of prosperity and salvation.

Bhavnath Mahadeo Fair near the Girnar hills of Junagadh district coincides with a massive puja of Lord Siva at midnight. Naga bawas arrive on elephant back, holding flags, spears and conch shells, and then walk around Mount Girnar before the puja. They are known to perform tantric feats (even lifting weights and pulling trucks with their private parts!). Folk dances and Bhawai drama are staged, while stalls sell local handicrafts and religious objects. (12-14 March 2002).

Holi, the festival of colours, marks the climax of spring. The previous night bonfires are lit in parts of North India symbolizing the end of winter (and conquering of evil). People have fun throwing coloured powder and water at each other and in the evening some gamble with friends. If you don't mind getting covered in colours, you can risk going out but celebrations can sometimes get rowdy. Some link the festival to worship of Kama the god of pleasure; some worship Krishna who defeated the demon Putana. *Holi* is particularly colourful at Jaipur, Jodhpur (where the royal family often celebrates it with guests), Jaisalmer, Udaipur and Bikaner but can get riotous. In rural areas like Daspan it is more subdued with folk dancing and music.

March-April

Preceding and following *Holi*, a series of tribal fairs are held in Chotta Udepur area of eastern Gujarat when there is music, dancing, bazaars and firewalking. Jaipur celebrates the *Elephant Festival*. The *Tilwara Fair* near Balotra is one of Rajasthan's largest camel and cattle fairs. *Dangs Durbar* is the meeting of tribal chieftains at Ahwa, with various dances, folk drama etc. Tribal groups gather to meet their former rulers at villages like Poshina in north Gujarat. (28 March-1 April 2002).

Chitra Vichitra Fair near Poshina, a fortnight after Holi, brings together various tribal groups for ancestor reverence, rituals, rejoicing, dancing and match making followed by eloping. The *Gaur Fair* near Abu Road are held at the same time. (11 April 2002).

Gangaur at Jaipur, Udaipur and other cities features colourful processions. At Udaipur, the procession arrives on foot at the Pichola Lake, and continues on boats. In Jodhpur colourfully dressed women carry pots of water to Girdikot. (15-16 April 2002, 4-5 April 2003).

April-June *Mewar Festival*, Udaipur, features cultural programs of the region. (15-16 April 2002).

Mahavir Jayanti celebrates the birth of the founder of the Jain religion. *Mahaveerji Fair* near Sawai Madhopur is an important Jain event with prayers.

A *Summer festival*, which includes traditional music, dance and crafts, is held at Mount Abu. (1-3 June).

July-August Raksha Bandhan (literally 'protection bond') commemorates the wars between *Indra* (the king of heaven) and the demons, when Indra's wife tied a silk amulet around his wrist to protect him from harm. The full-moon festival symbolizes the bond between brother and sister. A sister says special prayers and ties coloured threads around her brother's wrist while he in turn gives her a gift and promises to protect and care for her.

Teej, a fertility festival, celebrates the reunion of Siva and Parvati at the onset of the monsoon. There is a big procession with ornately dressed elephants. In the villages women wear bright clothes and green striped veils, and sit on swings decorated with flowers, singing songs to welcome the rains. (23-24 July 2001, 11-12 August 2002, 1-2 August 2003).

Independence Day is a national secular holiday. In cities it is marked by special events, and in Delhi there is an impressive flag hoisting ceremony at the Red Fort. (15 August).

August-September *Tarnetar Fair* is a betrothal fair held at the Triniteshwar Temple in Saurashtra, attended by herdsmen who come to find brides. (22-24 August 2001, 10-12 September 2002).

Janmashtami, the birth of Krishna, is celebrated at midnight at Krishna temples and at Dwarka it reaches the proportions of a fair (12 August 2001, 31 August 2002).

Ganesh Chaturthi, unlike most Hindu festivals, has a known origin. It was established just over 100 years ago by the Indian nationalist leader Tilak. The elephant-headed god of good omen (also called Ganpati) is shown special reverence. On the last of the five-day festival after harvest, clay images of the god are taken in procession with dancers and musicians, which are then immersed in the sea, river or pond. The Ganesh temple in Ranthambore receives a large influx of pilgrims on this day.

Gandhi Jayanti, Mahatma Gandhi's birthday is remembered with prayer meetings and devotional singing. (2 October).

Navratri in Gujarat and parts of Rajasthan is a colourful nine night event featuring music and dancing. It is marked by Garba, Dandia-ras and other dances as well as fasting, feasting and religious rites. Shakti temples at Ambaji and Pawagadh are visited by pilgrims in this period as it celebrates nine goddesses. Navratri culminates in *Dasara*. Various episodes of the Ramayana story or *Ramlila*, (see page 409) are enacted and recited, with particular reference to the battle between the forces of good and evil as in *Rama*'s victory over the demon king *Ravana* of Lanka with the help of loyal *Hanuman* (Monkey). Huge effigies of *Ravana* made of bamboo and paper are burnt on the 10th day of *Dasara* in public parks. Kota is well known for its Dasara fair. (17-25 October 2001, 7-15 October 2002).

Marwar Festival features folk music and dances of the region at Jodhpur (31 October 2001, 19 October 2002).

Diwali/Deepavali (from the Sanskrit *dipa* lamp) is the festival of lights. Some Hindus celebrate Diwali as Krishna's victory over the demon Narakasura, some Rama's return after his 14 years' exile in the forest when citizens lit his way with earthen oil lamps (see also page 404). *Rangolis* are painted on the floor as a sign of welcome. Fireworks have become an integral part of the celebration. Equally, Lakshmi, the Goddess of Wealth (as well as Ganesh) is worshipped by merchants and the business community who start the accounting year on the day. Most people wear new clothes; some play games of chance.

Kartik Poornima is one of the most important dates in the Hindu calendar. Pushkar, Chandrabhaga and Kolayat hold cattle and camel fairs There is a large two-week tribal fair at Shamlaji temple in north Gujarat during this period. (27-30 November 2001, 16-19 November 2002, 5-8 November 2003).

Vautha Camel Fair, at the confluence of six tributaries with River Sabarmati, features camel and donkey trading. Thousands of decorated camels and painted donkeys are brought for sale at the fair. Pilgrims bathe at the confluence of rivers. (1-4 November 2001, 20-23 November 2002).

Christmas (25) and *New Year's Eve* (31) are celebrated with music, dancing and other events in cities like Ahmadabad and Vadodara, and as a religious festival by Christians of Daman, Diu and elsewhere in these states. Hotel prices peak during this period and large supplements are added for meals and entertainment in the upper category hotels. Some churches mark the night with a Midnight Mass.

Muslim holy days

These are celebrated in cities with a significant Muslim population like Ahmadabad, Galliankot, Siddhapur and Dhoraji in Gujarat and Ajmer in Rajasthan. The dates are fixed according to the lunar calendar, see page 404. According to the Gregorian calendar, they tend to fall 11 days earlier each year, dependent on the sighting of the new moon.

Ramadan, the ninth month of the Islamic year, is a month of fasting. It is a period of atonement and recalls the "sending down of the Quran as a guidance for the people". All Muslims (except young children, the very elderly, the sick, pregnant women and travellers) must abstain from food and drink, from sunrise to sunset. *Id-ul-Fitr* is the three-day festival marks the end of Ramadan.

Essentials

Id-ul-Zuha/Bakr-Id is when Muslims commemorate Ibrahim's sacrifice of his son according to God's commandment; the main time of pilgrimage to Mecca (the Hajj). It is marked by the sacrifice of a goat, feasting and alms giving.

Muharram is when the killing of the Prophet's grandson, Hussain, is commemorated by Shi'a Muslims. Decorated *tazias* (replicas of the martyr's tomb) are carried in procession by devout wailing followers who beat their chests to express their grief. Hyderabad and Lucknow are famous for their grand *tazias*. Shi'as fast for the 10 days.

Purnima (Full Moon)

Many religious festivals depend on the phases of the moon. Full moon days are particularly significant and can mean extra crowding and merrymaking in temple towns throughout India, and are sometimes public holidays.

Entertainment

Despite an economic boom in cities like Delhi and Mumbai and the rapid growth of a young business class, India's night life remains meagre, focused on club discos in the biggest hotels. More traditional, popular entertainment is widespread across Indian villages in the form of folk drama, dance and music, each region having its own styles, and open air village performance being common. The hugely popular Hindi film industry comes largely out of this tradition. It's always easy to find a cinema, but prepare for a long sitting with a standard story line and set of characters and lots of action (see page 359). See also page 64 for spectator sports.

Sport and special interest travel

Camel safaris Today's camel safaris try to recreate something of the atmosphere of the early merchant camel trains that travelled through the desert. The Thar desert, in Rajasthan, with its vast stretches of sand, dotted with dunes and its own specially adapted shrubs and wildlife is ideal territory. The guides are expert navigators and the villages on the way add colour to an unforgettable experience, if you are prepared to sit out the somewhat uncomfortable ride (see page 245).

Jaisalmer has regular camel safaris ranging from short rides on the dunes to long hauls of six or seven days visiting villages, towns, dunes, wildlife areas and scenic places. Facilities vary: simple safaris allow you to spend the night on the dunes, in tents or village huts supplied with bed-rolls, and you get simple Rajasthani food; deluxe ('royal') safaris provide luxury self-contained tents, multi-cuisine meals and camel carts to transport your baggage.

Jaisalmer is the easiest place to organize a camel safari. Bikaner and Jodhpur have fewer tour operators and hotels offering safaris but these are often preferable as they are much less commercialized though they could be more pricey than those of Jaisalmer. If you want something more exclusive, and traverse areas where you do not keep bumping into tourists these could be a better options. Hotels in Manver, Osian, Gajner also arrange camel safaris. Others coincide with colourful fairs like those at Pushkar and Tilwara.

Horse safaris These are similar to camel safaris, with grooms (and often the horse owner) accompanying. The best months are November to March when it is cooler in the day (and often cold at night). The trails chosen usually enable you to visit small villages, old forts and temples, and take you through a variety of terrain and vegetation including scrub covered arid plains to forested hills. The charges can be a lot higher than for a camel safari but the night stays are often in comfortable palaces, forts or *havelis*.

The popular areas for horse safaris are the desert plains and Aravalli hills of Shekhawati, the Marwar plains south from Jodhpur to the hills of Ranakpur, and the Aravalli passes of the Mewar triangle and the Vindhya hills of southeastern Rajasthan. Heritage hotels of Dundlod and Nawalgarh (in Shekhawati), Udaipur, Bijaipur near Chittaurgarh, and Rohet near Jodhpur, are known for their horse safaris. Danta in the hills of north Gujarat, and Dasada, near the Rann of Kachchh, have introduced horse safaris in Gujarat. The safaris are only recommended for those who are reasonably adept at horse back riding for the trips can be long and tiring, the horses are quite spirited and require good handling. Most routes are planned to include interesting sight seeing destinations within a week or ten day horseback tour.

Jeep safaris

Besides game drives by jeep in sanctuaries and national parks, some hotels and tour operators now arrange jeep safaris, with accommodation in heritage hotels and camps along the way along lesser roads and cross-country trails.

Bird watching

The country's diverse and rich natural habitats harbour over 1,200 species of birds of which around 150 are endemic. Visitors to all parts of the country can enjoy spotting Oriental species whether it is in towns and cities, in the country side or more abundantly in the national parks and sanctuaries. On the plains, the cooler months (November to March) are the most comfortable for a chance to see migratory birds from the hills. Water bodies large and small draw visiting water fowl from other continents during the winter.

It is quite easy to get to some parks from the important tourist centres, for example Keoladeo Ghana, in Rajasthan, or Nal Sarovar, in Gujarat. *A Birdwatcher's Guide to India* by Krys Kazmierczak and Raj Singh, published by Prion Ltd, Sandy, Bedfordshire, UK, 1998, is well researched and comprehensive with helpful practical information and maps. Useful websites include www.orientalbirdclub.org and biks@giasdl01.vsnl.net.in for Bird Link, concerned with conservation of birds and their habitat. The Salim Ali Centre for Ornithology and Natural History is at centre@sacon.ernet.in

Yoga & meditation

There has been a growing Western interest in the ancient life-disciplines in search of physical and spiritual wellbeing, as practised in ancient India. Yoga is supposed to regulate the nervous system and aims to attain perfect equilibrium through the practice of *asanas* (body postures), breath control, discipline, cleansing, contemplation and awareness. It seeks to achieve moral purification through abstinence and restraint (dietary and sexual). Meditation which complements yoga to relieve stress, increase awareness and bring inner peace, prescribes *dhyana* (purposeful concentration) by withdrawing oneself from external distractions and focusing ones attention to consciousness itself. This leads ultimately to *samadhi* (release from worldly bonds). At the practical level *Hatha Yoga* has captured the Western imagination as it promises good health through postural exercises, while the search for inner peace and calm drive others to learn meditation techniques.

Centres across the country offer courses for beginners and practitioners. Some are at special resort hotels which offer all inclusive packages in idyllic locations, some advocate simple communal living in an ashram while others may require rigorous discipline in austere monastic surroundings. In Rajasthan, hotels in Pushkar such as *White House* can arrange lessons. Alternatively, enquire at the Vipasana Buddhist Meditation Centre at Dhamma Giri, PO Box 6, Igatpuri, Nasik, Maharashtra for their branch in Jaipur, which also has a Yoga and Naturopathy Centre at 'C Scheme' opposite Rajasthan University. You can contact *Om Shanti Bhavan* run by the Brahma Kumaris in Mount Abu. *Sariska Palace* provides courses in luxurious surroundings. In Gujarat, enquire at Akshardham at Gandhinagar, and at Sabarmati Ashram, Ahmadabad. The new *Sharma Resorts* on the Gandhidham-Bhuj road offers courses (as well as ayurvedic treatment).

Cycling Cycling offers a peaceful – not to mention healthy – alternative to cars, buses or trains. Touring on locally hired bicycles is ideal if you want to see village life in Rajasthan and Gujarat. As cycles are an important means of transport, it is easy to find repairers for punctures and other problems in towns and cities. These cycles are simple and do not have gears. If you bring mountain bikes and multi-geared cycles for touring with you, be warned that cycle thefts are not uncommon. Delhi based tour operators arrange deluxe cycle tours of Rajasthan and Gujarat with guide, back-up vehicles and accommodation in good hotels on the way. Mopeds are an alternative to cycling and these can be bought or hired in popular tourist destinations like Diu and Udaipur.

Biking For those keen on moving faster along the road, discover the joys of travelling on the two wheels of a motorbike. The 350 cc Enfield Bullets are particularly attractive. Vespa, Kinetic Honda and other makes of scooters in India are slower than motorbikes but comfortable for short hauls of less than 100 km and have the advantage of a `dicky' for spares, and a spare tyre. Scooters can be hired at Diu, Udaipur, Bikaner et cetera, to tour areas in and around the cities. See page 46.

Trekking Heritage hotels, resorts and tour operators offer treks in the Aravalli and Vindhya hills of Rajasthan. As the altitudes here are much lower than the Himalayas and the Western Ghats, the focus is on visiting tribal villages and seeing wildlife and birds along the trail, and perhaps a fort or a temple.

The easily accessible parts of the national parks, wildlife sanctuaries and reserved forests provide ample opportunity for walking but if you want to venture deeper you'll need to take a local guide as paths can soon become indistinct and confusing. Some areas require a permit to visit since the authorities wish to keep disturbance to wildlife and tribal communities to a minimum. The government Wildlife and Forestry Departments and private tour operators will be able to set you on the right path but you need to enquire, sometimes as much as a month, in advance. There are simple lodges and guest houses in most areas including tribal villages, but more comfortable jungle camps and luxury safari lodges also exist in the national parks, which can be used as a base for day treks.

Spectator sports

Soccer India's greatest popular entertainment has become sport, soccer being one. It is played from professional level to kick-about in any open space. Professional matches are played in large stadia attracting vast crowds.

Cricket Cricket has almost a fanatical following across the country. Reinforced by satellite TV and radio, and a national side that enjoys high world rankings and much outstanding individual talent, cricket has become a national obsession. Stars have cult status, and you can see children trying to model themselves on their game on any and every open space. The national side's greatest moment was, arguably, winning the 1983 World Cup. The low point in Indian cricket is the attention now focused on the role of "Bombay bookmakers" in the sport's current corruption enquiry, and the implication of leading players in match-fixing. When foreign national sides tour India, tickets are remarkably easy to come by (for Test matches at least), and are considerably cheaper than for corresponding fixtures back home. Tickets are often sold through local bank branches.

Health

Travellers to India are exposed to health risks not encountered in Western Europe or North America. Because much of the area is economically underdeveloped, serious infectious diseases are common, as they were in the West some decades ago. Obviously, business travellers staying in international hotels and tourists on organized tours face different health risks to travellers backpacking through rural areas. There are no absolute rules to follow; you will often have to make your own judgement on the healthiness of your surroundings. With suitable precautions you should stay healthy.

There are many well qualified doctors in India, most of whom speak English, but the quality and range of medical care diminishes rapidly as you leave the major cities. If you are in a major city, your embassy may be able to recommend a list of doctors. If you are a long way from medical help, some self-treatment may be needed. You are more than likely to find many drugs with familiar names on sale. Always buy from a reputable source, and check date stamping. Vaccines in particular have a much reduced shelf-life if not stored properly. Locally produced drugs may be unreliable because of poor quality control and the substitution of inert ingredients for active drugs.

Before you go

Take out good medical insurance. Check exactly what the level of cover is for specific eventualities, in particular whether a flight home is covered in case of an emergency, whether the insurance company will pay any medical expenses directly or whether you have to pay and then claim them back, and whether specific activities such as trekking or climbing are covered. If visiting for a while have a dental check up. Take spare glasses (or at least a glasses prescription) and/or lenses, if you wear them. If you have a long-standing medical problem such as diabetes, heart trouble, chest trouble or high blood pressure, get advice from your doctor, and carry sufficient medication to last the full duration of your trip. You may want to ask your doctor for a letter explaining your condition.

Self-medication may be forced on you by circumstances so the following text contains the names of drugs and medicines which you may find useful in an emergency or in out-of-the-way places. You may like to take some of the following items with you from home: **anti-infective ointment** eg cetrimide; **dusting powder** for feet, containing fungicide; **antacid tablets**; **antibiotics** (ask your GP); **anti-malarial tablets**; **painkillers** (paracetamol or aspirin); **rehydration salts** packets plus anti-diarrhoea preparations; **travel sickness tablets**; **first aid kit** including a couple of sterile syringes and needles and disposable gloves (available from camping shops) in case of an emergency.

Travelling with children

Children get dehydrated very quickly in hot countries and can become drowsy and uncooperative unless cajoled to drink water or juice plus salts. The treatment of diarrhoea is the same for adults, except that it should start earlier for children and be continued with more persistence. Colds, catarrh and ear infections are also common so take suitable antibiotics. To help young children to take anti-malarial tablets, one suggestion is to crush them between spoons and mix with a teaspoon of dessert chocolate (for cake-making) bought in a tube.

Vaccination & immunization

If you require travel vaccinations see your doctor well in advance of your travel. Most courses must be completed in a minimum of four weeks. Travel clinics may provide rapid courses of vaccination but are likely to be more expensive. The following vaccinations are recommended:

Essentials

Typhoid This disease is spread by the insanitary preparation of food. A single dose injection is now available (*Typhim Vi*) that provides protection for up to three years. A vaccine taken by mouth in three doses is also available, but the timing of doses can be a problem and protection only lasts for one year.

Polio Protection is by a live vaccine generally given orally, and a full course consists of three doses with a booster every five years.

Tetanus If you have not been vaccinated before, one dose of vaccine should be given with a booster at six weeks and another at six months. Ten yearly boosters are strongly recommended. Children should, in addition, be properly protected against diphtheria, mumps and measles.

Infectious hepatitis If you are not immune to hepatitis A already, the best protection is vaccination with *Havrix*. A single dose gives protection for at least a year, while a booster taken six months after the initial injection extends immunity to at least 10 years. If you are not immune to hepatitis B, the vaccine Energix is highly effective. It consists of three injections over six months before travelling. A combined hepatitis A & B vaccine is now licensed and available.

Malaria For details of malaria prevention, see below.

The following vaccinations may also be considered:

Tuberculosis The disease is still common in the region. Consult your doctor for advice on BCG inoculation.

Meningococcal Meningitis and Diphtheria If you are staying in the country for a long time, vaccination should be considered.

Japanese B Encephalitis (JBE) Immunization (effective in 10 days) gives protection for around three years. There is an extremely small risk in India, though it varies seasonally and from region to region. Consult a travel clinic or your family doctor.

Rabies Vaccination before travel gives anyone bitten more time to get treatment (so particularly helpful for those visiting remote areas), and also prepares the body to produce antibodies quickly. The cost of the vaccine can be shared by three persons receiving vaccination together.

Smallpox, **Cholera** and **Yellow Fever** Vaccinations are not required, although you may be asked to show a vaccination certificate if you have been in a country affected by yellow fever immediately prior to travelling to India.

You can get all your injections done at your local surgery for a fee but you will need to give them some notice. If you are in London, you have a choice. **Nomad**, c/o STA, 40 Bernard St, Russell Square, London WC1, T020-78334114, and 3-4 Wellington Terrace, Turnpike Lane, London N8, T020-88897014, operates a small clinic with a visiting pharmacist twice a week, free advice on preventative treatment; medicines and vaccinations are available at the Dispensary. **British Airways Travel Clinic**, Harrow, Middlesex, offers a similar service on weekdays. All this is cheaper at the **Hospital for Tropical Diseases**, 4 St Pancras Way, London, N1 0PE, T020-72889600, 0900-1630 (call for an appointment).

On the road

Intestinal upsets Intestinal upsets are due, most of the time, to the insanitary preparation of food. Do not eat uncooked fish, vegetables or meat (especially pork, though this is highly unlikely in India), fruit with the skin on (always peel fruit yourself), or food that is exposed to flies (particularly salads).

Shellfish eaten raw are risky and at certain times of the year some fish and shellfish concentrate toxins from their environment and cause various kinds of food poisoning.

Water purification

There are various ways of purifying water in order to make it safe to drink. Dirty water should first be strained through a filter bag, and then boiled or treated.

Bringing water to a rolling **boil** at sea level is sufficient to make water safe for drinking, but at higher altitudes you have to boil the water for longer to ensure that all the microbes are killed.

Various sterilizing methods can be used and there are propriety preparations containing **chlorine** (eg 'Puritabs') or **iodine** (eg 'Pota Aqua') compounds. Chlorine compounds generally do not kill protozoa (eg giardia). Prolonged usage of iodine compounds may lead to thyroid problems, although this is rare if used for less than a year.

There are a number of **water filters** now on the market, available both in personal and expedition size. There are two types of water filter, **mechanical** and **chemical**. Mechanical filters are usually a combination of carbon, ceramic and paper, although they can be difficult to use. Ceramic filters tend to last longer in terms of volume of water purified. The best brand is possibly the Swiss made Katadyn. Although cheaper, the disadvantage of mechanical filters is that they do not always remove viruses or protozoa. Thus, if you are in an area where the presence of these is suspected, the water will have to be treated with iodine before being passed through the filter. When new, the filter will remove the taste, although this may not continue for long. However, ceramic filters will remove bacteria, and their manufacturers claim that since most viruses live on bacteria, the chances are that the viruses will be removed as well. This claim should be treated with scepticism.

Chemical filters usually use a combination of an iodine resin filter and a mechanical filter. The advantage of this system is that according to the manufacturers' claims, everything in the water will be killed. Their disadvantage is that the filters need replacing, adding a third to the price. Probably the best chemical filter is manufactured by Pur.

Tap water should be assumed to be unsafe, especially in the monsoon; the same goes for stream or well water. Bottled mineral water is now widely available, although not all bottled water is mineral water; some is simply purified water from an urban supply. If your hotel has a central hot water supply, this is generally safe to drink after cooling. Ice for drinks should be made from boiled water but rarely is, so stand your drink on the ice cubes rather than putting them in your drink. For details on water purification, see box.

Heat treated **milk** is widely available, as is ice cream produced by the same methods. Unpasteurized milk products, including cheese, are sources of tuberculosis, brucellosis, listeria and other food poisoning germs. You can render fresh milk safe by heating it to 62°C for 30 minutes, followed by rapid cooling or by boiling. Matured or processed cheeses are safer than fresh varieties.

Diarrhoea is usually the result of food poisoning, occasionally from contaminated water. There are various causes: viruses, bacteria or protozoa (like amoeba and giardia). It may take one of several forms, coming on suddenly, or rather slowly. It may be accompanied by vomiting or by severe abdominal pain and the passage of blood or mucus with stools. How do you know which type you have and how do you treat them?

All kinds of diarrhoea, whether or not accompanied by vomiting, respond favourably to the replacement of water and salts taken as frequent small sips of some kind of rehydration solution. Proprietary preparations, consisting of sachets of powder which you dissolve in water (ORS, or Oral Rehydration Solution) are widely available, although it is recommended that you bring some of your own. They can also be made by adding half a teaspoonful of salt (3½ g) and four tablespoonfuls of sugar (40 g) to a litre of safe drinking water.

Essentials

If you can time the onset of diarrhoea to the minute, then it is probably viral or bacterial, and/or the onset of dysentery. The treatment, in addition to rehydration, is Ciprofloxacin (500 mg every 12 hours). The drug is now widely available. If the diarrhoea has come on slowly or intermittently, then it is more likely to be protozoal (ie caused by amoeba or giardia). These cases are best treated by a doctor, as should any diarrhoea continuing for more than three days. If medical facilities are remote a short course of high dose Metronidazole (*Flagyl*) may provide relief. This drug is widely available in India, although it is best to bring a course with you after discussion with your family doctor. If there are severe stomach cramps, the following drugs may sometimes help: *Loperamide* (*Imodium, Arret*) and *Diphenoxylate* with *Atropine* (*Lomotil*).

Thus, the lynch pins of treatment for diarrhoea are rest, fluid and salt replacement, antibiotics such as Ciprofloxacin for some bacterial types and special diagnostic tests and medical treatment for amoeba and giardia infections.

Salmonella infections and **cholera** can be devastating diseases and it would be wise to get to a hospital as soon as possible if these were suspected. Fasting, peculiar diets and the consumption of large quantities of yoghurt have not been found to be useful in calming travellers' diarrhoea or in rehabilitating inflamed bowels. As there is some evidence that alcohol and milk might prolong diarrhoea, they should probably be avoided during and immediately after an attack. Antibiotics to prevent diarrhoea are probably ineffective and some, such as Entero-vioform, can have serious side effects if taken for long periods.

Heat & cold Full acclimatization to high temperatures takes about two weeks. During this period it is normal to feel relatively apathetic, especially if the relative humidity is high. Drink plenty of water and avoid extreme exertion. When you are acclimatized you will feel more comfortable but your need for plenty of water will continue. Tepid showers are more cooling than hot or cold ones. Remember that especially in the mountains, deserts and the highlands, there can be a large and sudden drop between temperatures in the sun and shade and between night and day. Large hats do not cool you down but do prevent sunburn. Warm jackets or woollens are essential after dark at high altitude. Loose cotton is still the best material when the weather is hot.

The burning power of the tropical sun is phenomenal, especially at altitude. Always wear a wide brimmed hat and use some form of sun cream or lotion. Normal temperate suntan lotions (up to factor seven) are not much good. You will need to use the types designed specifically for the tropics or for mountaineers/skiers, with a protection factor between seven and 25 (dependent on skin type). Glare from the sun can cause conjunctivitis, so wear good quality UV protection sunglasses on beaches and snowy areas. There are several variations of 'heat stroke'. The most common cause is severe dehydration, so drink plenty of non-alcoholic fluid. Sun-block and cream is not widely available in India, so you should bring adequate supplies with you.

Insects These can be a great nuisance. Some of course are carriers of serious disease. The best way to keep mosquitoes away at night is to sleep off the ground with a mosquito net and to burn mosquito coils containing Pyrethrum (available in India). Aerosol sprays or a 'flit' gun may be effective, as are insecticidal tablets which are heated on a mat which is plugged into a wall socket. These devices, and the refills, are not widely available in India, so if you are taking your own make sure it is of suitable voltage with the right adaptor plug. Bear in mind also that there are regular power cuts in many parts of India.

A better option is to use a personal insect repellent of which the best contain a high concentration of Diethyltoluamide (DEET). Liquid is best for arms, ankles and face (take care around eyes and make sure you do not dissolve the plastic of your spectacles). These are available in India (eg *Mospel, Repel*), although it is recommended that you bring your own supply. Aerosol spray on clothes and ankles deter mites and ticks. Liquid DEET suspended in water can be used to impregnate cotton clothes and mosquito nets. MASTA recommends *Mosiguard* which does not contain DEET as an insect repellent.

If you are bitten, itching may be relieved by cool baths and anti-histamine tablets (care with alcohol or driving), corticosteroid creams (great care and never use if hint of infection or on the face) or by judicious rubbing or scratching. Calamine lotion and cream are of no real use, and anti-histamine creams may sometimes cause skin allergies so use with caution.

Bites which do become infected (common in India) should be treated with a local antiseptic or antibiotic cream such as Cetrimide, as should infected scratches. Skin infestations with body lice, crabs and scabies are unfortunately easy to pick up, particularly by those travelling cheaply or trekking to mountain grazing pastures. Use Gamma benzene hexachloride for lice and Benzylbenzoate for scabies. Crotamiton cream alleviates itching and also kills a number of skin parasites. Malathion 5% is good for lice, but avoid the highly toxic full strength Malathion used as an agricultural insecticide.

Malaria

In India malaria was once theoretically confined to coastal and jungle zones, but is now on the increase again. It remains a serious disease and you are strongly advised to protect yourself against mosquito bites and to take prophylactic (preventive) drugs. Certain areas are badly affected particularly by the highly dangerous falciparum strain. Mosquitoes do not thrive above 2,500 m, so you are safe at altitude. Recommendations on prevention change, so consult your family doctor or see the further information at the end of this section. However, the current combination of anti-malarial drugs for use in India requires a daily dosage of *Proguanil* (brands such as *Paludrine*) and a weekly dosage of *Chloroquine* (various brands). Start taking the tablets one week before exposure and continue to take them for four weeks after leaving the malarial zone. For those unable to use these particular drugs, your doctor may suggest *Mefloquine*, although this tends to be more expensive, less well tried, and may cause more serious side effects so it is best to try two doses before leaving.

The subject of malaria prevention is becoming more complex as the malaria parasite becomes immune to some of the older drugs. In particular, there has been an increase in the proportion of cases of falciparum malaria which is particularly dangerous. Some of the preventive drugs can cause side effects, especially if taken for long periods of time, so before you travel you must check with a reputable agency the likelihood and type of malaria in the areas you intend to visit. Take their advice on prophylaxis, but be prepared to receive conflicting advice. Do not use the possibility of side effects as an excuse not to take drugs.

You can catch malaria even when taking prophylactic drugs, although it is unlikely. If you do develop symptoms (high fever, shivering, severe headache, sometimes diarrhoea) seek medical advice immediately. The risk of disease is obviously greater the further you move from the cities into rural areas with primitive facilities and standing water.

Infectious hepatitis (jaundice)

Medically speaking there are two types. The less serious but more common is **hepatitis A**, a disease frequently caught by travellers, and common in India. The main symptoms are yellowness of eyes and skin, lack of appetite, nausea, tiredness and stomach pains. The best protection is careful preparation of food, the avoidance of contaminated drinking water and scrupulous attention to toilet hygiene.

The other, more serious version is **hepatitis B**, which is acquired as a sexually transmitted disease, from blood transfusions or injection with an unclean needle, or possibly by insect bites. The symptoms are the same as hepatitis A, but the incubation period is much longer.

You may have had jaundice before or you may have had hepatitis of either type without becoming jaundiced, in which case it is possible that you could be immune to either form. This immunity can be tested for before you travel. There are various other kinds of viral hepatitis (C, E etc) which are fairly similar to A and B, but currently vaccines do not exist for these.

AIDS

In India, AIDS is increasing in prevalence with a pattern typical of developing societies. Thus, it is not wholly confined to the well known high risk sections of the population ie homosexual men, intravenous drug abusers, prostitutes and the children of infected mothers. Heterosexual transmission is now the dominant mode and so the main risk to travellers is from casual unprotected sex. The same precautions should be taken as when encountering any sexually transmitted disease.

The AIDS virus (HIV) can be passed via unsterile needles which have previously been used to inject a HIV positive patient, but the risk of this is very small. It would, however, be sensible to check that needles have been properly sterilized, or better still, disposable needles used. The chance of picking up hepatitis B in this way is much more of a danger. If disposable needles are carried as part of a proper medical kit, customs officials in India are not generally suspicious.

The risk of receiving a blood transfusion with blood infected with the HIV virus is greater than from dirty needles because of the amount of fluid exchanged. Supplies of blood for transfusion are now usually screened for HIV in reputable hospitals, so the risk may be small. Catching the AIDS virus does not necessarily produce an illness in itself; the only way to be sure if you feel you have been at risk is to have a blood test for HIV antibodies on your return to a place where there are reliable laboratory facilities. The test does not become positive for many weeks and you are advised to be re-tested after 6 months.

Bites & stings

The best precaution against a snake bite is not to walk in snake territory with bare feet, sandals or shorts & not to touch snakes even if assured they are harmless. Make noise (with a stick) to scare snakes away in advance

If you are unlucky enough to be bitten by a venomous snake, spider, scorpion, centipede or sea creature, try (within limits) to catch the animal for identification. Failing this, an accurate description will aid treatment. See the information on rabies (below) for other animal bites. The reactions to be expected are fright, swelling, pain and bruising around the bite, soreness of the regional lymph glands (eg armpits for bites to hands and arms), nausea, vomiting and fever. If, in addition, any of the following symptoms supervene get the victim to a doctor without delay: numbness, tingling of face, muscular spasm, convulsions, shortness of breath or haemorrhage. Commercial snake bile or scorpion sting kits may be available but are only useful for the specific type of snake or scorpion for which they are designed. The serum has to be given by injection into a vein, so it is not much good unless you have some practice in making and giving such injections. If the bite is on a limb, immobilize the limb and apply a tight bandage (not a tourniquet) between the bite and the body. Be sure to release it for 90 seconds every 15 minutes. Do not try to slash the bite and suck out the poison because this will do more harm than good. Reassurance of the bitten person is important. Death from snake-bite is extremely rare. Hospitals usually hold stocks of snake-bite serum, though it is important to have a good description of the snake, or where possible, the creature itself.

If swimming in an area where there are poisonous fish such as stone or scorpion fish (also called by a variety of local names) or sea urchins on rocky coasts, tread carefully or wear footwear. The sting of such fish is intensely painful but can be helped by immersing the stung part in water as hot as you can bear for as long as it remains painful. This is not always very practical and you must take care not to scald yourself. At certain times of the year, coincidental with the best surfing season, stinging jelly-fish can be a problem.

Avoid spiders and scorpions by keeping your bed away from the wall, look under lavatory seats and inside your shoes in the morning. Dark dusty rooms are popular with scorpions. In the event of being bitten or stung, consult a doctor quickly.

Rabies is endemic in India. If you are bitten by a domestic or wild animal, do not leave things to chance. Scrub the wound immediately with soap and water/disinfectant. Try to capture the animal (within limits). Treatment depends on whether you have already been vaccinated against rabies. If you have (and this is worthwhile if you are spending lengths of time in developing countries) then some further doses of vaccine are all that is needed. Human diploid cell vaccine is best, but expensive; other, older types of vaccine such as that made of duck embryos may be the only type available. These are effective, much cheaper and interchangeable generally with the human derived types. If not already vaccinated then anti-rabies serum (immunoglobulin) may be required in addition. It is wise to finish the course of treatment whether the animal survives or not.

Other afflictions

Dengue fever is present in India. It is a viral disease, transmitted by mosquito bites, presenting severe headache, fevers and body pains. Complicated types of dengue known as haemorrhagic fevers occur throughout Asia, but usually in persons who have caught the disease a second time. Thus, although it is a very serious type, it is rarely caught by visitors. There is no treatment; you must just avoid mosquito bites as much as possible.

Athlete's foot and other fungal infections are best treated by sunshine and a proprietary preparation such as Canesten or Ecostatin.

Influenza and respiratory diseases are common, perhaps made worse by polluted cities and rapid temperature and climatic changes.

Intestinal worms are common, and the more serious ones such as hook worm can be contracted by walking barefoot on infested earth.

Prickly heat is a very common itchy rash, and can be avoided by frequent washing and by wearing loose clothing. It is helped by the use of talcum powder to allow the skin to dry thoroughly after washing.

Returning home

It is important to take your anti-malaria tablets for four weeks after you return. Malaria can develop up to one year after leaving a malaria area. If you do become ill with fever or the other symptoms listed above, make sure your doctor knows about your travel. If you have had attacks of diarrhoea, it may be worth having a stool specimen tested in case you have picked up amoebic dysentery, giardiasis or other protozoal infections. If you have been living rough, a blood test may be worthwhile to detect worms and other parasites.

Further information

The following organizations give information regarding well trained English speaking physicians throughout the world: **International Association for Medical Assistance to Travellers**, 745, 5th Avenue, New York, 10022; **Intermedic**, 777, Third Avenue, New York, 10017. Information regarding country by country malaria risk can be obtained from: **Malaria Reference Laboratory**, UK, T0891-600350; **Liverpool School of Tropical Medicine**, UK, T0891-172111 (both have recorded messages, premium rate); and **Centre for Disease Control**, Atlanta, USA, T404-3324555. The organization **MASTA** (Medical Advisory Service to Travellers Abroad), T020-78375540, F0113-2387575, www.masta.org and **Travax** (Glasgow, T0141-9467120 ext 247) will provide up to date country by country information on health risks.

Further information on medical problems abroad can be obtained from: *"Travellers' Health: How To Stay Healthy Abroad"*, edited by Richard Dawood (Oxford University Press), recently updated. A new edition of the HMSO publication "Health Information for Overseas Travel" is available. The London School of Hygiene and Tropical Medicine, Keppel Street, London, WC1E 7HT, UK, publishes a strongly recommended book titled *"The Preservation of Personal Health in Warm Climates"*.

This information has been compiled by Dr David Snashall, Senior Lecturer in Occupational Health, United Medical Schools of Guy's and St Thomas' Hospitals and Chief Medical Advisor, Foreign and Commonwealth Office, London. Added comments and recommendations specific to India are from Dr Martin Taylor, Kensington Street Health Centre, Bradford, West Yorkshire and Dr Anthony Bryceson, Emeritus Professor of Tropical Medicine at the London School of Hygiene and Tropical Medicine.

Further reading

The literature on India is as huge and varied as the subcontinent itself. India is a good place to buy English language books as foreign books are often much cheaper than the published price. There are also cheap Indian editions and occasionally reprints of out-of-print books. There are excellent bookshops in all the major Indian cities.

Art & architecture Burton, T Richard *Hindu Art*, British Museum PA. Well illustrated paperback; a broad view of art and religion. **Desai, VN** *Life at court: Art for India's rulers, 16th-19th centuries*, Boston, Museum of Fine Arts, 1985. **Fass, V** *The Forts of India*, London, 1986. **Gupta, ML** *Frescoes and Wall paintings of Rajasthan*, Jaipur, 1965. **Jain, J and M** *Mud architecture of the Indian desert*, Ahmadabad, AADI, 1992. **Jain-Neubauer, J** *The stepwells of Gujarat*, New Delhi, Abhinav, 1994. **Michell, George** *The Hindu Temple*, Univ of Chicago Press, 1988. An authoritative account of Hindu architectural development. **Michell, G & Martinelli, A,** *Royal Palaces of India*, Thames & Hudson, 1994. **Pramar VS,** *Haveli*, Ahmadabad, Mapin, 1989 and *Royal Families and Palaces of Gujarat*, Scorpion Cavendish,1998. Beautifully produced. **Sterlin, Henri** *Hindu India*, Köln, Taschen, 1998. Traces the development from early rock-cut shrines, detailing famous examples; clearly written, well illustrated. **Tillotson, Giles** *The Rajput Palaces*, Yale, 1987; *Mughal architecture*, London, Viking, 1990; *The tradition of Indian architecture*, Yale 1989. Superbly clear writing on development of Indian architecture under Rajputs, Mughals and the British. **Welch, SC** *Indian Art and culture 1300-1900*, New York, Metropolitan Museum of Art, 1985.

Current affairs & politics French, Patrick *Liberty or Death*, Harper Collins, 1997. Well researched and serious yet reads like a story. **Khilnani, Sunil** *The idea of India*, Penguin, 1997. Excellent introduction to contemporary India, described by the Nobel prize winner Amartya Sen as "spirited, combative and insight-filled, a rich synthesis of contemporary India". **Manor, James** (ed) *Nehru to the Nineties: the changing office of Prime Minister in India*, Hurst, 1994. An excellent collection of essays giving an insider's view of the functioning of Indian democracy. **Tully, Mark** *No full stops in India*, Viking, 1991. An often superbly observed but controversially interpreted view of contemporary India.

History: pre-history & early history Allchin, Bridget and Raymond *Origins of a civilisation*, Viking, Penguin Books, 1997. The most authoritative up to date survey of the origins of Indian civilizations. **Basham, AL** *The Wonder that was India*, London, Sidgwick & Jackson, 1985. Still one of the most comprehensive and readable accounts of the development of India's culture.

Edwardes, Michael *The Myth of the Mahatma.* Presents Gandhi in a whole new light. History:
Gandhi, Mohandas K *An Autobiography*, London, 1982. **Gascoigne, Bamber** *The* medieval &
Great Moghuls, London, Cape, 1987. **Nehru, Jawaharlal** *The discovery of India*, modern
New Delhi, ICCR, 1976. **Keay, John** *India: a History*, Harper Collins, 2000. A major new
popular history of the subcontinent. **Lt Col AF Pinhey**'s *History of Mewar* (with inter-
esting comments on Tod's authenticity), 1909 (reprinted 1996, Rs 300). **Robinson,**
Francis (ed) *Cambridge Encyclopaedia of India*, Cambridge, 1989. An introduction to
many aspects of South Asian society. **Schomer, K et al eds** *The Idea of Rajasthan:*
explorations in regional identity. 2 vols. Delhi, American Inst of Indian Studies, 1994,
Rs 750. **Sharma, GN** *Social life in medieval Rajasthan*, Agra, 1968. **Spear, Percival &**
Thapar, Romila *A history of India*, 2 vols, Penguin, 1978. **Tod, J** *Annals and antiquities*
of Rajasthan. 2 vols. London, 1829-32 (reprinted 1994 in 3 vols, Rs 600). **Wolpert,**
Stanley *A new history of India*, OUP, 1990.

Snell, Rupert and Weightman, Simon *Teach Yourself Hindi*. An excellent, accessible, Language
authoritative teaching guide with a cassette tape. **Yule, H and Burnell, AC** (eds), *Hob-*
son-Jobson, 1886. New paperback edition, 1986. A delightful insight into Anglo-Indian
words and phrases.

Chatterjee, Upamanyu *English August*, London, Faber, 1988. A wry account of a Literature
modern Indian Civil Servant's year spent in a rural posting. **Chaudhuri, Nirad** Four
books give vivid, witty and often sharply critical accounts of India across the 20th century: *The autobiography of an unknown Indian*, Macmillan, London; *Thy Hand, Great*
Anarch!, London, Chatto & Windus, 1987. **Holmstrom, Lakshmi** *The Inner Courtyard*.
A series of short stories by Indian women, translated into English, Rupa, 1992. **Granta**
57 *India! The Golden Jubilee.* A diverse collection on a wide range of topics. **Mehta,**
Gita *Raj*, Delhi, Penguin, 1990. **Naipaul, VS** *A million mutinies now*, Penguin, 1992.
Naipaul's 'revisionist' account of India turns away from the despondency of his earlier
two India books (*An Area of darkness* and *India: a wounded civilisation*) to see grounds
for optimism at India's capacity for regeneration. **Rushdie, Salman** *Midnight's chil-*
dren, London, Picador, 1981. A novel of India since Independence. At the same time
funny and bitterly sharp critiques of South Asian life in the 1980s. **Rushdie, Salman**
and West, Elizabeth *The Vintage book of Indian writing*, Random House, 1997. **Scott,**
Paul *The Raj Quartet*, London, Panther, 1973 and *Staying on*, Longmans, 1985. Outstandingly perceptive novels of the end of the Raj. **Seth, Vikram** *A Suitable Boy*, Phoenix House London 1993. Prize winning novel of modern Indian life. **Weightman,**
Simon (ed) *Travellers Literary Companion: the Indian Sub-continent*. An invaluable
introduction to the diversity of Indian writing.

Bomiller, Elizabeth *May you be the mother of 100 sons*, Penguin, 1991. An American Social history:
woman journalists' account of coming to understand the issues that face India's People
women today. **Cimino, RM** (ed) *Life at court in Rajasthan*, Florence, 1985. **Jain, KC** & places
Ancient cities and towns of Rajasthan, Delhi, 1976. **Lord, J** *The Maharajahs*, London,
1971. **Patnaik, N** *A desert Kingdom: the Rajputs of Bikaner*, London, Weidenfeld &
Nicholson,1990. **Robinson, A** (photographs by S Uchiyama), *Maharaja: the spectacu-*
lar heritage of Princely India. London, Thames & Hudson,1988. **Singhvi, AK & Kar, A**
Thar Desert in Rajasthan: land, man and environment, Bangalore, Geological Society
of India, 1991.

Theodore de Bary, W (ed) *Sources of Indian Tradition: Vol 1*, Columbia UP. Traces the Religion
origins of India's major religions through illustrative texts. **Jain, JP** *Religion and Culture*
of the Jains. 3rd ed. New Delhi, Bharatiya Jnanapith, 1981. **Doniger O'Flaherty,**
Wendy *Hindu Myths*, London, Penguin, 1974. A sourcebook translated from the

Sanskrit. **Qureshi, IH** *The Muslim Community of the Indo-Pakistan Sub-Continent 610-1947*, OUP, Karachi, 1977. **Vaudeville, C** *Myths, saints and legends in Medieval India*. Delhi, OUP, 1996. **Zaehner, RC** *Hinduism*, OUP.

Travel **Dalrymple, William** *City of Djinns*, Indus/Harper Collins 1993, paperback. Superb account of Delhi based on a year living in the city. **Davidson, R** *Desert places*, Viking, 1996. Crossing the desert on a camel's back with nomadic herders. **Hatt, John** *The tropical traveller: the essential guide to travel in hot countries*, Penguin, 3rd ed 1992. Excellent, wide ranging and clearly written common sense, based on extensive experience and research. **Keay, John** *Into India*, London, John Murray, 1999. A seasoned traveller's introduction to understanding and enjoying India; with a new foreword.

Wildlife & **Ali, Salim and Dillon Ripley, S** *Handbook of the birds of India & Pakistan* (compact
vegetation ed); also in five volumes. **Cowen** *Flowering Trees and Shrubs in India*. **Hawkins, RE** *Encyclopaedia of Indian Natural History*, Bombay Natural History Soc/OUP. **Kazmierczak, Krys & Singh, Raj** *A birdwatcher's guide to India*. Prion, 1998, Sandy, Beds, UK. Well researched and carrying lots of practical information for all birders. **Nair, SM** *Endangered animals of India*, New Delhi, NBT, 1992. **Prater, SH** *The Book of Indian Animals*. **Woodcock, Martin** *Handguide to Birds of the Indian Sub-Continent*, Collins.

Maps

The export of large
scale maps from India
is prohibited

For anyone interested in the geography of India, or even simply getting around, trying to buy good maps is a depressing experience. For security reasons it is illegal to sell large scale maps of any areas within 80 km of the coast or national borders.

The **Bartholomew** 1:4 m map sheet of India is the most authoritative, detailed and easy to use map available. It can be bought worldwide. **GeoCenter** World Map 1:2 m, covers India in three regional sections and are clearly printed. **Nelles'** regional maps of India at the scale of 1:1.5 m offer generally clear route maps, though neither the road classifications nor alignments are wholly reliable. The same criticism applies to the attractively produced and easy to read **Lonely Planet** *Travel Atlas of India and Bangladesh* (1995, 162 pp).

State maps and town plans are published by the **TT Company**. These are updated and improved from time to time. IMS (Indian Map Service) has a limited range of maps relating to Rajasthan. Their state map (1:1230,000), 1997, Rs 120, is the best available.

Sources of maps outside India: **Australia**: *The Map Shop*, 16a Peel St, Adelaide, SA 5000, T08-82312033. **Canada**: *Worldwide Books*, 552 Seymore St. Vancouver, BC. **Germany**: *Geo Buch Verlag*, Rosenthal 6, D-6000 München 2; *GeoCenter GmbH*, Honigwiessenstrasse 25, Postfach 800830, D-7000 Stuttgart 80; *Zumsteins Landkartenhaus*, Leibkerrstrasse 5, 8 München 22. **Italy**: *Libreria Alpina*, Via C Coroned-Berti, 4 40137 Bologna, Zona 370-5. **Switzerland**: *Travel Bookshop*, Rindermarkt, 8001 Zurich. **UK**: *Blackwell's*, 53 Broad St, Oxford, T01865-792792, www.bookshop.blackwell.co.uk *Stanfords*, 12-14 Long Acre, London WC2E 9LP, T020-78361321, www.stanfords.co.uk **USA**: *Michael Chessler*, PO Box 2436, Evergreen, CO 80439, T800-6548502, 303-6700093; *Ulysses*, 4176 St Denis Montreal, T0524-8439447.

The Survey of India publishes large scale 1:10,000 town plans of approximately 70 cities. These detailed plans are the only surveyed town maps in India, and some are over 20 years old. The Survey also has topographic maps at the scale of 1:25,000 and 1:50,000 in addition to its 1:250,000 scale coverage, some of which are as recent as the late 1980s. However, maps are regarded as highly sensitive and it is only possible to buy these from main agents of the Survey of India.

India on the web

www.tourindia.com The official government promotional site with useful information but no objective evaluation of problems and difficulties. Has separate state entries
within it. 'India Travel Online' is informative and issued fortnightly. General sites
www.indiacurrentaffairs.com/ Regularly updated cuttings from Indian national dailies.
www.fco.gov Advice from the Foreign Office, London.
www.travel.indiamart.com Commercial site – details of online bookings for selected
hotels.
www.india.org The sites on India section contains excellent information on the
structure of Indian government. Tourism Information is less useful.
www.123india.com Wide ranging current affairs and general India site.
www.tourismindia.com Yellow pages for major cities.
www.wunderground.com An excellent weather site, world wide, city specific and fast.

www.rajasthantourism.com, www.gujarattourism.com, www.ahmedabad.com, State specific
www.allindia.com/gujtourism sites

India on film

The Indian film industry is one of the largest in the world, each region having its own
regional language films. The Hindi film industry is based in Mumbai, specialising in
robust song and dance fantasies, all characterised as "Bollywood" movies.

In a wholly different wold as the films by producers such as **Satyajit Ray** (Apu trilogy
and many others), **Shyam Benegal** and **Aparna Roy**. **Mira Nair**'s *Salaam Bombay*
captured something of the social injustices of modern urban India.

India has been the focus for many foreign and overseas based Indian film makers.
Some have focused on the big political stories – **Richard Attenborough**'s, *Gandhi*, or
on video, the brilliant TV drama the *Jewel in the Crown*, evoking India at the end of the
British period.

Essentials

Delhi and around

3

Delhi and around

Delhi

Delhi can take you aback with its vibrancy and growth. Less than 60 years ago the spacious, quiet and planned city of New Delhi was still the pride of late colonial British India, while immediately to its north the crowded lanes of Old Delhi resonated with the sounds of a bustling medieval market. Today both worlds have been overtaken by the brash rush of modernisation. As Delhi's population surges towards 14 million its tentacles spread in all directions from both the ancient core of Shahjahan's city in the north and the late British capital of New Delhi to its south.

The drive from the airport gives something of the feel of this dynamism, the roads often crowded with traffic, new highrise buildings transforming the spacious outlines of Lutyens' New Delhi with its broad tree lined avenues, into a humming commercial hub centred around Connaught Place. Close to New Delhi Railway station the cheap hotels and guesthouses of Paharganj, heart of backpackerland, squeeze between clothmerchants and wholesalers, cheek by jowl in the narrow lanes opposite the station, the hub of New Delhi's network to the rest of India. In Old Delhi, further north, with the Red Fort and Jama Masjid, the old city is still a dense network of narrow alleys and tightly packed markets and houses. Your senses are bombarded by noise, bustle, smells and the apparent chaos of a much more traditional city. A 'third city', often scarcely seen, comprises the remorselessly growing squatter settlements (jhuggies) which provide the only shelter for at least one-third of Delhi's total population. To the south is yet another, newer, chrome and glass city, the city of the modern suburbs and urban 'farms', where the rural areas of Gurgaon have become the preserve of the prosperous, with shopping malls, banks, and private housing estates.

Outside the railway stations taxi drivers, rickshaw-wallahs and hotel touts overwhelm the traveller. Beggars, sometimes mutilated, compete for space and attention with trinket sellers and novelty vendors. Old and new, simple and sophisticated, traditional and modern, East and West are all juxtaposed.

Phone code: 011
Colour map 2, grid B5
Area: 434 sq km
Altitude: 216 m

Delhi & around

Ins and outs

Air Delhi is served by the **Indira Gandhi (IGI) Airport** to the southwest of the city. The Domestic **Terminal 1** is 15 km from Connaught Circus, the central hub of activity and the main hotel area in New Delhi. It handles flights from 2 separate sections: 'A' (exclusively for *Indian Airlines*) and 'B' (for others). The International **Terminal 2** is 23 km from the centre. During the day, the journey to Connaught Circus, can take from 30 to 45 mins from the Domestic Terminal and 45 mins to 1 hr from the International Terminal. A free shuttle runs between the terminals. To get to town take a pre-paid taxi or an airport coach unless your hotel sends its own bus. **Bus** The principal **Inter State Bus Terminus (ISBT)** is at Kashmir Gate (near the Red Fort), about 30 mins by bus from Connaught Place. Services connect it to the other Delhi ISBTs. **Rail** Travellers are likely to use the 2 main stations. The busy **New Delhi** station, about 1 km or a 20-min walk north of Connaught Place, is maddeningly chaotic and requires having all your wits about you. The overpoweringly crowded **Old Delhi (Main) Station**, 2 km north of Connaught Place, also has some important trains.

Getting there
See page 93 for further details

Getting around

The City Guide published by Eicher Goodearth, New Delhi, 1998 (Rs 345), is well illustrated & the best available

Auto-rickshaws and taxis are widely available, though few are prepared to use their meters, especially for foreigners. They offer the only realistic choice for getting about the city, which is much too spread out to walk, as city buses are usually packed and have long queues. From the New Delhi train station there is a road beginning from the southern end of platform 1 which runs parallel to Chelmsford Rd, to Connaught Place, which is a hassle-free alternative during the day (gate closed at night).

Orientation

Delhi is now a very spread out city which has pushed across the state border into Gurgaon District of Haryana

Connaught Place, the main commercial centre of New Delhi, is about 1 km south of New Delhi railway station and the main backpackers' area, Paharganj. Running due south of Connaught Place is Janpath with small shops selling a variety of craft products and hotels like the *Imperial* and *Le Meridien*. Running east west across Janpath is Rajpath with all the major state buildings at its western end. Immediately beyond them is the diplomatic enclave, Chanakyapuri. Most of the upmarket hotels are scattered across the wide area between Connaught Place and the airport to the southwest. As Delhi has spread southwards a series of new markets has grown up to serve extensive housing colonies such as South Extension, Greater Kailash and Safdarjang Enclave, where huge new commercial centres are being built. This development has brought one of the major historic sites, the Qutb Minar, within the limits of the southern city, about half an hour by taxi from Connaught Place. About 2 km northeast of Connaught Place are the Jama Masjid and the Red Fort, the heart of Shahjahanabad, or Old Delhi. It too has a thriving commercial centre, focused on Chandni Chowk, but set in a far more traditional complex of winding lanes and small shops.

★ Sights

Central New Delhi

A tour of New Delhi will usually start with a visit to **India Gate**. This war memorial is situated at the eastern end of Rajpath. Designed by Lutyens, it commemorates more than 70,000 Indian soldiers who died in the First World War. Rajpath leads west from India Gate towards Janpath. To the north are the **National Archives**, formerly the Imperial Record Office. To the south is the **National Museum**.

The Secretariats, standing on either side of Raisina Hill, has a north block housing the Home and Finance Ministries, and a south block for the Ministry of Foreign Affairs. These long classical buildings, topped by Baroque domes, were designed by Baker. In the **Great Court** between the Secretariats are the four **Dominion Columns**, donated by the governments of Australia, Canada, New Zealand and South Africa – ironically, as it turned out. In the centre of the court is the Jaipur column of red sandstone topped with a white egg, bronze lotus and six-pointed glass star of India. Across the entrance to the Great Court is a 205 m wrought iron screen. At the Secretariat and Rashtrapati Bhavan gates, mounted and unmounted troops parade in full uniform. ■ *Sat 1030, worth attending.*

Rashtrapati Bhavan, once the Viceroy's House, is the official residence of the President of India. Designed by Lutyens, it combines western and eastern styles. To the south is Flagstaff House which became the Prime Minister's residence in 1948. Re-named **Teen Murti Bhawan** it now houses the Nehru Memorial Museum (see page 85). The **Martyr's Memorial**, at the junction of Sardar Patel Marg and Willingdon Crescent, has 11 statues of national heroes headed by Mahatma Gandhi.

Northeast of the Viceroy's House is the **Council House**, now **Sansad Bhavan**. Inside is the library and chambers for the Council of State, Chamber of Princes and Legislative Assembly – the Lok Sabha.

Connaught Place and its outer ring, **Connaught Circus**, comprise two-storeyed arcaded buildings, arranged radially. In 1995 they were re-named **Rajiv Chowk** and **Indira Chowk** respectively, but are still widely known by their original names. They have become the main commercial centre of Delhi. Vendors of all sorts gather in the area as well as aggressive touts ready to take advantage of the unwary traveller by getting them into spurious 'official' or 'government' shops and travel agencies.

To the south in **Janpath** (the People's Way), the east and west Courts with their long colonnaded verandahs were hostels for members of the Legislative Assembly.

Jantar Mantar was built on the orders of the Mughal Emperor Muhammad Shah (ruled 1719-48) who entrusted the renowned astronomer Maharaja Jai Singh II with the task of revising the calendar and correcting the astronomical tables used by contemporary priests. Daily astral observations were made for years before it was built in 1725. Plastered brick structures were favoured for the site instead of brass instruments.

Beyond Delhi Gate the bank of the **Yamuna** is marked by a series of memorials to India's leaders. The most prominent memorial is that of **Mahatma Gandhi** at **Raj Ghat**. To its north is **Shanti Vana** ('forest of peace'), landscaped gardens where Prime Minister Jawaharlal Nehru was cremated in 1964, and subsequently his grandson Sanjay Gandhi in 1980, daughter **Indira Gandhi** in 1984 and elder grandson, Rajiv, in 1991.

The **Purana Qila** (Old Fort), now an attractive and quiet park, witnessed the crucial struggle between the Mughal Emperor Humayun and his formidable Afghan rival Sher Shah Suri. The massive gateways and walls were probably built by Humayun around 1534. The **Qila-i-Kuhna Masjid** (mosque of the Old Fort) is considered one of the finest examples of Indo-Afghan architecture with arches, tessellations and rich ornamentation in black and white marble against red sandstone. A small museum near the Humayun Darwaza houses finds from the excavations. ■ *0800-1830. Entrance by west gate. Guide books and postcards. Clean toilets.*

Though the fort is in ruins, the mosque is in good condition

South Delhi

The beautiful **Lodi Gardens**, with mellow stone tombs of the 15th- and 16th-century Lodi rulers are 1 km to the southwest of the Purana Qila.

Hazrat Nizamuddin, a shrine of Sheikh Nizamuddin Aulia (1236-1325), a Chishti saint, is at the east end of the Lodi Road. It is visited by pilgrims of all faiths and is particularly stirring when *Qawwalis* are sung at sunset after *namaaz* (prayers). Dress ultra-modestly if you don't want to feel uncomfortable.

Humayun's tomb, eclipsed later by the Taj Mahal and the Jama Masjid, is the best example in Delhi of the early Mughal style of tomb. The tomb has an octagonal plan, lofty arches, pillared kiosks and the double dome of Central Asian origin. Here also is the first standard example of the garden tomb concept: the *char bagh* (garden divided into quadrants) has water channels and fountains. The red sandstone dome has white marble to highlight the lines of the building and there is attractive inlay work, and some *jalis*. ■ *Daily, sunrise to sunset. US$10 foreigners, Rs 10 Indians, no longer free on Fri. Video cameras Rs 25. 15 mins by taxi from Connaught Circus.*

The spacious layout of New Delhi has been preserved despite the building boom

Delhi & around

New Delhi

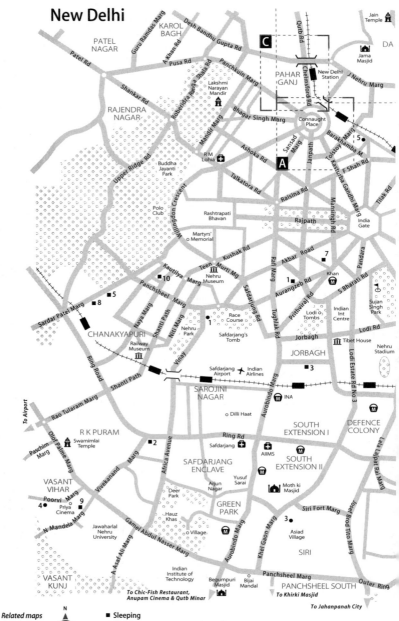

Delhi & around

Related maps
A Connaught Place, page 91
B Old Delhi, page 86
C Paharganj, page 88

N

0 metres 500
0 yards 500

■ **Sleeping**
1 Claridges
2 Hyatt Regency
3 Jorbagh 27
4 Legend Inn
5 Maurya Sheraton
6 Oberoi
7 Taj Mahal
8 Taj Palace
9 Vasant Continental
10 Youth Hostel & Moti Mahal Delux

Delhi & around

Hauz Khas, a large tank, was created by Ala-ud-din Khalji (ruled 1296-1313) for the inhabitants of **Siri**, the second capital city of Delhi. Fifty years later **Firoz Shah Tughluq** cleaned up the tank and raised several buildings on its banks. Firoz Shah's austere tomb, a *madrasa* (college) and some octagonal and square *chhattris*. Classical music concerts, dance performances and a son et lumiëre show are held in the evenings. ■ *1 hr cultural show, 1845, Rs 100 (check with Delhi Tourism). Upmarket restaurants and shops have opened.*

The Qutb Minar Complex

The Qutb Minar, built to proclaim the victory of Islam over the infidel (unbeliever), dominates the countryside for miles around. Visit the Minar first.

Qutb Minar (1) In 1199 work began on what was intended to be the most glorious tower of victory in the world and which was also to serve as the minaret attached to the Might of Islam Mosque. From here the muezzin could call the faithful to prayer. Later every mosque would incorporate its minaret. It is 73 m high and consists of five storeys. The calligraphy bands are verses from the Koran and praises to its patron builder. The staircase inside the tower to the balconies are closed.

Quwwat-ul-Islam Mosque (2) (The Might of Islam Mosque) This is the earliest surviving mosque in India. It was completed in 1198, using the remains of local Hindu and Jain temples. The screen (4) formed the façade of the mosque and, facing in the direction of Mecca, became the focal point. The sandstone screen is carved in the Indo-Islamic style, lotuses mingling with Koranic calligraphy.

- **Eating**
- 1 Basil & Thyme, Santushti Complex
- 2 Big Chill
- 3 Chopsticks & Ankur
- 4 McDonalds, TGI Friday & Baskin Robbins
- 5 Nathu's

Ala'i Minar (8) To the north of the Qutb complex is the Ala'i Minar, intended to surpass the tower of the Qutb, but not completed beyond the first storey.

Iltutmish's Tomb (3) Built in 1235, it is the first surviving tomb of a Muslim ruler in India. The idea of a tomb was quite alien to Hindus, who had been practising cremation since around 400 BC.

■ *Sunrise to sunset. US$10 foreigners, Rs 10 Indians; no longer free on Fri. Bus 505 from New Delhi Rly station (Ajmeri Gate), Super Bazar (east of Connaught Circus) and Cottage Industries Emporium, Janpath.*

Tugh luqabad

From the walls you get a magnificent impression of the strategic advantages of the site

Tughluqabad's ruins still convey a sense of the power and energy of the newly arrived Muslims in India. Ghiyas'ud-Din Tughluq (ruled 1321-25) built this massive fort around his capital city which stands high on a rocky outcrop of the Delhi Ridge. ■ *Sunrise-1700; free. Allow 1 hr. Very deserted so don't go alone. Take plenty of water. About 7½ km east from Qutb Minar. For return rickshaws, turn right at entrance and walk 200 m.*

Baha'i Temple (Lotus Temple)

Architecturally this temple is remarkably striking. Built out of white marble, it is in the characteristic Baha'i temple shape of a lotus flower surrounded by nine pools. The **Baha'i faith** was founded by a Persian, **Baha'u'llah** whose teachings were directed towards the unification of the human race. ■ *1 Apr-30 Sep 0900-1900, 1 Oct-31 Mar 0930-1730. Closed Mon. Visitors are welcome to services. Audio visual presentations in English, 1100, 1200, 1400, 1530. Getting there: Taxi or auto-rickshaw though Bus 433 from the centre (Jantar Mantar) goes to Nehru Place, within walking distance (1½ km) of the temple.*

Old Delhi

Shah Jahan (ruled 1628-58) decided to move back from Agra to Delhi in 1638. Within 10 years the huge city of **Shah Jahanabad**, now known as Old Delhi, was built. Chandni Chowk, its principle street, retains some of its former magic, though now it is a bustling jumble of shops, labyrinthine alleys running off a main thoroughfare with craftsmen's workshops, hotels, mosques and temples. Here goldsmiths, silversmiths, silk traders and embroiderers can all be found.

The Red Fort (Lal Qila)

The plan of Shah Jahan's city symbolized the link between religious authority enshrined in the Jama Masjid to the west, and political authority represented by the Diwan-i-Am in the fort, joined by Chandni Chowk, the route used by the Emperor.

Inside **Chatta Chowk** is the 'Covered Bazar', quite exceptional in the 17th century. Originally they catered for the Imperial household and carried stocks of silks, brocades, velvets, gold and silverware, jewellery and gems.

The **Swatantra Sangrama Sangrahalaya Museum** tracing India's history from the colonial period and focuses on the struggle for independence is interesting, educative and well organized. ■ *1000-1700, closed Fri.*

Between the first inner court and the royal palaces at the heart of the fort, stood the **Diwan-i-Am** (Hall of Public Audience), a showpiece intended to hint at the opulence of the palace itself.

The original **Life-Bestowing Gardens** (Hayat Baksh Bagh) were landscaped according to the Islamic principles of the Persian *char bagh*, with pavilions, fountains and water courses dividing the garden into various but regular beds.

Beyond is the single-storeyed **Diwan-i-Khas (5)** 'Hall of Private Audience', topped by four Hindu-style *chhattris* and built completely of white marble. The *dado* (lower part of the wall) on the interior was richly decorated with inlaid precious and semi-precious stones.

■ *Daily sunrise to sunset. US$5 foreigners, Rs 5 Indians; no longer free on Fri. The palaces within the fort may not open to visitors.*

The magnificent Jama Masjid, 1 km to the west of the Red Fort, is the largest mosque in India and the last great architectural work of Shah Jahan. The mosque is much simpler in its ornamentation than Shah Jahan's secular buildings – a judicious blend of red sandstone and white marble, which are interspersed in the domes, minarets and cusped arches. The minarets have great views from the top; well worth the climb for Rs 10. ■ *Visitors welcome from 30 mins after sunrise until 1200; and from 1345 until 30 mins before sunset. Free.*

Jama Masjid (The Friday Mosque)
Remove shoes & cover your head

Museums

The National Museum has a rich collection of the artistic treasure of Central Asia and India including ethnological objects from prehistoric archaeological finds to the late Medieval period. There is a research library. ■ *1000-1700, closed Mon. Janpath, T3019272. Foreigners Rs 150, students Rs 1, Indians Rs 10, camera Rs 300; free guided tours 1030, 1130, 1200, 1400. Films, 1430.*

   Nehru Memorial Museum and Library is the official residence of India's first Prime Minister, Jawaharlal Nehru, converted into a national memorial. Films and *Son et Lumière*. Very informative and vivid history of the Independence Movement. ■ *Museum 0930-1645, closed Mon. Library 0900-1900, closed Sun, free. Teen Murti Bhavan, T3014504.*

   Craft Museum, a large 'Village Complex', has over 20,000 pieces of traditional crafts from all over India – including terracottas, bronzes, enamel work, wood painting and carving, brocades and jewellery. Good crafts for sale. Interesting, evocative and highly recommended. ■ *1000-1700, closed Mon. Bhairon Rd, T3317641.*

   Rail Transport Museum preserves a memorable account of 144 years of the history of Indian Railways with 26 vintage locomotives. ■ *Apr-Sep 0930-1230, 1330-1930; Oct-Mar 0930-1230, 1330-1730, closed Mon and public holidays. Rs 5; camera Rs 10. Good booklet. Auto from centre Rs 40. T/F6880804. Chanakyapuri, southwest of Connaught Place.*

Essentials

Sleeping

Pre-paid taxis at airport may pretend not to know the location of your hotel so give full details. Cheaper **E, F** accommodation is concentrated around Janpath and Paharganj in New Delhi and Chandni Chowk in Old Delhi. Some have dormitory beds for under Rs 100. Taxes include a 10% luxury tax, 10% service charge andd 20% expenditure tax (where rooms are over Rs 1,200 per night). See page 38 for hotel classification. Hotels in New Delhi Centre are grouped under 'Central', 'Connaught Place' and 'Paharganj'.

Dial 1952, then old number, to get new phone number

LL *Radisson*, Mahipalpur, next to International Airport, T6129191, F6129090, raddel@del2.vsnl.net.in

Airport

Old Delhi

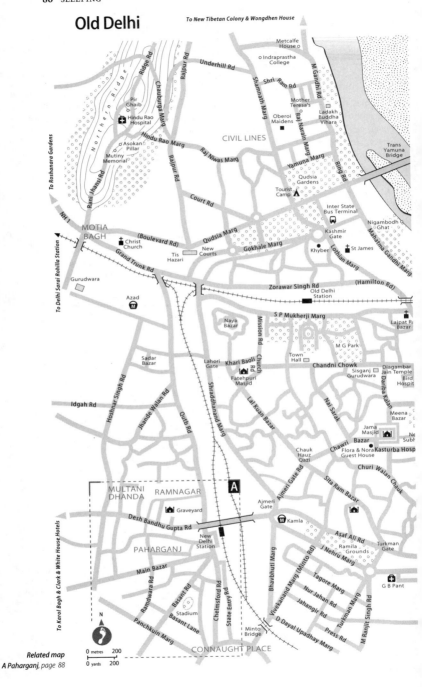

To New Tibetan Colony & Wongdhen House

Metcalfe House
Indraprastha College
Shri Ram Rd
Ridge Rd
Rajpur Rd
Underhill Rd
Shamnath Marg
M Gandhi Rd
Mother Teresa's
Ladakh Buddha Vihara
Pir Ghaib
Hindu Rao Hospital
Chauburja Marg
Oberoi Maidens
Raj Narain Marg
CIVIL LINES
Trans Yamuna Bridge
Northern Ridge
Asokan Pillar
Hindu Rao Marg
Raj Nivas Marg
Yamuna Marg
Ring Rd
Mutiny Memorial
Rajpur Rd
Qudsia Gardens
Mahatma Gandhi Marg
Rani Jhansi Rd
Court Rd
Tourist Camp
To Roshanara Gardens
Inter State Bus Terminal
Nigambodh Ghat
NH 1
MOTIA BAGH
(Boulevard Rd)
Qudsia Marg
Kashmir Gate
Christ Church
Grand Trunk Rd
Tis Hazari
New Courts
Gokhale Marg
Khyber
Lothian Marg
St James
To Delhi Sarai Rohilla Station
Gurudwara
Zorawar Singh Rd
(Hamilton Rd)
Old Delhi Station
Azad
S P Mukherji Marg
Lajpat Rai Bazar
Naya Bazar
Mission Rd
M G Park
Sadar Bazar
Lahori Gate
Khari Baoli
Church Rd
Town Hall
Chandni Chowk
Sisganj Gurudwara
Diagambar Jain Temple
Bird Hospital
Idgah Rd
Hoshiar Singh Rd
Jhande Walan Rd
Qutb Rd
Shraddhanand Marg
Fatehpuri Masjid
Lal Kuan Bazar
Nai Sarak
Dariba Kalan
Meena Bazar
Jama Masjid
New Subh
Chauk Hauz Qazi
Chawri Bazar
Flora & Nora Guest House
Kasturba Hosp
MULTANI DHANDA
RAMNAGAR
Churi Walan Chauk
Ajmeri Gate Rd
Sita Ram Bazar
A
Graveyard
Ajmeri Gate
Kamla
Asaf Ali Rd
Desh Bandhu Gupta Rd
New Delhi Station
Ramila Grounds
Turkman Gate
PAHARGANJ
Bhavbhuti Marg
J Nehru Marg
To Karol Bagh & Clark & White House Hotels
Main Bazar
Ramdwara Rd
Basant Rd
Tagore Marg
G B Pant
Vivekanand Marg (Minto Rd)
Nur Jahan Rd
Jahangir Rd
Turkman Marg
M Ranjit Singh Rd
Chelmsford Rd
State Entry Rd
Press Rd
D Dayal Upadhay Marg
Panchkuin Marg
Stadium
Basant Lane
Minto Bridge
N
CONNAUGHT PLACE

0 metres 200
0 yards 200

Related map
A Paharganj, page 88

Delhi & around

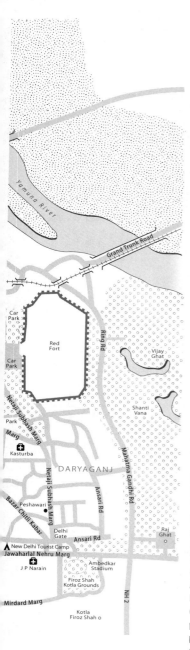

LL-L *Inter-Continental*, Barakhamba Rd, Connaught Place, T3320101, F3325335, newdelhi@interconti.com **LL-L** *Le Meridien*, Windsor Place, Janpath, T3710101, F3714545. **C-D** *Andraprastha* (ITDC), 19 Ashoka Rd, T3344511, F3368153. Excellent a/c *Coconut Grove* south Indian restaurant, (full tariff plus a day's refundable deposit in advance), good value.

Connaught Place LL-L *Park*, 15 Sansad Marg, T373247, F3732025, resv.del@park. sprintrpg.ems.vsnl.net.in **L-AL** *Imperial*, Janpath, T3341234, F3342255. 200 rooms, colonial feel, well tended gardens, good pool, **AL-A** *Hans Plaza*, 15 Barakhamba Rd (on 16th-20th floor), T3316868, F3314830. 'boutique hotel', quiet, superb views. **B** *Centrepoint*, 13 Kasturba Gandhi Marg, T3324805, F3329138. Well located, old charming building in a small park, large clean rooms, bath tubs though front rooms can be noisy. **B** *Marina*, G-59 Connaught Circus, T3324658, F3328609, marina@nde. vsnl.net.in 93 clean rooms, some large, others cramped but refurbished, good coffee shop. **B** *Nirula's*, L-Block, Connaught Circus, T3322419, F3353957. Good restaurant clean, comfortable, friendly, efficient. **B-C** *Fifty Five*, H-55 Connaught Place, T3321244, F3320769, hotelfiftyfive@hotmail.com 15 small, clean, simple rooms (some windowless), road can be a bit noisy, roof terrace for breakfast, helpful, very friendly staff. **B** *York*, K-10, Connaught Circus, T3323769, F3352419. 28 simple rooms on upper floor, restaurant (good snacks), quiet. **C-D** *YWCA International Guest House*, Sansad Marg (near Jantar Mantar), T3361561. 24 a/c rooms, centre 1 km, open to both sexes. **C-D** *YMCA Tourist Hostel*, Jai Singh Rd, T3746031, F3746032. Some a/c rooms with bath (B-Block, non a/c, shared bath), good pool (Rs 100 extra), luggage stored (Rs 5 per day), unhelpful reception, pay in advance but check bill, reserve ahead. **E-F** *Jain's Guest House*, 7 Pratap Singh Building, Janpath Lane. Rooms without bath, quiet, clean. **E** Off **Kasturba Gandhi**

See map, page 91

Central New Delhi
Airports about 15-23 km
Railway about 1-3 km

Delhi & around

Marg: **E-F** *Ringo Guest House*, 17 Scindia House, T3310605. Tiny rooms (some windowless) crowded dorm or beds on rooftop, no hot showers, basic toilets, lockers, good restaurant friendly.

There are several fairly cheap, noisy, basic hotels, often with shared baths. Inspect before deciding & avoid street-side rooms

Paharganj area C *City Palace*, 2014, Street 7, Chuna Mandi, T3542678. Pleasant new hotel, rooms (some windowless) with clean tiled baths, some a/c, 2 suites, restaurant on top. Peaceful, very friendly. **D** *Tourist Delux*, Qutb Rd, T7770985, F7777446. Comfortable a/c rooms, few **C** suites with bath tubs, vegetarian restaurant. **D-E** *Major Den's*, Lakshmi Narain St, off Rajguru Rd, T3629599. Clean, basic, quiet, good value. **D-**E *Mayur*, near *Namaskar*. New with TV and good showers. Good value. **D-E** *My Hotel*, 901 Gali Chandi Wali, T3616215. 42 pleasant rooms in a new, quiet hotel, some a/c (up to Rs 675), restaurant on top, cyber café. **D-E** *Saina International*, 2324 Chuna Mandi, near Imperial Cinema, T3529144, F7520879. Clean rooms, some a/c, hot water, open-air restaurant serves beer. **E** *Anoop*, 1566 Main Bazar, T735219. Rooms with bath, some air-cooled, very clean though basic, noisy at times, safe, good 24-hr rooftop restaurant. **E** *Hare Krishna*, 1572 Main Bazar, T7533017, harekrishnagh@hotmail.

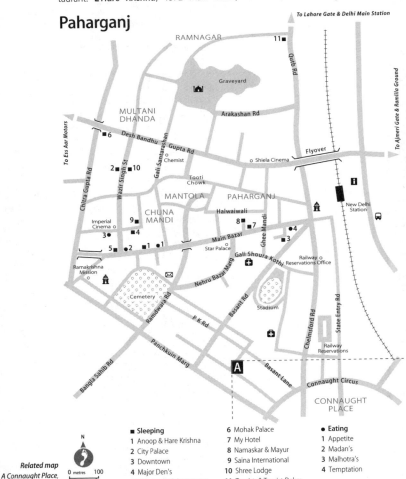

Paharganj

*Related map
A Connaught Place,
page 91*

■ **Sleeping**
1 Anoop & Hare Krishna
2 City Palace
3 Downtown
4 Major Den's
5 Metropolis & Restaurant

6 Mohak Palace
7 My Hotel
8 Namaskar & Mayur
9 Saina International
10 Shree Lodge
11 Tourist & Tourist Delux

● **Eating**
1 Appetite
2 Madan's
3 Malhotra's
4 Temptation

com Very clean rooms with bath (some windowless, stuffy), friendly, travel, restaurant (good selection of cheap pizzas). **E** *Metropolis*, 1634 Main Bazar, T7535766, F7525600. 13 rooms, some air cooled, good 4-bed dorm, clean, restaurant with wide choice but pricey. **E-F** *Downtown*, 4583 Dal Mandi, T3555815. Clean and quiet rooms, some with bath. **F** *Mohak Palace*, Multani Dhanda. Clean, friendly, safe to leave luggage. **F** *Namaskar*, 917 Chandiwalan, Main Bazar, T3621234, F7522233, namaskarhotel@yahoo.com Small rooms (2-4 beds) with bath and bucket hot water, clean but some windowless, newer **E** a/c rooms in extension (no generator), safe, quiet at night, stores luggage, 'poste restante'. **F** *Shree Lodge*, 2012-2015 Chuna Mandi, T3526864. Clean rooms, quiet.

LL *Taj Mahal*, 1 Mansingh Rd, T3016162, F3017299. Excellent restaurants and service lavishly finished. **LL** *Taj Palace*, 2 Sardar Patel Marg, T6110202, F6110808. Purpose-built for business travellers. **LL-L** *Maurya Sheraton Hotel* and *Towers*, Sardar Patel Marg, T6112233, F6113333. Splendid pool, avoid rooms near disco, good restaurants. **LL-L** *Oberoi*, Dr Zakir Hussain Marg, T4363030, F4364084. Immaculate, quietly efficient. **L-AL** *Claridges*, 12 Aurangzeb Rd, T3010211, F3010625. Colonial atmosphere, grand but frayed around the edges. **A-B** *Orchid*, G4 S Extn 1, T4643529, F4626924. 18 a/c rooms, crowded area, restaurants nearby, pleasant, helpful. **B** *Nirula's*, C-135 Sector 2, NOIDA, T85-526512, F85-551069 (also in Connaught Circus). Free transfer to town centre, pleasant atmosphere. **B** *Rajdoot*, Mathura Rd, T4699583, F4647442. 55 rooms, near Nizamuddin Rly, pool. **D-E** *Master Paying Guest*, R-500 New Rajendra Nagar (near Shankar & GR Hospital Rds), T5850914. Clean, rooms, shared facilities, rooftop for breakfast, secure. **Youth hostels F** *Youth Hostel*, 5 Naya Marg, Chanakyapuri, T3016285. Basic dorm (Rs 30), breakfast, prefer International YHA members, popular, recommended.

New Delhi
See map, page 82

Airports 9-17 km
Railway 5-9 km
Centre 5 km

AL-A *Oberoi Maidens*, 7 Sham Nath Marg, T3975464, F3980771. Colonial style in quiet area, spacious gardens with excellent pool. Personal attention. **A-B** *Broadway*, 4/15A Asaf Ali Rd, T3273821, F3269966. Indian business hotel, 32 clean but gloomy rooms, friendly, efficient, unique *Chor Bizarre* restaurant. **E** *Noor*, 421 Matia Mahal, Jama Masjid (1st left after *Flora's Restaurant*, then 3rd left), T3267791. 34 clean, quiet rooms, shared facilities (Indian WC), fans. **E** *Wongdhen House*, 15A New Tibetan Colony, Manju-ka-Tilla, by the Yamuna, T3916689, F3945962. Very clean rooms, safe, homely, good breakfast and Tibetan meals. **Camping F** *New Delhi Tourist Camp*, Nehru Marg, opposite JP Narayan Hospital, T3272898, F3263693. 130 tiny rooms (deluxe **E** rooms, cooler/TV Rs 35 extra) plus cheaper dorm beds, hot water, restaurant, exchange, pleasant gardens, EATS bus to airport (Rs 50), friendly atmosphere, secure. **F** *Tourist Camp*, Qudsia Gardens, opposite ISBT-, T2523121. Camping and huts, food available.

Old Delhi
See map, page 86

Airports 17-25 km
Old & New Delhi
Railways 1-3 km

LL *Grand Hyatt Delhi*, Nelson Mandela Rd, Vasant King Phase II, T6121234, F6895891, info@hyattdelhi.com New luxury hotel, choice of good restaurants, health club. **LL** *Hyatt Regency*, Bhikaiji Cama Place, Ring Rd, T6181234, F6186833. Rooms tiny for price. **A** *Vasant Continental*, Vasant Vihar, T6148800, F6873842. 110 rooms, convenient for airports (free transfer). **B-C** *Jorbagh '27'*, 27 Jorbagh, T4698647, F4698475. 20 a/c rooms, not plush but very quiet. **B-C** *Manor*, 77 Friends Colony, T6832171, F6840481. Boutique hotel, 'Beautiful, excellent service and restaurant'. **C** *Legend Inn*, E-4 East of Kailash, T6216111, F6483353. Comfortable a/c rooms, no restaurant, homely. **C-D** *Naari*, Vasant Kunj (easy access from airport), guest house for women in pleasant residential area, simple rooms with shower, some air-cooled, (reserve ahead T6138316, F6187401, naari@del3.vsnl.net.in

South Delhi
Airports 9-17 km
Railway 12 km
Centre 10 km

Several are 20 mins'
drive from the airport
(see map, page 82)

Delhi & around

Eating

● on maps
Price codes:
see inside front cover

The larger hotel restaurants are often the best for cuisine, décor and ambience. Buffets (lunch or dinner) cost Rs 500 or more. Alcohol is served in most top hotels, but only in some non-hotel restaurants.

Central New Delhi **Expensive** *Bukhara*, Maurya Sheraton, T6112233. Stylish Northwest Frontier cuisine. Amidst rugged walls draped with rich rugs.*Corbett's*, *Claridge's Hotel*, T3010211. Authentic North Indian. Animal park theme outdoor, jungle soundtrack, hidden animals delight children, good value. *Chinese*, does great soups. *Dum Phukt*, Maurya Sheraton, T6112233. North Indian. Slowly steam cooked to produce melt-in-the-mouth Nawabi dishes. *Las Meninas*, *Park Hotel*, 15 Sansad Marg, T3733737. Good Spanish dishes, pricey but generous *tapas* Rs 100-475. *Orient Express*, *Taj Palace Hotel*, T6110202. Continental. Recreated luxury of the famous train carriages. *Spice Route*, *Imperial Hotel*. Excellent Kerala, Thai, Vietnamese, spectacular décor. **Mid-range** *Basil and Thyme*, Santushti Complex, Chanakyapuri, T4673322. Continental. Pleasant setting, simple dÉcor, a/c, modestly priced Western snacks at lunch.

See map, page 91 **Connaught Place Area Expensive** *Amber*, N-Block, T3312092. Lightly spiced Indian. *Zen*, T3724458. Generous portions for Chinese. **Mid-range** *Berco's*, L-Block, T3318134. Chinese, Japanese. Generous helpings, fast service. *DVB*, 13 Regal Building. Newly renovated restaurant and English style, smart and cosy pub below. Round the world meals, good buffet (Rs 200), a la carte (Rs 150+), good music, great Espresso coffee. *Kwality*, Parliament St. International. Try spicy Punjabi dishes with various breads. *Mughal Hans*, at Hans Plaza, Karol Bagh. Indian. Smart, beautifully presented, delicious Mughal. *Potpourri*, Nirula's, L-Block. Indian and continental. Bright, clean and very popular –light meals, salad bar (safe!) beers, Defence Colony Flyover. *Rodeo*, A-12. Excellent Mexican and Italian. **Cheap** *Delhi Darbar*, 49 Connaught Circus. North Indian. Good mutton dishes, bar. *Don't Pass Me By*, by *Ringos*, 17 Scindia House. Chinese. Bit dingy, but good basic food and plenty of it. *Nathu's*, Bengali Market (east of Connaught Place) and also at 2 Sunder Nagar Market. Indian. Mainly vegetarian. Good *dosa idli, utthapam* and North Indian *chana bathura*, clean, functional canteen style.

Paharganj Rooftop restaurants tend to be pricier. *Appetite*, 1575 Main Bazar, T7532079. Chinese, Nepali, Italian. German bakery, good lassis. *Madan's*, 1601 Main Bazar. International. Egg and chips to *thalis*, not special but friendly, popular, good value. *Malhotra's*, 1833 Laxmi Narayan St. Good food, wide choice; also take-away. *Temptation*, at *Gold Regency*, 4350 Main Bazaar. Pleasant. Good western (veg burgers, cakes), internet, disco and bar.

Old Delhi & the North
See map, page 86
Expensive **Mid-range** *Khyber*, Rajendra Place, T5762501. Peshwari dishes. **Cheap** *Flora*, Daryaganj. North Indian. Optional floor cushions, excellent *kalmi* chicken kebab, *biryani* and breads, dark and gloomy but good food. *Peshawari*, 3707 Subhash Marg, Daryaganj. Northwest Frontier. Tiny, with tiled walls, serves delicious chicken, closed Tue.

South Delhi **Mid-range** In Asiad Village, Siri Fort Marg: *Ankur* Mughlai and Italian. Good food, bar. *Chopsticks*, T6493628. Chinese, Thai. Good value, pleasant ambience, bar, weekend buffet lunches Rs 270. *The Big Chill*, F-38 East of Kailash (off Lala Lajpat Rai Path near Spring Meadows Hospital), T6481020. 1230 till late. A bright, new café with a difference. Wholesome light meals, spectacularly successful home made ice creams and desserts. Great atmosphere, good prices.

Shopping

English language books can be bought, often at a great saving. **Connaught Place**: *Jain's Bookshop* in C-Block, is the government book agency; *Oxford Book and Stationery*, Scindia House, and *Bookworm*, B-29, have a wide selection, including art, Indology, fiction; *People Tree*, 8 Regal Bldg, Parliament St, is ecology oriented. **Old City**: *Manohar*, 4753/23 Ansar Rd, Daryaganj. A real treasure trove for books on India. *Motilal Banarsidass*, and *Munshiram Manoharlal*, Nai Sarak, Chandni Chowk, have books on Indology. **Khan Market**: *The Bookshop*, has a wide choice (also at Jor Bagh Market), as do *Bahri & Sons* opposite Main Gate. **South Extensions**: *Crossword*, Ebony, 2nd Floor, D-4, Part 2, very good selection in modern, spacious shop.

Books

Shops generally open from 1000-1930 (winter 1000-1900). Food stores, chemists stay open later

Delhi & around

Connaught Place

Sleeping
1 Centrepoint *D3*
2 Hans Plaza *C3*
3 Hotel 55 *A2*
4 Imperial *D2*
5 Jain's Guest House *C2*
6 Marina & Chemists *A1*
7 Nirula's, Ice Creams & Potpouri Restaurant *A3*
8 Park *C1*
9 Ringo Guest House & Don't Pass Me By Restaurant *C2*

10 YMCA Tourist Hostel *D1*
11 York *A3*
12 YWCA International Guest House *D1*

Eating
1 Amber *C2*
2 DVB *C2*
3 Delhi Darbar *A3*
4 Kwality *C2*
5 Wengers & Rodeo *B2*
6 Wimpy & Pizza King *C2*
7 Zen *A2*

Shopping
1 Bookworm *A2*
2 Central Cottage Industries Emporium *D2*
3 Hidesign *B1*
4 Jain's Bookshop *A2*
5 Khadi Gramodyog *B1*
6 Map Sales Office *C2*
7 Oxford Book & Stationery *C2*
8 The Shop *C1*

Clothing For **inexpensive** (Western and Indian) clothes, try bargaining in shops along Janpath and between Sansad Marg and Janpath. The underground a/c *Palika Bazar* (Connaught Circus) can be a hassle but has decent salwar kameez, leather jackets and trousers (bargain very hard). **Quality** clothes in the latest Western styles and fashionable fabrics are almost unobtainable; a modest selection (plus table linen and bedspreads) are sold at *The Shop*, Regal Building, Connaught Place; *Archana*, Gt Kailash I, which has several boutiques, and at *Fab India*, 14N, Gt Kailash I, which has excellent shirts, Nehru jackets, salwar kameez (also linen, furnishing fabrics etc). *Hauz Khas Village* and *Sunder Nagar Market* have some designer wear. For Indian style clothes and fabrics, try Janpath, the *Khadi shop*, near the Regal building, the state emporia on Baba Kharak Singh Marg, and the *Central Cottage Industries Emporium*. **Tailoring** Small shops charge around Rs 80-100 to copy a dress or shirt; trousers Rs 100-150. Nearly all big hotels have up-market boutiques and also fabric/tailor's shops (allow 24 hrs for stitching). *Khan Market*, has several tailors and cloth stores. *Shankar Market* near Connaught Place, has good suiting, corduroys, denim etc, and will suggest tailors.

Food **Spices** dried fruit, nuts etc are sold at *Khari Baoli*, Chandni Chowk, lined with colourful shops. Excellent Indian **teas** at *Central Cottage Industries Emporium*, Janpath, *Assam* and *W Bengal Emporia*. *Darjeeling Tea Bureau*, Kaka Nagar Market (opposite Delhi Golf Club), T4622442, F6843737, nathmulls@goldentipstea.com Charming, reliable and good selection.

Handicrafts **Carpets** can be found in most top hotel arcades and in shops round Connaught Place. *Government run, fixed* **Emporia** Most open 1000-1800 (close for lunch, 1330-1400). *Central Cottage Indus-* *price emporia are* tries Emporium, corner of Janpath and Tolstoy Marg, offers hassle-free shopping; they *often dull with* will pack and post overseas. *Khadi Gramodyog Bhawan*, Regal Building, for inexpensive *reluctant sales staff,* homespun cotton *kurta pajama* (loose shirt and trousers), cotton/silk waistcoats, fabrics *but give a newcomer* and Jaipuri paintings. State emporia along Baba Kharak Singh Marg include: *Bengal* (tea) *an idea of fair prices* *Delhi* (silk), *Bihar* (excellent Madhubani paintings, gems), *Gujarat* (good quilts, bedspreads), *Kashmir* (papier-mâché, shawls, carpets, wood carving), *Maharashtra* (bedspreads), *Assam* (blankets, silk, tea), *Rajasthan* (printed cotton, miniature paintings, jewellery), *Tripura* (wood sculptures, cane work), *Orissa* (silk *ikat*, stoneware, silver filigree), *UP*, *Andhra Pradesh* (dolls, printed fabric, cotton *ikat*), *Kerala* (sandalwood), *MP*. Small stalls along Janpath can be fun to explore but bargain hard. *Santushti*, Chanakyapuri, opposite *Hotel Samrat* has attractive a/c units in a garden setting. Shops sell good quality clothes, crafts, linen, saris, silver etc (1000-1800, except Sun, some close for lunch), Basil and Thyme serves trendy western snacks (busy 1300-1400); *Anokhi*, near the entrance, has good household gifts; *IK* sells quality silver gifts, jewellery and paintings. *Khazana*, at *Taj Mahal* and *Taj Palace hotels* (0900-2000; daily) is classy. **Handmade paper** *Frontline*, 78 Scindia House (off Janpath) and *Khadi Gramudyog*, Connaught Place. **Jewellery** Traditional silver and goldsmiths in Dariba Kalan, off Chandni Chowk (north of Jama Masjid). Cheap bangles and along Janpath; also at Hanuman Mandir, Gt Kailash I, N-Block, where you can get *henna* painted on the hand (Rs 25). *Jewel Mine*, 12A Palika Bazar, has silver, beads and semi-precious stones, fair prices, pleasant service. *Sundar Nagar* market (see below). **Leather** Cheap sandals from Janpath (Rs 100). *Khan Market* and *South Extension*, leather goods and shoes. *Central Cottage Industries Emporium*, Janpath. In Connaught Place: *Bharat*, opposite *Nirula's*. *Hidesign* at G49. **Marble** For inlay work, Agra is the place.

Markets *Basant Lok* Vasant Vihar, has a few up-market shops attracting the young. *Dilli Haat* *Beware of pick pockets* opposite INA Market, is a well designed open-air complex with rows of brick alcoves for craft stalls from different states, changed periodically; local craftsmen's outlets (bargaining possible), excellent occasional fairs (tribal art, textiles etc). Also good regional food – hygienic, safe 'street food'! Very pleasant, quiet, clean (no smoking) and uncrowded; no hassle. Entry Rs 5, open 1000-2200. *Hauz Khas village* has authentic, old village houses converted into designer shops selling handicrafts, ceramics, art and antiques in addition to luxury wear. *Sunder Nagar* has a few shops selling Indian hand-icrafts and jewellery (precious and semi-precious). *South Extension*, is good for clothes, shoes, jewellery, music etc. *Tibetan Market* stalls along Janpath have plenty of curios – most are new but rapidly aged to look authentic. Western travellers hankering for the familiar, and prepared to pay the price, will find a good range of eatables and toiletries in **Jorbagh and Gt Kailash Pt I-M** and in Main Bazar, Paharganj.

Transport: local

Non-polluting vehicles are widely available at about half the cost of taxis (Rs 4 per km); **Auto-rickshaw** agree fare in advance. **Cycle-rickshaws** are available in the Old City but are not allowed into Connaught Place.

The city bus service run by the Delhi Transport Corp connects all important points in **Bus** the city. Buses are often hopelessly overcrowded so only use at off-peak. For airport transport, see under 'air' below.

Private taxi: Full day local use with driver (non a/c) is about Rs 700-800, 80 km/8 hrs, **Car hire** driver overnight *bata* Rs 150 per day. Companies include: *Cozy Travels*, opposite 'Out' gate of New Delhi Rly Station, T3614991, F7534446, cozytravels@vsnl.net.com for Ambassador or similar, Rs 600 non-a/c, Rs 850 a/c. *Western Court Tourist Taxis*, 36 Janpath, outside *Hotel Imperial* T3321236; *Nature Tour*, 2591 Mandir Wali Gali, W Patel Nagar, T5709584, nature_tour_travels@yahoo.com *Budget*, 78/3 Janpath, T3715657, F3739182 and 82, Nehru Place, T6452634; *Europcar*, 14 Basant Lok, Vasant Vihar, T6140373, F6145383; M3 Connaught Circus, T6862248; *Hertz*, Barakhamba Rd, T3318695; Bhikaji Cama Place, T6197188, F6197206.

Karol Bagh shops: *Chawla Motorcycles*, 1770, Shri Kissan Dass Marg, Naiwali Gali; *Inder* **Motorcycle** *Motors*, 1744 Hari Singh Nalwa Gali, Abdul Aziz Rd, T5725879; *Nanna Motors*, 112 Press Rd (east of Connaught Circus), T3351769; *Ess Aar Motors*, Jhandewalan Extn, west of Paharganj.

In yellow-top taxis the meter is often not updated so ask for the conversion card. **Taxi** Add 25% night charge (2300-0500). These extras apply to auto-rickshaws as well. *Mega Cab* are to introduce a fleet of 500 new taxis running on eco-friendly com-pressed natural gas.

Transport: long distance

International flights arrive at the **Indira Gandhi International Terminal. Enquiries** **Air** T5622011: pre-recorded arrivals and departures, T144/5; reservations, T146. Money changing: Thomas Cook accepts only their own TCs. **Palam Domestic Terminal**. Enquiries T3295121: pre-recorded arrivals and departures, T142/3; private airlines, T149; reservations, *Indian Airlines* T141.

Delhi has daily flights to Agra US$55, Ahmadabad US$135, Jaipur US$90, Mumbai US$175, Rajkot US$150, Udaipur US$105, and non-daily flights to Jaisalmer US$135 and Jodhpur US$105.

Delhi & around

Transport to and from the airport Bus: Run by Ex-Servicemen's Airlink Transport Service (EATS), F Block Connaught Pl, T3316530, **Delhi Transport Corp (DTC)** and **Airports Authority of India (AAI)** from the 2 terminals go to Connaught Place, New Delhi Railway Station and ISBT (Kashmir Gate) via some hotels. One leaves from *Indian Airlines* office, Connaught Place, goes to the Domestic and then the International terminal, 0400,0530, 0730, 1000, 1400, 1530, 1800, 1900, 2200, 2330; Rs 50; Rs 10 luggage. There is a booth just outside 'Arrivals' at the International and Domestic terminals. A bus is a safe, economical option, particularly for the first-time visitor on a budget. At night, take a pre-paid taxi. **Free shuttle** between the 2 terminals every 30 mins during the day. Some hotel buses leave from the Domestic terminal. **Bus 780** runs between the **airport** and **New Delhi Railway station**.

Taxi: The International and Domestic terminals have **pre-paid taxi** counters outside the baggage hall which ensure that you pay the right amount (give your name, exact destination and number of all items of luggage). Most expensive are white 'DLZ' **limousines** and then white 'DLY' **luxury taxis**. Cheapest are 'DLT' **ordinary Delhi taxis** (black with yellow top Ambassador/Fiat cars, often very old). See page 33. Take your receipt to the ticket counter outside to find your taxi and give it to the driver when you reach the destination; you don't need to tip. From the International terminal **DLT taxis** Rs 200 for town-centre (Connaught Place area); night charges, double, 2300-0500.

Hotel booking service: The Government **Tourist Information** desk will book a hotel but not in the 'budget' category. **Indian Railways Counter**. Helpful computerized booking; easier and quicker than at a station.

Road Bus All road journeys in India are slow. The main roads out of Delhi are very heavily congested. Best time to leave is very early morning. **Inter-State Bus Termini (ISBT)**; these have bus services between them. Allow at least 30 mins for buying a ticket and finding the right bus. **Kashmir Gate**, T2968709, has a restaurant, left luggage (Rs 5 per day). **Delhi TC**, T2968836.

Train New Delhi Rly Station and **Hazrat Nizamuddin Station** (just north, and 5 km southeast of Connaught Place, respectively) connect Delhi with most major destinations. The latter has many important south-bound trains. **Old Delhi (Main) Station**, 6 km north of the centre, has broad and metre gauge trains. **Enquiries** T131, T3366177. Waiting rooms and rest rooms are for those 'in transit'. Authorized **porters** (*coolies*) wear red shirts and white *dhotis*. The number on the brass badge identifies each so it is best to make a note of it, and agree the charge, before engaging one. For **left luggage**, you need a secure lock and chain. **Reservations** T1330 or 3348686, Old Delhi T3975357. Allow time (1-2 hrs) and be prepared to be very patient as it can be a nightmare but don't be tempted to go to an unauthorized agents (see below). The Central Booking Office has counters for paying by credit cards (although these cannot be used for booking tickets on the tourist quota). **Computerized reservation offices** (in separate building in Connaught Circus); 0745-2100, Sun 0745-1400; fee Rs 20. The Sarojini Nagar office is quick, hassle free (especially the credit card counter). Alternatively, you can use a recommended travel agent for tickets/reservations and pay Rs 30-50 fee.

At **New Delhi Station**: International Tourist Bureau (ITB), 1st Floor, Main Building, T3734164, for foreigners, Mon-Fri 0930-1630; Sat 0930-1430. You need your passport and visa; pay in US$, or rupees (with an encashment certificate). Those with *Indrail* passes, should look for sign to confirm bookings. Get a copy of 'Trains at a glance' (Rs 25) if you plan to travel extensively by train. There is also a counter for foreigners and NRIs at Delhi Tourism, N-36 Connaught Place, 1000-1700, Mon-Sat. The airport counter (when open) is quick and efficient for tickets and reservations. **Exchange**: Thomas Cook, near Platform 12, New Delhi station, by VIP Parking, Ajmeri Gate, open 24 hrs. The **pre-paid taxi** and **auto-rickshaw** kiosks are next to the taxi rank as you come out of the station. See under airport taxis above. An auto to Connaught Place costs Rs 12, Old Delhi Station Rs 25. Rickshaw drivers/touts may say the ITB is closed/ has moved and suggest alternatives. Ignore them.

Stations from which trains originate are given codes: **OD** – Old Delhi, **ND** – New Delhi, **HN** – Hazrat Nizamuddin.

Agra: *Shatabdi Exp, 2002*, ND 0600, 2 hrs; *Taj Exp, 2180*, HN, 0715, 2¾ hrs. **Ahmadabad**: *Rajdhani* Tue, Thu, Sat. **Jaipur**: *Shatabdi Exp, 2015*, daily except Sun, ND, 0615, 4¾ hrs; *Delhi-Jodhpur Exp, 4859*, OD, 1655, 5½ hrs; *Chetak Exp, 9615*, DSR, 1410, 7½ hrs. **Mumbai** (Central): *Rajdhani Exp, 2952*, ND, 1600, 17 hrs; *Paschim Exp, 2926*, ND, 1700, 22 hrs; *Golden Temple Mail, 2904*, ND, 0755, 22 hrs; *Jammu Tawi-Bombay Exp, 2472*, Tue, Wed, Fri, Sat, ND, 2145, 20½ hrs. **Udaipur**: *Chetak Exp, 9615*, DSR, 1410, 20¼ hrs; *Ahamadabad Exp, 9943*, DSR, 2100, 21 hrs.

For special steam *Fairy Queen* and the diesel *Palace on Wheels* tours see page 47 under Rajasthan. The latter departs from Delhi Cantonment every Wed from Sep to Apr, US$270-325 each per night with 2 sharing a cabin.

Directory

Airline offices

Abbreviations used: A = Airport phone no. KG Marg = Kasturba Gandhi Marg

Domestic: Check in for all ***Indian Airlines*** flights at terminal 1-A. Check in for all other domestic airlines Terminal 1-B, J Class Tele Check-in T5665166. Arrivals for all domestic flights Terminal 1-C. ***Indian Airlines***, Safdarjang Airport, Aurobindo Marg, 24-hr daily (to avoid delays be there at 0830), T141, T4620566, 4624332 (2100-0700), closed Sun; pre-recorded flight information (English) T142. Reservations also 1000-1700, Mon-Sat, at PTI Building, Sansad Marg, T3719168; at *Ashok Hotel*, T6110101; A5665121 (and F-block, Connaught Place). ***Alliance Air*** is a subsidiary, Safdarjang Airport, T4621267, A5665854. **Private:** ***Jagson Airways***, 12 E Vandana Building, 11 Tolstoy Marg, T3328580, A5665375. ***Jet Airways***, 13 Community Centre, Yusuf Sarai, T T6853700; G-12 Connaught Place, T3320961, A5665404, Tele Check-in T6562266. ***Sahara***, 7th Flr, 14 KG Marg, T3326851, A5665234.

Tourist offices

Information offices: ***Govt of India Tourist Office***, 88 Janpath, T3320008 (0900-1800, closed Sun). ***Delhi Tourism***, N-36 Connaught Place, T3315322, F3313637. For hotel, transport and tours: 18, DDA SCO Complex, Defence Colony, T4623782, Coffee Home Annexe, Baba Kharak Singh Marg, T3365358. ***ITDC***, L-Block Connaught Place, T3320331. Counters at ITDC hotels (Ashok). **State tourist offices:** open 1000-1800, Mon-Fri. On Baba Kharak Singh Marg: ***Gujarat***, A-6, T3340305. ***Rajasthan***, Bikaner House, Pandara Rd, south of India Gate, T3381884.

Travel agents

See also page 31

We list a few. Some will get air and rail tickets/reservations for about Rs 50 ***American Express***, A-Block, Connaught Place, T3324119. ***Cozy Travel***, opposite 'Out' gate of New Delhi Railway Station, T3614991, F7534446, cozytravels@vsnl.net.com Prompt ticketing, tours. ***Creative Travel***, 27-30 Creative Plaza, Nanak Pura, Moti Bagh, T4679192, F6889764. ***Mahendra Travels***, 2 Scindia House on Janpath, T3737861, F3737862, Friendly, reliable, knowledgeable. ***Outbound***, 216A/11 Gautam Nagar, T6521308, F6522617, outbound@vsnl.com ***Paradise Holidays***, 20-B Basant Lok, Community centre, Vasant Vihar, T6145116, F6145112, paradise@del2.vsnl.in ***Peak Adventure***, T-305, DAV Complex, DDA Shopping Complex, Mayur Vihar Phase-1, T2711284,

F2711292, peakadv@nde.vsnl.net.in **Perfect Travel**, 108 Pragati Tower, 26 Rajindra Place, T/F5751536, perfect@giasdl01.vsnl.net.in **Royal Expeditions**, R-184, Gt Kailash I, T6238545, F6475954, www.royalexpeditions.com **STIC**, Hotel Imperial, Janpath, T3327582. Student specialists. **Thomas Cook**, Hotel Imperial, Janpath, T3342171; 85A Panchkuin Marg, T3747404; International Trade Towers, Nehru Place, T6423035. **Wanderlust**, M51/52 Palika Bhawan, opposite Hyatt Regency, T4102180, F6885188, www.wanderlustindia.com **Y's**, YMCA Tourist Hostel, Jaisingh Rd, T3361915.

Useful numbers Ambulance (24 hrs): T102. **Fire:** T101. **Police:** T100.

Agra

Phone code: 0562
Colour map 2, grid C6
Population: 956,000

Like Delhi, Agra stands on the right bank of the river Yamuna. The romance of the world's most famous building still astonishes in its power. In addition to the Taj Mahal, Agra houses the great monuments of the Red Fort and the I'timad-ud-Daulah, but to experience their beauty you have to endure the less attractive sides of one of India's least prepossessing towns. A big industrial city, the monuments are often covered in a haze of all too polluted air, while visitors may be subjected to a barrage of high power selling. Despite it all, the experience is still unmissable. The city is also the convenient gateway to the abandoned capital of Fatehpur Sikri, nearby.

Ins & outs
See page 106 for further details

Getting there By far the best way to see Agra on a day trip from Delhi is by using the Shatabdi Express train, which gives you 12 hrs in the city. Considering waiting time and delays, it is often faster than flying, and infinitely more comfortable than bus or car. There are frequent 'express' buses from Delhi and Jaipur, but it can take up to 5 tiring hours of often nightmare driving by bus or car. **Getting around** Buses run a regular service between the station, bus stands and the main sites and up to 2 km of the Taj Mahal. See 'Entrances' on page 101. Cycle-rickshaws and taxis can be hired to go further afield, or a bike if it's not too hot. **Climate** Best time to visit is between Nov and Mar.

Background In winter the river shrinks from its monsoon turbulence to a meagre trickle. The polluted condition of the river is a reminder of the fact that Agra today is one of Uttar Pradesh's largest and most industrialized cities. With minor interruptions Agra alternated with Delhi as the capital of the Mughal Empire.

Akbar lived in Agra in the early years of his reign. Ralph Fitch, the English Elizabethan traveller, described a 'magnificent city, with broad streets and tall buildings'. He also saw Akbar's new capital at Fatehpur Sikri, 40 km west, describing a route lined all the way with stalls and markets. Akbar moved his capital again to Lahore, before returning to Agra in 1599, where he spent the last six years of his life. **Jahangir** left Agra for Kashmir in 1618 and never returned. Despite modifying the Red Fort and building the Taj Mahal, **Shah Jahan** too moved away in 1638 to his new city Shah Jahanabad in Delhi, though he returned in 1650 to spend his last days in Agra as his son Aurangzeb's prisoner. **Aurangzeb**, the last of the Great Mughals, moved the seat of government permanently to Delhi. In the 18th century it suffered at the hands of the Jats, was taken, lost and retaken by the Marathas who, in turn, were ousted by the British in 1803.

When in Agra

■ Don't rush – sit around the gardens and soak up the atmosphere.

■ Every visitor to the Taj Mahal should also try to allow time for the Fort and the little gem, the I'timad-ud-Daulah.

■ Avoid visiting the monuments on Friday and during Urs in early January, marking Shah Jahan's death anniversary, when entry is free and it can get very crowded. Agra is becoming exceptionally popular around Christmas with Indian and foreign visitors. Very long queues form at the Taj Mahal and the Red Fort. Get there as early as you can and be patient.

■ You don't need a guide. They are generally more interested in getting you to a carpet or marble factory.

■ Many unofficial guides at the Taj will try to get money by showing you the 'best' place to photograph or 'yodeling' inside the tomb. Don't pay. For the truly amateur photographer – look out for reflections in the water – you'll be delighted by the effect. Many find the aggressive hawkers here particularly unpleasant. Con-men posing as students sometimes approach visitors: keep your distance.

■ In late winter and spring, **wild bees** often nest in the outer walls of some of Agra's major buildings. While there is no cause for alarm, they can sometimes be a nuisance under foot at the Taj Mahal and in the Red Fort.

★ Agra Fort (Red Fort)

On the west bank of the Yamuna River, Akbar's magnificent fort dominates the centre of the city. You can only enter now from the Amar Singh gate in the south. Although only the southern third of the fort is open to the public, this includes nearly all the buildings of interest.

The fortifications tower above the wide, deep moat gives it a feeling of great defensive power. The best route round is to start with the building on your right before going through the gate at the top of the broad 100 m ramp; the gentle incline made it suitable for elephants.

These buildings retain some distinctively Islamic Persian features – the geometrical planning of the pavilions and the formal layout of the gardens, for example. Tillotson points out that here 'Hindu motifs are treated in a new manner. The temple columns and corbel capitals have been stripped of their rich carving and turned into simpler, smoother forms. The *chhattris* have Islamic domes, the indigenous motifs are bound with Islamic components into a new style. The unity is assisted by the use of the cusped arch and the *Bangladar* roof'.

Jahangiri Mahal (1) Despite its name, this was built by Akbar (circa 1570) as women's quarters. It is all that survives of his original palace buildings. In front is a large **stone bowl** with steps both inside and outside, which was probably filled with fragrant rose water for bathing. The presence of distinctively Hindu features in the exterior does not indicate a synthesis of architectural styles at this early stage of Mughal architecture, as can be seen much more clearly from inside the Jahangiri Mahal Jodha Bai's Palace (2), on the south side, is named after one of Jahangir's wives.

Through the slits in the wall you can see the Taj

Turn left through to **Shah Jahan's Khas Mahal** (1636). The open tower allows you to view the walls and see to your left the decorated Mussaman Burj tower.

Anguri Bagh (3) (Vine Garden) The formal, geometric gardens are on the left. In the middle of the white marble platform wall in front is a decorative water slide. The surface was scalloped to produce a rippling waterfall, or inlaid to create a shimmering stream bed. Behind vertical water drops, there are little cusped arch niches into which flowers would be placed during the day and lamps at night. The open pavilion on your right has a superb view across to the Taj.

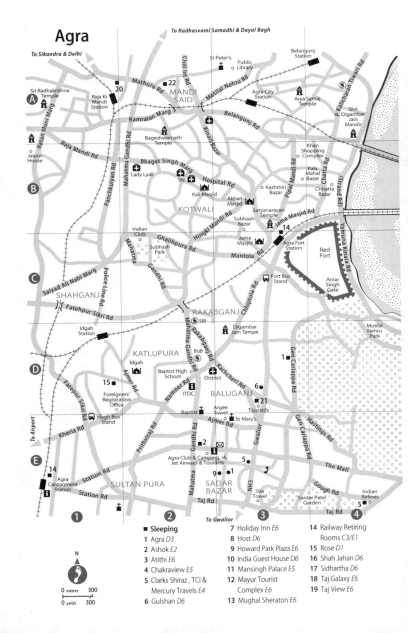

Agra

Golden Pavilions (4) The curved *chala* roofs of the small pavilions by the Khas Mahal are based on the roof shape of Bengali village huts constructed out of curved bamboo, designed to keep off heavy rain. These were probably ladies' bedrooms, with hiding places for jewellery in the walls.

Khas Mahal (5) The interior decoration of this gives an impression of how splendid the painted ceiling must have been. The metal rings were probably used for *punkhas*. Underneath are cool rooms used to escape the summer heat.

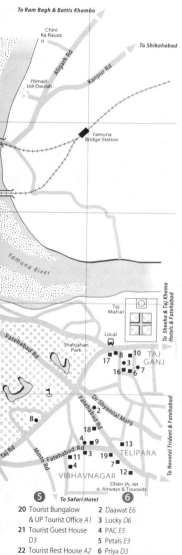

To Ram Bagh & Battis Khamba

Chini Ka Rauza

Aligarh Rd

To Shikohabad

Kanpur Rd

I'timad-Ud-Daulah

Yamuna Bridge Station

Yamuna River

Taj Mahal

Local

Shahjahan Park

Fatehabad Rd

To Sheeha & Taj Khema Hotels & Fatehabad

17   8   10   TAJ GANJ

16   6   7

Dr Shyamlal Marg

2

8   18

4   9   13

Fatehabad Rd

Taj Rd   Minto Rd

11   3   19   TELIPARA

4   7

12

VIBHAVNAGAR   Dhen IA, Jet Airways & Touraids

To Novotel Trident & Fatehabad

5   To Safari Hotel   **6**

20 Tourist Bungalow & UP Tourist Office *A1*
21 Tourist Guest House *D3*
22 Tourist Rest House *A2*

● **Eating**
1 Chung Wah *E3*

2 Daawat *E6*
3 Lucky *D6*
4 PAC *E5*
5 Petals *E3*
6 Priya *D3*
7 Shankar Vegis *D6*
8 Sonam *E5*
9 Zorba the Buddha *E3*

Mussaman Burj (6) On the left of the Khas Mahal is a beautiful octagonal tower with an open pavilion which could well have been used as the Emperor's bedroom. It has been suggested that this is where Shah Jahan lay on his deathbed, gazing at the Taj. The inlay work here is exquisite, especially above the pillars.

Sheesh Mahal (7) (Mirror Palace) Here are further examples of decorative water engineering in the hammams; the water here may have been warmed by lamps. The mirrors, which were more precious than marble, were set into the walls, often specially chiselled to accommodate their crooked shape.

Diwan-i-Khas (8) The Hall of Private Audience (1637) is next to the Mussaman Burj. The interior would have been richly decorated with tapestries and carpets. The double columns in marble inlaid with semi-precious stones in delightful floral patterns in *pietra dura* have finely carved capitals.

In front of the Diwan-i-Khas are two throne 'platforms' on a **terrace (9)**. The **black marble throne (10)** at the rear of the terrace was used by Jahangir when claiming to be Emperor at Allahabad. The Emperor sat on the white marble platform facing the **Machhi Bhavan (11)** or Fish Enclosure, which once contained pools and fountains.

Diwan-i-Am (12) Go down an internal staircase and you enter the Diwan-i-Am from the side. On the

Delhi & around

back wall of the pavilion are *jali* screens to enable the women of the court to watch without being seen. The throne alcove of richly decorated white marble used to house the Peacock Throne. 'The canopy was carved in enamel work and studded with individual gems, its interior was thickly encrusted with rubies, garnets and diamonds, and it was supported on 12 emerald covered columns' writes Tillotson. When Shah Jahan moved his capital to Delhi he took the throne with him to the Red Fort, only for it to be taken back to Persia as loot by Nadir Shah in 1739.

Nagina Masjid (13) From the corner opposite the Diwan-i-Khas two door-ways lead to a view over the small courtyards of the *zenana* (harem). Further round in the next corner is the Nagina Masjid, the private mosque of the ladies of the court. Beneath it was a *mina* bazar for the ladies to make purchases from the marble balcony above.

Looking out of the Diwan-i-Am you can see the domes of the **Moti Masjid** (Pearl Mosque, 1646-53), closed to visitors because of structural problems. In the paved area in front of the Diwan-i-Am is a large well and the tomb of **Mr John Russell Colvin**, the Lieutenant Governor of the Northwest Provinces.

The **bookshop** has a selection often sold at 25% discount. The **café** is a pleasant place for a drink or ice-cream before leaving the Fort.

■ *0700-1800. Fri free for Indians (often very crowded), though this is under review. Foreigners US$10, Indians Rs 15. Allow minimum of 1½ hrs for a visit. Guide books and good postcards. Reasonable toilet; the better toilet block built by a hotel chain is often locked.*

★ I'timad-ud-Daulah and the east bank

Beware, the monkeys here are aggressive & may attack without provocation

Sometimes called 'Baby Taj' set a startling precedent as the first Mughal build-ing to be faced with white marble inlaid with contrasting stones. Unlike the Taj it is small, intimate and has a gentle serenity.

The tomb was built for **Ghiyas Beg**, a Persian who had obtained service in Akbar's court, and his wife, see page 382. On Jahangir's succession in 1605 he became *Wazir* (Chief Minister). Jahangir fell in love with his daughter, **Mehrunissa**, who at the time was married to a Persian. When her husband died in 1607, she entered Jahangir's court as a lady-in-waiting. Four years later Jahangir married her. Thereafter she was known first as **Nur Mahal** ('Light of the Palace'), later being promoted to **Nur Jahan** ('Light of the World'), see page 382. Her niece Mumtaz married Shah Jahan

The plan
There is a good view from the roof of the entrance

Nur Jahan built the tomb for her father in the *Char Bagh* that he himself had laid out. It is beautifully conceived in white marble, mosaic and lattice.

Marble screens of geometric lattice work permit soft lighting of the inner chamber. The yellow marble caskets appear to have been carved out of wood. On the engraved walls of the chamber is the recurring theme of a wine flask with snakes as handles – perhaps a reference by Nur Jahan, the tomb's creator, to her husband Jahangir's excessive drinking. Stylistically, the tomb marks a change from the sturdy and manly buildings of Akbar's reign to softer, more feminine lines.

The main chamber, **Pietra dura**, richly decorated with mosaics and semi-precious stones inlaid in the white marble, contains the tomb of I'timad-ud-Daulah ('Pillar of the goverment') and his wife. Some have argued that the concept and skill must have travelled from its European home of

16th-century Florence to India. However,Florentine *pietra dura* is figurative whereas the Indian version is essentially decorative and can be seen as a refinement of its Indian predecessor, the patterned mosaic. See also page 103.

■ *0700-1800. Indians Rs 15 (currently free on Fri); foreigners US$10 includes still camera.*

The Persian Afzal Khan, who was a minister under Shah Jahan, is buried here, 1 km north of the I'timad-ud-Daulah. The chamber has been severely damaged. The outside is decorated with glazed (*chini*) tiles, showing strong Persian influence. A visit to the roof of the Chini ka Rauza shows how the false dome is carried on a drum base over the true dome, to aggrandize it. ■ *Sunrise to sunset. Free.*

Chini ka Rauza

At 3 km upstream from I'timad-ud-Daulah, Ram Bagh is believed to be the first Mughal garden in India. Reputed to have been laid out by Babur (ruled 1526-30) as a pleasure garden, it was the resting place of his body before its interment at Kabul. Now in ruins, it is being cleaned up and its layout restored. ■ *Sunrise to sunset. Rs 2.*

Ram Bagh

The unfinished **Radhasvami Samadhi** at Dayal Bagh is 3 km north of the City Station on the Dayal Bagh Rd. Work on this incredible cross between the Taj Mahal and London's Albert Memorial started in 1904 and continues. You can see marble cutting, sculpting and *pietra dura* work.

Delhi & around

★ The Taj Mahal

When the Taj Mahal was constructed, the Mughal Empire was already past its prime. The Taj, despite its unquestionable beauty, was an extravagance which the empire could not afford. Because of his profligate overspending of State funds, for the last eight years of his life, Shah Jahan was imprisoned by his son Aurangzeb and confined to his marble palace at the Agra Fort.

History
No photos inside the tomb (instant fines)

The white marble of the Taj is extraordinarily luminescent and even on dull days seems bright. The whole building appears to change its hue according to the light in the sky. In winter (December-February), it is worth being there at sunrise. Then the mists that often lie over the river Yamuna lift as the sun rises and casts its golden rays over the pearl white tomb. Beautifully lit in the soft light, the Taj appears to float on air. At sunset, the view from across the river is equally attractive.The Archaeological Survey of India explicitly asks visitors not to make donations to anyone including the custodians in the tomb who often ask for money.

Viewing
Visit at sunrise & sunset to avoid crowds & take photographs in peace (early morning can be misty). Opening times may alter, so check

To reduce damage to the marble by the polluted atmosphere, local industries are having to comply with strict rules now and vehicles emitting noxious fumes are not allowed within 2 km of the monument. People are increasingly using horse drawn carriages or walking. You can approach the Taj from three directions. The western entrance is usually used by those arriving from the Fort. At the Eastern entrance, rickshaws and camel drivers offer to take visitors to the gate for up to Rs 100 each; however, an official 'battery bus' ferries visitors from the car park to the gate for Rs 2 each.

Entrances

In the unique beauty of the Taj, subtlety is blended with grandeur and a massive overall design is matched with immaculately intricate execution. You will already have seen the dome of the tomb in the distance, looking almost like a

The approach

miniature, but as you go into the open square the Taj itself is so well hidden that you almost wonder where it can be. The glorious surprise is kept until the last moment, for wholly concealing it is the massive red sandstone gateway of the entrance, symbolizing the divide between the secular world and paradise.

The gateway, completed in 1648 though the huge brass door, is recent. The original doors (plundered by the Jats) were solid silver and decorated with 1,100 nails whose heads were contemporary silver coins. Although the gateway is remarkable in itself, one of its functions is to prevent you getting any glimpse of the tomb inside until you are right in the doorway itself. From here only the tomb is visible, stunning in its nearness, but as you move forward the minarets come into view.

The garden The Taj garden, well kept though it is nowadays, is nothing compared with its
You may see former glory. The guiding principle is one of symmetry. The *char bagh*, sepa-
bullocks pulling the rated by the watercourses (rivers of heaven) originating from the central,
lawnmowers around! raised pool, were divided into 16 flower beds, making a total of 64. The trees, all carefully planted to maintain the symmetry, were either cypress (signifying death) or fruit trees (life). The channels were stocked with colourful fish and the gardens with beautiful birds. It is well worth wandering along the side avenues for not only is it much more peaceful but also good for framing photos of the tomb with foliage.

The mosque On the east and west sides of the tomb are identical red sandstone buildings.
& its jawab On the west (left hand side) is a mosque. It is common in Islam to build one next to a tomb. It sanctifies the area and provides a place for worship. The replica on the other side is known as the **Jawab** (answer). This cannot be used for prayer as it faces away from Mecca.

The tomb The four **minarets** at each corner of the plinth provide balance to the tomb. Each has a deliberate slant outwards. Familiar with the disastrous effects of earthquakes on mosques in Gujarat to the south, the architects designed the minarets so they would fall away from the tomb, not onto it.

There is only one point of access to the **plinth** and tomb where, shoes must be removed (socks can be kept on; remember the white marble gets very hot) or cloth overshoes worn (Rs 2, though strictly free).

The **tomb** is square with bevelled corners. At each corner smaller domes rise while in the centre is the main dome topped by a brass finial. The dome is actually a double dome and this device, Central Asian in origin, was used to gain height. The resemblance of the dome to a huge pearl is not coincidental. The exterior ornamentation is calligraphy (verses of the Koran), beautifully carved panels in bas relief and superb inlay work.

The **interior** of the mausoleum comprises a lofty central chamber, a crypt (*maqbara*) immediately below this, and four octagonal corner rooms. The central chamber contains replica tombs, the real ones being in the crypt. The public tomb was originally surrounded by a jewel encrusted silver screen. Aurangzeb removed this, fearing it might be stolen, and replaced it with an octagonal screen of marble carved from one block of marble and inlaid with precious stones. It is a stupendous piece of workmanship. If you examine the flowers by placing a flashlight on the surface you can see how luminescent the marble is and the intricacy of the inlay work. This chamber is open at sunrise, but may close during the day.

Above the tombs is a **Cairene lamp** whose flame is supposed to never go out. This one was given by Lord Curzon, Governor General of India

(1899-1905), to replace the original which was stolen by Jats. The tomb of Mumtaz with the 'female' slate, rests immediately beneath the dome. If you look from behind it, you can see how it lines up centrally with the main entrance. Shah Jahan's tomb is larger and to the side, marked by a 'male' pen-box, the sign of a cultured or noble person. Not originally intended to be placed there but squeezed in by Aurangzeb, this flaws the otherwise perfect symmetry of the whole complex. Finally, the acoustics of the building are superb, the domed ceiling being designed to echo chants from the Koran and musicians' melodies.

The **museum** above the entrance has a small collection of Mughal memorabilia, photographs and miniatures of the Taj through the ages but has no textual information. Sadly, lights do not always work. ■ *1000-1700, closed Fri.*

Jami Masjid (1648), near the Fort railway, is attributed to Shah Jahan's dutiful elder daughter Jahanara. The fine marble steps and bold geometric patterns on the domes are quite striking. The large gardens have deer, black buck and monkeys.

■ *Open daily* **except Mon**, *Fri free for Indians (no access to underground tomb). 0600-1900. Rs 15 (Indians); foreigners US$10 plus Rs 500 'tax' (this allows Rs 40 reduction at the other Agra sites); includes still camera (video cameras may not be allowed). A torch is very useful for the crypt, though officially they are not allowed within the complex! Allow at least 1 hr.*

★ Sikandra

Akbar's tomb Following the Timurid tradition, Akbar (ruled 1556-1605) had started to build his own tomb at Sikandra. He died during its construction and his son **Jahangir** completed it in 1613. The result is an impressive, large but architecturally confused tomb. A huge gateway, the **Buland Darwaza**, leads to the great garden enclosure. The decoration on the gateway is strikingly bold, with its large mosaic patterns, a forerunner of the *pietra dura* technique. The white minarets atop the entrance were an innovation which reappear, almost unchanged, at the Taj Mahal. The walled garden enclosure is laid out in the *char bagh* style, with the mausoleum at the centre.

Morning is the best time to visit when few others are likely to be around

A broad paved path leads to the 22.5-m high tomb with four storeys. The lowest storey, nearly 100 m sq and 9-m high, contains massive cloisters. The entrance on the south side leads to the tomb chamber. Shoes must be removed or cloth overshoes worn; hire Rs 2. In a niche opposite the entrance is an alabaster tablet inscribed with the 99 divine names of Allah. The sepulchre is in the centre of the room, whose velvety darkness is pierced by a single slanting shaft of light from a high window. The custodian, in expectation of a donation, makes 'Akbaaarrrr' echo around the chamber.

Four kilometres south of Sikandra, nearly opposite the high gateway of the ancient **Kach ki Sarai** building, is a sculptured horse, believed to mark the spot where Akbar's favourite horse died. There are also *kos minars* (marking a *kos*, about 4 km) and several other tombs on the way.

■ *Sunrise-sunset; parking by the main entrance. Entry Rs 15 (Indians); foreigners US$10; includes still camera. Video Rs 25.*

UP Tourism, *Taj Khema*, east Gate, Taj Mahal, T330140. Coach Tours: **Tours** Fatehpur Sikri-Taj Mahal-Agra Fort (full day) 1000-1800, Rs 100 (including guide but not entry fee); Sikandra-Fatehpur Sikri (half a day) 0930-1400,

Rs 100 (excludes entry fees); Sikandra-Fatehpur Sikri-Taj Mahal-Agra Fort (full day), 0930-1800; Fatehpur Sikri (half a day) 1030-1400 which only gives 45 mins at the site; not worthwhile, better take a taxi if you can afford it. Some tours start and finish at Agra Cantt Rly Station, T368598.

Essentials

Sleeping
■ *on maps*
Price codes:
see inside front cover

Most are 5-10 km
from the airport &
2-5 km from
Agra Cantt Rly.
Top hotels offer
discounts May-Sep

LL-L *Mughal Sheraton* (Welcomgroup), Fatehabad Rd, T331701, F331730. 285 rooms, *Nauratna* restaurant (bland Mughlai), good live Indian music, beautifully designed in the Mughal tradition, rooftop observatory offers good views of the Taj. **L** *Clarks Shiraz*, 54 Taj Rd, T361421, F361428, clarkraj@nda.vsnl.net.in 237 rooms (bit tired), good rooftop restaurant with live music, distant view of the Taj from top floor, good shops, pleasant gardens and pool. **L** *Taj View* (Taj Group), Fatehabad Rd, T331841, F331860. 100 rooms, superior (even nos) have very distant Taj view, lacks character, good pool, *Khazana* shop. **L** *Mansingh Palace* (was *Mumtaz*, now Mansingh Group), 181/2 Fatehabad Rd, T331771, F330202. 50 comfortable rooms, many with view of the Taj a km away, rather soulless, Indian food good, disappointing breakfast buffet. **L** *Novotel Agra*, Tajnagri, Fatehabad Rd, T331818, F360217. 143 rooms (some for disabled), lowrise, immaculately clean but characterless. **L-AL** *Trident* (Oberoi), Fatehabad Rd, T331818, F331827, ttag@tridentag.com 143 very comfortable rooms, good pool, beautiful gardens, polite, friendly staff.

AL *Holiday Inn*, Sanjay Place, Hariparwat Chowk, MG Rd, T357642, F357625, hinnagra@sancharnet.in New location (8 km from Taj), 94 rooms, restaurant, business centre. **A** *Ashok* (ITDC), 6B Mall Rd (3 km Taj), T361225, F361620. 55 comfortable a/c rooms, good restaurant but a little dated, pleasant. **A** *Great Value Agra*, Bansal Nagar, Fatehabad Rd, T330225, F352645. Modern, comfortable. **A** *Howard Park Plaza*, Fatehabad Rd, T331870, F330408, howard@nda.vsnl.net.in 85 comfortable rooms, good buffet breakfast (Indian/western), service can be extremely slow.

C *Atithi*, Fatehabad Rd, T330879, F330878. 44 clean a/c rooms, clean pool. **C-D** *Chakraview*, Vibhav Nagar, 1 km from Taj, T332609. 11 rooms ('wall-to-wall marble!'), bath tubs, very helpful, friendly yet professional, good home-cooked food – takes time but all freshly prepared, very good value especially non-a/c rooms. **C-D** *Mayur Tourist Complex*, Fatehabad Rd, T332302, F332907. 30 rooms (most a/c) in pleasant bungalows, could be better maintained, restaurant, bar, pool, garden setting. **D-E** *Safari*, Shamsabad Rd, T360013. Clean, small rooms, simple rooftop restaurant, away from hectic Taj Ganj area. **D-E** *Tourist Bungalow* (UP Tourism), Station Rd opposite Raja-ki-Mandi station, T350120. Some a/c rooms, dorm and camping, clean but far from centre.

Many budget hotels
are in Taj Ganj (for
help, contact Mr A
Bansal of Agra Hotel &
Restaurants Assoc at
Hotel Sheela,
T331194)

E *Agra*, 165 Gen Cariappa Rd, T363312, F361146. 18 large rooms, bath, some a/c, Taj view from patio with seating, basic, old fashioned, good food, pleasant garden. **E** *New Bakshi House*, 5 Laxman Nagar, towards airport, T368035. Best room has a/c, good food, free pick-up, clean, well run, helpful owners. **E** *Taj Khema* (UP Tourism), near East Gate, T360140. 6 rooms (a/c dearer), 8 camping huts, good Indian restaurant, not well-kept. **E-F** *Jai Hind*, Naulakha Rd (off Taj Rd), T363503. Some air-cooled rooms, basic, friendly. **E-F** *Tourist Rest House*, Balugunj, Kachcheri Rd, T363961, F366910. Western toilet, hot showers, air-cooling inadequate in summer, a/c, pure-vegetarian restaurant, fairly basic, a bit dog-eared but friendly, helpful and knowledgeable manager, often full. In Taj Ganj: several cheap guesthouses include **E-F** *Host*, West Gate, T331010. Clean rooms with bath and hot water (Rs 175), some a/c with bath and balcony, rooftop restaurant with good views but food unpredictable. **E-F** *Sidhartha*,

250 m south from Taj West Gate, T331238, 264711. Rooms with bath and hot water (could be cleaner), good restaurant, pleasant courtyard and rooftop.

F *Gulshan*, South Gate. Mediocre rooms with bath, good, cheap food but slow service (no commission to rickshaws). **F** *India Guest House*, South Gate, T330909. 8 simple but clean rooms, some with coolers (Rs 80), shared toilets, average food, lovely family atmosphere. **F** *Shah Jahan*, T331159. Room with a view of the Taj (Rs 120), hot shower, simple, cheap, north Indian food, Taj view. **F** *Sheela*, East Gate, 2 mins walk from Taj, T331194. 20 decent rooms with bath ('nearest clean hotel to Taj'), fan, mosquito-proof (some **E** air-cooled with hot shower), pleasant garden, camping Rs 20, good restaurant, clean, peaceful, reliable laundry, secure (ask for gates to be unlocked for sunrise or else climb over spiked railings!), very helpful manager, excellent value (no commission to rickshaws), reserve ahead. Recommended. **F** *Youth Hostel*, Sanjay Place, MG Rd, T65812.

Camping In **C** *Mayur* **D** *Grand*. **E** *Agra* and *Tourist Bungalow* and **E** *Taj Khema* hotels. **E-F** *Akbar Inn*.

Expensive The top hotels are the most comfortable. *PAC* opposite *Atithir*. Chinese and Indian. Newish, large outdoor seating, clean, good food and service, breakfast to dinner, no beer. *Petals*, 19A Taj Rd, Sadar Bazar, T363087. Mughlai specially. Comfortable, modern, a/c, good food and service. *Priya*, 4/17 Baluganj, behind *Ratan Deep Hotel*. Indian, Chinese. A/c, good Indian, friendly, live *sitar* music. Wait. **Mid-range** *Maya*, Fatehabad Rd, Purani Mandi, Taj Ganj. Mixed. Good Punjabi *thalis* (Rs 75), garlic naan, pasta, 'special tea', friendly, prompt service, hygienic, tasty. *Sonam*, 51 Taj Rd. Indian, Chinese. A/c, good food, clean, bar, cheaper *thalis*, pleasant garden. *Tin Tin*, near Taj. Chinese. Friendly owners, good escape from hawkers. **Cheap** Near the **Taj**: *Daawat*, Fatehabad Rd, 5 mins walk from Taj. Indian. Pleasant garden area, beer. *Lucky*, good food, seasoned to your taste, pleasant, friendly. *Shivam*, in *Raj Hotel* near Taj south gate. Quality Indian, clean. **Vegetarian** *Shankar Vegis*, Chowk Kaghzi, 150 m south of Taj Gate. Occasional barbecues on rooftop, friendly 'special tea' (beer in teapots). *Zorba the Buddha* (Osho), behind Tourist Office, E13 Shopping Arcade, GC Shivhare Rd. A/c, no artificial colours, good cooking (spices on request), pleasant, very clean, not cheap, 1200-1500, 1800-2100.

Eating
● *on maps*
Price codes:
see inside front cover

Cases of deliberate 'food-poisoning' reported in some cheap Taj Ganj restaurants involving touts & unscrupulous private 'hospitals' who present highly inflated bills

Agra specializes in jewellery, inlaid and carved marble, carpets and clothes. The main shopping areas are Sadar Bazar (closed Tue), Kinari Bazar, Gwalior Rd, Mahatma Gandhi Rd and Pratap Pura. **Warning** You may order a carpet or an inlaid marble piece and have it sent later but it may not be what you ordered. Never agree to any export 'deals' and take great care with credit card slips (fiddles reported).

Books *Modern Book Depot*, Sadar Bazar. *Hotel Taj View* shop. **Carpets** Silk/cotton/wool mix hand knotted carpets and woven *dhurries* are all made in Agra. High quality and cheaper than in Delhi. *Mughal Arts Emporium*, Shamshabad Rd. Also has marble. Artificial silk is sometimes passed off as pure silk. **Handlooms and handicrafts** State Govt emporia in arcade at Taj entrance. Also *UP Handlooms* and *UPICA* at Sanjay Place, Hari Parbat. **Marble** Delicately inlaid marble work is a speciality. Sometimes cheaper alabaster and soapstone is used and quality varies. *Akbar International*, Fatehabad Rd. Good selection, inlay demonstration, fair prices. *Handicrafts Inn*, 3 Gorg Niketan, Fatehabad Rd, Taj Ganj. *UP Handicrafts Palace*, 49 Bansal Nagar. Very wide selection from table tops to coasters, high quality and good value. *Oswal*, 30 Munro Rd, Sadar Bazar, T363240. Watch craftsmen working here, or at *Krafts Palace*, 506 The Mall.

Shopping
Many rickshaws, taxi drivers & guides earn up to 40% commission by taking tourists to shops. Insist on not being rushed away from sights. To shop, go independently. To get a good price you have to bargain hard anyway

Delhi & around

Transport **Local** **Auto rickshaw**: point-to-point rates, eg Idgah Bus Stand to Taj Ganj Rs 40. **Bus**: City Bus Service covers most areas. Plenty leave from the Taj Mahal area and the Fort Bus Stand. Buses also go to the main sites. **Cycle hire**: Sadar Bazar, near Police station and near *Tourist Rest House*, Rs 15 per day. **Cycle rickshaw**: negotiate (pay more to avoid visiting shops!); Taj Ganj to Fort Rs 10; Rs 75-100 for visiting sights, PO, bank etc; Rs 150 for 10 hrs. **Taxis/car hire**: Tourist taxis from travel agents, remarkably good value for visiting nearby sights. Non-a/c car Rs 3 per km, full day Rs 400 (100 km), half day Rs 200 (45 km); a/c rates approximately double; to Fatehpur Sikri about Rs 650 return). *Budget* Rent-a-car, T361771; *UP Tours*, T351720.

Long distance **Air** Kheria airport is 7 km from city centre. Transport to town: airport bus to/from major hotels; auto-rickshaws charge about Rs 50; Taxis, Rs 75. *Indian Airlines*, Clarks Shiraz, T361180, airport T361241. Daily flights to **Delhi**. **NB** Long delays in flight departures and arrivals possible especially in winter when Agra and Delhi airports close for periods due to fog.

Most buses from Jaipur go on to a 2nd stop near Hotel Sakura: closer to most hotels & where there is less hassle from touts; auto from 1st stop to Taj Ganj, Rs 25

Road **Bus**: UPSRTC Roadways Bus Stand, Idgah, enquiry T367543; **Fort Bus Station** (opposite Power House), T364557; Ram Bagh Crossing (across river Yamuna). *Deluxe* buses from *Hotel Sheetal*, T369420. **Delhi** from tourist office, 0700, 1445, *Deluxe*, 4 hrs. Most long distance services leave from the **Idgah Bus Stand** including daily *Express* buses to: **Fatehpur Sikri**. Others hourly, (1 hr), very bumpy.

Train travel from Delhi is quicker & more reliable

Train Information and reservations: **Agra Cantt Rly Station**, enquiries T131, reservations T364519, open 0800-2000. Foreigners' queue at Window 1. **Pre-paid taxi/auto rickshaw** kiosk outside the station. Railway Stations: **Agra Cantt**, T131, T364516; **Agra Fort**, T132, T364163. Trains mentioned arrive and depart from Agra Cantt southwest of the city, about 5 km from the Taj Mahal. From **New Delhi**: best is *Shatabdi Exp, 2002*, 0600, 2¼ hrs (meals included); *Punjab Mail, 2138*, 0530, 3 hrs; *Kerala Exp, 2626*, 1130, 2¾ hrs; from **New Delhi (HN)**: *Taj Exp, 2180*, 0715, 2½ hrs; *Lakshadweep Exp, 2618*, 0955, 2½ hrs; *Gondwana Exp, 2412*, 1430, 2½ hrs; *Goa Exp, 2780*, 1500, 2½ hrs; *Mahakoshal Exp, 1450*, 1620, 3 hrs. To **New Delhi**: *Shatabdi Exp, 2001*, 2018, 2½ hrs; to **New Delhi (HN)**: *Intercity Exp, 1103*, 0600, 3½ hrs (2nd class only); *Taj Exp, 2179*, 1835, 3¼ hrs (CC/II). To **Jaipur** *Howrah-Jodhpur/Bikaner Exp, 2307*, 2000, 8 hrs (from Fort); *Marudhar Exp, 4853/63*, 0715, 6¾ hrs. **Mumbai** (CST): *Punjab Mail, 2138*, 0830, 23¼ hrs. **Sawai Madhopore** (for Ranthambore) at 0600, 0900, 1800.

Directory **Banks** *Andhra Bank*, Taj Rd, opposite *Kwality's* gives cash against card. *Canara*, Sadar Bazar and Sanjay Place, and others. **Communications** The Mall (24 hrs). At Taj Mahal and elsewhere, 1000-1700, closed Sun. **Post**: GPO opposite India Tourist Office, with Poste Restante. Internet: *Khurana Cyber Café*, 805 Sadar Bazar, opposite Cantt Hospital, T91562. **Hospitals and medical services** District, Chhipitola Rd/MG Rd, T363043. **Lady Lyall**, S Bhagat Singh Rd, T267987. SN, Hospital Rd, T361314. **Dr VN**, Kaushal, opposite Imperial Cinema, T363550. Recommended. **Amit Jaggi Hospital**, Vibhav Nagar, T330600. Clean, safe, but expensive and 'pays commission to rickshaws'. **Tourist offices** Govt of India, 191 The Mall, T363377. **Guides** available (about Rs 100), helpful and friendly Director and staff. Kheria (Agra) Airport counter, during flight times. **Uttar Pradesh**, 64 Taj Rd, T360517, and at *Tourist Bungalow*, Raja-ki-Mandi; T350120, Agra Cantt Railway Station, T368598. **Rajasthan**, T360017. **Useful addresses** Ambulance: T202. **Fire**: T201. **Police**: T200.

Rajasthan

Rajasthan

*The fortifications which stride across the arid ridges above Jaipur are a reminder of the fiercely contested political history of **northern Rajasthan**. Yet alongside its status as a battleground its dry hills and sometimes fertile valleys have also seen great prosperity, reflected in the palaces and country houses of the maharajas and the decorated houses and havelis of Shekhawati. All within easy range of Delhi, Jaipur and the towns of northern Rajasthan – from Ajmer in the south to Jhunjhunun in the north – are rich with living reminders of past wealth and culture. They are also surrounded by a natural world in which wild animals and birds continue to find a protected home in sanctuaries and wildlife parks, including the magnificent Bharatpur-Keoladeo Ghana National Park between Jaipur and Agra.*

*The stark ranges of the Aravallis cross **southeastern Rajasthan**, creating an often rugged landscape belying the fact that this is Rajasthan's wettest region. Valleys of intensive agriculture are interspersed with bare hills or the still forested game reserves such as Ranthambore, one of the best sites in the world to see tigers in the wild. But the southeast had its share of Rajput princely states, as former capitals like Kota and Bundi vividly testify.*

*In **southern Rajasthan**, Udaipur, whose shimmering Lake Palace is an image which represents Rajasthan around the world, centres on a region which has something of everything that is the state. From the hill station of Mount Abu, with its magical Jain Dilwara temples, to the fortress of Kumbhalgarh, the great Jain temple of Ranakpur, or small towns like Dungarpur, the Mewar Rajputs left their indelible imprint right across southern Rajasthan.*

*Jodhpur stands like the fortress gateway to desert Rajasthan in **the West**. The cities of Bikaner and Jaisalmer rise from the surrounding desert landscape, their forts, temples and* havelis *testimony to the medieval power and wealth of the desert trade which once gave them life. You can still ride on camel-back across the desert, but this region can lay claim to a far longer history than that of the silk route. The dried up valley of the Saraswati was once part of the first of India's great civilisations, centred on the Indus Valley, which gave Indian culture some of its most profound roots.*

Jaipur and Northern Rajasthan

4

Jaipur and Northern Rajasthan

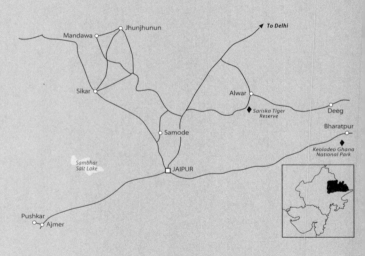

★ Jaipur

Jaipur, the colourful capital of a richly colourful state, is a highly distinctive planned city, made all the more attractive by the pink wash that most buildings are periodically given. It is deservedly included on the popular tourist 'Golden Triangle' of Delhi-Jaipur-Agra. It has some fine museums in the atmospheric Old City with its bazars, palaces and havelis, *as well as a couple of forts and the ancient city of Amber nearby which are well worth exploring. Its downside includes traffic jams, pollution, over-zealous rickshaw drivers and persistent hotel touts.*

Phone code: 0141
Colour map 4, grid A4
Population: 1,510,000
Altitude: 431 m

Getting there Sanganer Airport, 15 km south of town, has flights from **Ahmadabad**, **Aurangabad**, **Delhi**, **Jodhpur**, **Mumbai**, **Rajkot** and **Udaipur**. Airport buses, taxis and auto-rickshaws take about 30 mins to the centre. The railway station, to the west of town, now has improved links with major cities through upgrading to broad gauge. The Main Bus Terminal, a 15-min walk east of the station, is used by state and private buses. Buses from Delhi use the dramatically improved NH8, India's first toll "motor-way", and the journey now takes under 4 hrs by car. The alternative Gurgaon-Alwar-Jaipur route is more interesting but much slower. **Getting around** The Old City, to the northeast of town, holds most of the sights and the bazar within its walls. It's best explored on foot though to get there you can hire a rickshaw. The newer town has spread out and there are interesting places to visit in the neighbourhood which you may prefer to hire a taxi for as the city buses are overcrowded.

Ins & outs
See page 127 for further details

Most hotels are a short auto-rickshaw ride away from the station & bus terminal

Jaipur & Northern Rajasthan

History

Jaipur (City of Victory) was founded in 1727 by **Maharaja Jai Singh II**, a Kachhawaha Rajput, who ruled from 1699-1744. He had inherited a kingdom under threat not only from the last great Mughal Emperor Aurangzeb but also from the Maratha armies of Gujarat and Maharashtra. Victories over the Marathas and diplomacy with Aurangzeb won back the favour of the ageing Mughal so that the political stability Maharaja Jai Singh was instrumental in creating was protected, allowing him to pursue his scientific and cultural interests. Jaipur is very much a product of his intellect and talent.

A story relates an encounter between the **Emperor Aurangzeb** and the 10-year-old Rajput prince. When asked what punishment he deserved for his family's hostility and resistance to the Mughals, the boy answered "Your Majesty, when the groom takes the bride's hand, he confers lifelong protection. Now that the Emperor has taken my hand, what have I to fear?" Impressed by his tact and intelligence, Aurangzeb bestowed the title of *Sawai* (one and a quarter) on him, signifying that he would be a leader.

Jai Singh loved mathematics and science. A brilliant Brahmin scholar, Vidyadhar Bhattacharya from Bengal, helped him to design the city. Jai Singh also studied ancient texts on astronomy, had the works of Ptolemy and Euclid translated into Sanskrit, and sent emissaries to Samarkand to inform him on Mirza Beg's 1425 observatory, building masonry observatories at Delhi, Varanasi, Ujjain and Mathura, and most impressively at Jaipur.

Work began in 1727 and it took four years to build the main palaces, central square and principal roads. The layout of streets was based on a mathematical grid of nine squares representing the ancient Hindu map of the universe, with the sacred Mount Meru, home of Siva, occupying the central square.

Jaipur's Old City – town planning

In Jaipur the royal palace is at the centre. The three by three square grid was modified by relocating the northwest square in the southeast, allowing the hill fort of Nahargar (Tiger Fort) to overlook and protect the capital. The surrounding hills also provided good defence. At the southeast and

Jaipur & Northern Rajasthan

Jaipur

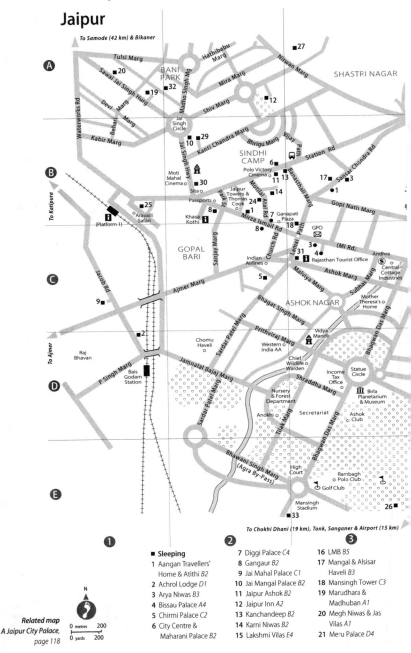

To Samode (42 km) & Bikaner

To Katipura

To Ajmer

To Chokhi Dhani (19 km), Tonk, Sanganer & Airport (15 km)

Related map
A Jaipur City Palace,
page 118

0 metres   200
0 yards   200

N

■ **Sleeping**
1 Aangan Travellers'
   Home & Atithi B2
2 Achrol Lodge D1
3 Arya Niwas B3
4 Bissau Palace A4
5 Chirmi Palace C2
6 City Centre &
   Maharani Palace B2

7 Diggi Palace C4
8 Gangaur B2
9 Jai Mahal Palace C1
10 Jai Mangal Palace B2
11 Jaipur Ashok B2
12 Jaipur Inn A2
13 Kanchandeep B2
14 Karni Niwas B2
15 Lakshmi Vilas E4

16 LMB B5
17 Mangal & Alsisar
   Haveli B3
18 Mansingh Tower C3
19 Marudhara &
   Madhuban A1
20 Megh Niwas & Jas
   Vilas A1
21 Meru Palace D4

southwest corners of the city were squares with pavilions and ornamental
fountains. Water for these was provided by an underground aqueduct with
outlets for public use along the streets. The main streets are 33-yards wide
(33 is auspicious in Hinduism); the lesser ones are graded in width down to

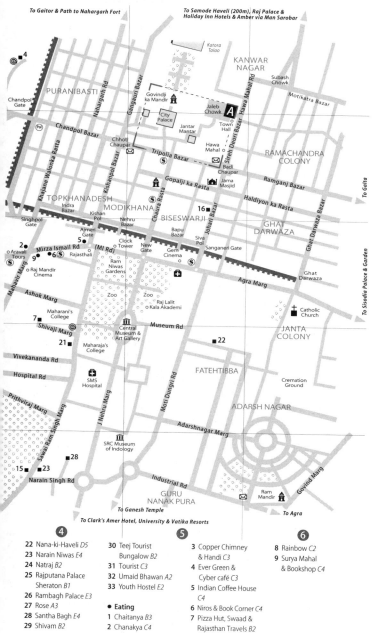

Jaipur & Northern Rajasthan

Things to do in Jaipur

- *Have a vegetarian thali at Chanakya, Handi or LMB.*
- *Bargain hunt in the bazar of the Old City.*
- *Marvel at the treasures at the City Palace Museum.*
- *Reach the Amber Fort Palace on elephant back.*
- *Gaze at the giant astronomical instruments at the Jantar Mantar observatory.*

4 m, all being in proportion to one another. The sidewalks were deliberately wide to promote the free flow of pedestrian traffic and the shops were also a standard size.

Built with ancient Hindu rules of town planning in mind, Jaipur was advanced for its time. Yet many of its buildings suggest a decline in architectural power and originality. The architectural historian, Giles Tillotson, argues that even in the earliest of them "traditional architectural details lack vigour and depth and are also flattened so that they become relief sculpture on the building's surface, and sometimes they are simply drawn on in white outline". In Jai Singh's day, the buildings were painted in a variety of colours, including grey with white borders. Pink, a traditional colour of welcome, was used in 1853 in honour of the visit by Prince Albert, and the colour is still used.

Architectural revival In addition to its original buildings, Jaipur has a number of examples of late 19th-century public and private buildings which marked an attempt to revive Indian architectural skills. A key figure in this movement was **Sir Samuel Swinton Jacob**, who transferred from the army to the Public Works Department and in 1867 he became Executive Engineer to the Maharaja of Jaipur, living there until 1902. A school of art was founded in 1866 by a group of English officers employed by Maharaja Sawai Madho Singh II (ruled 1880-1922) to encourage an interest in Indian tradition and its development.

In February 1876 the Prince of Wales visited Jaipur, and work on the **Albert Hall**, now the Central Museum, was begun to a design of Jacob. It was the first of a number in which Indian craftsmen and designers were actively employed in both building and design. This ensured that the Albert Hall was an extremely striking building in its own right, but it was not simply a British Indo-Saracenic building of the type becoming popular elsewhere in India. A number of crafts were revived, a process fostered by the 1883 Jaipur Exhibition which attracted over 250,000 visitors. ■ *Rs 30. No cameras.* The opportunities for training provided under Jacob's auspices encouraged a new school of Indian architects and builders. One of the best examples of their work is the Mubarak Mahal (1900), now Palace Museum, designed by Lala Chiman Lal.

Sights

★ Hawa Mahal The 'Palace of the Winds' (circa 1799) forms part of the east wall of the City Palace complex and is best seen from the street outside. Possibly Jaipur's most famous building, it is the pink sandstone eastern façade of a palace built for the ladies of the harem by Sawai Pratap Singh. The five storeys stand on a high podium with an entrance from the west. The elaborate façade contains 953 small casements in a huge curve, each with a balcony and crowning arch. The windows enabled cool air (*hawa*) to circulate and allowed the ladies who were secluded in the *zenana* to watch processions below without being seen. ■ *Rs 3 (Mon free); cameras Rs 30. 1000-1630, closed Fri. Enter from Tripolia Bazar (west of the GPO); for best views accept invitation from shop owners on*

The *havelis* of Jaipur

Jaipur's formal planning recognized the importance of the joint family as the traditional social unit around which the houses should be built. The normal building was the haveli *(Persian for 'enclosed space'), a three to five-storeyed house built around a shaded communal courtyard. To counter the heat and glare, the shops and houses were deep rather than wide. Large eaves*

and awnings provided shade. An outer gate and walls provided security and privacy.

A number of havelis *usually formed a* mohalla *(district) and about 400 of these a* chokra *(section). Each district housed a particular trade. Muslim jewel cutters still live in Johari Bazar, marble workers in Chandpol Bazar and Hindu cloth merchants in Nehru Bazar.*

---

upper floors across the street. The **museum** has second-century BC utensils and old sculpture.

The City Palace occupies the centre of Jaipur, covers one seventh of its area and is surrounded by a high wall – the *Sarahad*. To find the main **entrance**, from the Hawa Mahal go north about 250 m along the Sireh Deori Bazar past the Town Hall (Vidhan Sabha) and turn left through an arch – the *Sireh Deori* (boundary gate). Pass under a second arch – the *Naqqar Darwaza* (drum gate) – into **Jaleb Chowk**, the courtyard which formerly housed the Palace guard. Today it is where coaches park. This is surrounded by residential quarters which were modified in the 19th century under Sawai Ram Singh II. A gateway to the south leads to the Jantar Mantar, the main palace buildings and museum and the Hawa Mahal.

★ **The City Palace (1728-32)**

Its style differs from conventional Rajput fort palaces in its separation of the palace from its fortifications, which in other Rajput buildings are integrated in one massive interconnected structure. In contrast the Jaipur Palace has much more in common with Mughal models, with its main buildings scattered in a fortified campus. ■ *Rs 150, Indians Rs 35 (includes Sawai Man Singh II Museum and Jaigarh Fort, valid for 2 days). Camera: still, free; video (unnecessary) Rs 100; doorkeepers expect tips when photographed. Photography in galleries prohibited, only of façades allowed. Guide books, post cards and maps available. 0930-1700 (last entry 1630).*

Mubarak Mahal The main entrance leads into a large courtyard at the centre of which is the Mubarak Mahal, faced in white marble. Built in 1890, originally as a guest house for the Maharaja, the Mubarak Mahal is a small but immaculately conceived two-storeyed building, designed on the same cosmological plan in miniature as the city itself – a square divided into a 3 x 3 square grid (see page 113).

The **Textile and Costume Museum** on the first floor has fine examples of fabrics and costumes from all over India as well as musical instruments and toys from the royal nursery. In the northwest corner of the courtyard is the **Armoury Museum** containing an impressive array of weaponry – pistols, blunderbusses, flintlocks, swords, rifles and daggers. This was originally the common room of the harem. From the north facing first floor windows you can get a view of the Chandra Mahal (see below). Just outside the armour museum is **Rajendra Pol**, a gate flanked by two elephants, each carved from a single block of marble, which leads to the inner courtyard. There are beautifully carved alcoves with delicate arches and jali screens and a fine pair of patterned brass doors.

Jaipur & Northern Rajasthan

Diwan-i-Khas (Sarbato Bhadra) The gateway leads to the courtyard known variously as the Diwan-i-Am, the Sarbato Bhadra or the Diwan-i-Khas Chowk. Today the building in its centre is known as the Diwan-i-Khas (circa 1730). Originally the Diwan-i-Am, it was reduced to the hall of private audience (Diwan-i-Khas) when the new Diwan-i-Am was built to its southeast at the end of the 18th century. The courtyard itself reflects the overwhelming influence of Mughal style, despite the presence of some Hindu designs, a result of the movement of Mughal-trained craftsmen from further north in search of opportunities to practise their skills. In the Diwan-i-Khas (now known by the Sanskrit name Sarbato Bhadra) are two huge silver urns used by Sawai Madho Singh for carrying Ganga water to England, see page 119.

Diwan-i-Am (Diwan Khana) Art gallery Entered in the southeast corner of the Diwan-i-Am courtyard, the 'new' Hall of Public Audience built by Maharaja Sawai Pratap Singh (1778-1803) today houses a fine collection of Persian and Indian miniatures, some of the carpets the Maharajas had made for them and an equally fine collection of manuscripts. To its north is the Carriage Museum, housed in a modern building. In the middle of the west wall of the Diwan-i-Am courtyard, opposite the art gallery, is the **Ganesh Pol**, which leads via a narrow passage and the Peacock Gate into **Pritam Niwas Chowk**. This courtyard has the original palace building 'Chandra Mahal' to its north, the zenana on its northwest, and the Anand Mahal to its south. Several extremely attractive doors, rich and vivid in their peacock blue, aquamarine and amber colours, have small marble Hindu god watching over them.

Chandra Mahal Not always open to visitors. Built between 1727 and 1734 the *Moon Palace* is the earliest building of the palace complex. Externally it appears to have seven storeys, though inside the first and second floors are actually one high-ceilinged hall. On the ground floor (north) a wide verandah – the **Pritam Niwas** (*House of the beloved*) – with Italian wall paintings, faces the formal Jai Niwas garden. The main section of the ground floor is an Audience Hall.

The 2 top floor storeys give superb views of the city & Tiger Fort

The hall on the first (and second) floors, the **Sukh Niwas** (*House of pleasure*), underwent a Victorian reconstruction, above which are the **Rang Mandir** and the **Sobha Niwas**, built to the same plan. The two top storeys are

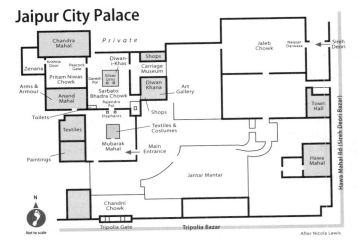

Jaipur City Palace

Private

Chandra Mahal

Zenana — Krishna Door — Peacock Gate — Diwan-i-Khas — Shops

Pritam Niwas Chowk — Ganesh Pol — Silver Urns — Carriage Museum — Jaleb Chowk — Naqqar Darwaza — Sireh Deori

Arms & Armour — Anand Mahal — Sarbato Bhadra Chowk — Diwan Khana — Art Gallery

Rajendra Pol — Shops — Town Hall

Toilets — Elephants

Textiles — Mubarak Mahal — Textiles & Costumes — Main Entrance — Hawa Mahal

Paintings

Hawa Mahal Rd (Sireh Deori Bazar)

Jantar Mantar

N

Not to scale

Chandni Chowk

Tripolia Gate — Tripolia Bazar

After Nicola Lewis

Sawai Madho Singh: devotion across the oceans

The present Maharaja's grandfather was an extremely devout Hindu. Any physical contact with a non-Hindu was deemed to be ritually defiling, so contact with the British carried awkward ritual problems. Whenever required to meet a British official, including the Viceroy, the Maharaja would wear white gloves, and after any meeting would ritually purify himself in a bath of Ganga water and have the clothes he wore burnt. When he went to England to celebrate Queen Victoria's Diamond Jubilee Sawai Madho Singh had a P&O liner refitted to include a Krishna temple and carried sufficient Ganga water with him in two 309 kg silver urns to last the trip.

much smaller, with the mirror palace of the **Chavi Niwas** succeeded by the small open marble pavilion which crowns the structure, the **Mukat Niwas**.

In the northeast corner of the Pritam Niwas Chowk, leading into the zenana, is the **Krishna door**, its surface embossed with scenes of the deity's life. The door is sealed in the traditional way with a rope sealed with wax over the lock.

North of the Chandra Mahal, the early 18th-century **Govind Deo Temple**, which was probably built as a residence, has been restored by an ancient technique using molasses, curd, coconut water, fenugreek, rope fibres and lime. The furniture is European – Bohemian glass chandeliers – the decoration Indian. Following the steps around you will see a *mandala* (circular diagram of the cosmos), made from rifles around the royal crest of Jaipur. The ceiling of this hall is in finely worked gold. Further on are the beautiful Mughal style fountains and the **Jai Niwas gardens** (1727), laid out as a *char bagh*, the **Badal Mahal** (circa 1750) and the **Tal Katora** tank. The view extends across to the Maharaja's private Krishna temple and beyond the compound walls to the Nahargarh (Tiger Fort) on the hills beyond.

★ **Jantar Mantar (Observatory)**

Literally 'Instruments for measuring the harmony of the heavens', the Jantar Mantar was built between 1728 and 1734. Jai Singh wanted things on a grand scale and chose stone with a marble facing on the important planes. Each instrument serves a particular function and each gives an accurate reading. Hindus believe that their fated souls move to the rhythms of the universe and the matching of horoscopes is still an essential part in the selection of partners for marriage. Astrologers occupy an important place in daily life and are consulted for all important occasions and decision-making. The observatory is a fascinating and attractive site to walk round, but it gets extremely hot in the middle of the day. ■ *0930-1630. Rs 5 (Mon free), camera Rs 50, video Rs 100 (stills better).*

Moving clockwise you will see the following instruments or **yantras**:
1 Small 'Samrat' is a large sundial (the triangular structure) with flanking quadrants marked off in hours and minutes. The arc on your left shows the time from sunrise to midday, the one on the right midday to sundown. Read the time where the shadow is sharpest. The dial gives solar time so as to adjust it to Indian Standard Time. Between one minute 15 seconds and 32 minutes must be added according to the time of year and solar position as shown on the board.
2 'Dhruva' locates the position of the Pole Star at night and those of the 12 zodiac signs. The graduation and lettering in Hindi follows the traditional unit of measurement based on the human breath calculated to last six seconds. Thus: four breaths = one *pala* (24 seconds), 60 palas = one *gati* (24 minutes), 60 gatis = one day (24 hours).

The Jaipur foot

The 'Jaipur foot' may sound like an affliction, but for thousands it represents a miraculous cure to the problems of living with an amputated leg.

Artificial feet were available long before orthopaedic surgeons in Jaipur began to work on a local solution to a specifically Indian problem. For while the surgeons had been fitting high quality western-designed artificial feet for some time, they found that patients would frequently give them up and return to crutches. They couldn't use the rigid wooden foot supplied, which had been designed to fit inside shoes and failed to meet the needs for flexibility essential for sitting cross-legged or for walking across fields and village tracks.

The answer was to adapt the foot with local skills and technology and a highly resilient, flexible and lightweight foot was developed. The work has been one of the many social service projects undertaken by the Bhagwan Mahaveer Viklang Sahayata Samiti *voluntary body to help people irrespective of caste, religion or politics. (Those interested may contact SMS Hospital, Jaipur.) Patients arrive at Jaipur from all over India, but the society now organizes camps in many parts of the country. The* Rotary Jaipur Limb Project, *started in UK in 1984 raises money to help establish Limb Camps in India and elsewhere.*

3 **'Narivalya'** has two dials: south facing for when the sun is in the southern hemisphere (21 September-21 March) and north facing for the rest of the year. At noon the sun falls on the north-south line.

4 **The Observer's Seat** was intended for Jai Singh.

5 **Small 'Kranti'** is used to measure the longitude and latitude of celestial bodies.

6 **'Raj'** (King of Instruments) is used once a year to calculate the Hindu calendar, which is based on the Jaipur Standard as it has been for 270 years. A telescope is attached over the central hole. The bar at the back is used for sighting, while the plain disk is used as a blackboard to record observations.

7 **'Unnathamsa'** is used for finding the altitudes of the celestial bodies. Round-the-clock observations can be made and the sunken steps allow any part of the dial to be read.

8 **'Disha'** points to the north.

9 **'Dakshina'**, a wall aligned north-south, is used for observing the position and movement of heavenly bodies when passing over the meridian.

10 **Large 'Samrat'** is similar to the small one (1) but ten times larger and thus accurate to two seconds instead of 20 seconds. The sundial is 27.4-m high. It is used on a particularly holy full moon in July/August, to predict the length and heaviness of the monsoon for the local area.

11 **'Rashivalayas'** has 12 sundials for the signs of the zodiac and is similar to the Samrat yantras. The five at the back (north to south), are Gemini, Taurus, Cancer, Virgo and Leo. In front of them are Aries and Libra, and then in the front, again (north-south), Aquarius, Pisces, Capricorn, Scorpio and Sagittarius. The instruments enable readings to be made at the instant each zodiacal sign crosses the meridian.

12 **'Jai Prakash'** acts as a double check on all the other instruments. It measures the rotation of the sun, and the two hemispheres together form a map of the heavens. The small iron plate strung between crosswires shows the sun's longitude and latitude and which zodiacal sign it is passing through.

13 **Small 'Ram'** is a smaller version of the Jai Prakash Yantra (12).

14 **Large 'Ram Yantra'** Similarly, this finds the altitude and the azimuth (arc of the celestial circle from Zenith to horizon).

15 'Diganta' also measures the azimuth of any celestial body.

16 Large 'Kranti' is similar to the smaller Kranti (5).

The small fort with its immense walls and bastions stands on a sheer rock face. The city at its foot was designed to give access to the fort in case of attack. You have to walk first through some quiet and attractive streets at the base of the hill, then 2 km up a steep, rough winding path to reach the top. Beautifully floodlit at night, it dominates the skyline by day. Much of the original fort is in ruins but the walls and 19th century additions survive, including rooms furnished for maharajas. This is a 'real fort', quiet and unrushed, and well worth visiting for the breathtaking views, to look inside the buildings and to walk around the battlements. ■ *1000-1630, Rs 2, camera Rs 30.* If you fancy a snack *Durg Café*, T383202, has good views and sells quite reasonable snacks, drinks and chilled beer but service is slow for meals. There is one simple **D** room with bath (T365256). *Padco Café*, on a terrace at the end of the ruins, has great views but dirty china and not much in the way of food and drink.

★ **Nahar-garh (Tiger Fort, 1734)**
Women alone have been taken advantage: you are urged to join a group

You can combine this visit with the **Jaigarh Fort** (see page 129), 7 km away (part of the same defensive network), along the flat-topped hill. A good road, originally a military one, connects the two. A covered aqueduct brought water to Jaigarh over the same distance. Taxis are available or you can walk. It is also a pleasant rickshaw journey from Amber. Tell the auto-rickshaw driver if you want to go to the bottom of the footpath or to take the road to the top (much further and more expensive).

Something of an architectural curiosity, the modern temple built by the Birla family in the southeast of the city is impressive in scale and in the eclecticism of its religious art.

Birla Mandir

From Galta Pol take a walk to the 'Valley of the Monkeys', east of Jaipur, to get a view of the city from the Surya Mandir (Sun Temple). Walk down the steps to the five old temples dedicated to Rama-Sita and Radha-Krishna, with some nice wall paintings. You can watch hundreds of monkeys that play in the water of the tank below. ■ *Galta Pol can be reached by taking a bus, or by walking the 2 km from the Hawa Mahal. It is about 600 m uphill and then downhill.*

Surya Mandir

Central Museum, Albert Hall, Ram Niwas Gardens Mainly excellent decorative metalware, miniature portraits and other art pieces in beautiful building. Also Rajasthani village life displayed through costumes, pottery, woodwork, brassware etc (first floor displays covered in dust and poorly labelled). ■ *1000-1630, closed Fri. Rs 3 (Mon free).*

Museums, parks & zoos

Sawai Man Singh II Museum Forms part of the City Palace. Excellent display of paintings, miniatures, textiles, costumes, armoury, maps, objects from royal court (16th-19th centuries); see above. ■ *Rs 110 (Indians Rs 35). 0900-1700, closed on holidays. T608055.*

Modern Art Gallery Collection of contemporary Rajasthani art. ■ *1000-1630, closed Fri. Ravindra Rang Manch, Ram Niwas Gardens.* Also in these gardens is the Zoological Garden, a crocodile farm. ■ *Rs 2.*

SRC Museum of Indology Collection of folk and tantric art including manuscripts, textiles, paintings. ■ *Rs 35 (groups of 10, Rs 10 each). 1000-1700. 'Nilambara', Prachya Vidya Path, 24 Gangwal Park.*

Jaipur & Northern Rajasthan

Tours RTDC City Sightseeing, half day: 0800-1300, 1130-1630, 1330-1830, Rs 75; Central Museum, City Palace, Amber Fort and Palace, Gaitore, Nawab ki Haveli, Jantar Mantar, Jal Mahal, Hawa Mahal; City Sightseeing, full day: 0900-1800, Rs 120; including places above plus Nahargarh Fort, Indology Museum, Dolls Museum, Galta, Sisodia Rani Garden. Jaigarh Fort. Nahargarh evening tour, 1800-2200, includes non-veg meal, folk dances. Book at Railway station, *Gangaur* or *Tourist Hotel*. Other operators also offer city sightseeing: half/full day, Rs 80-120. The tours are worthwhile, but may miss out promised sights and claim that they are closed. Some may find the guides' English difficult to follow and the obligatory trip to shops, tedious.

Essentials

Jaipur's popularity has meant that foreigners are being targeted by hotel and shop touts, so you need to be on your guard.

Sleeping
■ *on maps*
Price codes:
see inside front cover.
Auto-rickshaw
drivers often get
commissions as
hotel touts

MG Rd is Mahatma
Gandhi Rd, MI Rd is
Mirza Ismail Rd

LL-L *Jai Mahal Palace* (Taj), Jacob Rd, Civil Lines, T223636, F223660. 102 rooms (6 unique suites), imaginative, plush, good solar heated pool, gardens especially lovely, geared to package tours, good off-season discounts. **LL-L** *Rajvilas* (Oberoi), on Goner Rd, at the base of Amber fort, T680101, F680202, reservations@rajvilas.com 72 beautifully furnished a/c rooms (pricey villas with private pools, courtyard groups, 14 luxury a/c 'tents' with bath), ayurvedic 'spa' in a restored *haveli*, re-created fort-palace architecture in large gardens, orchards, pools and fountains, award winner. **LL-L** *Rambagh Palace* (Taj), Bhawani Singh Rd, T401140, F401122. 106 rooms, Maharaja Ram Singh's (1835-80) hunting lodge, extensively modified by Madhu Singh II (1880-1922), some excellent rooms, others disappointing, pleasant relaxing atmosphere, good food and service, superb gardens, indoor pool, good shops including books and silver. **L** *Raj Palace* (GKV Heritage), *Chomu Haveli*, Zorwar Singh Gate, Amer Rd, T630489, F382980 (office T/F373119). 25 spacious suites with modern baths (extra bed US$15), 5-storeyed *haveli* (1728) with character carefully restored, traditional courtyard, Darbar Hall, garden, well managed, friendly service. **L** *Rajputana Palace Sheraton* (Welcomgroup), Palace Rd, T401140, F401122, rajputana@welcomgroup.com Ultra modern '*haveli*'-style 216 rooms, lush garden and open courtyard for live entertainment, excellent bookshop, rather impersonal.

A *Clarks Amer*, JL Nehru Marg, T549437, F550013, clkamer@jp1.dot.net.in 202 rooms (a/c erratic), 8 km centre, less 'exotic' than 'palace hotels', friendly, good shops, garden, food occasionally inspired. **A** *Trident* (Oberoi), Amber Rd, opposite Jal Mahal, T672000, F672335. 138 a/c rooms, attractive overlooking lake or hills, fully equipped, excellent service. Highly recommended. **A-B** *Holiday Inn*, Amer Rd (just northeast of city), T672000, F672335. Clean, comfortable (good value in its class), well managed (staff badge says 'you are my first concern'!), friendly and helpful. **A-B** *Mansingh Tower*, Sansar Chandra Rd, T378771, F377582, mansinghjaipur@mailcity.com 91 rooms, no garden or pool but convenient for shops. Older *Mansingh* has had poor reports, ask for newer *Tower*.

B *Jaipur Ashok* (ITDC), Jai Singh Circle, Bani Park, T204491, F202099. 97 rooms, comfortable but unimaginative, good food, pool (Rs 150 non-residents). **B** *Jas Vilas*, next to *Megh Niwas*, C-9 Sawai Jai Singh Highway, Bani Park, T204638. An excellent new small hotel with 5 a/c rooms with bath (tub, power shower), internet, home-cooked meals, lawns, fine pool, friendly family. Recommended. **B** *Karauli House*, New Sanganer Rd, Sodala (towards the airport), T211532, F210512, www.karauli.com 6 rooms in a family 'retreat', large garden, pool, personal attention, home-cooked meals. **B** *Samode Haveli*, Gangapol, Old City, T632407, F632370, jagdish@jp1.vsnl.net.in 20 lovely rooms, charming 19th-century *haveli* with beautiful decorations (more personal in scale than Samode Palace), magnificent dining room (lunch/dinner, Rs 325/400), mid-day snacks, friendly atmosphere, good rooftop views over city at dawn and sunset. Highly recommended, reservations essential. **B** *Maharani Palace*, (Best Western), Station Rd, opposite Polo Victory, T2947028, F202112. Modern 60 room hotel with roof-top pool. **B-C** *Alsisar Haveli*, Sansar Chandra Rd, T364685, F364652. 30 comfortable a/c rooms, modern frescoes, excellent conversion of 1890s character home, attractive courtyards,average food (try *Chaitanya* nearby, listed below), beautiful new pool with glass mosaic, village safaris, 'super-quiet', friendly, very attentive and courteous service. Very highly recommended. **B** *Bissau Palace* (Heritage Hotel), outside Chandpol Gate (access through busy Old City), T304371, F304628, sanjai@jp1.dot.net.in 45 a/c rooms, some charming, in the home of the Rawal of Bissau (built 1919) with library and royal museum, interesting 'memorabilia' and antiques, bookshop, pleasant front garden, good views from terrace of city and nearby forts, tours, "excellent camel safaris", exchange etc from *Karwan Tours*, but temple music can irritate at times. Recommended for delightful atmosphere, charming hosts.

C *Chirmi Palace* (Heritage Hotel), Dhuleshwar Garden, Sardar Patel Marg, T680101, F364462, chirmi@vsnl.com 150-year-old *haveli* conversion, 15 spacious a/c rooms, traditional Rajasthani decor, attractive dining room, lawns, pool, e-mail, gentle staff. Recommended. **C** *LMB*, Johari Marg, Old City, T565844, F562176. 33 rooms, some a/c in incongruous, modern building, good veg restaurant, monkeys may be a nuisance! **C** *Megh Niwas*, C-9 Jai Singh Hwy, Bani Park, T322661, F321420. Comfortable rooms in former royal home (some air-cooled), family run, good pool. **C** *Meru Palace*, Sawai Ram Singh Rd, T371111, F378882, kotawaha@jp1.dot.net.in 48 rooms (some **B** suites), good veg restaurant, bar, exchange, marble building, not a palace but pleasant. **C** *Narain Niwas*, Narain Singh Rd, full of character but poor reports on rooms and food. **C** *Nana-ki-Haveli*, Fateh Tiba, Moti Dungri Rd, near Old City, T665502, F605481. 7 spacious a/c rooms in modernised 1918 garden house, very hospitable, friendly family, excellent home cooking. Recommended. **C-D** *Royal Castle*, A70 Jai Ambey Nagar, Tonk Rd, south of Jaipur, T551425, F721655, delta@jp1.dot.net.in Spacious rooms (some a/c), hot water, safe and quiet, family run, delicious home cooking, ask for free pick-up from airport/station. **C-D** *General's Retreat*, Sardar Patel Rd, T377134. 10 rooms with bath, some with kitchenettes, attractive bungalow of a retired general, pleasant gardens, restaurant. **C-D** *Mangal*, Sansar Ch Rd, T375126. 50 rooms (20 a/c), bar, gym, sauna, quiet, modern. **C-D** *Kanchandeep*, Vanasthali Marg (south of Central Bus Stand), T364507, F364518. 56 reasonable a/c rooms (prices vary) in modern 5-storey pink building, slightly brash, varied veg restaurant, attentive service. **C-D** *Santha Bagh*, Kalyan Path, Narain Singh Rd, T566790, F560332. 10 comfortable rooms (a/c or air-cooled), very friendly and helpful staff, excellent meals, lawn.

D *Achrol Lodge*, Jacob Rd, Civil Lines, T382154, F382810. 7 large rooms with big bath tubs, period furniture in old mansion, breakfast, large gardens, **F** camping (tents, overland trucks), friendly. Recommended. **D** *Arya Niwas*, Sansar Chandra Rd (behind Amber Tower), T372456, F361871, aryahotl@jp1.vsnl.net.in 50 very clean rooms but not always quiet, modernized and smart, good very cheap veg food, pleasant lounge, book shop, good travel desk, tranquil lawn, "very clean oasis", friendly, helpful management, book ahead (arrive by 1800), great value. Highly recommended. **D** *Bani Park Palace*, D160 Kabir Marg, T315384. Rooms vary (some **C** a/c) with bath. **D** *Gangaur* (RTDC), MI Rd, T371641. 63 rooms, some a/c, restaurant, good coffee shop, convenient for bus and rly. **D** *Jai Mangal Palace*, opposite Central Bus Stand, T378901. 115 rooms (30 a/c), pleasant restaurant, bar, pool, modern. **D** *Lakshmi Vilas*, Sawai Ram Singh Marg, T381567. 21 rooms, some a/c, Indian veg restaurant, quiet, large open grassy

Gangaur – Prayer for a good husband

Ishar and Gangaur are the mythical man and wife who embody marital harmony. Colourfully dressed young women carrying brass pitchers on their heads make their way through the streets to the temple of Gauri (another name for Parvati). Here they ceremonially bathe the deity who is then decked with flowers. Young women pray for good husbands, and the long life of their husbands (if they are already married). The festival ends with singing and rejoicing as it is believed that if a woman is unhappy while she sings she will be landed with an ill-tempered husband! The festivities end when Siva arrives, accompanied by elephants, to escort his bride Gauri home.

court. **D** *Madhuban*, D237 Behari Marg, Bani Park, T208427, F202344, madhuban@usa.net Clean quiet rooms in friendly cluster of bungalows around small courtyards, some **C** a/c, pleasant garden, helpful staff, good food, very good value (Alsisar family). Recommended. **D** *Natraj*, 20 Motilal Atal Rd, T361348, F371758. 17 clean rooms, some very pleasant, large, a/c, good veg restaurant. Recommended. **D** *Rajasthan Palace*, 3 Bhilwa Gardens (1 km from Sanganeri Gate), Moti Dungri Rd, T41542. Not a palace, 24 rooms (some **C** a/c) refurbished, 10 smaller **E** rooms with shared bath, around pleasant gardens. **D** *Teej* (RTDC), Jai Singh Hwy, T374373. 48 bland, clean rooms, some a/c, **F** dorm (Rs 50). **D** *Umaid Bhawan*, D1-2A Bani Park, T316184. 26 immaculate rooms with fan, hot shower, various categories, dorm bed (Rs 150), pool planned, small lawn, very quiet lane. Recommended.

D-E *Aangan Traveller's Home*, opposite All India Radio, 4 Park House Scheme, MI Rd, 500 m rly, T373449, F364596. 18 clean, comfortable room with bath (hot water), fairly new larger rooms above, all air-cooled or a/c, pleasant tiny garden, good food (non-residents phone first), very helpful and welcoming family (but "unexpected 10% luxury tax"). Highly recommended. **D-E** *Ashirwad*, 4 Bhilwa Gardens, Moti Dungri Rd. 9 rooms with bath, hot water, in family guest house, meals, gardens. **D-E** *Atithi*, 1 Park House Scheme, T378679. Very clean rooms, wonderful hot showers, relaxing roof terrace, internet, good veg food, helpful, friendly staff. Highly recommended. **D-E** *Diggi Palace*, Shivaji Marg, T373091, F370359. Pleasant rooms, some with shower, some have no windows, good restaurant, peaceful garden, good value. Recommended. **D-E** *Jaipur Inn*, B17 Shiv Marg, Bani Park, T201121, F204796, jaipurinn@hotmail.com. 18 rooms (shared bath), mosquito problem, some 'camp beds', **F** dorm (Rs 100), secure, very clean, spacious, food varies (chaotic breakfast, good Rs 80 veg buffet), pleasant rooftop for chilled beer and snacks, use of kitchen, internet, camping (see below), often full. Recommended. **D-E** *Karni Niwas*, C-5 Motilal Rd, T365433. Spotless rooms with hot shower, some large a/c, some with balconies, breakfast and snacks, internet (Rs 2 per min), very friendly and helpful owners. Highly recommended.

Several have dormitary beds Rs 50-80) **E** *City Centre*, near Central Bus Stand, T368320. Good size, clean room, western toilet, hot showers, good value, rickshaws reluctant (no commission). **E** *Evergreen*, Chameliwala Market, opposite GPO, MI Rd, T363446. 96 rooms (standard and prices vary), clean on 1st floor with showers (Rs 200), **F** dorm, good restaurant, good travel desk, peaceful garden, small pleasant pool, cyber café, full of cliquey backpackers, foreigners only, often full. **E** *Rose*, B6 Shopping Centre, Subhash Nagar, T305422. Clean rooms with bath, dorm, quiet location with small garden, open-air restaurant; **E** *Tourist Hotel* (RTDC), MI Rd, T360238. 47 simple rooms with bath, dorm (Rs 50), little atmosphere, beer bar, tours. **F** *Marudhara*, D250, Behari Marg, Bani Park. Rooms with bath (basic, dark, windowless), restaurant, garden, friendly service (Indian students there are interesting). **F** *Shakuntala*, 157 Durga Marg, Bani Park, T379225. Family run,

attentive service, meals available. **F** *Railway Retiring Rooms* and men's dorm.
F *Shivam* , A26, C1, Bharatia Path, Kanti Chandra Rd, Bani Park (behind *Ashok*),
T201008. Some rooms with hot shower, dorm in converted garage (Rs 60), mosquito
menace, hop over fence and use *Ashok's* pool (Rs 100)! **F** *Youth Hostel*, T373311, near
the Stadium, out of town. Discounts for YHA members.

Paying guests Mostly **D-E** (some have dorm beds); good home cooked meals are a
bonus. **E** *Shri Sai Nath*, 1233 Mali Colony, outside Chandpol Gate, T304975,
shreesainath@indya.com 8 clean, quiet rooms, meals on request, very hospitable
family, warm welcome, 'a real delight and very helpful'. **E** *Mandap Homestays*, Bhilwa
Garden, Moti Dungri Rd, T44389. 5 rooms with baths, bungalow of a former ruling family, large gardens.

The tourist office has a list of families

Camping (see above) **D** *Achrol Lodge*. Toilet and power connections, in large lawns.
D-E *Jaipur Inn*. In pleasant garden, own tent/van Rs 50 each. **F** *Youth Hostel*.

Expensive In top hotels: *Jaimahal Palace*. International. Beautiful surroundings, buffet breakfast and dinner recommended, but snack bar inadequate. *Rambagh Palace*.
International. Smart restaurant, attractive decor in coffee shop, popular for lunch,
pricey but generous.

Eating
● *on maps*
Price codes:
see inside front cover

Mid-range *Chaitanya*, Sansar Ch Rd (100 m from Alsisar, in shopping complex on
opposite side of road). Excellent vegetarian. *Chanakya*, MI Rd. Indian vegetarian. Good
food and service, pleasant atmosphere, very clean, huge tasty *thalis* (Rs 150). *Copper
Chimney*, MI Rd. International. A/c, open for lunch and dinner only, quality food, generous helpings, dimly lit. *Evergreen*, opposite GPO, MI Rd. Good Western, also cyber café.
Full of backpackers. Watch bill. *LMB*, Johari Bazar. Rajasthani vegetarian. A/c (50s fairground decor), but generous tasty *thalis;* sweets and *kulfis* outside (meal about Rs 150).
Mehfil, Anukampa Mansion-II, off MI Rd, T367272. Superb range of good quality
dishes, friendly service, great ambience. *Natraj*, M1 Rd. Rajasthani, some Chinese. A/c,
immaculate, veg snacks and silver-leaf sweets. *Niros*, MI Rd, T374493. International.
A/c, pleasant decor, wide choice. *Rainbow*, MI Rd. International. Good food, clean, some
drinks pricey. *Surya Mahal* MI Rd. Indian. Try *paneer butter masala* (*Bake House* cakes
inside not recommended but good ices next door). *Swaad*, B Ganpati Plaza, Motilal Atal
Rd, T360749. International. A/c, wide choice, good meals and snacks, excellent service,
beer downstairs. *Temptations*, New Colony. Vegetarian. A/c, varied menu.

Watch out for deliberate 'food-poisoning' scams in cheap restaurants involving touts & unscrupulous private 'hospitals'

Cheap Several good value pure vegetarian restaurants on Station Rd (near the Bus
Station) like **Shri Shanker**, with lively atmosphere, grubby looking but freshly cooked
(Rs 30); also on the Gaitor road towards Amber, serve large helpings for Rs 60. *Handi*,
back of Maya Mansion. Indian. Partly open-air, simple canteen style. *Laxmi*, Johari
Bazar. Indian vegetarian. Good food and sweets. *Sun City*, Gangapol. Good value meals
in an eccentric environment.

Cafés and fast food *BBs*, Bhandari Chambers, MI Rd. Western. A/c, clean, swanky,
main courses Rs 50. *Jai Mangal Palace*, opposite Central Bus Stand. Snacks. A/c, 'tasty
pakoras and huge pot of wonderful real coffee', bar. *Pizza Hut*, 109 Ganpati Plaza, MI
Rd, T360749. Italian. A/c, great pizzas. *Royal Fast Food*, Johari Bazar. South Indian.
Air-cooled, good snacks.

Raj Mandir Cinema. 'Experience' a Hindi film in shell pink interior. *Ravindra Rang
Manch*, Ram Niwas Garden. Sometimes hosts cultural programmes and music shows.
Also 'shows' at Theme Villages on the outskirts – see below. **Meditation** *Vipasana*

Entertainment

Centre, Dhammathali,Galta (3 km east of centre) runs courses for new and experienced students, T641520. **Sports and activities** Some hotels will arrange golf, tennis or squash. *Ashok Club* (formerly the British Officers' Club, with interesting memorabilia), Bhagwandas Rd, T381690, has a squash court (mediocre); temporary membership, Rs 350 per month. There is a polo ground near Rambagh Palace. *Ashok Hotel* and *Khetri House* (Rs 100).

Festivals All the Hindu festivals are celebrated (see page 58 and above). **14 Jan**: *Makar Sankranti* The kite flying festival is spectacular. Everything closes down in the afternoon and kites are flown from every rooftop, street and even from bicycles! The object is to bring down other kites, attempted to the deafening cheers of huge crowds. **Mar**: *Elephant Festival* (28 Mar 2002; 17 Mar 2003) at Chaugan Stadium, procession, elephant polo etc. **Apr**: *Gangaur Fair* (15-16 Apr 2002, 4-5 Apr 2003) about a fortnight after *Holi*, when a colourful procession of women start from the City Palace with the idol of Goddess Gauri. They travel from the Tripolia gate to Talkatora, and these areas of the city are closed to traffic during the festival. **Jul/Aug**: *Teej* (23-24 Jul 2001, 11-12 Aug 2002, 1-2 Aug 2003). The special celebrations in Jaipur have elephants, camels and dancers joining in the processions.

Shopping
You may find better bargains in other cities in Rajasthan, especially Jodhpur

Antiques and art In Chomu Haveli *Art Palace* specializes in 'ageing' newly crafted items – alternatives to antiques. Also found around **Hawa Mahal**. *Manglam Arts*, Amer Rd. Sells modern miniature paintings and silver. *Mohan Yadav*, 9 Khandela House, behind Amber Gauer, SC Rd, T378009. Visit the workshop to see high quality miniatures produced by the family.

Bazars Traditional bazars and small shops are well worth a visit; cheaper than MI Rd shops but may not accept credit cards. Most open 1030-1930; closed on Sun. *Bapu Bazar*, specializes in printed cloth. *Johari Bazar* for jewellery and *Khajanewalon-ka-Rasta*, off Chandpol bazar, for marble and stoneware. Try *Maniharon-ka-Rasta* for lac bangles which the city is famous for, *Tripolia Bazar* (3 gates). For inexpensive jewellery. *Chaupar* and *Nehru Bazars* for textiles. *Ramganj Bazar* has leather footwear while opposite Hawa Mahal you will find the famous featherweight Jaipuri *rezais* (quilts).

Blue pottery *Kripal Kumbha*, B-18, Shiv Marg, Bani Park. *Blue Pottery Art Centre*, Amer Rd, near Jain Mandir. For unusual pots. Recommended.

Books *Book Corner*, MI Rd by *Niro's Restaurant*. Good selection, largest at the University on Nehru Marg near Birla Temple. *Bookwise*, *Rajputana Sheraton Hotel*, vast range, excellent service, fair price, safe posting. Recommended.

Carpets *Channi Carpets and Textiles*, Mount Rd opposite Ramgarh Rd. Factory shop, watch carpets being handknotted, then washed, cut and quality checked with a blow lamp! *Kashmiri Carpet Museum*, 327 Old Amer Rd, near Zorawar Singh Gate. Excellent stock. *The Reject Shop*, Bhawani Singh Rd. For 'Shyam Ahuja' durrie collections, and *Art Age*, Plot 2, Bhawani Singh Rd. Watch *durrie* weavers. *Maharaja*, Chandpol (near *Samode Haveli*). Watch carpet weavers and craftsmen, good value carpets and printed cotton.

Fabrics *Chirag International*, 771 Khawasji ka Rasta, Hawa Mahal Rd, T608537. Wholesale warehouse, vast selection. *Ridhi Sidhi Textiles*, 9 East Govind Nagar, Amber Rd.

Handicrafts Jaipur specializes in printed cotton, handicrafts, carpets and durries; also embroidered leather footwear and blue pottery. *Gems & Silver Palace*, G11 Amber

Tower, Sansar Ch Rd. Good choice of 'old' textiles, reasonable prices, helpful owners. *Handloom Haveli*, Lalpura House, Sansar Ch Rd. *Handloom House*, Rituraj Building, MI Rd (near *Tourist Hostel*). *Rajasthali*, Govt Handicrafts, MI Rd, 500 m west of Ajmeri Gate. *Rajasthan Fabrics & Arts*, near City Palace gate. Exquisite textiles. *Anokhi*, 2 Yudhistra Marg, opposite Udyog Bhawan. Well-crafted, attractive block-printed clothing, linen etc. Recommended.

Jewellery Jaipur is famous for gold, jewellery and gem stones (particularly emeralds, rubies, sapphires and diamonds, but the last requires special certification for export). Semi-precious stones set in silver is more affordable (but check for loose settings, catches and cracked stones); sterling silver items are rare in India and the content varies widely. Bargaining is easier on your own so avoid being taken by a 'guide'. *Gem Testing Laboratory* off MI Rd near New Gate (reputable jewellers should not object). Check for members of 'Gems and Jewellery Association of Rajasthan'. You may be able to see craftsmen at work in *Johari Bazar*, especially in Gopalji-ki-Rasta. *NK Meghraj*, 239-240 Johari Bazar. *Bhuramal Rajmal Surana*, 1st floor, between nos 264 and 268, Haldiyon-ka-Rasta. Highly recommended. *Dwarka's*, H20 Bhagat Singh Marg, T360301. Crafts high quality gemstones in silver (975), gold and platinum in modern and traditional designs. *Beg Gems*, Mehdi-ka-Chowk, near Hawa Mahal. *Ornaments*, 32 Sudharma Arcade, Chameliwala Market, opposite GPO (turn left, first right and right again), T365051. Recommended for stones and silver (wholesale prices; made up in 24 hrs). **Warning** Never agree to 'help to export' jewellery. Report of misuse of credit card accounts at *Monopoli Gems* opposite Sarga Sooli, Kishore Niwas (1st fl) Tripolia Bazar, *Apache Indian Jewellers* (also operating as *Krishna Gems* or *Ashirwad Gems & Art*) opposite Samodia Complex, Loha Mandi, SC Rd.

For about Rs 40 you can have gems valued

Do not use credit cards to buy these goods

Photography Shops on MI Rd and Chaura Rasta.

Silverware *Amrapali Silver Shop*, Chameliwala Market, opposite GPO, MI Rd. *Arun's Emporium*, MI Rd; *Balaji's*, Sireh Deori Bazar (off *Johari Bazar*). *Silver and Art Palace*, Amer Rd. Also *Mona Lisa*, Hawa Mahal Rd and *Nawalgarh Haveli*, near Amber Fort Bus Stop.

Local **Auto rickshaw**: Station to city centre hotel, about Rs 25; **sightseeing** (3-4 hrs) Rs 200, 6-7 hrs, Rs 300. From railway and bus stations, drivers (who expect to take you to shops for commission) offer whole day hire including Amber for Rs 150; have your list of sights planned and refuse to go to shops. **Bus**: To **Amber** they originate from Ajmeri Gate, junction with MI Rd so get on there if you want a seat. **Cycle rickshaws**: (often rickety) station to central hotels, Rs 15; full day Rs 100. **Taxi**: unmetered taxis; 4 hrs Rs 350 (40 km), 8 hrs Rs 550 (city and Amber). Out of city Rs 5 per km; *Marudhar Tours* (see directory) recommended; or try **RTDC**, T315714.

Transport
City buses are cheap

Long distance **Air**: **Sanganer airport** has good facilities. Transport to town: taxi, 30 mins, Rs 250; auto rickshaw Rs 120. *Indian Airlines*, Nehru Pl, Tonk Rd, T743500; airport, T741333. They fly to **Aurangabad**, **Delhi**, **Jaisalmer**, **Jodhpur**, **Mumbai**, **Udaipur**. *Gujarat Airways*, T383181, fly to **Ahmadabad**. *Jet Airways*, T360763, airport T551352. They fly to **Delhi, Mumbai, Udaipur**.

Road Bus: **Central Bus Stand**, Sindhi Camp, Station Rd. Enquiries: Deluxe, T375834, Express, T363277 (24 hrs), Narain Singh Circle, T564016. State and private 'Deluxe' buses are very popular so book 2 days in advance. Deluxe buses depart from Platform 3 which has the reservation counter. Journeys can be very bumpy and tiring. Left luggage, Rs 10 per item per day. To **Agra** about hourly from bus station 6½ hrs with 1 hr lunch stop, Rs 100, pay when seat number is written on ticket; (230 km, 5 hrs, via

Avoid hotel touts & use the pre-paid auto-rickshaw counter to get to your hotel

Jaipur & Northern Rajasthan

Jaipur & Northern Rajasthan

Bharatpur) – you can get off at the 2nd (last) stop to avoid being hassled by rickshaw drivers; **Ajmer** (131 km, ½ hourly, 3 hrs); **Bharatpur** Rs 90; **Delhi** (261 km, ½ hourly, 5½ hrs, Rs 200); **Jaisalmer** (654 km, 2200, 14 hrs via Jodhpur, Rs 320). **Jodhpur** (332 km, frequent, 7 hrs, Rs 190); **Udaipur** (374 km, 12 hrs, Rs 230).

Train Enquiry, T131, T133, reservation T135. Computerized booking office in separate building to front and left of station; separate queue for foreigners. Persistent auto-rickshaw drivers, in addition to being hotel touts, may quote Rs 10 to anywhere in town, then overcharge for city tour. Use pre-paid rickshaw counter. **Abu Rd (for Mount Abu)** *Ahmadabad Mail, 9106,* 0440, 8½ hrs, *Aravali Exp, 9708,* 0700, 9½ hrs; **Agra Cantt:** *Marudhar Exp, 4854/4864,* 1505, 7 hrs. **Ahmadabad:** *Aravali Exp, 9708,* 0700, 14 hrs; *Ashram* Exp, 2916, 2050, 11½ hrs. *Rajdhani Exp, 2958,* Tue, Thu, Sat, 0045, 9 hrs. **Ajmer:** *Shatabdi Exp, 2015,* not Sun, 1045, 2 hrs;. *Aravali Exp, 9708,* 0700, 2½ hrs; **Bikaner:** *Bikaner Exp, 4737,* 2100, 10 hrs; *Intercity Exp, 2468,* 1500, 7 hrs. **Chittaurgarh:** *Jaipur-Purna Exp, 9769,* 1220, 7½ hrs; *Chetak Exp, 9615,* 2050, 8½ hrs. **Delhi:** *Jodhpur Delhi Exp, 4860,* 0600, 5 hrs; *Jaipur Delhi Exp, 2414,* 1620, 5½ hrs; *Ahmadabad Mail, 9105,* 2340, 5½ hrs. **Indore:** *Jaipur-Purna Exp, 9769,* 1220, 16½ hrs. *Jaipur Indore Exp 9308,* 1545, 16 hrs; **Jodhpur:** *Jodhpur Delhi Exp, 4859,* 2330, 6 hrs. **Mumbai (C):** *Jaipur Mumbai Exp 2956,* 1330, 18½ hrs; **Udaipur** *Chetak Exp, 9615,* 2220, 12 hrs. **Varanasi** via **Lucknow:** *Marudhar Exp, 4854/4864,* 1325, 20 hrs.

Directory **Airlines offices** *Air India,* MI Rd (opposite All India Rd), T368569. *Lufthansa,* T561360; others at Jaipur Tower, MI Rd, T377051. **Banks** Several on MI Rd. Open 1030-1430, 1530-1630; most change money. *Andhra Bank,* MI Rd. For Visa: *Indus Bank,* C-Scheme; *SBBJ,* both recommended. *Thomas Cook,* Jaipur Towers, 1st floor, MI Rd (500 m from rly station, T360801, 0930-1730, open Sun). No commission on own TCs, Rs 20 for others. Recommended. Often easier to use hotels, eg Rambagh Palace (0700-2000). *Karwan Tours,* Bissau Palace (sunrise until late). Jewellery shops opposite Hawa Mahal often hold exchange licences but travellers report misuse of credit cards at some. **Communications** *GPO,* MI Rd. Excellent parcel service. **Couriers:** *Blue Dart,* T365010, *Skypack* T373560. **Internet:** at Ganpati Plaza basement, Re 1 per min. *Cyber Café,* 15 Nandisha Inn, Sivaji Rd. Reliable. *Interphase* C-Scheme. At hotels: *Mewar* nr Central Bus Stand, T206042. Jaipur Inn, Rs 3 per min. Also 34 Station Rd (behind Polo Victory Cinema). **Hospitals and medical services** *Santokba Durlabhji,* Bhawani Singh Rd, T566251. *SMS,* Sawai Ram Singh Marg, T560291. **Tour companies and travel agents** *Aravalli Safari* opposite *Rajputana Palace Hotel,* Palace Rd, T373124, F365345. Very professional. *Chetan,* 17 Muktanand Nagar, Gopalpura Bypass, Tonk Rd, T9829007198 (M). Experienced, reliable, car tours. *Forts & Palaces Tours,* A-110 Bhan

Nagar, Queens Rd, T351117, F356959, www.palaces-tours.com Includes camel safaris, hotel reservations. *GITS*, knowledgeable owner. Special interest tours (eg textiles), good hotel rates. **Karwan Tours**, *Bissau Palace Hotel*, Chandpol Gate, T308103, F304854, karwantours@usa.net For camel safaris, tours, taxis, ticketing, exchange, very helpful. **Marudhar Tours**, H-20 Bhagat Singh Marg, C-scheme, T371768, F365042, marudhar@datainfosys.net.in, car hire, air/train tickets; **Rajasthan Travel**, 52 Ganpati Plaza, MI Rd, T365408. Ticketing, reliable guides, recommended. **Tourist offices** (closed on 2nd Sat of month) *Govt of India* T372200, and *Hotel Khasa Kothi*. *Rajasthan*, Paryatan Bhavan, *Tourist Hotel*, MI Rd, T365256, F376362. Counters at railway station, T315714 and Central Bus Stand. *Guides* for 4-8 hrs, about Rs 250-400 (Rs 100 extra for French, German, Japanese, Spanish). *Gujarat*, *Tourist Hotel*, opposite GPO, T362017. **Useful addresses Ambulance:** T102. **Fire:** T101. **Police:** T100. **Foreigners' Registration Office:** Hazari Garden, behind Hawa Mahal.

★ Amber (Amer)

As you take the winding road from modern Jaipur between the barren hills immediately to the north there is little hint of the magnificent fort and palace which once dominated the narrow valley. Today there is no town to speak of in Amber, just the palace clinging to the side of the rocky hill, overlooked by the small fort above, with a small village at its base.

Colour map 4, grid A4
11 km N of Jaipur

Some find it
rather touristy

Amber, which takes its name from Ambarisha, a king of the once famous royal **History** city of Ayodhya, was the site of a Hindu temple built by the Mina tribes as early as the 10th century. Two centuries later the Kachhawaha Rajputs made it their capital, which it remained until Sawai Jai Singh II moved to his newly planned city of Jaipur in 1727. Its location made Amber strategically crucial for the Mughal emperors as they moved south, and the Maharajahs of Amber took care to establish close relations with successive Mughal rulers. The building of the fort palace was begun by Raja Man Singh, a noted Rajput General in Akbar's army, in 1600, and Mughal influence was strong in much of the subsequent building.

In the high season this is one of India's most popular tourist sites, with a continuous train of colourfully decorated elephants walking up and down the ramp to the palace. One penalty of its popularity is the persistence of the vendors. From the start of the ramp you can either walk or ride (10 minutes) by elephant; the walk is quite easy and mainly on a separate path. Elephants carry up to four persons on a padded seat. The ride can be somewhat unnerving when the elephant comes close to the edge of the road, but it is perfectly safe. You have to buy a 'return ticket' even if you wish to walk down later (elephants get bad tempered as the day wears on). ■ *Rs 400 per elephant carrying four. There is no need to tip, though the driver will probably ask. Jeeps charge Rs 100 each way, or Rs 10 per seat.*

From the side of the main road you get a dramatic view of the hilltop palace. Across the **Maota Lake** to its north is Dilaram Bagh, a formal garden connected to the **Jaigarh Fort** by a path that joins the old military road. The road runs up the steep escarpment alongside a powerful defensive wall, to the long narrow fort running along the top. ■ *Boating on the lake, Rs 40.*

After passing through a series of five defensive gates, you reach the first court- **The Palace** yard of the **Raj Mahal** built by Man Singh I in 1600, entered through the **Suraj Pol** (Sun Gate). Here you can get a short ride around the courtyard on an elephant, but bargain very hard. There are some toilets near the dismounting platform. On the south side of this Jaleb Chowk with the flower beds, is a flight of steps leading up to the **Singh Pol** (Lion Gate) entrance to the upper courtyard of the palace. The monkeys here will try to steal any food you have visible.

On your right, after climbing the steps, is the green marble-pillared **Shila Mata** Temple (to Kali as Goddess of War) which contains a black marble image of the goddess Man Singh I brought back from Jessore (now in Bangladesh; the chief priest has always been Bengali). The silver doors with images of Durga and Saraswati were added by his successor. ■ *The temple only opens at certain times of the day and then, only allows a limited number of visitors at a time so ask before joining the queue!*

In the left hand corner of the courtyard, the **Diwan-i-Am** (Hall of Public Audience) was built by Raja Jai Singh I in 1639. Originally, it was an open pavilion with cream marble pillars supporting an unusual striped canopy-shaped ceiling, with a portico with double red sandstone columns. The room on the east was added by Sawai Ram Singh II. The **Ganesh Pol** (circa 1700-25), south of the chowk, colourfully painted and with mosaic decoration, takes its name from the prominent figure of Ganesh above the door. It separates the private from the public areas.

This leads onto the **Jai Singh I** court with a formal garden. To the east is the two-storeyed cream coloured marble pavilion – **Jai Mandir** (Diwan-i-Khas or Hall of Private Audience) below and **Jas Mandir** (1635-40) with a curved Bengali roof, on the terrace above. The former, with its marble columns and painted ceiling, has lovely views across the lake. The latter has colourful mosaics, mirrors and marble *jali* screens which let in cooling breezes. Both have **Shish Mahals** (Mirror Palaces) faced with mirrors, seen to full effect when lit by a match. To the west of the chowk is the **Sukh Niwas**, a pleasure palace with a marble water course to cool the air, and doors inlaid with ivory and sandalwood. The Mughal influence is quite apparent in this chowk.

Above the Ganesh Pol is the **Sohag Mandir**, a rectangular chamber with beautiful latticed windows and octagonal rooms to each side. From the rooftop there are stunning views over the palace across the town of Amber, the long curtain wall surrounding the town and further north, through the 'V' shaped entrance in the hills, to the plains beyond (particularly good for photographs). Beyond this courtyard is the **Palace of Man Singh I**. A high wall

Amber Palace

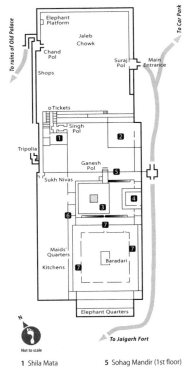

1 Shila Mata
2 Diwan-i-Am
   (Daftar Khana above)
3 Jai Singh I Garden
4 Jai Mandir
   (Jas Mandir, 1st floor)

5 Sohag Mandir (1st floor)
6 Palace of
   Man Singh I (1st floor)
7 Zenana

To Jaigarh Fort

Not to scale

separates it from the Jai Singh Palace. In the centre of the chowk which was once open is a **baradari** (12-arched pavilion), combining Mughal and Hindu influences. The surrounding palace, a complex warren of passages and staircases, was turned into *zenana* quarters when the newer palaces were built by Jai Singh. Children find it great fun to explore this part.

■ *0900-1630. Tickets in the Chowk, just below the steps up to Shila Mata. Rs 50; still camera Rs75, video Rs 150. Son et lumière is planned. Getting there: Take the green bus from the Hawa Mahal, Rs 5 or auto-rickshaw Rs 50 (Rs 125 for return, including the wait). Tourist information is at the new Elephant Stand, T530264. Guides, about Rs 250 for a half day (group of 4). ITDC plan to develop a Sound and Light show.*

The Old Palace

The palace at the base of the hill, to the north, started in the early 13th century, is of little interest today. The temples nearby include the **Jagatsiromani Temple** dedicated to Krishna, with carvings and paintings; it is associated with Mira Bai. Close by is the old temple to Narasinghji and *Panna Mian-ki-Baoli* (step well). Some of the *chhatris* on Delhi Road still retain evidence of paintings.

★ Jaigarh Fort

Above the Palace on the hill top stands the gigantic bulk of Jaigarh, impressively lit at night, its *parkotas* (walls), bastions, gateways and watchtowers a testimony of the power of the Jaipur rulers. It is well worth a visit.

The forbidding medieval fort was never captured and so has survived virtually intact which makes it particularly interesting. In the 16th-century

Jaipur & Northern Rajasthan

Around Amber

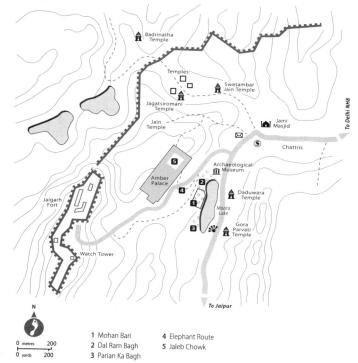

N

0 metres 200
0 yards 200

1 Mohan Bari
2 Dal Ram Bagh
3 Parian Ka Bagh
4 Elephant Route
5 Jaleb Chowk

well-planned **cannon foundry** you can see the pit where the barrels were cast, the capstan-powered lathe which bored out the cannon and the iron-workers' drills, taps and dies. The **armoury** has a large collection of swords and small arms, their use in the many successful campaigns having been carefully logged. There is an interesting photograph collection and a small café outside the armoury.

There are gardens, a granary, open and closed reservoirs; the ancient temples of Ram Harihar (10th-century) and Kal Bhairava (12th-century) are within the fort. You can explore a warren of complicated dark passageways among the palaces. Many of the apartments are open and you can see the collections of coins and puppets (shows on demand).

The other part of the fort, at a slightly higher elevation, has a tall watch tower. From here there are tremendous views of the surrounding hills. The massive 50 tonne **Jai Ban cannon** stands on top of one tower. Allegedly the largest cannon on wheels in the world, with an 8 m barrel, it had a range of around 20 km, but it was never used. Some 7 km further along the top of the hill is the smaller Nahargarh Fort overlooking Jaipur itself. See page 121.

Old Palace of Amber (1216) lies at the base of Jaigarh fort. A stone path (currently being restored) from the Chand Pol in the first courtyard of Amber Palace leads to the ruins.

■ *1000-1630. Rs 20, still camera Rs 20, vehicle entry Rs 50. Getting there: From Amber Palace, turn right out of the Suraj Pol and follow a stone road past the old elephant quarters. This is the start of the ascent – a steady climb of about 25 mins, or take a taxi. The road is protected throughout its length by a strong wall which zigzags up the hill to the fort's main gate. What appears at first to be two adjoining forts is in fact all part of the same structure which follows the contour of the hilltop. From Nahargarh to Jaigarh is an 8-km walk.*

Shopping At Amber near the baoli and temples, you can see demonstrations of block printing and other handicrafts, there is a small cafeteria for drinks and simple snacks, shops selling gems, jewellery, textiles, handicrafts and 'antiques' (objects up to 90 years old; genuine 100-year old antiques may not be exported). Amber is a tax holiday zone, and products manufactured by industries here are 10-15% cheaper than at Jaipur (though the benefit may not be passed on to the customer). Travellers warn that the privately owned *Rajasthan Small Scale Cottage Industries* on Jagat Shiromani Temple Road looks like a government fixed price shop but charges very high prices. The RTDC tour guide even recommends the shop.

Around Jaipur

Jal Mahal & Gaitore
8 km from Jaipur

The **Man Sarobar** lake has the attractive, Rajput style **Jal Mahal** (Water Palace, 1735) at its centre. Though often dry in the summer, during the monsoon the lake is transformed from a huge grassy field into a beautiful water hyacinth-filled lake. Opposite the lake at **Gaitore** are the marble and sandstone *chhatris* of the rulers of Jaipur, built by Jai Singh II and set in landscaped gardens.

Kanak Vrindavan

This attractive garden in Mughal style has fountains, pools and a pillared pavilion (1707) with a temple which has been restored by the Birlas. It is a popular picnic spot; kiosks sell soft drinks. ■ *0800-1700.*

Sanganer
12 km SW of Jaipur

The airport road gives access to this small town through two ruined triple gateways beyond which is the ruined palace and old Jain temples. The greater attractions of Sanganer are block-printing and paper-making. The latter uses waste cotton and silk rags which are pulped, sieved, strained and dried. Screen and block-printing is done in *Chipa Basti* where you can watch the printers in workshops and purchase samples, usually at a fraction of the price asked in Jaipur. *The Village Restaurant* is near the airport, T550860. Folk entertainment and a market is planned. There is a *Donkey Fair* at Looniyabas nearby in October where thousands of animals are traded. ■ *Getting there: Hourly buses from Jaipur.*

Theme villages & crafts On the outskirts of the city, these offer a chance to sample an authentic Rajasthani meal in pleasant 'rural' surroundings. **Chokhi Dhani**, 19 km south, on Tonk Road, has recreated a bazar atmosphere – an 'artificial village, but worthwhile for photo opportunity alone'. ■ *Rs 150 (can be set against any meal at the restaurant). Getting there: Buses from Station Rd, or taxi from Jaipur, Rs 300-400 return.*

Sleeping B-C *Chokhi Dhani*, T583534, F580118. 31 attractive standard and 34 'executive' huts (the 'Shekhavati haveli' with carved doors, open courtyard and frescoes, has 6 suites), very modern inside with a/c, TV, comfortable beds, marble bathrooms with hot showers/tubs (at odds with the thatched roof and tribal murals outside!) pool, gym, exchange (for residents).

Eating *Chokhi Dhani Restaurant.* A/c, interesting decor though very dimly lit. Buffet lunch, a la carte or multi-course Rajasthani meals (Rs 150) from leaf platters and pottery. Occasionally you can watch puppeteers, folk dancers, *nats* (fantastic acrobatics) and artisans at work on pottery, block printing, rolling lac into bangles and metal work. Camel, horse and boat rides for Rs 10. A craft bazar sells various handicrafts. Another restaurant *Highway Dhaba*, decorated with truck tyres everywhere, serves typical Punjabi food enlivened by *ghazals* and Punjabi music. There are a number of restaurants and beer bars on Jaipur-Sanganer highway. *Amrapalli Village Resort* serves veg food in pleasant environment.

Sisodia Rani-ka Bagh & Vidyadhar Bagh
8 km E of Jaipur on the Agra Rd
Built for Jai Singh's second wife, these gardens are attractively tiered with fountains, watercourses and pavilions with murals. ■ *0800-1800, Rs 10.* **Vidyadhar Bagh**, also on the Agra Road, is a beautiful garden laid out in honour of Jai Singh's friend and city planner Vidyadhar Bhattacharya. ■ *0800-1800, Re 1.* These are among the many landscaped gardens laid out by kings and courtiers in the 18th and 19th centuries. Accommodation can be found at *Chokhi Dhani Resort* (see above).

Ramgarh Lake & Jamwa Sanctuary
30 km NE (45 mins' drive)
This 15 sq km lake, of Jamwa Ramgarh, which attracts large flocks of waterfowl in winter, lies within a game sanctuary with good boating and bird watching. It was the venue for yachting and other sports in the 1982 Asian Games and is being developed as a water sports resort. Built to supply Jaipur with water it now provides less than 1% of the city's needs and in years of severe drought it may dry up completely. In the summer of 2000, at the end of a particularly hot dry spell, the lake's crocodiles were reported to be searching the few remaining mud pools in the rapidly drying lake bed. The 300-sq km Jamwa Sanctuary which once provided the Jaipur royal family with game still has some panthers, nilgai and small game. ■ *Public buses: For details contact Jaipur Tourist Office.*

Jaipur & Northern Rajasthan

Sleeping and eating A-B *Ramgarh Lodge* (Taj), overlooking the lake, T0141-381098. 17 rooms (2 enormous suites) in the royal hunting lodge with a museum and library, furnished appropriately, hunting trophies, limited restaurant, delightful walks, ruins of old Kachhawaha fort nearby. **D** *Jheel Tourist Village* (RTDC), T01426-52170. 10 rustic huts (Rs 400).

Sport Polo can be played at *Ramgarh Resort* (HRH), T01426-52170 (or T0141-374791). An exclusive facility for enthusiasts with a full size polo field near the lake, occasional matches and polo training camps run by World Cup Indian captain Lokendra Singh. Deluxe tented accommodation for participants. 50 rooms, restaurant, pool and riding stable are planned.

Bagru
35 km towards Ajmer on the NH8

In this small town *Chipa* printers continue the three centuries old tradition of hand block printing using natural dyes and treating the cotton cloth with 'Fuller's earth' from the riverside. They then soak the cloth in turmeric water to produce the traditional cream-coloured background before using hand carved wooden blocks for printing floral patterns. The dyes are specially prepared and fixed with gum – molasses and iron for black; red ochre and alum for red; indigo for blue. The very active *chipa mohalla* (printers' quarter), where the three dozen or so families devoted to printing live and work, makes an interesting excursion. If you want to stay *Aravalli Resorts*, on Ajmer Road, T864528, F351247, is a highway motel with two air conditioned rooms (10 more planned), lawn and restaurant. There is also a handicraft shop which has good Bagru printed textiles and light weight *razai* quilts.

Madhogarh
45 km SE of Jaipur, off the Jaipur-Agra Rd

Madhogarh is a small but impressive fort, with a strong medieval flavour. It is located on a hillock, and has huge walls, bastions, wells and turrets. The Rajput-Maratha battle of Tunga was fought at the nearby village, with the Jaipur army based at Madhogarh, during the mid-18th century. The *Madhogarh* is a Heritage Hotel with six quaint rooms (some in the tower) with views of the countryside. More rooms are planned. Good (though rather spicy) food, interesting temples nearby, family run, recently converted so still finding its feet. Great atmosphere on the ramparts in the evening when the family and guests enjoy tea. ■ *Getting there: A pleasant place to break journey between Jaipur and Ranthambore if you have your own transport.*

★ Samode

Phone code: 01423
Colour map 2, grid C4
42 km NW of Jaipur

At the head of the enclosed valley in the dry rugged hills of the northern Aravallis, Samode stands on a former caravan route. Today, the sleepy village, with its local artisans producing printed cloth and glass bangles, nestles within its old walls. The old painted havelis are still full of character.

Samode is well worth the short visit from Jaipur or en route to the painted towns of Shekhawati

The **Palace**, which dominates the village, is fabulously decorated with 300-year old wall paintings (hunting scenes, floral motifs etc) which still look almost new. Around the first floor of the Darbar Hall are magnificent alcoves, decorated with mirrors like *shish mahal* and *jali* screens through which the royal ladies would have looked down into the grand jewel-like Darbar Hall.

Towering immediately above the palace is **Samode Fort**, the Maharajah's former residence, reached in times of trouble by an underground passage. The old stone zig-zag path has been replaced by 300 steps. Though dilapidated, there are excellent views from the ramparts; a caretaker has the keys. The main fort gate is the starting point of some enticing walks into the

Aravallis. A paved path leads to a shrine about 3 km away. There are two other powerful forts you can walk to, forming a circular **walk** ending back in Samode. Allow three hours, wear good shoes and a hat, and carry water.

Samode Bagh, a large 400-year old Mughal-style formal garden with fountains and pavilions, has been beautifully restored. It is 3 km southeast of Samode (towards the main Jaipur-Agra road).

AL-A *Samode Palace*, T632407, F631397, reservations@samode.com 40 a/c rooms (more being added), tastefully modernized without losing any of the charm (but short of hot water), courtyard restaurant (international menu). The dining room serves buffets to groups, gardens, pool being added, magnificent setting, shop with good textiles, camel rides around village and to Samode Bagh (but some animals are in poor condition), generally friendly, really remarkable for its setting and atmosphere but somewhat impersonal, disappointing service (tip-seeking), Rs 100 entry for non-residents. Still highly recommended. Samode Haveli (T/F0141-632407) reserve and arrange taxi (Rs 950). **B** *Samode Bagh*, T0141-632407, F631397, 3 km away. 50 luxury tents equipped as colourful hotel rooms with fan, sit-out, and modern bathroom in the old walls, *Darbar* tent, al fresco meals, beautiful pool, tennis, lovely setting in peaceful walled Mughal gardens (see above), plenty of birdwatching, "amazing". Recommended. Reservations essential for both. **B-C** *Maharaja Palace*, modern hotel. 18 rooms (some a/c) in mock *haveli*, restaurant, garden with village style huts.

Sleeping
Try UCO Bank if short of money

A small artists' colony in the village produces good quality miniature **paintings** on old paper. Contact Krishan Kumar Khari, often found at the hotel entrance.

Shopping

Samode is a 1 hr drive from Jaipur. Buses from Chandpol Gate go to Chomu where you can pick a local bus to Samode.

Transport

★ Shekhawati

Covering an area of about 300 sq km on the often arid and rock-studded plains to the northwest of the Aravalli mountain range, Shekhawati is the homeland of the Marwari community. The area is particularly rich in painted havelis. *Sikar district in the southwest and Jhunjhunun in the northeast form an 'open-air art gallery' of paintings dating from the mid-19th century. Although a day trip gives you an idea of its treasures, it is better to spend two or three nights in Shekhawati to see some good examples of temples, frescoed forts, chhatris and step-wells at leisure. There are other diversions laid on such as horse or camel safaris and treks into the hills, for visitors who can spare a little more time.*

Getting there You can get to the principal Shekhawati towns by train but road access is easier. A car comes in handy to see the area, though there are crowded buses from Delhi, Jaipur and Bikaner to some towns. Buses leave every 30 mins from 0500-2000 from Jaipur's Main Bus Station and take about 3 hrs. You can get from one Shekhawati town to another by local bus which run every 15 to 20 mins, and take about an hour. **Getting around** Be prepared for very rough roads between the towns. Within each town it is best to enlist the help of a local person (possibly from the hotels listed below) to direct you to the best *havelis*. See below for unusual alternative safaris.

Ins & outs
Avoid visiting bazars alone: tourists have been harassed. Women alone may find young men's behaviour aggressive See page 144 for further transport details

The 'garden of Shekha' was named after Rao Shekhaji of Amarsar (1433-88) who challenged the Kachhawahas, refusing to pay tribute to the rulers at Amber. These Rajput barons made inroads into Muslim territory even during

History

Jaipur & Northern Rajasthan

Mughal rule, and declared Shekhawati independent from the Jaipur suzerainty until 1738. During this period the merchants lavishly decorated their houses with paintings on religious, folk and historical themes. As Mughal power collapsed Shekhawati became a region of lawless banditry. In the early 19th century the British East India Company brought it under their control, bringing peace but also imposing taxes and tolls on trade which the Marwaris resented. Many of the merchants migrated to other parts of the country to seek their fortune and those who flourished returned their wealth to their homeland and took over as patrons of the artists.

The *havelis* Ramgarh has the highest concentration of painted *havelis*, though they are not as well maintained as those of Nawalgarh which has the second largest selection. It is easier to visit havelis in towns that have hotels, like Nawalgarh, Mandawa, Dundlod, Mukundgarh, Mahansar, Fatehpur, Baggar and Jhunjunun, and where the caretakers are used to visitors, though towns like Bissau, Alsisar, Malsisar and Churu have attractive *havelis* as well.

The *havelis* are often occupied by the family or retainers who will happily show you around but many charge a fee of about Rs 20. Many *havelis* are in a poor state of repair with fading paintings which may appear monotonously alike to some. Some visitors find towns like Fatehpur and Mandawa very dirty, unkempt and disappointing.

Shekhawati (Jhunjhunun & Sikar districts)

Shekhawati *havelis*

The havelis in Shekhawati were usually built around two courtyards – one for general use, and the other a zenana courtyard for the women. The latter was also used for laundry and so often had a well and occasionally a play area for children. Security was a prime concern so a haveli was typically entered by a solid gate with a smaller door in it for regular use by residents. Watchmen had rooms on either side of the entrance. The baithak (reception room) had mattresses and bolsters for sitting on the floor while others were set aside for sleeping or storage. The havelis were enlarged as the families grew larger or wealthier, and with the onset of peaceful times, they became more palatial and lavished with decoration.

The haveli was made from brick or local stone. It was plastered in two layers with decorations on the second layer – a polished lime plaster finish often set with agate and other semi-precious stones. Murals were either painted on dry surfaces or on wet plaster. Mineral colours were derived from indigo, ochre, lead, copper, lapis lazuli, lime and even gold. Synthetic blue was imported and only the wealthiest could afford strong blue tones on their havelis. Some of the finest frescoes were near the door separating the courtyard from the main chambers and these were often restored or repainted during weddings and festivals. The subject of the paintings varied. The 10 avatars of Vishnu were popular, especially scenes from Krishna Lila and the Ramayana. The Mahabharata, the Ragamala (depicting musical modes of different seasons), folk tales, historic events, daily life in Shekhawati and floral and faunal themes were also popular, together with a fascination for portraying the British and their curious ways.

Trekking There are some interesting treks in the Aravalli hills near Nawalgarh starting from Lohargal (34 km), a temple with sacred pools. Local people claim that this is the place recorded in the *Mahabharata* where Bhim's mace is said to have been crafted. A four to five day trek would take in the Bankhandi peak (1,052 m), Krishna temple in Kirori Valley, Kot Reservoir, Shakambari mata temple, Nag Kund (a natural spring) and Raghunathgarh fort. The cost depends on the size of the group and the facilities provided. *Apani Dhani* arranges treks with stays at the temple guest houses and villages for US$ 50 per person per day for minimum of two persons.

Trekking & safaris

Horse safaris Dundlod Fort and Roop Niwas at Nawalgarh offer one week safaris with nights in royal tents (occasionally in castles or heritage hotels) to cover the attractions of the region. The most popular take in the Pushkar or Tilwara fairs. You can expect, folk music concerts, campfires, guest speakers, masseurs, and sometimes, even a barber, all with jeep support. You ride three hours in the morning and two hours in the afternoon, and spend time visiting eco-farms, rural communities and *havelis* en route.

Camel safaris *Roop Niwas Palace, Apani Dhani* (Nawalgarh), Dundlod and Mandawa offer these. On a five-day safari, you might cover Nawalgarh-Mukundgarh-Mandawa-Mahansar-Churu, crossing some of the finest sand dunes in Shekhawati; Nawalgarh to Fatehpur for three-day safaris, and one week country safaris to Tal Chapper Wildlife Sanctuary. The cost depends on the number in the group and the facilities provided ranging from Rs 800-1,500 per day. One-day safaris arranged by the heritage hotels cost about Rs 800 with packed lunch and mineral water.

Wildlife safari A possible day excursion from one of the castle hotels is a visit to **Tal Chappar** near Sujjangarh covering 71 sq km of desert scrubland with ponds and salt flats. It has some of the largest herds of Blackbuck antelope

Guiding light

It can be very difficult to find your way around so don't venture out without a local guide. Your hotel can provide one, or a local person will often volunteer for a small tip. If arriving by train, ask your hotel to send a jeep for transfer. Power cuts can cause real problems in hotels bringing to a halt, cooling in summer, heating (and hot water) in winter and lighting at night – always have a torch handy.

in India (easily seen at the watering point near the park gate itself), besides chinkara gazelle, desert cat, desert fox and other dryland wildlife. Huge flocks of demoiselle and common cranes can be seen at nearby lakes and wetlands where they feed on tubers and ground vegetation. Other birdlife include sandgrouse, quails, bar headed geese and cream coloured desert courser. The enthusiastic forest official, Laxman Singh, is a good guide to the area. A local NGO, Krishna Mirg, is active in tree plantation and in fund-raising for the eco-development of Tal Chappar, providing support fodder during dry months to blackbuck and cranes. The Forest Department *Rest House* offers a shady spot for packed meals during hot afternoons. Try *Hanuman* tea stall for delicious *chai* and the local sweet, malai laddoo. ■ *Getting there: the drive to Tal Chapper can be long and tiring on a bad last stretch of road, and it can be a full day trip with not much to see. If you are travelling between Bikaner and Shekhawati in a jeep, it is worth making a detour. Riaskhan (T01425-24391) has a fleet of open, convertible and hardtop (closed) jeeps for visitng Tal Chappar from Kuchaman, Sambhar or Roopangarh, at Rs1200-1500.*

Recommended reading   *The painted towns of Shekhawati* by Ilay Cooper, a great Shekhawati enthusiast (Mapin, Allahabad, 1994), has numerous colour photos and maps. *Shekhawati: Rajsthan's painted houses* by P Rakesh and K Lewis is also well illustrated.

Sikar District

Occupying the southwestern flank of the Shekhawati region, Sikar district has a number of picturesque forts, towns and villages.

Sikar
Colour map 2, grid C3
Population: 148,000

The late 17th-century fort was built when Sikar was an important trading centre and the wealthiest *thikana* (feudatory) under Jaipur. You can visit the old quarter and see the Wedgwood blue 'Biyani' (1920) and 'Mahal' (1845), Murarka and Somani *havelis* and murals and carvings in Gopinath, Raghunath and Madan Mohan temples. ■ *Getting there: From Jaipur take the NH11 to Ringas (63 km) and Sikar (48 km).*

Sleeping and eating   **E** *Aravalli Resort* NH11, 2 air-cooled rooms with bath (simple, shabby), inexpensive Indian restaurant, gift shop, popular tourist stop to pick up mineral water. *Natraj Restaurant*, Main Rd, does good meals and snacks, clean, reasonable. *Paradise*, inexpensive Indian food.

Lachhmangarh

Founded early 19th century, the town plan was based on Jaipur's model; this can be seen by climbing up to the old fort which has now been renovated by the Jhunjhunwala family. The fine *havelis* include one of the area's grandest – Ganeriwala with char chowks (four courtyards) – the 'Rathi' *haveli* near the Clock Tower in the market, and others in the Chowkhani.

Fatehpur, founded in the mid-15th century by a Kayamkhani Nawab, has very **Fatehpur**
attractive *havelis* along the Churu-Sikar road. Visit in particular the Devra *Good tie-and-dye*
(1885), Singhania (circa 1880), Goenka (circa 1880) and Saraogi. Later amus- *fabrics can be*
ing frescoes showing European influence can be seen in the Jalan and white *bought here*
Bharthia (1929) *havelis*.

Sleeping and eating D *Amar*, has clean rooms (price varies), good bar, quick service,
pool. **E** *Haveli* (RTDC), Sikar Rd, 500 m south of bus stand, T01571-20293, 8 clean
rooms, some a/c with bath, dorm (Rs 50), pleasant building, dull restaurant (mice and
birds tolerated in kitchen).

This is a little town in the middle of the sand dunes with the golden sandstone **Pachhar**
castle scenically situated on a lakeshore. A road north from Bagru on the NH8, *W of Jaipur*
also gives access. The place is pleasantly free from 'give me pen, give me
rupees' children.

Sleeping and eating C *Golden Castle Resort*, 16 very well-decorated rooms, Indian
meals, collection of portraits, paintings and weaponry, camel and jeep safaris.

Ramgarh was settled by the Poddars in the late 18th century. In addition to **Ramgarh**
their many *havelis* and that of the Ruias, visit the *chhatris* with painted *W of Ringas*
entrances near the bus stand, the temples to Shani (with mirror decoration)
and to Ganga. Ramgarh has the highest concentration of painted *havelis*,
though they are not as well maintained as those of Nawalgarh which has the
second largest selection. Look for handicrafts here.

Danta, nearby, originally a part of Marwar, was given to Thakur Amar Singhji **Danta**
in the mid-17th century. Two *kilas* (forts) and the residential wing (early
18th-century) combine Mughal and Rajput art and architectural styles.

Sleeping and eating C *Kila*, T0157-589362 (*Dera Heritage Hotel*, T0141-366276),
12 large rooms in residential wing below the 2 old forts, good restaurant (meals
Rs 160), peacocks at dawn, camel rides (Rs 250 per hr, Rs 550 per 3 hrs), horse safaris
(see above), Jeep safaris (minimum 4 persons), Rs 1,200 each per day.

Jhunjhunun District

At Fatehpur, a country road to the east takes you to Mandawa (22 km), a small, **Mandawa**
rather dirty bustling town. Founded in the mid-18th century, it has interesting *The havelis here are*
murals in the large rugged fort (circa 1755) built by Thakur Nawal Singh, which *past their prime but*
is now a hotel. The Goenka *haveli* – Ladhuram Tarkesvar (1878) and Dedraj *can be interesting*
Turmal (1898); the Ladia *havelis* – Gulab Rai (1870) and Sneh Ram (1906),
Nandlal Murmuria (1935), Bansidhar Newatia (1910) and the Mohanlal Saraf
(1870) *havelis* are interesting. The Siva temple here has a rock crystal lingam.
The Mandawa Haveli near Sonthaliya Gate (northeast of town) displays local
crafts, 0600-2200 daily. If you stay overnight in Mandawa you can visit the
Harlalka *baoli* (a working step well) early in the morning to watch oxen at work
on the ramp to raise water. If you are in Mandawa in October or November you
might catch the *Desert Music Festival*. There are some reasonably priced, good
quality miniatures on 'silk' at the *Mandawa Art School* at the castle gate, and fabrics and carpets at *CM Souvenirs*, Main Market.

Jaipur & Northern Rajasthan

Sleeping and eating B *Castle Mandawa* , T01592-23124, F23171. Huge castle with lots of character but parts rather run down. 70 a/c rooms, some in tower, complete with swing, most with 4-posters and period trappings but rooms vary so select with care ("cheerless, cold, hard beds"), excellent views, atmospheric but a overpriced, mixed reports, some disappointed with meals (Rs 400-450) "very commercial". Also **B** *Desert Resort*, T01592-23151, 1 km south. 60 rooms in 3 wings including a haveli, modern amenities (many renovated), pricey restaurant (Rs 250-450 and only buffets for tour groups), pool, shady garden, good views of countryside, camel rides. Contact Mandawa House, Jaipur, T0141-371194, F372084, www.india-travel.com **C** *Heritage Mandawa*, off Mukundgarh Rd, T01592-23742, F23743, 200 m from the main bazar street and the bus stand. 13 rooms with local 'ethnic' furnishings in an old haveli, attached baths (hot water, Western fixtures), dining hall (Rajasthani and Continental; set menu Rs 125-250), clean and pleasant, quite quiet, manager and staff very friendly and accommodating (good discounts in the low-season), camel rides, guides, taxis. **Camping** possible in grounds. Another *haveli* nearby has been recently converted to take guests. **C** *Mandawa Haveli*, T01592-23088 hotelmandawahaveli@yahoo.com, near Sonthaliya Gate. 7 rooms with modernized baths in a 3-storeyed, haveli with original 19th-century frescoes in courtyard, Rajasthani meals, museum and library. **D** *Rath*, on the eastern edge of town. 25 simple rooms with bath, dining hall, but leased privately in early 2001.

Directory Banks *SBBJ* and *Bank of Baroda*.

Mukundgarh Mukundgarh is the market for textiles and brass betel cutters. The town lies 10 km south of Jhunjhunun and 14 km from Mandawa. The Ganeriwala *havelis* (1860s and '70s) are worth visiting as well as the Jhunjhunwala (1859) haveli with Krishna stories and Sukhdev haveli (circa 1880).

Sleeping and eating B *Mukundgarh Fort* (Heritage Hotel), converted mid-18th-century fort, T0141-6968937, F6969831, 48 rooms (four suites) with frescoes along wide corridors, restaurant, bar and pool, a bit run down.

Nawalgarh Nawalgarh, some 25 km southeast of Mandawa, was founded in 1737 by
There are numerous Thakur Nawal Singh. The town has a colourful bazar and two forts (circa
fine havelis worth 1730). Nawalgarh fort has fine examples of maps and plans of Shekhawati and
visiting here Jaipur. The Bala Kila which has a kiosk with beautiful ceiling paintings is
Lone tourists have approached via the fruit market in the town centre and entered through the
been harassed in *Hotel Radha*. It also has the *Roop Niwas Palace* (now a hotel) and some
the bazar 18th-century temples with 19th- and early-20th- century paintings. There are other interesting temples in town including Ganga Mai near Nansa Gate.

The Anandilal Poddar Haveli, now converted to the Poddar Haveli Museum, is perhaps the best restored Haveli of Shekhawati. The 1920s haveli has around 700 frescoes including a Gangaur procession, scenes from the Mahabharata, trains, cars, the avatars of Vishnu, bathing scenes and British characters, some of the best frame the doors leading from the courtyard to the rooms. The upper storey of the Haveli is now a school but the ground floor has been opened as a museum. The photo-gallery records the life of Congressman and freedom fighter Anandilal Poddar, and the merchant-turned- industrialist Poddar family. There is a diorama of costumes of various Rajasthani tribes and communities, specially bridal attires, a gallery of musical instruments, The frescoes in the courtyard, which have been remarkably restored, are worth seeing. ■ *Rs 30 (foreigners) includes camera and guide.* Among the remarkable Murarka *havelis* are the 19th-century Kesardev Murarka which has a finely painted façade and the Radheshyam Murarka which was built in

The love story of Dhola and Maru

There are numerous versions of this romantic legend of the separation of a young couple and their subsequent reunion. The story which originated in northwestern Rajasthan, is the subject of many paintings.

Dhola, or Salhakumar, prince of Narvar, is married in infancy to Princess Maruni (Maru) of Pugal in Marwar, after their families meet by chance in Pushkar. However, the child bride returns home with her parents and only wakens to a longing for her husband when she reaches adolescence. The parents seeing their heartbroken daughter pining for her absent love, send minstrels to the court of Narvar but without luck. They learn that Prince Dhola has remarried and his new bride, Malvani of Malwa, has intercepted the messengers before they could reach Dhola. Although, the prince longs to find his first wife, Malvani uses every means to hold him back. However, at long last, Dhola escapes when his second wife falls asleep, having found a camel that will speed him to Pugal within a single day. He surmounts the many obstacles that are conjured up by the unscrupulous Malvani, and the couple are reunited. On the return journey, Maru is bitten by a venomous snake but Dhola remains with his dead wife. His prayers are answered when a passer-by performs a miracle and brings her back to life and the young couple are taken by the remarkable, fleet-footed camel back to the kingdom of Narvar. The tale ends happily – Maru assumes her rightful place and is adored by the people of Narvar, while Malvani emerges bitterly defeated by the gentle princess from the harsh and arid deserts of Marwar.

Jaipur & Northern Rajasthan

the early-20th century. The latter portrays processions, scenes from folk tales, Hindu and Christian religious paintings, sometimes interspersed with mirrorwork. Other fine *havelis* are those of the Bhagat, Chokhani, Goenka, Patodia, Kedwal, Sangerneria, Saraogi, Jhunujhunwala, Saha and Chhauchuria families. The paintings here depict anything from European women having a bath (Aath – "eight" – Haveli complex) to Hindu religious themes and Jesus Christ. Some of the *havelis* are complexes of several buildings which include a temple, dharamshala, cenotaph and a well). ■ *Most charge Rs 15-20 for viewing.*

Sleeping C *Roop Niwas Palace*, T01594-22008, F23388, 1 km north of town. 35 rooms (older ones are large, air-cooled and simply furnished with old fashioned Western bathrooms, the newer are a/c but smaller), most are in 3 storeys around court-yards and a few in garden-side annexe good food, large gardens (peacocks), pool, stables with camels and 35 horses ('dancing' horses arranged Rs 3,000), 'safaris', attractive, small 90-year old palace, warm and hospitable, Rajput family run, pleasant. Simple but recommended. **D** *Apani Dhani*, near Kisan Chhatrawas, 1 km from rly station, 500 m north of Bus Stand, T01594-22239. 10 'environmentally friendly' huts in an 'ecological farm', run by Ramesh Jangid (helpful and very knowledgeable), attractive, comfortable thatched cottages built traditionally using mud and straw, Indian toilets, home-grown veg, immaculately presented, relaxing atmosphere. Cheaper **E** *Jangid Tourist Pension*, T01594-22129, F22491, behind Maur hospital. Comfortable rooms with bath, good veg meals, tours, jeep/cycle hire, camel rides, cultural shows, quiet, clean, welcoming. These 2 lack character of the fort hotels but are highly recommended.

Eating *Roop Niwas*. Delicious meals (set menu – try *tandoori* chicken and *methi paneer*). Nearby. *DS Guest House* and *Shekhawati Garden* are popular for lunch and dinner. Both have **D-E** rooms.

Directory Banks *SBBJ* changes currency and TCs, but poor rate. *Roop Niwas* can sometimes help get better rates.

Parasarampura, about 12 km southeast of Nawalgarh, has a decorated *chhatri* to Sardul Singh (1750) and the adjacent Gopinath temple (1742); these are the earliest examples of Shekhawati frescoes painted with natural pigments (caretaker has keys).

Dundlod West of Nawalgarh, the best murals are in the **castle** (1750), now a Heritage Hotel. You enter the moated castle by the Suraj Pol and proceed through the Bichla Darwaza and Uttar Pol (north) before arriving at the courtyard. Steps lead up to the majestic Diwan Khana furnished with period furniture, portraits and hangings; there is a library with a collection of rare books of Indian history and the *duchatta* above, which allowed the ladies in *purdah* to watch court ceremonies unobserved. Ask for the key to the painted family *chhatris* nearby. ■ *Darbar Hall: Rs 20 for non-residents.* The Goenka *haveli* near the fort has three painted courtyards, and the Satyanarayan temple has religious paintings but both these may be closed in the low season. The interesting deep step well now has an electric pump.

Mukundgarh is the nearest station where you can get jeeps & taxis

Sleeping and eating **C** *Dundlod Fort* ('Castle' and 'Kila' combined), Heritage Hotel, in village centre, T/F01594-52519. 42 rooms, upgraded ones particularly good, others mediocre with poor bathrooms, good state rooms with some period furniture, **B** suites with terraces, good food (Rs 180-220), power cuts can be a problem but full of atmosphere and interesting murals, pool, library, tours (jeep around Shekhawati, Rs 1,300), camel/horse rides Rs 300-350 per hr (owners are keen horsemen), warm welcome, very hospitable and helpful.

Polo Centre: opportunity to see camel, horse & bicycle polo, tent pegging etc

Directory Banks *UCO Bank* changes currency.

Jhunjhunun Jhunjhunun was a stronghold of the Kayamkhani Nawabs until defeated by the Hindu Sardul Singh in 1730. The Mohanlal Iswardas Modi (1896), Tibriwala (1883) and the Muslim Nuruddin Farooqi *havelis* (which is devoid of figures) and the maqbara are all worth seeing. The *Chhe* (6) Haveli complex, Khetri Mahal (1760) and the Biharilal temple (1776), which has attractive frescoes (closed during lunch time), are also interesting. The Rani Sati temple commemorates Narayana Devi who is believed to have become a sati; her stone is venerated by many of the wealthy *bania* community and an annual Marwari fair is held (protesting women's groups feel it glorifies the practice of *sati*). Since 1947, 29 cases of *sati* have been recorded in the Sikar and its two neighbouring districts.

Sleeping and eating **B**-**C** *Jamuna Resort*, T01592-30871, F32603. 4 air-cooled cottage rooms with attractive mirror work and murals, 'Golden Room' with painted ceiling "like a jewel box", frescos, open-air Rajasthani veg/non-vegetarian restaurant, gardens, pool (open to hotel/restaurant guests only), pleasant and clean, local guided tours. Also **C**-**D** *Shiv Shekhawati*, Muni Ashram, Khemi Sati Rd, T01592-32651, F38168. 18 simple clean rooms, 8 a/c, all with bath and hot water, good veg restaurant, tourist office (guides). The owner of both, LK Jangid, is very knowledgeable. Recommended. **C**-**D** *Tourist Bungalow* (RTDC), 6 rooms, dining room, beer shop. **D**-**F** *Neelam*, T0159-238415, opposite Kethan Hospital. Small hotel off the highway with some a/c and air-cooled rooms with bath and TV, also economical rooms with shared facilities, restaurant serving snacks. **D**-**G** *Naveen*, Station Rd, T32527. A/c and aircooled rooms with attached baths, some much cheaper with shared baths popular with salesmen. **E-F** *Sangam*, near bus stand, T32544., F34063, clean rooms, better with bath at rear, veg meals. **E-F** *Shalimar* and **E-F** *Shekhawati Heritage* nearby are similar.

The grand haveli of the Makharias, 10 km north east of Jhunjhunun, has rooms along open corridors around grassy courtyards and wall paintings of gods and angels being transported in motor cars!

Baggar

Sleeping and eating B-C *Piramal Haveli*, T01592-22220, sales@neemrana.com, 100-year old home, restored sensitively, excellent vegetarian meals and attentive service, simple but overpriced, does not have as much atmosphere as castle hotels.

Founded in the mid-18th century, the town has a distinctly medieval feel. It has the Poddar haveli of Son Chand, the Rama Temple (ask for the key to the Golden Room; no photography) and the large Raghunath Temple with some of the finest paintings of the region. The fort (1768) has palaces and a baradari which were added later.

Mahansar
30 km NE of Jhunjhunun

Sleeping and eating C *Narayan Niwas Castle*, near bus stand, T01562-64322. Some airy rooms with potential, but poor bathrooms, attractive wall paintings, converted by Thakur Tejpal Singh, meals (cooked by his wife) "quite an experience", pleasant owners.

Set in semi-desert countryside, Churu, northwest of Baggar, was believed to have been a Jat stronghold in the 16th century. In the 18th century it was an important town of Bikaner state and has an 18th-century fort. The town

Churu

Jhunjhunun

Jaipur & Northern Rajasthan

thrived during the days of overland desert trade. The local Rajputs barons revolted only to be crushed by the royals of Bikaner. The town has some interesting 1870s Oswal Jain *havelis* like those of the Kotharis and the Suranas. Banthia (early-20th century), Bagla (1880), Khemka (1800s). There are also the Bajranglal mantri haveli and the Poddar haveli and numerous towers, temples, wells and reservoirs which are interesting.

Transport

Road **Bicycle**: *Apani Dhani,* Nawalgarh, arranges cycle tours in Shekhawati. **Bus**: To **Nawalgarh** from Delhi, best from ISBT daily at 0800, 2200 and 2300, 8 hrs. From **Jaipur** frequent buses from 0630-1830 (Express in the morning), 3½ hrs. Also to **Sikar** from Jaipur and Bikaner. **Taxi**: From Jaipur, diesel Ambassador, Rs 1,200 for day tour of parts of Shekhawati; with detours (eg Samode), up to Rs 1,500; Rs 1,700 including 1 night. A/c cars can be twice as much. Local hire is possible in Mandawa, Mukundgarh and Nawalgarh. **Jeeps**: For hire in Samode, Nawalgarh, Mandawa and Dundlod, about Rs 1,200 per day.

Train From **Jaipur**, 3 trains run daily to stations in Shekhawati. *Shekhawati Exp* (Delhi-Jaipur): To **Mukundgarh** from Delhi, 2315, 7½ hrs; from Jaipur, 1015, 1330, 1805, 4 hrs. To **Nawalgarh** from Delhi, 2230, 8½ hrs. To **Jhunjhunun** from Delhi, dep 2315, 7½ hrs, arriving in Sikar after 2 hrs; from Jaipur, dep 1805, 5 hrs, continues to Delhi, 6 hrs. To **Sikar** from Bikaner, dep 2025, 7 hrs.

Alwar

Phone code: 0144
Colour map 2, grid C4
Population: 211,000

Alwar has fascinating monuments including the Bala Quilla fort overlooking the town and the Moti Doongri fort in a garden. The former, which was never taken by direct assault, has relics of the early Rajput rulers who had their capital near Alwar, the founders of the fort. Over the centuries it was home to the Khanzadas, Mughals, Pathans, Jats and finally the Rajputs. There are also palaces, and colonial period parks and gardens.

Background As Mughal power crumbled Rao Pratap Singhji of Macheri founded Alwar as his capital in 1771. He shook off Jat power over the region and rebelled against Jaipur suzerainty making Alwar an independent state. His successors lent military assistance to the British in their battles against the Marathas in 1803 AD, and in consequence gained the support of the colonial power. The Alwar royals were flamboyant and kept a fleet of custom-made cars (including a throne car and a golden limousine), and collected solid silver furniture and attractive walking sticks.

Sights Alwar is protected by the hilltop **Bala Quilla** which has the remains of palaces, temples and 10 tanks built by the first rulers of Alwar. It stands 308 m above the town, to the northwest, and is reached by a steep four-wheel drive track (with permission from the police station). There are splendid views.

The **Vinai Vilas Mahal**, the City Palace (1840), with intricate *jali* work, ornate *jarokha* balconies and courtyards, houses government offices on the ground floor, and a fine **museum** upstairs. The palace is impressive but is poorly maintained, with dusty galleries (you may find children playing cricket in the courtyard). The Darbar Room is closed, and the throne, miniatures and gilt edged mirrors can only be viewed through the glass doors and windows or by prior permission of the royal family (which is not easily obtained). The museum is interesting, housing local miniature paintings, as well as some of the Mughal, Bundi and other schools, an array of swords, shields, daggers, guns and armour, sandalwood carvings, ivory objects, jade art, musical instruments and princely relics. There are over 7,000 manuscripts in various Asian languages (part housed in the Oriental Research Institute, also in the Palace) ■ *Rs 3, 10.30-16.30, closed Fri.* This was a garden palace with exotic floral species, and can be seen from the road, as also the old railway station and the Fateh Jang Gumbad. The Company garden has a domed greenhouse, called Simla, in a public park.

Next to the city palace are the lake and royal cenotaphs. On the south side of the tank is the Cenotaph of Maharaja Bakhtawar Singh (1781-1815) which is of marble on a red sandstone base. The gardens are alive with peacocks and other birds. To the right of the main entrance to the palace is a two-storey processional elephant carriage designed to carry 50 people and be pulled by four elephants.

The **Yeshwant Niwas**, built by Maharaja Jai Singh in the Italianate style, is also worth seeing. Apparently on its completion he disliked it and never lived in it. Instead he built the **Vijay Mandir** in 1918, a 105-room palace beside Vijay Sagar, 10 km from Alwar. Part of it is open to the public with prior permission from the royal family or their secretary but is worth seeing from the road, with its façade resembling an anchored ship. ■ *1000-1630, closed Fri. Rs 3.* When not in Delhi, the royal family now live in Phool Bagh, a small 1960s mansion opposite the New Stadium.

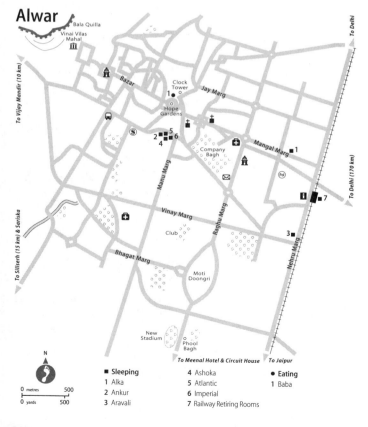

Alwar

Bala Quilla
Vinai Vilas Mahal ⛪
To Vijay Mandir (10 km)
To Silliserh (15 km) & Sariska
To Delhi
To Delhi (170 km)
Bazar
Clock Tower
Jay Marg
Hope Gardens
Company Bagh
Mangal Marg
Manu Marg
Vinay Marg
Raghu Marg
Nehru Marg
Club
Bhagat Marg
Moti Doongri
New Stadium
Phool Bagh
To Meenal Hotel & Circuit House
To Jaipur

1
2 5 6
4
1
3
7

N
0 metres 500
0 yards 500

■ Sleeping	4 Ashoka	● Eating
1 Alka	5 Atlantic	1 Baba
2 Ankur	6 Imperial	
3 Aravali	7 Railway Retiring Rooms	

Jaipur & Northern Rajasthan

Jaipur & Northern Rajasthan

Excursions At **Siliserh**, 15 km to the west, runs an aqueduct which supplies the city with water. The lake, a local picnic spot, has boats for hire. You can stay at **C-D** *Lake Palace(RTDC), T0144-86322, 10 rooms, five a/c, restaurant, modest but superb location.*

Kesroli, 10 km northeast, has a seven-turreted 16th-century fort atop a rocky hillock, now sympathetically (though more modestly) restored into a hotel by the owners of *Neemrana.* It is a three-hours' drive from Delhi and convenient for an overnight halt. Turn left off NH8 at Dharuhera for Alwar Road and you will find it. **B** *Hill Fort Kesroli* (Heritage Hotel), Alwar Road T0144-89352, sales@neemrana.com Around a courtyard are 22 comfortable, if eccentric, airy rooms, reasonable restaurant and service, relaxing, and in a lovely isolated rural location. **Kushalgarh Fort** is en route to Sariska. Near Kushalgarh is the temple complex of Talbraksha (or Talvriksh) with a large population of rhesus macaque monkeys. Guides report panthers having been seen near the *Cafeteria Taal* here, probably on the prowl for monkeys near the canteen.

Sleeping **D** *Alwar*, 26 Manu Marg, T20012, F332250, ukrustagi@hotmail.com Set on the main
■ *on maps* road with an attractive garden, 10 rooms (some a/c) with attached baths (hot show-
Price codes: ers), TV, refrigerator and phone, restaurant (closed on Mon), arrangements for swim-
see inside front cover ming and tennis at nearby club, efficient service, popular. **D-E** *Ankur*, Manu Marg, T333025. 9 rooms of varying quality (Rs 150-600) **D-E** *Ashoka*, Manu Marg, T21780. 35 rooms, clean and comfortable, deluxe rooms have TV, running hot water and western toilets, cheaper rooms have Indian toilets and hot water in buckets, restaurant (Rs 35 *thalis*), good value. **D-E** *Atlantic*, Manu Marg, T343181. 11 rooms with attached baths, only **D** a/c and deluxe rooms have Western toilets. **D-E** *Imperial Guest House*, Manu Marg, T21430. Air-cooled rooms (a/c rooms with colour TV), vegetarian restaurant (south Indian snacks). **D-E** *Meenal* (RTDC), near Circuit House, T347352. 6 rooms with bath (2 a/c), restaurant, bar. **E** *Aravali*, Nehru Marg, near the station, T332883, F332011. Some air-cooled rooms (around Rs 250), **F** dorm, reasonable restaurant, bar, swimming arranged on request. **E** *Alka*, Mangal Marg, T332796. Basic rooms. **E** *Saroop Vilas Palace*, near Moti Doongri, T331218. Renovated royal mansion taken over by private entrepreneur, 5 rooms with attached baths (western toilets, plans for running hot water), vegetarian restaurant (set menu Rs 60, or a la carte), non veg meals on order (Rs 100-150). *Railway Retiring Rooms*, T332222.

Eating *Baba*, Hope Circle. Popular for 'milk cake' (*kalakand*) and other Rajasthani sweets.
● *on map, page 145* *Narulas*, Kashiram Circle. Indian/Chinese/Continental. A/c restaurant, popular for
Price codes: Punjabi non veg and veg dishes, "best in town". Moti Doongri Park has a number of
see inside front cover stalls selling cheap south Indian snacks in the evening. You can also get inexpensive Chinese and north Indian.

Tourist office *Rajasthan*, Tourist Reception Centre, Nehru Marg, opposite railway station, T347348.

Transport **Road Bus**: There are regular buses to/from Delhi (4½-5 hrs) and Jaipur. Frequent service to Bharatpur (2½ hrs), Deeg (1½ hrs) and Sariska (1 hr). **Train New Delhi**: *Shatabdi Exp*, *2016*, not Sun, 1941, 2½ hrs. **Delhi**: *Jodhpur Delhi Exp*, 4860, 0835, 3 hrs; *Jaipur-Delhi Exp*, *2414*, 1845, 3 hrs.

Directory **Communications** Internet: near the bus and railway station and on Manu Marg.

Sariska Tiger Reserve

Phone code: 0144
Colour map 2, grid C4

The 480 sq km sanctuary is a dry deciduous forest set in a valley surrounded by the barren Aravalli hills. The princely shooting reserve of the Maharajah of Alwar in the Aravallis was declared a sanctuary in 1955 and is a tiger reserve under Project Tiger.

The main rhesus monkey population live at Talvriksh near Kushalgarh, whilst at Bhartri-Hari you will see many langurs. The chowsingha, or **four-horned antelope**, is found at Sariska. Other deer include chital and sambar. You may see nilgai, wild boar, jackals, hyenas, hares and porcupines, though tigers and leopards are rarely seen, since the reserve is closed at night to visitors. During the monsoons the place is alive with birds but many animals move to higher ground. There are ground birds such as peafowl, jungle fowl, spur fowl and the grey partridge. Babblers, bulbuls and tree pies are common round the lodges.

The **Kankwari Fort** (20 km), where Emperor Aurangzeb is believed to have imprisoned his brother **Dara Shikoh**, the rightful heir to the Mughal throne, is within the park. The old **Bhartrihari** temple (6 km) has a fair and six hour dance-drama in September to October. **Neelkanth** (33 km) has a complex of sixth to 10th-century carved temples.

Sariska Tiger Reserve

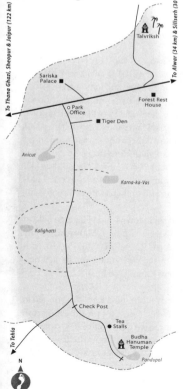

After Prosenjit Das Gupta

Not to scale

The park is open all year round. During the monsoon travel through the forest may be difficult. The best season to visit is between November and April. In the dry season, when the streams disappear, the animals become dependant on man-made water holes at Kalighatti, Salopka and Pandhupol.

Sariska, the gateway for the Sariska National Park, is a pleasant, quiet place to stay and relax. Excursions by jeep are possible to forts and temples nearby. **Bhangarh** (55 km), on the outskirts of the reserve, is a deserted city of some 10,000 dwellings established in 1631. It was abandoned 300 years ago, supposedly after it was cursed by a magician.

■ *Rs 200 (foreigners); vehicle Rs 125 per trip. Early morning jeep trips from Sariska Palace Hotel or Tiger Den go into the park as far as the Monkey Temple, where you can get a cup of tea and watch monkeys and peacocks. Jeep-hire for non-standard trips in the reserve, Rs 700 for 3 hrs, excluding entry fees. Further information from Wildlife Warden, Sariska, T332348.*

B *Sariska Palace*, T41322, F6172346, sariska@del2.vsnl.net.in (40 km from Alwar rly). 101 refurbished a/c rooms,

Sleeping & eating

(annexe lacks the charm of the Lodge), restaurant and bar (generally only open for residents), gym, pool, new ayurvedic and yoga centre, tours, converted royal hunting lodge full of photographs and stuffed tigers, reports of "noisy guests partying until late". **C-D** *Tiger Den* (RTDC), in the sanctuary, T41312. Superbly located tourist bungalow with views of hill and park, 30 rooms with attached baths (hot showers) but shabby and dirty public areas, vegetarian restaurant (Indian buffets Rs 130-150), bar (no snacks, carry your own to have with beer/drinks) shop sells cards and souvenirs, nice garden. **C-D** *Tiger Resort*, near Park check post, T86268. 8 rooms (some a/c) with attached baths (hot showers), TV, phones, some rooms with shared bath, dorm beds (Rs 250), run by retired army officer's family, restaurant (set menu meals Rs 120-140, western breakfast Rs 75), laundry, fishing, basic rock climbing, boating and horse/camel riding arranged, nature treks, 4 WD jeep safaris in park and to fort (with police permission), travel desk. **C-D** *Tiger Haven*, on the Viratnagar Rd, is a new hotel. **D** *Forest Rest House*, Main Rd, opposite turning to Kushalgarh. Simple rooms.

Transport   **Air** Nearest airport at Jaipur (110 km). **Train** Nearest at Alwar (36 km), with buses to the sanctuary.

Jaipur to Agra

From Jaipur the road east along the NH11 runs to **Kanota** (14 km). The 200-year old castle surrounded by orchards and gardens, has been converted into a distinctive hotel. **C** *Royal Castle* has 12 clean, well-decorated, comfortable rooms, a good restaurant, a collection of arms and carriages, a library of rare books, manuscripts and paintings, and horse and camel rides. Recommended. Contact: T0141-561291, F561045.

Mohanpura, 27 km from Jaipur and 1 km to the left off the NH11 is **B** *The Retreat* (Heritage Hotel), behind Govt Nursery, T0141-304371, F304628. Two cottage like rooms or deluxe tents among orange and lemon groves, former hunting lodge of Bissau royal family retaining rustic flavour, traditional buffets, pool, camel rides in dunes and through villages (worthwhile if you are not visiting western Rajasthan), "after Princess Diana and Prince Charles had a cup of tea in the Retreat many English and American tourists want to go there"! Make your reservations at the *Bissau Palace Hotel* in Jaipur.

Bhandarej, 62 km from Jaipur, south of NH11 after Dausa, has the **B** *Bhadrawati Palace*, T0141-372919, 35 rooms with bath in converted palace, gardens, pool, wide choice in restaurant; also orchard with camping facilities, 5 km from palace.

The NH11 then goes through a series of small towns and villages to **Sakrai** (77 km) where there is a good road side RTDC *restaurant*. **Mahuwa**, exactly half way between Jaipur and Agra, has **E** *Motel* (RTDC), T07461-33210, with five simple rooms, a fast food restaurant, toilets, basic motor repair facilities. Here a road south leads through Hindaun to Karauli (64 km).

Karauli   Noted for its pale red sandstone, widely used for building, Karauli, founded in 1348, was the seat of a small princely state which played a prominent part in support of the Mughal Emperors. The impressive **City Palace** has some fine wall paintings, stone carvings and a fine Darbar Hall. Fairs are held at nearby temples lasting a week to a fortnight: *Sivaratri* (28 February 2002), *Kaila Devi* (18 September 2001, 9 April 2002, 7 October 2002).

Essentials **B** *Bhanwar   Vilas   Palace* (Heritage   Hotel),   T07464-20024, www.karauli.com 21 comfortable rooms in converted palace, most air-cooled (cheaper in cottage), restaurant (Indian, Rajasthani), pool, tours, camping. All trains except *Rajdhani Express* stop at Gangapur City, 30 km away. **Mahavirji**, associated with the 24th Tirthankar Mahavir, is an important Jain pilgrimage centre.

Deeg

For a typical dusty and hot north Indian market town, Deeg gained the somewhat surprising reputation as the summer resort of the Raja of Bharatpur. Located on the plains just northwest of Agra, the Raja decided to develop his palace to take full advantage of the monsoon rains. The fort and the 'Monsoon' pleasure palace have ingenious fountains and are of major architectural importance.

Phone code: 05641
Colour map 2, grid C6
Population: 38,000

Badan Singh (1722-56), a Sinsini Jat, began the development of the town as capital of his newly founded Jat Kingdom. The central citadel was built by his son **Suraj Mal** in 1730. In the late 18th century the town reverted to the Raja of Bharatpur. The British stormed the fort in December 1804, after which the fortifications were dismantled. **History**

The rubble and mud walls of the square **fort** are strengthened by 12 bastions and a wide, shallow moat. It has a run-down *haveli* within. The entrance is over a narrow bridge across the moat, through a gate studded with anti-elephant spikes. Negotiating the thorny undergrowth, you can climb the ramparts which rise 20 m above the moat; some large cannons are still in place on their rusty carriages. You can walk right around along the wide path on top of the walls and climb the stairs to the roof of the citadel for good views all round. **Sights**

The palaces are flanked by two reservoirs, Gopal (west) and Rup Sagar (east), and set around a central square formal garden in the style of a Mughal *char bagh*. The main entrance is from the north, through the ornamental, though unfinished, Singh (Lion) Pol; the other gates are Suraj (Sun) Pol (southwest) and Nanga Pol (northeast). The impressive main palace **Gopal Bhavan** (1763), bordering Gopal Sagar, is flanked by Sawon and Bhadon pavilions (1760) named after the monsoon months (mid-July to mid-September). Water was directed over the roof lines to create the effect of sheets of monsoon rain. Outside, overlooking the formal garden, is a beautiful white marble *hindola* (swing) which was brought as booty with two marble thrones (black and white) after Suraj Mal attacked Delhi.

To the south, bordering the central garden, is the single-storey marble **Suraj Bhavan** (circa 1760), a temple and **Kishan Bhavan** with its decorated faÁade, five arches and fountains. The water reservoir to its west was built at a height to operate the fountains and cascades effectively; it held enough water to work all the fountains for a few hours though it took a week to fill from four wells with bullocks drawing water up in leather buckets. Now, the 500 or so fountains are turned on once a year for the *Monsoon festival* in August. All these are gravity fed from huge holding tanks on the Palace roof, with each fountain jet having its own numbered pipe leading from the tank. Coloured dyes are inserted into individual pipes to create a spectacular effect. The (old) **Purana Mahal** beyond, with a curved roof and some fine architectural points was begun by Badan Singh in 1722. It now houses government offices but the wall paintings in the entrance chamber of the inner court, though simple, are worth seeing.

Keshav Bhavan, a *baradari* or garden pavilion, stands between the central garden and Rup Sagar with the **Sheesh Mahal** (Mirror Palace, 1725) in the southeast corner. **Nand Bhavan** (circa 1760), north of the central garden, is a large hall 45 m long, 24 m wide and 6 m high, raised on a terrace and enclosed by an arcade of seven arches. There are frescoes inside but it has a deserted feel. The pavilion took the monsoon theme further; the double-roof was ingeniously used to create the effect of thunder above-water channelled through hollow pillars rotated heavy stone balls which made the sound! On a sunny day the fountains are believed to have produced a rainbow.

The **'Monsoon' Pleasure Palaces**, to the west of the fort were begun by Suraj Mal. ■ *0800-1200 and 1300-1900. Free.*

Sleeping & eating Avoid spending a night here but if you have to you have the choice of the **D** *Deeg Motel* (RTDC), Agra Rd. 2 dirty rooms, restaurant, or **F** *Dak Bungalow*, next door, T2366. Basic and filthy.

Bharatpur

Phone code: 05644
Colour map 2, grid C6
Population: 157,000
40 km S of Deeg

A popular halting place on the 'Golden Triangle', Bharatpur, at the confluence of the Ruparel and Banganga rivers, is known for its **Keoladeo Ghana Bird Sanctuary**. *The old fort is rarely visited by foreign travellers but is worthwhile. The Bharatpur ruling family was Jat and constantly harassed the later Mughals. Under Badan Singh they controlled a large tract between Delhi and Agra, then led by Suraj Mal they seized Agra and marched on to Delhi in 1763.*

The fort & palaces
Bottled water difficult to find

Built by **Suraj Mal**, the **Lohagarh** Fort appears impregnable. The British initially repulsed in 1803 took it in 1825. There are double ramparts, a 46-m wide moat and an inner moat around the palace. Much of the wall has been demolished but there are the remains of some of the gateways. Inside the fort are three palaces (circa 1730) and Jewel House and Court to their north. The

Bharatpur

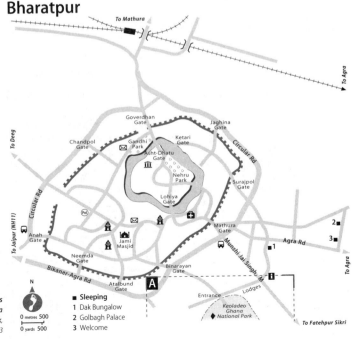

Related maps
A Keoladeo Ghana
National Park,
page 153

N
0 metres 500
0 yards 500

■ Sleeping
1 Dak Bungalow
2 Golbagh Palace
3 Welcome

museum in the Kachhari Kalan exhibits archaeological finds from villages nearby, dating from the first to 19th centuries as well as paintings and artefacts; the armoury is upstairs. ■ *1000-1630, closed Fri. Rs 3*. **Peharsar**, 5 km from centre, with a carpet weaving community, is very interesting to visit. ■ *Rs 30 to 'headman' secures a tour.*

A *Moti Mahal Palace-Golbagh* (Taj), being renovated, 86 rooms, no pool but squash. **Sleeping**
C *Chandra Mahal*, Peharsar, Jaipur-Agra Rd, Nadbai, T/F05643-3238. Simply furnished,19th-century Shia Muslim haveli with character, quality set meals (from Rs 250), jeep-hire, good service, rupee payment only. E *Welcome*, Golbagh Palace Rd, off Agra Rd, T23077. Basic, clean, good food, friendly management.

Brij Festival, a few days before Holi, honours lord Krishna with folk dances and drama **Festivals**
relating the love story of Radha-Krishna. (around **24 Mar** 2002).

Local Auto-rickshaw From railway station (6 km) to park Rs 50; from bus stand **Transport**
(4 km), Rs 20. **Air** Nearest airport is at Agra (55 km). **Road Bus**: From **Agra** (55 km, *Buses tend to get very*
1½ hrs, Rs 12), **Deeg** Rs 15; **Delhi** (185 km, 6 hrs, Rs 70) and **Jaipur** (175 km, 5 hrs, Rs 60) *crowded but give*
arrive at Anah Gate just off NH11 (east of town). **Train Delhi (ND)**: *Paschim Exp, 2925*, *an insight into*
0630, 4 hrs; *Golden Temple Mail, 2903*, 1540, 3½ hrs; *Mumbai-Firozepur Janata Exp*, *Indian rural life*
9023, 0800, 5½ hrs. **Sawai Madhopur**: *Paschim Exp, 2926*, 1955, 2½ hrs; *Golden Temple Mail, 2904*, 1055, 2½ hrs.

Banks *SBBJ* near Binarayan Gate, may ask to see proof of purchase, or refuse to **Directory**
change TCs.

★ Bharatpur-Keoladeo Ghana National Park

Once the hunting estate of the Maharajas of Bharatpur, with daily shoots recorded of up to 4,000 birds, the 29-sq km piece of marshland, with over 360 species, is one of the finest bird sanctuaries in the world. It has been designated a World Heritage site.

Getting there The park is 4 km south of Bharatpur town. See transport, above. **Ins & outs**
Getting around Good naturalist guides cost Rs 75 per hr per group or Rs 35 per hr per *Allow a full day,*
person at entrance, or contact *Nature Bureau*, Haveli SVP Shastri, Neemda Gate, *though you can*
T/F25498. Official cycle-rickshaws at the entrance are numbered and work in rotation, *spot many species*
Rs 30 per hr for 2 (drivers may be reluctant to take more than one). Well worthwhile as *in just 2 hrs.*
some rickshaw-wallahs are very knowledgeable and can help identify birds (and know *It is best to carry*
their location): a small tip is appropriate. The narrower paths are not recommended as *your own pair*
the rough surface make them too noisy. It is equally feasible to just walk or hire a bike. A *of binoculars*
boat ride is highly recommended for viewing; boatmen are equally knowledgeable;
hire one from the *Rest House* near jetty. **Climate** Winters can be very cold and foggy,
especially in the early morning. It is especially good Nov-Feb when it is frequented by
Northern hemisphere migratory birds.

The late Maharaja Brajendra Singh converted his hunting estate into a bird **History**
sanctuary in 1956 and devoted many of his retired years to establishing it. He
had inherited both his title and an interest in wildlife from his deposed father,
Kishan Singh, who grossly overspent his budget – 30 Rolls Royces, private jazz

Jaipur & Northern Rajasthan

band and extremely costly wild animals including "dozens of lions, elephants, leopards and tigers" for Bharatpur's jungles.

Wildlife A handful of rare Siberian Crane visit annually. The ancient migratory system, some 1,500 years old, is in danger of being lost since young cranes must learn the route from older birds (it is not instinctive). These cranes are disappearing – eaten by Afghans and sometimes employed as fashionable 'guards' to protect Pakistani homes (they call out when strangers approach). September to October is the breeding season but it's worth visiting any time of the year.

Among other birds to be seen are egrets, ducks, coots, storks, kingfishers, spoonbills, Sarus cranes, birds of prey including Laggar falcon, greater spotted eagle, marsh harrier, Scops owl and Pallas' eagle. Shortage of water may result in migrants failing to arrive. There are also chital deer, sambar, nilgai, feral cattle, wild cats, hyenas, wild boar and monitor lizards, whilst near Python Point, there are usually some very large rock pythons.

Birds can be watched from a short distance from the road between the boat jetty and Keoladeo temple, especially Sapan Mori crossing, since they have got accustomed to visitors. Dawn (which can be very cold) and dusk are the best times; trees around Keoladeo temple are favoured by birds for sleeping in, so are particularly rewarding at dawn. Midday may prove too hot so take a book and find a shady spot. Carry a sun hat, binoculars and plenty of drinking water.

■ *Rs 100 (foreigners) payable each time you enter, professional video camera Rs 1,500, car Rs 75. Café provides good lunch stop.*

Further information It is worth buying the *Collins Handguide to the Birds of the Indian Sub-continent* (available at the Reserve and in booksellers in Delhi, Agra, Jaipur etc), well illustrated. Also *Pictorial Guide to the birds of the Indian Sub-Continent* by Salim Ali and S Dillon, Ripley and *Bharatpur: Bird Paradise* by Martin Ewans, Lustre Press, Delhi, are also extremely good.

Essentials

Sleeping
■ *on maps*
Price codes:
see inside front cover

Inside the park B *Bharatpur Forest Lodge* (ITDC), 2½ km from gate, T22722, F22864, 8 km rly and bus stand, book in advance. 18 comfortable rooms, 10 a/c with balconies, pricey restaurant, grotty bar, very friendly staff, peaceful, boats for bird watching, animals (eg wild boar) wander into the compound. Entry fee each time you enter park. Also the cheaper E *Shanti Kutir Rest House*, near boat jetty, T22265. 5 clean rooms in old hunting lodge.

Outside the park B *Laxmi Vilas Palace* (Heritage Hotel), Kakaji ki Kothi, Agra Rd, 2½ km from town (auto-rickshaws outside), T23523, F25259. 22 good rooms around a courtyard (avoid downstairs, rather damp), good food and service, attractive 19th-century hunting lodge decorated in period style (jackals spotted), pleasantly old fashioned, welcoming friendly staff, "took good care of children when we went birding". Recommended. C-D *Pratap Palace*, near Park Gate, T24245, F20593. 24 rooms (8 a/c) with bath, 4 F with clean shared bath (Rs 150), mediocre restaurant, helpful management, good value. C-D *Saras* (RTDC), Fatehpur Sikri Rd, T23700. 25 simple clean rooms, some a/c (limited hot water), dorm (Rs 50), restaurant (indifferent food), lawns, tourist information, camping, rather dull.

D-E *Eagle's Nest*, at NH11 crossing, T25144. Some a/c rooms (overpriced), hot water, new restaurant, can be noisy. **D-E** *Sunbird*, near Park gate, T25701. Clean rooms with hot shower, better on 1st floor, pleasant restaurant but very salty food, friendly staff, bike hire, good value. Highly recommended. **D-F** *Nightingale* and *Tented Camp*, near Park gate, T27022. Deluxe 2-bed tents with bath, others with shared bath, good food,

Some budget hotels have tented accommodation

Keoladeo Ghana National Park

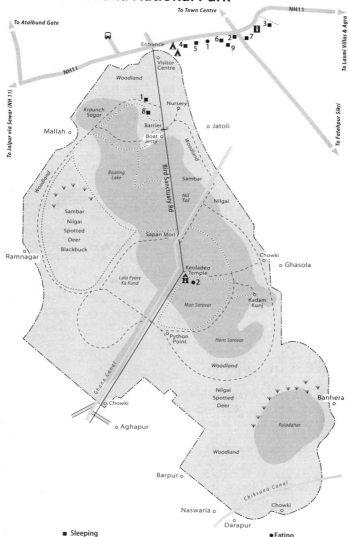

Jaipur & Northern Rajasthan

■ **Sleeping**
1 Bharatpur Forest Lodge
2 Eagle's Nest
3 Falcon Guest House & Jungle Lodge
4 Nightingale
5 Pelican & Sunbird

6 Pratap Palace & Moon Dance Restaurant
7 Saras & Spoonbill
8 Shanti Kutir Rest House
9 Tourist Guest House

● **Eating**
1 Bambinoo
2 Snack Bar

contact *Asian Adventures* T/F011-8525014 or *North West Safaris*, T/F079-6560962, ssibal@ad1.vsnl.net.in **E** *Falcon Guest House*, off NH11. Very clean well kept rooms, some a/c with bath, owned by naturalist, good information, bike hire, quiet, very helpful, warm welcome, off-season discount. Highly recommended. **E** *Jungle Lodge*, Shankar Colony (next to *Falcon*), T25622. Very clean rooms, excellent meals for residents (huge portions, cheap), quiet, friendly family, 'no Indians' policy. **E** *Kiran Guest House*, 364 Rajendra Nagar, 300 m from park gate, T23845. Clean rooms, excellent meals, peaceful, safe, homely, helpful and knowledgeable family. Recommended. **E** *Pelican*, near Park gate, T24221. 9 clean rooms with fan, best No 8 with hot (salty!) shower (ask for towel), quite modern with tiny balcony, restaurant, friendly, bike hire (Rs 40 per day), good info. **E** *Spoonbill*, near *Saras*, T23571. Good value rooms with shared facility (hot water in buckets), dorm (Rs 60), run by charming ex-Army officer, courteous and friendly service, good food, bike hire. Highly recommended. **F** *Tourist Guest House*, behind *Moondance*. 2 rooms with bath, 1 shared, dorm (Rs 30), basic but acceptable.

Eating Inside the park Expensive *Forest Lodge* with overpriced buffets feeding the many
● *on maps* tour groups. Also a dirty **Snack Bar** serving only drinks and biscuits. **Outside the**
Price codes: **park** All offer some Indian and Western dishes. **Expensive** *Laxmi Vilas*, wide choice
see inside front cover but some find it disappointing ("standard fare doled out to Westerners").
Mid-range *Eagle's Nest*, new 100-seater restaurant with the promise of a/c to come.
Moon Dance tent, near *Pratap Palace*. Good food, lively atmosphere, beer.
Cheap *Bambino*, near Park Gate. Open-air in a garden. *Pelican*, good choice, chicken,
vegetarian, Israeli dishes, 'westernized'. *Spoonbill*, good food obliging (beer and special *kheer* on request). Recommended.

Transport **Bicycle hire** Near *Saras* or ask your hotel; Rs 40 per day; hire on previous evening for an early start next day.

Directory **Tourist offices** *Rajasthan*, *Hotel Saras*, T22542. *Wildlife office*, Forest Rest House, T22777. Guides available. **Tour operator** *GTA*, near Tourist Lodge, Gol Bagh Rd, T28188, F25259, vfauzdar@yahoo.com Knowledgeable English speaking guides, Rs 300 for 2 hrs.

West of Jaipur

The drive along the NH8 from Jaipur to Ajmer is worth taking. After crossing relatively low lying land to Kishangarh the road enters the Aravalli hills. The direct railway line from Jaipur to Jodhpur passes by the Sambhar salt lake, a site of special wetland interest identified by the Slimbridge Waterfowl Trust, and Makrana, where the white marble used in the Taj Mahal was quarried.

Sambhar Lake The salt lake, one of the largest of its kind in India, until recently attracted
Colour map 2, grid C3 thousands of flamingoes and an abundance of cranes, pelicans, ducks and other waterfowl. About 120 species of birds have been checklisted. However, the poor monsoons of 1999 and 2000, have caused the lake to dry up leaving only a few marshy patches. Visitors have returned seeing less than 100 flamingoes, a few other species of waterfowl, and some ground birds like the Syke's Crested lark. It is a good idea to check the situation before visiting. Nilgai, fox and hare are spotted in the lake environs. The saline marshes are used for production of salt. The Sakambari Temple nearby, dedicated to the ancestral deity of the Chauhans, is believed to date from the sixth century. You can stay at **C** *Sambhar Lake Resorts* which can be booked in Jaipur, T0141-378184. It

has 10 cottage rooms, bath with hot showers (but need improving), friendly staff, pool and bar proposed, camel rides and jeep safaris across the saline marshes and sand dunes, also arranges short rail journey on diesel locomotive driven trolleys that carry salt from the pans to the towns. Rs 1150 includes meals and safaris. Day visit (Rs 500) includes veg lunch, tea and a tour of the salt marshes by camel cart or rail trolley. ■ *Getting there: Train to Phulera, 7 km from Sambhar village, 9 km from the lake. Jeeps charge Rs 50 for the transfer.*

Kuchaman

Kuchaman Fort is a unique experience

Kuchaman is a large village with temples and relics. It is a popular tea and snacks stop for travellers between Shekhawati and Ajmer. Before the eighth century Kuchaman lay on the highly profitable Central Asian caravan route. Here Gurjar Pratiharas built a massive clifftop fort with 10 gates leading up from the Meena bazaar in the village to the royal living quarters. The Chauhans drove the Pratiharas out of the area and for some time it was ruled by the Gaurs. From 1400, it has been in the hands of the Rathores who embellished it with mirrors, mural and gold work in superb palaces and pavilions such as the golden Sunheri Burj and the mirrored Sheesh Mahal, both in sharp contrast to the fort's exterior austerity. The Sariska Palace Group have taken over the fort, and restored and renovated the property at an enormous cost. Cars have to be parked in the courtyard after the first couple of gates, and four-wheel drive jeeps take guests to their rooms after checking in at the reception. You can visit the Krishna temple with a 2,000-year old image, and the Kalimata ka Mandir which has an eighth-century black stone deity, shop in the Meena Bazar or watch local village crafts people.

Sleeping and eating AL *Kuchaman Fort* (Heritage Hotel), T01586-20882, F20476, sariska@del2.vsnl.net.in, 51 superb a/c rooms in a part of the fort, attractively furnished, restaurant, bar, jacuzzi, gym, luxurious pools (including a 200-year old cavernous one underground), camel/horse riding, royal hospitality.

Kishangarh

Population: 22,000

Kishangarh was a small princely state, founded by Kishan Singh in 1603 as an independent state with a fort facing lake Gundalao. Local artists known for their depiction of the Krishna legend and other Hindu themes were given refuge here by the royal family during the reign of the Mughal emperor, Aurangzeb, who, turning his back on the liberal views of earlier emperors, pursued an increasingly zealous Islamic purity. Under their patronage the artists reached a high standard of excellence and they continue the tradition of painting Kishangarh miniatures here which are noted for sharp facial features and elongated almond-shaped eyes. Most of those available are cheap copies on old paper using water colours instead of the mineral pigments of the originals. Powerloom weaving is a major industry, together with marble carving and polishing (India's best marble is quarried at nearby Makrana). The 1870 garden palace, **B** *Phool Mahal Old City*, T01463-47405 (or Delhi T011-6237000), set next to the medieval moat of Kishangarh fort has patios facing Gundalao lake with plenty of water birds, island pavilion. There are 14 a/c rooms, viewing of royal family's miniature collection. ■ *Getting there: Kishangarh is an important railway junction between Jaipur and Ajmer.*

The fort palace stands on the shores of Lake Gandalan. Its Hathi Pol (Elephant Gate) has walls decorated with fine murals and, though partly in ruins, you can see battlements, courtyards with gardens, shady balconies, brass doors and windows with coloured panes of glass. The temple has a fine collection of miniatures.

Jaipur & Northern Rajasthan

A saint of the people

Khwaja Mu'inuddin Chishti probably came to India before the Turkish conquests which brought Islam sweeping across northern India. A sufi, unlike the Muslim invaders, he came in peace. He devoted his life to the poor people of Ajmer and its region. He was strongly influenced by the Upanishads; some reports claim that he married the daughter of a Hindu raja.

His influence during his lifetime was enormous, but continued through the establishment of the Chishti school or silsila, which flourished 'because it

produced respected spiritualists and propounded catholic doctrines'. Hindus were attracted to the movement but did not have to renounce their faith, and Sufi khanqah (a form of hospice) were accessible to all.

Almost immediately after his death Khwaja Mu'innuddin Chishti's followers carried on his mission. The present structure was built by Ghiyasuddin Khalji of Malwa, but the embellishment of the shrine to its present ornate character is still seen as far less important than the spiritual nature of the Saint it commemorates.

Roopangarh   About 20 km from Kishangarh, Roopangarh was an important fort of the Kishangarh rulers founded in 1649 AD on the old caravan route along the Sambhar Lake. The fort stands above the centre of the village which is a centre for craft industries – leather embroidery, block printing, pottery and handloom weaving can all be seen. The Sunday market features at least 100 cobblers making and repairing *mojdi* footwear. Some 12 km away is the old town of Salemabad with a stepped *kund* (tank) and Nimbarak Tirth temple which attract Hindu pilgrims.

Sleeping and eating **B** *Roopangarh Fort* (Heritage Hotel), T01463-7217. 20 large, high-ceilinged rooms , rich in character, Marwar decor and cuisine, 18th-century miniatures; excursions to Makrana and Sambhar salt lake, good sunrise and sunset views.

Ajmer

Phone code: 0145
Colour map 4, grid A2
Population: 401,000
Altitude: 486 m

Situated in a basin at the foot of Taragarh Hill (870 m), Ajmer is surrounded by a stone wall with five gateways. Renowned throughout the Muslim world as the burial place of Mu'inuddin Chishti who claimed descent from the son-in-law of Mohammad, seven pilgrimages to Ajmer are believed to equal one to Mecca. Every year, especially at the annual Islamic festivals of Id and Muharram, thousands of pilgrims converge on this ancient town on the banks of the Ana Sagar Lake.

Ins & outs
See page 160 for further details
Getting there Visitors come to Ajmer for its own sake and also en route to Pushkar. The railway station has several cheap hotels and eating places just across the busy main road. Buses for Pushkar use the stand nearby; the main State and Private Bus Stands are chaotic and dirty, and are about 2 km away. **Getting around** The main sights and congested bazars, which can be seen in a day, are within 15-20-mins walk of the railway station but to get to Ana Sagar, hail an auto-rickshaw. Shuttle buses run between the main bus stand and the railway station.

History   According to tradition Ajmer was founded in 145 AD by Raja Ajaipal, one of the Chauhan kings. In the 11th and 12th centuries it was attacked by Mahmud of Ghazni and Muhammad Ghuri. Born in Afghanistan, Mu'inuddin Chishti visited Ajmer in 1192 and died here in 1235. His tomb became a place of pilgrimage.

The houses of Mewar, Malwa and Jodhpur each ruled for a time until Akbar annexed it in 1556 and made the dargah a place of pilgrimage. He built a palace, later occupied by Jahangir who laid out the beautiful Daulat Bagh garden by the artificial lake Ana Sagar which dates from circa 1135. Jahangir also received the first British ambassador from King James I in the Daulat Bagh in 1616. Shah Jahan, Aurangzeb's successor, embellished the garden with five fine marble pavilions.

After the Mughals, Ajmer returned to the House of Jodhpur and later to the Marathas. The British annexed it in 1818 and brought it under their direct rule.

The **Dargah of Khwaja Mu'inuddin Chishti** (1143-1235) is the tomb of the Sufi saint (also called 'The Sun of the Realm') which was begun by Iltutmish and completed by Humayun. Set in the heart of the old town, the entrance is through the bazar. Access to the main gate is on foot or by tonga or auto. The Emperor Akbar first made a pilgrimage to the shrine to give thanks for conquering Chittor in 1567, and the second for the birth of his son Prince Salim. From 1570 to 1580 Akbar made almost annual pilgrimages to Ajmer on foot from Agra, and the *kos* minars (brick marking pillars at about two-mile intervals) along the road from Agra are witness of the popularity of the pilgrimage route. It is considered the second holiest site after Mecca. On their first visit, rich Muslims pay for a feast of rice, ghee, sugar, almonds, raisins and spices to be cooked in one of the large pots in the courtyard inside the high gateway. These are still in regular use. On the right is the Akbar Masjid (circa 1570), to the left, an assembly hall for the poor. In the inner courtyard is the white marble Shah Jahan Masjid (circa 1650), 33 m long with 11 arches and a carved balustrade on three sides. In the inner court is the *Dargah* (tomb), also white marble, square with a domed roof and two entrances. The ceiling is gold-embossed velvet, and silver rails and gates enclose the tomb. At festival times the tomb is packed with pilgrims, many coming from abroad, and the crush of people can be overpowering.

Nearby is the **Mazar** (tomb) of Bibi Hafiz Jamal, daughter of the saint, a small enclosure with marble latticework. Close by is that of Chimni Begum, daughter of Shah Jahan. She never married, refusing to leave her father during the seven years he was held captive by Aurangzeb in Agra Fort. She spent her last days in Ajmer, as did another daughter who probably died of tuberculosis. At the south end of the *Dargah* is the *Jhalra* (tank).

The **Arhai-din-ka Jhonpra Mosque** ('The Hut of two and a half days') lies beyond the Dargah in a narrow valley. Originally a Jain college built in 1153, it was partially destroyed by Muhammad of Ghori in 1192, and in 1210 turned into a mosque by **Qutb-ud-din-Aibak** who built a massive screen of seven arches in front of the pillared halls, allegedly in two and a half days (hence its name). The temple pillars which were incorporated in the building are all different. The mosque measures 79 x 17 m with 10 domes supported by 124 columns and incorporates older Hindu and Jain masonry. Much of it is in ruins though restoration work was undertaken at the turn of the century; only part of the 67 m screen and the Jain prayer hall remain.

Akbar's Palace is in the city centre near the east wall. It is a large rectangular building with a fine gate. Today it houses the **Government museum**.

The ornate **Nasiyan Jain Temple** (Red Temple) on Prithviraj Marg has a remarkable museum alongside the Jain shrine, which itself is open only to Jains. Ajmer has a large Jain population (about 25% of the city's total). The Shri Siddhkut Chaityalaya was founded in 1864 in honour of the first Jain Tirthankar, Rishabdeo, by a Jain diamond merchant, Raj Bahadur Seth

Sights *From Station Rd, a walk through the bazars, either to the Dargah/Masjid area or to Akbar's Palace/ Nasiyan Temple area, can be interesting*

This temple is well worth visiting

Jaipur & Northern Rajasthan

Moolchand Nemichand Soni (hence its alternative name, the Soni temple). The opening was celebrated in 1895. Behind a wholly unimposing exterior, on its first floor the Svarna Nagari Hall houses an astonishing reconstruction of the Jain conception of the Universe, with gold plated replicas of every Jain shrine in India. Over 1,000 kg of gold is estimated to have been used, and at one end of the gallery diamonds have also been placed behind decorative coloured glass to give an appearance of backlighting. Encased in a huge room behind glass (which fails to protect it from dust), the whole of the reconstruction can be seen from different external galleries. The holy mountain, Sumeru, is at the centre of the continent, and around it are such holy sites as Ayodhya, the birthplace of the Tirthankar, recreated in gold plate, and a remarkable collection of model temples. Suspended from the ceiling are *vimanas* – airships of the gods – and silver balls. On the ground floor, beneath

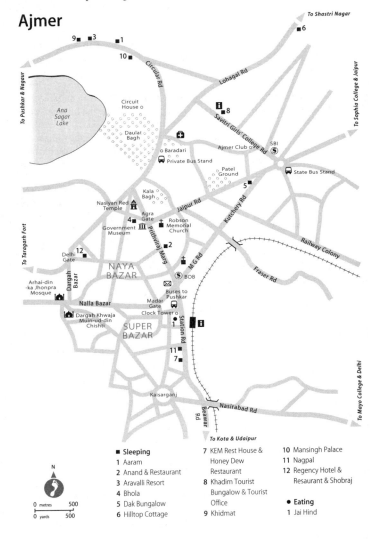

Ajmer

■ Sleeping	7 KEM Rest House &	10 Mansingh Palace
1 Aaram	Honey Dew	11 Nagpal
2 Anand & Restaurant	Restaurant	12 Regency Hotel &
3 Aravalli Resort	8 Khadim Tourist	Resaurant & Shobraj
4 Bhola	Bungalow & Tourist	
5 Dak Bungalow	Office	● Eating
6 Hilltop Cottage	9 Khidmat	1 Jai Hind

the model, are the various items taken on procession around the town on the Jain festival day of 23 November each year. The trustees of the temple are continuing to maintain and embellish it. The walls and ceilings of the main hall have been completely re-painted in traditional style, and the surrounding galleries are undergoing a similar programme of renovation. ■ *0800-1700. Rs 5. Copies of Mughal miniature paintings on silk are available outside.*

Mayo College (1873), only 4 km from the centre, was founded to provide young Indian princes with a liberal education, one of two genuinely Indo-Saracenic buildings designed by De Fabeck in Ajmer, the other being the **Mayo Hospital** (1870). The College was known as the 'Eton' of Rajputana and was run along the lines of an English Public School. Access is no longer restricted to Rajput princes.

Excursions

Ana Sagar, an artificial lake (circa 1150) was further enhanced by Emperors Jahangir and Shah Jahan who added the *baradari* and pavilions. The **Foy Sagar**, 5 km away, another artificial lake was a famine relief project.

Taragarh (Star Fort), built by Ajaipal Chauhan in 1100 with massive 4½ m thick walls, stands on the hilltop overlooking the town. There are great views of the city but the walk up the winding bridle path, tiring. A jeepable road, however, has reduced the climb on foot and made access easier. Jeeps charge Rs 500 for the trip. Tea and snacks are sold in stalls at viewpoints. Along the way is a graveyard of Muslim 'martyrs' who died storming the fort.

Of course Ajmer is a good base from which to visit **Pushkar** some 11 km to the west. Buses leave from outside the railway station.

The government museum in **Akbar's Palace**, built in 1570 and restored in 1905. Fine sculpture from sixth to 17th centuries; paintings; old Rajput and Mughal armour and coins are sometimes on view. ■ *1000-1630, closed Fri. Rs 3. No photography.*

Museum

The *Urs Festival* commemorating Khwaja Mu'inuddin Chishti's death in 1235 is celebrated with six days of almost continuous music, and devotees from all over India and the Middle East make the pilgrimage. *Qawwalis* and other Urdu music developed in the courts of rulers can be heard. Roses cover the tomb. The festival starts on sighting the new moon in *Rajab*, the seventh month of the Islamic year. The peak is reached on the night between the fifth and sixth days when tens of thousands of pilgrims pack the shrine. At 1100 on the last morning, pilgrims and visitors are banned from the dargah, as the *khadims*, who are responsible through the year for the maintenance of worship at the shrine, dressed in their best clothes, approach the shrine with flowers and sweets.

Festivals
On the final day, women wash the tomb with their hair, then squeeze the rose water into bottles as medicine for the sick

Essentials

A *Mansingh Palace*, Ana Sagar Circular Rd, Vaishali Nagar, T425855. 60 rooms, modern and the most comfortable in town. **C-D** *Aaram* off Ana Sagar Circular Rd, opposite *Mansingh*, T425272. 22 rooms, a/c, restaurant, small garden, decent, modern. **C-D** *Khadim* (RTDC), Savitri Girls' College Rd, near bus station, T627490. 49 rooms, 11 a/c (**C** suites), dorm (Rs 50), good restaurant, bar, Tourist Information, car hire, pleasant setting, popular and good value. **C-E** *Nagpal*, opposite railway station, T429603. 16 rooms vary widely, some with bath (a/c up to Rs 1000). **D** *Hilltop Cottage*, 164 Shastrinagar (hard to find), near shopping centre, T620823. Neither a cottage nor on a hilltop but a family home taking guests, clean, comfortable rooms (Rs 400; Rs 700 with bath and hot water), meals, good situation in residential area with hills nearby for walks. **D** *New Park*,

Sleeping
■ *on maps*
Price codes:
see inside front cover

Prices rise sharply, as much as 10 times, during the week of the Pushkar mela. Many hotels are booked well in advance

Panch Kund Rd, T72464, F72199. 32 clean and comfortable rooms, attached baths (a/c or air-cooled) simple decor, superb views of hills and dunes, outdoor dining area, own farm produce, pool. **D** *Regency*, Delhi Gate, near Dargah, T620296, F621750, bahulbali@jp1.dot.net.in 20 clean, comfortable, air-cooled or a/c rooms (Rs 400-750), TV, phone, a/c restaurant, bar, travel, in very crowded area but set back from road.

The tourist office, T52426, has a list of Paying Guest accommodation

D-E *Haveli Heritage Inns*, Kutchery Rd. 6 new rooms in century old haveli (Rs 350-600), 6 more planned, clean, comfortable, family run, good home cooking, lots of historic associations with Gandhi, Nehru etc, located on busy main road but with a pleasant courtyard. **D-E** *Shobraj*, Delhi Gate, T32300. 22 rooms, 5 a/c, centre of old town in busy area, popular restaurant. **E** *Anand*, Prithviraj Marg, T23099. Clean rooms with shower (no hot water), some renovated, friendly service. **E** *Aravalli Resort*, near bus stand (next to RTDC), T627089. 4 rooms (Rs 300), clean and comfortable. **E** *Bhola*, Prithviraj Marg, T423844. Simple clean rooms, good vegetarian restaurant. **E** *Khidmat* (RTDC), Ana Sagar Circular Rd, 5 km from rly, T52705. 10 good-value rooms including some 6-bed, dorm (Rs 50), open-air restaurant. **E-F** hotels offering rooms with bath, by the station include: *KEM*, Station Rd, T429936. 45 rooms, 1st class rooms are clean and acceptable. The 2nd class rooms are unkind to your noise and not recommended, popular with pilgrims.

Eating

● *on maps*
Price codes:
see inside front cover

Expensive *Mansingh Palace*, Ana Sagar Circular Rd. International. Relatively pricey, unexciting food. **Cheap** *Amba*, opposite station. Good snacks, *idli-wada*, Rs 10, pizza Rs 25. *Honey Dew*, Station Rd. Indian, Continental. Pleasant shady garden, good Indian snacks all day, disappointing Western. *Jai Hind* in alley by clock tower, opposite rly station. Best for Indian vegetarian. Delicious, cheap meals. *Mamata*, Shastri Nagar Shopping Centre. Fast food, snacks. *Regency*, Delhi Gate. Indian, Continental. Bright, decent surroundings, good food. Recommended. *Tandoor*, Jaipur Rd, 1 km from bus station. Dinner in the garden with log fires, a/c section for lunch, good food (try *paneer butter masala* and *tandoori* chicken), cake shop, icecreams, also snacks to takeaway, cyber café. Recommended. *Son halwa*, a local sweet speciality, is sold near the *dargah* and at the market near Station Road (try *Azad*).

Shopping

Fine local silver jewellery, tie-and-dye textiles and camel hide articles are best buys. The shopping areas are Madar Gate, Station Rd, Purani Mandi, Naya Bazar and Kaisarganj. Some of the alleys in the old town have good shopping. *Arts and Art's*, Bhojan Shala, near Jain Temple.

Transport

Ajmer Station is seemingly overrun with rats & is not a great place to wait for a night train. Mansingh Palace Hotel allows short-stay rates, useful if you have a wait of several hrs

Road **Auto rickshaw**: to Pushkar, Rs 60 after bargaining. **Bus**: Enquiries, T427603. Buses every 30 mins to **Agra**, **Delhi**, **Jaipur**, 3 hrs; **Jodhpur**, 5 hrs; **Bikaner**, 7 hrs; **Chittaurgarh** (190 km), **Udaipur** (302 km) via Chittaurgarh, **Kota** via Bundi. Buses for **Pushkar** (Rs 4) which leave from near the station, are very crowded. **Jeep**: Good option to get to Pushkar but difficult to get. **Train** Reservations, T431965, 0830-1330, 1400-1630, enquiries, T131. Adequate station restaurant. **Ahmadabad**: *Aravali Exp, 9708*, 1005, 11½ hrs; *Ahmadabad Mail, 9106*, 0735, 10 hrs; *Ashram Exp, 2916*, 2325, 8½ hrs, last 3 via **Beawar**, 1 hr; **Chittaurgarh**: *Ahmadabad Exp, 9943*, 0750, 5 hrs; *Chetak Exp, 9615*, 0150, 4½ hrs. **Jaipur**: *AjmerJaipur Exp, 9652*, 0640, 3 hrs. *Aravali Exp, 9707*, 1733, 2½ hrs; *Shatabdi Exp, 2016*, 1530, not Sun, 2 hrs. **Delhi**: *Ahmadabad Delhi Mail, 9105*, 2033, 9 hrs; *Shatabdi Exp, 2016* not Sun, 1530, 6½ hrs; (OD) *Ashram Exp, 2915*, 0215, 8 hrs; **Jaipur**: *Aravali Exp, 9707*, 1735, 2½ hrs. **Jodhpur**: *Jodhpur Mail, 4893*, 0545, 6 hrs. **Udaipur**: *Ahmadabad Exp, 9943* , 0750, 8½ hrs.

Directory

Banks *Bank of Baroda*, opposite GPO, accepts Visa, Mastercard; *State Bank of India* near Bus Stand, changes cash, TCs. SBI, near bus stand. Also government approved money changers in Kavandas Pura main market. **Tourist offices** Alongside *Khadim*

Hotel, T52426. 0800-1200, 1500-1800, closed Sun, very helpful. Approved guide (4-8 hrs, about Rs 250-400) and tourist taxi hire. Counter at rly station, near 1st class main gate, entrance on right from car park.

The NH8 south of Ajmer is relatively quiet. After 38 km, you come across D *Fort Kharwa* which is an interesting place to stay. Built in 1568, the fort overlooks a lake with good birdlife. Good value. The road continues south through dry rocky hills, with occasional date palms and open savanna or agricultural land. Just south of **Bhim** the *Hotel Vijay* is modest but quite clean.

Ajmer to Udaipur

The road from Ajmer passes the village of Nausar and a striking 2 km long pass through the Nag Pahar (Snake Hill) which divides Pushkar from Ajmer.

Ajmer to Pushkar

Pushkar

Pushkar lies in a narrow dry valley overshadowed by impressive rocky hills which offer spectacular views of the desert at sunset. The lake at its heart, almost magically beautiful in the really early morning or late evening light, is one of India's most sacred lakes. The celebrated Pushkar Fair transforms the quiet village to a colourful week of heightened activity. The once peaceful lakeside village on the edge of the desert has been markedly changed by the year-round presence of large numbers of foreigners who were originally drawn by the famous fair. Some travellers fail to see its attraction now because of the continuous hassle from beggars, shopkeepers, holy men and millions of flies.

Phone code: 0145
Colour map 4, grid A2
Population: 11,500

Getting there Most visitors arrive by bus which heads for the Central (Marwar) Bus Stand overrun by aggressive hotel touts and porters, but you can ask to be dropped before hand on entering the town from Ajmer. **Getting around** Pushkar is small enough to explore on foot. Hire a bike to venture further.

Ins & outs
See page 166 for further details

Sights

Pushkar Lake is believed to mark the spot where a lotus thrown by Brahma landed. Ghats lead down to the water to enable pilgrims to bathe. Fa Hien, the Chinese traveller who visited Pushkar in the fifth century AD commented on the number of pilgrims and although several of the older temples were subsequently destroyed by Aurangzeb, many remain.

The **Brahma temple**, at the far end of the lake, is a particularly holy shrine and draws pilgrims throughout the year. Although it isn't the only Brahma temple in India, as people claim, it is the only major pilgrim place for followers of the Hindu God of Creation. It is said that when Brahma needed a marital partner for a ritual, and his consort Saraswati (Savitri) took a long time to come, he married a cow-girl, Gayatri, after giving her the powers of a goddess (Gayatri because she was purified by the mouth of a cow or *gau*). His wife learnt of this and put a curse on him – that he would only be worshipped in Pushkar. ■ *0600-1330, 1500-2100 (changes seasonally).*

There are 52 ghats around the lake, of which the Brahma Ghat, Gan Ghat and Varah Ghat are the most sacred, and dozens of other temples, most of which are open 0500-1200, 1600-2200. The medieval **Varah temple** is dedicated to the boar incarnation of Vishnu. It is said the idol was broken by Emperor Jahangir as it resembled a pig. The **Mahadev Temple** is said to date from 12th century while the **Julelal Temple** is modern and jazzy. Interestingly

Jaipur & Northern Rajasthan

enough the two wives of Brahma have hilltop temples on either side of the lake, with the Brahma temple in the valley. A steep 3-km climb up the hill which leads to the **Savitri Temple** (dedicated to Brahma's first wife). It offers excellent views after a long, steep climb. A welcome sight in the mornings is a vendor selling chilled Pepsi.

The **Main (Sadar) Bazar** is full of shops selling typical tourist, as well as pilgrim knick-knacks and is usually very busy. At full moon, noisy religious celebrations last all night so you may need your ear plugs here.

Kartik Purnima is marked by a vast **cattle and camel fair** (27-30 November 2001, 16-19 Nov 2002, 5-8 Nov 2003), see box. Pilgrims bathe in the lake, the night of the full moon being the most auspicious time, and float 'boats' of marigold and rose petals in the moonlight. Camel traders often arrive a few days early to engage in the serious business of buying and selling and most of the animals disappear before the official starting date. Arrive three days ahead if you don't want to miss this part of the fair. The all-night drumming and singing in this Tent City can get very tiring. Travellers warn of pickpockets and 'purse slashers'.

Excursions **Merta City**, the fortified town west of Pushkar, is associated with Mira Bai of Chittaurgarh, who was renowned as a poet. The station is at Merta Road, where there is **D** *Raj Palace Motel*, T1590-20202, clean rooms with bath, friendly family, recommended.

Khejarla, a small village south of Merta City, is another convenient place to break your journey. The massive turreted fort gives good views over the

Pushkar

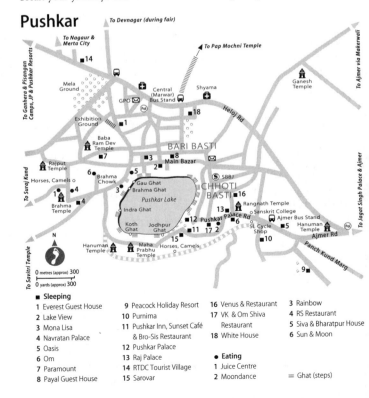

■ Sleeping
1 Everest Guest House	9 Peacock Holiday Resort
2 Lake View	10 Purnima
3 Mona Lisa	11 Pushkar Inn, Sunset Café
4 Navratan Palace	& Bro-Sis Restaurant
5 Oasis	12 Pushkar Palace
6 Om	13 Raj Palace
7 Paramount	14 RTDC Tourist Village
8 Payal Guest House	15 Sarovar

16 Venus & Restaurant	3 Rainbow
17 VK & Om Shiva	4 RS Restaurant
Restaurant	5 Siva & Bharatpur House
18 White House	6 Sun & Moon

● **Eating**
1 Juice Centre
2 Moondance

≡ Ghat (steps)

★ The draw of cattle and camels

The huge Mela is Pushkar's biggest draw. Over 200,000 visitors and pilgrims and hordes of cattle and camels with their semi-nomadic tribal drivers, crowd into the town. Farmers, breeders and camel traders buy and sell. Sales in leather whips, shoes, embroidered animal covers soar while women bargain over clay pots, bangles, necklaces and printed cloth.

Events begin four to five days before the full moon in November. There are horse and camel races and betting is heavy. In the Ladhu Umt race teams of up to 10 men cling to camels, and one another, in a hilarious and often chaotic spectacle. The Tug-of-War between Rajasthanis and foreigners is usually won by the local favourites. There are also sideshows with jugglers, acrobats, magicians and folk dancers. At nightfall there is music and dancing outside the tents, around friendly fires – an unforgettable experience.

surrounding arid countryside. Nearby is a small shrine on a large rock with a *Surya-Naka* stone with a small 'D' shaped hole – those who can wriggle through it prove they have no sin! There is an unfinished step well which a mystic abandoned having built single-handed over just two nights. You can stay at **D** *Fort Khejarla*, T02930-8311. Simple rooms in the old part, meals (Rs 180), excursions to Raika and Bishnoi tribal villages. Contact Curvet India, Delhi T011-6840037.

Essentials

B-C *Pushkar Resorts*, Motisar Rd, Ganhera (3 km away), T772017, F772946, pushres@ datainfosys.net Pushkar's up-market resort, 40 individual cottages with TV, phone, large garden, delicious meals (home grown produce), pool, sports (putting green, golf practice tees), book/handicraft shop, unique camel *kafila* (caravan) tours, desert jeep safaris, great location, enthusiastic staff. **C** *Jagat Singh Palace*, Ajmer Rd, T772953, F772952, hppalace@datainfosys.com 36 a/c rooms in new building imitating a Rajput fort, impressive, colourful interiors, attractive vegetarian restaurant, exchange, garden, gym, pool planned. **C-D** *Oasis*, near Ajmer Bus Stand, T772100. 35 rooms with bath, some a/c (Rs 500-1050), 24 hr coffee shop, exchange, garden with shady trees and potted plants, pool. **C-D** *Pushkar Palace* (Heritage Hotel), T772001, F772226. A renovated old palace (motto: 'shuned the sway but not the sword'!?) 44 rooms, best on lakeside with a/c and bath on 1st and 2nd floors (some small; few **E** damp, very basic with shared bath), unfortunately "drums and mullah wake you up from 0330", pleasant terrace and garden overlooking lake, good restaurant, camel and horse safaris, safe, cash only, book ahead. **C-D** *Peacock Holiday Resort*, 1 km centre, near Ajmer Bus Stand, T772093, F772516. 40 rooms, some a/c (Rs 450-1100), pleasant shady courtyard and small clean pool, exchange, jacuzzi, friendly staff, adequate food, travel, camel safaris, less than immaculate but very popular, crowded during camel fair despite price rise, year round camp site for overlanders and campers with facilities Rs 50 (see also below). **C-D** *JP's Tourist Resort* at Ganhera, T772067, F772026. 28 clean 'traditional' thatched cottage rooms to suites (Rs 400-1000), colourfully decorated with sculptures, *mandapa* paintings, bathrooms need improving, al fresco meals (eggs served), pleasant sit-outs in garden and orchards among dunes.

D *Navratan Palace*, near Brahma temple, T772145, F772225. 15 clean rooms, some a/c with hot showers (Rs 300-600), comfortable though not particularly attractive, pool, small garden with views. **D** *Pushkar Inns*, on the lake. Aircooled rooms with bath (Rs 450), some shared, could be cleaner, popular Sunset café and German bakery, lake

Sleeping
■ *on maps*
Price codes:
see inside front cover

The town suffers from early morning temple bells. During the fair, hotel charges can be 10 times the normal rate. Booking in advance for Mela essential for the better places

Jaipur & Northern Rajasthan

Persistent Pandas

Pandas – *priests with responsibility for particular families or local communities* – meet pilgrim buses and arrange the necessary rituals, keeping records of who has attended. If you receive a 'blessing', temple priests may charge for a coconut they use; they may also ask for a minimum 'donation' and then try to increase this ("Is that all you can give for your dead family member?"). Once a donation has been paid, a red braid (a **Pushkar passport**) is tied round the wrist which then protects you from further demands. Since it is difficult to escape this 'ceremony', it is perhaps best not to resist. Go along and enjoy it though your 'donation' may never reach the temple. Pay a modest Rs 15-20 even when the figure suggested may well be Rs 500-1,000!

and hill views, camping /trailer parking. **D** *Sunset Café* by *Pushkar Palace,* overlooking lake. 10 rooms (some with tubs) but their cakes have deteriorated. **D-E** *Sarovar* (RTDC), on lakeside, T772040. 38 clean rooms (best with lake view, in old part), some a/c with bath and cheap 6-bed dorm, set around courtyard in former lakeside palace, some rooms have splendid views, indifferent vegetarian restaurant, attractive gardens. **D-F** *Paramount*, Bari Basti, T772428, F772244. 16 clean, comfortable rooms, some with bath (Rs 100-350), better with balcony Rs 600, 3 new a/c, elevated site with splendid views.

Some budget hotels offer views of the lake from communal rooftops; to escape the noise of the Main Bazar, choose one in a back street of Bari Basti or near Ajmer Bus Stand. Rooms with shared facilities often around Rs 80 but can soar to Rs 400 during *mela*. **E** *Everest Guest House*, short walk from Marwar Bus Stand, T772080. Some rooms with bath and **F** dorm, quiet, clean. **E** *Holiday Resort*, Ajmer bus station, T772130. 8 rooms with bath, fairly clean, marble floors, pleasant garden, *Mansarovar* thali restaurant. **E-F** *Payal Guest House*, opposite Municipal Office, Main Bazar, T772163. Reasonable rooms, some with bath, small courtyard garden. **E-F** *VK*, near *Pushkar Palace*, T772174. Clean, decent rooms (Rs 100) some with bath and 24-hr hot water (power shower!), excellent *Om Shiva* garden restaurant nearby, friendly and helpful. Recommended. **E-F** *White House*, in narrow alley near Marwar Bus Stand, T/F772950, hotelwhitehouse@usa.net Rooms with hot showers (Rs 150), small with shared facilities (Rs 50/100), larger with balcony (Rs 350), good hill and dune views from terrace and upstairs, large grounds (orchards, home grown vegetables), restaurant with good choice (no-egg flour 'omelettes'!), internet, gym, yoga, billiards, travel desk, clean and well run, friendly.

F *Girdhar Palace*, Ajmer Rd, T773285. 10 comfortable rooms in old haveli, some with Indian WC, homecooked meals. **F** *Lake View*, well-placed, T772106. Rooms with shared facilities (Rs 150), some have no window, 3 with bath, arrive at 1000 for better room. **F** *Mona Lisa*, near Ram Ghat, T772356. Pleasant atmosphere, hot showers, friendly. **E-F** *Om*, Ajmer Rd, near Tourist Bungalow and Bus Stand, T772672. Basic rooms in old house, some with cold showers (Rs 100-300), meals (Rs 30), buffet breakfast, nice garden with restaurant but dirty pool. **F** *Poonam Palace*, Shiv Chowk, near Marwar Bus Stand (away from lake). Clean rooms with bath, roof terrace (fire lit on chilly nights), nice garden, peaceful, friendly (card says 'not recommended by Lonely Planet so why not try my place'!). **F** *Pushkar Lake*, Chhoti Basti, T772317. 10 comfortable rooms with baths (hot showers), popular restaurant (Rs 100-150), 2 with shared facilities, small garden, café. **F** *Rainbow*, Mahadev Chowk, T772167. 13 rooms with bath and hot water, rooftop restaurant with good views but noisy area. **F** *Raj Palace*, opposite Old Rangnath Temple, Chhoti Basti, clean rooms with cupboard size baths (free hot buckets), good beds, average restaurant, enthusiastic young staff. **F** *Shyam Krishna Guest House*, Chhoti Basti, T772461. Part of 200-year old temple complex with 10 rooms around a courtyard (Rs 150 with bath, Rs 100 shared), some with *jali* work on upper floor, more being added, Brahmin family run, popular with artists and those keen to learn Indian music etc. **F** *Venus*, Main Market, Ajmer road T772323. 15 simple rooms with bath and hot shower (Rs 100/150), clean, very popular roof restaurant, meals in the garden, see eating.

During the fair It is best to visit early in this week when toilets are still reasonably clean. RTDC erects a remarkable *Tourist Village*, for 100,000 people – conveniently placed, deluxe/super deluxe tents (Rs 2,000-3,500 with meals), ordinary/dorm tents (Rs 200 per bed), 30 'cottages', some deluxe (Rs 4000; Rs 350-850 off-season). Beds and blankets, some running water, Indian toilets are standard. Meals are served in a separate tent (or eat delicious cheap, local food at the tribal tented villages near the show ground). Reservation with payment, essential (open 12 months ahead); contact RTDC, Chandralok Building, 36 Jan Path, New Delhi 110001, or at Jaipur.

Others, privately run charge about US$ 150-250 including meals for Regular and 'Swiss' double tent (US$15 extra bed): *Pushkar Palace*, T772001, F772226. Sets up 50 'Swiss' tents and 50 Deluxe. *Colonel's Desert Camp*, T772407, Motisar Rd, Ghanera. Tents with toilet and shower, contact Wanderlust, T011-6875200, F6885188. *Peacock International Camp Resort*, T772093, F772516. Among orchards with pool at Devnagar (2 km from Mela Ground), free transport. *Royal Tents Camp* (WelcomHeritage) comfortable tents with verandah, flush toilet, hot water in buckets or "shower of sorts", Rajasthani cuisine, very well organized. Reserve through WelcomHeritage or T0291-510101, F510100). *Wanderlust Desert Camp*, T011-6875200, F6885188, travel.wander@axcess.net.in 120 Swiss tents with bath, electricity, varied meals. Some private camps are some distance from fair ground and may lack security.

Long stay budget travellers have encouraged western and Israeli favourites like falafel and apple pie, while Nepali and Tibetan immigrants have brought their own specialities. Roadside vendors offer a variety of filling *thalis* for under Rs 15. Non-vegetarian dishes are only offered out of town.

Eating
No meat, fish or eggs are served in this temple town Alcohol & 'narcotics' are banned. Take special care during the fair: eat only freshly cooked food & drink bottled water

Mid-range *Bro-Sis*, Pushkar Palace Road. Western snacks. Good value service and surroundings, fruit juice (Rs 25), veg burrito (Rs 65), burger (Rs 60). *Moondance*, just by the turning to Pushkar Palace. Western. Run by friendly Nepalese. Recommended. *Pushkar Palace*, recommended for evening buffet (Rs 110).

Cheap *Karmima*, and other small places opposite *Ashish-Manish Riding*, offer home cooked *thalis* (Rs 15/20) and excellent fresh, pure orange/sweet lime juice. *Om Shiva*, 20 m from *VK Hotel* in a garden. Good breakfasts (brown bread, garlic cheese, pancakes, fruit), buffets (Rs 45) or a la carte, well presented and hygienic. Another *Om Shiva* opposite *State Bank of Bikaner & Jaipur*, which is inferior. *Rainbow* (above *Krishna*), Brahma Chowk. Wide choice (pizzas, jacket potatoes, enchiladas, humus, falafel, Indian dishes), fruit crumble with choc sauce and ice cream (dirty toilet). *RS*, near Brahma Temple. Good Indian, some Chinese and western (Rs 40-50). Recommended. *Sun and Moon*, Brahma Temple Rd. Very good food, friendly, great garden to relax in (hammocks). Recommended. *Sunset Café* by *Pushkar Palace* overlooking lake. Breakfasts, snacks. *Venus*, Ajmer Rd. Mixed menu. A la carte (good sizzlers) in the garden, also *thalis* (Rs 35), on the rooftop. *Halwai ki gali* and other sweet shops sell *malpura* (syrupy pancake), as well as usual Rajasthani/Bengali sweets.

Jaipur & Northern Rajasthan

Sport **Riding** Horses Rs 150-200 per hr, camel Rs 30-50 per hr, at most hotels and near Brahma temple. Lessons: Rs 150 per hr (minimum 10 hr over 5 days) from *Ashish-Manish*, opposite Brahma Temple, *Sunset Café* and others. **Swimming** *Sarovar*, *Oasis*, *Peacock* hotels, non-residents pay Rs 40-50.

Shopping **Books** Several have second-hand copies; shop around as prices vary. **Cloth** *Essar*,
There is plenty to shop 6, Sadar Bazar, opposite Narad Kunj. Excellent **tailoring** (jacket Rs 250-300
attract the western including fabric). *Harish*, Brahma Temple Rd, for light weight *razai* quilts, bedsheets,
eye; check quality & cloth bags. **Paintings** Miniatures on silk and old paper are everywhere. *JP Dhabai's*,
bargain hard opposite Shiva Cloth Store near *Payal Guest House,* Main Bazar. Offers fine quality
(painted with a single squirrel hair!) at a price. Recommended. **Hairdressing and massage** Many hotels now offer health clubs, barbers, massages, yoga. *Shri Ram Janta*, Chhoti Basti Ghat, No 12, offers "bone crack", with "turbo-powered hands"! (Rs 50) – also henna, haircuts, hand painting.

Transport **Local Cycle/motorbike hire**: *Michael Cycle SL Cycles*, Ajmer Bus Stand Rd, very helpful, Rs 3 per hr, Rs 25 per day; also from the market. *Hotel Oasis* has Vespa scooters, Rs 300 per day. **Long distance Road** Rs 10 entry 'tax' per vehicle. **Auto-rickshaw**: To Ajmer Rs 60 after bargaining. **Bus**: Frequent service to/from **Ajmer** Rs 4. Direct buses to **Jodhpur** via Merta (8 hrs) but it is quicker to return to Ajmer and take an express bus (4-5 hrs) from there ('First class' passengers travel on the roof!). *Pushkar Travels*, good minibuses; avoid *Shrinath Travels*, overcrowded, often late, charges last minute premiums. **Car**: Delhi, 10 hrs; **Jaipur, 3 hrs.**

Directory **Banks** *SBBJ* changes TCs; Hotels *Peacock* and *Oasis* offer exchange for a small commission. **Communications** Internet: near *Oasis Hotel*, Ajmer Bus Stand, expensive. Post: One at the Chowk with a very helpful Postmaster, east end of Main Bazar. **Hospital and medical services** *Shyama*, Heloj Rd, T72087. **Tour companies and travel agents** At *Pushkar Palace Hotel*, *Pushkar Travels*, excellent service, good buses, ticketing Rs 50.

Southeastern Rajasthan

5

Southeastern Rajasthan

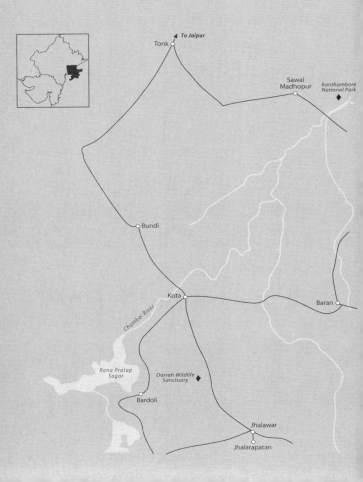

Kota

Kota, below a deep gorge of the Chambal River, was once on a major trade route
from Delhi to Gujarat. An army headquarter town in a region known for its stone
quarries, it is now a rapidly expanding industrial area for processing chemicals,
with hydro-electric and nuclear power plants nearby, but it still retains some
parks, gardens, wide tree-lined streets and princely architecture. For most tour-
ists, however, Kota remains little more than a base for visits to the historic monu-
ments of Hadoti in Jhalawar, Bundi and Baran.

Phone code: 0744
Colour map 4, grid B4
Population: 537,000

Getting there Trains link Kota Junction station with Jaipur, Delhi (via Sawai
Madhopur) and Mumbai. The station is 4 km north of the bus station at the town centre; shuttle buses run between the two. Regular buses run to Bundi and Jhalawar.
Getting around Autos, cycle rickshaws and fixed-route tempos ferry passengers
around town. Parts of the palace in the old fortified town, including the museum, are
worth exploring on foot.

Ins & outs
See page 172 for
further details

Cave paintings date the occupation of the area along the Chambal River to
prehistoric times. It was ruled by Bhil chieftains until the 13th century, when
Jait Singh of Bundi, a Hada Chauhan, usurped their territory. Kota became an
independent state from Bundi when Rao Madho Singh was installed as ruler
in 1631 with the blessings of the Mughal emperor Shah Jahan.

History

Sights

At the south end of the town, near the barrage, is the vast, strongly fortified
City Palace (1625) which you enter by the south gate. The city palace within
contains some striking buildings with delicate ornamental stonework on its
balconies and façade, though parts are decaying. The **Hathi Pol** (Elephant
Gate 1625-48), decorated with more recent murals, shows a royal wedding
procession, while the **Hawa Mahal** (1864) is modelled on the one in Jaipur.
The **Bhim Mahal**, an early 18th-century Darbar Hall, is covered with Rajput
miniatures documenting the town's history and local legends and intricate
mirror work and ivory inlaid doors. The best preserved murals in the chambers upstairs and in the Arjun mahal can be visited with permission from the
Madho Singh Museum in the palace. These murals reflect the Kota School of
art which focused on portraiture (especially profiles), hunting scenes, festivals
and the Krishna Lila. Although the rulers of this region, the Hadotis, claim to
be *Agnivanshi* (born from the flames), you will see the Sun insignia of the
Suryavanshi on ceilings and walls. The excellent **Madho Singh Museum** has a
collection of arms and armour (including swords with pistols attached),
stuffed animals, sculpture, miniature paintings and princely relics. ■ *Daily*
except Fri, 1100-1700. Rs 40 for foreigners, camera Rs 40, video Rs 70.
   The **Jag Mandir** Island Palace (closed to visitors) in the centre of the lake,
was commissioned in 1740 by Maharani Brij Kumari of Kota, daughter of the
Maharana of Mewar (which may explain the resemblance to the Jag Mandir
palace on Udaipur's Lake Pichola).
   The **Chattra Vlas Park**, near the Chambal Tourist Bungalow, has a good
view of the lake and the island palace, besides *chhatris* which are attractive
though somewhat neglected.
   The government **Brij Vilas Palace Museum** near the park, has a large collection of architectural fragments and individual sculptures salvaged from the

The 15th-century
Kishore Sagar
tank between the
station & the palace
occasionally has
boats for hire

ruins of medieval temples of southeastern Rajasthan, besides pre-historic rock inscriptions, coins, weapons, miniature paintings, manuscripts and costumes. ■ *1000-1700. Rs 2. Photography prohibited.*

The **Chambal Gardens** by Amar Niwas, south of the fort, is a pleasant place for a view of the river. The pond is stocked with gharial fishing-eating crocodiles which have become rare in Rajasthan. A variety of birds, including occasionally flamingoes can be seen at the river and in nearby ponds.

Nearby, **Adhar shila** is an unusual rock formation that seems to be suspended in the water without any support on the river bed. Local people believe it is the result of a miracle of a Muslim saint whose dargah is next to the rock.

Upstream at **Bharatiya Kund** is a popular swimming spot whilst the Kota **barrage** controls the river level and is the headworks for an irrigation system downstream. Photography of the barrage gates is prohibited but you can photograph the view from the bridge.

The **Umed Bhawan** (1904), 4 km north of town, was built for the Maharao Umaid Singh II and designed by Sir Samuel Swinton Jacob in collaboration with Indian designers. The buff-coloured stone exterior with a stucco finish has typical Rajput detail. The interior, however, is Edwardian with a fine drawing-room, banquet hall and garden.

Excursions **Kansua**, on the outskirts of town, is a 17th-century Siva temple set by a kund. There is an interesting Sivalinga with a honeycomb of about a 100 tiny lingas.

Khaitoon (pronounced Khetun), about 12 km from Kota, is famous for *Doria* saris which are woven on traditional pit handlooms with a distinctive

Kota

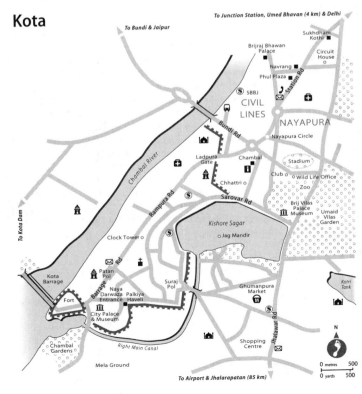

checked pattern using silk and cotton threads and pure gold *zari*. Prices range from Rs 500 for simple cotton ones, to Rs 25,000 for silk with a high gold content in the zari. About 2000-2500 men and women work at home on weaving Doria saris. The more intricate saris can take almost a month to be ready for the market.

Alaniya, about 25 km from town, has prehistoric rock paintings portraying animistic figures that resemble tiger, bull and herbivores, in ancient shelters by a small river. Alaniya station is off the Kota-Jhalawar highway, and you may have difficulty finding the man with the keys to open the railway crossing gates leading to the rock shelters. Taxi drivers confuse this with Alaniya dam, a popular birdwatching and picnic spot, a couple of kilometres further south on the same highway.

Sleeping
■ *on map*
Price codes:
see inside front cover

B *Brijraj Bhawan Palace*, Civil Lines, T450529, F450057. 6 a/c rooms with verandahs, fixed Indian meals, old British Residency with character (regal memorabilia), most of the buildings date from the early 1900s, well-kept grounds by river, but restrictions on meal times and visiting parts of building, feels unwelcoming. **B** *Umed Bhavan* (WelcomHeritage), Palace Rd (see above), T325262, F451110. 24 large, comfortable rooms, sympathetic conversion of grand building once owned by the former Maharaja of Kota, behind woods (langurs, deer, parakeets, peacocks), modernized but not plush, billiards, tennis. **C** *Palkiya Haveli*, near Suraj Pol, T328797, F327275. 10 a/c rooms (well restored, carved wood furniture, murals) with bath, near City Palace, good fixed meals, garden, very peaceful (full of birds) despite walled town location, family run, knowledgeable host, local tours arranged. Recommended. **C** *Sukhdham Kothi*, Civil Lines, T320081, F327781. 14 comfortable rooms (size varies), some a/c, in modernized 19th-century *haveli*, fixed meals, garden, family run.

D *Chambal* (RTDC), 2 km from bus stand, T327695. 12 simple rooms, some a/c, dorm (Rs 50), a bit run down, restaurant (limited menu), tourist office, pleasant gardens. **D-E** *Navrang*, Nayapura, Civil Lines, T323294, F450044. 21 decent, clean rooms, aircooled or a/c, TV, **C** suites, impossibly slow restaurant, recommended. **D-E** *Phul Plaza*, Nayapura, Civil Lines, T329350, F322614. Some clean, decent rooms, most a/c, **C** suites cheap vegetarian restaurant. **D-E** *Surya Royal*, Jhalawar Rd, T324240. 35 rooms, most air cooled or a/c with hot showers, **C** suites, restaurant, popular, fairly modern, business hotel. **D-E** *Everest*, Jhalawar Rd, T327747, F320647, 20 rooms, some a/c with Western toilets (Rs 200-725), fairly modern, popular with Indian businessmen. **E** *Vandana*, Jhalawar Rd, T326841, F329605. Good value, decent, aircooled and a/c (some **D**). **F** budget hotels near the bus stand and station can be noisy and dirty.

Eating
● *on map*
Price codes:
see inside front cover

Mid-range *Payal*, Nayapura. Good Indian. Also some Chinese, and Indianized Continental. *Venue*, Civil Lines. A/c, good Indian but very spicy, disappointing western. **Cheap** *Hariyali*, Bundi Rd. Good Punjabi, some Chinese/Continental. Pleasant garden restaurant, outdoors or under a small shelter, very popular but transport can be difficult. In Nayapura *Priya*, and *Maheswari*, are popular for Indian vegetarian. *Jain*, a popular *dhaba*, is cheaper. **Snacks and drinks** *Palace View* serves outdoor meals/snacks. Handy for visitors to the City Palace. *Chowpatty* is popular for omelettes and south Indian snacks, fresh juice, tea, ice creams etc. In Ghumanpura Market: *Jodhpur Sweets* sell Saffron *lassis* and flavoured milks (pista, almonds etc). Also good *kulfis* and home made ices in Sindhi shops. **Fast food** Near the bus syand excellent food served cheerfully.

Festivals

Gangaur (15-16 Apr 2002, 4-5 Apr 2003) and *Teej* (23-24 Jul 2001, 11-12 Aug 2002, 1-2 Aug 2003) are colourful festivals. *Dasara Mela* (24-26 Oct 2001, 13-15 Oct 2002, 3-5 Oct 2003). Great atmosphere, with shows in lit up Palace grounds.

Southeastern Rajasthan

Shopping   Cloth markets, eg Rampura, sell fine Kota *doria* saris.

Transport   **Air** No flights at present. **Road Bus**: At least hourly bus to **Bundi** (45 mins) and a few daily to **Ajmer**, **Chittaurgarh**, **Jhalarapatan** (2½ hrs); also to **Gwalior**, **Sawai Madhopur** and **Ujjain**. **Train** From Kota Junction: **Bharatpur**: *Golden Temple Mail, 2903*, 1130, 4 hrs (and Mathura, 5 hrs) . **Mumbai** (Central): *Rajdhani Exp, 2952*, 2050, 11½ hrs; *Paschim Exp, 2926*, 2355, 15½ hrs; *Golden Temple Mail, 2904*, 1455, 15½ hrs; **New Delhi**: *Rajdhani Exp, 2951*, 0430, 5½ hrs; *Golden Temple Mail*, 2903, 1130, 7½ hrs; *Dehra Dun Exp, 9019*, 1955, 10½ hrs – all via **Sawai Madhopur**, 1½ hrs.

Directory   **Banks** 1000-1400 Mon-Fri, 1000-1200 Sat. *Punjab National*, Airport Crossing, *SBBJ*, IL Township, *SBI*, Chawani Chauraha. **Communications** Internet: Opposite *Umed Bhavan Palace*. **Hospitals and medical services** *MBS Hospital*, T450241. **Tourist offices** *Rajasthan*, *Hotel Chambal*, T327695. **Police** T450066.

Around Kota

From Kota a picturesque route skirts the Rana Pratap Sagar and Gandhi Sagar lakes to Chittaurgarh and Udaipur. The views are very attractive and there are some beautiful picnic spots along the way. It is 180 km to Neemuch and a further 56 km to Chittaurgarh(see page 195).

Bardoli   Bardoli (Barolli) has some of the finest examples of 10th-century Pratihara temples in India, just east of the bus stand. The restored **Ghatesvara Temple** has an elaborately carved *sikhara* over the sanctuary and a columned porch. Inside are sculptures of Siva dancing flanked by Brahma and Vishnu with river goddesses and dancing maidens beneath. One of the sanctuary's five stone lingas resembles an upturned pot or *ghata* which gives the temple its name. The **Mahishashurmardini Temple**, immediately southwest, with a smashed image of Durga in the sanctuary, also has a finely carved tower. **Trimurti Temple** to the southeast is derelict but houses a large triple-headed Siva image.

Baran   The historic Baran township is the base for some interesting sightseeing
72 km E of Kota   attractions. **Krishan Vilas**, 19 km from Baran, has numerous ruins of a well planned medieval city, including ninth-11th-century sandstone structures with fine carvings. Pre-historic rock paintings can be seen here and early tools have been unearthed. Numerous Hindu and Jain temples, stepwells and inscriptions are other attractions.

   Shergarh, in Baran district, has a number of monuments including a seventh-century Naga fort, Sher Shah's fort, as well as fine *havelis* in the heart of forested countryside. There are good treks and pleasant lakes for picnics. Unfortunately, the road is terrible and the 125 km drive from Kota takes five hours. Palkiya Haveli in Kota arranges safaris to Shergarh with a night's stay in one of the famous Shergarh *havelis*.

★ Ranthambhore National Park

Phone code: 07462   *The park is one of the finest tiger reserves in the country where most visitors*
Colour map 4, grid A5   *spending a couple of nights are likely to spot one of these majestic animals. Once the private tiger reserve of the Maharaja of Jaipur, in 1972 the sanctuary came under the **Project Tiger** scheme. It covers about 400 sq km and runs from the*

*easternmost spur of the Aravallis to the Vindhya range. Within the park is both the old fort and the wildlife sanctuary, also known as **Sawai Madhopur**, after the town which has some Jain temples with gilded paintings. Set in dry deciduous forest, the area covers rocky hills and open valleys dotted with small pools and fruit trees. The path to the fort zig-zags up the steep outcrop in a series of ramps and through two impressive gateways.*

Ins and outs

It is 10 km east of Sawai Madhopur town with the approach along a narrow valley; the main gate is 4 km from the boundary. See page 176 for further details. **Getting there**

Entrance is only by jeep (or "Gypsys") or open bus (Canter) on 3 hr tours from 0630-0930 and 1500-1800 (0700-1000, 1430-1730 in winter). The park has good roads and tracks. Padam Talao by the Jogi Mahal is the park's favourite water source; there are also water holes at Raj Bagh and Milak. Fourteen jeeps and eight Canters are allowed in at any one time to minimize disturbance. Jeeps and Gypsys can be very difficult to get in the peak season as they are usually reserved ahead by local tour operators for clients, sometimes up to 8 weeks ahead, so request one at the time of booking your lodge giving passport details! Canters usually have space. The Project Tiger Office T20223, and Tourist Office, T20808, are 500 m from the railway station. **Getting around** *Passengers for both Canters & Gypsys are collected from hotels*

Jeep hire costs Rs 850 for up to 5 passengers (photography best with two passengers). Jeep entry fee is Rs 125; a guide Rs 350; individual entry fee Rs 25 (Indians) Rs 200 (foreigners) Rs 2,325 for five. Camera free, video Rs 250 (each game drive), professional movie/video Rs 5,000. 16 and 20-seater Canters: about Rs 150 per person plus entry Rs 200 (foreigners) and camera fees. Book in the Project Tiger Office behind the tourist office near the bridge by the Sawai Madhopur railway station, intermittently between 0530-1500. The Canter can be good value and you are as likely to see tiger or leopard in a Canter as in a Gypsy, however some special interest travellers (birders, photographers) find that the Canter tour catering to diverse tourist interests does not allow enough time for photography or observation. **Costs**

The park is open Oct-May, 0600-0900, 1500-1800. The climate ranges from 49°C to 2°C. It can be very cold at dawn in winter so go well prepared. The best time to visit is Nov-Apr if possible avoid weekends when there are larger numbers of noisy visitors. The park is open Oct-Jun. **When to go**

Tiger sightings are reported almost daily, usually in the early morning, especially from November to April. Travellers see them "totally unconcerned, amble past only 30 ft (10 m) away"! Sadly, poaching is prevalent, and the tiger population has been depleted to around 30. The lakeside woods and grassland provide an ideal habitat for herds of chital and sambhar deer and sounders of wild boar. Nilgai antelope and chinkara gazelles prefer the drier areas of the park Langur, mongoose and hare are prolific. There are also sloth bear, a few leopards, and the occasional rare caracal. Crocodiles bask by the lakes, and some rocky ponds have fresh water turtles. Extensive birdlife include spurfowl, jungle fowl, partridges, quails, crested serpent eagle, woodpeckers, flycatchers etc. There are also water birds like storks, ducks and geese at the lakes and waterholes. **Wildlife**

Ranthambhore Fort dominates the landscape. The fort is believed to have been settled from the eighth century and over the next six centuries changed **Fort**

Southeastern Rajasthan

hands a number of times. The earliest historic record is of it being wrested by the Chauhans in the 10th century. In the 11th century, after Ajmer was lost to Ghori, the Chauhans made it their capital. Hamir Chauhan, the ruler of Ranthambhore in the 14th century gave shelter to enemies of the Delhi sultanate, resulting in a massive siege and the Afghan conquest of the fort. The fort was later surrendered to emperor Akbar in the 16th century when Ranthambhore's commander saw resistance was useless, finally passing to the rulers of Jaipur. The forests of Ranthambhore historically guarded the fort from invasions but with peace under the Raj they became a hunting preserve of the Jaipur royal family. The fort wall runs round the summit and has a number of semi-circular bastions, some with sheer drops of over 65 m and stunning views. Inside the fort you can see a Siva temple (where Rana Hamir beheaded himself rather than face being humiliated by the conquering Delhi army), ruined palaces, pavilions and tanks. Mineral water, tea and soft drinks are sold at the foot of the climb to the fort and next to the Ganesh temple near the tanks. ■ *Free. The entrance to the fort is before the gate to the park proper and is open from dawn to dusk though the Park Interpretation Centre near the small car park may not be open.*

The Ranthambhore Foundation at Sherpur village, T20286, works closely with the local community in the spheres of agro forestry, animal husbandry, primary health care, alternative energy etc.

Recommended reading *Of tigers and men,* by Richard Ives. Doubleday, 1995, describes the park. *The Ultimate Ranthambhore Guide* compiled by S Sippy and S Kapoor, 2001, sold locally, Rs 125. An informative, practical guide stressing conservation. *Wild tigers of Ranthambhore,* by Thapar and

Ranthambore National Park

■ Sleeping	4 Hammir	8 Sawai Madhopur Lodge
1 Ankur Resorts	5 Oberoi	9 Sher Bagh
2 Anurag Resort	6 Ranthambore Bagh	10 Tiger Moon Resort
3 Castle Jhoomar Baori	7 Regency	

Rathore. OUP, 2000. *Tiger-wallahs* by Geoffrey C Ward. Harper Collins, 1993. Includes some who have worked to save the park.

Most down to **B** category are geared for tour groups so may neglect independent travellers.

Sleeping
Book well ahead. Hotels tend to be overpriced for facilities provided, rooms can be dusty & electricity erratic. Carry a torch

Ranthambhore Rd AL *Sawai Madhopur Lodge* (Taj), T20541, F20718. 20-mins drive from park, 16 a/c rooms (6 tents Oct-Mar), dated hunting lodge but comfortable, good buffet watched over by tigers' heads, pool unusable (green algae), front desk lacks sparkle, park tour by jeep Rs 1420 each. **AL** *Sher Bagh Tented Camp*, Sherpur. Comfortable, well organized. A new **AL** *Oberoi Camp* is scheduled to open. **B** *Tiger Den*, Khilchipur, T52070, F20702, www.tigerdenindia.cjb.net 20 cottage rooms. **B** *Tiger Moon Resort*, near Sherpur on the edge of the park (12 km rly), T52042. 32 stone, and 5 simple bamboo 'cottages', all with modern fittings, hot water, some tents are added in the peak season, buffet meals, bar, library, pool, expensive safaris, pleasant "jungle ambience". **B-C** *Castle Jhoomar Baori* (RTDC), 8 km rly (rickshaws/jeeps, Rs 100 from station; rickshaws stop short (you must walk 8 mins up steep hill), T20495, F21212. A former royal hunting lodge, 11 large rooms (but rats have been reported in window air-coolers), rather dirty, poor restaurant, good hilltop site with fantastic views, some arrogant staff. **B-C** *Regency*, contact *Asian Adventures*, T011-91524874, F91524878, wildindiatours@vsnl.com A/c rooms in cottages. **C-D** *Ankur Resorts*, 2 km rly, T20792, F20697. 15 simple rooms and 10 cottages with bath, tents in high season, in garden setting, fairly clean, fixed meals, friendly, helpful. **C-D** *Hill View*, T22173, F21212. Attractive, large garden complex set in hills with great views, 20 cottage rooms (claustrophobic, but plans for a/c when prices will rise), attached baths, fixed meals. **B-C** *Ranthambhore Bagh*, T217281, F22879, www.ranthambhore.com 12 clean, simple doubles with hot showers (inspect for creaky beds!), 10 dearer luxury tents also with attached baths, pleasant lawns, good meals (around bonfire at night), safaris, treks, excursions (report of unsatisfactory management). **D** *Anurag Resort*, T20451, F20697. Single-storey bungalow with a garden has 17 tired, aircooled rooms with bath (poorly maintained), dorm beds (Rs 75), camping, restaurant, large lawns, log fires at night, naturalist, jungle visits, helpful owner. **D** *Hammir*, T20562, F21842. 6 new rooms added (rest are a bit shabby), restaurant (beer served), pool planned, exchange (poor rate), wildlife videos, library, friendly and cheerful.

Sawai Madhopur The small hotels in noisy market areas are rather seedy but can be handy for the railway station (which has *Retiring Rooms* for Rs 110, dorm beds, Rs 35). **E** *Chinkara*, Civil Lines, T22642. Family run, rooms in a surgeon's home, a bit neglected but in a quiet area. **E-F** *Rajeev Resort*, 16 Indira Colony, Civil Lines, T21413. 11 fairly

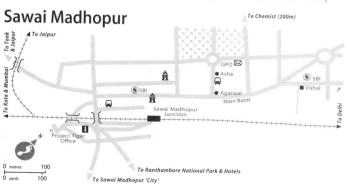

Sawai Madhopur

To Chemist (200m)

To Tonk & Jaipur
To Jaipur
To Kota & Mumbai

GPO
Asha
SBI
Agarwal
Main Bazar
SBI
Vishal
To Delhi

Sawai Madhopur Junction

Project Tiger Office

| 0 | metres | 100 |
| 0 | yards | 100 |

To Ranthambore National Park & Hotels
To Sawai Madhopur 'City'

Southeastern Rajasthan

decent rooms (some with western toilets), and larger 4-bedded rooms, simple meals to order. **F** *Swagath*, near railway station, T20601. 13 rooms in a rather ordinary guest house, 5 with bath (Western toilets, hot showers), singles with shared bath, Rs 50. **F** *Vishal*, Main Bazaar, opposite SBI, T20504. 7 passable rooms some with bath (hot water in buckets).

Eating   **Cheap** *Asha*, next to bus stand, and *Agrawal* are both recommended. Some near the
● *on map*   rly station serve good *thalis* but are dirty.

Shopping   **Art** *ranthambhore School of Art*, opposite *ranthambhore Regency Hotel*. Mainly tigers and wildlife; expensive. *Dastkar*, near Kutalpura, is reviving traditional art and crafts.

Transport   **Road** The park is midway between Bharatpur and Kota so if you have a car it is well worth stopping. The Bus Stand is 500 m from rly station. The road from Sawai Madhopur to Bundi via **Lakheri** is appalling and best avoided (3½hrs). **Bus**: To **Sawai Madhopur** from Kota and Jaipur are slow (4 hrs); trains are better. **Train** Sawai Madhopur Junction (14 km from main park gate), T20222. It is on the main Delhi-Mumbai line (Western Rly). The non-stop *Jaipur-Mumbai, 2956* dep Jaipur at 1350, 1½ hrs. **Jaipur**: *Mumbai-Jaipur Exp, 2955*, 1035, 2 hrs; **Kota**: *Golden Temple Mail, 2904*, 1320, 1½ hrs; *Mumbai Exp, 2956*, 1550, 1½ hrs. **Mumbai Central**: *Jaipur Mumbai Exp, 2956*, 1550, 16 hrs; *Paschim Exp, 2926*, 2220, 17½ hrs; *Golden Temple Mail, 2904*, 1320, 15 hrs. **New Delhi** (via Bharatpur and Mathura) *Golden Temple Mail, 2903*, 1300, 6 hrs; *Dehra Dun Exp, 9019*, 2140, 8 hrs.

Directory   **Banks** *Bank of Baroda*, *SBBJ* and *State Bank of India* offer exchange in Sawai Madhopur Town. **Communications** Internet: Cyber café on Ranthambhore Rd near entrance to Ankur Resort entrance. **Conservation Group** *Tiger Watch*, T20811. **Tour operator** *Forts and Palaces*, Dang walon ka mohalla, Sawai Madhopur, T34042, jaipur@palaces-tours.com

Tonk   Before Independence, Tonk was a tiny Princely State ruled by Muslim
Population: 100,200   Nawabs. The **Sunehri Kothi**, a late 19th-century addition to the palace built by the Nawab, is a mixture of predominantly local architectural styles with European style additions such as imitation Ionic columns and false marbling. Some of the 'doors' are also simply painted. The **Amirgarh Fort** was built by Amir Khan.

At **Uniara**, half way between Tonk and Sawai Madhopur, is the attractive **C** *Uniara Fort* (Heritage Hotel), with modern amenities but still retaining a medieval ambience.

★ Bundi

Phone code: 0747   *Bundi, in a beautiful narrow valley above which towers the Taragarh Fort, can*
Colour map 4, grid B4   *easily be visited on a day trip from Kota. The drive into the town is particularly*
Population: 65,000   *pleasing as the road runs along the hillside overlooking the valley opposite the fort.*
Completely unspoilt and rarely visited, it is worth spending a day or two here to soak in the atmosphere.

Ins & outs   **Getting there** Bundi is best reached by bus or car from Kota, Chittaurgarh, Ajmer or
See page 180 for   Sawai Madhopur. **Getting around** The town itself has a compact, if crowded, centre.
further details   From the bus stand to the south, a few mins' walk through the interesting bazar brings you to the start of the climb to the hillside palace and the fort beyond. For visiting

sights around Bundi, autos and cycle-rickshaws are available or you can hire a bike from town.

Formerly a small state founded in 1342, Bundi's fortunes varied inversely with those of its more powerful neighbours. Neither wealthy nor powerful, it nevertheless ranked high in the Rajput hierarchy since the founding family belonged to the specially blessed Hada Chauhan clan. After Prithviraj Chauhan was defeated by Muhammad Ghuri in 1193, the rulers sought refuge in Mewar. However, adventurous clan members overran the Bhils and Minas in the Chambal valley and established the kingdom of Hadavati or **Hadoti** which covers the area around Bundi, Kota and Jhalawar in southeastern Rajasthan. It prospered under the guidance of the able 19th century ruler Zalim Singh, but then declined on his death. The British reunited the territory in 1894.

The **Taragarh Fort** (1342) stands in sombre contrast to the beauty of the town and the lakes below. There are excellent views but it is a 20-minute difficult climb (not recommended in summer); good shoes help. The eastern wall

Bundi

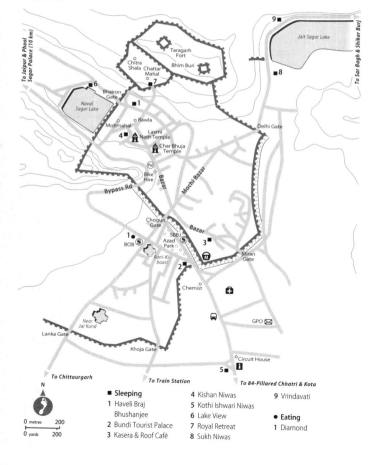

Southeastern Rajasthan

■ Sleeping	4 Kishan Niwas	9 Vrindavati
1 Haveli Braj Bhushanjee	5 Kothi Ishwari Niwas	
2 Bundi Tourist Palace	6 Lake View	● Eating
3 Kasera & Roof Café	7 Royal Retreat	1 Diamond
	8 Sukh Niwas	

0 metres 200
0 yards 200

To Chittaurgarh
To Train Station
To 84-Pillared Chhatri & Kota

Opium poppies

Crossing the high plateau between Bundi and Chittaurgarh the landscape is suddenly dotted with tiny patches of papery white flowers. These two Rajasthani districts, along with the neighbouring districts of Madhya Pradesh, are India's opium poppy growing belt, accounting for over 90% of production. As early as the fifteenth century this region produced opium for trade with China. Today the whole process is tightly monitored by the Government. Licences to grow are hard won and easily lost. No farmer can grow more than half a bigha of opium poppy (less than one twentieth of a hectare), and each must produce at least 6 kg of opium for sale to the Government.

Failure to reach this tough target results in the loss of the licence to grow. Laying out the field, actual cultivation and sale are all government controlled. Between late February and early April the farmers harvest the crop by incising fine lines in one quarter of each poppy head in the evening, and collecting the sap first thing in the morning. The harvesting has to be so precise that each evening a different quarter of the seed head will be cut on a different face - north, south, east or west. Finally the Government announces the collection point for the harvested opium just two or three days in advance, and farmers have to travel miles to the centre selected for weighing and final payment.

is crenellated with high ramparts while the main gate to the west is flanked by octagonal towers. The **Bhim Burj** tower dominates the fort and provided the platform for the Garbh Ganjam, a huge cannon. A pit to the side once provided shelter for the artillerymen, and there are several stepped water tanks inside.

To visit the Badal Mahal & rooms of the Chattar Mahal ask permission at the Rawla office behind the Ayurvedic Hospital below the palace

The **palace** complex below Taragarh which was begun around 1600 is at the northern end of the bazar. The buildings, on various levels, follow the shape of the hill. A steep, rough stone ramp leads up through the **Hazari Darwaza** (Gate of the Thousand) where the garrison lived; you may need to enter through a small door] within the darwaza. The palace entrance is through the **Hathi Pol** (Elephant Gate, 1607-31), which has two carved elephants with a water clock. Steps lead up to **Ratan Daulat** above the stables, the unusually small Diwan-i-Am which was intended to accommodate a select few at public audience. A delicate marble balcony overhangs the courtyard giving a view of the throne to the less privileged, who stood below. The **Chattar Mahal** (1660) the newer palace of green serpentine rock, is pure Rajput in style and contains private apartments decorated with wall paintings, glass and mirrors. The **Badal Mahal** bedroom has finely decorated ceilings. The **Chitrashali**, a cloistered courtyard (open to the public, free entry) with a gallery running around a garden of fountains, has a splendid collection of miniatures showing scenes from the Radha Krishna story. Turquoise, blues and greens dominate (other pigments may have faded with exposure to sunlight) though the elephant panels on the dado are in a contrasting red. The murals (circa 1800) are some of the finest examples of Rajput art but are not properly maintained. There is supposed to be a labyrinth of catacombs in which the state treasures are believed to have been stored. Each ruler was allowed one visit but when the last guide died in the 1940s the secret of its location was lost!

At night, the palace is lit up & the bazar comes alive

There are several 16th-17th-century stepwells and 'tanks' (*kunds*) in town. The 46-m deep **Rani-ki-baori** with beautiful pillars and sculptures of Vishnu's 10 *avatars*, is the most impressive.

Sukh Niwas (Mahal), a summer pleasure palace, faces the **Jait Sagar** lake where Kipling spent a night in the original pavilion. It is now an Irrigation Department bungalow (see sleeping below). Further out are the 66 royal memorials at **Sar Bagh** (where the caretaker expects Rs 10 tip to open the complex) and the **Shikar Burj** (Hunting Tower) once used as a royal residence. The **84-pillared chhatri** on the Kota road has fine carvings.

The square artificial **Naval Sagar** lake has in its centre a half-submerged temple to Varuna, the god of water. The lake surface beautifully reflects the entire town and palace. West of the Naval Sagar is **Phool Sagar Palace** (10 km), which was started in 1945 but was left unfinished (prior permission needed to view).

On the road to Chittaurgarh are two interesting sites. **Bijolia**, 48 km southwest, has three of its original 100 Siva temples still standing, one with a large statue of Ganesh. At **Menal** (a further 48 km), there is a cluster of Siva temples believed to date from the time of the Guptas. They are associated with the Chauhans and other Rajput dynasties. Though neglected the temples have some fine carvings and a panel of erotic sculptures somewhat similar to those at Khajuraho in Madhya Pradesh. Behind is a deep, wooded ravine with a seasonal waterfall. You can stay at the **E** *Menal Motel* (RTDC), where there is one simple room, handy for a cup of tea or a simple meal. At **Begun**, 10 km south of Katoda, Thakur Hari Singh has converted his old haveli into a palace hotel.

Excursions

Essentials

B *Ishwari Niwas Palace*, opposite *Circuit House*, T443541, F442486. 20 air-cooled rooms (period furnishings) with bath around a courtyard, tired looking old mansion but pleasant interiors, home cooked meals, friendly, peaceful, Rajput family (only owner speaks English), good local tours including exclusive places owned by Maharao and other Rajputs in Bundi which require special permission to visit. **B-C** *Haveli Braj Bhushanjee* below Fort, opposite Ayurvedic Hospital (entrance in alley), T442322, F442142, res@kiplingsbundi.com 18 quaint rooms (each different) with clean bath (hot showers), in 19th century 4-storey haveli with plenty of atmosphere and interesting memorabilia, home-cooked Brahmin vegetarian meals (no alcohol), pleasant terrace, good fort views, pick-up from station on request, good craft shop below. Recommended. **D** *Royal Retreat*, below Fort, T444426, F443278, jpbundi@ yahoo.com Looks run down but quite clean and well kept inside, open courts, 5 largish rooms most with bath (others **E**), family run, good veg restaurant, café (popular with fort visitors), rooftop dining with views, good craft shop, internet. Recommended. **D-E** *Sukh Niwas* Guest House (Irrigation), contact tourist office, in case rooms are available. **D-E** *Vrindavati* (RTDC), 300 m from Sukh Mahal, on Jait Sagar Lake, T442473. 7 rooms in old bungalow in attractive garden with beautiful views, tents, simple meals to order, helpful staff. **E** *Lake View Paying Guest House*, Bohra Meghwan ji ki Haveli, Balchand Para, just below the palace, by Nawal Sagar, T442326, lakeview@yahoo.com 4 simple clean rooms (shared bath) in 150-year old *haveli* with some wall painting, private terrace shared with monkeys and peacocks, lovely views from rooftop, warm welcome, very friendly hosts. Recommended.. **E-F** *Kasera*, Haveli Dev Baxjiki, near Ojha Temple, Nagadi Bazar (old part of town), T444679. 14 rooms, some with air-cooler and hot shower, other singles (Rs 50), good vegetarian meals in rooftop restaurant, 350-year-old *haveli*, pleasant family. **E-F** *Kishan Niwas*, near Laxmi Nath Temple, Nahar ka Chohtta, by the Moti Mahal, T445807, F443278. Simple, clean rooms with bath (hot water), good home cooking, Mr Singh is very friendly and helpful. **F** *Bundi Tourist Palace*, near bus stand, T442650. 6 rather small rooms in a guest house, shared bath, aircoolers Rs 20, hot water Rs 5 per bucket.

Sleeping
■ *on map, page 177*
Price codes:
see inside front cover

Southeastern Rajasthan

Eating
● *on map, page 177*
Price codes:
see inside front cover

In hotels *Diamond*, Suryamahal Chowk. Very popular locally for cheap vegetarian meals, handy when visiting stepwells; (*Sher-e-Punjab* nearby, serves non-vegetarian). *Kasera*. Indian vegetarian. Good home cooking and special lassi and cane juice. *Sathi Cold Drinks*, Palace Rd. Excellent *lassis*; (try saffron, spices, pistachio and fruit).and an excellent place for a refreshment and a late-afternoon chat.

Festivals

Bundi is particularly colourful and interesting during *Gangaur* (15-16 Apr 2002, 4-5 Apr 2003)) and *Kalji Teej Fair* (6-7 Aug 2001, 25-26 Aug 2002).

Transport

Road Buses to Ajmer (165 km), 5 hrs; Kota (37 km), 45 mins, Chittaurgarh (157 km), 5 hrs; Udaipur (120 km), 3 hrs. **Train** T22582. The station south of town has a train each way between Kota and Neemuch via Chittaurgarh.

Directory

Banks Exchange can be a problem; try *Bank of Baroda*. **Communications** Internet: at *Royal Retreat*. **Hospitals** T32833, City T32827. SS Nursing Home T32333. **Tourist office** At Circuit House, T22697, has a list of paying guest accommodation.

South of Kota

Jhalawar

Jhalawar was the capital of the princely state of the Jhalas which was separated from Kota by the British in 1838. It lies in a thickly forested area on the edge of the Malwa plateau with some interesting local forts, temples and ancient cave sites nearby. Rarely visited by foreigners,the town is very pleasant to wander around. The **Garh Palace** in the town centre, now housing government offices, has some fine wall paintings which can be seen with permission. The **museum** here, established in 1915, has a worthwhile collection of sculptures, paintings and manuscripts. ■ *1000-1630, closed Fri. Rs 3*. Bhawani Natyashala (1921) was known for its performances ranging from Shakespearean plays to Shakuntala dramas. The stage with a subterranean driveway allowed horses and chariots to be brought on stage during performances.

The ruined **Gagron Fort** (eighth-14th centuries), 12 km north, is an example of a *Jal* (water) *durg* (fort) with rivers on three sides.

Sleeping and eating **D** *Purvaji* in the town centre, delightful old *haveli*, family interesting to talk to, delicious and simple homecooked meals.

Jhalarapatan

The small walled town, 7 km south of Jhalawar, has several fine 11th-century Hindu temples, the **Padmanath Sun Temple** on the main road being the best. The 30-m high temple with fine carvings on its 52 pillars had the *chhatris* added later by the Jhalas. The **Shantinath Jain temple** has an entrance flanked by marble elephants. There are some fine carvings on the rear façade and silver polished idols inside the shrines. Some 7 km away, **Chandrawati**, on the banks of the Chandrabhaga River, has the ruins of some seventh-century Hindu temples with fragments of fine sculpture.

Festival *Chandrabhaga Fair* (28-30 **Nov** in 2001, 18-20 **Nov** in 2002, 7-9 **Nov** in 2003). The cattle and camel fair has all the colour and authenticity of Pushkar without its commercialization. Animals are traded in large numbers in the fields, pilgrims come to bathe in the river as the temples become the centre of religious activity and the town is abuzz with all manner of vendors.

Transport Buses from Kota to Jhalawar; then auto-rickshaw or local bus for sights. Ujjain-Jhalawar road is appalling.

Southern Rajasthan

182

Southern Rajasthan

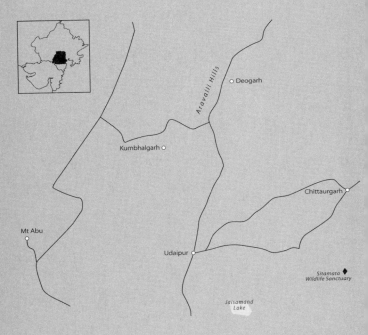

Udaipur

Set in the Girwa valley amidst the Aravalli hills of south Rajasthan, Udaipur is a beautiful city, regarded by many as one of the most romantic in India. In contrast to some of its desert neighbours it presents an enchanting image of white marble palaces, placid blue lakes, attractive gardens and green hills that keep the wilderness at bay. High above the lake towers the massive palace of the Maharanas. From its rooftop gardens and balconies, you can look over Lake Pichola, at the summer palace, 'adrift like a snowflake' in its centre. Around the lake, the houses and temples of the old city stretch out in a pale honeycomb making Udaipur an oasis of colour in a stark and arid region.

Phone code: 0294
Colour map 4, grid B1
Population: 308,000
Altitude: 577 m

Getting there The airport, about 30-45 mins by taxi or City Bus from town, has flights from several cities. The main Bus Stand is east of Udai Pol, 2-3 km from most hotels, while Udaipur City Railway Station is another 1 km south. Both have auto-rickshaw stands outside as well as pushy hotel touts. Remember, Udaipur station to the north, is inconvenient. **Getting around** The touristy area around the Jagdish temple and the City Palace, the main focus of interest, is best explored on foot but there are several sights further afield. City buses and unmetered auto-rickshaws cover the whole city and surrounding area. There are taxis too though some travellers prefer to hire a scooter or bike. Be prepared for the crowds, dirt and pollution and the persistent hotel touts who descend on new arrivals. It is best to reserve a hotel ahead or ask for a particular street or area of town.

Ins & outs
See page 194 for further details

The legendary **Ranas of Mewar** who traced their ancestry back to the Sun, first ruled the region from their seventh-century stronghold Chittaurgarh. The title 'Rana', peculiar to the rulers of **Mewar** (also used in Nepal), was supposedly first used by Hammir who reoccupied Mewar in 1326. In 1568, **Maharana Udai Singh** founded a new capital on the shores of Lake Pichola and named it Udaipur (the city of sunrise) having selected the spot in 1559. On the advice of an ascetic who interrupted his rabbit hunt, Udai Singh had a temple built above the lake and then his palace around it.

In contrast to the house of Jaipur, the rulers of Udaipur prided themselves on being independent from other more powerful regional neighbours, particularly the Mughals. In a piece of local princely one-upmanship, **Maharana Pratap Singh**, heir apparent to the throne of Udaipur, invited Raja Man Singh of Jaipur to a lakeside picnic. Afterwards he had the ground on which his guest had trodden washed with sacred Ganga water and insisted that his generals take purificatory baths. Man Singh reaped appropriate revenge by preventing Pratap Singh from acceding to his throne. Udaipur, for all its individuality, remained one of the poorer princely states in Rajasthan, a consequence of being almost constantly at war. In 1818, Mewar, the Kingdom of the Udaipur Maharanas, came under British political control but still managed to avoid almost all British cultural influence.

History of 'The city of sunrise'

Sights

Udaipur is a traditionally planned fortified city. Its bastioned rampart walls are pierced by massive gates, each studded with iron spikes as protection against enemy war elephants. The five remaining gates are: **Hathi Pol** (Elephant Gate – north), **Chand Pol** (Moon Gate – west), **Kishan Pol** (south), the main entrance **Suraj Pol** (Sun Gate-east) and **Delhi Gate** (northeast). On the

The Old City

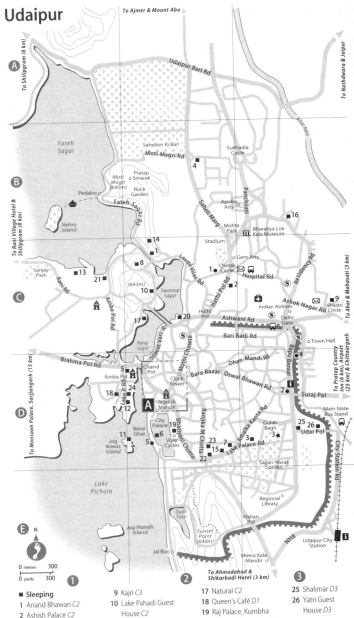

Udaipur

Related map
A Udaipur
(Jagdish Mandir Area),
page 191

■ Sleeping
1 Anand Bhawan *C2*
2 Ashish Palace *C2*
3 Chandra Prakash
  & Gulmohar *D3*
4 Chandralok *B2*
5 Dream Haven *D2*
6 Fateh Prakash & Shiv
  Niwas *D2*
7 Haveli *D2*
8 Hilltop Palace *C2*

9 Kajri *C3*
10 Lake Pahadi Guest
  House *C2*
11 Lake Palace *D2*
12 Lake Pichola, Lake
  Shore, Wonder View
  & Bharti Restaurant *D2*
13 Lakend *C1*
14 Laxmi Vilas Palace *C2*
15 Mahendra Prakash *D2*
16 Mewar Inn *B3*

17 Natural *C2*
18 Queen's Café *D1*
19 Raj Palace, Kumbha
  Palace & Mona Lisa *D2*
20 Rajdarshan & Delhi
  Darbar Restaurant *C2*
21 Ram Pratap Palace *C1*
22 Rang Niwas Palace &
  Palace View Restaurant *D2*
23 Ranjit Niwas *D2*
24 Sarovar *D2*

25 Shalimar *D3*
26 Yatri Guest
  House *D3*

● Eating
1 Berrys *C2*
2 Chief *D3*
3 Garden Hotel
  & Hariyali *D3*
4 Park View *D3*
5 Sunset Terrace *D2*

west side, the City is bounded by the beautiful Pichola Lake and to the east and north, by moats. To the south is the fortified hill of Eklingigarh. The main street leads from the Hathi Pol to the massive City Palace on the lake side.

The walled city is a maze of narrow winding lanes flanked by tall white-washed houses with doorways decorated with Mewar folk art, windows with stained glass or *jali* screens, majestic *havelis* with spacious inner courtyards and shops. Many of the houses here were given by the Maharana to retainers – barbers, priests, traders and artisans while many rural landholders (titled *jagirdars*), had a *haveli* conveniently located near the palace.

The 18th to 19th-century-*haveli* with 130 rooms was built as a miniature of the city palace with cool shady courtyards containing some peacock mosaic and fretwork, carved pillars made from granite, marble and the local blueish grey stone and lime plastered walls. The museum has a beautiful collection of folk costumes, turbans, hookahs, local art and utensils.

The **Jagdish Mandir**, 150 m north of the palace (1651), was built by Maharana Jagat Singh. The temple, currently being renovated, is a fine example of the Nagari style. A shrine with a brass *Garuda* stands outside and stone elephants flank the entrance steps; within is a black stone image of Vishnu as Jagannath, the Lord of the Universe.

This impressive complex of several palaces is a blend of Rajput and Mughal influences. Between the **Bari Pol** (Great Gate, 1600) to the north, and the **Tripolia Gate** (1713), are eight *toranas* (arches), under which the rulers were weighed against gold and silver on their birthdays, which was then distributed to the poor. Beyond the Tripolia the **Ganesh Deori Gate** (entry tickets) leads south to the fine Rai Angan (Royal Courtyard, 1571), with the Jewel Room. From here you can wander through a number of picturesque palace enclosures of the *Mardana*, some beautifully decorated.

★ **City Palace**
Half of it, with a great plaster façade, is still occupied by the royal family

The attractive **Mor Chowk** court, intended for ceremonial *darbars,* was added in the mid-17th century, which has beautiful late 19th-century peacock mosaics. The throne room is to its south, the **Surya Chopar,** from which the Rana (who claimed descent from the Sun) paid homage to his divine ancestor. To the Chowk's north, the **Chhoti Chitra Shali** has interesting blue tiles while the **Manak Mahal** (Ruby Palace)was filled with figures of porcelain and glass in the mid-19th century. The **Moti Mahal** (Pearl Palace) is a *sheesh mahal* decorated with mirrors which was added on the third level and has the small prayer room with illustrations of the Krishna legend. On either side of the Chowk are the women's quarters with shuttered windows which allowed the ladies to view the proceedings below. At the top level the breezy pavilions which open out to superb views, is the **Chini ki Chitra Mahal** (1711-34) which has fine ornamentation of Dutch and Chinese-made tiles counter-pointed with mirror work. To the north, the **Bari Mahal** or Amar Vilas (1699-1711) was added on top of a low hill. It has a pleasant garden with full grown trees around a square water tank in the central court. The cloisters with cusped arches have wide eaves and is raised above the ground to protect the covered spaces from heavy monsoon rain. This was an intimate 'playground' where the royal family amused themselves and were entertained.

At the far end is the **Queen's Palace**, now exhibiting palanquins, howdahs and photos of British Residents. An exhibition traces the progress of a project to record the history of the Udaipur dynasty.

On the west side of the Tripolia are the **Karan Vilas** (1620-28) and **Khush Mahal**, a rather grotesque pleasure palace for European guests, whilst to the south lies the **Shambhu Niwas Palace** the present residence of the Maharana.

Maharana Fateh Singh added to this the opulent **Shiv Niwas** with a beautiful courtyard and public rooms, and the **Fateh Prakash Palace**. Here the **Darbar Hall**'s royal portrait gallery displays swords still oiled and sharp. The Bohemian chandeliers (1880s) are reflected by Venetian mirrors, the larger ones made in India of lead crystal. Both, now exclusive hotels (see below), are worth visiting.

The **Crystal Gallery** on the first floor has an extensive collection of cut-crystal furniture, vases etc, made in Birmingham, England in the 1870s, supplemented by velvet, rich 'zardozi' brocade, objects in gold and silver and a precious stone-studded throne. ■ *Open to guests only at lunch and dinner. Rs 200 for a guided tour with a talk on the history of Mewar, followed by a cup of tea; cold reception reported by some.*

Part of the City palace is a **government museum** with second century BC inscriptions, fifth- to eighth-century sculpture and 9,000 miniature paintings of 17th- and 19th-century Mewar schools of art but also a stuffed kangaroo and Siamese twin deer. ■ *1000-1630, closed Fri. Rs 3.*

■ *From Ganesh Deori Gate: Rs 60 (more from near Lake Palace Ghat). Camera Rs 75; video Rs 300. 0920-1730, last entry 1630. From 'Maharajah's gallery', you can get a pass for Fateh Prakash Palace, Shiv Niwas and Shambu Niwas, Rs 75. Guided tour (about 1 hr), about Rs 100 each. A shop sells guide books etc (Mewar Paintings recommended). There is a post office and an exchange counter for cash, Visa or Mastercard.*

Lake Pichola Fringed with hills, gardens, havelis, ghats and temples, Lake Pichola is the scenic focus of Udaipur though parts get covered periodically with vegetation. Set in it are the Jag Niwas and the Jag Mandir Palaces. The **Jag Mandir** in the south is notable for the Gul Mahal, a domed pavilion started by Karan Singh (1620-28) and completed by Jagat Singh (1628-52). It is built of yellow sandstone inlaid with marble around an attractive courtyard. Maharajah Karan Singh gave the young Prince Khurram (later Shah Jahan), refuge here when he was in revolt against his father Jahangir in 1623, cementing a friendly relationship between the Mewar Maharaja and the future Mughal Emperor. Refugee European ladies and children were also given sanctuary here by Maharana Sarap Singh during the Mutiny. There is a lovely pavilion with four stone elephants on each side (some of the broken trunks have been replaced with polystyrene!). You get superb views from the balconies.

An enjoyable **boat trip** around the lake including a visit to Jag Mandir island, operates from Bansi Ghat (City Palace) Jetty. It's especially attractive in the late afternoon light. ■ *Apr-Sep 0800-1100, 1500-1800, Oct-Mar 1000-1200, 1400-1700. The 1 hr boat trip, on the hour, Rs 200, landing on Jag Mandir 30 minute boat ride, Rs 100.*

★ The Lake Palace The **Jag Niwas** island has the Dilaram and Bari Mahal Palaces. They were built by **Maharana Jagat Singh II** in 1746 and cover the whole island. Once the royal summer residences (now a hotel), they seem to float like a dream ship on the blue waters of the lake. The courtly atmosphere, elegance and opulence of princely times, the painted ceilings, antique furniture combined with the truly magical setting make it one of the most romantic in India. There area superb views. ■ *Visiting for non-residents: boat ticket from Bansi Ghat jetty with buffet meal, Rs 500-625 (see eating); some have found the meals disappointing. Tour operators make block bookings so book in advance or try your luck at the jetty.*

Friend or foe?

Travellers often risk being befriended by someone who will show them the city free of charge – "I just want to practise the language" or "I like to meet foreigners".

Don't be tempted to accept as you will end up in yet another shop, in front of another cup of tea, where your 'friend' will hope to pick up a good commission.

The **Jal Burj** is on the water's edge, south of the town. A pleasant two-hour walk to the south of the city takes you to the Sunset Point which has excellent views. The path past the café (good for breakfast) leads to the gardens on the wall; a pleasant place to relax. Although it looks steep it is only a 30-minute climb from the café.

From the small **Dudh Talai** (Milk Lake), nearby, there is an attractive walk to the main lake (especially pleasant in the evening; large fruit bats can also often be seen). A left turn up a new road leads to a new Manikya Lal Verma Park (still unfinished in early 2001) which has a 'musical fountain' which is switched on in the evening. ■ *Rs 5 day time, Rs 10 evening.*

The **Fateh Sagar Lake**, north of Lake Pichola, was constructed in 1678 during the reign of Maharana Jai Singh and modified by Maharana Fateh Singh. There is a pleasant lakeside drive along the east bank but, overall, it lacks the charm of the Pichola. Nehru Park on an island (accessible by ferry) has a restaurant.

Other sights in the city

Overlooking the Fateh Sagar is the **Moti Magri** (Pearl Hill). There are several statues of local heroes in the attractive rock gardens including one of Maharana Pratap on his horse Chetak, to which he owed his life. Local guides claim that Chetak jumped an abyss of extraordinary width in the heat of the battle of Haldighati (1576) even after losing one leg. To find out more look at *Hero of Haldighati.* ■ *Rs 10, camera free.*

Sahelion ki Bari (Garden of the Maids of Honour'), north of the city, is attractive and restful. This ornamental pleasure garden is a great spot. In a pavilion in the first courtyard opposite the entrance, a children's museum has curious exhibits including a pickled scorpion, a human skeleton and busts of Einstein and Archimedes! Beautiful black marble kiosks decorate the corners of a square pool. An elegant round lotus pond has four marble elephants spouting water. To the north is a rose garden with over 100 varieties. ■ *0900-1800. Rs 2, plus Rs 2 for 'fountain show'.*

At **Ahar** (3 km east) are the remains of the ancient city which has some Jain *chhatris* set on high plinths in the Mahasati (royal cremation ground). A small **museum** contains pottery shards and terracotta toys from the first century BC and 10th-century sculptures. ■ *1000-1630, closed Fri and holidays. Rs 3.* Nearby are the temples of Mira Bai (10th century), Adinatha (11th century) and Mahavira (15th century).

Bharatiya Lok Kala Museum, north of Chetak Circle, is responsible for the preservation of Rajasthani folk arts, but it is poorly maintained. ■ *0900-1800. Rs 10; camera Rs 50, T529296.*

Museums

The 18th-century **Bagore-Ki-Haveli**, at Gangor Ghat, has been recently renovated by the West Zone Cultural Centre. Several rooms display typical furnishings, utensils, costumes, musical instruments et cetera with interesting informative general notes. Examples of contemporary art and exquisite marble carving are also displayed. Worth a visit. ■ *Rs 2. 1000-1700. Nightly music and dance performances 1900-2000, Rs 25.*

Southern Rajasthan

Parks & zoos **Nehru Island Park** in Fateh Sagar and **Sahelion ki Bari** (see above). **Gulab Bagh** a rose garden on Lake Palace Road (see Restaurants below). Also contains a zoo (unremarkable) and toy train.

Excursions

Monsoon Palace There are good views from the deserted palace on a hilltop. The unfinished building on **Sajjangarh**, at an altitude of 335 m, which looks picturesque from the west facing battlements, was named after Sajjan Singh (1874-84) and was planned to be high enough to see his ancestral home, Chittaurgarh. Normally, you need a permit from the police in town to enter though many find a tip to the gateman suffices. It offers panoramic views of Udaipur (though the highest roof is spoilt by radio antennas); the windows of the Lake Palace can be seen reflecting the setting sun. The palace itself is very run down but the views from the hill top are just as good. A visit in the late afternoon is recommended; take binoculars. ■ *No formal entry fee but caretaker expects a tip (about Rs 20 per person). Getting there: It is 15 km west of the city. Taxis minimum Rs 300 (tourist taxis Rs 450 including road toll), auto-rickshaws Rs 200 return, including road toll at the foot of the hill (start from Udaipur by 1700 for sunset). Allow about 3 hrs for the round trip. It is possible to walk there from Udaipur, passing through a wildlife park which surrounds the hill (entrance Rs 40).*

Shilipgram 'Crafts Village' This craft village, near Havala (5 km) beyond Fateh Sagar on the Rani Road, has traditional huts from Rajasthan, Gujarat, Maharashtra and Goa faithfully replicated. The collection of colourful folk art, folk music and dancing makes for an interesting outing though it is getting touristy. Crafts demonstrations and sales are held mostly at weekends but it is nearly deserted on week days and so can be disappointing. *Shilpi Café and Beer Bar* is good for snacks. The main attraction is the spotless, well managed swimming pool where you can swim for Rs 100 (loungers, Rs 50). Short camel rides are offered but are not recommended for women alone ("camel driver may climb up behind you and behave most unpleasantly"). Allow two hours for a visit at weekends. ■ *Rs 10. Daily, 1000-1800 in season; some evenings only otherwise. Getting there: Take a taxi or auto-rickshaw. If you cycle, you can have a break and cold drink at the boat jetty on Nehru Island.*

Bari Lake (Tiger Lake), 12 km northwest, past Shilipgram, a clean lake in a quiet spot, is good for a swim and a picnic.

Fort and wildlife sanctuary (64 km) and the superb Jain temples, at **Ranakpur** to the northwest, can be visited allowing a whole day (see page 203) and is highly recommended. Good value tours are available during the season. They are also en route to Deogarh and Jodhpur with interesting places to stay overnight.

Jaisamand Lake, 51 km, and **Sitamata Sanctuary**, which has with excellent birdwatching, are to southeast of Udaipur (see below).

Tours **Rajasthan Tourism** Fath Memorial, Suraj Pol. City sightseeing: half day
Rickshaw tours (0800- 1230) Rs 60 (reported poor). Excursion: half day (1400-1900),
may mean lots Haldighati, Nathdwara, Eklingji, Rs 90. Chittaurgarh (0800-1800), Rs 230
of shop stops (with lunch); Ranakpur, Kumbhalgarh (0800- 1900) Rs 230; Jagat-Jaisamand-Chavand-Rishabdeo (0800-1900) Rs 230 (with lunch).

Udaipur, Fabled City of Romance, 1997, Rs 265, an excellent picture book with well written text is available locally.

Recommended reading

Essentials

LL-L *Lake Palace* (HRH), Pichola Lake, T528800, F528700, jaideep.khanna@ tajhotels.com 84 rooms, most with lake view, superb situation (see sights above), an experience, excellent suites and service (see eating). **LL-L** *Fateh Prakash* (HRH), City Palace, T528016, F528006, sales@hrhindia.com 9 rooms (US$150) and 7 suites (US$300), period furniture, restaurant (see below), facilities of *Shiv Niwas*, good service (residents may ask for a 'Pass' at entrance of City Palace, for a short cut to hotel). **L** *Shiv Niwas* (HRH), City Palace (right after entrance), T528016, F528006, sales@hrhindia.com 19 rooms (US$125), 17 suites (US$300-600), some with superb lake views, very comfortable, good restaurant, very pleasant outdoor seating for all meals around a lovely marble pool (non-residents pay Rs 300 to swim), tennis, squash, excellent service, beautiful surroundings, reserve ahead in season. **L-AL** *Trident* (Oberoi), overlooking Lake Pichola, peaceful far side, T432200, F432211, www.oberoihotels.com Tastefully decorated, all facilities, good pool, varied restaurants, polite but friendly, lush gardens, unpretentious, relaxing, own ferry to city Palace. Recommended.

AL *Laxmi Vilas Palace* (ITDC), T529711 F526273, on hillock above Fateh Sagar, 5 km station. 54 rooms (45 a/c), built as royal guesthouse, still atmospheric, good pool (non-residents, Rs 175), tennis. **A-B** *Hilltop Palace*, 5 Ambavgarh near Fateh Sagar, T432245, F432136. 55 rooms (large rooms upstairs with balcony), restaurant (visit for a view from the roof!), bar, exchange, pool, good food, friendly and efficient service. Recommended. **B** *Vishnupriya* (Quality Inn), 9 Garden Rd, near Gulab Bagh, T420314. 51 comfortable rooms, business facilities, outdoor pool. **B** *Rajdarshan*, 18 Pannabai Marg, inside Hathipol against the walls, by the lake edge, T526601, F524588. 52 rooms, very good restaurant, bar, exchange, pool, good views from balconies though sacred peepul tree may block out your view! Pleasant service. **B** *Shikarbadi* (HRH), Govardhan Vilas, Ahmadabad Rd (5 km from centre), T583201, F584841. 26 good, re-furbished a/c rooms, **C** 9 deluxe tents, pool, horse riding (Rs 150 per 40 mins), attractive 100 year old royal hunting lodge and stud farm with lake, lovely gardens, deer park, far from city. Recommended. **B-C** *Rang Niwas Palace*, Lake Palace Rd, T523891, F520294. 24 well-renovated rooms with bath, some a/c, and some in annexe, restaurant, very pleasant pool (non-residents Rs 100), gardens, very helpful staff, old-world and charming but near busy road junction.

C *Chandralok*, Saheli Marg, T560011, F560032. 14 a/c well-kept rooms, restaurant, bar. **C** *Lake Pichola*, overlooking lake, T431197, F430575. 20 rooms, some a/c, poorly maintained, tired old baths, fantastic views from some rooms, boat rides, friendly, relatively cheap food, jewellery shop sells conservative styles at reasonable prices. **C** *Sarovar*, 1 Panchdevri Marg, Hanuman Ghat outside Chandpol, T432801, F431732, sarovar@bppl.net.in 21 rooms on 3 floors in a new hotel, 13 overlook Lake Pichola (3 **B** are a/c), clean and comfortable, rooftop restaurant serves , sunbathing terrace, free use of good pool near Shilipgram. **C-D** *Anand Bhawan* (RTDC), Fateh Sagar Rd, T523256, F523247. 24 a/c rooms (lake facing deluxe rooms best), hilltop location with spectacular views, pleasant gardens, 1930s royal guesthouse, but getting increasingly run down with unsatisfactory service, unhelpful management. **C-D** *Ashish Palace*, 125 Chetak Marg, T525558, F525458. 32 good rooms (most a/c) with bath, restaurant, friendly and helpful manager, crowded area but convenient for sightseeing, GPO, Tourist Office. **C-D** *Caravanserai* (Jaiwana Haveli, part mid-18th century), 14 Lal Ghat (wrought iron gates lead

Sleeping
■ *on maps*
Price codes:
see inside front cover

Frenzied building work continues to provide more hotels while restaurants compete to offer the best views from the highest rooftop. Most hotels can arrange puppet shows, folk concerts etc if guests are ready to share costs

Southern Rajasthan

into small garden), T411103, F521252. 24 rooms, cramped rooms and baths, (better in rear of main building, larger and with views), average food, bar, exchange, lots of stairs. **C-D** *Kankarwa Haveli*, 26 Lalghat, T411457, F521403; 3 mins from bazar but quiet, impressive views from terrace, 14 excellent very clean rooms (Rs 400-1,000) with modern baths, some face lake, in renovated 250-year old *haveli* on lake shore, breakfast and snacks on the roof terrace, meals on request, family run, very friendly, reserve direct. Highly recommended. **C-D** *Lakend*, Alkapuri, Fateh Sagar, T431400, F431406. 85 rooms, some a/c, pool, modern with large lakeside garden, reasonably attractive rooms with balconies, very peaceful, excellent views (plans to extend into luxury hotel). **C** *Ram Pratap Palace*, on Fateh Sagar, T431701, F431700. Good rooms, some a/c, most with lake views in new attractive hotel, lawns, peaceful, very friendly. Recommended. **C-D** *Vinayak*, 39-40 Kalaji Goraji, T522166, near Gulab Bagh. Very central, beautiful gardens, quiet, big rooms, friendly management, popular with Indian guests. Recommended. **C-D** *Wonder View*, 6 vdevri Marg, near *Lake Pichola Hotel*, T522996, F415287. 8 rooms on 4 floors (newish matchbox-like building) but with fabulous views especially from rooftop with restaurant (food arrives slowly from ground floor kitchen!), very friendly, excellent taxis, peaceful and relaxed part of town. Highly recommended.

D *Damanis*, near telegraph office, T525675. Simple, unimpressive building but modern facilities, 35 rooms, a/c or aircooled, with bath, phone, TV. **D** *Fountain* Sukhadia Circle, T560290, F527549. 30 rooms, most a/c with TV, lawn, very popular. **D** *Jagat Niwas*, 24-25 Lalghat (on the lake), T420133, F520023. 21 individual, very clean rooms, most with bath (best **C**), in beautifully restored 17th-century îfairy taleî haveli, very good restaurant, helpful staff, good travel desk, excellent service. Highly recommended. The *haveli* has now been split in two, with cheaper rooms in the neighbouring *Hotel Jagat Niwas Palace*. **D** *Kajri* (RTDC), Shastri Circle, T410501. 53 rooms, some a/c and dorm, deluxe overlooking garden best, restaurant (dull, mediocre food), bar, travel, Tourist Reception Centre. **D** *Pratap Bhawan*, 12 Lal Ghat, T560566, F415015, pratapbhawan@usa.net 8 large, very clean rooms with baths in a lovely guest house, lake-facing terrace restaurant, excellent, home-cooked meals, warm welcome from retired army colonel and his wife. Highly recommended. **D** *Pratap Country Inn*, Airport Rd, Titadhia Village, T583138, F583058. 20 rooms, few a/c, restaurant, horse and camel safaris, riding, pool (sometimes empty), old royal country house in attractive grounds, 6 km centre (free transfer from rly station). **D** *Rani Village*, Rani Rd, Sanjay Park (near Fateh Sagar), T430880, F431094. 6 rooms, *Feast* restaurant, pleasant garden, peaceful surroundings. Away from centre but recommended. **D** *Sai Niwas*, 75 Navghat, T421586, F450009, www.hotelsainiwas.com Redecorated in Rajasthani style, rooms with bath and hot water, beautiful roof-terrace with good views of lake.

Paying guest accommodation list at Tourist Reception Centre, Fateh Memorial

Budget hotels Lal Ghat area: **D-E** *Jheel Guest House*, 56 Gangor Ghat (behind temple), T28321. Pleasant rooms, dearer in new extension with bath and hot water and some views, best view rooms Rs 400 (No 1 has enormous mirrors!), good rooftop restaurant. **D-E** *Mughal Palace*, T417954, shanu_21@yahoo.com Clean rooms with bath, Indian terrace restaurant, individually decorated home, solar power, internet, specially for artists, exhibitions. **D-E** *Ratan Palace*, 21 Lal Ghat (down alley going south past *Lalghat GH*), T561153. Spotless rooms with bath (size varies), constant hot water, 'unfinished' feel, rooftop restaurant (poor lighting, lacks ambience) with views, very helpful, friendly manager, efficient travel bookings, îattracts more mature travellersî, good value. Recommended. **E** *Evergreen*, 32 Lal Ghat. 7 rooms, good rooftop restaurant, clean, quiet and relaxed, western visitors only, îbit of a 'scene'î, staff usually friendly but can be off-hand. Not recommended for tours or safaris; **E** *Lake Ghat*, 4/13 Lalghat, 150 m behind Jagdish Mandir T521636. Some good rooms, clean, friendly, superb view from terraces, good food. **E** *Relish*, 60 Gadiya Devra, excellent rooftop restaurant with 6 clean rooms with bath. **E-F** *Badi Haveli*, near Jagdish Temple, T412588. 8 rooms with bath, some good, restaurant, travel (Ranakpur and Kumbhalgarh, 0800-1900, Rs 250), terraces with lake view, pleasant atmosphere, very friendly owner. Recommended. Next door, **E-F** *Lalghat Guest House*, 33 Lal Ghat, T525301. Best rooms with marble bath recommended (Rs 300), cheaper have no window, **F** dorm (Rs 80) good clean beds with curtains (!), spotless baths, breakfast, snacks, drinks, good views from terraces, very relaxed, good travel desk. Recommended. **E-F** *Lehar*, rooms with bath, best with lake view. ìNot as cute but less crowded than Badi Haveliî. **F** *Gyaneshwar Lodge*, Gangor Ghat Rd, Lalghat Corner. Friendly with cheap veg food at *Namaste* restaurant. **F** *Nukkad Guest House*, 56 Ganesh Ghat (signposted from Jagdish Temple). 9 small, simple rooms (Rs 50-80), some with bath, in typical family house, home cooked meals, rooftop, very friendly and helpful, clean. Highly recommended.

Bhatiyani Chotta: D-E *Raj Palace*, at 103, T527092. Clean rooms with bath (best **C**) and dorm, restaurant, garden, highly recommended for comfortable beds, excellent service, city tour, Rs 120. **E** *Kumbha Palace*, at 104, T422702. 8 rooms, clean, good linen, quiet, very good rooftop restaurant (see below), atmospheric, good views, attractive, riding (Rs 600). Recommended. **F** *Mona Lisa*, at 104, T561562. Some rooms air-cooled, with bath, good breakfast, garden, newspaper, pleasant and quiet, family run, good value. Recommended.

Lake Palace Rd area: D-E *Mahendra Prakash*, T529370. 15 large, spotless but simple rooms (hot water), some a/c, pleasant patio garden, excellent pool, owner/manager of the Maharana's family, friendly, excellent service. Recommended. **D-E** *Haveli*, T528294. Some rooms with bath tub, courtyard, clean, very helpful manager. **E** *Gulmohar*, 9 Sheetla Marg, T422857. 16 rooms in new hotel, pleasant and obliging staff, near Gulab Bagh but can be noisy. **E** *Lake Shore*, on Lake Pichola (no commission so ask rickshaw for Lake Pichola Hotel and walk 50 m). Run down (awaiting new management) may still produce classy (if pricey) meals, given adequate notice, on superb terrace, garden, very relaxing (real French café atmosphere!), good views of ghat. **E** *Ranjit Niwas*, Kalaji Goraji Temple Rd, T525774. 14 rooms some with hot shower, some cheaper and **F** dorm, in quiet residential area, small garden, good views from rooftop, village safaris organized. Recommended for friendly atmosphere and location. **F** *Chandra Prakash* (near Sajjan Niwas Garden), T422909. Some rooms with bath, clean, quiet, food good value, helpful manager. Recommended.

Jagdish Mandir area

■ **Sleeping**
1 Badi Haveli & Lehar
2 Caravanserai
3 Evergreen & Lalghat Guest House
4 Gokul
5 Gyaneshwar Lodge
6 Jagat Niwas & Kankarwa Haveli
7 Jheel
8 Lake Ghat
9 Nukkad
10 Pratap Palace
11 Ratan Palace & Sai Niwas
12 Relish

● **Eating**
1 Heaven
2 King Roof Café
3 Mayur

Southern Rajasthan

Elsewhere: **E** *Dream Haven*, 22 Bhim Parmeshver Marg, just over Chandpol, on the edge of the lake. 6 clean, simple rooms with bath, family run, no frills but excellent rooftop restaurant. **E** *Dream Palace*, Saheliyon ki bari Rd, T527227. Decent rooms (some **D** a/c), modern facilities, restaurant, small garden but pleasant hotel. **E-F** *Lake Pahadi Guest House*, on Swaroop Sagar, T27039. Good value rooms, enterprising manager. **E-F** *Island Tower*, 10 Nag Marg, outside Chand Pol. 14 clean rooms (avoid street side Rs 200 with shower), roof restaurant with brilliant views, quiet. peaceful, friendly, helpful, geared to tourist needs. Recommended. **E-F** *Natural*, 55 Rang Sagar (between New and Chandelle bridges), T527879, hotelnatural@ hotmail.com. 16 rooms with hot showers, sunny balconies facing lake, good restaurant (see below), good puppet show (1930), peaceful, "a home from home". Recommended. *Mewar Inn*, 42 Residency Rd (pleasantly away from centre), T522090, F525002, mewarinn@hotmail.com. Rooms vary, some with (brief!) hot shower best (Rs 99), very clean but street side incredibly noisy, no commission to rickshaws (if they refuse to go; try a horse carriage!), *Osho* veg restaurant, good cheap bike hire, rickshaw to town Rs 10-20, very friendly, YHA discounts. Recommended. **F** *Queens Café*, 14 Bajrang Marg (from Jagdish Temple, cross Chand Pol, then first left, continue for a few minutes to find the hotel on your right), T430875. 2 decent rooms, shared bath, roof terrace with good views, home cooked meals (including continental Swiss), informal, welcoming family.

Near the bus stand: **D-E** *Pathik*, City Station Rd, T483080. 17 rooms most a/c, with bath (hot water), TV, phone, restaurant. travel desk, crowded area, lots of bus traffic. **E** *Yatri Guest House*, 3/4 Panchkuin Rd, Udaipol, T27251. Simple rooms, helpful, knowledgeable owner. **F** *Shalimar*, Udaipol Rd, T29319. Good value. **F** *Railway Retiring Rooms*.

Eating
● *on maps,*
pages 184 & 191
Price codes:
see inside front cover

Try the local daal,
bhati, choorma
The larger hotels
have bars

Expensive In plush Heritage hotels (see above) – worth simply for the visit but remember non-vegetarian buffet food kept warm for long periods can be risky: *Shiv Niwas*. "Exemplary a la carte", buffet (Rs 650), good food followed by disappointing desserts, eat in the bar, or dine in luxury by the pool listening to live Indian classical music (Rs 1,000); bar expensive but the grand surroundings are worth a drink. *Lake Palace*, buffet lunch 1230-1430 (Rs 500), dinner 1930-2030 (Rs 670) often preceded by puppet show at 1800, expensive drinks (check bill). *Fateh Prakash*'s beautiful *Gallery Restaurant*. Superb views but pretty tasteless continental food, English cream teas. Tea also at *Darbar Hall* (see above).

Mid-range *Jagat Niwas*, 24-25 Lal Ghat, T415547. Mainly Indian. *Jarokha* rooftop restaurant with fabulous lake views, excellent meals, breakfast, teas, ices. *Sai Niwas*, 75 Nav Ghat. International. Excellent views from roof terrace, good evening meal, freshly cooked, attentive service. **Elsewhere**: *Berrys*, near Chetak Circle. International. Standard menu, comfortable, open 1000-2300. *Bharti*, Bhim Prameshwar Marg, Lake Pichola Hotel Rd. International (including Swiss, Mexican). Good food, friendly. Another at Suraj Pol, T561771. Indian breakfast, dinner. Beautiful gardens, clean, highly recommended. *Kumbha Palace*, 104 Bhatiyani Chotta, T422702. Excellent Indian and western food. Rooftop, simple seating under awning (chocolate cake, baked potato, pizzas, milk shakes), friendly, helpful service. *Natural*, 55 Rang Sagar, T431983. International including Tibetan, Italian and Mexican. Good buffet breakfasts, home-baking, peaceful rooftop. Recommended. *Park View*, opposite Town Hall, City Station Rd. Good North Indian. Comfortable.

It is perhaps best to
avoid Blue Shore

Cheap Lal Ghat area: No alcohol near the temple; usual fare includes pancakes, macaroni etc for the homesick westerner; some still show the locally shot Octopussy! *Evergreen*, 32 Lal Ghat. International. *Natural View* on rooftop with good lake views. *Gokul*,

A classic car collection

The Garden Hotel *was the former royal garage of the Maharanas of Mewar before it was converted into a restaurant. The original fuel pumps can still be seen in the forecourt where 19 cars from the ancestral fleet have been displayed. The impressive collection includes a 1920s Rolls Royce, custom built for a disabled member of the Mewar family, 1930s models of Rolls and Cadillacs, and two 1940s Chevrolet trucks, one of which was used as a school bus to take boys to the Maharana of Mewar's school!*

Gadiya Devra. Good, cheap breakfasts. **Heaven**, street corner near Lal Ghat. International. A long climb up to rooftop, stunning uninterrupted lake views, usual fare (also cheap rooms). **King Roof Café**, Gangor Ghat. North Indian. Delicious spicy dishes, comfy chairs, usual rickety bamboo and matting for shade, most hospitable owner. **Mayur**, Mothi Chowtha, opposite Jagdish Temple. Mainly Indian. Pleasant for veg thali (Rs 45) snacks and Octopussy, but slow service, also exchange after hours (good rate if you walk away!), internet. **Maxim's**, nearby, is part art gallery (silk paintings). Slow service but good food. **Purohit**, Anand Plaza. Good *dosas*.

City Palace and Lake Palace Rd area: **4 Seasons**, near City Palace, and **Green Rose Café**. Western and Indian (mild). Very good food (but irregular hours). Both recommended. **Garden Hotel**, opposite Gulab Bagh, Gujarati/Rajasthani. Air-cooled, excellent veg *thalis*, Rs 45 (try *khadhi*, *khaman*, *makkhan buda*), busy at lunch but not for dinner, interesting building, elderly waiters (will show you around kitchen). Recommended. **Hariyali**, near Gulab Bagh, has good North Indian. In a pleasant garden setting. **Samore Garden** has a wide international menu. **Sunset Terrace**, Bansi Ghat, Lake Pichola. Very pleasant, superb views of City Palace Complex.

Elsewhere: **Delhi Darbar**, Hathipol, good Mughlai. **Dream Haven**, 22 Bhim Parmeshver Marg, across Chandpol. Excellent, never ending *thalis* (Rs 25) on rooftop "watch the sun go down over the lake listening to the drum from the Jagdish Mandir". **Natraj**, near Town Hall. Rajasthani. Excellent *thalis* in family run simple dining hall, very welcoming. **Neelam**, City Station Rd. Average Indian. A/c, a good place to relax while waiting.

Entertainment

Bharatiya Lok Kala Museum, T529296. The 20-min puppet demonstrations during the day are good fun. Evening puppet show and folk dancing, 1800-1900, Sep-Mar, Rs 30, camera Rs 50. Recommended (often free afternoon rehearsals). **Meera Kala Mandir**, south of rly station, T583176. Daily except Sun, 1900-2000, Rs 60; cultural programme, a bit touristy and amateurish. See 'Shilipgram' above.

Festivals

Mewar Festival (15-16 **Apr** 2002, 4-5 Apr 2003). *Ashwa Pujan* at the City Palace (25 **Sep** 2001).

Shopping

The local handicrafts are wooden toys, colourful portable temples (kavad), *Bandhani* tie-and-dye fabrics, embroidery and *Pichchwai* paintings. Paintings are of 3 types: *miniatures* in the classical style of courtly Mewar; *phads* or folk art; and *pichchwais* or religious art (see Nathdwara below). The more expensive ones are 'old' – 20-30 years – and are in beautiful dusky colours; the cheaper ones are brighter.

Main shopping centres: Chetak Circle, Bapu Bazar, Hathipol, Palace Rd, Clock Tower, Nehru Bazar, Shastri Circle, Delhi Gate, Sindhi Bazar, Bada Bazar

Books *Mewar International*, 35 Lalghat. 'One-Stop-Shop' for wide selection of English books, exchange, films. **Sai**, 168 City Palace Rd, 100 m from palace gate. Good English books (new and second-hand), internet, exchange, travel services. **Suresh**, Hospital Rd, good fiction, non-fiction and academic books. **Pustak Sadan** (Hindi sign), Bapu

Southern Rajasthan

Bazar, near Town Hall. Good for Rajasthani history. **Clothing** Good in Hathipol but shop around; prices vary. *Fabric Ashoka*, opposite entrance to *Shiv Niwas*. Good quality but very expensive. *Monsoon Collection*, 55 Bhatiyani Chotta, quick, quality, tailoring, recommended. *Shree Ji Saree Centre*, Mothi Chowtha, 200 m from Temple. Good value, very helpful owner. Recommended. *Udaipur New Tailors*, inside Hathipol. Gents tailoring, reasonably priced, excellent service. **Handicrafts and paintings** Some shops sell old pieces of embroidery turned into bags, cushion covers etc. Others may pass off recent work as antique. *Ashoka Arts*, *Uday Arts*, Lake Palace Rd and *Apollo Arts*, 28 Panchwati. Paintings on marble paper and 'silk', bargain hard. Hathipol shop has good silk scarves (watch batik work in progress). Gallery Pristine, Kalapi House, Bhatiyani Chotta, Palace Rd, original 'white on brown' paintings, pleasant ambience. *Gem-arts*, near Chetak Circle. *Jagdish Emporium*, City Palace Rd. For traditional Udaipur and Gujarati embroideries. *Gangour*, Mothi Chowtha. Quality miniature paintings. *KK Kasara* opposite Nami Gali, 139 Mothi Chowtha. Good religious statues and jewellery. *Shivam Ayurvedic*, Lake Palace Rd, also art store, interesting, knowledgeable owner. *Sisodia Handicrafts*, entrance of Shiv Niwas Palace. Miniature 'needle paintings' of high quality – see artist at work, no hard sell. **Photography** Shops on City Station Rd and Bapu Bazar. *Deluxe Camera* 109 Bapu Bazar, 3rd flr. Good repairs. **Opticians** *Bharat Opticals*, 106 Bapu Bazar, T561197. Spectacles (including frames) Rs 800-1,000), 3 hrs. Recommended.

Sports **Riding** On elephant, camel or horse: travel agencies (eg *Namaskar*, Parul in Lalghat) arrange elephant and camel rides, Rs 200 per hr but need sufficient notice. Horse riding through hotels (Shikarbadi, Pratap Country Inn and some castles around Udaipur). **Swimming** Some hotel pools are open to non-residents: *Lakshmi Vilas* (Rs 175); *Rang Niwas* (Rs 100); **Shiv Niwas** (Rs 300). Also at Shilipgram Craft Village, Rs 100. **Vintage and classic cars** At the *Garden Hotel* opposite Gulab Bagh (see box). Guided tour, Rs 100.

Transport **Local** **Auto-rickshaw**: Rs 5, then Rs 3 per km; about Rs 50 per hr. **Bicycle hire**: Rs 25 per day, well maintained, comfortable, from *Vijay Cycles* half way down Bhatiyani Chotta; also shops near *Kajri Hotel*, Lalghat and Gangor Ghat area, which also have scooters (Rs 125 per day). Motorbike hire: scooters and bikes can be hired from a small courtyard behind Badi Haveli (Jagdish Temple area). **Taxi**: RTDC taxis from Fath Memorial, Suraj Pol. Private taxis from airport, rly station, bus stands and major hotels; negotiate rates. *Taxi Stand*, Chetak Circle, T525112. *Tourist Taxi Service*, Lake Palace Rd, T524169.

Long distance **Air**: Dabok airport is 25 km east, T655453. Security check is thorough; no batteries or knives allowed in hand luggage. Transport to town: taxis, Rs 190. *Indian Airlines*, Delhi Gate, T410999, 1000-1315, 1400-1700. Airport, T655453, enquiry T142. Reserve well ahead. *Indian Airlines* flights to **Aurangabad**; **Delhi**, US$90; **Jaipur, Jaisalmer, Jodhpur, Mumbai**. *Jet Airways*, T565105, airport T656288: **Delhi via Jaipur, Mumbai**. *U.P. Air*, daily to **Delhi, Jaipur, Mumbai, Rajkot**.

Road **Bus**: Main State Bus Stand, near rly line opposite Udai Pol, T484191; reservations 0700-2100. State RTC buses to **Agra** 15 hrs; **Ahmadabad** 252 km, 7 hrs; **Bhopal** 765 km, 15 hrs; **Bikaner** 13 hrs; **Delhi** 635 km, 17 hrs; **Indore** 635 km; **Jaipur** 405 km, 10 hrs; **Jaisalmer** 14 hrs; **Jodhpur** 8 hrs (uncomfortable, poorly maintained road); **Mount Abu** 270 km, 0800, 1030 and 1500, 7 hrs), Rs 50 (Tourist bus, Rs 75, not much faster); **Mumbai** 802 km, very tiring, 16 hrs; **Pushkar** (Tourist bus, 7 hrs, Rs 90); **Ujjain** (7 hrs). Private buses and Luxury coaches run mostly at night. **Ahmadabad** *Bonney Travels*, Paldi, Ahmedabad, has a/c coaches with reclining seats (contact *Shobha Travels*, City Station Rd), dep 1400 (6½ hrs), Rs 225, with drink/snack stops every 2 hrs. Highly recommended. *Shrinath* and *Punjab Travels* have non a/c buses to **Ahmedabad** and **Mount Abu**. **Jaipur**: several 'deluxe' buses (computerized booking) with reclining seats, Rs 200, more expensive but better. **Jaisalmer**: change at Jodhpur, Rs 160. **Jodhpur**: several options but best to book a good seat, a day ahead, RS90. Tour operators have **taxis** for Kumbhalgarh and Ranakpur.

Train Udaipur City station, 4 km southeast of centre, T131. **Ahmadabad**: *Ahmadabad Exp, 9943*, 2115, 9½ hrs. **Ajmer**: *Delhi SR Exp, 9944*, 0800, 13 hrs; *Chetak Exp, 9616*, 1810, 8½ hrs. **Delhi (SR)**: *Delhi SR Exp, 9944*, 0800, 23½ hrs; *Chetak Exp, 9616*, 1810, 17½ hrs (best to change at Jaipur at 0715 to faster *Intercity* for Delhi Junction station). **Jalgaon**: (day and night trains) to visit Ajanta, Aurangabad, Ellora. **Jaipur**: *Delhi SR Exp, 9944*, 0830, 15 hrs; *Chetak Exp, 9616*, 1810, 11½ hrs.

Banks Foreign exchange at: *Andhra Bank*, Shakti Nagar. Cash advance against Visa/Mastercard, efficient. *Bank of Baroda*, Bapu Bazar. For Amex. *Bank of Bikaner & Jaipur*, Chetak Circle. *Thomas Cook*, inside City Palace. But poor rates. *Trade Wings*, Polo Ground Rd, *Vijaya Bank* at City Palace entrance. **Communications** Internet: *Mayur*, Mothi Chowtha. *Mewar*, Raj Palace Hotel, Bhatiyani Chotta, T410364. *One Stop Shop*, near *Lal Ghat Guest House*. Sai, 168 City Palace Rd. Thomas Cook in City Palace Courtyard. Cyber Café near *Jagat Niwas*. **Post**: The GPO is at Chetak Circle. Posting a parcel can be a nightmare and mean endless queuing. **Poste Restante:** Shastri Circle Post Office. **Hospitals and medical services** *General Hospital*, Chetak Circle. *Aravali Hospital* (private), 332 Ambamata Main Rd, opp Charak Hostel, T430222, very clean, professional. Recommended. Several **Chemists** on Hospital Rd. **Tour companies and travel agents** *Aravalli Safari*, 1 Sheetla Marg, Lake Palace Rd, T420282, F420121. Very professional. Recommended. *Forts & Palaces*, 34-35 Shrimal Bhawan, Garden Rd, T417359, jaipur@palaces-tours.com *Parul*, *Jagat Niwas Hotel*, Lalghat, T522990, parul@ad.vsnl.net.in Air/train, palace hotels, car hire, exchange. Highly recommended. *Rajasthan Travels*. Excellent service. *Srinath Travel*, T529391. Direct buses to Mount Abu, Mumbai etc. Recommended. *Tourist Assistance Centre*, 3 Paneri House, Bhatiyani Chotta, T528169, F561938. Guides. **Tourist offices** *Rajasthan*, Tourist Reception Centre, Fath Memorial, Suraj Pol, T411535. 1000-1700. **Guides** 4-8 hrs, about Rs 250-400. Also from Tourist Assistance Centre (see above). Counters at City Railway Station, T412984. 0800-1200 and at Dabok Airport at flight times, T655433. **Useful addresses** Ambulance: T23333. **Fire:** T27111. **Police:** T3000.

Directory

Southern Rajasthan

Chittaurgarh (Chittor)

Chittaurgarh Fort stands on a 152 m high rocky hill, rising abruptly above the surrounding plain. The walls, 5 km long, enclose the deserted ruins while the slopes are covered with scrub jungle. The modern town lies at the foot of the hill with access across a limestone bridge of 10 arches over the Gambheri River.

Phone code: 01472
Colour map 4, grid B2
Population: 72,000

One of the oldest cities in Rajasthan, Chittaurgarh was founded formally in 728 by Bappu Rawal, who according to legend was reared by the Bhil tribe. However, two sites near the River **Berach** have shown stone tools dating from half a million years ago and Buddhist relics from a few centuries BC. From the 12th century it became the centre of Mewar. Excavations in the **Mahasati** area of the fort have shown four shrines with ashes and charred bones, the earliest dating from about the 11th century AD. This is where the young **Udai Singh** was saved by his nurse **Panna Dai**; she sacrificed her own son by substituting him for the baby prince when, as heir to the throne, Udai Singh's life was threatened.

History

Sights   The **fort** dominates the city. Until 1568 the town was situated within the walls. Today the lower town sprawls to the west of the fort. The winding 1½ km ascent is defended by seven impressive gates: the **Padal Pol (1)** is where Rawat Bagh Singh, the Rajput leader, fell during the second siege; the **Bhairon** or Tuta (broken) **Pol (2)** where Jaimal, one of the heroes of the third siege, was killed by Akbar in 1567 (*chhatris* to Jaimal and Patta); the **Hanuman Pol** and **Ganesh Pol**; the Jorla or Joined) Gate whose upper arch is connected to the **Lakshman Pol**; finally the **Ram Pol** (1459) which is the main gate. Inside the walls is a village and ruined palaces, towers and temples.

Rana Kumbha's Palace (3)   On the right immediately inside the fort are the ruins of the palace (1433-68), originally built of dressed stone with a stucco covering. It is approached by two gateways, the large **Badi Pol** and the three-bay deep **Tripolia**. Once there were elephant and horse stables, *zenanas* (recognized by the *jali* screen), and a Siva temple. The *jauhar* committed by Padmini and her followers is believed to have taken place beneath the court-yard. The north frontage of the palace contains an attractive combination of canopied balconies. Across from the palace is the archaeological office and the

Chittaurgarh

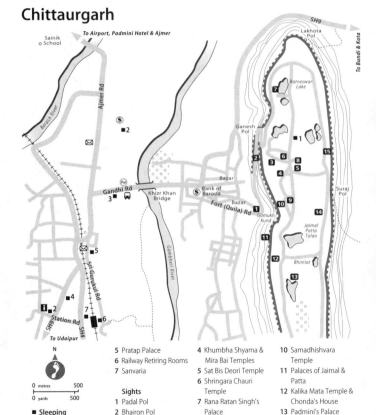

N

0 metres 500
0 yards 500

■ **Sleeping**
1 Birla Rest House
2 Janta Avas Grih
3 Natraj
4 Panna
5 Pratap Palace
6 Railway Retiring Rooms
7 Sanvaria

Sights
1 Padal Pol
2 Bhairon Pol
3 Rana Kumbha's Palace, Nau Lakha Bandar & Archaeological Office
4 Khumbha Shyama & Mira Bai Temples
5 Sat Bis Deori Temple
6 Shringara Chauri Temple
7 Rana Ratan Singh's Palace
8 Fateh Prakash Palace & Museum
9 Vijay Stambha & Mahasati
10 Samadhishvara Temple
11 Palaces of Jaimal & Patta
12 Kalika Mata Temple & Chonda's House
13 Padmini's Palace
14 Adbhutanatha Temple
15 Kirti Stambha

The *jauhar* – Rajput chivalry

On three occasions during Chittaurgarh's history its inhabitants preferred death to surrender, the women marching en masse into the flames of a funeral pyre in a form of ritual suicide known as jauhar *before the men threw open the gates and charged towards an overwhelming enemy and annihilation.*

The first was in 1303 when Ala-ud-din Khalji, the King of Delhi, laid claim to the beautiful Padmini, wife of the Rana's uncle. When she refused, he laid siege to the fort. The women committed jauhar, *Padmini entering last, and over 50,000 men were killed in battle. The fort was retaken in 1313.*

In 1535 Bahadur Shah of Gujarat laid claim to Chittaurgarh. Every Rajput clan lost its leader in the battle in which over

32,000 lives were lost, and 13,000 women and children died in the sacred jauhar *which preceded the final charge.*

The third and final sack of Chittaurgarh occurred only 32 years later when Akbar stormed the fort. Again, the women and children committed themselves to the flames, and again all the clans lost their chiefs as 8,000 defenders burst out of the gates. When Akbar entered the city and saw that it had been transformed into a mass grave, he ordered the destruction of the buildings.

In 1567 after this bloody episode in Chittaurgarh's history, it was abandoned and the capital of Mewar was moved to Udaipur. In 1615 Jahangir restored the city to the Rajputs.

Nau Lakha Bhandar (The Treasury; *nau lakha* – 900,000). The **temple** to Rana Kumbha's wife **Mira Bai (4)** who was a renowned poetess is visible from the Palace and stands close to the Kumbha Shyama Temple (both circa 1440). The older 11th-century Jain **Sat Bis Deori (5)** with its 27 shrines, is nearby. The **Shringara Chauri Temple (6)** (circa 1456), near the fort entrance, has sculptured panels of musicians, warriors and Jain deities.

Rana Ratan Singh's Palace (7) is to the north by the Ratneshwar Lake. Built in stone around 1530 it too had stucco covering. Originally rectangular in plan and enclosed within a high wall, it was subsequently much altered. The main gate to the south still stands as an example of the style employed.

The early 20th-century **Fateh Prakash Palace (8)** built by Maharana Fateh Singh (d1930) houses an interesting **museum** (1000-1630; closed Friday). To the south is the **Vijay Stambha (9)** (1458-68), one of the most interesting buildings in the fort, built by Rana Kumbha to celebrate his victory over Mahmud Khilji of Malwa in 1440. Visible for miles around, it stands on a base 14 m sq and 3 m high, and rises 37 m. The nine-storeyed sandstone tower has been restored; the upper section retains some of the original sculpture. For Re 0.50 you can climb to the top. Nearby is the **Mahasati** terrace where the ranas were cremated when Chittaurgarh was the capital of Mewar. There are also numerous *sati* stones. Just to the south is the **Samdhishvara Temple (10)** to Siva (11th and 15th centuries), with some good sculptured friezes. Steps down lead to the deep **Gomukh Kund**, where the sacred spring water enters through a stone carved as a cow's mouth (hence its name).

Of the two **Palaces of Jaimal and Patta (11)**, renowned for their actions during the siege of 1567, the latter, based on the *zenana* building of Rana Kumbha's Palace, is more interesting. You then pass the **Bhimtal** before seeing the **Kalika Mata Temple (12)** (originally an eighth century Surya temple, rebuilt mid-16th) with exterior carvings and the ruins of **Chonda's House** with its three-storey domed tower. Chonda did not claim the title when his father, Rana Lakha, died in 1421.

Southern Rajasthan

Padmini's Palace (13) (late 13th century, rebuilt end of the 19th) is sited in the middle of the lake surrounded by pretty gardens. Ala-ud-din Khilji is said to have seen Padmini's beautiful reflection in the water through a mirror on the palace wall. This striking vision convinced him that she had to be his.

You pass the deer park on your way round to the **Suraj Pol** (Sun Gate) and pass the **Adbhutanatha Temple** to Siva **(14)** before reaching the second tower, the **Kirti Stambha (15)**, a Tower of Fame (13th, 15th centuries). Smaller than the Vijay Stambha (23 m) with only seven storeys, it is dedicated to Adinath, the first Jain Tirthankar. Naked figures of Tirthankars are repeated several hundred times on the face of the tower. A narrow internal staircase goes to the top.

Of particular interest are the number of tanks and wells in the fort that have survived the centuries. Water, from both natural and artificial sources, was harnessed to provide an uninterrupted supply to the people.

Visiting the fort on foot means a circuit of 7 km; allow four hours. The views from the battlements and towers are worth the effort. The Archaeological Survey Office is in the fort, opposite Rana Kumbha's Palace; guide books are not always available so ask at *Panna Hotel*.

Tours **Rajasthan Tourism** run two daily tours, 0800-1130, 1500-1830, in summer (May-June), 0700-1030, 1600-1930. Tours start from *Panna*, Udaipur Road. Guide fees: Highlights of Chittaurgarh fort, Rs 250 for half day; Rs 450 for full day including surrounding excursions.

Sleeping **C-D** *Padmini*, Chanderiya Rd, near Sainik School, T41718, F40072. 16 clean rooms,
■ *on map, page 196* 6 a/c, good Indian restaurant, quiet, airport transfer from Udaipur. **C-D** *Pratap Palace*,
Price codes: Sri Gurukul Rd, near Head Post Office, T40099, F41042, pratapp@jp1,dot.net.in Pleas-
see inside front cover ant, dated but fairly clean rooms, some a/c, good food in restaurant or in the pleasant
Chittaurgarh has few garden, jeep and horse safaris visiting villages. **D-F** *Chetak*, opposite railway station
hotels. Udaipur has a (a short walk past transport offices), T41588. Modern hotel, 23 clean, fairly pleasant
better choice rooms (various categories), only 'deluxe' have Western toilets and hot showers.
D-F *Meera*, near the railway station, T40266. Modern hotel, 22 a/c and non a/c rooms with TV and phone, restaurant (Gujarati/north Indian) and bar, laundry, car rental and travel assistance . **D-E** *Panna* (RTDC), Udaipur Rd, near rly station, T40842, F43942. 31 simple rooms, some a/c best with fort view (4 with Western toilets), others with Indian toilet (no shower), dorm (Rs 50), veg dining hall, bar, run down but attentive service. Indian business hotel, popular with those visiting quarries/mines.. **E** *Janta Avas Grih* (RTDC), Station Rd, T41089. 4 simple, refurbished rooms with bath, restaurant, Tourist Office. **E-F** *Railway Retiring Rooms* (1 a/c), T42008. Book ahead. **F** *Sanvaria*, small guest house near the Kirti Stambh in the Fort has been opened by the dharamshala group. (better than the Sanvaria near the railway station), T40597. Very basic.

Eating Best in hotels. *RTDC Café* near the Vijay Stambha is handy for visitors to the fort.

Festival *Mira Utsav* is held in Oct.

Transport **Local** The fort is over 6 km from station. **Auto and cycle rickshaw**: Negotiate fares.
Bottled water at **Bicycle**: for hire opposite railway station, Rs 2 per hr. **Long distance** **Road** **Bus**:
Chittaurgarh station is Enquiries, T41177. Roads are poor and even the relatively short ride to Udaipur can
often tampered with; be excruciatingly uncomfortable. Daily buses to Bundi (4 hrs), Kota (5 hrs), Ajmer (5
take extra care hrs) and Udaipur; 2½ hrs along a picturesque route passing fields of pink and white poppies, grown legally for opium. **Train**: Enquiries, T41009. A 117 km branch line runs from **Chittaurgarh** to **Udaipur**. At **Mavli Junction** (72 km) another branch runs down the Aravalli scarp to **Marwar Junction** (150 km). The views along this line are

very picturesque indeed. By taking this route you can visit Udaipur, Ajmer and Jodhpur in a circular journey. **Ajmer**: *Purna-Jaipur Exp, 9770*, 0550, 4½ hrs. *Ahmadabad DSR Exp, 9944*, 1500, 6 hrs. **Indore**: *Jaipur-Purna Exp, 9769*, 2015, 7½ hrs; **Jaipur**: *Purna Jaipur Exp, 9770*, 0550, 8½ hrs; *Chetak Exp, 9616*, 2200, 8½ hrs; both continue to **Delhi** 15-16 hrs. **Udaipur**: *Chetak Exp, 9615*, 0650, 3½ hrs; *DSR Ahmadabad Exp, 9943*, 1345, 4½ hrs, (continues to Ahmadabad, 17 hrs).

Tourist offices *Rajasthan, Janta Avas Grih*, Station Rd, T41089.　　**Directory**

Bassi

The town, 28 km from Chittaurgarh, is famous for handicrafts and miniature wooden temples painted with scenes from the epics. The palace, a massive 16th-century fort, has been opened as a hotel, **D** *Bassi Palace*, T01472 25321. The 20 rooms are in a modern annexe, simple Indian meals.

Bijaipur

Bijaipur is a feudal village about 50 km south of Chittaurgarh. The 16th-century castle, set among the Vindhya hills, has a splendid location near the Bassi-Bijaipur wildlife sanctuary which is home to panther, antelope and other wildlife. The forests are interspersed with lakes, reservoirs, streams and waterfalls with good birdlife in the winter months. The ruined Pannagarh fort facing a lily covered lake is believed to be one of the oldest in Rajasthan.

Sleeping and eating **B** *Castle Bijaipur* (Heritage Hotel), www.castlebijaipur.com 24 simple rooms decorated in traditional style with comfortable furniture and modern bathrooms in castle and a new wing, lawns and gardens, great hill views from breezy terrace, delicious Rajasthani meals, also tea on medieval bastion, jeep/ horse safaris with camping, jungle trekking. Reserve at T/F01472-40099.

Jaisamand Lake
52 km SE of Udaipur

Before the building of huge modern dams in India Jaisamand was the second largest artificial lake in Asia (15 km by 10 km). Dating from the late 17th century, it is surrounded by the summer palaces of the Ranis of Udaipur. The highest two of the surrounding hills are topped by the **Hawa Mahal** and **Ruti Rani** palaces, now empty but worth visiting for the architecture and the view. A small sanctuary nearby has deer, antelope and panther. Tribals still inhabit some islands on the lake. Crocodiles, keelback water snakes and turtles bask on other islands.

Sleeping and eating **B** *Jaisamand Island Resort*, Baba Island, T02906-2222. 40 well equipped a/c rooms, restaurant (international menu), pool, garden, excellent location, great views, mixed reports on food and service.

Bambora

The imposing 18th-century hilltop fortress of Bambora (45-minutes' drive southeast of Udaipur) has been converted to a heritage hotel by the royal family of Sodawas at an enormous restoration cost yet retaining its ancient character. The impressive fort is in Mewari style with domes, turrets and arches. ■ *Getting there: from Udaipur, go 12 km east along the airport road and take the right turn towards Jaisamand Lake passing the 11th-century Jagat Temple (38 km) before reaching Bambora.*

Sleeping **B** *Karni Fort*, (Heritage Hotel), T512101, F512105, www.karnihotels.com Beautifully decorated rooms (circular beds!), marble bathrooms, modern facilities, impressive interiors, enthusiastic and friendly manager, exceptional marble swimming pool, folk concerts. Reservations T0291-433320, F433495 welcome@ndf.vsnl.net.in **E** *Bungalow* (previously RTDC). 4 rooms, shared bath, dorm.

Southern Rajasthan

Southern Rajasthan

Bhindar The town, once ruled by Maharana Pratap's younger brother, Shakti Singh, has the ruins of a 1578 castle with faded frescoes of later centuries, *zenanas* and beacon towers which are open to visitors, though the town itself is charmless. **C** *Bhindar Castle Resort*, T02957-20209 ranbin@bppl.net.in Six small, simple rooms in 20th-century wing, dorm beds, simple homecooked Rajasthani meals, pleasant courtyard garden, family hospitality but not very well run, folk entertainment, jeep to Sitamata, extremely noisy location, reservations, T079-6560962, F02712-23729. ■ *Getting there: Bhindar is off the highway, south of Chittaurgarh and about 60 km from Udaipur.*

Sitamata
Wildlife
Sanctuary
117 km from Udaipur

The reserve of dense deciduous forests covers over 400 sq km and has extensive birdlife (woodpeckers, tree pies, blue jays, jungle fowl). It is one of the few sanctuaries between the Himalayas and the Nilgiris where giant brown flying squirrels have been reported. Visitors have seen hordes of langur monkey, nilgai in groups of six or seven, four-horned antelope, jackal and even panther and hyena, but the thick forests make sighting difficult. There are crocodiles in the reservoirs.

Sleeping and eating B-C *Fort Dhariawad*, T02950-2250. 16 rooms and 4 suites in restored and converted, mid-16th century fort, (founded by one of Maharana Pratap's sons) and some in contemporary cottage cluster, meals (international menu), period decor, medieval flavour, great location by sanctuary (flying squirrels, langur monkeys in garden, crocodiles in reservoir), tribal village tours, jeeps to park, horse safaris, treks. **D** *Forest Lodge*, Dhariawad. Rather expensive considering lack of amenities, but fantastic location and views, a paradise for birders.

Rishabdeo
63 km S of Udaipur
along the NH8

Rishabdeo, off the highway, has a remarkable 14th-century Jain temple with intricate white marble carving and black marble statuary, though these are not as fine as at Dilwara or Ranakpur. Dedicated to the first Jain Tirthankar, Adinath or Rishabdev, Hindus, Bhils as well as Jains worship there. An attractive bazar street leads to the temple which is rarely visited by tourists. Special worship is conducted several times daily when Adinath, regarded as the principal focus of worship, is bathed with saffron water or milk. The priests are friendly; a small donation (Rs 10-20) is appreciated. You can stay at **E** *Gavri* (RTDC), T02907-2245, eight simple rooms, dorm.

★ Dungar-
pur
Phone code: 02964
Population 50,000
24 km SE of Kherwara

Dungarpur is a birdwatchers' paradise with lots of ducks, moorhens, waders, ibises at the lake, tropical green pigeons & grey hornbills in the woodlands

Dungarpur (the 'City of Hills') dates from the 13th century. The district is the main home of the Bhil tribal people (see page 420). It is also renowned for its stone masons, who in recent years have been employed to build Hindu temples as far afield as London. The attractive and friendly village has one of the most richly decorated palaces in Rajasthan, the Juna Mahal. Surrounded on three sides by Lake Gaibsagar and backed by picturesque hills, the more recent **Udai Bilas Palace** (now a heritage hotel) was built by Maharawal Udai Singhji in the 19th century and extended in 1943. The huge courtyard surrounds a 'pleasure pool' from the centre of which rises a four-storeyed pavilion with a beautifully carved wooden chamber.

The **Juna Mahal**, above the village, dates from the 13th century when members of the Mewar clan at Chittaur moved south to found a new kingdom after a family split. It is open to guests staying at Udai Bilas and by ticket for non residents, obtainable at the hotel. The seven-storeyed fortress-like structure with turrets, narrow entrances and tiny windows has colourful and vibrant rooms profusely decorated over several centuries with miniature wall paintings (among the best in Rajasthan), and glass and mirror inlay work.

There are some fine *jarokha* balconies and sculpted panels illustrating musicians and dancers in the local green-grey parava stone which are strikingly set against the plain white walls of the palace to great effect. The steep narrow staircases lead to a series of seven floors giving access to public halls, supported on decorated columns, and to intimate private chambers. There is a jewel of a *Sheesh Mahal* and a cupboard in the Maharawal's bedroom on the top floor covered in miniatures illustrating some 50 scenes from the *Kama Sutra*. Windows and balconies open to the breeze command lovely views over the town below. The fort ruins cling to the hilltop above the palace, which is now dominated by a microwave telecommunications tower. They make an ideal picnic spot, offering panoramic views over the town.

Rajmata Devendra Kunvar State **museum** has a large gallery of sculptures of 6th-7th century, 11th-12th century and 16th-18th century periods, excavated from the surrounding region of Vagad. ■ *1000-1630, closed Fri. Rs 3.*

Some interesting temples nearby include the 12th-century Siva temple at Deo Somnath, 12 km away, and the splendid complex of temple ruins profusely decorated with stone sculptures.

Sleeping and eating B *Udai Bilas Palace*, 2 km from town, T30808, F31008, www.udaibilaspalace.com 20 unique a/c rooms (including 10 suites of which 3 are vast 'grand suites') mirror mosaics, some "dated" with art deco furniture, marble bathrooms some with modern furniture in old guest house, all with either a lake or garden view, good food (lunch Rs 380) a 'Country House' style hotel (guests dine together at one table) where Harshvardhan Singh is a charming host, beautiful new swimming pool, boating, TCs and credit cards accepted, idyllic setting, very relaxing. Highly recommended. **E-F** *Vaibhav*, Saghwara Rd, T30244. Simple rooms, tea stall style restaurant, owner very friendly and helpful. Also *Pushpanjali* and *Gayatri* (*Pratibha Palace* not recommended).

Festivals *Baneshwar Fair* (25-27 **Feb** 2002; 14-16 Feb 2003). The tribal festival at the Baneshwar Temple, 70 km from Dungarpur, is one of Rajasthan's largest tribal fairs when Bhils gather to the temple in large numbers for ritual bathing at the confluence of rivers. There are direct buses to Baneshwar during the fair. The temporary camp during the fair is best avoided. *Vagad Festival* in Dungarpur during this period offers an insight into local tribal culture. Both festivals are uncommercialized and really authentic. Details from *Udai Bilas*.

Transport Buses to/from Udaipur (110 km), 3 hrs Ahmadabad (170 km), 4 hrs by car.

Deogarh (Devgarh) is an excellent place to break journey between Jaipur or Pushkar, and Udaipur to visit sights nearby. It is a very pleasant, little frequented town with a dusty but interesting bazar. Its elevation makes it relatively cool and the countryside and surrounding hills are good for gentle treks. There is an old fort on a hill as well as a magnificent palace on a hillock in the centre with murals illustrating the fine local school of miniature painting. Raghosagar lake, which is very pleasant to walk around, has an island with a romantic ruined temple and tombs (poor monsoons for three years had left the lake dry in 2001). It attracts numerous migratory birds and is an attractive setting for the charming 200-year-old palace, *Gokal Vilas*, the home of the present Rawat Saheb Nahar Singhji and the Ranisahiba. Their two sons have opened the renovated 17th-century Deogarh Mahal Palace to guests. The Rawat, a knowledgeable historian and art connoisseur, has a private collection of over 200 paintings which guests may view.

★ **Deogarh**
2 km off the NH8 about half way between Ajmer & Udaipur Altitude: 700 m

Southern Rajasthan

Sleeping and eating A-B *Deogarh Mahal*, T02951-52555, F52777, deogarh1@ detainfosys.net.in, in superb old fort. 36 rooms, atmospheric suites furnished in traditional style with good views (the Raja's room – "like sleeping in a jewel box"), attached baths, excellent lotus shaped pool, jacuzzi, Mewari meals, home grown produce (room service 50% extra), bar, good gift shop, log fires, folk entertainment, boating, bird watching, jeep safaris, talks on art history, hospitable and delightful hosts. Outstanding hotel, highly recommended, reserve well ahead. *Devigarh*, a 7-storey fort palace (similar to Udaipur's City Palace) has been acquired by the Poddars, an industrial family of Shekhawati origin, and converted to a heritage hotel with modern facilities. **E** *Deogarh Motel* (RTDC), T02951-52011. 4 clean rooms with bath, reasonable refreshments.

Rajsamand Lake   At **Kankroli**, 56 km north of Udaipur on the NH8, is the Rajsamand Lake. The **Nauchoki Bund**, the embankment which contains it, is over 335-m long and 13-m high, with ornamental pavilions and toranas, all of marble and exquisitely carved. Behind the masonry bund is an 11-m wide earthen embankment, erected in 1660 by Rana Raj Singh who had defeated Aurangzeb on several occasions. Kankroli and its beautiful temple are on the southeast side of the lake.

Kumbhalgarh and its surroundings

Little known Kumbhalgarh (63 km from Udaipur) is one of the finest examples of defensive fortification in Rajasthan. You can wander round the palace, the many temples and along the walls to savour the great panoramic views. It is two hours north of Udaipur through the attractive Rajasthani countryside. The small fields are well kept, wherever possible irrigated from the streams, Persian wheels and 'tanks' that are dotted across the landscape. In winter, wheat and mustard grow in the fields, and the journey there and back is just as magical and fascinating as the fort itself. A round trip from Udaipur could also take in Eklingji, Nagda and Nathdwara, or be extended to Ghanerao and Ranakpur.

Eklingji   The white marble **Eklingji Temple** has a two-storey *mandapa* to Siva, the family deity of the Mewars. It dates from 734 AD but was rebuilt in the 15th century. *22 km from Udaipur*   There is a silver door and screen and a silver *nandi* facing the black marble Siva. The evenings draw crowds of worshippers and few tourists. ■ *0500-0700, 1000-1300 and 1700-1900. No photography.* Nearby is the large but simple **Lakulisa Temple** (972), and other ruined semi-submerged temples. The back street shops sell miniature paintings (see page 416). It is a peaceful spot attracting many waterbirds. ■ *Getting there: Occasional buses go from Udaipur to Eklingji (22 km) and Nagda which are set in a deep ravine containing the Eklingji Lake. RTDC run tours from Udaipur, 1400-1900.*

Heritage Resort is a pleasanter place to stay for seeing Udaipur

Sleeping and eating B *Heritage Resort*, T0294-440382, fabulously located by the lake ringed by hills. Excellent a/c rooms, contemporary building in traditional design, good food, pool, boating, riding, good walking and cycling. Recommended. **F** *Guest House*, very basic.

Nagda   At Nagda, are three temples: the ruined 11th-century Jain temple of **Adbhutji** and the Vaishnavite **Sas-Bahu** ('Mother- in-law'/'Daughter-in-law') temples. The complex, though comparatively small, has some very intricate carving on pillars, ceiling and *mandapa* walls. You can hire bicycles in Eklingji to visit them.

This is a centre of the Krishna worshipping community of Gujarati merchants who are followers of Vallabhacharya (15th century). Non-Hindus are not allowed inside the temple which contains a black marble Krishna image, but the outside has interesting paintings. The **Shrinathji temple** is one of the richest Hindu temples in India. At one time only high caste Hindus (Brahmins, Kshatriyas) were allowed inside, and the **pichhwais** (temple hangings) were placed outside, for those castes and communities who were not allowed into the sanctum sanctorum, to experience the events in the temple courtyard and learn about the life of lord Krishna. You can watch the 400-year old tradition of pichhwai painting which originated here. The artists had accompanied the Maharana of Mewar, one of the few Rajput princes who still resisted the Mughals, who settled here when seeking refuge from Aurangzeb's attacks. Their carriage carrying the idol of Shrinathji was stuck at Nathdwara in Mewar, 60 km short of the capital Udaipur. Taking this as a sign that this was where God willed to have his home, they developed this into a pilgrim centre for the worship of lord Krishna's manifestation, Shrinathji. Their paintings, Pichhwais, depict Lord Krishna as Shrinathji in different moods according to the season. The figures of lord Krishna and the *gopis* (milkmaids) are frozen on a backdrop of lush trees and deep skies. The Bazar sells *pichchwais* painted on homespun cloth . with mineral and organic colour often fixed with starch.
■ *Getting there: Several buses from Udaipur from early morning.*

Nathdwara
48 km from Udaipur

Sleeping and eating   **C-D** *Pratap Palace* (Heritage Resort), 5 km from temple, rooms and suites with hot water and Western toilets in a restored haveli, carved balconies, pool, gym, camel/jeep/horse safaris, treks, royal family run. **D-E** *Gokul* (RTDC), near Lalbagh, 2 km from bus stand, T02932-30917, 6 rooms and dorm (Rs 50), restaurant. **D-E** *Yatika* (RTDC), T02932-31119. 5 rooms and dorm (Rs 50).

★ Kumbhalgarh Fort

Kumbhalgarh Fort, off the beaten tourist track, was the second most important fort of the Mewar Kingdom after Chittaurgarh. Built mostly by Maharana Kumbha (circa 1485), it is situated on a west facing ridge of the Aravalli hills, commanding a great strategic position on the border between the Rajput kingdoms of Udaipur (Mewar) and Jodhpur (Marwar). It gives superb views over the lower land to the northwest, standing over 200 m above the pass leading via Ghanerao towards Udaipur.

Altitude: 1,087m

Passing though charming villages and hilly terrain, the route to the fort is very picturesque. The final dramatic approach is across deep ravines and through thick scrub jungle. Seven gates guarded the approaches while seven ramparts were reinforced by semicircular bastions and towers. The 36 km-long black walls with curious bulbous towers exude a feeling of power as they snake their way up and down impossibly steep terrain. They were built to defy scaling and their width enabled rapid deployment of forces. The walls enclose a large plateau containing the smaller Katargarh Fort with the decaying palace of Fateh Singh, a garrison, 365 temples and shrines, and a village. The occupants (reputedly 30,000) could be self-sufficient in food and water, with enough storage to last a year. The fort's dominant location enabled defenders to see aggressors approaching from a great distance. Kumbhalgarh is believed to have been taken only once and that was because the water in the ponds was poisoned by enemy Mughals during the reign of Rana Pratap.

The approach
It is accessible enough to make a visit practicable & getting there is half the fun

Southern Rajasthan

The gates The first gate **Arait Pol** is some distance from the main fort; the area was once thick jungle harbouring tigers and wild boar. Signals would be flashed by mirror in times of emergency. **Hulla Pol** (Gate of Disturbance) is named after the point reached by invading Mughal armies in 1567. **Hanuman Pol** contains a shrine and temple. The **Bhairava Pol** records the 19th-century Chief Minister who was exiled. The fifth gate, the **Paghra** (Stirrup) **Pol** is where the cavalry assembled; the Star tower nearby has walls 8-m thick. The **Top-Khana** (Cannon Gate) is alleged to have a secret escape tunnel. The last, **Nimbu** (Lemon) **Pol** has the Chamundi temple beside it.

The palace It is a 30-minute walk (fairly steep in parts) from the car park to the roof of the Maharana's darbar hall. Tiers of inner ramparts rise to the summit like a fairytale castle, up to the appropriately named **Badal Mahal** (19th century) or Palace in the Clouds, with the interior painted in pastel colours. Most of the empty palace is usually unlocked (a *chaukidar* holds the keys). The views over the walls to the jungle-covered hillsides (now a wildlife reserve) and across the deserts of Marwar towards Jodhpur, are stunning. The palace rooms are decorated in a 19th-century style and some have attractive coloured friezes, but are unfurnished. After the maze-like palace at Udaipur, this is very compact. The **Maharana's palace** has a remarkable blue darbar hall with floral motifs on the ceiling. Polished *chunar* – lime – is used on walls and window sills, but the steel ceiling girders give away its late 19th-century age. A gap separated the *mardana* (men's) palace from the *zenana* (women's) palace. Some of the rooms in the *zenana* have an attractive painted frieze with elephants, crocodiles and camels. A circular Ganesh temple is in the corner of the *zenana* courtyard. A striking feature of the toilets was the ventilation system which allowed fresh air into the room while the toilet was in use. ■ *US$5 (some feel it is not worth the money).*

Other temples The **Neelkantha, Kumbhaswami temples** and Raimal's *chhatri* nearby, are worth visiting. The **Mahadeva Temple** (1458) in a gorge below contains black marble slabs inscribed with the history of Mewar.

Kumbhalgarh Wildlife Sanctuary The sanctuary to the west of the fort covering about 600 sq km has a sizeable wildlife population but you have to be extremely lucky to spot any big game in the thick undergrowth. Some visitors have seen bear, panther, wolf and hyena but most have to be contented with seeing nilgai, sambhar deer, wild boar, jackal, jungle cat, and birds (grey jungle fowl, red spurfowl, grey hornbill, painted francolin, quails, flycatchers, woodpeckers). Crocodiles and water fowl can be seen at Thandi Beri Lake. Jeep and horse safaris can be organized from several hotels in the vicinity including *Aodhi*, Ranakpur, Ghanerao, Narlai. The rides can be quite demanding as the tracks are very rough. A small patch of the sanctuary facing the temple has been set aside for deer in an enclosure. There is a four-wheel drive jeep track, and a trekking trail through the safari area can be arranged through Shivika Lake Hotel, Ranakpur (see below). Spotted deer and nilgai are easily seen, plus plenty of birdlife. Panthers sometimes trespass in to hunt young animals. You can good views from the hilltop.

The tribal Bhils and Garasias (the latter found only in this belt) can be seen here, living in their traditional huts. The Forest Department may permit an overnight stay in their *Rest House.* **Kelwara** Village, 6 km from the fort is attractive, with steep, narrow streets devoid of cars.

Sleeping A *Aodhi* (HRH), isolated, 2 km from fort gate, T02954-42341, F42349. 26 renovated rooms, modern stone 'cottages' (hot water bottles in bed), heaters in winter, Room 19 recommended (after a long climb "spacious, double bed size window seat, views of pool from on high"), good restaurant (a fine meal when Udaipur Maharana is in residence, pool for the really hardy only in winter, disastrous laundry, very helpful staff , TCs exchanged, fabulous views, very quiet, superb horse safaris (US$200 per night), trekking, tribal village tours. Highly recommended. **B** *Kumbhalgarh Fort*, en route Kelwara to Kumbhalgarh, T02954-42057, 24 rooms with modern facilities, superb location with hill, lake and valley views, garden, tented dining area, bar, exchange, pool, cycle hire, riding. **C** *Ratnadeep*, Kelwara, in the middle of a bustling village, T02954-42217, F42340. 8 clean rooms, some a/c, modern with TV, Western toilets, small lawn, camel, horse and jeep safaris. **D** *Forest Department Guest House*, near the Parsram Temple, about 3 km by road and 3 km off the road (access by 4WD jeep or trek) from Aodhi. Basic facilities but some fantastic views. Worth a visit for the views over the Kumbalgarh sanctuary towards the drylands of Marwar which rival if not surpass the ones from the fort. **F** *Government Rest Houses* and school hostels nearby may have rooms available.

Eating Expensive *Aodhi*, thatched restaurant with central barbecue area. Good Indian (try *laal maas*, a mutton dish), wide choice, authentic 7-course Mewari meal but service can be very slow. **Mid-range** *Ratnadeep*, a la carte veg menu. **Cheap** A shack makes tea and sells chocolates, film rolls, mineral water, biscuits near the fort gate.

Transport From Udaipur, a **taxi** for 4, Rs 900, can cover the fort and Ranakpur in 11 hrs; very worthwhile. For the fort: **buses** (irregular times) from Chetak Circle, Udaipur go to **Kelwara**, Rs 20, 3 hrs (cars take 2 hrs); from there a local bus (Rs 2) can take you a further 4 km up to a car park; the final 2 km climb is on foot; the return is a pleasant downhill walk of 1 hr. **Jeep taxis** charge Rs 50-100 from Kelwara to the fort (and say there are no buses). Return buses to Jaipur from Kelwara until 1730.

Ghanerao

Ghanerao with its red sandstone *havelis* has a number of old temples, *baolis* and marble *chhatris*, 5 km beyond the Reserve, was founded in 1606 by Gopal Das Rathore of the Mertia clan. The village lay at the entrance to one of the few passes through the Aravallis between the territories held by the Rajput princes of Jodhpur and Udaipur. The beautiful 1606 castle has marble pavilions, courtyards, faded paintings, wells, elephant stables and walls marked with canon balls. The present Thakur Sajjan Singh who has opened his castle to guests, organizes two to three day treks to Kumbhalgarh Fort, 18 km (50 km by jeepable road) and Ranakpur temples.

The **Mahavir Jain Temple**, 5 km away, is a beautiful little 10th-century temple. It is a delightful place to experience an unspoiled rural environment.

Sleeping and eating C *Royal Castle*, Ghanerao, Dist Pali, T02934-84035 (or T0294-561849). Decidedly rustic 'castle', 20 simple rooms with renovated baths (geysers), pricey **B** suites, restaurant (simple food), bit run down but has nostalgic appeal of faded glory, charming hosts, expensive local guide (bargain hard if buying paintings), jeeps and camping arranged. **C** *Kotri Rawla*, T02934-6324 (or T0294-560822), 8 rooms, 2 suites in 17th-century royal 'bungalow', excellent horse safaris, run by thakur Mahendra Singh, an expert on Marwari horses and his son, a well known polo player. **D** *Ajit Bagh*, near Ghanerao, a walled orchard with 5 pleasant cottages, unfortunately now very run down; 4 km from castle, **E** *Bagha-ka-Bagh* (Tiger's Den). Spartan hunting lodge among tall grass jungle near wildlife sanctuary gate, 10 very basic rooms, 5 with bucket hot water, dorm, generator for electricity, breathtaking location, wildlife (including panther, nilgai), rich birdlife, 5 day treks including Kumbhalgarh, Ranakpur. Contact *North West Safaris*, T/F079-6560962, ssibal@ad1.vsnl.net.in

Rawla Narlai
25 km from Kumbhalgarh Fort
1 hr's drive from Ranakpur

This Hindu and Jain religious centre has a 17th-century fort with interesting architecture, right in the heart of the village, which is ideal for a stop over. **C** *Fort Rawla Narlai*, T02934-82425, has 18 rooms individually decorated with antiques in the renovated fort, new showers, good simple meals under the stars, helpful, friendly staff, attractive garden setting, good riding, contact, *Ajit Bhawan*, T0291-511410.

★ Ranakpur
Colour map 4, grid B1
90 km from Udaipur
25 km SW of Kumbhalgarh.
A visit here is highly recommended

Shoes & socks must be removed at the entrance (no tips)

You can approach Ranakpur through the wildlife reserve in 1½ hours. One of five holy Jain sites and a popular pilgrimage centre, it has one of the best known Jain temple complexes in the country. Though not comparable to the Dilwara temples in Mount Abu, it has very fine ornamentation and is in a wonderful setting with peacocks, langurs and numerous birds. The semi-enclosed deer park with spotted deer, nilgai and good birdlife next to the temple, attracts the odd panther!

The **Adinatha** (1439), the most noteworthy of the three main temples here, is dedicated to the first Tirthankar. The sanctuary is symmetrically planned around the central shrine and is within a 100-m sq raised terrace enclosed in a high wall with 66 subsidiary shrines lining it, each with a spire; the gateways consist of triple-storey porches. The sanctuary with a clustered centre tower contains a *chaumukha* (four-fold) marble image of Adinatha. The whole, including the extraordinary array of engraved pillars (1,444, and all different), carved ceilings and arches are intricately decorated, often with images of Jain saints, friezes of scenes from their lives and holy sites. The beautiful lace-like interiors of the corbelled domes are a superb example of western Indian temple style. The **Parsvanatha** and **Neminath** are two smaller Jain temples facing this, the former with a black image of Parsvanatha in the sanctuary and erotic carvings outside. The star-shaped **Surya Narayana Temple** (mid-15th century) is nearby.
■ *Daily; closes for lunch about 1300 when the dharamshala serves very good food. Non-Jains may visit the Adinatha only between 1100 and 1700 except lunchtime. Black clothing is not permitted. The head priest, 'a very busy man', helps to show people around. Photos (1200-1700) with permission from Kalyanji Anandji Trust office next to the temple, camera Rs 40, video Rs 150 photography of the principal Adinatha image is prohibited. Unofficial 'guide' may ask for baksheesh.*

Sleeping **B** *Ranakpur Hotel* (HRH), on the highway near the temple, T0294-528008, F528006. A new resort style hotel and restaurant with comfortable rooms. **B** *Maharani Bagh* (WelcomHeritage), Ranakpur Rd (4 km north), Sadri, T02934-3705, marwar@del3.vsnl.net.in 19 well-furnished modern bungalows with baths in lovely 19th-century walled orchard of Jodhpur royal family full of bougainvillaea and mangos, outdoor Rajasthani restaurant (traditional Marwari meals Rs 300), pool, jeep safaris, horse riding. **C** *Shivika Lake Hotel*, near the lake in pleasant jungle setting. 8 simple but comfortable rooms with baths, hot water (Rs 750), 2 tents with shared bath (Rs 450), cottages planned, delicious Rajasthani food, views of lake and wooded hills, treks, excellent jeep safaris with spotter guide in Kumbhalgarh sanctuary (Rs 350; discount if you see nothing!), camping trips, personal attention, friendly and cheerful hosts. Reservations: *North West Safaris* T079-6302019, F6300962, ssibal@ad1.vsnl.net.in **D-E** *Hotel Castle*, cottage rooms in a pretty jungle setting, moderately priced lunch stop en route. **D-E** *Shilpi* (RTDC), on a hillock, T02934-3674. 12 cleanish rooms, best with hot water, dorm (dirty), veg meals. **F** *Dharamshala*, with some comfortable rooms, simple and extremely cheap veg meals.

Eating None near the temple, only tea stall, but decent, cheap lunches (Rs 10-15), around noon for lunch, before sunset for dinner. *Roopam*, Ranakpur-Maharani Bagh road, near *Shivika*. Good Rajasthani food. Pleasant village theme setting, modern facilities, popular. *Shivika Lake*, part open-air restaurant by lake with hill views. Delicious Rajasthani lunches (Rs 150-250) non-spicy curries possible, barbecued chicken, excellent breakfasts, tea by the lake, family run, shabby but clean. The temple serves decent meals (Rs 15) around noon and just before sunset.

Transport Road Bus: From **Udaipur**, 6 daily (0530-1600), slow, 4 hrs from **Jodhpur** (doesn't stop long enough to see the temples so break your journey here) and **Mount Abu**. **Train**: Palna Junction on the Ajmer-Mount Abu line is 39 km away.

★ Mount Abu

Mount Abu, Rajasthan's only hill resort, away from the congestion and traffic of the tourist centres on the plains, stretches along a 20-km long plateau. Many of the rulers from surrounding princely states had summer houses built here. Today, it draws visitors from Rajasthan and neighbouring Gujarat who come to escape the searing heat of summer and also to see the exquisite Dilwara Jain temples. There is attractive countryside to explore as it is well wooded with flowering trees with numerous orchids during the monsoon and a good variety of birdlife.

*Phone code: 02974
Colour map 3, grid B5
Population: 15,600
(swells considerably during season)
Altitude: 1,720 m
Winters can be cold*

Getting there The nearest railway station is at Abu Road, 27 km away. It is often quicker to take a bus that will go all the way to Mount Abu, instead of going to Abu Road by train and then taking a bus up the hill. **Getting around** The compact area by Nakki lake with several hotels, restaurants and shops, is pedestrianized. Taxis are available at a stand nearby to get you to more distant hotels and also visit the Dilwara Temples if you don't feel up to the uphill hike.

Ins & outs
See page 214 for further details

Mount Abu was the home of the legendary sage **Vasishtha**. One day Nandini, his precious wish-fulfilling cow, fell into a great lake. Vasishtha requested the gods in the Himalaya to save her so they sent *Arbuda*, a cobra, who carried a rock on his head and dropped it into the lake, displacing the water, and so saved Nandini. The place became known as Arbudachala, the 'Hill of Arbuda'. Vasishtha also created the four powerful 'fire-born' Rajput tribes, including the houses of Jaipur and Udaipur at a ritual fire ceremony on the mount. **Nakki Talao** (Lake), sacred to Hindus, was, in legend, scooped out by fingernails (*nakki*) of gods attempting to escape the wrath of a demon.

Background

Abu was leased by the British Government from the Maharao of Sirohi and was used as the HQ for the Resident of Rajputana until 1947, and as a sanatorium for troops. There are rowing boats for hire and a pleasant walk around the lake past the Raghunath Temple. The Toad Rock is here too; the other rock formations (Nandi and Camel) are not as obvious. A local curiosity is a *baba gari* (a sort of pram), which is used as a small cart to transport goods, and occasionally children!

Sights

★ Dilwara Jain Temples

A notice warns 'Any lady in monthly cycle if enters any of the temples she may suffer'! Leather items not allowed.

5 km from town centre

Set in beautiful surroundings of mango trees and wooded hills, the temples have superb marble carvings. The complex of five principal temples is surrounded by a high wall, dazzling white in the sunlight. There is a resthouse for pilgrims on the approach road. **Chaumukha temple**, the grey sandstone three-storey building, is approached through the entrance on your left. Combining 13th- and 15th-century styles, it is generally regarded as inferior to the two main temples. The colonnaded hall (ground floor) contains four-faced images of the Tirthankar Parsvanatha (hence *chaumukha*), and figures of *dikpalas* and *yakshis*. Along the entrance avenue on the right is a statue of Ganesh.

Adinatha Temple (Vimala Shah Temple) lies directly ahead; the oldest and most famous of the Dilwara group. Immediately outside the entrance to the Temple is a small portico known as the *Hastishala* (elephant hall), built by Prithvipal in 1147-59 which contains a figure of the patron, **Vimala Shah**, the Chief Minister of the Solanki King, on horseback. Vimala Shah commissioned the temple dedicated to Adinatha in 1031-32. The riders on the 10 beautifully carved elephants that surround him were removed during Alauddin Khilji's reign. Dilwara belonged to Saivite Hindus who were unwilling to part with it until Vimala Shah could prove that it had once belonged to a Jain community. In a dream, the goddess **Ambika** (Ambadevi or Durga) instructed him to dig under a *champak* tree where he found a huge image of Adinatha and so won the land. To the southwest, behind the hall, is a small shrine to *Ambika*, once the premier deity. ■ *1200-1800 for non-Jains. Cameras Rs 5.*

In common with many Jain temples the plain exterior conceals an wonderfully ornately carved interior. It is an early example of the Jain style in West India, set within a rectangular court lined with small shrines and a double colonnade. The white marble of which the entire temple is built was brought not from Makrana, as many guidebooks suggest, but from the relatively nearby

Dilwara Temples, Mount Abu

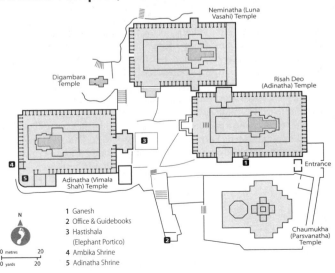

Neminatha (Luna Vasahi) Temple

Digambara Temple

Risah Deo (Adinatha) Temple

Adinatha (Vimala Shah) Temple

Entrance

Chaumukha (Parsvanatha) Temple

N

0 metres 20
0 yards 20

1 Ganesh
2 Office & Guidebooks
3 Hastishala (Elephant Portico)
4 Ambika Shrine
5 Adinatha Shrine

marble quarries of **Ambaji** in Gujarat, 25 km south of Abu Road. Hardly a surface is left unadorned. *Makaras* guard the entrance, and below them are conches. The cusped arches and ornate capitals are beautifully designed and superbly made.

Lining the walls of the main hall are 52 shrines. Architecturally, it is suggested that these are related to the cells which surround the walls of Buddhist monasteries, but in the Jain temple are reduced in size to house simple images of a seated Jain saint. Although the carving of the images themselves is simple, the ceiling panels in front of the saints' cells are astonishingly ornate. Going clockwise round the cells, some of the more important ceiling sculptures illustrate: **Cell 1** lions, dancers and musicians; **2-7** people bringing offerings, birds, music making; **8** Jain teacher preaching; **9** the major auspicious events in the life of the Tirthankars; and **10** Neminath's life, including his marriage, and playing with Krishna and the gopis. In the southeast corner of the temple between cells **22** and **23** is a large black idol of Adinath, reputedly installed by Vimal Shah in 1031.

By cell **32** Krishna is shown subduing Kaliya Nag, half human and half snake, and other Krishna scenes; **38**, the 16 armed goddess Vidyadevi (goddess of knowledge); **46-48** 16 armed goddesses, including the goddess of smallpox, Shitala Mata; and **49** Narasimha, the 'man-lion' tearing open the stomach of the demon Hiranya-Kashyapa, surrounded by an opening lotus.

As in Gujarati Hindu temples, the main hall focuses on the sanctum which contains the 2½ m image of **Adinatha**, the first Tirthankar. The sanctum with a pyramidal roof has a vestibule with entrances on three sides. To its east is the *Mandapa*, a form of octagonal nave nearly 8 m in diameter. Its 6-m wide dome is supported by eight slender columns; the exquisite lotus ceiling carved from a single block of marble, rises in eleven concentric circles, carved with elaborately repeated figures. Superimposed across the lower rings are sixteen brackets carved in the form of the goddesses of knowledge.

Risah Deo Temple, opposite the Vimala Visahi, is unfinished. It encloses a huge brass Tirthankar image weighing 4.3 tonnes and made of *panchadhatu* (five metals) – gold, silver, copper, brass and zinc. The temple was commenced in the late 13th century by Brahma Shah, the Mewari Maharana Pratap's chief minister. Building activity was curtailed by war with Gujarat and never completed.

Luna Vasihi or **Neminatha Temple** (1231) to the north of the Adinatha Temple, was erected by two wealthy merchants Vastupala and Tejapala, and dedicated to the 22nd Tirthankar; they also built a similar temple at Girnar. The attractive niches on either side of the sanctum's entrance were for their wives. The craftsmanship in this temple is comparable to the Vimala Vasihi; the decorative carving and *jali* work are excellent. The small domes in front of the shrine containing the bejewelled Neminatha figure, the exquisitely carved lotus on the *sabhamandapa* ceiling and the sculptures on the colonnades are especially noteworthy.

There is a fifth temple for the **Digambar** ('sky-clad') Jains which is far more austere.

■ *Free (no photography). Shoes and cameras, leather items and backpacks (against tokens, Re 1 per item) are left outside; tip expected. 1200-1800 for non-Jains; some guides are excellent. It's a 1-hr uphill walk from town, or share a jeep, Rs 5 each. Good* masala chai *available nearby.*

Southern Rajasthan

Walks **Trevor's Tank**, 50 m beyond the Dilwara Jain temples, is the small wildlife sanctuary covering 289 sq km with the lake which acts as a watering hole for animals including sloth bear, sambhar, wild boar, panther. Most of these are nocturnal but on your walk you are quite likely to see a couple of crocodiles basking on the rocks. The birdlife is extensive with eagles, kites, grey jungle fowl, red spurfowl, francolin, flycatchers, bulbuls etc seen during walks on the trails in the sanctuary. There are superb views from the trails that lead through the park. *Rs 5. Car/jeep taken up to the lake Rs 125.*

Adhar Devi, 3 km from town, is a 15th-century Durga temple carved out of a rock and approached by 220 steep steps. There are steep treks to Anandra point or to a Mahadev temple nearby for great views.

Around Nakki Lake Honeymoon Point, and Sunset Point to the west, give superb views across the plains. They can both be reached by a pleasant walk from the bus stand (about 2 km). You can continue from Honeymoon Point to Limbdi House. If you have another 1½ hours, walk up to Jai Gurudev's meditation eyrie – gurus always choose good views! If you want to avoid the crowds at Sunset Point, take the Bailey's Walk from the Hanuman Temple near Honeymoon Point to Valley View Point which joins up with the Sunset Point walk. You can also walk from the Ganesh temple to the Crags for some great views.

Spiritual University movement The headquarters of the Spiritual University movement of the **Brahma kumaris** is **Om Shanti Bhavan** (T38268) with its ostentatious entrance on Subhash Rd. You may notice many residents dressed in white taking a walk around the lake in the evening. It is possible to stay in simple but comfortable rooms with attached baths and attend discourses, meditation sessions, yoga lessons etc; good vegetarian meals are provided. The charitable trust runs several worthy institutions including a really good hospital.

Museums **Art Museum and Gallery** has a small collection which includes some textiles and stone sculptures (ninth to 10th centuries). ■ *1000-1700, closed Fri. Free. Raj Bhavan Rd.* The **Spiritual Museum**, near the pony stand by the lake, offers courses. ■ *0800-2000.*

Excursions The **Aravalli hills**, part of the subcontinent's oldest mountain range look more like rocky outcrops, in places quite barren save for date palms and thorny acacias. From Mount Abu it is possible to make day-treks to nearby spots.

Achalgarh (11 km) has superb views. The picturesque **Achaleshwar Temple** (ninth century) is believed to have Siva's toeprint, a brass Nandi and a deep hole claimed to reach into the underworld. On the side of Mandakini tank near the car park is an image of Adi Pal, the Paramara king and three large stone buffaloes pierced with arrows. In legend, the tank was once filled with *ghee* and the buffaloes (really demons in disguise), came every night to drink from it until they were shot by Adi Pal. A path leads up to a group of carved Jain temples (10-minutes' climb).

Guru Shikhar is the highest peak in the area (1,720 m) with a road almost to the top. It is about 15 km from Mount Abu and taxis take about an hour. To get to the small Vishnu temple you need to climb 300 steps or hire a palanquin. Good views especially at dawn. There is an RTDC *Café* and *chai stalls*.

Gaumukh (Cow's Mouth), 8 km southeast, is on the way to Abu Rd. A small stream flows from the mouth of a marble cow. There is also a Nandi bull, and the tank is believed to be the site of Vasishtha's fire from which the four great Rajput clans were created. An image of the sage is flanked by ones of Rama and Krishna.

The **Arbuda Devi Temple** carved out of the rocky hillside is also worth walking to for the superb views over the hills.

Rajasthan Tourism, T3129, and Rajasthan SRTC, T3434, run daily tours to Dilwara, Achalgarh, Guru Shikhar, Nakki Lake, Sunset Point, Adhar Devi and Om Shanti Bhavan, 0830-1300, 1330-1900, Rs 80. *Gujarat, Maharajah and Green Travels* also offer similar tours for Rs 40-60; Ambaji-Kumbhairyaji tours Rs 120.

Essentials

Prices (as given) shoot up during Diwali, Christmas week and summer (20 Apr to 20 Jun) when many **D-F** hotels triple their rates; meals, and ponies and jeeps cost a lot more too. Off-season discounts of between 30 and 50% are usual, sometimes even 70% in mid-winter. **A-B** *Cama Rajputana Club Resort* (Heritage), T38205, F38412. Refurbished old club house (1895) for Mount Abu's royal and British residents, guests become temporary members, 40 rooms in split level cottages with views, 2 period suites, lounge with fireplaces and old club furniture, average restaurant (Gujarati flavour to western dishes),

Sleeping
■ on map, page 212
Price codes:
see inside front cover

Touts can be a nuisance to budget travellers at the bus stand

Mount Abu

Southern Rajasthan

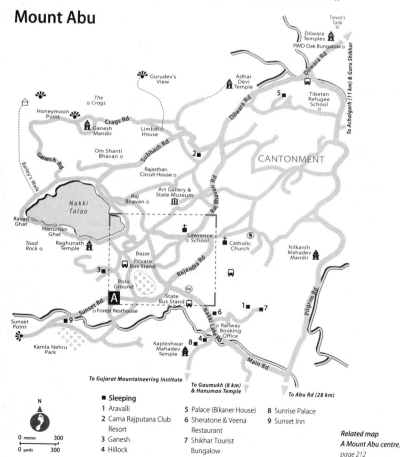

■ Sleeping
1 Aravalli
2 Cama Rajputana Club Resort
3 Ganesh
4 Hillock
5 Palace (Bikaner House)
6 Sheraton & Veena Restaurant
7 Shikhar Tourist Bungalow
8 Sunrise Palace
9 Sunset Inn

Related map
A Mount Abu centre,
page 212

eco-friendly (recycled water, alternative energy, drip irrigation), beautifully landscaped gardens, billiards, tennis etc, efficient service, T079-5503565. **A-B** *Hillock*, opposite petrol pump, T38463, F38467. 36 rooms, restaurant, exchange, garden, modern, small pool, clean and well presented if slightly anonymous. **A-B** *Hilltone*, set back from road near petrol pump, T38391, F38395. 68 rooms (some a/c, heaters), good Handi (a style of cooking using baking/steaming in covered pots) restaurant, exchange, pool, garden, quiet, one of the most popular of the modern hotels.

B *Connaught House* (WelcomHeritage), Rajendra Marg, uphill opposite bus stand, T38560. British resident of Jodhpur's colonial bungalow, 14 pleasantly old fashioned rooms (royal memorabilia), modern rooms in quieter new cottage, comfortable place to stay, restaurant (average a la carte, good Rajasthani meals on order for Rs 200), trekking with guide (Rs 2000+), gardens filled with birds, interesting old retainer of the Jodhpur family full of tales, efficient management, reservations: T011-6561875, F6868994, welcom@ndf.vsnl.net.in **B** *Palace Hotel* (Heritage), Bikaner House, Dilwara Rd, 3 km from centre, T38673, F38674. 38 large renovated rooms with period and reproduction furniture in Swinton Jacob's imposing 1894 hunting lodge, also new annexe, atmospheric public rooms, grand dining hall (good English breakfast, Rajasthani meals with game dishes, memorable a la carte; expensive set menu), tennis etc, distinctively civilized character but large complex with average service, very quiet, set in sprawling grounds and backdrop of hills (bears come searching for honey combs at night!). **B-C** *Sunrise Palace*, Bharatpur Kothi, near petrol pump, T43573, F38775. 16 large rooms in a grand building though a bit musty (could do with a clean), good small restaurant, open-air barbecue, converted mansion, elevated with excellent views over town.

Mount Abu centre

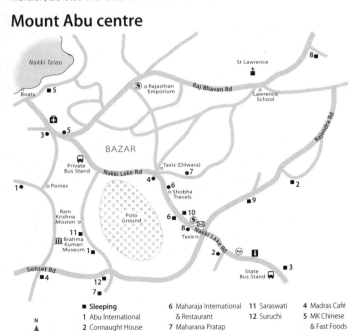

■ Sleeping	6 Maharaja International	11 Saraswati	4 Madras Café
1 Abu International	& Restaurant	12 Suruchi	5 MK Chinese
2 Connaught House	7 Maharana Pratap		& Fast Foods
3 Hilltone Madhuban &	8 Mount	● **Eating**	6 Neelam
Tourist Guest House	9 Rajendra	1 Haveli	7 Sher-e-Punjab
4 Kesar Bhavan Palace	10 Samrat International	2 Kanak	8 Veena
5 Lake View	& Navjivan	3 King's Food	

C *Chacha Inn*, T43374, F38624. Attractive though a bit brash, with lots of artefacts on display, 22 good rooms with modern facilities, 6 a/c, some with balconies offering hill views, restaurant, bar, exchange, garden, log fires on request, car parking. **C** *Kesar Bhavan Palace*, Sunset Rd, facing polo ground, T38647. 19th-century residence of the Sirohi royal family (Mt Abu's oldest royal property), renovated rooms in main palace and 10 attractive rooms with period furniture in stable wing, comfortable, modernized, balconies good views, western breakfast, meals brought in to order, family run, environment friendly (energy saving devices), T07965-60962, F02712-23729. **C** *Aravalli* opposite RTDC's *Shikhar*, T43316. 40 rooms (12 in cottages, 10 in new wing) on different levels with hill views, restaurant, very well maintained, landscaped terraced garden, pool, gym, good off-season discount. **C** *Madhuban*, near the bus stand, T38822, F38900, hotmadhuban@yahoo.com 10 spacious, clean rooms with tiny marble baths, room service food, good discounts. **C** *Sunset Inn*, Sunset Rd, 1 km centre, T43194, F43515. 40 spacious rooms, some a/c, modern facilities, veg restaurant, outdoor dining, garden, wooded site, pleasant atmosphere, popular. **C** *Suruchi Hill Resort*, opposite Polo ground, T43577, F38573. 43 good rooms (some a/c), attached baths, simple and clean with TV and phone, vegetarian restaurant, 70% off-peak discount. **C-D** *Shikhar* (RTDC), elevated above the petrol pump, T38129. 82 simple rooms with bath (Rs 400-1200), some 'deluxe' in annexe and good value cottages (avoid old rooms), dorm, Indian restaurant, bar, garden, pretty views but stiff climb up.

D *Abu International*, opposite polo ground, T38177. 43 rooms, simple, clean, Indian restaurant. **D** *Lake Palace*, facing lake, T37254, F38817. 13 rooms (some a/c), garden restaurant, beautifully situated with great lake views from terrace, rear access to hill road for Dilwara. Recommended. **D** *Maharaja International*, near Bus Stand, T43161, F38637. 53 comfortable rooms with hot shower, good restaurant, galleries with views, friendly staff, travel ticketing. **D** *Maharana Pratap*, tucked away off the main road near Polo ground, T38667. Rooms with attached baths, modern facilities, big off-season discounts. **D** *Mount*, Dilwara Rd, T38150. 7 rooms with unmodernized bath in a British officer's bungalow, charm very faded, none too clean. **D** *Samrat International*, near bus stand, T43173, F38467. 50 rooms, *Takshila* veg restaurant, exchange, travel, shares reception area with slightly cheaper **D** *Navjivan*, T38153. **D-E** *Sheratone*, near Bus Stand, T43544. 40 rooms, modern hotel, clean, characterless, but enthusiastic owner.

E *Ganesh*, west of the polo ground, uphill behind Brahma Kumari, T43591. Simple rooms, plenty of hot water, very quiet, helpful owner. **E** *Lake View*, beautiful location on a slope facing the Lake, T38659. 15 rather shabby rooms with Indian wc, odd bug/mouse problem overcome by helpful and friendly staff. **E** *Mamta Palace*, Sunset Rd, T43356, F37110. Rooms on several floors in an uninspiring building but clean and comfortable with baths (hot showers), TV and phone; excellent value. **E** *Saraswati*, west of Polo Ground, T38887. 36 rooms (some with balconies), better in annexe, good views from upstairs, simple, clean, large rooms with bath and hot water, Indian meals, other guests often noisy. **F** *Arbuda*, Nakki Lake Rd, T43358. Rooms with Indian wc, fairly clean though a little musty smelling, well-maintained restaurant (*thalis* vegetarian Punjabi/Chinese). **F** *Rajendra*, Rajendra Rd (from bus stand, turn right at post office), T38174. Well designed, clean rooms with bath (bucket hot water), thalis, huge balcony, friendly management.

List of families taking paying guests from tourist information, or ask at Connaught House (above)

Gujaratis visit Mount Abu in large numbers, some come to escape the state's prohibition on alcohol. **Expensive** *Handi* at *Hilltone Hotel*. Gujarati, Punjabi, Western. Plenty of choice, very comfortable but pricey, open 0900-2300. This, and other large hotels have bars. **Mid-range** *Neelam*, near bus stand. Indian meals (Rs 50-75), Chinese dishes, Western snacks. *Shere-e-Punjab*, among the best in town for veg/non veg

Eating
● *on map, page 212*
Price codes:
see inside front cover

Southern Rajasthan

Indian (also some Chinese/western). **Cheap** Small roadside stalls sell tasty local vegetarian food. You can also get good *thalis* (Rs 30-40) at simple restaurants but nightmar-
ish service as they are unused to foreigners. *Bhavani*, by the bus stand. Good for
daal-bhatti-choorma, Rajasthani snacks and *rabri*. *Kanak* and *Purohit*, near Bus Stand.
Great Gujarati *thalis* and South Indian snacks (Rs 30-50). Quick service, popular. *King's
Food*, near *MK*, Nakki Lake Rd. Very popular for North Indian veg meal (Rs 40); also Chinese and South Indian, western snacks. *Madras Café*, Nakki Lake Rd. Indian. Veg 'hot
dog', *thalis*, juices, real coffee and milk shakes in a garden, meals indoors. *Maharaja*,
near bus stand. Gujarati. Simple, clean, produces excellent value *thalis*. *MK* on the
lakeside. Clean tables but a bit musty smelling, non-veg meals (Rs 100), Western
snacks. *Uncle Fast Food*, Raj Bhawan Rd. Fresh and cheap snacks, immaculately clean.
Veena near taxi stand. Brews real coffee, serves traditional Indian meals and a few
Western favourites, very clean, outdoors, loud music.

Festivals An annual *Summer Festival*, **1-3 Jun**, features folk music, dancing, fireworks etc.
Diwali is especially colourful.

Shopping Readymade Indian clothing and silver jewellery are particularly good value.
Shopping is less *Saurashtra* and *Rajasthan* emporia, Raj Bhavan Rd, opposite the bus stand. *Khadi*
hassle here than in *Gramudyog*, opposite pony hire. Handloom fabric, carved agate boxes, marble figures.
the tourist towns; *Chacha Museum*. Good metal, wood, stone crafts, paintings and odd curios (fixed
most are open price but may give a discount). *Roopali*, near Nakki Lake, has silver jewellery.
0900-2100 daily For *Garasia* tribal jewellery try stalls near the GPO.

Sports **Mountain sports** For rock climbing, rapelling, contact Mountaineering institute,
near *Gujarat Bhawan Hostel*. Equipment and guide/instructors are available.
Swimming, **tennis**, **billiards** Non-residents can pay to use facilities at the *Cama
Rajputana* and *Bikaner House Palace* hotels.

Transport **Local** Toll on entering town, Rs 5 per head. **Bus**: For Dilwara and/or Achalgarh; check
time. **Baba garis**: To Sunset Point, Rs 50-60. **Pony hire**: Short rides from Rs 5. **Taxi and
jeep**: With posted fares for sightseeing; about Rs 700 per day; anywhere in town Rs 30;
to Sunset Point Rs 50.

Frequent rockfalls **Long distance Air** The nearest airport is at Udaipur. **Road Bus**: State Bus Stand,
during the monsoon Main Rd (opposite Tourist Office); Private Bus Stand, north of Polo Ground (towards
makes the road from Lake). To **Abu Rd**: hourly bus (45 mins-1 hr) Rs 10. **Ahmadabad**: several (7 hrs, Rs 100)
Mount Abu via Palanpur for Bhuj (3 hrs); **Delhi**: overnight. **Jaipur** (overnight, 9 hrs), **Jodhpur** am
hazardous; avoid and pm (6 hrs). **Mumbai, Pune**: early morning (18 hrs). **Udaipur**: 0830, 1500, 2200 (5-6
night journeys hrs, Rs 80). **Vadodara**: 0930, 1930 (5 hrs). *Shobha* and *Gujarat Travels* run private buses.
Taxi (for sharing) **Abu Rd** Rs 250; **Dilwara** stand is near the bazar. **Train** Western Rly
Out Agency near Petrol Pump has a small reservation quota, 0900-1600, Sun
0900-1230. Book onward reservations well in advance; you may have to wait 2-3 days
even in the off-season. Abu Rd is the railhead with frequent buses to Mount Abu.
To **Ahmadabad**: *Ashram Exp, 2916*, 0423, 3½ hrs; *Ahmadabad Mail, 9106*, 1305, 4½ hrs;
Aravali Exp, 69708, 1615, 4½ hrs (continues to Mumbai, further 8½hrs). **Jaipur**: *Aravalli
Exp, 9707*, 1110, 9 hrs; *Ahmadabad-Delhi Mail, 9105*, 1430, 9 hrs. **Jodhpur**: *Ranakpur
Exp, 4708*, 0440, 5½ hrs; *Surya Nagri Exp, 4846*, 0150, 5½ hrs. **Delhi**: *Ahmadabad Delhi
Mail, 9105*, 1430, 15¾ hrs; *Ashram Exp, 2915*, 2123, 13¾ hrs.

Directory **Banks** *State Bank of India*, Raj Bhavan Rd. Terrible rate so come prepared. **Communications GPO:** is on Raj Bhavan Rd. **Tourist offices and travel agents** *Rajasthan
Tourism*, opposite bus stand, T38151. 0800-1100, 1600-2000 (1000-1330, 1400-1700

off-season), **guides** 4-8 hrs, about Rs 250-400. *Shobha Travels*, T38302, and *Gujarat Travels*, Main Bazaar.

Around Mount Abu

Sheoganj has a major textile market for Rajasthani bridal dresses, sarees etc. **Sheoganj**
You can stay at **C-D** *Woodland Hotel* by the Jawai River (dry except in monsoon) on the highway but with views of Jawai river and rock formations.
There are 21 rooms, most a/c, modern comforts, Indian restaurant
(non-vegetarian on request) jeep safari (panthers, nilgai, hyena etc), camel
rides, campfires on sand dunes ('for a glimpse of desert scapes'), cultural
programmes. **Mansarovar** has a **E-F** *Midway Motel* with decent rooms and
cheap food.

The **Sirohi** royal family set up Mount Abu and later leased it to the British.
Just south of Sirohi is a large zinc smelting factory, while across to the east can
be seen the almost camouflaged walls of a fort, another in the chain which
marked the borders of Marwar and Mewar territory.

The large panther population in the surrounding hills of Bera and the Jawai **Bera**
River area draws wildlife photographers. Antelopes and jackals also inhabit the *34 km from Sirohi*
area. Visit the **Jawai Dam** (150 km from Mt Abu towards Jodhpur) to see historic embankments, numerous birds and basking marsh crocodiles. A bed for
the night is provided by **A** *Leopard's Lair* in a colourful Raika village near the
lake and fine jungle. T02933-43478. There are seven a/c rooms in well designed
stone cottages, modern amenities, delicious meals included (fresh fish from
lake), bar, pool, garden, riding (horse, camel), birdwatching, panther viewing
'safaris' with owner. ■ *Getting there: Trains from Mumbai and Ajmer via Abu Rd
(Aravalli and Ranakpur Exp) stop at Jawai Dam and Mori Bera.*

Jalor is an **historic citadel**. In the early 14th century, during court intrigues, **Jalor**
the Afghani Diwan of Marwar, Alauddin Khilji, took over the town and set up *160 km N of*
his own kingdom. Later, the Mughal emperor Akbar captured it and returned *Mount Abu*
the principality to his allies, the Rathores of Marwar by means of a peaceful
message to the Jalori Nawabs, who moved south to Palanpur in Gujarat. The
medieval fort straddles a hill near the main bazaar and encloses Muslim,
Hindu and Jain shrines. It is a steep climb up but the views from the fort are
rewarding. The old Topkhana at the bottom of the fortified hill has a a mosque
built by Alauddin Khilji using sculptures from a Hindu temple. Of particular
interest are the scores of domes in different shapes and sizes, the symmetry of
the columns and the delicate arches. Jalor bazaar is good for handicrafts, silver
jewellery and textiles, and is still relatively unaffected by tourist pricing.

Bhenswada is a small, colourful village on the Jawai river, 16 km east of Jalor. It **Bhenswada**
has another Rajput country estate whose 'castle' with a Hawa Mahal, Zenana
Chowk and Sirai Mahal, has been converted into an attractive hotel. The jungles and hills nearby have panther, nilgai, chinkara, blackbuck, jungle cat,
jackal, porcupines and spiny tailed lizards. **C** *Rawla Bhenswada*,
T02978-22080, has 12 comfortable rooms with bath, painted exterior, attractive unique interiors (swings and silver settees for beds), inspired decor
('Badal Mahal' with cloud patterns, 'Hawa Mahal' with breezy terrace etc),
breakfast treats of masala cheese toast or vegetarian *parathas*, delicious
Marwari meals ("among the best in Rajasthan"), parakeet-filled orchards,
courtyard lawns, pool, interesting visits to Rabari herdsmen and Bhil tribal

hamlets, night safaris, hospitable family. Highly recommended. Reservations: *North West Safaris*, T079-6302019, F6300962, ssibal@ad1.vsnl.net.in
■ *Getting there: Trains and buses from Abu Rd.*

Bhinmal
95 km NW of Mount Abu

Bhinmal has some important archaeological ruins, notably one of the few shrines in the country to Varaha Vishnu. It is also noted for the quality of its leather embroided *mojdis*. Nearby at **Vandhara** is one of the few marble *baolis* (step wells) in India, while the historic **Soondha Mata** Temple is at a picturesque site where the green hills and barren sand dunes meet at a freshwater spring fed by a cascading stream. The Navratri festival is held in September.
■ *Getting there: Trains to Bhinmal: from Jodhpur, 1530, 2230 (4½ hrs); to Jodhpur, 0530, 2030, from Ahmadabad, 2130 (12 hrs); to Ahmadabad, 1940.*

Daspan
25 km N of Bhinmal

Daspan is a small village where the restored 19th-century castle built on the ruins of an old fort provides a break between Mount Abu and Jaisalmer. Special Navratri celebrations are held here. Yo can stay at **D** *Castle Durjan Niwas*, T02969-73523 (or T0291-616992, F616991), 11 rooms, pleasant open sitting areas, folk entertainment, very knowledgeable owners, camel rides (Rs 200 per hour; Rs 800 per day).

Western Rajasthan

7

Western Rajasthan

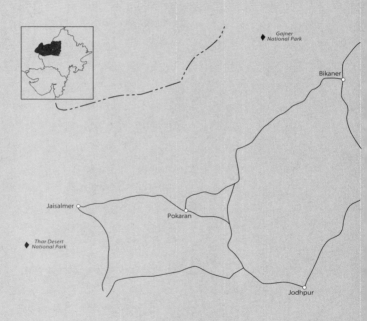

★ Jodhpur

The second city of Rajasthan, once the capital of Marwar, Jodhpur sprawls around the massively impressive clifftop Meherangarh Fort, one of the most rewarding in the state. The outer city, covering a large area, has the added bonus of the vast Umaid Bhavan Palace with its art deco interior. The city centre is very busy with a lot of action and is not too touristy.

Phone code: 0291
Colour map 3, grid A5

Getting there Jodhpur has air links with Delhi, Jaipur, Mumbai and Udaipur, and is also an essential stop for most visitors to Jaisalmer and western Rajasthan. The airport is 5 km south of town. Be prepared for beggars and hordes of rickshaw drivers on arrival at the station; rickshaw to old town Rs10-15, fort Rs 20-25. **Getting around** A pleasant way to explore the Old City is by hiring a bike. If you are really fit you can attempt cycling up to see Meherangarh – worth it for the free-wheel back down!

Ins & outs
See page 228 for further details

The **Rathore** Rajputs had moved to Marwar – the 'region of death' – in 1211, after their defeat at Kanauj by Muhammad Ghori. In 1459 Rao Jodha, forced to leave the Rathore capital at Mandore, 8 km to the north, chose this place as his capital because of its strategic location on the edge of the Thar Desert. The Rathores subsequently controlled wide areas of Rajasthan. Rao Udai Singh of Jodhpur (died 1581) received the title of Raja from Akbar, and his son, Sawai Raja Sur Singh (died 1595), conquered Gujarat and part of the Deccan for the Emperor. Maharaja Jaswant Singh (died 1678), having supported Shah Jahan in the Mughal struggle for succession in 1658, had a problematic relationship with the subsequent Mughal rule of Aurangzeb, and his son Ajit Singh was only able to succeed him after Aurangzeb's own death in 1707. In addition to driving the Mughals out of Ajmer he added substantially to the Meherangarh Fort in Jodhpur. His successor, Maharaja Abhai Singh (died 1749) captured Ahmadabad, and the State came into treaty relations with the British in 1818.

History

Jodhpur lies on the once strategic Delhi-Gujarat trading route and the Marwaris managed and benefited from the traffic of opium, copper, silk, sandalwood, dates, coffee and much more besides. Trade provided the essential economic base for the military power of the state.

Sights

Jodhpur is well worth visiting. If you can spare no more than a day, try to see Meherangarh Fort and Museum, the nearby Jaswant Thada (cenotaphs) and Umaid Bhavan Palace.

The Old City, surrounded by a huge 9½-km long wall which has 101 bastions and seven gates, above which are inscribed the name of the place to which the road leads, is a labyrinthine maze of narrow streets. Some of the houses and temples are of richly carved stone, in particular the red sandstone buildings of the Siré (Sardar) Bazar. Here the **Taleti Mahal**, one of three concubines' palaces in Jodhpur, has the unique feature of balconies (*jarokhas*) decorated with temple columns. Although it was added to by Ajit Singh, it is probably the oldest remaining palace in Jodhpur and dates from the early 17th century. The **Kunjebehari Temple** dedicated to Krishna and the **Raj Mahal** garden palace are both on the banks of the **Gulab Sagar** to the east of the fort.

The Old City

The new city Beyond the walls is the new city, which is of interest too. Overlooking the **Umaid Sagar** is the **Umaid Bhawan Palace** on Chittar Hill. Building started in 1929 as a famine relief exercise when the monsoon failed for the third year running. Over 3,000 people worked for 14 years, building this vast 347 room palace of sandstone and marble. The hand hewn blocks which are interlocked into position, use no mortar. It was designed by HV Lanchester, with the most modern furnishing and facilities in mind, and completed in 1943. The interior decoration was left to the artist Julius Stephan Norblin, a refugee from Poland. He painted the frescoes in the Throne Room (East Wing). For Tillotson, it is "the finest example of Indo-Deco... The forms are crisp and precise, and the bland monochrome of the stone makes the eye concentrate on their carved shapes." The royal family still occupy part of the palace. Part is a museum and part a luxury hotel (see below), and the interior produces a remarkable sensation of separation from the Indian environment in which it is set. There is a subterranean swimming pool decorated with signs of the zodiac; the murals are Norblin's. Lanchester deliberately avoided any attempt to re-capture Mughal style on the grounds that Rajasthan had never been fully under Muslim influence. Thus the "dripstones or *chajjis* are ribbed, recalling those of ancient Indian temples" and the dining hall is "a reinterpretation of a Buddhist Chaitya hall".

Just southeast of Raikabagh Station are the **Raikabagh Palace** and the **Jubilee Buildings**, public offices designed by Sir Samuel Swinton Jacob in the Indo-Saracenic style. On the Mandore Rd, 2 km to the north, is the large **Mahamandir Temple**.

★ Meherangarh

The 'Majestic Fort' sprawls along the top of a steep escarpment with a 37-m sheer drop to the south. Originally started by Rao Jodha in 1459, it has walls up to 36-m high and 21-m wide, towering above the plains. Most of what stands today is from the period of Maharajah Jaswant Singh (1638-78). On his death in 1678, Aurangzeb occupied the fort, bringing the first major period of fort extension to an end. However, after Aurangzeb's death Meherangarh returned to Jaswant Singh's son Ajit Singh and remained the royal residence until the Umaid Bhavan was completed in 1943.

The summit has three areas: the palace (northwest), a wide terrace to the east of the palace, and the strongly fortified area to the south. There are extensive views from the top. One approach is by a winding path up the west side (possible by rickshaw), but the main approach and car park is from the east. The climb is quite stiff; the disabled may use the elevator.

The gateways There were originally seven gateways. The first, **Fateh Gate**, is heavily fortified with spikes and a barbican that forces a 45° turn. The smaller **Gopal Gate** is followed by the **Bhairon Gate**, with large guardrooms. The fourth, **Toati Gate**, is now missing but the fifth, **Dodhkangra Gate**, marked with cannon shots, stands over a turn in the path and has loopholed battlements for easy defence. Next is the **Marti Gate**, a long passage flanked by guardrooms. The last, **Loha (Iron) Gate**, controls the final turn into the fort and has handprints (31 on one side and five on the other) of royal *satis*, the wives of Maharajas, see page 410. It is said that six queens and 58 concubines became *satis* on **Ajit Singh's** funeral pyre in 1724. *Satis* carried the Bhagavad Gita with them into the flames and legend has it that the holy book would never perish. Within the fort area are two small tanks – the **Rani Talao** and the **Gulab Sagar** (Rose-Water lake). The main entrance is through the **Jay (Victory) Pol**.

From the **Loha Gate** the ramp leads up to the **Suraj (Sun) Pol**, which opens onto the **Singar Choki Chowk**. This is the main entrance to the museum, and a guide takes visitors round the inner buildings.

Used for royal ceremonies such as the anointing of rajas, the north, west and southwest sides of the Singar Choki Chowk date from the period immediately before the Mughal occupation in 1678. The southeast wing is later – the capitals of the pillars were typical of Maharajah Ajit Singh's period (1707-24). The upper storeys of the chowk were part of the *zenana*, and from the **Jhanki Mahal** ('glimpse palace') on the upper floor of the north wing the women could look down on the activities of the courtyard. The upper storeys of the Jhanki Mahal itself comprise a long gallery whose arcades are flanked by a further narrow gallery from which *jarokhas* project over the courtyard. Thus the chowk below has the features characteristic of much of the rest of the *zenana*, *jarokhas* surmounted by the distinctive Bengali style eaves, and beautifully ornate *jali* screens. These allowed cooling breezes to ventilate rooms and corridors in the often stiflingly hot desert summers.

Also typical of Mughal buildings was the use of material hung from rings below the eaves to provide roof covering, as in the columned halls of the

Meherangarh Fort

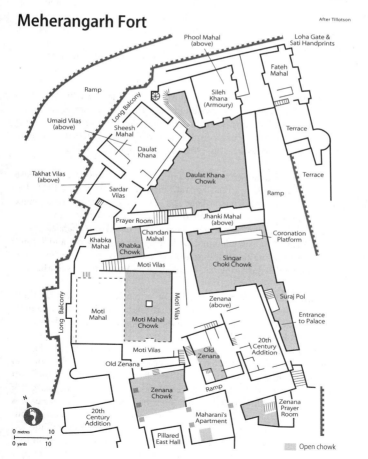

After Tillotson

Phool Mahal (above)
Loha Gate & Sati Handprints
Fateh Mahal
Ramp
Sileh Khana (Armoury)
Long Balcony
Umaid Vilas (above)
Sheesh Mahal
Terrace
Daulat Khana
Takhat Vilas (above)
Daulat Khana Chowk
Terrace
Sardar Vilas
Ramp
Prayer Room
Jhanki Mahal (above)
Chandan Mahal
Coronation Platform
Khabka Mahal
Khabka Chowk
Moti Vilas
Singar Choki Chowk
Moti Vilas
Long Balcony
Moti Vilas
Zenana (above)
Suraj Pol
Moti Mahal
Moti Mahal Chowk
Entrance to Palace
Moti Vilas
20th Century Addition
Old Zenana
Old Zenana
20th Century Addition
Zenana Chowk
Ramp
Zenana Prayer Room
20th Century Addition
Maharani's Apartment
Pillared East Hall

0 metres 10
0 yards 10

N

Open chowk

True blue Brahmins?

As you approach the fort you will notice the predominance of blue houses which are often inaccurately referred to as "Brahmin houses" – the colour being associated with the high caste. In fact they are blue due to termites (white ants). It appears that the white lime-wash used originally did not deter the pests which caused havoc, making

unsightly cavities in local homes. The addition of chemicals (eg copper sulphate), which resulted in turning the white lime to a blue-wash, was found to be effective in limiting the pest damage and so was widely used in the area around the fort. This also happens to be a part of town where large numbers of the Brahmin community live.

Daulat Khana and the **Sileh Khana** (the armoury), which also date from Ajit Singh's reign. The collection of Indian weapons in the armoury is unequalled, with remarkable swords and daggers, often beautifully decorated with calligraphy, and a wide range of other weapons. **Abai Singh's** tent from his highly successful Deccan campaign is also displayed. Along the ramparts antique cannonry can be seen. Shah Jahan's (later Aurangzeb's) red silk and velvet tent lavishly embroidered with gold thread, used in the Imperial Mughal campaign, is in the **Tent Room**. The **Jewel House** has a wonderful collection of jewellery, including diamond eyebrows held by hooks over the ears. There are also *palanquins*, *howdahs* and ornate royal cradles, all marvellously preserved and maintained.

The **Phool Mahal** (Flower Palace), above the Sileh Khana, was built by Abhai Singh (1724-49) as a hall of private audience. The stone *jali* screens are original and there are striking portraits of former rulers, a lavishly gilded ceiling and the Jodhpur coat of arms displayed above the royal couch; the murals of the 36 musical modes are a late 19th-century addition.

The **Umaid Vilas**, which houses Rajput miniatures, is linked to the **Sheesh Mahal** (Mirror Palace), built by Ajit Singh between 1707 and 1724. The room, which has characteristic large and regularly sized mirror work, unlike Mughal 'mirror palaces', looks out to the northwest. Immediately to its south, and above the Sardar Vilas, is the **Takhat Vilas**. Added by Maharajah Takhat Singh (1843-73), it has wall murals of dancing girls, love legends and Krishna Lila, while its ceiling has two unusual features: massive wooden beams to provide support and the curious use of colourful Belgian Christmas tree balls.

The **Ajit Vilas** has a fascinating collection of musical instruments and costumes. On the ground floor of the Takhat Vilas is **Sardar Vilas**, and to its south the **Khabka and Chandan Mahals** (sleeping quarters), which also have the Ionic columns typical of Ajit Singh's period. The **Moti Vilas**, wings to the north, east and south of the Moti Mahal Chowk, date from Jaswant Singh's reign. The women could watch proceedings in the courtyard below through the *jali* screens of the surrounding wings. Tillotson suggests that the **Moti Mahal** (Pearl Palace), although placed in the *zenana* of the fort, was such a magnificent building that it could only have served the purpose of a Diwan-i-Am (Hall of Public Audience). He argues that its common attribution to Sawai Raja Sur Singh (1595-1629) is a century too early, the real builder being Ajit Singh, who probably had to demolish buildings on the west of the square to make room for it. The Moti Mahal is fronted by excellently

Bishnois

The Bishnois *(Vishnois), follow '29'
(bish-noi) principles of a non-violent
Vaishnava sect, founded in the 15th century
by Jambeswarji. They are known for their
reverence for wildlife and their careful
environmental management, protecting,*
*especially, green vegetation and preserving
the blackbuck antelope from extinction.
They are a gentle community of potters,
weavers, leather embroiderers and camel
herders. Some groups are being helped to
overcome their addiction to opium.*

carved 19th-century woodwork, while inside waist-level niches housed oil
lamps whose light would have shimmered from the mirrored ceiling. A palm-
ist reads your fortune at Moti Mahal Chowk (museum area). ■ *10 mins for
Rs 50 (mornings), 30 mins, Rs 250 (afternoons); reported as uncannily accurate
about the past!*

■ *1000-1700 (museum only, closed 1300-1430). Foreigners Rs 110, Indians,
Rs 20. Guide Rs 50. Camera Rs 50. Video Rs 100. You are requested not to tip
guides, but contribute to the Staff Welfare Fund at the booking office if you wish.
Allow at least 2 hrs. Near the ticket office on the terrace there is a pleasant restaurant, popular with travellers. Just below the fort, on the road leading to Jaswant
Thada, there is a 'water hut' where you can often get a free fresh cup of tea but
watch out, the kind of old man may also offer you strong* bhang.

On the way to Meherangarh is the cremation ground of the former rulers. **Jaswant Thada**
These distinctive memorials in white marble commemorate Jaswant Singh II
(1899) and houses portraits of successive rulers of Marwar. ■ *1000-1300,
1400-1700. Rs 10.*

★ **Mehrangarh Fort Palace Museum**, in a series of palaces, beautifully **Museums**
designed and decorated windows and walls. Magnificent collection of the
Maharajas' memorabilia – superbly maintained and presented (see above).
   The **Old Fort Museum** is fascinating. *Palanquins,* royal *howdahs* lavishly
upholstered and one of silver, a golden throne, shoes with pearls, paintings,
mirrors, cribs, weapons and a magnificently embroidered royal desert tent,
among the exhibits. ■ *Summer 0800-1800, winter 0900-1700. Closed 1230-
1430, so be there by 1100 if visiting in the morning. Tours with English speaking
guides provided.*
   Umaid Bhawan Palace Museum includes the Darbar Hall with its flaking
murals; good collection of miniatures, armour and old clocks. Some are disappointed. ■ *0900-1700. Rs 50 (Indians Rs 10). Umaid Bhawan Palace Hotel.*
   Government Museum, a time-capsule from the British Raj (little added
since Independence). Some moth-eaten stuffed animals and featherless birds,
model aeroplanes, images of Jain Tirthankars, textiles, local crafts, miniature
portraits and antiquities. A small **zoo** in gardens has a few rare exotic species.
■ *1000-1630, closed Fri. Rs 3. Umaid Park.*

Excursions

A village safari, visiting **Bishnoi** villages, is recommended. Most tours include **Village safaris**
the hamlets of Guda, Khejarali, Raika cameleers' settlement and Salawas
(see below). Tours by *Ajit Bhawan, Madho Niwas* (T434486), *Poly Travels,
Jhalamandgarh* and *Rohetgarh*. About Rs 450 for four.

Mandore
8 km N of Jodhpur

Mandore, the old 14th-century capital of Marwar, sits on a plateau. Set around the old cremation ground with the red sandstone *chhatris* of the Rathore rulers, the gardens are usually crowded with Indian tourists at weekends. The **Shrine of the 33 Crore Gods** (330 million) is a hall containing huge painted rock-cut figures of heroes and gods. The largest *deval*, a combination of temple and cenotaph, is Ajit Singh's (died 1724). A small **museum** in the Janana Mahal contains some fine sculpture and miniature paintings. ■ *1000-1630; closed Fri.* The remains of an eighth-century Hindu temple is on a hilltop nearby. ■ *Getting there: frequent Local/City bus, 100 m from the station and Paota Bus Stand.*

Bal Samand Lake
5 km N of Jodpur

This is the oldest artificial lake in Rajasthan. Dating from 1159, it is surrounded by parkland laid out in 1936 where the 19th-century *hawa mahal* was turned into a royal summer palace. Although the interior is European in style, it has entirely traditional red sandstone filigree windows and beautifully carved balconies. **AL-A** *Bal Samand Palace* (WelcomHeritage), T0291-545991, extensive grounds, on lakeside, 36 rooms in palace and renovated stables (suites **LL**) restaurant (mainly buffet), pool, boating, pleasant orchards which attract nilgai, jackals, peacocks; reservations: Jodhpur T433316, F635373.

Tours

City sightseeing: half day (0830-1300, 1400-1800). Fort and palaces, Jaswant Thada, Mandore Gardens, Govt Museum, colourful bazar around Old City clock tower.

Essentials

Sleeping
■ *on map*
Price codes:
see inside front cover

See also page 229
for out of town
alternatives

LL-L *Umaid Bhawan Palace*, 5 km centre (car to town Rs 250; rickshaw Rs 30), T510101, F510100. 95 a/c rooms (suites up to US$990), unusual pool, luxurious ambience, expensive bufffet and meals in impressive dining hall, snacks in pleasant *Pillars* overlooking lovely garden, non-residents' pay Rs 350 'cover charge' adjusted against meals. Luxury tented camp (en suite toilet) on fort ramparts in high season. **L** *Taj Hari Mahal*, 5 Residency Rd, T439700, F614451. 93 rooms blending traditional and modern. **B** *Ajit Bhawan* (Heritage Hotel), Airport Rd, near Circuit House, T511070, F510674. 54 air-cooled rooms with bath, best in cottages in 'village' complex (a real farmyard), decor overdone (Indian kitsch), few cheaper small rooms, good pool, good Indian buffets, well-kept garden, pool, 'village safari' (see excursions above), charming though group-oriented. Recommended. Part now '*Ranbanka*', T512801, F512800, with 30 renovated rooms, pool and gardens, under new management. **B** *Durjan Niwas* (HRH), Daspan Vihar, Ratanada, T649546, F616991, sales@hrhindia.com 15 comfortable rooms (20 more planned) with balcony, pool planned, old house of Thakur family. **B** *Utambar House*, Raikabagh, T622274, info@indiatravelite.com, 2 a/c suites, good homecooked meals, hospitable family (good guides), car hire arranged, good contacts with handicrafts producers. **B-C** *Ratanada Polo Palace*, Residency Rd, T431910, F433118. 50 rooms (vary), poolside dinner with folk music, tennis.

C *Karni Bhawan* (Heritage Hotel), Palace Rd, Ratanada, T512101, F512105, www.karnihotels.com 30 rooms, some a/c (**B** suites), each with a seasonal or festival theme with decor and period furniture to match, in a 1940s red sandstone building, expensive village theme restaurant (live folk music at dinner), peaceful lawns, pool, unpretentious. **C** *Raj Basera*, Residency Rd, T431973, F616434. 17 rooms in 'rustic' cottages, among shady trees, quiet, average food. **C** *Rajputana Palace*, Panch Batti Circle, Airport Rd, T431672, F438072. 24 rooms in renovated building. **C** *Sandhu Palace*, 169

£4000 worth of holiday vouchers to be won!

... that can be claimed against any exodus, Peregrine or Gecko's holiday, a choice of around 570 holidays that set industry standards for responsible tourism in 90 countries across seven continents.

exodus

The UK's leading adventurous travel company, with over 25 years' experience in running the most exciting holidays in 80 different countries. We have an unrivalled choice of trips, from a week exploring the hidden corners of Tuscany to a high altitude trek to Everest Base Camp or 3 months travelling across South America. If you want to do something a little different, chances are you'll find it in one of our brochures.

Peregrine

Australia's leading quality adventure travel company, Peregrine aims to explore some of the world's most interesting and inaccessible places. Providing exciting and enjoyable holidays that focus in some depth on the lifestyle, culture, history, wildlife, wilderness and landscapes of areas that are usually quite different to our own. There is an emphasis on the outdoors, using a variety of transport and staying in a range of accommodation, from comfortable hotels to tribal huts.

Gecko's

Gecko's holidays will get you to the best places with the minimum of hassle. They are designed for younger people who like independent travel but don't have the time to organise everything themselves. Be prepared to take the rough with the smooth, these holidays are for active people with a flexible approach to travel.

To enter the competition, simply tear out the postcard and return it to Exodus Travels, 9 Weir Road, London SW12 0LT. Or go to the competition page on www.exodus.co.uk and register online. Two draws will be made, Easter 2001 and Easter 2002, and the winner of each draw will receive £2000 in travel vouchers. The closing date for entry will be 1st March 2002. If you do not wish to receive further information about these holidays, please tick here. ☐ No purchase necessary. Plain paper entries should be sent to the above address. The prize value is non-transferable and there is no cash alternative. Winners must be over 18 years of age and must sign and adhere to operators' standard booking conditions. A list of prizewinners will be available for a period of one month from the draw by writing to the above address. For a full list of terms and conditions please write to the above address or visit our website.

To receive a brochure, please tick the relevant boxes below (maximum number of brochures 2) or telephone (44) 20 8772 3822.

exodus	Peregrine	Gecko's
☐ Walking & Trekking	☐ Himalaya	☐ Egypt, Jordan & Israel
☐ Discovery & Adventure	☐ China	☐ South America
☐ European Destinations	☐ South East Asia	☐ Africa
☐ Overland Journeys	☐ Antarctica	☐ South East Asia
☐ Biking Adventures	☐ Africa	☐ India
☐ Multi Activity	☐ Arctic	

Please give us your details:

Name: --

Address: --

Postcode: --

e-mail: --

Which footprint guide did you take this from?
----

getaway tonight on
www.exodus.co.uk

exodus
The Different Holiday

exodus
The Different Holiday

getaway tonight on

www.exodus.co.uk

exodus
The Different Holiday

2

exodus

9 Weir Road
LONDON
SW12 0BR

BUSINESS REPLY SERVICE
Licence No SW4909

Ajeet Colony, opposite Circuit House, T510154, F511611, Sandhu_Palace@vsnl.net.in 20 a/c or aircooled rooms (some with balcony), in a 3-storey modern house, rooftop restaurant, pleasant. **C-D** *Adarsh Niwas*, opposite rly station, T627313, F740005. 35 rooms, some a/c, with bath and TV, suites best, good *Kalinga* restaurant. **C-D** *Devi Bhavan*, 1 Ratanada Rd, T434215. 8 rooms with bath, delightful suburban garden, excellent Indian dinner (Rs 150), tours, safaris, Rajput family home. Highly recommended. **C-D** *Jug Villa*, Shikargarh on the outskirts. Pleasant a/c cottages, good Gujarati *thalis* (around fire in the garden at night), large lawn, good views of fort at sunset, book through *North West Safaris*, T/F079-6560962, ssibal@ad1.vsnl.net.in **C-D** *Newton's Manor*, 86 Jawahar Colony, opposite Ratanada Polo Palace, Central School Rd, T430686, F610603. Renovated a/c rooms, touches of Victoriana, breakfast and dinner on request, exchange. **D** *Akshey*, behind station, opposite Raikabagh Palace (quick

Jodhpur

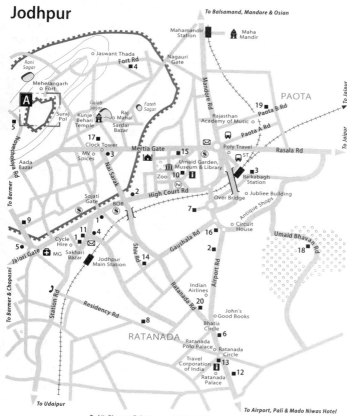

Western Rajasthan

■ **Sleeping**
1 Adarsh Niwas & Kalinga Restaurant

2 Ajit Bhawan Palace & Tandoori Nights
3 Akshey
4 Chauhan's
5 Cosy Guest House
6 Devi Bhavan
7 Durag Niwas & Durag Vilas
8 Durjan Niwas
9 Fort View
10 Ghoomar

11 Govind
12 Karni Bhawan
13 Newton's Manor
14 Raman Guest House
15 Rawat
16 Sandhu Palace
17 Sri Amar Bhawan Haveli
18 Umaid Bhawan Palace
19 Umang International
20 Youth Hostel

● **Eating**
1 Agra Sweet Home & Uttam
2 Jodhpur Coffee House & Poonam Vegetarian
3 Mishrilal
4 Rawat Mishtan Bhandar
5 Shandar

Related map
A Meherangarh Fort,
page 221

access to centre through rear door), T421549. Some modern a/c rooms, cheap dorm, poorly run restaurant, pleasant garden, peaceful, good value. **D** *Ghoomar* (RTDC), High Court Rd, T40810. 75 rooms, dorm (Rs 50), restaurant, bar, tourist information, travel, garden, not very clean (especially dorms), rather dull, 'super deluxe' a/c rooms slightly better. **D** *Umang International*, 1306 Paota, B Rd, T544485, F540225. 5 rooms, air-cooled or a/c, large, clean, comfortable, homely, very good service and veg food (no alcohol), quiet with pleasant garden, new 2-storey house with a wildly ornamental gate, an 'oasis', Highly recommended.

The tourist office has a list of Paying Guest accommodation, T645083

D-E *Indrashan*, 593 High Court Colony (3 km southeast), T440665, F438593, comfortable, friendly. Mr Chandra Shekhar Singh also offers interesting home stays. Recommended. **D-E** *Durag Vilas*, 1 Old Public Park, near Circuit House, T621300. 6 very clean, quiet, air-cooled rooms with shower, 1 **C** a/c, travel bookings, desert safaris, family run, friendly, helpful, free lift from station/airport. Recommended. Next door, cheaper and longer established *Durag Niwas*, 1 Old Public Park, T639092, duragniwas@usa.net 10-mins walk from bus station (phone for free lift). Pleasant rooms (may need to bargain), good cheap food,, very quiet, clean and friendly. Recommended. **D-E** *Blue House (R)*, Sumer Bhawan, Moti Chowk, T/F619133, bluehouse36@hotmail.com 7 clean rooms, 5 with bath (hot water all day), home cooked meals, great views from roof top restaurant. **D-E** *Mandore Guest House*, opposite Mandore Gardens, 8 km north (15 mins bus from centre), T545210, F546959, poly@nda.vsnl.net.in (Poly Travels). 10 simple air-cooled 'bungalows' with bath (hot water), spotlessly clean, deluxe tents, home-cooked meals included, peaceful gardens, bonfires, internet, welcoming family, excellent value. **D-E** *Raman Guest House*, opposite Keshar Bagh, Shiv Rd, T513980. Simple a/c rooms, attached bath, rooftop restaurant, quiet location. **D-E** *Sri Amar Bhawan Haveli*, opposite Turjika Jhalra, Makrana Mohalla, T614615. 7 simple clean rooms (some pricey) in traditional old haveli, beds on roof (Rs 50), cheerful decor, good views from breezy roof terrace, 'auntie's' good food, quiet, helpful manager, village safari is touristy. **D-F** *Chauhan's Guest House*, Fort Rd, inside Nagori Gate, T541497. Rooms vary, (some a/c with hot shower, Rs 450), half-day rates, relaxing café, interesting family, cultural centre (Hindi/painting taught), shop, book exchange.

Guest houses & cheaper E & F hotels often have shared baths

E *Govind*, Station Rd, 200 m to right from station, opposite GPO, T622758. 14 clean rooms (Rs 250), some **D** a/c, rooftop restaurant with good Indian and Continental, good fort views, camel safaris, bus and rail ticketing, internet, friendly, very helpful owner, an oasis. Highly recommended. **E** *Rawat*, north of Umaid Public Park, T642622. Very quiet, large clean rooms, some a/c, but poor food and slow service. **E-F** *Raman Guest House*, opposite Kesar Bagh, Shiv Rd, T513980. Clean though simply furnished rooms with attached bath (hot water), family atmosphere, traditional meals. **F** *Cosy Guest House* (was Joshi's Blue House), Novechokiya Rd (north from Jalori Gate), Brahm Puri, Chuna ki Choki, just west of the fort, T612066. 6 simple clean rooms, 3-bed dorm (Rs 40), all day bucket hot water, good home-cooked meals (other restaurants 15 mins walk), bus bookings, rooftop views of fort and old city, quiet, very friendly and homely, no commission to rickshaws. Highly recommended. **F** *Fort View*, Lakshmi Bhavan, near Jalori Gate, T439923. Simple rooms from Rs 70 some with bath (best on roof Rs 140), good Indian veg meals to order, pleasant though dusty rooftop, friendly welcoming owner (accept a local tour if he offers one). Highly recommended (tailor opposite also recommended). **F** *Gangaur Homestay*, Khagal Phulla Rd, T625190. Few rooms with bath, very friendly, excellent home cooking. **F** *Railway Retiring Rooms*, Jodhpur Rly Station dorm, reasonable restaurant, see 'Waiting Room' under Transport. **F** *Youth Hostel*, Ratanada, T620150. Dorms (Rs 25, non-members Rs 45), rooms with shared bath, canteen meals.

Expensive The best restaurants are in hotels (non-residents should reserve): *Ajit Bhawan*, T612410, evening buffet (Rs 250), excellent meal in garden on a warm evening with entertainment, but poor atmosphere if eating in dining hall ('canteen') in winter. *Umaid Bhavan's*, T633316, palatial, formal *Marwar Hall*, Rs 350 entrance refunded against bill (try fish and chips, Rs 300), occasional barbecues, friendly staff. Beautiful coffee shop on terrace overlooking lovely garden. *Madho Niwas*, New Airport Rd, Ratanada, T434486, to sample real homecooked Marwari food, though described as "OK but expensive"), reserve ahead. *Dhanni* in *Karni Bhawan* T33320, average food but very pleasant setting in a recreated village with huts, buffet with barbecue, musicians and bonfire.

Eating
● *on map, page 225*
Price codes:
see inside front cover

Mid-range *Kalinga*, below *Adarsh Niwas*, opposite station. Western and Indian. A/c, good food (try *daal makhani* and aubergine dishes), friendly service, handy for breakfast. **On the Rocks**, near *Ajit Bhavan*. Good Indian and Continental.

Cheap *Daal-bhatti, lassi* and *kachoris* are sold around Jalori and Sojati Gates. *Jodhpur Coffee House*, Sojati Gate. Good South Indian snacks, good thalis, Rs 18. *Kashmiri*, near Anand Cinema. Excellent hot and spicy Indian food. *Poonam*, High Court Rd. Pure veg Indian. "Gorgeous 4-ft masala *dosas*", friendly waiters (but tip-seeking). *Shandar*, Jalori Gate. Indian vegetarian. Good food and sweets. *Tandoor*, Ratanada Rd. Mughlai. Good tikkas and tandoori chicken. *Tandoori Nights*, next to *Ajit Bhawan*. Mughlai. Excellent meals, braziers at table for winter nights outdoors. *Rajasthali*, Station Rd. Marwari thalis. *Uttam*, High Court Rd, near Sojati Gate. Good a/c *thali* restaurant friendly, fast service. Recommended.

Sweets and drinks *Mishrilal*, main entrance to Sardar Bazar. Splendid creamy and saffron flavoured *makhania lassi* – the best in town! *Rawat Mishtan Bhandar*, near Rly Station. Tempting Indian sweets and drinks. *Agra Sweet Home*, near Sojati Gate, *Janata*, Nai Sarak and *Laxmi* Ratanada, are also recommended. Juice stall at northern gate does great fresh carrot and orange juice.

In *Umaid Palace*, *Ashok* and *Ghoomar* and in *Kalinga Restaurant* (see above).

Bars

Several are special to Rajasthan. **Jul/Aug**, *Nag Panchami*, when reverence for the *Naga* (*naag*), the cobra, is shown by people all over the country. The day is dedicated to *Sesha*, the thousand-headed god or *Anant* ('infinite') Vishnu, often depicted reclining on a bed of serpents in between great acts or incarnations. In Jodhpur huge effigies of the serpent are displayed in a colourful fair. In other parts of India idols of hooded serpents are fed with milk and sweets. The *Marwar Festival* (31 **Oct**-1 Nov 2001, 19-20 Oct 2002, 8-9 Oct 2003), held at full moon, includes music, puppet shows, turban tying competitions, camel polo and ending with a fire dance on the dunes at Osian.

Festivals

Jodhpur is famous for its Jodhpuri coats and once popular *jodhpurs* (riding breeches), tie-and-dye fabrics, lacquer work. The main areas are: **Sojati Gate** for gifts, **Station Rd** for jewellery, **Tripolia Bazar** for handicrafts, **Khanda Falsa** for tie-and-dye, **Lakhara Bazar** for lac bangles. Shoes are made in **Mochi Bazar**, **Sardarpura** and **Clock Tower**, *bandhanas* in **Bambamola**, and around **Siwanchi** and **Jalori Gates**. *Durries* are woven at **Salavas** village, 18 km away.

Shopping

Antiques Shops on road between Umaid and Ajit Bhawans, flourishing trade though pricey. Don't forget that the export of items over 100-years-old is prohibited. **Books** *John's Good Books*, Bhati Circle, Circuit House Rd, T437638, small but quite good selection. *Sarvodaya*, near *Adarsh Niwas Hotel* and *Universal Book Depot*, Jalori Gate.

Western Rajasthan

Free book swap at *Chauhan's Guest House*, Main Fort Rd, inside Nagori Gate. **Handloom and handicrafts** *Rajasthan Khadi Sangathan*, BK ka Bagh. Recommended. *Khadi Sangh*, Station Rd and *Marasthaly*, High Court Rd, for quality and fair prices. *Bhagatram Ishwarlal*, *Lucky Silk* and *Prakash* are good for silk; *National Loom* on three floors and *Maharani Art Exports*, Tambaku Bazar, have high quality textiles. *Abani*, near *Tourist Bungalow*. *Arvind, Haswani* and *Lalji*, Umaid Bhawan Rd, have good local crafts. **Tailors** *Roshan*, Kapara Bazar, 1st flr, opposite *Kasper ki Darga*, T622920, recommended for men's traditional and modern clothes. **Photography** Shops in High Court Rd, Sojati Gate and in Jalori Gate. *Kala Colour Lab*, opposite MG Hospital is recommended. **Spices** *Mohanlal Verhomal*, 209B, Kirana Merchant (from Clock Tower enter veg market, then turn right), T615846, mvspices@datainfosys.net Sought after for their hand mixed spices (allow 40 mins!), efficient postal service. Recommended.

Transport

Local **Auto-rickshaw**: Rly station to fort should be about Rs 20 (may demand Rs 50; try walking away). **Car hire**: From tourist office, T45083, whole day about Rs 450; half day Rs 275. **Cycle hire**: Shops on the road opposite the station (near *Kalinga Restaurant*). **Mini-buses**: Cover most of the city except fort and *Umaid Bhavan Palace*. **Taxi**: Railway station.

Long distance **Air**: Transport to town: by taxi, Rs 170-200; auto rickshaw, Rs 100-120. *Indian Airlines*, near Bhati Cross Roads, T510757. 1000-1300, 1400-1700; airport, T512617. They fly a few times a week to **Delhi, Jaipur, Mumbai Udaipiur**.

Earplugs are recommended on video coaches. Allow time to find the correct bus; match number on ticket with bus registration plate

Road A convenient bus route links Jodhpur with Ghanerao and Ranakpur, Kumbhalgar and Udaipur. **Bus**: RST Bus Stand: near Raikabagh railway station, T44686. 1000-1700; bookings also at tourist office. State RTCs' daily services: **Ahmadabad**, 11 hrs; **Jaipur**, frequent, 8 hrs; **Abu Rd** 7 hrs; **Ajmer**, 4½ hrs; **Jaisalmer**, 0630 (dep Jaisalmer, 1400), 5-6 hrs, Rs 80; faster than train but scenically tedious; **Pali**, 4 hrs, Rs 27; **Udaipur**, 8-9 hrs, best to book a good seat a day ahead. Private operators: *HR Travels*, *Sun City Tours*, and *Sethi Yatra*, opposite main railway station. **Private Bus stand** 100 m west of main station. Deluxe video coaches and express buses between Jodhpur and **Delhi, Ahmadabad, Bikaner, Bhilwara**: most depart 0600 and 2200. **Jaipur**: 5 hrs; **Jaisalmer**: about hourly from 0600 ('when full'), 4-5 hrs, Rs 75-90 (tickets from travel agents); comfortable buses on good road, but beware of touts on arrival at Jaisalmer; decide on hotel in advance.

Train Jodhpur Station enquiries: T32535. Open 0800-2400. Reservations: T20842. Open 0900-1300, 1330-1600. Advance reservations, next to GPO. Tourist Bureau, T25052 (0500-2300); hotel booking (of your choice) unsatisfactory (may say 'full' when not and suggest another). The International Tourist Waiting Room for passengers in transit (ground floor), with big sofas and showers; if the western toilets are dirty, use spotless Indian toilets in 2nd Class Waiting Room on the 1st floor of the station foyer. **Abu Rd (Mount Abu)**: *Ranakpur Exp, 4707*, 1515, 5½ hrs. **Agra**: *Marudhar Exp, 4854/4864*, 0700, 14 hrs *Jodhpur-Howrah Exp, 2308*, 1715, 12¾ hrs (continues to Kolkata, further 21 hrs). **Ahmadabad**: *Surya Nagri Exp, 4845*, 1855, 9½ hrs. **Barmer**: *Barmer Exp, 4807*, 0805, 4½ hrs. **Delhi** (no 1st Class): *Mandore Exp, 2462*, 1930, 11 hrs (OD); *Jodhpur Delhi Exp, 4860*, 2300, 12½ hrs (OD) **Jaipur**: *Inter-City Exp, 2467*, 0545, 6 hrs; *Mandore Exp, 2462*, 1930, 5 hrs; *Marudhar Exp, 4854/4864*, 0700, 5 hrs. **Jaisalmer**: *Jodhpur Jaisalmer Exp*, and *4810 Exp*, 2315, 6½ hrs. Winter nights are cold so take a sleeping bag or blanket or order bedding. This is a dusty journey. **Varanasi** via Lucknow: *Marudhar Exp, 4854/4864*, 0700, 19 hrs (Lucknow), 26 hrs (Varanasi).

The Maharaja's railway carriages

In 1886 the Jodhpur Railway first introduced camel drawn trains until steam engines were acquired. The railway network had expanded to cover 2,400 km by 1924, stretching from Jodhpur to Hyderabad in Sind (now in Pakistan) across the desert. The Maharaja's luxurious personal saloons which date from 1926 are beautifully finished with inlaid wood and silver fittings and are on display near the Umaid Bhawan Palace.

Banks Open 1030-1400. *Bank of Baroda*, by *Arun Hotel*, Sojati Gate. For VISA. *Punjab National Bank*, Ratanada. For TCs. *State Bank of India*, High Court Rd. Currency and TCs. **Communications** Internet: *Amardeep*, Sardarpura, 3 km southwest of railway station, above *Marudhar Jewellers*. *Poly Travels* (see below). **GPO:** South of Jodhpur station, 1000-2000, Sat 1000-1600. **Hospital and medical services** In Jalori Gate, T24479, and Sivanchi Gate Rd, T22567. **Dispensary:** Paota, Residency. Open 0800-1200, 1700-1900, Sun 0800-1200. **Tour companies and travel agents** *Aravali Safari*, 4 Kuchaman House Area, Airport Rd, T35944, F34146. Professional. Recommended. *Forts & Palaces*, 15 Old Public Park, Raikabagh, T511207, jaipur@palaces-tours.com *Poly Travels* (Mr Gehlot), 10D Bus Stand, Paota, T545210, F546959, poly@nda.vsnl.net.in Recommended for visiting Bishnoi villages, friendly, knowledgeable and helpful. *Rajasthan Tours*, Airport Rd, T36294. *Travel Corp of India*, Airport Rd, T39052. **Tourist offices** *Rajasthan*, by *Ghoomar Hotel*, High Court Rd, T44010. 0800-1200, 1500-1800. *International Tourist Bureau* at railway station, T39052. **Useful addresses** Ambulance: T102. **Fire:** T101. **Police:** T20200.

Directory

Western Rajasthan

South of Jodhpur

The small, unimpressive looking 18th-century castle, 12 km south of Jodhpur in a semi-rural setting, has been renovated and restored and converted into a hotel. This is a good alternative to staying in Jodhpur but you need your own transport. It is a convenient base to explore the colonies of Bishnoi and Raika potters' and weavers' settlement. The castle, **C** *Jhalamandgarh*, T0291-740481, F741125, has 12 rooms (some a/c), good-sized and very comfortable with carved beds, hot showers (but watch out for power cuts), good Indian/western breakfast (try the stuffed parathas), delicious food (Rajasthani buffets Rs 300), Marwari kebab barbecues in the garden, dinner on terrace with views of the city lit up at night, camel/horse 'village safaris', family run. To make a reservation contact *North West Safaris*, T079-6302019, F6560962, ssibal@ad1.vsnl.net.in

Jhalamand

In Khejarali Bishnois prevented a grove of *khejri* trees from being chopped down by the soldiers of the royal army by 'hugging' the trees and refusing to let any to be cut. More than 300 Bishnoi men and women lost their lives before the Maharajah of Jodhpur heard about this symbolic sacrifice, and had the forest declared a protected area. Even today, shooting and tree felling are not permitted here. **Guda Lake** nearby attracts large flocks of waterfowl, especially wintering demoiselle and common cranes, at sunrise and sunset. The Forest Department has created a viewing post here from where the lake can be seen with its birdlife. Blackbucks, chinkaras, nilgai, monitor lizard and hare can be watched coming to the water's edge for a drink. Desert fox, Desert cat and jackal have also been spotted. There are some colourful Bishnoi, Raika and potters' villages around Guda sanctuary.

Khejarali

Salawas This village, about 30 minutes' drive south from Jodhpur, is well known for its pit loom weaving. The villagers produce *durries*, carpets, rugs, bed covers and tents using camel hair, goat hair, wool and cotton in colourful and interesting patterns. You can visit the weavers' co-operative *Roopraj Durrie Udyog*, where you can buy authentic village crafts, but watch out for high prices and pushy salesmen. ■ *Getting there: Buses from Jodhpur.*

Luni The tiny bustling village of Luni, about 40 km south of Jodhpur, sits in the shadow of the 19th-century red sandstone Fort Chanwa which has been converted to a hotel. With its complex of courtyards, water wheels, and intricately carved façades, the fort and its village offer an attractive and peaceful alternative to the crowds of Jodhpur. **C** *Fort Chanwa* (Heritage Hotel), T0291-432460, has 20 good rooms, not large but well furnished, individually designed (best in the keep), excellent Rajasthani meals in impressive dining room (Rs 300), pleasant lawn for drinks, pool, well managed but a bit impersonal. Recommended. You can visit craft villages (eg Salawas), watch good handloom weaving and bargain to buy). Contact Dalip Bhawan, 1 PWD Rd, Jodhpur, T/F32460. ■ *Getting there: Trains and buses from Jodhpur.*

Rohet
50 km from Jodhpur
Once a picturesque hamlet settled by the Bishnoi community, now Rohet is a busy highway village full of puncture shops and tea stalls. At the end of the village a lake attracts numerous winter migrants in addition to resident birds. The small castle, *Rohetgarh*, beside the lake, has a collection of antique hunting weapons. Again the castle has been converted into a hotel. **B** *Rohetgarh* (Heritage Hotel), T02936- 68231. 20 rooms (18 a/c, some rather small) with carved wooden and marble furniture, attached baths (avoid rooms near outdoor restaurant – noisy when waiters have their late night meal), excellent Rajasthani food ("among the best in Rajasthan"), ordinary architecture but in beautiful environment, pleasant courtyard and lake view terraces, good pool, friendly reception from hospitable family, efficient service, riding, jeep/camel/horse safaris to Bishnoi, Raika and artisans' villages, boating. Reservations: T0291-431161, F649368. ■ *Getting there: Frequent buses from Jodhpur.*

Sardar Samand
60 km SE of Jodhpur
The lake nearby is a beautiful setting for the royal 1933 art deco hunting lodge, **C** *Sardar Samand Palace* (WelcomHeritage) which with its annexe has 19 comfortable rooms, Rajasthani restaurant, pool, extensive grounds, lovely walks, tennis, squash, riding and boating. The lake attracts pelicans, flamingos, cranes, egrets and kingfishers – good for birdwatching. The wildlife sanctuary has blackbuck, gazelle and nilgai. Call T0291-510101, F510100 for reservations.

Pali &
Sodawas
90 km from Jodhpur
Pali is a textile town known for its screen printing and other textile units. Nearby, Sodawas stands amidst fields of mustard and wheat. **B** *Karni Fort* is a colonial period palatial home with 10 rooms, attached baths, good regional and Western food, riding and horse safaris. Advance bookings only, contact Karni Bhawan in Jodhpur (see page 224). **C** *Sodawas Kot*, T0291-32220, F393805, 10 rather overpriced, spartan rooms (Indian toilets)in Rajput family home, Rajasthani meals, good stables, horse and village safaris.

Balotra The small textile town southwest of Jodhpur is known for its traditional weaving using pit looms and block prints. Nearby is the beautiful Jain temple with elephant murals at **Nakoda**, which also hosts a remarkable camel and **cattle fair** which takes place on the river bed in March/April. Kanana, near Balotra, celebrates Holi with stage shows and other entertainment (27-19 Mar 2002).

You can stay at *Dharamshala* at Nakoda which has clean rooms with bath (Indian wc) or the **E-F** guest houses at Balotra.

The Mallinathji **cattle fair** is a major event (4-12 April 2002). Over 80,000 animals are brought making it Rajasthan's largest, including Kapila (Krishna's) cows and Kathiawari horses.

Tilwara
127 km from Jodhpur

North of Jodhpur

Surrounded by sand dunes, this ancient town in the Thar desert contains the largest group of eighth to 10th-century Hindu and Jain temples in Rajasthan. The typical **Pratihara Dynasty Temple Complex** is set on a terrace whose walls are finely decorated with mouldings and miniatures. The sanctuary walls have central projections with carved panels and above these rise curved towers. The doorways are usually decorated with river goddesses, serpents and scrollwork. The 23 temples are grouped in several sites north, west and south of the town. The western group contains a mixture of Hindu temples, including the **Surya Temple** (early eighth century) with beautifully carved pillars. The Jain **Mahavira Temple** (eighth to 10th centuries) is the best preserved, 200 m further on a hillock, rising above the town. The **Sachiya Mata Temple** (11th-12th century) is a living temple of the Golden Durga. Accommodation is at **AL** *Camel Camp*, on the highest sand dunes at Osian, T0291-37023. A complex of 10 double bedded luxury tents with modern conveniences (attached baths, hot showers), restaurant, bar, US$100 per tent inclusive of meals and camel safaris, ask in advance for jeep/camel transfers from the main road or station to avoid a steep climb up the dunes. Also some **E** and **F** guest houses in town.■ *Getting there: Jodhpur-Jaisalmer train stops at Osian. Also, 4 daily buses from Jodhpur, 2 hrs. Worth visiting; allow 1 hr there.*

Osian

Western Rajasthan

On the edge of the desert, Khimsar was founded by the Jain saint Mahavir 2,500 years ago. The remote, battle scarred, 16th-century moated castle had a *zenana* added in the mid-18th century and a regal wing added in the 1940s. **AL** *Khimsar Fort* (WelcomHeritage), T01585- 62345, F62228 (or reserve at WelcomGroup offices). There are 48 large, comfortable a/c rooms in this lovely fort, for atmosphere ask for old wing, good restaurant, modern pool, large gardens, "fire dances at the illuminated medieval fort ruins really captivating".

Khimsar
80 km NE of Jodhpur
(60 km from Osian)

Nagaur, which was a centre of Chishti Sufis, has attracted interest as it preserves some fine examples of pre-Mughal and Mughal architecture. The dull stretch of desert is enlivened by Nagaur's fort palace, temples and *havelis*. The walls are said to date from the 11th-12th century Chauhan period. Akbar built the mosque here and there is a shrine of the disciple of Mu'inuddin Chishti of Ajmer (see page 157). The fort which has palaces of the Mughal emperors and of the Marwars being restored with help from the Paul Getty Foundation, has excellent wall paintings and interesting ancient systems of rainwater conservation and storage, ably explained by a very knowledgeable curator. For further information take a look at *Nagaur: sultanate and early Mughal history and architecture of the district of Nagaur* by M and NH Shokoohy. The popular *Cattle and Camel Fair* (19-22 Feb 2002; 08-11 Feb 2003) is held just outside the town during which there are camel races, cock fights, folk dancing and music. The fields become full of encampments of pastoral communities, tribal people and livestock dealers with their cattle, camels, sheep, goat and other animals. Utensils, saddles and handicrafts are also sold during the fair.

Nagaur
Population: 67,000
137 km N of Jodhpur

If staying in town you may find the early morning (0400) prayer calls from the mosque & bhajan singing at dawn at the temples a major detraction

A *Fort* (WelcomHeritage) in Fort, T0291-510101, F510100, has been beauti-fully converted, Rajasthani meals, reservations T0291-45591, F542240. There is also **A** *Royal Camp* (WelcomHeritage) during the camel fair (plans to remain open Oct-Mar). Delightful deluxe two-bed furnished tents (hot water bottles, heaters etc), Western flush toilets, hot water in buckets, dining tent for buffets. Several **D-E** guest houses in town with Indian toilets and hot water. **E** *Kurja* (RTDC), 2 rooms, dorm. Places serve good but extremely spicy north Indian vegetarian food. Rajasthan Tourism arrange tented accommo-dation for visitors.

Bikaner

Phone code: 0151
Colour map 1, grid B5
Population: 415,000
Altitude: 237 m

Bikaner is an oasis town among scrub and sand dunes. The rocky outcrop in a barren landscape provides a dramatic setting for the Junagarh Fort, one of the finest in western Rajasthan. The old walled city retains a medieval air, while out-side the walls, palaces and mansions survive. Well off the usual tourist route, Bikaner is en route to Jaisalmer from Jaipur or Shekhawati.

Ins & outs
See page 238 for
further details

Getting there   Bikaner is a full day's drive from Jaipur but it may be worth stopping a night in Samode or the Shekhawati region (see page 135). The railway station is central and has services from Delhi (Sarai Rohilla), Jaipur and Jodhpur. The New Bus Stand is 3 km to the north but you can ask to be dropped in town (unless you arrive from the north). **Getting around**   The fort and the Old City are within easy walking distance from the station. Autos and cycle-rickshaws transfer passengers between the station and the New Bus Stand.

Background   Bikaner was set up as an independent kingdom in 1488 by Rao Bhikaji, the younger son of Jodhpur's founder, Rao Jodha. Protected by the harsh desert countryside, and by the military rulers who even humbled Aurangzeb's pow-erful Mughal army, it developed as a major centre in the cross-desert caravan trade. Even today, Bikaner's Marwari traders are noted throughout North India for their business acumen.

Like other desert trading cities, Bikaner would have decayed into a small town of little significance with the development of the sea ports but for the foresight of **Maharajah Ganga Singhji** who introduced wide ranging eco-nomic reforms which ensured the survival of the city. Among his greatest achievements was the 1927-28 **Bikaner Gang Canal** which turned 285,000 ha of arid scrub into cultivable land. The failure of the monsoon in 1998 and 1999 caused severe drought conditions in and around Bikaner in April and May 2000 and there was severe hardship across the region.

Sights

There is enough of interest in Bikaner to make it worth spending at least a cou-ple of days exploring. The atmospheric **Old City** enclosed within high walls, with its merchant *havelis*, temples and bazars, is worth seeking out. Enter through the Kote gate and you will still see camels, bullocks and donkeys pull-ing carts through narrow winding lanes. Some visitors however are disap-pointed by the dirt and smell and some women on their own have complained of unpleasant experiences.

This fort (1588-93) is one of the finest examples in Rajasthan of the paradox between medieval military architecture and beautiful interior decoration. Started in 1588 by Raja Rai Singh (1571-1611), a strong ally of the Mughal Empire, who led Akbar's army in numerous battles, it had palaces added for the next three centuries.

You enter the superbly preserved fort by the yellow sandstone **Suraj Pol** (Sun Gate, 1593) to the east. The pale red sandstone perimeter wall is surrounded by a moat (the lake no longer exists) while the *chowks* have beautifully designed palaces with balconies, kiosks and fine *jali* screens. The interiors are beautifully decorated with shell-work, lime plaster, mirror-and-glass inlays, gold leaf, carving, carpets and lacquer work.

The walls of the **Lal Niwas**, which are the oldest, are elaborately decorated in red and gold. Karan Singh commemorated a victory over Aurangzeb by building the **Karan Mahal** (1631-9) across the *chowk*. Successive rulers added the **Gaj Mandir** (1745-87) with its mirrored Shish Mahal, and the **Chattra Niwas** (1872-87) with its pitched roof and English 'field sport' plates decorating the walls.

The magnificent Coronation Hall, adorned with plaster work, lacquer, mirror and glass, is in Maharaja Surat Singh's **Anup Mahal** (1788-1828). The decorative façades around the Anup Mahal Chowk, though painted white, are in fact stone. The fort also includes the **Chetar Mahal** and **Chini Burj** of Dungar Singh (1872-87) and **Ganga Niwas** of Ganga Singh (1898-1943) who did much to modernize his state and also built the Lalgarh Palace to the north. Mirror work, carving and marble decorate the ornate **Chandra Mahal** (Moon Palace) and the **Phul Mahal** (Flower Palace), built by Maharaja Gaj Singh. These last two are shown to foreigners at the end as a 'special tour' when the guide expects an extra tip! The royal chamber in the Chandra Mahal has strategically placed mirrors so that any intruder entering could be seen by the Maharaja from his bed.

The fort **museum** has Sanskrit and Persian manuscripts, miniature paintings, jewels, enamelware, silver, weapons, *palanquins, howdahs* and war drums. During the Second World War, Ganga Singhji was a signatory to the Versailles treaty, and pictures of his life and rule, the bi-plane he received as a war memento, and other princely relics of the period can be seen in the fort. **Har Mandir**, the royal temple where birth and wedding ceremonies were celebrated, is still used for Gangaur and other festivities. The well nearby is reputedly over 130-m deep.

■ *Open all week, except during important festivals. 1000-1630 (last entry). Rs 50 (Indians Rs 10). Camera, Rs 30. Video Rs 100. Guided tours in Hindi and English (guides simply mention names and objects so you lose little by joining one in Hindi; most speak some English; an extra tip is needed to open 'locked rooms'. Private guides near the gate offer in-depth tours; Rs 80 for over 2 hrs. The Urmul Trust charity shop at the entrance has good local village crafts, a city map and guide.*

The red sandstone Lalgarh Palace stands in huge grounds to the north of the city, surrounded by rocks and sand dunes. Designed by Sir Swinton Jacob in 1902, the palace complex, with extensions over the next few decades, has attractive courtyards overlooked by intricate *zenana* screen windows and *jarokha* balconies, columned corridors and period furnishings. The banquet hall is full of hunting trophies and photographs. His highness, Dr Karni Singh of Bikaner, was well known for his shooting expertise – both with a camera and with a gun (he represented India in the Olympics). The Lalgarh is now a hotel, as are the Laxmi Niwas, with impressive carved exteriors and gold

Junagarh Fort
The ramparts offer great views of the elephant/horse stables and temples, the old city with the desert beyond & the relatively more recent city areas around the medieval walls

Lalgarh Palace
The bougainvillaea, parakeets & peacocks add to the attraction of the gardens in which the Bikaner State Railway Carriage is preserved

Western Rajasthan

polished interiors, and the Maan Bilas, an outhouse in the palace grounds in the same complex, as well as the *art deco* Karni Bhawan, the former royal guest house, nearby (see sleeping below). ■ *1000-1700, closed Wed. Rs 40.* You can visit Lalgarh for a meal and to see the **Sadul Museum** which houses old maps, photos and royal memorabilia. ■ *1000-1700, closed Wed. Rs 20. Hotel cloak rooms.* The **Anup Sanskrit Library** is open on request (ask hotel manager).

There are some exquisite **havelis** in Bikaner belonging to the Rampuria, Kothari, Vaid and Daga merchant families. The sandstone carvings combine traditional Rajasthani *haveli* architecture with colonial influence. Ask for Rampuria Street and the Purana Bazar and wander through lanes lined with fine façades. Among them is Bhanwar Niwas which has been converted into a heritage hotel.

Ganga Golden Jubilee Museum This museum has a fine small collection of pottery, paintings and weapons. Some pre-Harappan exhibits and a group of terracottas from the Gupta (fourth to fifth century) and Kushan periods. Separate section of local crafts and a gallery of artefacts. There are excellent examples of Bikaner miniature paintings which are specially prized because of their very fine quality. You can also see petrified wood fossils from the desert. ■ *1000-1630, closed Sun and government holidays. Rs 3. Public Park.*

Excursions

Bhand Sagar
A longer excursion to Kalibangan to the north, is described on page 239

Bhand Sagar, 5 km southwest, has a group of Hindu and Jain temples which are believed to be the oldest structures of Bikaner still in existance, dating from the days when it was just a desert trading out-post of Jodhpur. The white painted, sandstone Bandeshwar Temple with a towering *shikhara* roof and painted sculptures, murals, mirrorwork inside, is the most interesting. The Sandeshwar Temple, dedicated to Neminath, has gold leaf painting, *meenakari* work and marble sculptures. There are numerous steps but wonderful views. ■ *Free but caretakers may charge Rs 10 for cameras. Getting there: They are hard to find and difficult to approach by car but rickshaw wallahs know the way.*

Devi Kund Sagar Devi Kund Sagar, 8 km east, is the site of the Bhika rulers' *devals*, marking the funeral pyres; Surat Singh's has ceiling decorations of Rajput paintings. Great sunset views from the *devals* over the lake are sadly marred by poles and wires.

Gajner National Park Gajner National Park, 30 km west of Bikaner, was a private preserve which once provided the royal family of Bikaner with game. This birder's paradise is surrounded by 13,000 ha of scrub forest which harbours large colonies of nil-gai, chinkara, blackbuck, wild boar and desert reptiles. Throughout the day, a train of antelope, gazelle and pigs can be seen arriving to drink at Gajner Lake. Winter migratory birds include the Imperial black-bellied sand grouse, cranes and migratory ducks. Some visitors have spotted Great Indian bustard at the water's edge. There is an RTDC picnic spot by the lake from where visitors can view the birds. It is worth stopping for an hour's mini-safari if you are in the vicinity. Within the park is **A** *Gajner Palace* (HRH) beautifully set by the lake, T01534-55063, F0151-522408, sales@hrhindia.com There are 40 renovated a/c rooms in the palace and its wings (most with brass beds and fireplaces), full of character (Edwardian Raj nostalgia, period furniture, old lithographs, painted ceilings), billiards, tennis, pool planned, jeeps to scrub forest (Rs 1000), cycle hire (Rs 200), horse and camel rides, boating, good walking (great views from *Shabnam Cottage* on a hilltop), attractive red sandstone façades, latticework, pleasantly unfrequented and atmospheric (visitors welcome, Rs 100), friendly manager and staff.

Kolayat is an important Hindu pilgrimage centre around a sacred lake with 52 ghats and a group of five temples built by Ganga Singhji. The oasis village comes alive at the November full moon when a three-day festival draws thousands of pilgrims who take part in ritual bathing. The **cattle and camel fair** (27-30 November 2001, 16-19 November 2002, 5-8 November 2003) is very colourful and authentic but it can get quite riotous after dark. Since facilities are minimal, it is best to arrive before the festival to find a local family with space to spare, or ask a travel agent in Bikaner. An HRH bungalow and garden is available to those staying at their Bikaner or Gajner hotels (take a letter) to use the terrace and dining room for a picnic and the clean (Indian) toilets. ■ *Getting there: by car or rail.*

Kolayat
50 km SW via Gajner

Kolayat is regarded as one of the 58 most important Hindu pilgrimage centres

Karni Mata Mandir is a 17th-century temple, 33 km south at Deshnoke. The massive silver gates and beautiful white marble carvings on the façade were added by Ganga Singh (1898-1943), who dedicated the temple to a 15th-century female mystic Karniji, worshipped as an incarnation of Durga. A gallery describes her life. Mice and rats, revered and fed with sweets and milk in the belief that they are reincarnated saints, swarm over the temple around your feet. ■ *Closed 1200-1600. Free, camera Rs 40. Take socks as the floor is very dirty. Reasonable toilets, Indian style, Rs 2. Yatri Niwas nearby has simple rooms. Rajasthani food is sold by the temple. The train leaves Bikaner, 1000, returns 1230. Buses from Bikaner New Bus Stand or Ganga Shahar Rd, hourly, Rs 7 (share auto-rickshaw from Station Rd to Bus, Rs 3). On return journey, for Station Rd, get off at Thar Hotel and walk or take auto-rickshaw. Taxi about Rs 200 return.*

Karni Mata Mandir
Spotting the white rat at this temple is supposed to bring good luck

About 75 km south of Bikaner, this picturesque village with attractive huts, some painted and surrounded by sand dunes, is popular for camel safaris. You can stay at *Dr Karni Singh's Rest House*, T01532-33006, which has simple but comfortable rooms in a bungalow and three huts, attached baths with hot water in buckets (Rs 350, breakfast Rs 75, lunch/dinner Rs 150), camel safaris Rs 1500 per day with tented facilities in the desert.

Kakoo

This research farm, 9 km southeast, claims to be the only one in Asia. Camel rides may be available but there are no refreshments. Good views can be enjoyed from the top of the tower. ■ *1500-1700, closed Sun. Photography 'prohibited' but camel drivers ask to be photographed! Getting there: A pleasant cycle ride along a very quiet road, or hire a rickshaw.*

Camel Research Farm

Essentials

AL *Lalgarh Palace* (WelcomHeritage), 3 km railway, T540201, F522253, welcom@ndf.vsnl.net.in 38 large a/c rooms, attractive red sandstone façade, built in 1902, museum in poor state of repair (interesting if shown around by retainer), beautiful decorations (see above), sports, good pool, mixed reports on staff and slow service. In the grounds: **AL-A** *Laxmi Niwas*, Lalgarh Complex, T202777, F525219, laxminiwaspalace@123india.com 31 large rooms with fabulous carvings, painted ceilings, (19 new rooms planned), gardens, courtyard with fountains, billiards, lattice work balconies, restaurant, enthusiastic Bengali manager. **A** *Karni Bhawan Palace* (HRH), Gandhi Colony near Lalgarh Palace, T524701, F522408, sales@hrhindia.com 20 comfortable a/c or air-cooled rooms, some in annexe, well-renovated good restaurant (Marwari and simple

Sleeping
■ *on map, page 237*
Price codes:
see inside front cover

Taxis can be difficult to get from the Lalgarh Palace area in the evening

Western Rajasthan

continental), attentive service, art deco mansion. **A-B** *Bhanwar Niwas*, Rampuria St, Old City (500 m from Kote Gate), ask for *Rampuria Haveli Hotel* (difficult to find), T529323, F200880. 20 rooms around a courtyard, early 20th-century *haveli*, Indian kitsch decor, excellent vegetarian dinner, bar in an old *baori*, 'a wonderful place'.

B *Bhairon Vilas*, near fort, T544751, F523642. Restored 1800s aristocratic *haveli*, great atmosphere, 18 attractive rooms, some with period furniture, excellent rooftop restaurant (Rajasthani, some Punjabi, Chinese, Western) with live entertainment, good views, lawn. Recommended. **B** *Maan Vilas* (HRH), Lalgarh Complex, T524711, F522408, sales@hrhindia.com 9 comfortable garden facing rooms in a well restored and renovated outhouse, lawns. **B** *Heritage Resort*, along the Jaipur highway, 9 km from 'mile' stone, T752234, F207674. 36 cottage rooms, pleasant location, sprawling garden, bar, restaurant, outdoor coffee shop, swimming pool, sports, own vehicle essential.

C *Sagar*, next to *Lalgarh Palace*, T201877, F521877. 32 good a/c rooms (being extended) in modern building, popular restaurant, exchange, internet. **C** *Basant Vihar Palace*, Ganganagore Rd, T528299. Rooms in attractive early-20th century palatial sandstone mansion built by Maharajah Ganga Sinhji, magnificent darbar hall, pool, large gardens with old lily ponds. **C** *Meghsar Castle*, 9 Gajner Rd, T527315. 10 aircooled rooms in modern hotel but in traditional Rajput sandstone style, very attractive garden, friendly manager. Recommended. Next door **C** *Kishan Palace*, Gajner Rd, T527762, F522041, is similar. **C-D** *Palace View*, outside *Lalgarh Palace*, T527072. 16 clean, comfortable rooms (some a/c), good views of palace and gardens, restaurant (good 'unlimited' breakfast, wide choice), pleasant small garden, courteous, hospitable family. Recommended. **C-D** *Bharat Niwas*, near PBM Hospital, Sadul Colony, T523025, F523674. 24 rooms, a/c or air-cooled, good food, internet, clean, good atmosphere, friendly. **C-E** *Harasar Haveli*, opposite stadium, T209891, F523150, harasar-haveli@yahoo.com 16 rooms in converted mansion, some with verandahs and good views (Rs 250-850), dining room with period memorabilia, garden, exchange, internet, clean and friendly. **C-E** *Marudhar Heritage*, Bhagwan Mahaveer Marg, near Station Rd, T522524. Good rooms, aircooled or a/c (Rs 350-999), bath with hot showers (am), TV, very clean and comfortable, generous *thalis* (Rs 50), friendly owner.

Budget hotel rooms usually have shared bath; often serve Indian veg food only. The tourist office has a list of Paying Guest accommodation

D *Shivam*, Sadulganj, T203112, F525150. Good rooms in a nice bungalow in residential locality, restaurant, small garden, courteous owner, friendly. **D** *Thar*, Hospital Rd, Ambedkar Circle (up a flight of steps from shopping complex), T543050, F525150. 35 clean rooms with bath (7 a/c) most with balconies, also dorm, Indian restaurant, coffee shop, good service, desert camping possible. **D-E** *Desert Winds*, by MN Hospital, near Karni Stadium, 1 km Bus Stand, T542202. 6 clean, comfortable rooms, good food, pleasant balcony and garden, friendly family; **D-E** *Dhola Maru* (RTDC), near Puran Singh Circle, T529621. 25 rooms with bath, dorm (Rs 50), some a/c, restaurant, bar, adequate.

E-F *Deluxe*, Station Rd, T523292. Some air-cooled rooms with shower, bucket hot water, inspect first, restaurant (mainly *dosas*), eager-to-please management, popular but noisy. **E-F** *Kalinga*, near *Lalgarh Palace*, T209751. Economical rooms for Rs 150-250, small baths with hot water and western toilets, meals from Sagar hotel/ Niroj nearby. **F** *Delight Rest House*, behind Deluxe, T542313. Simple rooms with shared baths Rs 60-100, also some better rooms **F** *Shanti Niwas*, Ganga Shahar Rd, near Station, T542320, F524231. Rather dated rooms, some with bath (hot water), noisy and not too clean, inspect first. **F** *Railway Retiring Rooms* and dorm are good value, reservations T524660. **F** *Vijay Guest House* opposite Sophia School, Jaipur Rd, T231244, F525150. 3 clean rooms with shower (Rs 100), 3 with shared bath (Rs 50), use of fridge, delicious home cooked *thali*/set meals (Rs 30-100), travel information, camping (Rs 50) and caravan parking, pleasant garden, quiet very hospitable and knowledgeable host, great value. Highly recommended. Vijay's camel safaris also come highly recommended (see below).

Mid-range *Amber*, Indian, some western dishes. Most popular in town but reports of complacency and falling standards. **Cheap** In hotels: for Rajasthani meals, order ahead at *Vijay*; *Sagar* and *Thar* also have good restaurants. *Anand* serves *thalis*. *Kesria*, Jaipur Rd. Pleasant countryside location, popular on breezy summer evenings but disappointing food. *Moomal*, JNV Colony. Indian. A/c, popular, good value. *Niroj*, near government bus stand. Popular for Indian-Chinese-Continental food, bar. *Teja Garden*, Jaipur Rd. Pleasant outdoor garden restaurant, average food. *Vijay Guest House*, delicious home-cooked vegetarian *thalis* (Rs 30), non-veg set menu (Rs 60-100). **Fast food** Try the local specialities – *Bikaneri bhujia/sev/namkeen* – savoury (with spicy options) snacks made from dough (gram/pulses). Sweets (including Rajasthani *ghevar* and Bengali *rasgulla*) are best at *Bikharam Chandiram*, *Aggarwal*, *Girdharalal* and *Haldiram*, all in Station Rd, Kote Gate area. *Chhotu Motoo* at *Joshi*. Fresh Rajasthani sweets and snacks. Visit Purana Bazaar for ice-cold lassis by day, hot milk (milk, sugar, cream, whipped up with a flourish) at night. *Jamani Doodh Bhandar*, Vaidya Chowk, is popular.

Eating
● on map, page 237
Price codes:
see inside front cover

You can dine in style at the first four hotels listed. Plenty of veg restaurants on Station Rd

Outside hotels *Niroj* is near the government bus stand.

Bars

Western Rajasthan

Bikaner

■ Sleeping
1 Bhairon Vilas
2 Bhanwar Niwas
3 Bharat Niwas
4 Chhotu Motoo
5 Deluxe & Delight
6 Desert Wind
7 Dhola Maru
8 Harasar Haveli
9 Inder Restaurant
10 Lalgarh, Laxmi Niwas, Maan Vilas
11 Marudhar
12 Meghsar Castle
13 Palace View, Kalinga
14 Sagar
15 Shanti Niwas & Adarsh
16 Shri Ram
17 Thar

● Eating
1 Amber
2 Kesria

N
0 metres 200
0 yards 200

Camel safaris
These have to be arranged through private operators

A popular route is Raiser to Katriasar sand dunes on the Jaipur road, facing a fire dancers' village. *Camel Man* (see tour companies), arranges excellent camel safaris, jeep tours and cycling in the desert using light weight 'igloo' tents, clean mattresses and sheets, good food and guidance. You can see antelopes, colourful villages and potters at work. There are 1-2 hr-camel rides to villages around Bikaner, 4 hr-camel safaris breaking for lunch on the dunes, full day safaris with lunch, tea, dinner and log fire in the desert, 2-day safaris from Raisar, with tented stay at Surdhana, returning to Bikaner via Balakya Dhora sand dunes and Shivbari temple, and 5-day safaris from Bikaner to Khichan connecting to buses from Phalodi to Jaisalmer. Rs 500 per person per day, with a full time cook; Rs 800 with elaborate arrangements. *Virendra Singh Tanwar*, T0151-525594, offers up-market camel safaris from Bikaner towards Jaisalmer. *Gorbandh Safari*, T540123, F524806 or c/o *Aravalli Tours*, Rs 1600 per person (toilet tent between five two-person tents), *Fata Morgana*, T200561, 20 years experience, professional.

Festivals *Camel Fair* (27-28 **Jan** in 2002; 17-18 **Jan** in 2003) and *Diwali* (**Oct/Nov**) are especially spectacular in Junagarh Fort, in the Old City near Kote Gate and some smaller palaces.

Shopping Bikaner is famous for *Usta* work (camel leather painted in colours) which includes footwear, purses and cushions. You can also get local carpets and woodwork. The main shopping centres are on KEM (MG) Rd (from near the fort) and around, Kote Gate in the Old City, Modern Market. *Cottage Industries Institute*, near Junagarh Fort. *Rajasthali* counter at Information Centre. **Photography** Shops on MG Rd.

Transport From **Delhi** (435 km); **Jaipur** (330 km); **Jodhpur** (250 km); **Jaisalmer** (320 km); **Ajmer** (280 km); **Mumbai** (1,250 km).

Local Auto-rickshaw: Between station and bus stand or Lalgarh Palace, Rs 25. **Camel**: Local rides through travel agents (12-day Jaisalmer trip can be expensive). **Cycle**: For hire near *Amber* opposite railway station. **Taxi**: Unmetered, at station, bus stand or through hotels.

Long distance Air: No service at present. **Road Bus**: The New Bus Stand is 3 km north of town. Private buses leave from south of the fort. *Rajasthan Roadways*, enquiries, T523800; daily deluxe buses to **Ajmer, Jodhpur, Jaisalmer** (8 hrs), **Udaipur**. 2 daily to **Delhi** via Hissar (12 hrs). *Rajasthan Tourism*, T27445, deluxe coach to **Jaipur**, 7 hrs. **Train**: Enquiries, T61131, reservations, 0800-1400, 1415-2000, Sun 0800-1400. For tourist quota (when trains are full) apply to Manager's Office by Radio Tower near *Jaswant Bhawan Hotel*. **Delhi**: *Bikaner-DSR Exp*, *4790*, 0830, 10½ hrs; *Bikaner-DSRi Mail*, *4792*, 1945, 10 hrs. From Delhi (SR), the overnight train (*DSR Bikaner Mail*, *4791*, 2125, best 2nd class sleeper), gives very good sunrise views. **Jaipur**: *Intercity Exp*, *2466*, 0540, 5 hrs. **Jodhpur**: *KJC Exp*, *4667*, 1230, 5½ hrs; *Ranakpur Exp*, *4707*, 0935, 5½ hrs (continues to Ahmadabad, further 10 hrs) and Mumbai (Bandra), another 10½ hrs.

Directory **Banks** *Bank of Baroda*, Ambedkar Circle, changes TCs and currency. *State Bank of Bikaner & Jaipur*, Ambedkar Circle, also near fort's Suraj Pol. Changes TCs but may charge up to 10% commission! *Harasar Haveli Hotel* charges 1%. **Communications** **Internet**: *Meghsar Castle, Hotel Sagar* and *Harasar Haveli*, Rs 2 per min; others at Sadulganj, Sagar Rd, Jaipur Rd and Gajner Rd, and near the fort. **Post**: GPO is behind Junagarh Fort. **Hospital** *PBM Hospital*, Hospital Rd, T524175. **Tour companies and travel agents** *Aravalli Tours*, opposite Municipal Council Hall, Junagarh Rd, T571124. Efficient. Recommended. *Camel Man*, Vijay Guest House, opposite Sophia School, Jaipur Rd, T529344, F525150. Offers good value, reliable, friendly and professional safaris (see above) and tourist guides. Recommended. *Forts & Palaces*, Jodhasar

House, Hanuman. Hatha, T205985, jaipur@palaces-tours.com *Travel Plan*, Bhanwar Niwas, Rampuria St, T529323. **Tourist offices** Rajasthan, *Dhola-Maru Tourist Bungalow*, Poonam Singh Circle, T527445. 0800-1800, Oct-Mar, car-hire. **Useful addresses** Ambulance: T61902. **Police:** T100.

One of North India's most important early settlement regions stretches from the Shimla hills down past the important Harappan sites of Hanumangarh and Kalibangan, north of Bikaner.

Kalibangan & Harappan sites

Late Harappan sites have been explored by archaeologists since 1962. They were identified in the upper part of the valley, the easternmost region of the Indus Valley civilization. Across the border in Pakistan are the premier sites of Harappa (200 km) and Moenjo Daro (450 km). Here, the most impressive of the sites today is that of **Kalibangan** (west off the NH15 at Suratgarh). On the south bank of the Ghaggar River it was a heavily fortified citadel mound, rising about 10 m above the level of the plain.

There were several pre-Harappan phases. Allchin and Allchin record that the bricks of the early phase were already standardized, though not to the same size as later Harappan bricks. The ramparts were made of mud brick and a range of pottery and ornaments have been found. The early pottery is especially interesting, predominantly red or pink with black painting.

Transport Road Bus: Local buses to Kalibangan from Suratgarh, which can be reached by bus from Bikaner, Hanumangarh, Sirsa (Haryana) or Mandi Dabwali (Punjab). **Train** The broad gauge line connects **Suratgarh** with **Anupgarh**, about 15 km from the Pakistan border, where it terminates. Kalibangan is about half way to Anupgarh. The nearest station is Raghunathgarh, but travel from there to Kalibangan is difficult (check at Suratgarh or Anupgarh). From **Suratgarh** to **Anupgarh**: *Passenger*, 0755, 2¾ hrs. Trains from **Suratgarh: Bikaner (Lalgarh Junction)**: *Chandigarh Exp*, *4887*, 0835, 3¾ hrs. **Bhatinda**: *Chandigarh Exp*, *4888*, 1955, 3¾ hrs.

Western Rajasthan

This lovely village has superb red sandstone *havelis* of the Oswal Jains. Beyond the village are sand dunes and mustard fields, and a lake which attracts ducks and other waterfowl. The once small quiet village has grown into a bustling agricultural centre and a prominent bird feeding station. Jain villagers put out grain behind the village for winter visitors; up to 8,000 demoiselle cranes and occasionally Common eastern cranes can be seen together in December and January on the feeding grounds. There isn't anywhere to stay in Khichan but there is **E-F** *Hotel Sunrise* (RTDC), halfway to Phalodi, which has a few basic rooms (mostly with Indian toilets). Road side eating places in Phalodi serve extremely spicy north Indian food.

Khichan

4 km from Phalodi, SW of Bikaner, just off the NH15

Pokaran, between Jaisalmer and Jodhpur, stands on the edge of the great desert with dunes stretching 100 km west to the Pakistan border. It provides a mid-way stopover between Bikaner/Jodhpur and Jaisalmer, for tourists as it did for royal and merchant caravans in the past. Pokaran was a major principality under the Maharajahs of Jodhpur-Marwar in the 16th century. The Mughal Emperor Humayun is said to have stopped at Pokaran when retreating from Sher Shah's forces that took over his capital at Delhi. The impressive yellow sandstone Pokaran fort, overlooking a confusion of streets in the town below, has a small museum with an interesting collection of medieval weapons, costumes and paintings. It was built by the Marwar *thakur* Rao Maldeo (1532-84) with some masonry from an older Satelmer Fort nearby which is in ruins. There are good views from the fort ramparts of the countryside and the

Pokaran

Population: 15,000

town. Pokaran is also well known for its potters who make red-and-white pottery and terra cotta horses/elephants.

Ramdeora, the Hindu and Jain pilgrim centre nearby, has Bishnoi hamlets and a preserve for blackbuck antelope, Indian gazelle, bustards and sand grouse. *Ramdeora Fair* is an important religious event (27 Aug 2001, 15 Sep 2002). **Khetolai** is the site of India's first nuclear test explosion held underground on 18 March 1974, and further tests in May 1998. The road west out of Pokaran to Jaisalmer (112 km) is quite decent with little traffic, with the possibility of some wildlife viewing along the way. Sand sometimes obscures the road.

Sleeping and eating C *Fort Pokaran*, T029942-22274, F22279. 14 quaint rooms with bath (need improving), old four-posters, some carved columns, warm hospitality, good hot lunches Rs 200-250 (order ahead if passing through town). **D** *Godavan* (RTDC), on NH15, T029942-22275. 2 rooms and 4 huts, mediocre restaurant (slow service), clean toilet, pool. Pick up fresh *pakoras* from highway stalls on the outskirts or delicious *gulab jamuns* from the local *halwai* (sweet shop). **In Manvar (near Dechhu):** **B-C** *Manver Desert Camp*, 6 km south of Pokaran. Beautifully designed cottages with attractive interiors, some a/c, restaurant (a good place to break journey for a beer and lunch between Jodhpur and Jaisalmer), book shop, handicrafts. The **B** *Tented Resort*, 2½ km on a sand dune off the road, has very good 2-bed tents with attached hot showers and flush toilets, meals (Rs 300-375), camel and jeep safaris and visits to Bishnoi villages arranged for Rs 400-1200 depending on duration. Chinkara, desert fox and desert birds are seen around the camp. Reservations: 02928-66137.

Shergarh   Some 120 km from Jodhpur along the Jaisalmer Highway, Shergarh has the
(Garah)   largest expanse of sand dunes in the region with traditional villages nearby. At the war memorial between Balesar and Dechu, a detour to Khirjan goes to Shergarh (15-minutes drive).

★ Jaisalmer

Phone code: 02992
Colour map 1, grid C2
Population: 39,000
Altitude: 250 m
275 km from Jodhpur

The approach to Jaisalmer across the hot barren desert is magical as the city shimmers like a mirage. With the crenellated golden sandstone town walls and narrow streets lined with exquisitely carved buildings, through which camel carts trundle leisurely, it has an extraordinary medieval feel and an incredible atmosphere. The fort inside, perched on its hilltop, contains some gems of Jain temple building, while beautifully decorated merchants' havelis are scattered through the town. Jaisalmer gives convenient access to the surrounding desert wilderness, sand dunes and oasis villages ideal for camel rides and safaris. A few travellers have found the people unfriendly.

Ins & outs   **Getting there** The nearest airport is at Jodhpur. Trains from Jodhpur arrive at
See page 249   Jaisalmer railway station, to the east of town. Phone ahead and ask your hotel if they
further details   offer a pick-up. Most long-distance buses arrive at the station bus stand and then go to Amar Sagar Pol which is about 15-mins walk from the fort gate. **Getting around** Unmetered jeeps and auto-rickshaws can be hired at the station (and in the walled town) but they are no help inside the fort so you may have to carry your luggage some distance uphill if you choose a fort hotel. You can hire a bike for the day from Gopa Chowk (Rs 25) though the whole town is really best explored on foot. **Climate** Best time to visit is Jan-Feb, the air is clean and the nights are cool.

Founded by Prince Jaisal in 1156, Jaisalmer grew to be a major staging post on **History**
the trade route across the forbidding Thar desert from India to the West.
The merchants prospered and invested part of their wealth in building beautiful houses and temples with the local sandstone. The growth of maritime trade
between India and the West caused a decline in trade across the desert which
ceased altogether in 1947. However, the wars with Pakistan (1965 and 1971)
resulted in the Indian government developing the transport facilities to the
border to improve troop movement. This has also helped visitors to gain
access. Today, the army and tourism are mainstays of the local economy but
the town is relatively free of hassle from hawkers.

Sights

The walled town, mostly to the north of the inner fort, is enclosed by a wall
built in 1750. There are four major gateways or *pols*: Malka, Amar Sagar,
Baron and Gadisagar; the others have been sealed. Amar Sagar Pol to the west,
the main entry point, leads to Gandhi Chowk. The fort entrance, beyond the
Central Market and Gopa Chowk. Most of the hotels and restaurants are clustered around the two chowks and inside the fort. To retain its attraction, all,
including new structures, are built out of the local honey-coloured sandstone.

On the roughly triangular-shaped Trikuta Hill, the fort stands 76 m above the   **The fort**
town, enclosed by a 9-m wall with 99 bastions (mostly 1633-1647). You enter   *'Sunset Point' just*
the fort from the east from Gopa Chowk. The inner, higher fort wall and the   *north of the fort, is*
old gates up the ramp (Suraj, Ganesh, Hawa and Rang Pols) provided further   *popular at sundown*
defences. The Suraj Pol (1594), once an outer gate, is flanked by heavy bas-   *for views over*
tions and has bands of decoration which imitate local textile designs. Take a   *Jaisalmer*
walk through the narrow streets within the fort, often blocked by the odd goat   *Best light for*
or cow, and see how even today about a 1,000 of the town's people live in tiny   *photography in*
houses inside the fort often with beautiful carvings on doors and balconies. It   *late afternoon*
is not difficult to get lost!

As with many other Rajput forts,
within the massive defences are a
series of palaces, the product of successive generations of rulers' flights
of fancy. Often called the Golden
Fort because of the colour of the
sandstone, it dominates the town.
The stone is relatively easy to carve
and the dry climate has meant that
the fineness of detail has been preserved through the centuries. The *jali*
work and delicately ornamented balconies and windows with wide eaves
break the solidity of the thick walls
which gives protection from the heat,
while the high plinths of the buildings
keep off the sand.

Rajmahal Palace The Juna Mahal
(circa 1500) of the seven-storey palace with its *jali* screens is one of the
oldest Rajasthani palaces. The rather

Jaisalmer Fort

0 metres 100
0 yards 100

N

■ **Sleeping**
1 Deepak
2 Fort View & Kanchan
  Shree Restaurant
3 Jaisal Castle
4 Laxmi Niwas (New)
5 Laxmi Niwas &
  Surya Restaurant
6 Paradise
7 Sandrella
8 Simla
9 Sri Nath Palace
10 Suraj
11 Surya

● **Eating**
1 8th July
2 Vyas

Gopa Chowk
Entrance
Rajmahal Palace
Jain Temple
Market

plain *zenana* block to its west, facing the *chauhata* (square) is decorated with false *jalis*. Next to it is the *mardana* (men's quarters) including the Rang Mahal above the Hawa Pol, built during the reign of Mulraj II (1762-1820) which has highly detailed murals and mirror decoration. Sarvotam Vilas is ornamented with blue tiles and glass mosaics. The adjacent Gaj Vilas (1884) stands on a high plinth. Mulraj II's Moti Mahal has floral decoration and carved doors. ■ *0800-1300, 1500-1700. Rs 20 (Indians Rs 10), camera Rs 50.*

The open square beyond the gates has a platform reached by climbing some steps. This is where court was held or royal visitors entertained. There are also fascinating **Jain temples** (12th-16th centuries). Whilst the Rajputs were devout Hindus they permitted Jainism to be practised. *0700-1200. Camera Rs 50. Leather shoes not permitted.* The **Parsvanatha** (1417) has a fine gateway, an ornate porch and 52 subsidiary shrines surrounding the main structure. The brackets are elaborately carved as maidens and dancers. The exterior of the **Rishbhanatha** (1479) has more than 600 images as decoration whilst clusters of towers form the roof of the **Shantinatha** built at the same time. The **Ashtapadi** (16th-century) incorporates the Hindu deities of Vishnu, Kali and Lakshmi into its decoration. The **Mahavir Temple** has an emerald statue. ■ *View 1000-1100.* The **Sambhavanatha** (1431) has vaults beneath it that were used for document storage. The *Gyan Bhandar* here is famous for its ancient manuscripts. ■ *1000-1100.*

Havelis   There are many exceptional *havelis* (mansions of rich merchants) both in the fort and the walled town. Many have beautifully carved façades, *jali* screens and oriel windows overhanging the streets below. The ground floor is raised above the dusty streets and each has an inner courtyard surrounded by richly decorated apartments. An unofficial 'guide' will usually show you the way to them for about Rs 20.

Inside Amar Sagar Pol (gate), the former ruler's 20th-century palace **Badal Mahal** with a five-storeyed tower, has fine carvings. **Salim Singh-ki haveli** (17th-century), near the fort entrance, is especially attractive with peacock brackets. It is often referred to as the Ship Palace because of its distinctive and decorative upper portion. Often closed, you may get a view from a house opposite.

Nathumal-ki haveli (1885), nearer Gandhi Chowk, was built for the Prime Minister. Partly carved out of rock by two craftsmen, each undertaking one half of the house, it has a highly decorative façade with an attractive front door guarded by two elephants (mid-afternoon best for photos). Inside is a wealth of decoration; notice the tiny horse-drawn carriage and a locomotive showing European influence! ■ *When the havelis are occupied, you may be allowed in on a polite request. Otherwise, your guide will help you gain access for a small fee.*

Patwon-ki haveli (1805), further east, is a group of five built for five brothers. Possibly the finest in town, they have beautiful murals and carved pillars. A profusion of balconies cover the front wall and the inner courtyard is surrounded by richly decorated apartments. The main courtyard and some roofs are now used as shops. ■ *Rs 5 to view the gold ceilings and enjoy the view from the rooftop, best 1030-1700.* Gorbandh Palace proposes to open a rooftop restaurant.

Mandir Palace, the beautiful 1825 mansion of Maharaj Hukum Singh, a close relative of the Maharajah of Jaisalmer, with intricate carvings, is now a hotel. ■ *Non-residents may visit Rs 10.* The restored **Maharani's Palace** is expected to open as an exhibition centre.

The Gadi Sagar (Gadisar or Gharisar) tank, southeast of the city walls, was the oasis which led Prince Jaisal to settle here. Now connected by a pipe to the Indira Gandhi Canal, it has water all year. It attracts migratory birds and has many small shrines around it and is well worth visiting, especially in the late afternoon (see museums below). The delightful archway is said to have been built by a distinguished courtesan who built a temple on top to prevent the king destroying the gate.

Gadi Sagar tank

The **Government Museum**, near *Moomal Hotel*, houses fossils, sixth-12th-century inscriptions, 12th-century sculpture, embroideries, block prints and stoneware. ■ *1000-1630, Mon free, closed Fri. Rs 3*. **Folklore Museum**, on Gadi Sagar, has a small private collection of Mr NK Sharma including miniature paintings, handicrafts, utensils, attires of various communities of western Rajasthan, historic photographs, camel decorations and a section on the love story of princess Moomal and king Mahendra. Highly recommended. ■ *0800-1200, 1500-1800. Rs 10 (Indians Rs 5), camera Rs 20*. The **Palace Museum** is next to the Palace.

Museums

Excursions

Bada (Barra) Bagh, 6 km north of Jaisalmer, is an attractive oasis with mango trees and other vegetation not normally seen in the desert. The reservoir and systems of sanitary drainage may interest some! There is a viewpoint from the royal *chhatris* (memorials) here but the intrusive tall army watch posts spoil sunset views. ■ *Rs 10. Auto-rickshaws, Rs 40 return*. Suman Motel *with rooms and vegetarian restaurant nearby.*

Bada (Barra) Bagh

The pleasant Amar Sagar, 5 km northwest, was once a formal garden with a pleasure palace of Amar Singh (1661-1703) on the bank of a lake which dries up during the hot season. The Jain temple there has been restored. ■ *Camera Rs 50, video Rs 100.*

Amar Sagar

Lodurva, 15 km northwest of Jaisalmer, contains a number of Jain temples that are the only remains of a once flourishing Marwar capital. Rising honey-coloured out of the desert, they are beautifully carved with *jali* outside and are well maintained and well worth a visit. ■ *Camera Rs 50*. The road beyond Lodurva is unsealed. **E-F** *Sam Dhani*, on Lodurva Road, is 45 km from town. There are eight huts with bath (hot water), some air-cooled, dorm beds (Rs 50), meals with advance notice. Contact *Hotel Moomal,* Jaisalmer, T52392.

Lodurva

Kuldhara, 17 km from Jaisalmer, off the Sam Road, was once flourishing township on the shores of River Kak. An artificial reservoir, deep cylindrical wells and a 14th-century stepwell have been found amid the ruins of this deserted town of over 700 houses. It gives an insight into the Paliwal Brahmins who moved to this arid region in the twelfth century. Unlike other Brahmin communities, the Paliwals were farmers and bankers, and on these grounds the Parihar Rajputs of Marwar in the 12th century imposed taxes from which other Brahmins were exempt, and they moved from Pali to Jaisalmer and set up more than 84 villages. In the 18th century, disgruntled with the tyrannical minister, Salim Singh (the builder of the famous *haveli*), and his plans to tax them, the Paliwals abandoned the villages and moved to other areas. Kuldhara is an interesting place to see their houses, with space for cows/

Kuldhara

Western Rajasthan

bullock carts and sometimes rooms with wooden ceilings. A *chhatri* and a finely carved Krishna Temple, dated to the 18th century and recently restored, can be seen here.

Kabha Kabha, south of Kuldhara, is another enchanting deserted colony of the Paliwals, but permission is needed to visit from the Collector's office. Besides the many houses and chhatris in the town, you can climb to the recently restored fort on an elevation for superb views of the ruins and the sand dunes, to the picturesque thatched roof huts of the nearby Sodha Rajput village.

Sam dunes Sam dunes (or *Sain*), 40 km west of Jaisalmer, is popular for sunset camel rides. It is not really a remote spot in the middle of the desert but the only real large stretch of sand near town. The proper dunes only cover a small area yet are still quite impressive. Right in the middle of the dunes 'Sunset view' is like a fairground, slightly tacky with lots of day-trippers; the only escape from this and the camel men is to walk quite a way away! It is possible to stay over at **Mr Sodha's D-E** RTDC Huts facing the dunes, though they can get very busy in the late afternoon and sunset but is very pleasant at night and early morning. ■ *Rs 2; car Rs 10 (camera fees may be introduced). Camel rates usually start at Rs 50 per hour but can be bargained down.*

Khuri Khuri, 40 km southwest of Jaisalmer, is a small picturesque desert village of decorated mud thatched buildings which was ruled by the Sodha clan for four centuries. Visitors are attracted by shifting sand dunes, some 80-m high, but the peace of the village has been spoilt by the growing number of huts, tents and guest houses which have opened along the road and near the dunes; persistent hotel and camel agents board all buses bound for Khuri. Mr Sodha's **D-E** *Khuri Guest House*, near bus station, T02992-8444, has rooms in traditional round house style, delicious cooking, safaris, attentive hosts. Mr Singh's **D-E** *Mama's*, T02992-8423, has simple but comfortable thatched huts, some with fans, delicious Rajasthani meals, folk entertainment, camel safaris (but agree price beforehand). ■ *Best months Nov-Feb. Rs 3 (may be increased in line with Desert National Park; car Rs 10. Getting there: buses from Jaisalmer take 1½ hours. Jeep for 4, Rs 450 for sunset tour.*

Thar Desert National Park Thar Desert National Park is near Khuri, the core being about 60 km from Jaisalmer. The park was created to protect 3,000 sq km of the Thar Desert, the habitat for drought resistant, endangered and rare species which have adjusted to the unique and inhospitable conditions of extreme temperatures. The desert has undulating dunes and vast expanses of flat land where the trees are mostly leafless, thorny and have very long roots, eg *khejri* (*Prosopis cineraria*), which dominates. There is also *khair* (*Acacia katechu*), *thor* and *rohira*. Fascinating for birdwatching, it is one of the few places in India where the **Great Indian bustard** is proliferating (it can weigh up to 14 kg and reach a height of 40 cm). In winter it also attracts the migratory houbara bustard. You can see imperial black-bellied and common Indian sand grouse, five species of vultures, six of eagle, falcons, and huge flocks of larks at Sudasari, the core of the park, 60 km from Jaisalmer. Chinkaras are a common sight, as are Desert and Indian foxes. Blackbuck and Desert cat can be seen at times. Closer to sunset, you can spot desert hare in the bushes.

While most hotels will try to sell you a tour by a four-wheel drive vehicle, this is no longer necessary. You can hire any jeep or high clearance car (Ambassador, Sumo) for the trip to the park. Off-the-road journeys are by

On a camel's back

Camel safaris draw many to Jaisalmer. They give an insight into otherwise inaccessible desert interiors and a chance to see rural life, desert flora and wildlife. The 'safari' is not a major expedition in the middle of nowhere. Instead, it is often along tracks, stopping off for sightseeing at temples and villages along the way. The camel driver/owner usually drives the camel or rides alongside (avoid one sharing your camel), usually for two hours in the morning and three hours in the afternoon, with a long lunch stop in between. There is usually jeep or camel cart backup with tents and 'kitchen' close by, though thankfully out of sight. It can be fun, especially if you are with companions and have a knowledgeable camel driver.

They vary greatly in quality with prices ranging from around Rs 350 per night for the simplest (sleeping in the open, vegetarian meals) to those costing Rs 4,500 (deluxe double-bedded tents, attached western baths). Safaris charging Rs 750-1500 can be adequate (tents, mattresses, linen, cook, jeep support, but no toilets). It is very important to ascertain what is included in the price and what are extras.

The popular 'Around Jaisalmer' route includes Bada Bagh, Ramkunda, Moolsagar, Sam dunes, Lodurva and Amar Sagar with three nights in the desert. Some routes now include Kuldhara's medieval ruins and the colourful Kahla village, as well as Deda, Jaseri lake (good birdlife) and Khaba ruins with a permit. Most visitors prefer to take a two days/one night or three days/two nights camel safari, with jeep transfer back to Jaisalmer. A more comfortable alternative is to be jeeped to a tented/ hut camp in the desert as a base for a night and enjoy a camel trek during the day without losing out on the evening's entertainment under the stars. Thar Safaris, T52722, charges Rs 2750 (with mobile tents Rs 1300); Safari Tours, T51058, has Rawla Kanoi with 'desert huts' and tents with shared facilities, about 8 km from Sam, for Rs 2000 per night; Royal Desert Safaris, T52538 has its own Swiss-cottage tent site near the dunes charges Rs 4500 with meals from Trio (Rs 1850 per day. TGS too offers Swiss-cottage tent stays and camel rides at dunes near Sam, besides camel safaris. Sahara Travels, Comfort Tours (Gorbandh Palace), Aravalli Safaris, Travel Plan, also offer reliable safaris. . A short camel ride in town up to Sunset Point (or at Sam/Khuri) is one alternative to a 'safari' before deciding on a long haul, and offers great views of upper levels of havelis too! – watch out for low slung electric wires. For some, "half an hour is enough on a tick-ridden animal". See also page 250.

camel or camel cart (park tour Rs 50 and 150 respectively). **E** Rest huts facing the park, with western toilets, no electricity, great view (water holes nearby) but food can be a problem. Permission is needed from the Collector as well as the Director, DNP, Barmer Road, Jaisalmer for a fee (Rs 100 per person, likely to increase soon). ■ *Temp range: 50°C to -4°C. Rainfall: 150 mm. Best season: Oct-Mar.*

At Akaal, about 17 km south of town on the motorable (NH15) Barmer Rd, **Wood Fossil** you can see five pieces of 180 million-year-old fossils of trees in glass display **Park** cases. ■ *No entry fee but donation expected.*

Rajasthan Tourism, T52406. City sightseeing: half day, 0900-1200. Fort, **Tours** havelis, Gadisagar Lake. Sam sand dunes: half day, 1500-1900.

Western Rajasthan

Essentials

Sleeping
■ on maps, page 241
& below
Price codes:
see inside front cover

If you are hassled by hotel touts on arrival at the station, take their jeep to a hotel and decide afterwards. Some hotels close in Apr-Jun. Very low room prices may be conditional on taking the hotel's camel safari (check beforehand); refusal may mean having to move out. Hot water usually 0700-1000, 1700-2000.

The new **A** *Rawal-Kot* (WelcomHeritage), Jodhpur Rd, 8 km from town. 31 large, comfortable, a/c or aircooled rooms, attractively furnished, good restaurants, no pool, modern yet creating a medieval atmosphere, good views of fort, friendly. **A-B** *Rang Mahal*, 5 Sam Rd, 2½ km from fort, T50907, F51305. 53 spacious rooms with balconies, desert architecture, extensive a la carte. **B** *Gorbandh Palace* (HRH), Sam Rd, 2½ km from town, T53801, F53811, jaisalmer@hrhindia.com 67 rooms around a courtyard in a plush hotel, traditional decor, central a/c, also luxury tents, good but pricey set meals, noisy entertainment, very pleasant pool, book/handicrafts shop, airport, station transfer. Reservations also at T0294-528008, F528012. Recommended. **B** *Dhola Maru*. 15 km northeast of fort, T52863, F52761. 42 a/c rooms in attractive sandstone building but standards slipping and mixed reports of unhelpful staff, informative lectures by owner though. **B** *Heritage Inn*, 43 Sam Rd, T52769, F51638, channicarpets@vsnl.com 51 good-sized rooms, single-storey sand stone desert architecture, restaurant, bar, pleasant interior, garden, well-managed. **B** *Himmatgarh Palace*, 1 Ramgarh Rd, 2½ km from town, T52002, F52005. 40 a/c rooms (slow to cool), in attractive sandstone building, deluxe rooms with fridge, pool, great views from garden. **B** *Narayan Niwas Palace*, opposite Jain Temple, Malka Rd, T52753, F52101. A converted

Jaisalmer

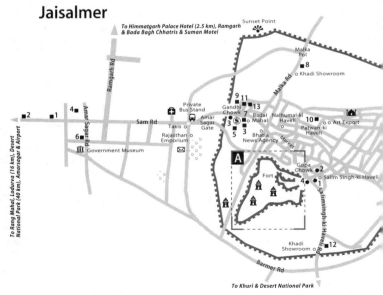

*Related map
A Jaisalmer Fort,
page 241*

■ **Sleeping**	5 Mandir Palace	10 Rajdhani
1 Gorbandh Palace	6 Moomal	11 Renuka
2 Heritage Inn	7 Nachana Haveli	12 Rama Guest House
3 Jaisal Palace	8 Narayan Niwas	& Golden City
& Kalpana Restaurant	& Narayan Vilas	13 Swastika
4 Jawahar Niwas	9 Ringo	

Western Rajasthan

caravanserai with 43 rooms, some a/c, modernized with bath (good hot showers, tubs), others spartan and windowless, overpriced, simple interiors, good Indian food in dining hall, pleasant courtyards. **B** *Rajwada*, Jodhpur-Barmer Link Rd, T53233, F53733. 69 a/c rooms in large modern fort-like hotel with carved balconies, traditional 18th-century décor, swimming pool, billiards, gardens. **B-C** *Jawahar Niwas*, Bada Bagh Rd, T52208, F52611. Small but attractive carved *haveli*, 11 renovated period furnished rooms in the main palace, 7 cheaper rooms in annexe, garden tented restaurant, pool by 2001, superb views, quiet, friendly helpful staff. **B-C** *Mandir Palace*, Gandhi Chowk, T52788, F53077. 11 disappointing overpriced rooms (see sights).

C *Nachana Haveli*, Govardhan Chowk, T52110, F52778: Converted 18th-century Rajput *haveli* with carved balconies and period artefacts, 7 huge aircooled rooms with small attached baths, around courtyard, better **B** rooms (spacious, high ceilings, period furniture, marble bathrooms), rather crowded area of town but convenient near market, rooftop restaurant, family run. Recommended. **C-D** *Jaisal Palace*, near Gandhi Chowk, behind SBI, T52717, F50257, hoteljaisalpalace@yahoo.com 14 simple clean rooms with bath, 6 a/c, 8 aircooled, 1st floor balconies with views, good food on roof terrace, train/ bus bookings, overpriced phone calls. **C-D** *Moomal* (RTDC), Amar Sagar Rd, T52392. 51 rooms, a/c, some cheaper in round huts and dorm, mediocre restaurant, bar, tours, friendly and helpful. **D** *Haveli*, opposite LIC office, T52552. Sandstone single storey building, 16 good, clean rooms, attached baths (hot shower), rooftop restaurant, travel assistance but exploitative prices in peak season. **D** *Narayan Vilas*, T52283. 16 rooms (some a/c) in older wing of *Narayan Niwas Palace*, rooms vary considerably so choose with care, family run, friendly and helpful owner, pleasant but not efficiently run, stable offers horse riding if you don't fancy camels. **D** *Rama Guest House*, Salim Singh-ki Haveli Marg, Dibba Para, T52570. 12 rooms, Indian restaurant, good views from rooftop, pleasant, relaxed, new management. Recommended. **D** *Rawal Kot*, Fort Rd, T/F50444. 31 rooms in modern hotel built like a *haveli* with pleasant courtyards, a/c restaurant, rooftop restaurant with barbecue, good views from terrace. **D** *Saroj Palace*, opposite the collector's office, T53575, F52575. 16 clean, comfortable rooms (6 a/c, rest aircooled), attached bath, friendly owner, rooftop restaurant with good views.

There are several budget hotels around the fort and near Amar Sagar Pol – check rooms first. Some allow travellers to sleep on the roof for Rs 30-50. The tourist office has a Paying Guest accommodation list.

In and around the fort: **D-F** *Paradise*, opposite Royal Palace, T52674. 24 basic rooms, best **C** with hot showers, most with balcony and views, camping on roof terrace – Rs 60 for tent, Rs 40 for bed, safe lockers, limited room-service, good value

To Mohangarh (NH15)

To Rawalkot Hotel (10 km) & Jodhpur

Kishanghat Pol

State Bus Stand

Auto Stand

Gadi Sagar Pol

Barmer Rd

Desert National Park Office

Folklore Museum

Tilon-ki Pol

To Narayan Bagh Resort (10 km) & Wood Fossil Park (17 km)

Gadi Sagar

● **Eating**
1 Monika
2 Natraj, Karan Palace & Samrat
3 Sky, Trio & Thar Safari
4 Treat

camel safaris, some reports of being hassled. **D-E** *Suraj*, behind Jain temple, T51623. 5 rooms with bath (unsatisfactory plumbing) in beautiful old *haveli*, some with view. **E** *Sri Nath Palace*, *haveli* opposite Jain Temple, T52907. Avoid top floor (no toilet), restaurant, helpful, friendly owners, good camel safaris. Recommended. **D-F** *Simla*, 5 clean rooms in old haveli, attractive wall hangings, 1 large with bath (Rs 800), others minute with bath downstairs, no safari pressure, expensive jeep tour (Rs 350, ½ day). **E** *Swastika* , opposite SBI, near Amar Sagar Pol, T52483. 9 clean, well kept rooms, most with bath, dorm, internet, bus/train bookings, family run. Recommended. **E-F** *Deepak*, behind fort Jain temples, T 52665. 25 rooms (most with hot showers, western toilets), best 8, 9 and 12, good vegetarian food (Brahmin), beds on rooftop, superb views, internet, travel ticketing, helpful owners, mixed reports about camel safaris. Recommended. **E-F** *Fort View*, Gopa Chowk, 50 m from fort entrance, T52214. 20 rooms, some with bath, cheap dorm, restaurant serves good snacks, travel. **E-F** *Laxmi Niwas*, T52758, in fort (signposted). 6 simple but clean rooms with bath in newer section at east end of fort, better upstairs, with good views from terrace, good breakfast; also cheaper 5 homely rooms with common bath in older section (west of fort), warm welcome. **F** *Pooja*, east of fort, towards Gadi Sagar Pol. Simple rooms in an old carved *haveli*, shared bath, hot water in bucket, sleep cheaply on roof terrace. **F** *Raj Palace*, near fort, T53264. 12 clean rooms, restaurant serves snacks, restored 18th-century building, cheerful, young manager, very helpful. **F** *Sandrella*, Main Bazar. Free hot water in buckets, free jeep from bus or railway station, very friendly, good away-from-the-crowd 2-day safaris Rs 750, Indian/Australian venture.

It is advisable to avoid 'Peacock'

Elsewhere: **E-F** *Golden City*, Dibba Para, near first fort gate, T51664, hotelgoldencity@ hotmail.com Clean, comfortable air cooled rooms with hot shower, 3 **D** a/c, rooftop restaurant with good views, free station transfer, exchange, internet, family atmosphere. **E-F** *Ringo Rooftop* , Mainpura St, Gandhi Chowk, T51627, bhatinarendra@ hotmail.com Comfortable rooms in family home, most with hot showers, some with tubs and a/c (Rs 40-275), rooftop restaurant, superb views over town from upper storeys, young enthusiastic graduates but disorganized. **F** *Karan Palace*, opposite Salim Singh ki Haveli, T50961. Basic doubles with bath (bucket hot water), best with balcony. **F** *Rajdhani*, towards Patwon-ki Haveli, T52746. Clean rooms with hot shower, rooftop snacks, reliable safari, friendly. **F** *Renuka*, opposite SBI, Chainpura St, T52757, F40323. 15 rooms (upstairs better), 8 with hot showers (Rs 80-200), roof top restaurant with good views, friendly, helpful, clean, peaceful, free station pick up (call ahead), popular, safaris (no hard sell). Recommended. **F** *Samrat*, near Salim Singh-ki-Haveli, T51498. 9 pleasantly furnished clean rooms, some with bath and balcony (Rs 30 to 200 with a/c), dorm (Rs 10), rooftop restaurant, helpful, family run, travel tickets, laundry, cycle hire. Recommended.

Eating

● on maps, pages 241& 246
Price codes:
see inside front cover

Many offer a varied menu, keen to cater for the western palate

In and around the fort Mid-range: *Cinera*, above *Grand View*, Central Market (off Gopa Chowk). Good varied menu (try vegetables in mango sauce!), friendly staff, great views of fort, especially at sunset. *8th Jul*, just inside fort (another opposite Fort Gate). Vegetarian. Pleasant rooftop seating – popular for breakfast, pizzas, food average, pleasant for evening drink, mixed reports on service. *Monika*, Asni Rd. Good Rajasthani *thalis*, non-veg a la carte (Rs 150). Attracts foreigners, rather tatty and musician can get tedious. *Natraj*, next to Salim Singh-ki-Haveli. Mixed. Spacious rooftop with good views and a/c room, beer bar, wide choice (meat dishes Rs 80-100), veg delights Rs 20-35, desserts Rs 20), good Indian and Chinese, clean toilet! Recommended. *Surya*, near Laxmi Niwas. Mixed. Good food, colourful, atmospheric, sit on cushions overlooking the city, reasonable prices. **Cheap**: *Vyas*, Fort. Simple, good *thalis* (Rs 20-30).

Gandhi Chowk Mid-range: *Sky*. Mainly Indian, 'English' breakfasts and some Italian. On rooftop, Rajasthani dancers and musicians, colourful and noisy! *Top Deck*. Good meat dishes (lamb steaks, southern fried chicken, Rs 60). *Trio*. The best in town, partly open-air, tented restaurant with small terrace, choice of cushions or chairs, excellent 'proper' tea, good atmosphere and creative food, friendly service, musicians at dinner expect tips, view of Mandir Palace and fort illuminated, usually crowded, Rs 200+ each. Recommended. **Cheap**: *Manbhavan*, Hanuman Circle. Rooftop restaurant, good Indian (Rajasthani, Gujarati, Bengali, south Indian). *Ringo Rooftop* (separate from hotel). Good north Indian including meat dishes. Superb views of fort.

Snacks and drinks *Chai* stalls at Gopa Chowk make good 'Indian' tea before 1730. Hot and crisp *kachoris* and *samosas* opposite Jain temples near Narayan Niwas, are great for breakfast or high tea; *aloo parathas* to order. *Doodh bhandars* in Hanuman Chauraya sell a delicious mix of creamy milk, cardamom and sugar, whipped up with a flourish, between sunset and mid-night. *Dhanraj Bhatia*, Scrumptious Indian sweets including Jaisalmeri delights (try *godwa*). *Kanchan Shree*, Jagani Para, near *Fort View*. Still among the best for drinks. *Lassis* (19 varieties) and ice cream floats. *Mohan Juice Centre*, near *Sunil Bhatia Rest House*. Delicious lassis, good breakfasts. Recommended.

'Gorbadh' has the best stocked bar. 'Jawahar Niwas' is reasonable

Bars *Gorbandh Palace*, has a well stocked bar, *Jawahar Niwas, Naryan Niwas* and other **B** hotel offer a reasonable choice.

Entertainment Cultural Centre off the Jaisalmer-Barra Bagh Rd Evening music and dances Rs 10, timings at Tourist office. **Swimming**: *Gorbandh Palace* (non-residents Rs 350); also *Heritage inn* and *Fort Rajwada*.

Festivals **Feb** 3-day *Desert Festival* (Feb: 25-27 in 2002; 14-16 in 2003) with *Son et Lumière* amid the sand dunes at Sam, folk dancing, puppet shows and camel races, camel polo and camel acrobatics, Mr Desert competition. You can also watch craftsmen at work. Rail and hotel reservations can be difficult. **Feb/Mar** *Holi* is especially colourful but can get riotous.

Shopping Jaisalmer is famous for its handicrafts – stone carved statues, leather ware (includes slippers), brass enamel engraving (includes camel seats), shawls, tie-and-dye work, embroidered and block printed fabrics, but garments are often poorly finished. Nost shops open 1000-1330 and 1500-1900. Traders are more relaxed and welcoming here, and expect you to bargain.

Look in Sirê Bazar, Sonaron-ka-Bas and the narrow lanes of the old city including *Kamal Handicrafts*, and *Damodar* in the fort. In Gandhi Chowk check out *Rajasthali* (closed Tue), *Khadi Emporium* at the end of the courtyard just above *Narayan Niwas Hotel*, *Jaisalmer Art Export*, behind Patwon-ki Haveli (doesn't look like a shop) has high quality textiles. **Books** *Bhatia News Agency*, Court Rd. Good selection including travel guides, second hand books bought and sold. **Paintings** Hari Ram Soni is an artist in Taloti Vyaspara. **Tailors** *Mr Durga*, small shop near fort entrance (between *New Tourist* and *Srilekha Hotels*), *Nagpur*, Koba Chowk, and *Raju*, Kachari Rd, outside Amar Sagar Pol. All do excellent western style tailoring. Shirts made to measure, around Rs 200.

Transport **Long distance Air**: No flights from the nearest airport at Jodhpur. *Alliance Air* from Delhi, 1030, via Jaipur; to Delhi, 1330. **Road Bus**: State (Roadways) buses, from near the station, T53141 and near Amar Sagar Pol. Services to Ajmer, Barmer, Bikaner (330 km on poor road, 9 hrs, Rs 100), Jaipur (638 km); for Mount Abu; carry drinking water (unavailable on the road). Jodhpur (285 km) hourly service, 5½ hrs, Rs 80, RTDC coach,

Jaisalmer is on NH15 (Pathankot-Samakhiali)

Western Rajasthan

Camel safari – the experience

The tour, lasting three days and two nights, circuits around Jaisalmer via Mool Sagar, the Sam sand dunes and Lodruva. En route you pass through a few Muslim, Rajput and tribal villages, occupied and abandoned. You see fields of hardy millet and come across flocks of sheep and goats with their tinkling bells. Supper is around a fire (a home-cooked meal is sometimes simply warmed up) before spending the first night on a mattress under the stars. Next morning, after breakfast (tea, toast and boiled egg or sometimes porridge, pakoras, toast and jam) the safari proper begins, starting with a gentle walk working up to a fast trot (make sure you have proper stirrups fitted). Midday meal (chapati and daal) will be cooked by the camel driver on an open

fire. When you stop to camp for the night, you may be joined by a member of the travel company from Jaisalmer. He will have brought out another meal on a motorbike to be warmed up over the camp fire. Next morning after breakfast you resume the gentle journey back to town. A leisurely stop for a freshly prepared lunch around midday allows you to return to base around 1600 – just two days after you started. Carry biscuits and bottled water though hawkers selling soft drinks, water, beer and chocolate materialize in the desert at contrived drink stops. Please encourage camel drivers not to litter the desert. Hygiene conditions are far from ideal – 'washing up' is in sand – so travellers often return feeling unwell.

departs from Jaisalmer, 1400 (departs from Jodhpur 0630). **To Udaipur**: (663 km), tiring 14 hrs. Private deluxe coaches from outside Amar Sagar Pol, to Jodhpur and Bikaner. Operators: *Marudhara Travels*, Station Rd, T52351, *National Tours*, Hanuman Choraha, T52348. Touts may board buses outside town to press you to take their jeep; it is better to walk 10-15-min from Amar Sagar Pol and choose a hotel. **Train** Foreign Tourist Bureau with waiting room, T52354. **To Jodhpur**: *Jaisalmer Jodhpur Exp, 4609, 4809 Exp*, 2225, 7 hrs, a/c sleeper, Rs 510. Can get very cold (and dusty) so take sleeping bag, or book bedding. From Jodhpur, *4810,* dep 2315, 6½ hrs.

Directory **Banks** Open from 1030-1430, Mon-Fri, 1030-1230, Sat, closed Sun. On Gandhi Chowk: *Bank of Baroda* and *SBBJ*, TCs and cash against credit cards; *State of Bank of India*, Nachana Haveli, currency only. **Communications** Internet: *Joshi Travel*, opposite post office, Central Market, Gopa Chowk, T/F50455 joshitravel@hotmail.com Cyber café with fast connection, modern equipment Rs 300 per hr, also STD, fax etc. Others Rs 2 per min but have problems connecting. **Post:** GPO is near the police station, T52407. With poste restante. **Hospitals and medical services** *SJHospital*, Gandhi Marg, T52343. Over stretched. **Tour companies and travel agents** *Aravali Safari*, near Patwon-ki Gali, T52632. Professional. Recommended. *Sahara Travels*, Gopa Chowk, right of the 1st fort gate, T52609. Mr (Desert) Bissa's reliable camel safaris with good food; *Fort View*, *Paradise*, *Suraj* hotels (½ day, *chhatris*, jain temple, good fort views etc). Also *Safari Tours*, Gandhi Chowk, T/F51058, and *Thar Safari*, Gandhi Chowk, near *Trio*, T52722, F53214. Recommended for reliable tours. *Tourist Guide Service*, near Patwon-ki Haveli, T52450. Avoid *Travellers Agency* (of *Puskhar Palace*), near *Skyroom* restaurant; *Adventure Tours* (*New Tourist Hotel*). Some travellers cheated when buying bus/train tickets – given only a reservation slip. **Tourist offices** Rajasthan, near TRC, Station Rd, Gadi Sagar Pol, T52406, 0800-1200, 1500-1800. Counter at railway station. **Useful addresses** Collector/magistrate: T52201; Fire: T52352. Police: T53322.

Barmer This dusty desert town, 153 km south of Jaisalmer, is surrounded by sand dunes and scrublands. It is a major centre for wood carving (surprisingly in a desert region), *durrie* rug weaving, embroidery and block printing (you can watch printers in Khatriyon ki galli). The 10th-11th-century **Kiradu temples** are also noteworthy. Although the five temples are now badly damaged they represented an important stage in the development of western Indian architecture. Someshvara (1020), the most intact, has some intricate carving but the dome and the tower have collapsed. It retains some basement reliefs showing naturalistic scenes and stories from the epics. The early 10th-century Vishnu temple has some ornate central pillars. You can stay at *Midway* (RTDC) and **E-F** Indian style. In March the *Thar festival* is held, organised by Rajasthan Tourism to highlight desert culture and the Kiradu temples. Cultural shows arranged and handicrafts are displayed in the evening. ■ *Getting there: It is a hot and dusty bus journey to Jaisalmer, 4 hrs; Mount Abu, 6 hrs.*

Dhorimmana

The area further south of Barmer has some of the most colourful and traditional Bishnoi villages and a large population of chinkaras and desert wildlife. The village women wear a lot of attractive jewellery but may be reluctant to be photographed so it is best to ask first. Accommodation is provided by *PWD Rest houses* which have clean and comfortable rooms (Indian toilets) at Barmer and Dhorimmana.

Western Rajasthan

Gujarat

Gujarat

Northern Gujarat, with its small plains and low hills, is a transition zone to Rajasthan, yet around the rapidly modernizing industrialised city of Ahmadabad, the cultural distinctiveness of Gujarat is readily apparent. The city witnessed the assertion of Muslim political power and cultural influence. The artistic treasure of the Sidi Sayid mosque is just one illustration. Yet as the great Sun Temple at Modhera shows Hindu culture was also richly developed. There are also great medieval monuments such as the Jain temples of Kumbhariya, Taranga, and Patan, and the marvellous stepwell at Adalaj.

The route south from Ahmadabad crosses the fertile alluvial plains of the Sabarmati and Mahi rivers before entering the Konkan region. The plains gradually give way south to broken hills while inland, parallel ridges reach between 500-600 metres where strategically placed old forts were sited. Paddy fields dominate further south, but ragi (finger millet) and pulses are also grown. *Vadodara* was one of India's most powerful princely states, set on these fertile lowland plains. Not far to the west rise the Western Ghats, offering a protective rim.

Southern Gujarat runs as a narrow coastal strip through Surat, one of India's oldest centres of sea borne trade, to the former Portuguese enclave of Daman. Modern Surat is an industrial town, but Daman retains a powerful sense of the lost Portuguese empire in microcosm. Inland, the colourful Dangs tribal district is centred around the state's only hill station at Saputara.

The **Saurashtra** peninsula has an identity rooted in its physical geography. Its long coastal fringe, stretching from the Gulf of Cambay in the east to the Gulf of

Kachchh in the west, has made much of its living from coastal trade, but also has some of the world's most beautifully undeveloped and unspoilt beaches. Diu, one of the smallest of Portuguese enclaves, retains its distinctive atmosphere. Immediately inland are some of India's most remarkable religious sites, including the Jain temples on the hills of Palitana and Girnar. Inland again, the dry, gently rolling scrub forest is home to a range of bird and wildlife, including blackbuck and the Gir lion.

With its capital Bhuj and many of its outlying villages devastated by the January 2001 earthquake, life in **Kachchh** *is slowly returning to normal. The scenic Maliya bridge, across salt marshes often filled with birds, gives a beguilingly attractive impression of this gateway to Kachchh, yet the environment is one of the harshest and least forgiving in India. Despite the difficulties, local people have developed an astonishingly colourful identity, with tribal groups such as the Rabaris, Ahirs and Meghwals among others developing their own distinctive dress styles and crafts. For many tourism was becoming a vital source of earning, and many are desperately anxious for visitors to return.*

Ahmadadbad and Northern Gujarat

8

Ahmadabad and Northern Gujarat

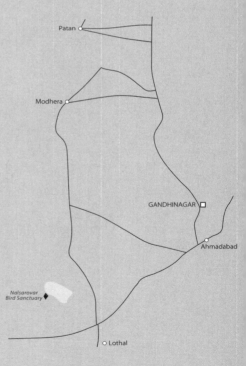

Ahmadabad

Ahmadabad, the former state capital (Gandhinagar is the new capital), is a very congested city which spreads out along both banks of the Sabarmati River in a rather chaotic fashion. The Old City, however, has a maze of narrow winding alleys with carved wooden house fronts and thriving bazars. The Calico Museum and Mahatma Gandhi's Sabarmati Ashram are well worth visiting.

Phone code: 079
Colour map 5, grid A6
Population: 3,298 mn
Altitude: 53 m

Getting there The airport is 13 km northeast of town. Regular City buses collect passengers from the airport and arrive at Lal Darwaza, close to many budget hotels. Taxis charge Rs 180-230, and autos about Rs 90-100, to transfer. Train travellers arrive at the Junction Station to the east of the Old City, while long distance buses use the Rajpur Gate Terminus to the south. There are taxis and autos at both to get you to a hotel. **Getting around** Ahmadabad is far too sprawling to be able to cover all the sights on foot so you will need to struggle with local buses or hire an auto-rickshaw or taxi.

Ins & outs
See page 272 for further details

Ahmadabad retains a highly distinctive feel born out of a long and continuously evolving social history. Recent developments in urban design have contributed important new experiments to its architectural tradition. It was founded in 1411 by Ahmad Shah I, then King of Gujarat. He made Asaval, an old Hindu town in the south, his seat of power then expanded it to make it his capital. Almost constantly at war with the neighbouring Rajputs, fortifications were essential. The **Bhadra** towers and the square bastions of the royal citadel were among the first to be built. The city walls had 12 gates, 139 towers and nearly 6,000 battlements. At the end of the 16th century, some western travellers considered it comparable to the finest European city.

Background

With a long tradition in craftsmanship under Gujarati Sultans and Mughal Viceroys, Ahmadabad was one of the most brilliant Indian cities. Its jewellers and goldsmiths are renowned, copper and brassworkers produce very fine screens and *paan daans* (betel boxes). Carpenters produce fine *shisham* wood articles. There are skilled stonemasons, lacquer artists, ivory/bone carvers, hand-block printers and embroiderers producing exquisite pieces with beads and mirrors. These complement the modern industries such as pharmaceuticals and textiles.

Although most of the Old City walls have gone, many monuments remain, some of them striking examples of Indian Islamic architecture. The provincial Gujarati style flourished from the mid-15th century, and in addition to the religious buildings many of the houses have façades beautifully decorated with wood carving. The Swami Narayan Temple, Kalipur, Rajani Vaishnav Temple and Harkore Haveli, near Manek Chowk as well as *havelis* on Doshiwadani Pol, illustrate traditional carving skills. Sadly, much of the old carving has been dismantled to be sold off to collectors.

The Old City

The 'new' city, lying on the west bank, has the site of Mahatma Gandhi's famous Sabarmati Ashram from where he began his historic Salt March in protest against the Salt Law in 1915. Modern Ahmadabad has its own share of showpieces designed by famous architects, among them Le Corbusier, Louis Kahn, Doshi and Correa. The School of Architecture, the National Institute of Design and the Indian Institute of Management (IIM) are national centres of learning.

The 'new' city

Sights

In the **Jami Masjid**, Ahmadabad has one of the best examples of the second period of Gujarat's provincial architectural development. In 1411, Ahmad Shah I, the founder of a new dynasty, laid the foundations of the city which was to be his new capital.

Things to do in Ahmadabad

- Follow the Heritage trail.
- Sample an *thali* meal at *Agashiye*.
- Go to Sabarmati Ashram.
- Join the kite fliers in mid-January.
- Visit the Calico Museum.

By 1423 the Jami Masjid, regarded by many as one of the finest mosques in India, was completed. He encouraged others to construct monumental buildings as well. As a result there are over 50 mosques and tombs dating from his period within the city. Mahmud I Begarha (ruled 1459-1511) established the third phase of Gujarati provincial architecture, building some of India's most magnificent Islamic monuments.

The citadel The citadel of the planned city formed a rectangle facing the river. A broad street was designed to run from Ahmad Shah's fortified palace in the citadel to the centre of the city, lying due east.

The ancient citadel built by Ahmad Shah I in 1411, now known as the **Bhadra** (see above), lies between the Nehru and Ellis bridges. It is named after an incarnation of the Hindu goddess Kali. In the east face is the **Palace**, now the post office, and other public buildings occupy the site, with the civil court to the south. **Sidi Sayid's Mosque** (circa 1570) formed part of the wall on the northeast corner but now stands isolated in a square. Ten windows of very fine stone tracery with patterns of branching tree are famous here. Note particularly those on the west wall. A notice prohibits women but visitors may have no problem getting permission.

In the southwest corner of the Bhadra is **Ahmad Shah's Mosque** (1414), built as a private chapel and one of the oldest mosques in Ahmadabad. The façade is plain and the minarets unfinished. The internal pillars and the stone latticed ladies' gallery are thought to be part of a Hindu temple that stood here. By the entrance to the mosque is the **Ganj-i-Shahid**, the place where Muslims killed during the storming of the town, are buried.

It is welcomingly quiet & peaceful inside

Jami Masjid Ideally, Ahmad Shah would have wished the main entrance to this mosque to face the processional route from the citadel to the centre of the city. Such a plan was impossible because the essential orientation of the Qibla wall to Mecca meant that the main entrance to the mosque itself had to be in its east wall. The mosque was aligned so that the present Mahatma Gandhi Road passed its north entrance. This is still the point at which you enter by a flight of steps which are not immediately visible until you are there. The vegetable and fruit market near the south entrance is worth visiting for the artistic display of stallholders wares.

The façade The beauty of the sanctuary is emphasized by the spacious courtyard paved in marble, with a tank in the middle. The façade has a screen of arches flanked by a pillared portico. The two 'shaking minarets', once 26 m high, were destroyed by earthquakes in 1819 and 1957.

The sanctuary The tradition of the Hindu temple *mandapa* is developed in the Jami Masjid's remarkable sanctuary. Over 300 graceful pillars are organized in 15 square bays. The whole rises from a single storey through the two-storeyed side aisles to the three-storey central aisle or nave. This comprises two-pillared galleries resting on the columns of the lower hall, screened for the women. Such a development was itself an innovation, but the central

Ahmadabad's 'pols'

The old parts of the city are divided into unique, self-contained pols, or quarters, fascinating to wander round. Huge wooden gates ('pol' literally means gate) lead off from narrow lanes into a section of houses with decorative wooden screens and brackets where small communities of people practising a craft or skill once lived. Merchants, weavers, woodworkers, printers and jewellers – each had their pol, their houses along winding alleys which met in common courtyards and squares.

While some of these pols are said to date from the Mughal period, they gained special importance in the 18th century when the power struggle between the Marathas, the British and the Mughals created unrest in cities like Ahmadabad resulting in the erection of huge gates. Many of the merchants houses, havelis, with their intricately carved wooden façades and balconies can be seen along the alleys. The pols are worth visiting especially during Uttarayana when crowds gather on the terraces for kite flying.

Today, these old quarters are being developed rapidly, with tower blocks rising up from just inside the old city walls.

octagonal lantern, rising through both storeys and covered by a dome, was also strikingly original. The gentle lighting effect is achieved by filtering light through the perforated stone screens.

Teen Darwaza Immediately to the east of the entrance to Ahmad Shah's mosque is the triumphal archway also known as the **Triple Gateway** (or Tripolia), which once led to the outer court of the royal citadel. Now crowded by shops, its effect is considerably diminished.

Royal tombs To the east of the Jami Masjid in Manek Chowk, is the Tomb of **Ahmad Shah I** (died 1442) on a square plan with *jali* screens, which was built by his son Muhammad Shah (died 1451) in the square Ahmad Shah had designed for the purpose. Across the street, in a state of disrepair, are the large marble tombs of the **Queens of Ahmad Shah**, with a decorative carved façade.

To the east and southeast are several buildings from the third Gujarati Muslim period. Some 500 m southwest of the Queens' Tombs is **Dastur Khan's Mosque** (1486) with a cloistered courtyard and very fine carved stone screens. To the southeast again, toward the Astodia Gate, is **Rani Sipri's Mosque** (1514). Small but beautifully proportioned, it has two 15-m minarets. Rani Asni's *rauza* (tomb) with *jali* screens stands in front of the mosque.

Northeast of the Astodia Gate and a short distance south of the railway station are **Sidi Bashir's Shaking Minarets**, two tall towers connected by a bridge which was once the entrance to the old mosque (now replaced by a modern one). The minarets were believed to 'shake' or vibrate in sympathy as they are cleverly built on a flexible sandstone base to protect against earthquake damage. **Bibi-ki-Masjid** (1454), Gomtipur, southeast of the railway station, also has a shaking minaret. If you climb up the 78 steps to a parapet 25-m high, and hold on to the minaret, your guide can make it gently sway by putting his weight against it! The old **English Cemetery** is close to Jamalpur Gate.

Sayid Usman's mausoleum Across the Gandhi bridge, immediately west of **The north** Ashram Road, the *rauza* (circa 1460) is one of the first examples of the Begarha style. Northwest of the Old City near Shahpur Gate, the **Mosque of Hasan Muhammad Chishti** (1565) has some of the finest tracery work in Ahmadabad.

There are several **Jain temples** in the city. The highly decorated, white marble **Hathi Singh Temple** (1848) just north of the Delhi Gate, dedicated to Dharamanath, the 15th Jain Tirthankar, is perhaps the most visited. Along the streets of Ahmadabad, it is quite common to see Jain *parabdis* (bird sanctuaries).

The **Rani Rupmati Masjid** (early 16th-century), in Mirzapur district, southwest of Delhi Gate and just south of the *Grand Hotel*, incorporates Hindu and Islamic design. Rupmati was Princess of Dhar (MP) and the Sultan's Hindu wife. The carvings in the gallery and the *mihrabs* are particularly attractive. Note how the dome is raised to allow light in around its base. Rupmati's tomb (mid-15th century) lies to the northeast.

Ahmadabad

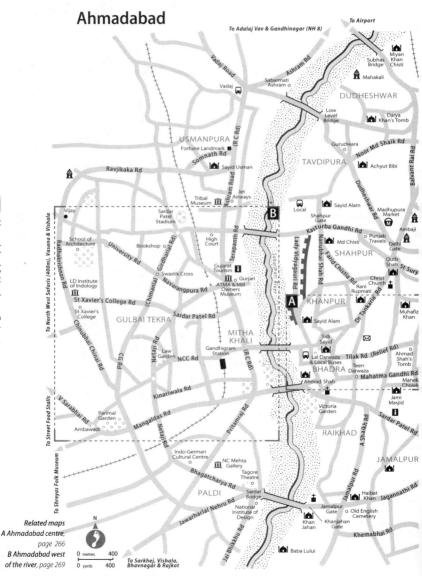

Ahmadabad & Northern Gujurat

Related maps
A Ahmadabad centre, page 266
B Ahmadabad west of the river, page 269

0 metres 400
0 yards 400

To Sarkhej, Vishala, Bhavnagar & Rajkot

East of the Rani Masjid is the **Mosque of Muhafiz Khan** (1465), which is beautifully proportioned and superbly carved. To the southeast is the **Pinjrapol**, or Asylum for Animals. This is a simple enclosure surrounded by stalls for the animals.

Baolis At **Asarva**, about 1 km northeast of Daryapur Gate, are the *baolis*, which in Gujarat are highly distinctive and often serve a dual purpose of being a cool, secluded source of water during the summer and a place of religious sanctity. At **Dada Hari** (1499) there is a spiral staircase leading down to three lower platforms and a small octagonal well at the bottom. It is best seen in mid-morning light. A short distance to the north is the even older **Mata Bhavani** well with Hindu carvings, which reputedly dates from the Solanki period (1063-93). The most highly decorated, however, is at **Adalaj Vav**, 19 km away (see page 274).

The **British Cantonment** lies about 4 km to the northeast of the city, where there is an Anglican Church and a few public buildings. On the west bank of the Sabarmati there is the **Ahmadabad Textile Mill Owners' Association** (ATMA) and the **museum**, both of which were designed by Le Corbusier.

Gandhi's Ashram, 6 km north of the centre, was founded in 1917 (originally known as Satyagraha and then Harijan Ashram), and was the starting point for Gandhi's celebrated, 385 km Salt March to Dandi in March 1930. He vowed not to return to the Ashram till India gained independence. Gandhi and 81 supporters began the march; by the end of it there were 90,000 protesters marching against the unpopular British Salt Tax Laws. Salt manufacture, a government monopoly, was chosen for the protest as it was a commodity every peasant used and could understand. At Dandi beach on 6 April Gandhi went down to the sea and made a small amount of salt, for which he was promptly arrested. In the following months, thousands of Indians followed his example and were arrested by the British. The **Sangrahalaya** includes a library, archives and a picture gallery depicting Gandhi's life in photographs and

★ **Sabarmati Ashram**

Ahmadabad & Northern Gujarat

paintings. A five-minute film on his life is shown several times daily. The peace, quiet and simple style of the Ashram is impressively maintained. Some of the original ashram's work, such as a school for Harijan girls, continues. **Hridaya Kunj**, Gandhi's home for 15 years, containing simple mats, desk, spinning wheel and some personal belongings, overlooks the central prayer corner and the river and remains undisturbed, as does the unfurnished room of his wife Kasturba. ■ *0830-1900 (1 Apr-30 Sep), otherwise 0830-1830. Last admission: 30 mins before closing, free. Daily Son et Lumière Sun, Wed, Fri (English 2100), closed during monsoons, Rs 5. Donations for upkeep are gratefully received and an ornately printed receipt provided.*

Nearby at Wadaj, **Kumbharwada** is a potters' village where you can watch the craftsmen at their wheels.

Kankaria Lake   Kankaria Lake, southeast of the city, is remarkable. The artificial lake, dating from 1451, has 34 sides, each 60 m long. It is a popular picnic spot with a large zoo. The Natural History Museum next to it has a collection of stuffed birds, some interesting *dioramas*. ■ *Open sunrise to sunset.*

Museums
Regarded as one of the finest museums of its kind in the world. The setting is superb.

★ **Calico Museum**, a part of the Sarabhai Trust, is in an attractive old *haveli*, 3 km north of Delhi Gate. Some exhibits date from the 17th century and include rich displays of heavy brocades, fine embroideries, saris, carpets, turbans, Maharajahs' costumes and a royal Mughal tent. It illustrates weaving techniques but not weaving equipment. Secular pieces are housed in traditional old *havelis* which have been reassembled around the chowk. ■ *Daily except Wed and holidays. Free. Tours from 1030-1230 (religious textiles), 1500-1645 (secular textiles); report 15 mins before; they are different and complementary. Guided tour of the garden is by appointment only. Open for research. The guides are friendly and charming. The museum shop sells cards of exhibits, reproductions and books.* Moti Manor Hotel *is the only place nearby, for lunch.*

LD Institute of Indology Museum, Gujarat University Campus, contains over 3,300 pieces of medieval sculpture, many of 11th-13th century, an outstanding Jain section (MSS, idols et cetera) and archaeological finds. The **NC Mehta Gallery** within the museum has a vast collection of miniatures from the Rajasthan, Mewar, Mughal, Kangra and other schools on three floors. The series of 150 paintings on the Gita Govinda theme and a set from the Gujarat Sultanate period are rare exhibits. ■ *Museum opens at 1030 and gallery at 1100 until 1800, closed Mon, entry free. Summer timings change so check before visiting.*

Shreyas Museum, near Shreyas Railway Crossing, has a comprehensive collection of contemporary rural textiles from all parts of Gujarat (managed by Sarabhai Trust) with excellent beadwork, embroideries, utensils, religious objects and bullock cart accessories. Children's section upstairs exhibits folk art (dance costumes, masks, puppets). The guided tour also takes you around the campus. ■ *Winter, 1030-1730, summer 0830-1300, closed Mon, Diwali, Christmas and during school summer vacation. Rs 35 (foreigners); Indians pay less.*

Sanskar Kendra Museum, Paldi, is an award-winning design by Le Corbusier, with ramps of steps leading up from a fountained pool, houses an excellent collection of old and contemporary art, superbly exhibited.

Piles and piles of textiles

The Calico mills of the Sarabhai family, founded in the late 1800s, was one of the earliest textile manufacturing units in Ahmadabad. As an important industrialist for several decades, Vikram Sarabhai (who was also a leading scientist), collected valuable pieces of textiles to inspire his designers. This collection was opened to the public at 'the Retreat', the family residence. The complex includes a botanically interesting garden, Shahi Bagh, with trees grown by Ambalal Sarabhai in the early-20th century still standing. There are buildings created by Le Corbusier and other famous architects, and reconstructed wooden haveli façades and jarokha balconies salvaged from houses that were marked for demolition, in the courtyard.

*The museum has separate sections for religious and secular textiles. The **religious galleries** exhibit outstanding medieval Jain manuscripts, 14th-19th-century Jain icons, a Jain shrine, a fine collection of pichhwais (see page 415) from the Shreenathji temple at Nathdwara, and pattachitras.*

*The **secular section** has a royal gallery. It contains Indian textiles that featured in trade, including a silk sarong (double ikat), woven in Gujarat for the Indonesian market, chintz for the East India Company, window curtains made for the Portuguese and fabrics believed to be of Indian origin salvaged from the Egyptian pyramids. Historic pieces of tie-and-dye, embroidery and beadwork from Gujarat, phulkari embroideries of Punjab, patola silk sarees from Patan, Pashmina shawls from Kashmir, Chamba rumals from Himachal, silk fabrics from Orissa and South India, a temple chariot from Tamil Nadu and kalamkaris are among the important exhibits. In the garden are temple curtains called mata-ni-pachedi of the Waghri tribe.*

Tribal Research Institute Museum, Gujarat Vidyapith, Ashram Road, has re-creations of tribal hamlets of Gujarat, besides weapons, implements, wall art, terracotta figurines and textiles. ■ *1130-1930, Sat 1130-1430, closed Sun.*

Amdavad-ni-Gufa, University Campus. These 'caves' were an inspirational venture by the architect Doshi and the artist MF Hussain to display their work. Tribal paintings and other works of art are being added.

The following all exhibit contemporary art: **Contemporary Art Gallery**, near Orient Club, **Gujarat Kala Mandir**, near Law College Bus Stand, all near Ellis Bridge, **Jyoti Art Gallery**, 587 Tilak (Relief) Road, T336996, and **Hutheesing Centre**, opposite Gujarat University. **National Institute of Design**, Paldi, shows students' work. ■ *1400-1700, closed Sun.*

Kamala Nehru Zoological Park, Kankaria, was masterminded by the late Reuben David, a 'captive breeding' genius. He had a fascination with albinos; note the albino porcupine, squirrel, deer et cetera here. **Sundervan**, Satellite Road, off M Dayanand Road, is a pleasant nature orientation park. There are snake demonstrations with illustrate their importance to the environment, a walk-in aviary and a library. ■ *Daily except Mon.*

Parks & zoos

Vishala, Sarkhej Road, Vasana, 5 km, is a purpose-built collection of tradi-tional Gujarati village huts, where you can eat accompanied by music and watch some traditional dancing after dinner. Light is provided in the evening entirely by lanterns. You sit cross-legged at low tables (low stools also pro-vided), eat off green leaves or metal *thalis*, and drink from clay tumblers. A fixed menu, full dinner costs under Rs 120 and lunch costs Rs 80. An

Excursions

Ahmadabad & Northern Gujarat

improved dining area has hospitable and friendly staff. Air-cooled seating for lunch and snacks. The **Utensils Museum**, renovated and expanded in a courtyard with a pool, has a very well displayed collection of milking vessels (cattle, camel), Rajasthani pottery, Hindu prayer lamps, jewel boxes and betel nut crackers. ■ *1700-2300 weekdays, 1000-1300, 1700-2200 Sun. Fix a return price with the auto-rickshaw.*

Indroda Village Deer Park is next to Sarita Udyan by Sabarmati River. It's a large park but has inappropriate enclosures (plains antelope in forest setting!). There is also an interesting reptile collection and well marked nature trails through forests where you may spot nilgai, porcupine, jackal, crested honey buzzard, paradise fly-catcher et cetera. Films, library, tented campsite.

Tours Ahmadabad Municipal Transport Service, Lal Darwaza, where you can reserve the following: **Tour 1** 0830-1830: Sidi Sayid mosque, Shaking minarets, Huteehsinh Jain temples, Gandhi Ashram, Gujarat Vidyapith, ISKCON temple, Sundarvan, Shreyas museum, Gandhinagar (also Akshardham) and Adalaj stepwell; Rs 160 a/c coach. **Tour 2** 0900-1700, slightly different, Rs 125 (non-a/c). **Tours 3, 4** 0930-1300, 1330-1730, split the sights; Rs 75, Rs 85 a/c.

Heritage Walking Tours Excellent tour with qualified architects/conservationists; starts at Swaminarayan Temple, Relief Road, Kalupur, and covers Juma Masjid, Rani no Haziro, temples, wooden havelis, *pols*, artisans' workshops et cetera. The guides are generally volunteers knowledgeable about architecture, social patterns of a haveli and related subjects. March-August

Ahmadabad centre

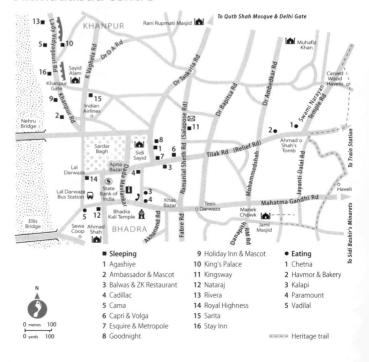

■ Sleeping		● Eating
1 Agashiye	9 Holiday Inn & Mascot	1 Chetna
2 Ambassador & Mascot	10 King's Palace	2 Havmor & Bakery
3 Balwas & ZK Restaurant	11 Kingsway	3 Kalapi
4 Cadillac	12 Nataraj	4 Paramount
5 Cama	13 Rivera	5 Vadilal
6 Capri & Volga	14 Royal Highness	
7 Esquire & Metropole	15 Sarita	
8 Goodnight	16 Stay Inn	----- Heritage trail

0730 to 1030, September-February 0800-1030. Rs 50. Check ahead at CRUTA, at the temple complex, T337058. Guaranteed departures. Highly recommended. Gujarat Tourism: Saurashtra Darshan, Friday; North Gujarat-Rajasthan Tour, Saturday; among others.

Essentials

AL *Taj Residency Ummed*, Airport Circle, Hansol, T2864444, F2864454. 88 rooms and some expensive suites, tastefully decorated with traditional embroideries and art pieces, usual facilities, good pool, improved restaurant, hotel sometimes overbooked. **A-B** *Comfort Inn*, Airport Rd, T2862591, F2861627, cisunset@satyam.net.in 33 rooms, modern facilities, airport pick up. **A-B** *Cama Park Plaza*, Khanpur Rd, T5505281, F5505285, camahotel@vsnl.com 50 a/c rooms, totally renovated and upgraded on 1st and 2nd floors with long bathrooms, some with river-view, less expensive rooms on 3rd floor, new restaurant, (speciality restaurants planned), pool, good coffee shop, upmarket crafts and textiles shop, friendly new management. **A-B** *Fortune Landmark*, Ashram Rd, T7552929. One of the best but on busy main road, massive, varied rooms, good restaurants (buffet breakfast to set you up for the day), health club (gym, ayurvedic massage). **A-B** *Holiday Inn*, Khanpur Rd near Nehru Bridge, T5505505, F5505501. 63 rooms, good restaurants, dance floor, good indoor pool. Recommended. **A-B** *Inder Residency*, opposite Gujarat College, Ellis Bridge, T6425050, F6560407. 79 rooms, modern, very comfortable, very good Indian restaurant (avoid Western), pool. Recommended.

B *Klassik Gold*, CG Rd, T6445508. 33 rooms, excellent restaurant, efficient management, best in category. Recommended. **B** *Moti Manor* (Best Western), Shahibagh Under Bridge, T2869701, F2866414. 28 good rooms (day rate Rs 1000), excellent restaurant, near Calico Museum, friendly owner. **B** *Radisson* (was Shalin), Gujarat College Cross Roads, T6426967, F6560022. Reopened after renovation. 68 rooms (some non-smoking), pool. **B** *Royal Highness*, Lal Darwaja, T5507450. Good hotel but on extremely crowded intersection. **B-C** *Days Inn Chicago*, Ashram Rd, T6578126, F6577226, chicago@ad1.vsnl.net.in Good rooms, modern but rather crowded locality. **B-C** *Nalanda*, Mithakhali 6 Rds, T6426262, F6426090, www.hotelnalandaonline.com 38 clean rooms (standard rooms small; bath tubs and fridge in best), very good restaurant. Recommended but lacking in atmosphere. **B-C** *Rock Regency*, Law Garden Rd, T6562333. 38 rooms, good décor, adequate veg restaurant, near shops.

C *Karnavati* (Quality Inn), Shri Cinema Building, Ashram Rd, T6582162. 48 rooms, good restaurant. **C** *Mascot*, Khanpur Rd, T5503848, F5503221. Very comfortable, good value. Recommended. **C** *Nest*, 37 Sardar Patel Marg, behind Telephone Exchange, Navrangpura, T6426255, F6426259. 48 rooms, modern facilities. **C** *President*, CG Rd, Swastik Char Rasta, T6421421, F6421414. 58 good rooms, friendly staff, average décor, excellent restaurants. **C** *Rivera*, Khanpur Rd, T5504201, F5502327. 69 clean, comfortable rooms (some overlook river), restaurant, free airport transfer, lawn, quiet, good value. Recommended. **C-D** *King's Palace*, opposite *Cama*, T/F5500275. 37 very clean rooms in new hotel, some a/c, good value (Rs 600-800), good restaurant, friendly staff.

Khanpur: **D** grade hotels with some a/c rooms with shower and TV. Those without restaurants provide good room service. **D** *Ambassador*, Khanpur Rd, T5502490, F5502327. 17 rooms with bath, restaurant, basic but clean. **D** *Stay-Inn*, near Gate, T5500724, F5504053. 14 colourful, clean rooms, friendly, eager to please.

Tilak (Relief) Rd: Most **D** hotels in between *Chetna Restaurant* and Sidi Sayid Mosque are similar in standard and facilities; most rooms have phone and bath with hot water,

Sleeping
Most near the centre, about 3 km from railway. (Airport 10 km)

Old street names continue to be used: Relief Rd is now Tilak Rd; Khanpur Rd is Lady Vidyagauri Rd

Budget travellers may not find any room with bath for under Rs 150

Ahmadabad & Northern Gujarat

some a/c, though room sizes and prices differ. **D** *Balwas*, 6751 Relief Rd, near Electricity House, T5507135. 21 clean rooms, 6 small at rear (side entrance), some economical non-a/c **E**, good restaurant attached but crowded, noisy area and "overcharges on bus tickets". **D** *Capri*, Relief Rd opposite Electricity House, T5507143, F5506646. 28 clean, adequate rooms with bath but a bit overpriced. **D** *Goodnight*, Dr Tankaria Rd, opposite Sidi Sayid Mosque, Lal Darwaza, T5506997. 35 clean rooms, good restaurant, good service. **D** *Kingsway*, near GPO, T5501215. 33 Large rooms with fan, bath (hot water), modern, small breakfast menu and snacks. **D** *Marvel*, opposite Bhagwati Emporium. Clean carpeted rooms, restaurant has varied menu. **D** *Prime*, 2nd Flr, 'Vishal', Relief Rd, opposite Punjab Bank (entrance in underground bicycle park, lift to Reception), T352582. Clean, smallish rooms. **D-E** *Metropole*, Hanuman Lane, opposite Electricity House, T5507988. 19 clean rooms (small singles) some a/c, good room service. **E** *Volga*, near Electricity House, T5509497 F5509636,Volga@icenet.net Decent rooms, car rentals, Internet. **F** *Cadilac*, opposite Electricity House, Lal Darwaza, T5507558. Good value rooms with shared facilities, helpful travel desk. **F** *Sarita*, near Khanpur Gate, T5501569. Clean, large rooms with bath, some a/c, fairly quiet.

West of the river: **D** *Dimple International*, Panchkuva, T2141849, F2113276. 30 rooms with modern facilities. **D** *Panshikura*, near Town Hall, Underbridge, Ellis Bridge, T402960. 24 a/c rooms, quieter at rear, excellent restaurant. **D** *Poonam Palace*, off Ashram Rd, near Dipali Cinema. Recommended. **D-E** *Moti Mahal*, near Kalupur Gate and rly station, T2121881, F2144132. 15 modern rooms with bath, some a/c, excellent restaurant (good biriyanis) **E** *Esquire*, opposite Sidi Sayid Mosque. Is clean and popular. **E** *Nataraj*, Dada Mavlankar Rd, near Ahmad Shah Mosque. Simple rooms with bath, hostel-like but good value. **E** *Railway Retiring Rooms*, Junction station. **E** *Swagat*, near Arya Samaj, Rajpur-Kankaria Rd, T2111314.

Eating: **Mid-range** *Agashiye*, opposite Sidi Sayid Mosque, Lal Darwaja. Attractive Gujarati
centre *thali* restaurant on the terrace of a 1920s heritage building. Unique atmosphere, local music (Rs 170-200). Varied snacks and mini-meals in garden at the *Green Rock* (try *appam, uttapam,* about Rs 50). Book and poetry readings, classic films etc, planned. *Bhagyodaya*, GPO Rd (opposite *Kingsway*). Good food, varied choice, pleasant outlook. *Goodnight*'s *Food Inn* downstairs serves good Indian (unlimited *thali*!) but freezing a/c. *Paramount*, MG Rd near Bhadra. Indian. Famous for mutton/chicken biryanis, tikkas, a/c but lacks atmosphere. **Cheap** *Chetna*, by Krishna Cinema, Relief Rd (upstairs). Unlimited Gujarati *thalis*. *Iqbal Madari*, Khanpur, excellent samosas. *Sarav*, opposite Sayid Mosque. Good Indian.

Eating: **Expensive** *Khyber*, pleasant rooftop restaurant with city views, open after dark at *For-*
elsewhere *tune Landmark*. Great atmosphere, live music, specialises in kebabs, sizzlers, tandoori and western style grills/roasts, about Rs 450 each. Restaurant downstairs for good buffets, breakfast (cereal, lamb's liver, cold cuts, variety of breads, choice of eggs, Indian options) Rs 150, lunch Rs 175, dinner Rs 275. *Colours of Spice*, Swastik Crossroads. International (including Thai/Indonesian), pleasant a/c interior, reasonable food, courteous service, about Rs 300 each. *Silver Leaf*, Cama Park Plaza. Good Continental (ask for favourite pasta and other western dishes), excellent club sandwiches, good coffee (Rs 400 for 2).

Mid-range *Black Knight*, CG Rd, good Indian, Chinese, Continental, medieval European theme décor. *China Town*, Stadium Circle. Good Chinese (including non-vegetarian). Try fish Manchurian or chicken in hot garlic. Rs 300 for two. *Mirch Masala*, CG Rd, very spicy. North Indian (Rs 450 for 2), Bollywood theme in Juhu beach-shack mock-up with filmland posters and music to match, also tempting and hygienic (usually forbidden!) 'street snacks'. *Rajwadu*, Jivraj Park. A rural theme restaurant. Rajasthani/Gujarati dinner, delightful open-air setting, water courses, gardens, folk entertainment, large meals in brass/copper vessels, refills galore, a bit like a Bollywood film set but very pleasant, not quite as authentic as *Vishala* but more comfortable and accessible. (Rs 150-200 each). **Sheebah**, opposite Telephone Exchange, Navrangpura. International, a/c, excellent north Indian (try fish, paneer or chicken *tikkas*, tandoori or butter chicken, sheek kebabs, Rs 450 for 2), friendly. Continental and Chinese fast food counter (to avoid excess spices, request when ordering). Highly recommended. Avoid cake shop. **Ten, the Restaurant**, Swastik Crossroads, CG Rd. Indian and Continental, a/c, one of the best in town, ship-breakers yard décor, friendly, occasional live Indian music. Great fish meuniére, fried fish, methi chicken, kebab platters, but avoid Chinese (Rs 450 for 2). For dessert try the 10-special pudding. Good take-away cake shop. **Tomato**, CG Rd. Western, a/c 1950s American diner theme, Rock-and-Roll era décor and music (owner's collection), good atmosphere, young crowd, good (though not always authentic) Mexican/Italian (Rs 500 for 2). Also coffee shop serving great coffee, nachos, tacos, sandwiches. **Toran** at *Panshikura Hotel*. Indian, excellent food and value, high reputation locally.

Cheap *Thalis* are around Rs 50 ('Kathiawadi' has more chilly and garlic, while 'Gujarati' is sweetened with sugar and jaggery). **Purohit**, Ashram Rd, near *Air India*. Indian, large

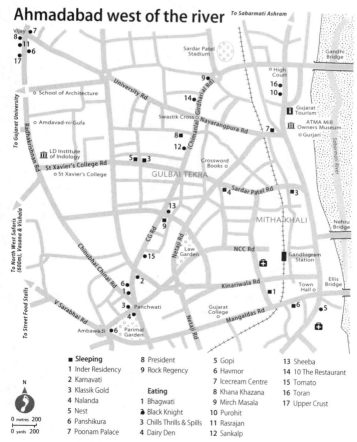

Ahmadabad west of the river

To Sabarmati Ashram

Sleeping
1 Inder Residency
2 Karnavati
3 Klassik Gold
4 Nalanda
5 Nest
6 Panshikura
7 Poonam Palace
8 President
9 Rock Regency

Eating
1 Bhagwati
2 Black Knight
3 Chills Thrills & Spills
4 Dairy Den
5 Gopi
6 Havmor
7 Icecream Centre
8 Khana Khazana
9 Mirch Masala
10 Purohit
11 Rasrajan
12 Sankalp
13 Sheeba
14 10 The Restaurant
15 Tomato
16 Toran
17 Upper Crust

0 metres 200
0 yards 200

The magic of *ikat* weaving

The highly skilful technique involves tie-dyeing the warp threads before weaving to create designs on the finished fabrics. Single ikat silk weaving is practised in various parts of Gujarat including Rajkot (where the Rashtriya Shala is working to revive traditional weaves), and in the towns and villages of Surendranagar district. In double ikat, which is twice as complex, both the warp and the weft threads are tie-dyed before being set on

the loom. This requires amazing precision, especially at the intersection of the warp and weft threads, and consequently it can take months to finish a single sari. The result is a richly patterned fabric, with both sides identical, which is considered highly collectable by textile connoisseurs. The double ikat method is exclusive to a few weavers of Patan in Gujarat (where patola saris are woven on traditional frameless looms), Indonesia and Japan.

helpings, generous refills. Highly recommended. **Gopi**, Ashram Rd. A/c, mildly spiced *thalis* specially for foreigners, good service, family run, popular. **La-Bela**, Mirzapur. Mutton/chicken curry and other dishes cooked up by a family. Lady owner treats visitors like part of her family. **Navrang**, Vijay Crossroads. Punjabi *thalis*, a/c. **Sankalp**, CG Rd. South Indian, rooftop terrace garden with fountain, good *dosas*. **Shiv Sagar** off CG Rd. *Thalis* (Rs 60), less spicy than elsewhere.

Seriously cheap Very cheap Indian meals and snacks are available at Bhatiar Gali, Law Garden, Raipur Gate and IIM Rd; the last popular with students (Chinese, South Indian etc, under Rs 30). **Azad Halwai**, Revdi Bazar. North Indian sweets, try brunch of *Daal-Pakwan*, a Sindhi favourite. **Mehta**, Ellis Bridge, excellent *thalis* and snacks. **New Swagath**, Babha Complex, opposite Gujarat Vidyapith. Good South Indian, *Puri-bhaji* (delicious spiced-up bubble 'n' squeak). **Tulsi**, near Gujarat University. Excellent value north Indian *thalis* and a la carte (about Rs 45), a/c. **Vallabha**, 1 Jeet Complex, opposite 'Shilip', C G Rd. Excellent Gujarati *thalis*.

Cafés and fast food Panchwati: **Bhagwati Chaats**, great Indian snacks and sweets, try *paneer tikkas, gulab jamuns* and *jalebis* (Rs 60 for 2 pieces); **Chills, Thrills, Frills**, veg/cheese burgers, excellent coffee, grilled and toasted sandwiches, vegetarian sizzlers, ice creams, thick shakes, disappointing pizzas, young crowd (Rs 150 for 2). **Cellad Eatery**, Swastik Crossroads. Buffet (Rs 120) includes soup and variety of salads, some main dishes, also a la carte option of sandwiches and snacks. **Dominos**, Stadium Circle. Good pizzas with variety of veg and non veg toppings but mainly for take-away (only a few tables outdoors, served in paper boxes), also desserts and side dishes. **Masty**, Panjarapol Cross-roads. Cheap Indian/Chinese. **Periera Takeaways** and **Icy Pick**, both near Vijay Crossroads. Cold meats, kebabs, tikkas. **Pizza Hut**, Swastik Crossroads. Young trendy crowd, a/c. Good salad bar and delicious icecreams but disappointing pizzas, pure vegetarian only. Ask for `meal deals'. **Rasrajan**, Vijay Crossroads (a/c). Self service, a/c upstairs. good vegetarian salad bar (cottage cheese, pineapple and pasta salads, Rs 45 per bowl), Indian and Chinese veg meals (about Rs 100 for 2), also sandwiches, good Indian sweets ("try *ras-malai*, it melts in the mouth") and pista milkshakes but cakes and icecreams are disappointing. Breakfast, Rs 40. Snack counter outdoors in the evening. **Real Taste**, near Commerce College. Cheap Chinese, vegetarian. **Upper Crust** Vijay Crossroads, (a/c). Good breads, chicken or paneer rolls, cakes and desserts, *kathi kabab* rolls, sizzlers, Sunday breakfast (Rs 50) with French toast, Spanish omelette etc. Rs 150-200 for a meal for 2. **UNO**. Good pizzas (fresh dough, deep-pan or normal crust), variety of toppings. Also, **Ehras**, Jamalpur, kebabs. **Honest Pau Bhaji**, Panchawati and Panjrapole. **Khana Khazana**, Ellis Bridge and Vijay Crossroads. Famous for mutton 'chops'.

Drinks *Lucky*, Lal Darwaza, and stalls near IIM, ID and Times of India Building are known for their masala tea. Ellis Bridge area, for refreshing fresh coconut milk. *Girish*, CG Rd, near Jami Masjid and elsewhere, and *Jamalpur*, Revdi Bazar, for fresh fruit juices and good milkshakes.

Ice creams Ahmadabad is famous for its icecreams. Everywhere in the city Vadilal icecreams (one of India's biggest brands - candy, cup, litre packs) are available. Also Baskin Robbins. Try *Dairy Den* at Municipal Market and Panchwati. For softies, sundaes and thick shakes. *Havmor* branches at Vijay Crossroads, Stadium, Jahanvee and Panchwati. Good sundaes, milkshakes, creamy icecreams rich in nuts/fruits/chocolate, and also serves snacks. Shreyas Crossing is a massive ice cream market *Patel* Panchwati, and *Rajasthan*, near Shreyas Railway Crossing. Fresh home-made ice cream. *Asarfi*, White House, Panchwati. *Vadilal* all over town. *Amul* St Xaviers School Rd, and *Dehrani-Jethani*, Stadium Rd. **Sweets** *Kamal*, Revdi Bazar, near the station. For excellent Indian sweets. *Kamdhenu*, near VS Hospital. For good Gujarati sweets. *Jai Sitaram* , near Paldi Railway Crossing. Delicious *kesar pedas* (saffron-flavoured milk sweets), *elaichi pedas* (with cardamom), they keep well; take some home!

India's ice cream capital!

Bars Prohibition is in force. Ask for a 'liquor permit' on arrival in India; getting one in the city is very tortuous. Ask at the airport tourist counter. There are plans to allow some larger hotels and popular tourist destination to issue 'spot' permits.

Entertainment

Clubs Better hotels can help with temporary membership at clubs with good facilities (tennis, swimming, billiards, library, restaurants etc). *Ahmadabad Gymkhana*, Army Cantt, Shahibagh has old world charm ('colonial' lounge). Others include *Sports Club of Gujarat*, Navrangpura Stadium and *Ellisbridge Gymkhana*, Law Garden. Several new 'Country clubs' along the highway (eg *Greenwoods, Sun 'n Step*) offer accommodation.

Festivals

14-15Jan: *Makar Sankranti* marks the end of winter. It is celebrated with kite flying by people of all ages, accompanied by colourful street markets and festivities. Kites come in all colours, shapes and sizes, the best varieties reputedly being available in Manek Chowk and Tankshala, Kalupur. The flying continues after sunset, when the kites are lit with candles. See box. **Sep/Oct:** *Navratri*, honouring Goddess Amba (*Shakti*), has special significance here and at Vadodara (17-25 Oct 2001; 7-14 Oct 2002). Nine days of music and traditional 'Garba Ras' dancing (sadly often to Westernized disco rhythm in some parts of the city). The custom of women balancing clay pots while they dance is still practised.

Shopping

Shops usually open from 0900-1900, most close on Sun. Manek Chowk is the main bazar. Other centres are Relief Rd, Ashram Rd, Lal Darwaza & Kapasia Bazar

Art Galleries include *Coq d'art*, Gulbai Tekra. Sells oil paintings. *Sun*, near A-one School, Gurukul Rd. Has Mahendra Mistry's works on devotional and cultural themes. Vinod Patel's pichhwais, miniatures and ivory paintings at *Thaltej Tekra*. Visit Law Gardens after 1600 to browse through stalls of artists and craftsmen.

Books *Art Book Centre*, Madalpur, near Inder Residency, specialises in books on art, architecture, handicrafts and tribes. *Book Shelf*, 16 City Centre, near *10-the Restaurant*, CG Rd, Navrangpura, T441826. A/c, good choice. *Books Plaza*, near Raymond show room, CG Rd. Excellent range, also CDs. *Crossword*, B6 Sri Krishna Centre, Mithakhali 6 Rds, T6425186. A/c, also CDs and café. *Kitab Kendra*, Sahitya Seva Sadan, near Gujarat College Crossroads. *Mapin*, Darpana Academy, Usmanpura, Ashram Rd. Specialist books on Indian arts. *Natraj*, Ashram Rd, with branches all over the city. Good range of books and CDs.

Food Supermarkets, bakeries and cold storages at Vijay Crossroads and Drive-in Rd.

Ahmadabad & Northern Gujarat

Handicrafts Good bargains at **Satellite Road**, where Kachhi and Saurashtrian arti-sans sell embroideries, block prints and handicrafts – appliqué bedspreads, wall hang-ings, embroidered folders, patchwork handbags etc, but bargain hard. *Treasure*, near Judge's bungalow, Satellite Rd, is a gallery for art, handicrafts and artefacts. Brassware and wood carvings are sold at Manek Chowk. Go to the huge **Sunday Market** on the river bank at Ellis Bridge in the morning to pick up 'antiques', handicrafts and sec-ond-hand books. *Dani Limda* for antiques and curios. Government *Garvi* and *Gujari*, Ashram Rd. Embroidered dresses, block-printed bedspreads, lacquered Sankehda fur-niture etc are well displayed, open 1030-1400, 1500-1900, closed Wed. *Kamdhenu* Ambawadi, has showrooms of several State Handicraft Co-ops. *Honeycomb*, at *Cama Hotel* and *Shringar* nearby, for up-market 'antiques'. *Bukhara-no-Khancho*, Shahpur, for warehouse prices for furniture and textiles (if you can put up with rudeness). **Ratanpole Rd** is the main silver market.

Photography Numerous 1-hr processing shops. *Dolphin*, Ambawadi, T6465665. Hand and computerised processing. *Rangoli*, near Gujarat Vidyapith, Ashram Rd, recom-mended developing. *Sukruti Q Lab*, Ashram Rd, T6587335. Transparencies (35 and 120 mm), also black and white. *Camera Clinic*, Vijay Plaza, Kankaria. Good camera repairs.

Textiles Gujarat's famous embroideries, *bandhani* and block prints are sold at *Rani-no-Haziro* and *Dalgarwad*, near Manek Chowk in the walled city. There many good value 'Khadi Bhandars' and *Handloom Houses* for textiles on Ashram Rd, between Gandhi Ashram and Natraj Theatre. *Revdi Bazar* and **Sindhi Market** have semi-wholesale textile shops. *Sewa*, east of Ellis Bridge. A commendable women's co-op producing very fine shadow embroidery and clothes. **CG Rd** is the up-market shopping area for high quality jewellery and garments.

Transport

Local Auto-rickshaws: Minimum Rs 4 (ask to see rate card). About Rs 2 per km inflated to Rs 5-10 for foreigners. Night charges are quite high. **Bus**: City service avail-able from main bus station, Lal Darwaza, railway station and all major points in the city. **Motorbikes**: *Shaikh Agency*, Swastik Supermarket, Ashram Rd. **Tourist taxis**: for hire from *TCGL*, T6589683 or *Sai*, 23 Aniket, Navrangpura; Rs 500 (4 hrs), Rs 900 (8 hrs).

Long distance Air: International flights to **Abu Dhabi, Bangkok, Copenhagen, Dhaharan, Dubai, Geneva** and **Hong Kong**. *Indian Airlines*, Lal Darwaza, near Roopalee Cinema, T5503061. 1000-1315, 1415-1715. Airport T140. **Delhi, Mumbai, Kolkata, Chennai** via **Bangalore, Hyderabad, Jaipur**. *Gujarat Airways*, T7868770: **Indore** and **Jaipur, Pune, Vadodara**. *Jet Airways*, T7543304: **Mumbai, Delhi**.

Arrive early to find your bus **Road Bus**: Central Bus Station, Geeta Mandir, T344764. Reservations 0700-1900. Advance booking for night services 1500-2300, luxury coach services 1030-1800. ST buses to **Mehsana** (Rs 20) on very poor road, **Mumbai** (492 km, 11 hrs), **Palitana** 217 km, **Porbandar** 394 km, **Rajkot** 216 km, **Sasan Gir** 217 km, **Surat** 120 km, and **Vadodara** 113 km. **Udaipur** 287 km. **Private operators** coaches, from suburban stands, often run at night. *Punjab Travels*, K Gandhi Rd, Delhi Darwaza, T449777, and Embassy Market, Ashram Rd. *Vyas* , Relief Rd, T33180. *Pawan*, Pritamnagar 1st Dhal, Ellis Bridge. *Tanna*, Paldi, for Bhavnagar. *Shajanand*, Shefali Complex, Paldi, for buses to **Diu**, Rs 90; **Mt Abu**, 7 hrs (via Khed Brahma).

Train Ahmadabad is on a broad gauge line to **Mumbai** (Platforms 1-4, near the main entrance) and a metre gauge line to **Delhi** (Platforms 7-12). Platforms 5 and 6 serve both, according to demand, and has 3 rails! Many meter services have been termi-nated. Ahmadabad Junction (Kalupur) Station, enquiries T131. Computerized reservations at Junction and Gandhigram stations: 1st Class 0730-1530, 2nd Class 0700-1430, 1500-2000, T135. If you don't have a reservation, last-minute berths can be booked for some trains at a temporary counter on the platform; premium charged. When booking ticket, confirm from which station train departs.

Agra Cantt: *Ahmadabad Gorakhpur Exp, 5045*, 0545, Tue, 25 hrs. **Ajmer**: *Aravali Exp, 9707*, 0620, 11 hrs; *Ahmadabad Delhi Mail, 9105*, 0955, 10½ hrs; *Ashram Exp 2915*, 1745, 7 hrs. **Bangalore**: *Ahmadabad Bangalore Exp* 1800, Sun, 13¾ hrs. **Bhavnagar**: *Bhavnagar Exp 9936*, 0705, 5½ hrs; *Shetrunji Exp, 9910*, 1710, 5½ hrs; *Link Exp, 9948*, 2155, 7 hrs. **Bhopal**: *Rajkot-Bhopal Jabalpur Exp, 1269/1263*, 1900, 14 hrs. **Chennai**: *Navjivan Exp, 6045*, 0630, 22¾ hrs. **Delhi** (OD)(: *Delhi Mail, 9105*, 0955, 20 hrs; *Ashram Exp, 2915*, 1745, 16½ hrs. **Jaipur**: *Aravali Exp, 9707*, 0620, 13¾ hrs; *Delhi Mail, 9105*, 0955, 13½ hrs; *Ashram Exp, 2915*, 1745, 11 hrs. **Kolkata** (H): *Howrah Exp, 8033*, 0920, 20 hrs. **Jamnagar**: *Jamnagar Exp, 9153*, 1815, not Mon, 6 hrs; *Mumbai Porbandar Saurashtra Exp, 9215*, 2015, 7½ hrs; *Mumbai Okha Saurashtra Mail, 9005*, 0550, 7½ hrs (all stop at **Wankaner**, 3 hrs before **Jamnagar**, and **Rajkot**, 2 hrs before Jamnagar). **Jodhpur**: *Ranakpur Exp, 4708*, 0030, 10 hrs (continues to **Bikaner**, 6 hrs). **Junagadh**: *Veraval Girnar Exp, 9946*, 2155, 8½ hrs; *Veraval Somnath Mail, 9924*, 2300, 10 hrs (both continue to **Veraval**, 2 hrs). **Mehsana**: *Aravali Exp, 9707*, 0620, 1¾ hrs; *Delhi Mail, 9105*, 0955, 2 hrs; *Ashram Exp, 2915*, 1745, 1½ hrs. **Mumbai** Central: *Shatabdi Exp, 2010*, 1435, not Fri, 7½ hrs; *Janata Exp, 9144*, 2105, 9½ hrs; *Gujarat Mail, 2902*, 2210, 8¾ hrs. **Porbandar**: *Mumbai Porbandar Saurashtra Exp, 9215*, 2015, 10½ hrs. **Rajkot**: See Jamnagar. **Udaipur City**: *DSR Express, 9944*, 2240, 9 hrs. **Vadodara**: *Gandhidham Vadodara Exp, 9104*, 0518, 2 hrs; *Ahmadabad Vadodara Exp, 9130*, 1445, 2½ hrs. **Varanasi**: *Sabarmati Exp, 9167*, 1955, Tue, Thu, Sat, 17¾ hrs. **Wankaner**: See Jamnagar.

Airline offices Domestic airlines under transport. *Air India*, Premchand House, near **Directory** High Court, T425644. *Air France*, T442391. *British Airways*, T465621. *Delta*, T448143. *Ethiopian Airlines*, T406077. *Gulf Air*, T463812. *Kuwait Airways*, T465848. *Kenya Airways*, T406027. *Lufthansa*, T464122. *Malaysian*, T425840. *Singapore Airlines*, T461335. *Swissair*, T449149. *United*, T401909. **Banks** *Bank of Baroda* and *Andhra Bank*, both on Ashram Rd, advance money against VISA, and encash TCs. Some on CG Rd and Ashram Rd, change TCs and currency. *Amex, Wall St Finance, Foreign Exchange Bureau*, all on CG Rd, and *Thomas Cook* near the High Court involve less paper-work and open till late. **Communications** Internet/email: *Bhavsons*, Ellis Bridge, Ashram Rd, email only; also fax shop, behind *Holiday Inn* Khanpur Rd. *Cyber Café*, Shri Krishna Centre, Mithakhali. *Log-In*, 92 Kamdhenu Complex, Polytechnic Rd, Ambawadi, T6302019, also printouts. *Random Access*, Ambawadi, cyber café, 10 terminals. **Post**: GPO off Relief Rd (special frank). Others at Navrangpura, Ellis Bridge, Gandhi Ashram, Gandhi Rd, Gujarat University, IIM, Madhavpura market, Polytechnic and Ambawadi ñ all with Speed Post. **Couriers**: *DHL*, Anand Market, Shahibagh Rd. *Blue Dart*, Embassy Centre, Ashram Rd. *Skypak*, near Lal Bungalow, CG Rd, are very reliable. **Cultural centres** West of Ellis Bridge, *Alliance Française*, behind Gujarat College, T441551 and *British Library*, near Law Garden, T350686, a/c; clean toilets. *Indo-German Centre*. **Medical services** Civil Hospital, Asarwa, T376351; **ESIC General**, Bapunagar, T363734; **Maninagar Sarbhai General**, Ellis Bridge; **Victoria Jubilee**, Panchkuwa Darwaza, T361080. **Tour operators** *Florican Tours*, opposite Electricity House, Lal Darwaza, T5506590, F6426545, for bookings for Poshina. *North West Safaris*, 91-92 Kamdhenu Complex, opposite Sahajanand College, T6302019, F6300962, ssibal@ad1.vsnl.net.in Knowledgeable, efficient. Highly recommended. *Sita*, Suflam Building, Mithakhali, Ashram Rd, T409105. *TCI*, near Natraj Theatre, behind Handloom House, Ashram Rd, T407061. **Tourist offices** *Gujarat (TCGL)*, HK House, opposite Bata, Ashram Rd, T6589172, F6582183, tcgl.ahm@rmt.sprintrpg. ems.vsnl.net.in; 1030-1830, closed Sun, 2nd and 4th Sat each month. Ahmadabad

'Dairy Den', Plat 1, Junction station, fast food, 24 hrs, grilled sandwiches, burgers, pizzas, ices. Western Railway dishes up passable Chinese & Indian

Ahmadabad & Northern Gujarat

Municipal Corp, near Khamasa Gate. 1100-1800. Also at airport, T367568, 0600-2200, and railway station, 0800-2000, Sun 0800-1400. **Useful addresses** Ambulance: T102. **Fire:** T101. **Police:** T100. **Foreigners' Regional Registration Office:** Police Commissioner's Office, Shahi Bagh.

Around Ahmadabad

Sarkhej
8 km SW

Sarkhej was once a country retreat of the Muslim rulers. The *Rauza* (1445-51) is a fine mausoleum complex, one of the largest in India, with a mosque, palace, pavilions and tombs, all grouped around a large tank. The style shows distinct Hindu influence. The Dutch established an indigo factory nearby. ■ *Getting there: 1 km west off the NH8A in the midst of the crowded village.*

★ Adalaj
17 km N Ajmer Rd (near Gandhinagar cross-road)

A visit here is highly recommended

The **Vav** (*baoli*), in a garden setting in the hamlet of Adalaj (1502), is one of the finest step wells in India, showing a combination of Hindu, Muslim and Buddhist styles. A long flight of steps descends over 30 m to the water. It has four floors, each cooler than the one above. Ornately carved pillars, niches and cross beams create large octagonal landings (now inaccessible) which served as resting places. Remains of the bullock ramp used for drawing water are still visible. Queen Rupabai is believed to have had it built to provide the traveller with a cool and pleasant refuge from the summer heat (some believe she drowned herself, rather than be forced to marry a second time). ■ *Getting there: Taxi drivers pretend not to know of it because of poor access road!*

Eating On Gandhinagar Highway *Bageshree* for Gujarati *thalis* in lovely garden setting; and *Gokul* with a village theme, *havelis* and huts, folk concerts, Gujarati *thalis*. *Punjab Malwa*, dhaba for cheap meals. *Sanja Chulla*, Punjabi dhaba style, meals around log fire in winter, charpois. *Saffrony Food Court* sells Indian snacks.

Gandhinagar

Phone code: 02712
Colour map 5, grid A6
Population: 123,400
23 km N of Ahmadabad;
7 km E of Adalaj

When Bombay state was divided along linguistic lines into Maharashtra and Gujarat in 1960, a new capital city was planned for Gujarat named after Mahatma Gandhi. As with Chandigarh, Le Corbusier was instrumental in the design. The 30 residential sectors around the central government complex are similarly impersonal. Construction began in 1965 and the Secretariat was completed in 1970. It is now an established town with over a quarter of a million people. Gandhinagar has become a popular place for day trippers from Ahmadabad with good multiplex theatre complexes, parks, gardens and the Indroda deer park.

Akshardham, in Sector 20, a temple with a cultural complex and entertainment park, is run by volunteers. The pink sandstone main building, floodlit at dusk, houses a 2-m gold leaf idol and some relics of Sri Swaminarayan, who led a Vedic revivalist movement 200 years ago. The three halls feature a variety of informative sound and light presentations relating to Sri Swaminarayan, the *Vedas* and the Hindu epics. Sahajanabad Vun, the garden for meditation, is impressive and has 'singing fountains' and a restaurant. ■ *0900-1830 (Nov-Feb); 1000-2000 (Mar-Oct), part closed on Mon; tickets, Rs 25. Temple Information Counter and shop has maps, guide books and post cards.*

Sleeping **C** *Haveli*, Sector 11, opposite Sachivalaya, T24052, F24057. 84 rooms, restaurants (good South Indian dining hall), exchange, car hire, free airport transfer, day rates available, smart entrance but rooms and toilets below standard. **F** Govt *Pathik Ashram*, Sector 11. **F** *Youth Hostel*, Sector 16, T22364. 2 rooms, 42 beds in 6-bed and 8-bed dorms, very good, no reservations.

Mid-range *Relief*, excellent Indian and Continental. Recommended. **Cheap** **Eating** *Premawati*, Akshardham Complex. Veg Gujarati food, Indian snacks, lime tea and delicious ice creams *Torana*, Sector-28, Punjabi. South Indian snacks, in a garden. *Chills, Thrills & Spills*, Sector-21 Shopping Centre. Pizzas, sandwiches, ice creams, veg *thalis*. *Sher-e-Punjabi*, North Indian veg and non veg. Sector 21 has street-side vendors who offer good snacks. Ask for the `Bhatiar' couple who make *bajra ka rotla* (millet *chapatis*) and chicken curry, meat samosas and daal in a little shack, not too far from Akshardham.

Train and **buses** to Ahmadabad. ST Bus Station, Sector 11, T22842. **Transport**

Forest Office, Nursery G4, Sector 17, (behind Town Hall), T21217. **Tourist** **Directory** **office** *Gujarat Tourism*, Nigam Bhavan, Sec 16, T22523, F22189.

A former Nawabi capital, Balasinore is now a crowded town centred around a **Balasinore** lake, and has some old Islamic architecture. It has come into international geolog- *86 km E of* ical limelight after dinosaur fossils were found nearby; eggs and fossils are still *Ahmadabad* being excavated. The **B** *Balasinore Garden Palace* (Heritage Hotel), T02690-62008, has four rooms (signs of damp) in an early 20th-century building, delicious Mughlai meals, one of few Nawab family run heritage hotels, pleasant orchard garden, personal attention, tours of 650 million year old dinosaur site and tribal villages, but overpriced at Rs 2,500. ■ *Getting there: Buses from Kakhal.*

Gandhinagar

Ahmadabad & Northern Gujarat

Vautha

Less colourful than Pushkar fair it is also far less touristy

Here the *Vautha Mela*, starting at *Kartik Purnima*, is held at the confluence of Sabarmati and Vatrak rivers (1-4 November 2001; 20-23 November 2002). About 4,000 donkeys, painted in vivid colours, and over 2,000 camels are traded. There is a great atmosphere on the river banks early in the morning, and in addition to the haggling over animals there are craft sales. Gujarat Tourism puts up twin bedded tents with catering. ■ *Getting there: It is 46 km south of Ahmadabad and 26 km from Dholka, on the railway. Special buses run to Vautha during the fair for both.*

Lothal 'Mound of the dead'

87 km SW of Ahmadabad

Southeast of Moenjodaro, 720 km as the crow flies, Lothal has some of the most substantial remains of the Harappan culture in India dating from circa 2500-1700 BC. Once a port sandwiched between the Sabarmati River and the Bhogavo River, it is now 10 km inland from the Gulf of Khambhat on a flat, often desolate looking plain. Thorn scrub and parched soils surround the site, and even in February a hot desiccating wind picks up flurries of dust.

Ins & outs

Carry bottled water

Getting there Trains and buses from Ahmadabad or Bhavnagar go close to Lothal; see Transport below. It can be a long, hard day. Hiring a taxi or motorbike makes it easier. **Getting around** You visit the site on foot but there is no shade and no proper drinks outlet.

The site

Closed on Fri

Lothal's location and function as a port have led most authorities to argue that it was settled by Harappan trading communities who came by sea from the mouths of the Indus. Others suggest that the traders came by an overland route. The site is surrounded by a mud-brick embankment 300 m north-south and 400 m east-west. Unlike the defensive walls at Harappa and Moenjodaro, the wall at Lothal enclosed the workers' area as well as the citadel. The presence of a dry dock and a warehouse further distinguish it from other major Harappan sites.

The dry dock This massive excavated structure runs along the east wall of the city. A 12-m wide gap in the north side is believed to have been the entrance by which boats came into the dock, while a spillway over the south wall allowed excess water to overflow. The city wall at this point may have been a wharf for unloading. Excavations of the warehouse suggest that trade was the basis of Lothal's existence. The building at the southwest corner of the wharf had a high platform made of cubical mud-brick blocks, the gaps between them allowing ventilation. Over 65 Indus Valley seals discovered here show pictures of packing material, bamboo or rope, suggestive of trade; one from Bahrain is evidence of overseas trade.

The city Excavations show a planned city in a grid pattern, with an underground drainage system, wells, brick houses with baths and fireplaces. The raised brick platform to the southeast may have been a kiln where seals and plaques were baked. Objects found include painted pottery, terracotta toys, ivory, shell, semi-precious stone items, bangles and even necklaces made of tiny beads of gold. Rice and millet were clearly in use, and there is some evidence that horses had been domesticated. The cemetery to the northwest had large funerary vessels indicating pit burials.

Ahmadabad & Northern Gujarat

Archaeological Museum exhibits some artefacts (copper and bronze implements), terracotta pottery, beautifully made beads, seals etc. Small but interesting, and well presented. A few books and postcards are for sale. ■ *1000-1700. Closed on Fri. Rs 2.*

Museum

There are a few **buses** from Ahmadabad and Bhavnagar: Change at Dholka. Luxury (*Tanna Travels*) and State buses can drop you at Gundi railway crossing; from there *chhakras*, motorbike trailers, charge Rs 5 each for the drop to Lothal. Get back on the highway to get a bus back to Ahmadabad or Bhavnagar. Ideally hire a car from Ahmadabad (Rs 800-1000). From **Ahmadabad**, travel 52 km to Bagodra on the NH8A, then turn left on SH1 towards Bhavnagar (73 km), go across the level crossing and immediately turn left. Lothal is signposted as 7 km (appalling section). From **Bhavnagar** follow the SH1 via Vallabhipur and Barwala. The turn off is 127 km from Bhavnagar. Some **trains** from Ahmadabad to Bhavnagar stop at Lothal-Burkhi station; shared *chhakras* drop you at Lothal or Utelia for a few rupees.

Transport

The alluvial Bhal plains along the Gulf of Khambhat are excellent wheat and cotton producing centres. Wheat harvesting and cotton picking can be seen here in late-winter (around February). There are salt works along the coast.

Around Lothal

Gundi, 4 km away, has ashrams dedicated to promoting rural development, where you can watch hand spinning and weaving and buy wool and cotton textiles from the co-operatives.

Utelia, 7 km away (3 km from the highway), is a very quiet peaceful yet colourful village where you can watch diamond cutting and visit hot springs. The postmaster's son is a good local guide. **C** *Palace Utelia* is an imposing mansion with 14 large comfortable rooms decorated in traditional Gujarati style. Rustic looking but very well maintained, excellent baths, balconies with views, beautifully presented food (expensive drinks - 'invited us for beer, and then billed us for it!'). Safaris overpriced check details beforehand. Reservations: *North West Safaris*, T079-6302019, F6300962, ssibal@ad1.vsnl.net.in

The lake and the Surendranagar Reservoirs southwest of Ahmadabad were declared a bird sanctuary in 1969. Early morning and from late afternoon is the best time for viewing. Avoid the rains from June to mid-September. Uniquely in Saurashtra, Nalsarovar is surrounded by reed beds and marshes though the lake often dries out before the rains. Bharwad herdsmen and their water buffaloes live on the reed islands – you can get hot millet buttered chapatis and chutney with sweet tea or lassi from some shacks. Padhar fisherfolk who live around the lake are good artisans (shell toys, embroideries et cetera) and known for their graceful dancing simulating waves and fishes. *Forest Dept Bungalows* provide two or three simple rooms with views of lake. ■ *Best season: Nov-Feb. Increased entry fees now control visitor numbers. Try a boat ride for birding (Rs 25 per person per hour) for an experience. Contact Forest Office at Gandhinagar.* ■ *Getting there: Direct buses from Ahmadabad (0700, 1500) take 2 hrs. Otherwise change buses at Sanand (38 km NW of Nalsarovar); last return from park at 1800.*

Nalsarovar Bird Sanctuary

The sanctuary is noted for waterbirds including migratory ducks, flamingos & geese

Situated on the banks of the artificial Ramsagar Lake with impressive old embankments, Limbdi was the capital of a former princely state. Attractive French Regency-style buildings in the market include the pretty *Yashwant Mahal*, *Darbargadh* and *Digbhuvan* **palaces** and the 19th-century clock tower. The town, 1 km from NH8A, specializes in ivory bangles and brass ware, especially boxes. The **Ramsagar Lake**, near Limbdi, is a beautiful reservoir, with attractively carved 19th-century embankments. The town was

Limbdi

109 km SW of Ahmadabad

Ahmadabad & Northern Gujarat

severely damaged in 2001 earthquake and may not be ready for visiting until 2002. ■ *Getting there: buses run along the NH8A. Also on the very slow Bhavnagar-Surendranagar railway.*

Sleeping and eating Motels near the highway include: **C-D** *Awantika*, NH8, 4 simple clean rooms (2 a/c), owned by former royal family, good vegetarian food (South Indian breakfast, Gujarati *thalis*, North Indian), pleasant dinners in a small garden.

Wadhwan Wadhwan, northwest of Limbdi, was a princely state of the Jhalas, a Rajput clan. The fortified old township has plenty of interesting architecture including two old stepwells with attractive carvings, some fine 11th-16th-century temples and a lake facing Hawa Mahal which was never completed. It is an ideal place to watch (and shop for) *bandhani*, wood and stone carving, silver and brass work, and textiles.

The opulent 19th-century Raj Mahal (*Bal Vilas*) occupied by the royal family, surrounded by parkland, has a grand Durbar hall with chandeliers, frescoes, carved furniture, crystal and velvet curtains, and a Sheesh Mahal library and billiard room. The living quarters of the royal family's ancestors have been left untouched. The vast landscaped gardens have tennis courts, lily ponds, fountains and a pillared courtyard with a swimming pool. Maharajah Chaitanya Dev is a keen restorer of classic cars and has a personal vintage car collection with a rare 1918 Crossley and a 1936 Mercedes convertible seven seater among other prized possessions.

Surendr- The larger town nearby has antique and curio dealers who hunt out interesting **anagar** pieces as well as embroidered textiles of Kachchh and Saurashtra, from former ruling families, landowners and villagers. Be aware that genuine antiques may not be exported. You can stay here at **D** *Shiv International* which is popular with business travellers, has a/c rooms and mod cons. **F** *Krishna* (ask locally) has clean rooms with bath and massive colour TV, very good value.

North of Ahmadabad

The fertile irrigated land immediately north of Ahmadabad becomes increasingly arid northwards towards Rajasthan. When approaching Mehsana there are signs of the growing economy, including natural gas, fertilizers, milk products and rape seed oil processing as well as a few modern places serving drinks and snacks.

Mehsana The town, 80 km north of Ahmadabad, has an impressive Jain temple, built in **(Mahesana)** the 1980s but in the traditional architectural style. Mehsana is used by visitors to Modhera and Patan for an overnight stop. Women travellers have reported being hassled by men near the bus station.

Sleeping **A-C** *Water World Resort*, 25-min drive out of town, T02762-82351, F82352. A/c cottages, modern, Mughal garden with a/c 'royal tents', vegetarian restaurant, bar, wave pool and sports complex, artificial lake. **D-E** *Vijay Guest House*, NH8, T02762-20041, near bus stop, on left going north. Good clean rooms with bath, some a/c, quieter at rear, friendly staff but no English spoken. Others are Indian style: **E** *Apsara*, *Janta Supermarket*, opposite bus station, T02762-20027. Reasonable rooms, some a/c, *thali* meals. **D-E** *Natraj*, 1 km from bus stand. 12 rooms ranging from basic dorm to comfortable a/c with bath, very good veg restaurant. **F** *Railway Retiring Rooms*, decent rooms (Rs 40) with bath.

Eating Cheap: *Kudarat*, near *Vijay* (Hindi sign with a triangular tree symbol), best of the highway cafés. South Indian and Punjabi. Open-air, so you may have a monkey for company. *Sher-e-Punjab*, by a petrol station, east of NH8, does good omelettes. Others in town.

Transport Road Auto-rickshaws: Rs 5 from town to *Vijay*. **Bus**: To Ahmadabad on a very poor road (2½ hrs) and to Patan. To **Modhera**: bus from ST Bus Stand (infrequent and uncertain timetable), ¾ hr, Rs 8; or bus from NH8/SH41 junction (Modhera Rd) but often full. Last return from Modhera, 1730 (sometimes delayed by up to 2 hrs). **Train** Rajasthan and Delhi bound trains from Ahmadabad stop at Mehsana

★ Modhera

Virtually a deserted hamlet, Modhera has the remains of one of the finest Hindu temples in Gujarat. Quite off the beaten track, it retains a great deal of its atmosphere and charm.

Colour map 5, grid A6
25 km W of Mehsana

The partially ruined **Surya** (Sun) **Temple** (1026), built during the reign of Bhimdev I and consecrated in 1026-27, two centuries before the Sun Temple at Konark, is a product of the great Solanki period (eighth-13th centuries). Despite the temple's partial destruction by subsequent earthquakes, which may have accounted for the collapse of its tower, it remains an outstanding monument, set against the backdrop of a barren landscape. Superb carvings of goddesses, birds, beasts and blossoms decorate the remaining pillars. Over the last 20 years the complex has undergone major restoration by the Archaeological Survey of India which is continuing as funds permit. Unlike the Temple at Konark, the main temple stands well above the surrounding land, raised by a high brick terrace faced with stone.

The temple

A rectangular pool (*kund*, now dry), over 50-m long and 20-m wide, with flights of steps and subsidiary shrines, faces the front of the temple. It is a remarkable structure, and although many of the images in the subsidiary shrines are badly weathered it is still possible to gain an impression of the excellence of the carving as well as of the grandiose scale on which the whole plan was conceived. On the west side of the tank a steep flight of steps leads up to the main entrance of the east *mandapa* through a beautifully carved *torana*, of which only the pillars now remain. The **sabha mandapa**, a pillared hall, is 15 sq m. Note the cusped arches which became such a striking feature of Mughal buildings 600 years later. The corbelled roof of this entry hall, which has been reconstructed, is a low stepped pyramid. Beautiful columns and magnificent carvings decorate the hall. The western part of the temple contains the raised **inner sanctuary** within its oblong plan. The upper storeys have been completely destroyed, though it clearly consisted of a low pyramidal roof in front of the tall *sikhara* (tower) over the sanctuary itself. Surya's image in the sanctuary (now missing) was once illuminated by the first rays of the rising sun at each solar equinox (proof of the mathematical and astronomical knowledge of the designers). Images of Surya and Agni are among the better preserved carvings on the external walls which also contain some erotic scenes. Unlike the exterior, the interior walls were plain other than for niches to house images of Surya. ■ *Getting there: for transport see Mehsana above. Visit early in the day.* Gujarat Tourism Toran Restaurant *serves drinks and snacks. A* Classical Dance Festival *is held in Jan (18-20, 2002). See under Festivals.*

Ahmadabad & Northern Gujarat

Patan
Hardly ever visited by foreigners 35 km NW of Mehsana

Patan has over 100 beautifully carved Jain temples and many attractive tradi-tionally carved wooden houses. It remains a centre for fine textiles, particu-larly silk *patola* saris produced by the characteristic *ikat* technique. Only two extended families can be seen at work on double ikat weaving.

In the eighth century, Patan, was the capital of the Hindu kings of Gujarat. Mahmud of Ghazni sacked it in 1024, and it was taken by Ala-ud-din Khalji's brother Alaf Khan in 1306. Little remains of the old city except some of the walls.

★ The spectacular **Rani ki Vav** (late 11th century), named after a Solanki queen, is one of the largest stepwells in India with superb carvings on seven storeys. Flights of steps lead down to the water level, lined by stringcourses of sculptured voluptuous women, Vishnu avatars and goddesses. Solar disc symbols of the sun-worshipping Rajputs can be seen on the structures. Directly above the now silted well is an exquisite carving of Vishnu reclining on a serpent. Chambers and galleries facing the well suggest that the queen and princesses could have used this area to enjoy the cool air wafting from the water ■ *US$5 (foreigners)*. The Sahasralinga Talao has a cluster of Solanki period (11th-12th century) shrines facing a small lake. Excavations are in progress to find more relics of the days when Patan was the seat of power of Gujarat (eighth-15th century).

Sleeping and eating A new **E** *Lodge* has opened at the crossroads on the main road leading into town. **E-F** *Neerav*, near bus and railway station, has rooms with bath (bucket hot water and room service, mornings only), some a/c with TV, clean and com-fortable, Gujarati *thali* and North Indian food, best but noisy area. **F** *Toran Tourist Bun-galow* (Gujarat Tourism), 2 simple rooms (Rs 200), cafeteria, convenient for stepwell and Patola silk weavers. **F** *Aram Griha* (Govt), simple rooms.

Transport Bus: To/from Mehsana and Modhera. **Train**: To/from Mehsana.

Vadnagar
40 km NE of Mehsana

The town, has the finest example of the *torana* arches that characterise North Gujarat. Beautiful sculptures decorate two of the original four 12th-century arched gateways on *kirti stambha* pillars. The Solanki period city gates are beautifully sculpted, the best being near the lake. The impressive 17th-century Haktesvar Temple, the most important Siva temple in Gujarat, has fine carvings, erotic sculpture and a silver shrine. Tana-Riri, two poet-ess-singers from Vadnagar, are said to have saved Tansen from the burning effects of the Deepak Raga (Song of Fire). Tansen had been persuaded to sing the raga in the court of Akbar by courtiers who were jealous of his skill, but the sisters saved him by singing the Maldaar Raga (Song of Rain). Akbar invited the sisters to sing in his court, but rather than refuse to sing for a Muslim emperor (which was against their custom) they immolated themselves. Their shrine can be seen at Vadnagar. ■ *Getting there: Buses and trains (45 mins - 1 hr) from Mehsana.*

Taranga
Panthers have been sighted near the temple complex

Named after Tara Devi, Taranga, 60 km northeast of Mehsana, has a fabulous complex of well preserved 12th-century Jain temples surrounded by spectac-ular hills with some dramatic formations. The large central sandstone temple to Adinatha is beautifully carved with sensual dancing figures, Hindu deities and Jain *Tirthankaras*. Inside is a bejewelled central statue carved out of a sin-gle piece of alabaster and the temple's intricately decorated pillars, brackets and ceiling. There is a scenic trek from the main Adinath temple, passing some dramatic rock formations, to the hilltop Shilp Temple where one of the Jain saints meditated. There is a bungalow with four rooms in a 100-year old home set on a hill with village and woodland views, Rajput family run, delicious food, 1000-acre farm with Marwari/Kathiawadi horses, riding, horse safaris. Recommended. There are cheap Gujarati *thalis*, Rs 9 (for Jains), Rs 15 (for non-Jains!). ■ *Getting there: Buses, and slow train (3 hrs) from Mehsana.*

Close to the Rajasthan border, en route to Mount Abu, Ambaji is known for   **Ambaji**
its marble mines. You can see marble artisans at work at this temple town (and at Khedbrahma nearby) where *Bhadra Purnima* fair is held with processions of flag bearing pilgrims followed by musicians and dancers (2 September 2001, 20 September 2002). A picturesque rope-way goes to Gabbar hill, a holy pilgrimage for Hindus (Rs 25). ■ *Ahmadabad-Mt Abu buses stop at Ambaji.*
   The five 11th- and 12th-century Jain temples at Kumbhariya, just east of Ambaji, are worth visiting for their exquisite marble carvings. ■ *0630-1930; aarti worship 0900-0930 and 1900, tea canteen, Jain thalis for Rs 12, reasonably clean Indian toilets, also bath cubicles with hot water buckets. Getting there: Jeeps (Rs 50) from Ambaji bus stand, Rs 5 for sharing.*

Enroute from Taranga to Ambaji, the princely state of Danta was known for   **Danta**
its cavalry. Even today the family keeps 15 Marwari and some Kathiawadi horses on their 1,000-acre stud farm. Set near the Balaram-Ambaji wildlife sanctuary, Danta is being developed by the former ruling family into an adventure destination for trekking and riding with well marked trails. It is dominated by the medieval Parmara Rajput fort. The jungles and rocky hills harbour panther, nilgai and four-horned antelopes, and there is extensive birdlife. **B** *Bhavani Villa* is on a hilltop and tourists are welcomed like family guests. There are four new a/c rooms facing the hills, two private guest rooms in family's colonial period mansion when required, delicious, well presented Rajput meals, friendly hosts, great place for nature lovers (view of jungles, panther sometimes seen from the room), nature trails (quails, francolin and other birdlife), game drives, riding (Rs 250 per hour), horse safaris (Rs 5000 per person). Reservations: *North West Safaris*, T079-6302019, F6300962.

An alternative route from Ahmadabad to Mount Abu, slightly longer but on   **Routes**
better roads, takes you past Himmatnagar, to Idar Fort, the scene of many battles with dramatic river sculpted rocks. **Khedbrahma**, just north of Idar, has one of the few Brahma temples in the country.

Vijaynagar, east of Khedbrahma, is known for an ancient temple complex – known as *polo* – set in wooded hills. Although most of the temples are in ruins, several interesting decorative features of the eighth-12th century period can still be seen. **C** *Polo Retreat*, near Saneshwar temple T02775-54278, has eight cottage rooms with baths, homecooked meals, family run.

Shamlaji, on the NH8, east of Himmatnagar, has a beautiful Vishnu temple. A large Bhil tribal fair is held during *Kartik purnima* and features ritual bathing in the tank. (28 Nov 2001, 20 Nov 2002)

The small 15th-century **Poshina fort**, 45 km south of Abu Road, stands on   **Poshina**
the Aravalli hills, at the confluence of two holy rivers (Sai and Panhari) with views over the hills. It was the capital of the North Gujarat branch of Vaghela Rajputs. There are ancient Jain and Siva temples nearby as well as tribal villages where you can watch arrowmaking, basketwork, silversmiths and potters. The area is home to Bhils who follow traditions said to date from 2000 BC, colourful

Garasias in their artistic jewellery and Rabaris who herd camels, cattle and goats. The busy and interesting market centre is well worth stopping at if you are travelling through although the last stretch of the approach road is very poor. *Chitra Vichitra Fair* is held a fortnight after *Holi* (11 April 2002), at **Gunbakhari**, 8 km away. It is attended by Bhils, Garasias and Rabaris (some of whom are now abandoning their traditional dhotis and turbans, to the disappointment of visitors). The night before the fair is dedicated to ancestor worship with mourning at the river. The fair is very colourful with much revelry, dancing and singing, food stalls etc. Matchmaking is often followed by elopements. The *Ambamahuda Fair* at the same time at Poshina itself is smaller but is also rewarding.

Sleeping and eating B *Darbargarh* (Heritage Hotel), in 17th-century wing of the fort complex, pleasant with open courtyards and hill views, old world charm, now renovated with antiques, Rajasthani miniatures and rare Tanjore paintings (rather haphazardly), 15 comfortable, air-cooled rooms (some complaints about cleanliness), spicy Indian meals, camel rides, folk entertainment, friendly hosts, owner is very knowledgeable about local tribes, crafts etc, good village safaris ("fantastic tribal shrine with terracotta horses in the open"), advance reservations, *Florican Tours*, T5506590, F6426545. *Tents* (Gujarat Tourism) during fair. Delicious flavoured *lassi* near the village entrance but ask to prepare with your own mineral water.

Transport Ahmadabad-Ambaji buses stop at Kheroj from where it is possible to get shared jeeps to Poshina (12 km)

Palanpur
N of Mehsana
on NH14

The *maqbara* with fine mausolea in this old Nawabi capital stands rather neglected. The palace is now the court. Look in to see the fabulous ceiling paintings and sandalwood carvings. The 1915 Kirti Stambha has the 700-year long history of the Nawabs of Palanpur inscribed on it. ■ *Getting there: Trains between Ahmadabad and Delhi stop at Palanpur. See also under Bhuj. Direct buses go to Mt Abu; Ambaji (also share jeeps, Rs 20); Poshina through attractive countryside and tribal areas, 1200 (1 hr), Rs 7.*

Sleeping and eating D *Cappal*, NH14, T02742-50666, F50888. 27 rooms with baths (some suites with TV and fridge), a/c veg restaurant. **D** *Lajwanti*, T02742-57200, and **D** *Greenwoods*, T02742-80464 are similar. **E** *Savera* on the highway, motel rooms and veg restaurant. **F** *Railway Retiring Rooms*, clean, spacious with bath (Rs 100). *Sona*, opposite, T02742-52049, for good cheap food and *thalis*, friendly service.

Balaram
Phone code: 02742

Balaram, 3 km off the highway, 14 km north of Palanpur, has one of the best palace hotels in Gujarat. About 20 km from there, the **Jessore Bear Sanctuary** in the Aravallis has sloth bear (occasionally spotted), panther, nilgai, sambhar, four-horned antelope et cetera, but these are best seen by climbing Jessore hill. Contact Forest Office, T57084.

Sleeping and eating B *Balaram Palace Resort*, Chitrasani, splendid riverside location surrounded by hills. Impeccably restored 1930s palace, 17 a/c rooms (interiors too modern and characterless for some) choose between 4 colonial rooms with old fireplaces and rooms upstairs with views. The Nawab Suite has huge arched windows, excellent terrace restaurants, lovely formal Nawabi garden, fountains, period swimming pool fed by natural cascading spring, good gym, bike hire. Recommended. Contact T079-6582191, F6578412, bprhot@ad1.vsnl.net.in

Vadodara and the Old Forts

Vadodara and the Old Forts

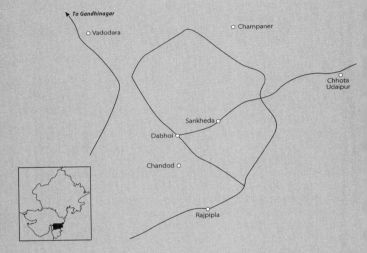

★ Vadodara

Formerly Baroda, Vadodara was the capital of one of the most powerful princely states. It is now a rapidly expanding industrial town, yet the older part is pleasant and interesting to wander through.

Phone code: 0265
Colour map 6, grid B1
Population: 1.115 mn

Getting there The airport, with flights from Ahmadabad, Delhi and Mumbai, is 6 km away with taxis and auto-rickshaws to town. Better hotels offer free airport transfer. The Railway and the Long Distance bus stations are to the northwest of town, close to hotels. From the railway station, walk under the bridge; then for 5 mins to find several to the left of the main road and in the streets behind. **Getting around** The local bus station is just opposite the railway station. There are taxis and autos to take you to the town centre and the sights.

Ins & outs
See page 288 for
further details

The Gaekwad (meaning 'Protector of Cows'), stood high in the order of precedence among rulers, being one of only five to receive a 21-gun salute. He was reputedly so rich that he had a carpet woven of diamonds and pearls, and cannons cast in gold.

History

Sights

The **Laxmi Vilas Palace** (1880-90) was built by RH Chisholm. The magnificent palace is somewhat neglected but the interiors are decorated with Venetian mosaic, Italian marble, porcelain, antique furniture, European stained glass, sculptures, a royal armoury et cetera. It now has a sports club with polo and golf with plans to open as a 17 room Heritage Hotel. ■ *Rs 100 (no photography)*. Nearby is the **Naulakhi Well**, a well-preserved *baoli* which has galleried levels.

Just to the south of the Palace is the **Maharajah Fateh Singh Museum** with a prized collection of paintings by the 19th-century Indian artist Raja Ravi Verma (see below). Further south, beyond the railway, the **Pratap Vilas** (circa 1910, known as Lalbagh palace), with a baroque façade, is now the Railway Staff College. Permission from Principal is needed to visit the small rail museum. The beautiful **Shiv Mahal** palace, near the race course, is being renovated.

In the town centre, the **Kirti Mandir** (early 20th century), the Gaekwad *samadhi* (memorial ground) has murals by Nandlal Bose and marble busts. The **Kothi Building** (late 19th century) is to the west and now houses the Secretariat. Across the road is the **Nyaya** (Law) **Mandir** (1896), not a temple but the High Court, in Mughal and Gothic styles. The **Jama Masjid** is next door.

Further along the road away from the lake is the **Mandvi** (1736), a square Muslim Pavilion and the spacious **Nazar Bagh Palace** (1721), which has a Shish Mahal (mirror palace), and is rather dilapidated now. The **College of Fine Art** is an institute of national renown.

Half-way down Raj Mahal Road are the remarkable buildings of the Khanderao Market. One of the old painted *havelis*, the four-storey **Tambekarwada**, residence of the Diwan of Vadodara (1849-54), acquired by the Archaeological Survey, is well worth visiting. It is between Raopura Road and Dandia Bazar. Rickshaw-wallahs appear not to know it so ask near the GPO and walk for two minutes.

A caretaker unlocks the first & second floors of the haveli 'free' then 'reluctantly' accepts a small tip

Maharajah Sayajirao Museum (Vadodara Museum) and **Art Gallery**, Sayaji Bagh, in the Victoria Diamond Jubilee Institute, was designed by RF

Museums

Chisholm. Archaeology, art, ethnology and ancient Jain sculptures; also Industrial arts, Mughal miniatures and European paintings. ■ *1000-1700, Sat 1000-1645.* **Maharajah Fateh Singh Museum**, Nehru Road, Laxmi Vilas Palace grounds, has good displays of royal state collection of European art (copies of some Murillo, Titian, Raphael, Rubens), Ravi Verma, Chinese and Japanese statuary and porcelain and European porcelain. ■ *1000-1730 (1600-1900 Apr-Jun), closed Mon, Rs 15, guide book Rs 35.* **Archaeology and Ancient History**, MS University, contains Buddhist antiquities, archaeological finds from North Gujarat, and good pre-history of Gujarat. ■ *1400-1700. Closed Sun and public holidays.*

Parks & zoos **Sayaji Bagh** is an extensive park, popular for evening strolls. **Planetarium** has an English show daily except Thursday, 35 minutes, which is fairly interesting, plus the bonus of air-conditioning. The **zoo** has been improved to house some mammals, reptiles and birds. **Kammati Bagh** is also beautiful.

Tours Gujarat Tourism (TCGL): **1** Saurashtra Darshan (five days). **2** North Gujarat and Rajasthan (five days). **3** Madhya Pradesh (four days). **4** Rajasthan (eight days).

Municipal Corp Tourist Office, T329656: **1** Tuesday, Wednesday and Friday, 1400-1800. Rs 50 (minimum 10). EME Temple, Sayaji Garden, Kirti Mandir, Geeta Mandir, Vadodara Dairy, Fatehsingh Museum, Aurobindo Society. **2** Saturday, Sunday, Monday (July-September), 1700-2100. Rs 50 (minimum 10). Nimeta (picnic spot), Ajwa (Brindavan pattern garden). **3** Saturday, Sunday, Monday (October-June) 1400-2100. Rs 70 (minimum 20); covers Tours 1 and 2. To Ajwa, Nimeta, Champaner and Pawagadh. Rs 125-150 including lunch and guide.

Essentials

Sleeping **AL-A** *Vadodara* (Welcomgroup), RC Dutt Rd (west from station), T330033, F330050. 102 rooms, some cramped, golf arranged. Private clients pay 30% higher than business travellers. **B-C** *Express*, RC Dutt Rd near *Vadodara*, T330750, F330980. Central a/c, 65 rooms, restaurants (excellent *thalis*), cake/Indian sweet shop, good travel desk, helpful staff, day tariff, unimpressive exterior but pleasant atmosphere.

C *Rama Inn* (Best Western), Sayajiganj, T362831. 74 modern rooms, half a/c, near Rly, 'wine shop', small gym (sauna extra), small pool. **C-D** *Aditi*, Sardar Patel Statue, Sayajiganj, T361188. 64 clean rooms, some a/c, mediocre restaurant. **C-D** *City Resort*, NH-8, T791922, near the airport. 10 a/c rooms, garden, pool, tennis, car needed (no rickshaws there). **C-D** *Express Alkapuri*, 18 Alkapuri, 500 m from *Express*, T337899, F330980. 40 a/c rooms (vary), restaurant, free airport transfer, day tariff. **C-D** *Kaviraj*, RC Dutt Rd, T323401. 30 rooms, some a/c, some with hot water, restaurant, 'Wine shop' issues permits (closes 1830). **C-D** *Sayaji*, Sayajiganj, T363030l. 53 a/c rooms, restaurants, pleasant rooftop dining (good *thalis*), business centre. **C-D** *Surya*, Sayajiganj, T361361. 82 rooms (most a/c), restaurant (wide choice, good *thalis* and 'high tea' buffet), friendly. **C-D** *Surya Palace*, opposite Parsi Agiari, Sayajiganj, T363366. 105 a/c rooms (wide range), extensive buffet lunch in a/c restaurant, efficient business services. **C-D** *Yuvraj*, near ST stand, T795252. 45 a/c rooms, restaurant, pool, gym, business centre. **D** *Ambassador*, Sayajiganj, near railway station, T362726. Good sized rooms with bath, some a/c, travel desk, good value.

D-E *Utsav*, Prof Amnekrao Rd, T435859. 28 a/c rooms, restaurants, exchange, good value, courtesy coach. **E** *Rajdhani*, Dandia Bazar, T421113. 22 rooms, some a/c, restaurant (good *thalis* and Chinese), helpful travel desk. Cheap hotels near the railway. **E** *Apsara*, Sayajiganj near rly station, T362051. All rooms with bath and phone, some a/c, popular. **E-F** *Green*, opposite Circuit House, T323111. 22 rooms, in old building, a bit run-down, but clean and good value for budget travellers, surprisingly free from fly nuisance. **E** *Railway Retiring Rooms*, (Rs 225) for double with bath, noisy but clean and convenient.

Expensive *Vadodara*, has extensive menu, polished service, plush and pricey, but try lunch buffet, alcohol against passport or permit. **Mid-range** *Havmor*, Yash Kamal Building, Tilak Rd. International, a/c. Huge portions. *Kansa*, Sayajiganj. Gujarati and Rajasthani *thalis*. Traditional décor, turbaned waiters. *Kwality*, Sayajiganj. Wide choice, including good Italian and Peshwari dishes served indoors or in garden. *Oriental Spice*, Tilak Rd, Sayajiganj. Chinese. Recommended. *Pizza King*, Alkapuri. Italian, justly popular. *Sayaji*, buffets, good choice, Rs 180. *Surya Palace*, sumptuous buffets. Indian and international, and a wide range of western and Indian desserts. *Volga* Alankar Cinema, Sayajiganj. Good Mughlai kebabs and Chinese. **Cheap** *Gokul*, Kothi Char-rasta. Indian. Good Gujarati *thalis*, small place, large local clientele. *Sahayog*, 1st left past *Express Hotel*. Good South Indian *thalis* (Rs 45) and Punjabi. Recommended. **Fast food** *Kalyan*, Fatehganj and Sayajiganj. Vegetarian, plus varied (including Mexican). Choice of the young. Others are mushrooming around this University town. Bengali sweets, nuts, savouries to take away, opposite *Express* hotel. **Paan** *Richa*, near *Express* makes excellent *Singhoda* with 'peanut marzipan cold filling'. Try after a *thali* – you'll be surprised!

Eating

Many hotels have good restaurants

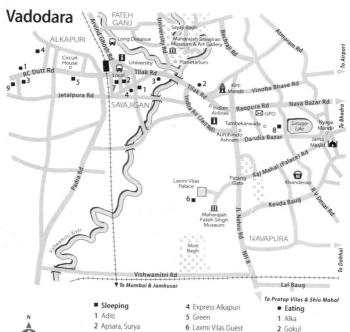

Vadodara

■ Sleeping	4 Express Alkapuri	● Eating
1 Aditi	5 Green	1 Alka
2 Apsara, Surya & Tradewings	6 Laxmi Vilas Guest House	2 Gokul
3 Express, Richa Paan shop & Sahayog Restaurant	7 Rama Inn & Ambassador	3 Havmor
	8 Utsav	4 Kalyan
	9 Vadodara	

0 metres 500
0 yards 500

Entertainment Look out for exhibitions, concerts, dance and theatre performances in the cultural capital of the state. MS University's Fine Arts College holds exhibitions. **Nightclub**: *Generation 1000* nightclub/discotheque, snacks and soft drinks. **Sports Boating**: at Sursagar Lake provided by Municipal Corp. **Swimming**: Lal Bagh and Sardar Bagh pools, Alkapuri; also at *Vadodara* and *Surya Palace* hotels.

The bullock train – the oldest narrow gauge!

The Vadodara-Dabhoi-Chandod line is the world's oldest surviving narrow gauge railway. The 19th-century line was commissioned for bullock drawn locomotives in 1863. Later turned to steam, it is now run by a diesel engine. There are some vintage locomotives including steam engines in the Dabhoi station yard dating back to 1902.

Festivals *Navratri* is very colourful when local Garba, Dandia and Raas performances are held, and pilgrims head for Pawagadh (17-25 Oct 2001; 7-14 Oct 2002). *Ganesh Chaturthi* is celebrated by the large Maharashtrian population here.

Shopping Vadodara is a centre for silver jewellery. Shopping areas are Raopura, Mandvi, Teen Darwaza, National Plaza, Leheripura Mandir Bazar and Alkapuri Arcade. *Khadi Bhandar*, Kothi Rd, for handlooms and local handicrafts. **Silks & saris**: *Kala Niketan* opposite *Hotel Vadodara,* and *Chimanlal Vrajlal*, National Plaza, MG Rd.

Transport **Local** **Auto-rickshaw**: minimum Rs 4. **Bus**: from opposite the rly station. **Taxi**: minimum Rs 10 (metered). **Tourist taxi**: from tourist office and travel agents, *Hotel Vadodara*. Non a/c Ambassador, Rs 4 per km, airport drop Rs 150, airport pick-up Rs 200, 80 km per 8 hrs, Rs 700-900. *Wheels*, TCI, T437866. **Long distance** **Air** *Indian Airlines*, Fatehgunj, T794747, 1000-1330, 1415-1700, airport, T443262. Mumbai, Delhi. *Gujarat Airways*, Vanijya Bhavan, Race Course, T330864: Mumbai, Ahmadabad. *Jet Airways*, 11 Panorama Complex, Alkapuri, T337051, airport, T551588. Mumbai. **Road** **Bus**: State Transport (SRTCs) to Ujjain (403 km), Mumbai (425 km), Pune, Udaipur and Mt Abu, among others. Central Bus Stand, opposite rly station, T327000. Reservations 0700-2200. Advance booking 0900-1300, 1330-1700. **Train** Vadodara is on the Western Railways' Delhi-Mumbai broad gauge line. Sayajiganj enquiries, T131. Reservations T135. 0800-2000 (2nd Class) and 0800-1800 (1st Class). Ahmadabad: many including *Gujarat Queen Exp, 9109*, 0813, 2¼ hrs; *Gujarat Exp, 9011*, 1303, 2¼ hrs; *Vadodara Ahmadabad Exp, 9129*, 1810, 2½ hrs. **Mumbai Central**: *Golden Temple Mail, 2904*, 2349, 6¼ hrs; *Kutch Exp, 9032*, 0508, 6½ hrs; *Paschim Exp, 2926*, 0852, 6¼ hrs; *Gujarat Exp, 9012*, 0907, 7¼ hrs. New Delhi: *Bandra Dehra Dun Exp, 9019*, 0615, 24 hrs; *Paschim Exp, 2925*, 1755, 16¾ hrs; *Rajdhani Exp, 2951*, 2153, 11 hrs. See narrow-gauge railway under Dabhoi. Porbandar: *Mumbai Porbandar Saurashtra Exp, 9215*, 1655, 14 hrs.

Directory **Airline offices** *Air India*, *British Airways* and *Japan Airlines* have offices on RC Dutt Rd. **Banks** *Bank of Baroda*, only Sayajiganj branch changes money; also *Trade Wings* on same street, fast and efficient. **Communications** Post: GPO in Raopura. **Medical services** Sayaji Hospital, Sayajiganj; Maharani Jamunabai Hospital, Mandvi. **Tour operators** *Prominent*, 7/12 Race Course Circle, T300120, F342333, recommended for ticketing. *Sita*, Sapna Centre, Alkapuri, T311280, F314334. *TCI*, Vishwas Colony, near Alkapuri petrol pump, T322181. *Travel House*, Hotel *Vadodara*, RC Dutt Rd, T320891. *Tradewings*, Sayajiganj, T327127, changes money (even on Sat). **Tourist offices** Gujarat Tourism, Narmada Bhawan, C-Block, Indira Ave, T427489, F431297; 1030-1810, closed Sun, instant reservations for Tourism and other hotels in Gujarat. Vadodara Tourist, Municipal Corp opposite railway station, T329656. 0900-1800. **Useful addresses** Forest Office T429748. Foreigners' Regional Registration Office: Collector's Office, Kothi Kacheri.

Forts near Vadodara

A enjoyable day trip by car from Vadodara could include Champaner with its strik-ing islamic monuments, Pawagadh on a nearby hilltop, and Dabhoi Fort, one of the first examples of Gujarati Hindu military architecture.

Champaner, on the plains, was the old capital of the local Rajputs who lost it in 1484 to Mahmud Beghara, who renamed it Muhammadabad and took 23 years to build his new city. In his campaign in Gujarat, the Mughal Emperor Humayun personally led a small team that scaled the walls of the city using iron spikes and then let the rest of the army in through the main gate. With the col-lapse of the Empire, Champaner passed to the Marathas.

Champaner
47 km NE of Vadodara

In the **old city**, which has been likened to the abandoned capital of Fatehpur Sikri, the remains of many 15th-16th-century mosques and palaces show a blend of Islamic and Jain traditions, a unique style encouraged by Champaner's relative isolation. The **Jami Masjid** (1523), a large, richly orna-mented mosque is exemplary of the Gujarati style with interesting features such as oriel windows. Few older structures of the Chauhan Rajputs remain – **Patai Rawal** palace, the domed granary **Makai Kota**, the 11th-12th-century Lakulisha Temple and some old wells.

Pawagadh Fort, 4 km southwest of Champaner, dominates the skyline and is visible for miles around. According to myth Pawagadh was believed to have been part of the Himalaya carried off by the monkey god Hanuman. Occupying a large area, it rises in three stages; the ruined fort, the palace and middle fort, and finally the upper fort with Jain and Hindu temples, which are important places of pilgrimage. Parts of the massive walls still stand. The ascent is steep and passes several ruins including the Buria Darwaza (Gate), and the Champavati Mahal, a three-storey summer pavilion. The temple at the summit had its spire replaced by a shrine to the Muslim saint Sadan Shah.

Sleeping and eating On the **Machi** plateau, Gujarat Tourism's **E** *Hotel Champaner* reached by road (near the cable car to Pavagadh). 32 rooms and dorm. The *cafeteria* is pleasant, with good views. Like other entrances to pilgrim spots, Machi has a plethora of food stalls and cheap guest houses.

Transport Shared jeeps and ST buses go up to **Machi** plateau where cable cars start for the ascent to the monuments on the hill; Rs 25 each (only hand baggage of 5 kg allowed), 0900-1700 with a break for lunch. Alternatively you can climb the steep steps all the way up to Pawagadh.

The town was fortified by the Solanki Rajputs from 1100 and the fort was built by a King of Patan in the 13th century. Dabhoi is regarded as the birthplace of the Hindu Gujarati architectural style. The fort with its four gates, a reservoir fed by an aqueduct and farms to provide food at times of siege. The **Vadodara Gate** (northwest) is 9-m high with pilasters on each side and carved with images depicting the reincarnation of Vishnu. The **Nandod Gate** (south) is similarly massive. The **Hira Gate** (east) with carvings, is thought to have the builder bur-ied beneath it. **Mori Gate** (north) lies next to the old palace and on the left of this is the **Ma Kali Temple** (1225), shaped like a cross, with profuse carvings. ■ *Getting there: Dabhoi is on the old narrow gauge line from Vadodara.*

Dabhoi Fort
29 km SW of Vadodara

Vadorada & the Old Forts

Chandod
17 km S of Dabhoi

This is the meeting place of the Narmada's two tributaries with picturesque bathing ghats and several temples. You can get mechanized country style river boats to visit temples, passing some spectacular ravines and water sculpted rocks. **D-E** *Sarita Haveli* (19th-century) is a 10-minute walk from the river, simple rooms, some air conditioning, dorm beds (Rs 150-650), marble and stone sculptures, library, period furniture, homecooked Indian food in courtyard, bullock cart tours of Juna Mandwa village, walking tours in the ravines, friendly, a bit shabby but good-value.

Sankheda
20 km E of Dabhoi

Sankheda, off the Indore road, is famous for its distinctive colourful lacquered wood furniture which is sold in sections to be assembled into chairs and tables. There are also attractive small temples. *Sher-e-Punjab* does good omelettes and spicy North Indian food.

Rajpipla
90 km SE of Vadodara

A former Rajput princely state in the Satpura hills, Rajpipla is a popular base for visiting nearby sights. The 'Indo Saracenic' **Vadia Palace** (1930s) is now Forest Department offices (T20013). Interesting murals inside include a frieze in the Bar of drunken monkeys, of dancing girls in the Ball Room, and of Krishna Lila in the Sitting Room. The bathing ghats on the Narmada are nearby, as is the frescoed temple of Hapeswar and the **Shoolpaneshwar Sanctuary** to the southeast. The sanctuary has sloth bear, panther, deer, antelope etc, but is best known for its population of crested hawk eagles, crested serpent eagles, shikra hawks and other birds of prey, as well as for the Malsamot waterfall. There are several Hindu ashrams in the area which attract interested westerners. **C-D** *Rajvant Palace*, part of a beautiful 1915 palace on River Karjan, T02640-20071, has 24 rooms, air conditioned suites (lack maintenance), average food, pool, large landscaped grounds, hill views, boating, tribal museum, good value, busy at weekends. *Kirti Bhuvan* is being converted.

Chhota Udepur
100 km E of Vadodara

Picturesque Chhota Udepur (Chotta Udaipur), centred around a lake, was once the capital of a Chauhan Rajput princely state. The town has palaces and numerous colonial period buildings. It is the capital of a colourful tribal district where Bhils and Ratwas live in secluded hamlets of a handful of mud huts each. The huts are decorated with wall paintings called *pithoras* (tigers and other animals are favourite subjects) and protected from evil spirits by small terracotta devotional figures.

There are colourful weekly tribal *haats* or **markets** in nearby villages which offer an insight into tribal arts, crafts and culture (though now you are as likely to find perfumes and cosmetics, as arrow heads and pottery!). The one in town is held by the lake on Saturdays. The government-run tribal **museum** in *Diwan Bungalow* has interesting examples of *pithoras*, folk costumes, artefacts, aboriginal weapons and handicrafts, but the labelling is in Gujarati and the attendant knows little English. West of Chotta Udepur is the tribal institute at Tejgadh, which is working to document aboriginal languages and culture in the entire country.

The imposing Rajput **Kusum Vilas** palace, set in 40-acre grounds, though Mughal in architectural style, has some impressive European decorative features inside. The large Mughal-style gardens have fountains, ponds, European marble statuary, a colonnaded art deco swimming pool and tennis courts, while the garages have old cars, and interesting carriages.

Dasara Fair here is famous. Other fairs held around *Holi* (March/April) in nearby villages like Kawant, with dancing, music, gymnastics and craft stalls, offer a glimpse of tribal life.

Sleeping and eating B-C *Prem Bhuvan*, 7 rooms with bath (hot showers) in the renovated *Kusum Vilas* outhouse, modernized interiors, (5 more are being renovated), pool, sports, set meals, (packages Rs 1500-2000). **C** *Tribal Huts*, set beside a stream. Simple cottages designed along the lines of tribal huts but with aircooler and modern bathrooms, economical restaurant. *Gita, Shradha* and *Bhagwati Lodge*, near the bus station, offer spartan rooms (Indian squat toilets, hard beds). *Bhagwati* is popular for Gujarati *thalis*. There are some eating places on Station Rd and around the lake.

Tejgadh

A tribal institute en route to Vadodara from Chotta Udepur is working to document aboriginal languages and culture in the entire strip from Nagaland in the east through Bihar, Orissa and Madhya Pradesh to Gujarat in the west, and from Rajasthan in the north to Andhra Pradesh in the south.

Jambughoda Sanctuary

The park has a population of panther (though rarely seen), four-horned antelope, sloth bear and other wildlife. The forest has fine walks and is good for birding. *Jambughoda Palace* facing the hills. Five fairly simple rooms with modern baths, good Indian food, jeep safaris and treks, hospitable owners.

Khambhat (Cambay)
Population: 89,800

Situated at the mouth of the Mahi River, Khambhat was Ahmadabad's seaport but later declined as it got silted up. Well known to Arab traders, it was governed until 1400 by the kings of Anhilwara (Patan). An English factory was established in the Nawab's Kothi in 1600 in the wake of Dutch and Portuguese ones. The **Jama Masjid** (1325) is built from materials taken from desecrated Hindu and Jain temples. The enclosed façade to the sanctuary is similar to that of the Quwwat-ul-Islam mosque at Delhi (see page 83). The design heavily influenced the Gujarati architectural style. The stone carvers, polishers and enamellers produce attractive jewellery and souvenirs; Dhuvaran hill has agate and jasper mines. **E** *Premalaya*, originally the Nawab's bungalow, now a government guesthouse, has air-conditioned rooms, pleasant dining room and galleries with seaviews, good value.

Vadodara & the Old Forts

Southern Gujarat

10

Southern Gujarat

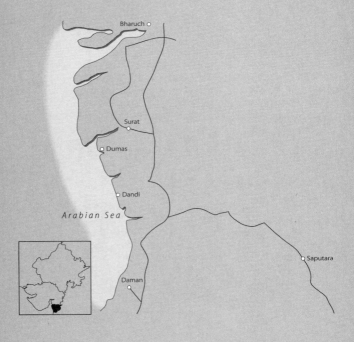

Surat

Situated on the banks of the Tapti River, Surat was already an important trading centre by 1600 but went into decline in the 19th century. Today it is again a rapidly growing industrial and commercial city, but there is little to attract a tourist. Parts of the city have seen a major cleaning and greening exercise in recent years although the area around the railway station remains unpleasantly congested.

Phone code: 0261
Colour map 6, grid C1
Population: 1.517 mn

Getting there The railway, and the confusion of ST and Private bus stations, are all a couple of kilometres east of the busy central Chowk. Sufi Baug with some hotels and restaurants are within easy reach for all arrivals. **Getting around** The city is very spread out but there are auto-rickshaws a-plenty. From the station area they ask around Rs 10 to the Chowk and Rs 25 to the Athwa gate.

Ins & outs
See page 297 for further details

The **Parsis**, driven from Persia, first arrived in India in the late eighth century and many moved from their first settlement on the west coast of the peninsula to Surat in the 12th century. The Mughals, under Akbar, took the town and during their reign, the Portuguese, British, Dutch and French in turn established trading outposts here. The British were the first to establish a 'factory' having arrived in 1608, and Surat remained their headquarters until it moved to Bombay in 1674. Surat's name is associated with 'Saurashtra' peninsula (The Good Land), across the gulf. During the 17th and 18th centuries, trade flourished and made Surat the mercantile capital of West India. The first dock was built in 1720 and by 1723 there were two shipyards. The tide turned, however, in the next century, when a fire destroyed the city centre to be followed by floods when the River Tapti burst its banks. This led many Parsis to move to Mumbai. Surat specializes in jewellery and diamond cutting. It also produces gold and silver thread, *kinkhab* brocades, wood and ivory inlay work. Silk weaving is a cottage industry producing the famous *Tanchoi* and *Gajee* saris.

Background

The **castle**, now full of offices, on the banks of the Tapti near the old bridge, provides a good vantage point for viewing the city and surrounding countryside. The **museum** nearby has an interesting collection of textiles, furniture, paintings, stamps, coins and ceramics. ■ *Wed-Sat 1045-1345, 1445-1745; Tue, Sun 1445-1745; Mon closed.* Photography is prohibited. The tombs in the Dutch, English and Armenian **cemeteries**, however, are rather neglected and overgrown though some like the Aungier mausoleum and Oxinden mausoleum are imposing. The strong Muslim influence is evident in several 16th- and 17th-century **mosques**. There are two Parsi **Fire Temples** (1823) and the triple-domed **Swami Narayan Temple**. The Chintamani Jain temple, probably dating from the 15th century, has some fine wood carvings.

Sights

Beaches Dumas, 16 km away, is a popular sea shore picnic spot. Hazira beach is a popular place for locals to enjoy the sea breezes but has been developed into a major coastal industrial zone. Along the Surat-Dumas road, **Hajira**, 28 km, has casuarina groves while **Ubhrat**, 42 km, with a palm-shaded beach was the seaside resort of the Maharajah of Baroda. His palatial property here was converted to a Gujarat Tourism Holiday Home (closed at present).

Excursions

Navsari, 39 km from Surat, has a historic Parsi fire temple which is one of the most important Zoroastrian pilgrim places in India. You cannot enter the temple but the building and garden are worth seeing from outside.

Southern Gujarat

Some 13 km from Navsari is **Dandi**, where Gandhiji ended his Salt March from Ahmadabad to the south Gujarat coast, and picked up a handful of salt. The mass movement generated by the Salt March is said to have broken the back of the British Empire in India. There is a monument raised at the spot where Gandhiji gathered salt and a photo gallery depicting a sequence of events in Gandhi's life.

Karadi is nearby where Gandhi was arrested after the Dandi March, his hut there is still preserved and there is a small Gandhi Museum. You can stay at *Guest House*, very peaceful and friendly, contact '*Om Shanti*', Matwad T83253, (English spoken).

Sleeping **A** *Holiday Inn* (was Rama Regency), Athwa Lines, Parle Pt, T226565, F227294. 140 rooms, good restaurant (breakfast included), modern, attractive location, riverside pool, health club, efficient, courteous staff, the most pleasant stay in town. **B** *Lord's Park Inn*, Ring Rd, T418300, F413921, lordsint@bom6.vsnl.net.in 102 rooms, a popular new business hotel. **B-C** *Embassy*, Sufi Baug, near station, T443170, F443173. 60 a/c rooms, some with tubs, popular restaurant (North Indian, Gujarati *thalis*), wheelchair facility, modern, pleasant. **B-D** *Central Excellency*, opposite railway station, T425324, F441271. 46 rooms (mostly a/c) with TV, fridge and other modern facilities, travel desk. **C** *Yuvraj*, opposite railway station, near Sufi Baug, T413001, F413007. 35 rooms, central a/c, good restaurant, rooftop garden café, modern with business services. **C-D** *Tex Palazzo*, Ring Rd, T623018, F620980. 39 rooms, half a/c, restaurants, on a crowded main road. **D** *Oasis*, near Vaishali Cinema, Varacha Rd, T641124. 25 rooms, some a/c, restaurants, garden, permit room, pool, favoured by diamond merchants! **D** *Bellevue*, Sumul Dairy Rd, near railway station, T437807, F412640. 34 modern rooms with baths, some **C**, business hotel, cyber café next door. **D** *Everyday Inn*, near Civil Court, T665154, F664230. 8 a/c doubles with bath (hot water) and TV in a house by the main road. **D-E** *Pritpar*, opposite District Court, T669857. Small hotel on a busy main road, 7 simple rooms with TV. Opposite the station: **D-E** *Dreamland*, T427664, 423235. 35 comfortable rooms but a bit run down, some a/c, South Indian restaurant. **E** *Sarvajanik*, T426434. Clean rooms with bath, hot water. **E-F** *Simla*, T431782. 50 simple rooms with Indian toilets, rather dingy/ **F** *Vihar*. Has rooftop views of the city, friendly and safe.

Eating **Expensive** *Holiday Inn*'s *Haveli* popular for Indian food, *Marina* for continental and Chinese restaurants (Rs180 for non-residents for buffet with a variety of hot items and

Surat

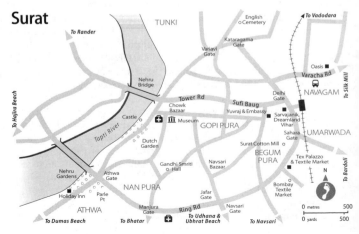

breads). *Riverside Café* does excellent international buffets (Rs 250) and good variety for breakfast, Indian or Western (Rs 180 for non-residents). **Mid-range** *Tex Palazzo*. Wide choice, good *thalis* in a revolving restaurant but the views aren't spectacular. *Yuvraj*, rooftop garden café (buffet breakfast). **Cheap** *Saatvik* opposite railway station. Excellent, unlimited Gujarati *thalis*, Rs 45. *Satlaj* and *Sher-e-Punjab* near the railway station. For good North Indian. A/c but rather dingy. **Fast food** Lots of places for pizza, Indian snacks, sandwiches and ice cream on Ring Rd and Athwa Lines. **Sweets** Surat is famous for its *Nan-katai* (a bit like shortbread) and twisty biscuits, best bought at Parsi bakeries like *Mehr* and *Mazda* in Bhagat Talao area and *Dotiwala* at Parle Pt.

Train Ahmadabad: *Shatabdi Exp, 2009,* 0955, not Fri, 3½ hrs; *Gujarat Exp, 9011,* 1045, **Transport** 4¾ hrs; *Mumbai Porbandar Saurashtra Exp, 9215,* 1408, 5¼ hrs. *Exp* **Chennai**: *Navjivan Exp, 6045,* 1040, 30 ½ hrs. **Kolkata**: *Ahmadabad Howrah Exp, 8033,* 1350, 15¾ hrs. **Mumbai Central**: *Kranti Rajdhani, 2954,* 0635, 3¾ hrs; *Paschim Exp, 2926,* 1055, 4¼ hrs; *Janata Exp, 9024,* 1444, 6 hrs. **New Delhi**: *Janata Exp, 9023,* 1325, 24 hrs; *Paschim Exp, 2925,* 1542, 19 hrs. **Porbandar**: *Mumbai Porbandar Saurashtra Exp, 9215,* 1408, 16½ hrs. **Rajkot and Jamnagar**: *Mumbai Porbander Saurashtra Exp, 9215,* 1408, 11¾ hrs (Rajkot), 13¾ hrs (Jamnagar); *Janata Exp, 9017,* 2132, 10½ hrs (Rajkot), 12½ hrs (Jamnagar). **Vadodara**: Frequent, 2 hrs.

Banks Exchange at **State Bank of India**, Chowk Rd. Also registered money changers **Directory** like *Trade Wings* and *Travel Exchange Bureau*. **Communications** Internet: *Cyber Cafés*, at Belgian Sq, Athwa Lines, Ambaji Rd and *Bellevue Hotel* near the station.

The lowland along the Narmada Plain is intensively cultivated under irriga- **Routes** tion, but is relatively poor away from the river. To the south, the Tapti has cut down 3-4 m into the floodplain as a result of geologically recent uplift of the land. There are several decent motels between Surat and Bharuch. In **Kadodra**, 48 km south of Bharuch, is the F *Manisha Guest House* and restaurant, and the *Alpa Restaurant*. There are also good wayside food stalls.

At the mouth of the Narmada River, Bharuch (Broach), which flourished in **Bharuch** the first century AD, is one of the oldest seaports in Western India. Mentioned as Barugaza by the Romans around 210 AD it was ruled by a Gurhara Prince and much later came under the rule of the Solanki Rajputs.

The **Bhrigu Rishi Temple** from which the town got its name 'Bhrigukachha', is on the bank of the river Narmada. It subsequently developed at the lowest crossing of the river, a point of strategic importance. During the rule of Muslims from Sind (1297 to 1772) the British and the Dutch established factories in 1614 and 1617. Aurangzeb ordered the fortifications to be destroyed in 1660 which paved the way for successful attacks by the Marathas in 1675 and 1686 who rebuilt the walls.

The **fort** overlooks the Narmada. Within it are the Collector's Office, Civil Courts, the old Dutch factory, a church, the Victoria Clocktower and other buildings. Below the fort is the **Jama Masjid** (early 14th-century), which was built from a demolished Jain temple but in accordance with conventional mosque design. Just over 3 km west of the fort are some early **Dutch tombs**, overlooked by some Parsi Towers of Silence. Today Bharuch is well known for its textile mills and long staple cotton. **Suklatirtha**, about 10 km upstream has a *Holiday Home*.

Southern Gujarat

Saputara

Saputara, a pleasant hill resort created after independence in the Sahayadri hills, is Gujarat's only hill station. Set in a tribal region, there is an attractive lake and forests nearby. It is a relaxing place to enjoy walks, scenic places and folklore.

Ins & outs
The resort gets very crowded during weekends & holidays

Getting there State buses run from Surat (135 km) and Nashik (Maharashtra, 80 km). Trains on the Mumbai-Ahmadabad line get you as far as Billimora (110 km), with buses to Saputara. **Getting around** The resort is ideal for walking. **Climate** Best season Nov-May (monsoon Jun-Oct).

Sights
The name Saputara is derived from the snake deity which is worshipped here by the tribal people

The hub of activity at Saputara is the lake which has boating facilities and lake view eating places.

The plateau is rather barren and not particularly appealing but there are some lovely **walks** around the hill resort. You can find attractive quartzite rocks, orchids and wild flowers on the trails. There are good views of the valley from Sunset Point (with a 10-minute ropeway service) and from Valley View Point which involves a strenuous 1½ km climb. There are also some old **Maratha hill forts** which involve steep climbs (only recommended for serious trekkers). The Hatgadh fort offers superb views and a chance to see rock chats, martens and wolf snakes in cracks on the fort walls. Carry water.

The Dangs district comprises more than 300 villages with a population of over 150,000, more than 94% of them belonging to tribal communities. The Bhils, Kunbis, Warlis and Gamits depend on the forest for their livelihood, obtaining timber, honey and lac. They are known for their traditional musical instruments and vigorous dances performed wearing wooden masks. Most villages have a shrine to Wagha-Deva, the tiger God, sculpted on stone. The **Dangs Cultural and Ecological Museum**, with a stone serpent at the entrance, offers an insight into the tribal area and the natural history of the Dangs. There are interesting *dioramas*, folk costumes, tribal weaponry and musical instruments. The Artists' Village conducts workshops of bamboo crafts, *papier maché* and pottery.

Festivals The *Dangs Darbar* held at **Ahwa**, 32 km north, is celebrated with a tribal fair (28 March-1 April 2002). Tribal chieftains called Bhil Rajas and Kunbi Rajas, who still receive privy purses from the government, are honoured during this festival. For *Nag Panchami* tribal huts are decorated with paintings.

Excursions Based at Saputara you can make a trip to **Vansda**, a former princely state capital surrounded by a national park. A whole range of animals from rusty spotted cat and giant squirrel to panther were seen here in the past but today you have to be extremely lucky to spot anything except the occasional hare, jungle cat or jackal.

The **Mahal Bardipura Forest** is not rich in interesting wildlife but has a good tract of deciduous, semi-evergreen and bamboo for treks. Both it, 60 km north of Saputara, and the Purna Wildlife Sanctuary, near Ahwa, are worth visiting. There are a few tiger, panthers, deer, antelope, hyena, and porcupine. You will see giant wood spiders, lots of butterflies, land crabs and other invertebrates. Local birdlife has been depleted by the tribal people (who eat even the smallest of them) though you may spot Gray hornbill, Racket tailed drongo, Gold fronted chloropsis and Paradise flycatcher. Permits are needed for both; ask at Toran Hill Resort.

B *Patang*, T37631, comfortable a/c rooms. **B-C** *Vaity*, Chimney Ropeway near Sunset **Sleeping**
Pt, T37210, F37213. Superbly situated on a hill with a panoramic views, clean, comfortable rooms, lawn, friendly staff, guides for surrounding excursions on weekdays.
B-C *Shavshanti Lake Resort*, Nageshwar Mahadev Rd, T37292, F37245. 25 rooms with
modern facilities. **C-D** *Anando*, T37202. 23 rooms with baths set on different levels facing the lake, vegetarian restaurant, good views. Gujarat Tourism's **C-D** *Toran Hill
Resort*, near Bus Stand T/F37226. Cottages and log huts (Rs 600+), dorms, restaurant
(book at any Tourism office). **D** *Chitrakut*, T37221. Well situated with view of hills, average rooms with bath. **E** *Purohit*, T37218, rooms (Rs 200-300). Other cheaper places
near the bus stand. **E** *Shilpi*, T37231. 10 rooms, clean and comfortable, attached baths,
set back from main road towards the hills, restaurant (meals included). **F** *Vaishali*,
T37208. Rooms for Rs 150-200.

Restaurants serve North Indian meals and Gujarati *thalis*. *Vaity*, offers the widest choice **Eating**
including non-veg, with a good view and some outdoor seating. *Toran*, *thalis* at
Rs 25-35. Roadside stalls can prepare delicious chicken and vegetarian dishes if you
ask ahead.

Road From the NH8, the turn off for cars is at Chikhli to the west. Petrol is only avail- **Transport**
able at Waghai (51 km northwest), and at a pump 40 km from Saputara, on the Nashik
road. From Mumbai, there are private luxury buses (***Modern Travels***) on alternate days
during the season. **Train** From Ahmadabad (400 km) or Mumbai (255 km) to
Billimora and then local bus or taxi; or a narrow gauge train to **Waghai**.

Daman

The forbidding black stone walls of the fort, pierced by impressive gateways, *Phone code: 02636*
conceal the Portuguese township of Moti Daman from the outside world. *Colour map 6, grid C1*
Only inside the gates is the extent of the continuing Portuguese influence *Population: 26,900*
apparant, the Rosario Chapel and the Church of Bom Jesus still testimony to
the catholic faith of the Portuguese while the former Governor's Palace is a
reminder of the Portuguese colony's secular purpose. That purpose was
partly sea borne trade and defence of its maritime interests, and the estuary
retains a sense of the vital link between the town and its harbour, with the
smaller fort of St Jerome across the Daman Ganga mouth.

Southern Gujarat

Getting there The nearest railway station is at Vapi (13 km southeast) on the **Ins & outs**
Mumbai-Ahmadabad line. From there you can get taxis for transfer (Rs 20 entry fee) *See page 302 for*
or walk 600 m for a bus. Long distance buses run from Mumbai and Surat. All, including *further details.*
those from Vapi, arrive at the main bus stand in Nani Daman. **Getting around** The settlement north of the river, still known as Nani (small) Daman, is where most of the *Avoid the Indian*
accommodation is. To the south, within walking distance across the river, Moti (large) *holiday periods as*
Daman has a few colonial remains. Bicycles can be hired in Nani Daman bazar. *Daman can get very*
overcrowded

The 380-sq km enclave of Daman, along with Diu and Goa, were Portuguese **History**
possessions until taken over by the Indian Government in 1961. Its association with Goa ceased when the latter became a 'State' in 1987. It is now a
Union Territory with its own Pradesh Council. Daman developed at the
mouth of the tidal estuary of the Daman Ganga River as a trading centre from
1531. Much of its early commerce was with the Portuguese territories in East
Africa. Later (1817-1837), it was a link in the opium trade chain until this was
broken by the British.

Sights

Moti Daman retains something of the Portuguese atmosphere. The land-ward (east) side has a moat and drawbridge. The shaded main street inside the **fort** wall runs north-south between attractive arched gateways which have Portuguese arms carved on them. One shows a saint carrying a sword but the sculpted giants on the doorways are modelled on the guardian *dwarpalas* at entrances to Hindu temples.

The former **Governor's Palace** and other administrative buildings are along the main road while towards the south end is the old **Cathedral Church of Bom Jesus**, started in 1559 but consecrated in 1603. Large and airy when the main south door is open, the chief feature is its painted and gilt wooden altar reredos and pulpit. Much of the ornamentation, notably the gold crowns of the saints, have been stolen. On the west side of the small square is the old **jail**, still in use. To the south, against the fort wall, is the **Rosario Chapel**, for-merly the Church of the Madre Jesus, with a unique feature in Indian churches of carved and gilded wooden panels illustrating stories from the life of Christ. These include the adoration of the Magi, Jesus teaching in the synagogue as a child, and Mary's ascension. The carved ceiling features charming cherubs. The statue of Mary of the Rosary was placed on the altar by a Portuguese com-mander as thanksgiving for surviving an attack by Sivaji, and the original statue of Mary the Mother of Jesus was moved to its present position on the west wall of the nave.

Jampore beach, planted with casuarina groves, 3 km south of Moti Daman, has a sandy beach with safe swimming but is otherwise not particu-larly appealing.

Nani Daman, north of the river, is reached by a bridge across Daman Gan-ga which gives attractive views of Moti Daman's walls and the country fishing boats on either bank. The smaller **fort** here encloses a church (now used as a school) and a cemetery. Some of the old houses retain beautifully carved wooden doors and lintels. The crowded town is thick with bars (trading on Gujarat's prohibition of alcohol) and has some basic hotels and restaurants.

A resort area, 5 km further north, has a cluster of better hotels by the rather unattractive **Devka beach** where bathing is unsafe.

Excursions **Udvada**, further north, near the entrance to Daman from NH8, has the most important of the eight prin-ciple Zoroastrian temples in the country. Non-Zoroastrians are not allowed in the fire temple but from outside you can see the historic façade, and the smoke from the sacred flames rising from the chim-neys. Near the temple are a number of old Parsi homes with trellised ter-races and intricate doors. *Hotel Majestic* offers simple rooms.

Tithal near Valsad, about 35 km from Vapi, is a popular beach resort for people of south Gujarat. The

Daman Union Territory

beach is not remarkable but there are some safe areas for swimming, the casuarinas groves offer shady places to enjoy the sea breezes, and the long stretch of firm sand is good for walking. **D** *Hotel Tithal* and Gujarat Tourism's **D** *Toran*, offer simple rooms near the beach, but are not really recommended. Most people prefer to visit for the day from Daman or Surat. An open-air cafeteria with good sea views towards the end of the beach offers good Gujarati snacks and simple meals. A Katchchhi *bhojnalaya* on the road to the beach does inexpensive *thalis*.

Essentials

Seaface Rd C-D *Gurukripa*, T255046. 25 large a/c rooms with bath, good restaurant (wide choice of Punjabi, Gujarati, some Chinese), roof garden, car hire. **C-D** *Suruchi Beach Resort*, Daman-Vapi Rd, T55134. 53 a/c rooms with a range of modern facilities, rooftop restaurant, with river views, pool, lawn, but not near a beach and no sea views. **D** *Sovereign*, T55023. 24 a/c rooms, clean, secure, friendly, veg restaurant (good Gujarati *thali*), chilled beer, travel desk. Recommended. There are plenty of cheap places on the seafront. **E** *Sanman*, Tin Batti, T255730. Rooms facing a busy main road, some a/c. **Sleeping**

Daman town

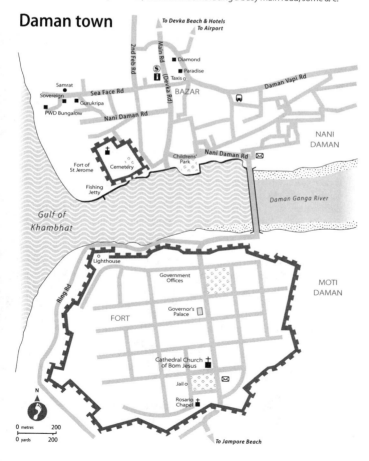

To Devka Beach & Hotels
To Airport

2nd Feb Rd

Main Rd
(Devka Rd)

■ Diamond
■ Paradise

Taxis

BAZAR

Daman Vapi Rd

Samrat
Sovereign
Sea Face Rd
Gurukripa

PWD Bungalow

Nani Daman Rd

NANI DAMAN

Fort of
St Jerome
Cemetery

Childrens'
Park
Nani Daman Rd

Fishing
Jetty

Daman Ganga River

*Gulf of
Khambhat*

Lighthouse

Ring Rd

Government
Offices

MOTI DAMAN

Governor's
Palace

FORT

Cathedral Church
of Bom Jesus

Jail

Rosario
Chapel

N

0 metres 200
0 yards 200

To Jampore Beach

Southern Gujarat

Jampore Beach **D** *China Town*, T254920. 20 rooms (some a/c), few with sea view but short beds, shower and toilets could improve, friendly helpful staff, good restaurant serves Chinese/Indian food (fresh Pomfret and other fish, prawns/shrimps in season), bar does pinacoladas with fresh coconuts, both handy for visitors to beach.

Devka Beach **B-C** *Cidade de Daman*, T250590. 72 breezy, a/c rooms in impressive hotel, pool, popular for conferences. **B-C** *Silver Sands*, T54376 silversa@bom3.vsnl. net.in 32 rooms with modern facilities, pool, bar, disco, across the road from the beach **C** *Dariya Darshan*, T54476, F54826. 38 modern a/c rooms, well fitted (TV, fridge), good outdoor restaurant (but piercingly loud Hindi film music heard throughout hotel), bar, pool, gym. **C** *Miramar*, T544971, F54934, miramar@cybervapi. 58 rooms (some a/c), some in cottages, sea-facing outdoor restaurant plays loud Indian film music, a/c indoors, discotheque, holiday camp atmosphere. **C** *Princess Park*, T254323, F250800. 27 rooms, some a/c, modern facilities, restaurant, good outlook facing the sea. **C-D** *Jazira*, T54330. 26 rooms, outdoor restaurant, car rental. **C-D** *Sandy Resort*, T254751, F254744. 46 rooms, some a/c (best upstairs), restaurant, disco, pool, the quietest and most pleasant here but across the road from the beach. **C-D** *Shilton*, T254558, F255193. 27 rooms (18 a/c), modern facilities, outdoor restaurant and bar, a little musty smelling. **C-E** *Summer Hotel*, T54474. 12 cottages and 7 rooms at the end of an alley across the road from the beach, the more expensive rooms have TV and phone, modern facilities but the approach is quite dark at night. **E** *Rahee Guest House* (PWD), Marwad Rd, between Nani Daman and Devka Beach, T254614. 15 rooms in neglected old building, some with bath and hot water, cheaper with Indian WCs.

Elsewhere **D-E** *Diamond*, near Taxi Stand, T34235. 25 large rooms, some a/c with TV, restaurant, friendly, clean but favoured by ants. **D-E** *Paradise*, Navi Ori, T34404. Rooms vary, some with bath.

Eating **Mid-range** *Gurukripa*, good for Punjabi and Gujarati. *Sovereign* does good *thalis*. *Duke*, Devka Beach. Parsi and Tandoori food outdoors (also rooms to let in the old Parsi bungalow next door, Rs 400). *Damanganga Lake Garden* on the Daman-Vapi Rd, Popular lake facing restaurant, with gardens all round and fountains. Unusual, though garish, bar has a Mughal theme with miniature paintings of royal drinking parties on the bar stools, tables and chairs. Good atmosphere and reasonable food. *Kadliya Lake Resort* is an island restaurant created by Daman Tourism, with lawns, gardens, cascades, fountains and boating facilities. The food upstairs is not bad and there is a bar and snacks place downstairs by the lake, but the service is slow and suffers an occasional scourge of flies and mosquitoes from the lake. Entry fee Rs 10, camera Rs 10, car parking Rs 10. **Cheap** *Jampore Beach Resort*, a cafeteria, offers meals/snacks upstairs with a view of the sea, also outdoor dining area, hammocks for relaxing, and a bar. See *China Town*, above. *Samrat*, Seaface Rd. Simple and clean, does excellent *thalis*.

You will find cheap Chinese food at night outside the main gates of Moti Daman fort

Transport **Road Bus**: For the bus stand turn right out of Vapi station, walk 500 m along main road to a T-junction; the stand is nearby, on the left. **Taxi**: Into Daman but shared with 8 others can be a squeeze (Rs 10 each); Rs 80 per taxi. By car, turn off the NH8 at Karmbeli between Bhilad and Vapi. **Train** Not all trains stop at **Vapi**. *Gujarat Exp 9011*, 0545, 3 hrs; *Saurashtra Exp 9215*, 0745, 3½ hrs.

Directory **Bank and money changers** *State Bank of India*, Kabi Kabarda Rd. **Communications Post:** GPO near bridge to Moti Daman. **Tourist offices** On Main Devka Rd, Dena Bank Building, T35014.

Southern Gujarat

The Union Territory of *Dadra and Nagar Haveli* was formerly administered **Dadra &** by the Portuguese from Goa who acquired it from the Marathas in 1779. **Nagar Haveli** Local tribal people (Konkans, Warlis, Dhodias) live in small clusters of huts in the villages.

Silvassa, which takes its name from the Portuguese selva (forest) is the capital **Silvassa** of the Union Territory. **Van Vihar** (Khanvel) is the setting of the *Forest Rest* *Population: 13,900* *House* with its lawns and terraced gardens down to the river. There is a deer park and a tribal museum. ■ *Getting there: The nearest railway station is Vapi which has trains from Mumbai Central; From Vapi, it is 1 hr by rickshaw or bus.*

Sleeping and eating C *Ras Resorts*, 128 Silvassa-Naroli Rd, T02632373 or Mumbai T4948271, F4950325. 60 a/c rooms, exchange, pool and other sports. **C-D** *Chowda Complex*, Khanvel. Two categories of cottages, luxury and economy. **E** *Khanvel Forest House*, in beautiful setting, with cook who will prepare meals, primarily for government officers, reserve in advance if available. **F** *Silvassa Circuit House* and **F** *Govt Rest House*. Several other small hotels and guest houses with restaurants.

11

Saurashtra

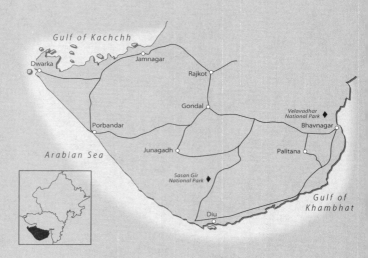

Rajkot

Rajkot is a bustling commercial city with a large number of shopping complexes and accompanying heavy road traffic, but there are also some fine late 19th-century colonial buildings and institutions since the British Resident for the Western Indian States lived here. It has seen rapid industrialization in the last two decades, based especially in the processing of agricultural products.

Phone code: 0281
Colour map 5, grid B4
Population: 550,000
Altitude: 120 m

Getting there The airport, 4 km north, has airlines' buses for transfer to town. The ST bus station is just south of the busy Dhebar Chowk at the centre, while more comfortable prvate long distance coaches arrive at the operators just behind the bus station. Most hotels are central but 2-3 km from the Junction station. **Getting around** It is possible to walk to the few sights in town quite easily from the centre. There are auto-rickshaws and taxis if you prefer.

Ins & outs
See page 309 for further details

Sights

Although there is an early Palaeolithic site at Rajkot, there is very little evidence of the settlement. Rajkot was the capital of the Jadejas, who ruled earlier from a place named Sardhar on the Rajkot-Bhavnagar road, and later set up this new city which became the headquarters of the British representatives in Saurashtra. The British impact can be seen in the impressive **Rajkumar College** in its vast grounds, a famous public school founded in 1870, and the richly endowed **Watson Museum**. The **Memorial Institute** has the crumbling Lang Library in the Jubilee Gardens in the Old Civil Lines.

Rajkot was the early home of Mahatma Gandhi. **Gandhi Smriti** (Kaba Gandhino Dela) is in Ghee Kanta Road, between MG Road and Lakahjiraj Road (rickshaw-wallahs know the way). **Rashtriya Shala**, where Mahatma Gandhi went to school, is now trying to promote one of Gandhi's greatest ideals – handloom and handicrafts. Among the textiles being promoted is Patola *ikat* silk weaving.

The **Watson Museum**, in Jubilee Gardens, has exhibits from the Indus Valley civilization, medieval sculpture, pottery and crafts, and colonial memorabilia. ■ *0900-1230, 1430-1800, closed Wed, 2nd and 4th Sat, each month. Rs 2, camera charges Rs 2 per photo.* **Gandhi Museum**, Dharmandra Road, in the Gandhi family home (1880), contains photographs and a few personal effects. Descriptions are mainly in Hindi and Gujarati; guides speak no English.

Museums

Tarnetar, 75 km away, has a betrothal fair which centres around the Trineteshwar Mahadev Temple whose pond is considered auspicious as the place where Arjuna is said to have won the hand of princess Draupadi in marriage. Religious rites, *bhajans* and ritual bathing are a feature of the fair, as are handicraft and food stalls. Bharwad and other herdsmen sport colourful dress and ornaments during the fair to attract a suitable match. They carry *chhattris* (umbrellas) with mirrorwork to signify bachelorhood. The fair is held on 22-24 August 2001 and 10-12 September 2002. Gujarat Tourism has a tent village.

Excursion

Saurashtra

Sleeping

There are nondescript cheap hotels near the station & bus stand

B-C *Kavery*, near GEB, Kanak Rd, T239331, F231007, kavery@planetace.com 33 a/c rooms, good hotel with modern facilities, restaurant, laundry, exchange. **C** *Aditya*, opposite Rajshri Cinema, T222003, F229901. New city centre hotel, 40 rooms, most with a/c, some dearer suites, restaurant, laundry, travel desk. **C** *Silver Palace*, Gondal Rd, T45005, F 450925 has some a/c rooms. **C-D** *Galaxy*, Jawahar Rd, T222304, F224105. 37 very well furnished, clean rooms, most a/c, pleasant roof-garden, exchange (including TCs, credit cards), well run, courteous and efficient, no restaurant but excellent room service to bring in food, access by lift only. Highly recommended. **D** *Samrat International*, 37 Karanpura, T222269, F232274. 32 decent rooms, some **C** a/c, vegetarian restaurant, exchange. **D** *Tulsi*, Kante Shree Vikas Guru Rd, T231731, F231735. 33 rooms, some a/c, excellent but bit pricey *Kanchan* restaurant, exchange, clean, modern hotel. **D-E** *Jayson*, Canal Rd, T226404. 18 rooms, half a/c, laundry, liquor shop, exchange. **E-F** *Babha Guest House*, Panchnath Rd, T220861. Small, good value rooms, some a/c, excellent veg *thalis*. Several **F** guesthouses near the shopping complex in Lakhajiraj Rd including *Himalaya*, T231736. Cleanish rooms with bath (bucket hot water), good value, very popular. *Railway Retiring Rooms* on 1st Flr, 3 clean rooms (1 a/c), 4-bed dorm, reasonable veg restaurant, good value.

Eating

Mid-range *Havmor*, near *Galaxy Hotel*. Good food (varied menu, mainly Chinese) but overpriced. *Lakshmi Lodge*, in road opposite *Rainbow*. Good *thalis*. *Lords Banquet*, for multi-cuisine. *Rainbow* Lakhajiraj Rd. Good, South Indian, very busy in the evenings when you may have to queue outside. *Step-In*, Galaxy Centre, Jawahar Rd. Pizzas, Indian fast food and ice creams. *Village-The Motel*. Indian, a rustic 're-creation', traditional meals and folk entertainment; cottages planned.

Rajkot

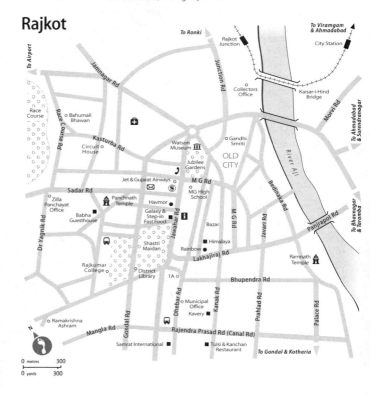

Saurashtra

Shopping complex in Lakhajiraj Rd, a bazar to its east, and a fruit market just north of **Shopping**
Jubilee Gardens.

Long distance Air: *Indian Airlines*, *Angel's Hotel*, Dhebar Chowk, T234122, airport **Transport**
T453313, and *Jet Airways*, 10 Sterling Apts, Jawahar Rd, T479623, airport T442930, fly
to **Mumbai** daily. **Road**: ST buses to Junagadh (2 hrs), Veraval (5 hrs), Jamnagar (2 hrs)
and Dwarka and Ahna. *Eagle Travels* run private luxury buses daily to Ahmadabad and
Mumbai. **Train**: from Junction Station. **Ahmadabad**: *Rajkot Ahmadabad Exp, 9154*,
0630, 4¼ hrs; *Porbandar Mumbai Saurashtra Exp, 9216*, 0050, 6½ hrs (continues to
Vadodara, 3¾ hrs); *Janata Exp, 9018*, 1440, 5¼ hrs (continues to **Vadodara**, 2½ hrs).
Mumbai (Central): *Okha Mumbai Saurashtra Mail, 9006*, 1735, 14½ hrs; *Porbandar
Mumbai Saurashtra Exp, 9216*, 0050, 18½ hrs. **Mail Porbandar**: *Saurashtra Exp, 9215*,
0200, 4¾ hrs; *Porbandar Exp, 9264*, 0915, Mon, Thu, 5 hrs; **Vadodara**: same as Mumbai,
7¼-9 hrs; **Veraval**: *Rajkot-Veraval Mail 9838*, 1110, 5¼ hrs.

Communications Post: GPO on MG Rd. **Tourist offices** *Gujarat*, Bhavnagar House, **Directory**
Jawahar Rd, behind *Bank of Saurashtra* (sign in Hindi), T234507. Limited information,
no map. *Department of Information*, Jubilee Gardens, T231616. Both open
1030-1400, 1430-1800, closed Sun, 2nd and 4th Sat. Helpful.

On the bend of Machchu River, Wankaner (*wanka* – curve, *ner* – river), **Wankaner**
another capital of the Jhala Rajputs, was founded in 1605. The old ruler, Amar *Population: 36,600*
Sinhji was known for his flamboyant lifestyle but he also introduced many
wide-ranging reforms (farmers' co-operatives, education, roads, tramways
and internal security). He was also responsible for building the **Ranjitvilas
Palace** (1907 extension to the 1980s British Residents' bungalow), visible for
miles across the plains. It is built in a strange mix of styles (Venetian façades,
a Dutch roof, *jarokha* balconies, a 'Mughal' pavilion, minarets, English
clocktower et cetera) yet all integrates remarkably well. The garage has an
interesting collection of models from the 1930s and 40s and a 1921 Silver
Ghost, jeeps, wagons and old buggies. Kathiawadi horses in the stables. A part
of the palace is now a museum brim full of royal memorabilia of a bygone lifestyle. There is an interesting stepwell with marble balustrade staircases, cool,
subterranean chambers and marble statues of Vishnu and a fountain.

Sleeping and eating C-D *Royal Oasis*, T02828-20000, F20002, guesthouse of the
Ranjitvilas among large fruit orchards with original 1930s art deco features, interesting
rooms but mosquitoes can be a problem, pool reopened, meals at the palace (slow
erratic service, "arrives cold") but worth it as presided over by Maharajah Pratap Singh
in his 90s, who is a fund of historic anecdotes. The palace **C-D** *Residency*, the
late-1800s colonial bungalow beside *Ranjitvilas*, 4-posters, planters' chairs, Burma teak
tables and Edwardian tubs but greatly neglected. Attractive art deco mansion in a
33-acre orchard but slack management ("30 minutes wait for tea/coffee, shabby
housekeeping").

Transport Bus: Frequent to/from Rajkot. **Train**: From **Ahmadabad** *Saurashtra Mail,
9005*, 0550, 4 hrs. To **Ahmadabad** *Ahmadabad Exp, 9154*, 0712, 3½ hrs; *Saurashtra Mail,
9006*, 1820, 4 hrs.

The picturesque town by river Machchu is well known for clock assembly, **Morvi**
pottery and ceramic tiles manufacture. The tiny princely state, Morvi, dom- *Population: 120,100*
inated access to the peninsula. Making use of the trade route, it developed *29 km away*
into a modern state under Thakur Sahib Waghaji (ruled 1879-1948). His

Saurashtra

aggressive reforms made it one of the most affluent princely states of Saurashtra.

A suspension bridge connects the two palaces

The **Darbargadh** palace with a riverside façade, inspired by the merchant mansions of Venice and built in the 1880s, was badly damaged in the 2001 earthquake. It is undergoing repairs and is expected to reopen in 2002 as a heritage hotel. The **Nazzar Bagh** palace, where the king's harem of eight queens lived is now an Engineering college. The **Mani Mandir** with fabulous domes, carved balconies and sculptures has a temple and 220 rooms for pilgrims. The family now resides in the 1930s and 40s **New Palace** (1931-44) containing late art-deco features; permission to visit is not readily given.

Sleeping and eating B *Darbargadh Palace* (Heritage Hotel). Rooms facing courtyard, outdoor restaurant (Rs 200-300 lunch/dinner). **D-E** *Thacker Lodge*, on the main Bhuj Rd, T31928, F31578. Newer wing has a/c rooms with baths (western toilets, hot showers), good value though garishly done up, 1 **C** suite. The old wing with traditional architecture has cheap rooms (small, hard beds) with Indian style toilets. The downstairs restaurant serves good lunch and dinner, Gujarati *thalis* (eat what you want and pay accordingly!), Indian snacks, *dosas* also offered at night. *Friends Foods*, Shakti Plot, Main Rd. Cheap, friendly, good food.

Halvad

Due to severe earthquake damage, Halvad is not expected to be ready for visitors until 2002

This was the 15th-century capital of the Jhala Rajputs. The old fortifications (circa 1470s) are now little more than crumbling ruins. The present palace (17th century) has ornately carved *jarokhas* around a forecourt. The grand central courtyard has an elaborate six-storeyed pavilion in a pleasure pool, and pillared galleries with exquisite wood carvings. The cremation grounds of the Jhala Rajputs have beautiful *chhattris* and carved *pallias* (funereal Hero Stones).

Enjal, just to the north, is the entrance to the Sanctuary. The Taj Group is converting the *Rannside Desert Lodge* to a Safari Resort.

Dhrangadra

Again severely damaged in 2001 it may be ready for visitors in 2002

The small village town of Dhrangadra is the government Forest Department's headquarters for the Little Rann of Kachchh Wild Ass Sanctuary (T02754-23016). The forest office arranges guides for visitors, see page 352.

Dhrangadra was also the capital of a very progressive princely state, which had English and vernacular schools in 1855 and free education in the early 1900s. The 18th-century **palace**, now partly government offices, has impressive domes, arches and carved balconies around courtyards.

The **royal palace**, the present residence, has splendid devotional carvings and friezes from the Ramayana and Mahabharata framed by Gothic arches, set in what were once formal gardens. The outhouses have workshops of sculptors and metal workers.

The **Salt Monopoly Act** introduced by the British in the 1920s, which caused the salt satyagraha that ultimately broke the back of British rule in India, affected Dhrangadra adversely as salt was a major stock-in-trade for the state. The chemical works using salt and selling by-products, started by the royal family, now employs around 2,500 people. It is possible to visit the Wild Ass Sanctuary. Wildlife guide at *DP Arts*, is very knowledgeable and friendly. Full day jeep tour of Little Rann (wild asses, salt mining communities, bird sanctuary), Rs 1,800 for two, including delicious and copious homecooked lunch.

Sleeping E *PWD Rest House* has some rooms (Rs 60). Avoid the only **F** *Hotel* (ask locally), next to temple where loud chanting starts at 0400, 'like a men's hostel with long queue for dirty toilet on roof'. *DP Arts*, T02754-50560, has rooms 'full of mosquitoes and not very private'.

Saurashtra

Transport The *Kutch Express* **train** Mumbai-Ahmadabad-Vadodara and Gandhidham, and the Bhuj-Surat luxury **bus** stop here.

Jasdan, about 60 km southeast of Rajkot en route to Bhavnagar, is where the local royal family ruled from for three centuries. It is known for its distinctive brass-lined jewellery boxes and chests.

Jasdan
In the heart of the small Ghim forest tract

The small, 7 sq km private **Hingolgadh Sanctuary** just northeast of Jasdan, stretching over forest covered hills, protects gazelle and nilgai. There are jungle cats and many scrubland birds, particularly good in the monsoons. Though not as impressive as the larger Gujarat sanctuaries, this remains open when the others close after the monsoons. The hilltop **castle** commands wonderful views over the forest.

Nearby, the **Botad Panjarapole** (Jain animal sanctuary) has grasslands where the several hundred blackbuck antelopes have got accustomed to human visitors.

Bhavnagar

Bhavnagar was ruled by progressive rulers since it was founded in 1723. Surrounded by flat and richly cultivated land, it is now a major industrial town and cotton export centre, and is rapidly becoming one of India's most important ship-building ports. However, most of its character is preserved in the bazars of the Old City where you can pick your way through the crowded lanes amongst the old merchants' havelis.

Phone code: 0278
Colour map 5, grid B6
Population: 405,200

Getting there The airport is 5 km southeast of town; auto-rickshaws to town insist on Rs 60-70. Hotels are scattered around with no budget option close to the ST bus station and only one within easy reach of the railway. Private bus operators have offices spread around town. **Getting around** It is best to hire an auto or taxi to see the town.

Ins & outs
See page 314 for further details

The Gohil Rajputs came to Gujarat from Rajasthan in the 1240s and set up rule along the coast of southeastern Saurashtra. In 1723, Bhav Singhji founded Bhavnagar as a port city and it soon replaced nearby Sihor as the capital of the Gohil Rajput state. Bhavnagar was one of the most affluent states of Saurashtra. The city was developed by a series of progressive rulers, from the flamboyant Maharaja Takth Sinhji, who commissioned European architects to build grand palaces and public buildings, to the humble Bhav Sinhji, who introduced educational and judicial reforms. Krishnakumar Sinhji was one of the first Indian princes to hand over his state unconditionally to the nation.

History

Saurashtra

Sights

The palace-like **Takhtsinghji Hospital** (1879-83) was designed by Sir William Emerson (President of RIBA), better known for the Victoria Memorial, Kolkata and the Crawford Market, Mumbai. The 18th-century **Darbargadh** (Old Palace, extended 1894-5), in the town centre, now has the State Bank but is scarcely visible in the incredibly overcrowded and dirty Darbargadh Bazar. The unremarkable marble **Takhteshwar Temple** on a hillock has good views over the city and the distant coastline. It is a popular place at sunrise or sunset. Gandhiji studied in Shamaldas Arts College and Sir PP Institute, which were founded in 1885 as Saurashtra's first arts college, and has an impressive campus.

Victoria Park, 2 km from centre, is a former royal hunting preserve. Far removed from the image conveyed by its name of a manicured British city park, it has rolling scrub-forests and marshes rich in birdlife. Nilgai, hyena, jackal, jungle cat and monitor lizard can all be seen. A pleasant stroll from the Nilambagh Palace, it is a great place for walks. **Gaurishankar Lake**, a popular escape from the city with parks and steps along the embankments, is good for winter birdwatching when cranes, pelicans and ducks arrive. Plovers, terns et cetera nest on the islands.

The **Bhav Vilas Palace**, a royal summer retreat and gymkhana, overlooks the large reservoir. The friendly owner (the late Maharajah's younger brother), when at home, often welcomes visitors in to see the antiques, his collection of hunting photos and trophies (cheetah coursing, falconry, pigsticking), and his own wildlife films.

Museums The complex includes the **Barton Museum** (1895), in an impressive crescent-shaped building, which has a collection of coins, carvings, geological and archaeological finds, farming implements, arms and armour, some handicrafts, miniature paintings and excellent bead and silk embroidery. ■ *0900-1300, 1400-1800. Rs 2, photography prohibited.* The better known **Gandhi Smriti** upstairs is dedicated to Mahatma Gandhi. He was at university here, his old college is now an Ayurvedic education centre. Photographs portray his life and the freedom struggle. There are also letters and marksheets showing his scores at university. The top floor is dedicated to arts and crafts of India. ■ *0830-1230, 1500-1900. Free. All are closed Sun, and 2nd and 4th Sat each month. Ask for a leaflet in English at entrance (small fee). Postcards, booklets and local handicrafts are sold at a shop here.*

Excursion **Ghogha** is a minor port, 15 minutes from town, with good birdlife on the way. Juna Bunder has a century old lock gate which still operates. Boats can take you to Piram island to see sea turtles.

Essentials

Sleeping **B** *Neelambagh Palace*, Ahmadabad Rd, T429323, F428072, www.fhraindia.com/hotel/bhavnagar/nilambag 1850s palace, 27 upmarket a/c rooms, long bathrooms with tubs (main palace better than cottage annexe), beautiful lobby with intricate wood carving, chandeliers, royal portraits, grand banquet hall now restaurant, vast gardens with peacocks, beautiful stepped pool, good atmosphere. **B** *Dil Bahar*, Waghawadi Rd, opposite Victoria Park, T568391. 2 km out of town with extensive views across the thickets of jungle to the hills. Former 1937 royal hunting lodge of the naturalist, late Dharamkumar Sinhji retaining art deco features. 4 a/c rooms (no TV or phone in rooms) with period furniture (ask to see the 'Indian' room), good food (Indian, Continental), long pool (Apr-Jun), memorabilia, historic photos, friendly staff, homely, peaceful, advance bookings: *North West Safaris*, T079-6302019, F6300962, ssibal@ad1.vsnl.net.in **B-C** *Sun'n'shine*, Panwadi, T516131, F516130. Attractive new hotel with fountains in the lobby but located on busy main road, 28 comfortable rooms, 18 more being added, popular vegetarian restaurant, health club (gym, sauna), travel desk, internet.

C *Blue Hill*, 500 m from bus, Pill Gardens, T426951, F427313. 40 a/c rooms with bath, **B** suites (traditional Gujarati lacquered furniture, best with Jacuzzi), a/c vegetarian restaurant, roof garden, popular with businessmen, comfortable hotel with a view of gardens (storks nest on the nearby trees in winter). **C-D** *Jubilee*, next to *Blue Hill*, T430045, F421744. 33 a/c rooms (recently renovated and upgraded), 10 newer dearer, restaurants, exchange, car hire. **C-D** *White Rose*, Vithalwadi, Ahmadabad Rd, T514022, F413403. 30 rooms, some a/c, restaurant modern facilities, restaurant, popular business hotel. **D** *Satkar*, Station Rd, T414821, F414894. 13 rooms with attached baths, some a/c, comfortable but not spectacularly clean. Small hotel in crowded area but convenient for the railway station. **E** *Royal*, near Alka Cinema, T425281. Non a/c rooms (Rs 375), crowded area. **E-F** *Vrindavan*, Darbargadh, T518928, F513022. Part of the old Darbargadh complex (18th-19th-century) converted to a budget hotel, 100 rooms, some with baths but only a few have western toilets, varied prices, some **D** a/c, also Rs 50 dorm beds, a/c Gujarati restaurant (*thali*, Rs 50), rather noisy surroundings, helpful owner. **F** *Mini*, Station Rd, T424415, F421246. Small hotel with clean rooms (check for ventilation), some a/c, TV (Rs 25), excellent value, very helpful and friendly manager, bus tickets, ISD phone, Internet, good restaurant and cycle hire down the road. **F** *Paradise*, Station Rd, T423291. Guest house with 20 spartan rooms, some with baths (Indian toilets), Rs 40 dorm beds, restaurant, popular with salesmen. **F** *Shital*, Amba Chowk, half-way between railway and bus station, entrance in alley at back, T428360. Some with bath, and dorm (Rs 35), good value. Recommended.

Eating

Expensive *Nilambagh's* in impressive Banquet Hall (chandeliers, Belgian mirrors, Burma teak furniture, paintings). Wide choice. Good tandoori food (try paneer tikka, chicken tandoori, chicken tikka, naan), disappointing soups, avoid Rs 400/450 buffets offered when there are groups. Garden restaurant at night is pleasant, except for loud Hindi film music. *Dil Bahar*, homecooked Continental and Gujarati. Set meals (Rs 250) on prior notice (T568391), among antiques, hunting trophies. **Mid-range** *Greenland*, Krishnanagar, near Barton Museum. North Indian and ice creams in a pleasant garden setting. *Live-in*, Waghawadi Rd. Roof garden, Indian/Chinese vegetarian. *Manali*, in *Apollo*. A/c, very good Indian and Chinese but modest helpings, very popular but rumours that it may close. *Murli*, Panwadi Chowk, T431037. Excellent *thalis*, the "only decent place in town!". *Nilgiri* at Blue Hill. Excellent Indian vegetarian (try *palak paneer* and cheese naan), also idli, dosa, a/c. *Rangoli*, Bhavnagar-Ahmadabad Rd.

Bhavnagar

Punjabi food in the garden, pleasant and clean but transport can be a problem. **Cheap** Gujarati *thali* places in the main market area include *Evening Point*. Traditional Kathiawadi *thali* in a rustic setting. *Tulsi*, Kalanala. A/c, excellent North Indian veg, also some Chinese and Western. *Woodland*, *Hotel Jubilee*, does excellent South Indian, North Indian dishes, Gujarati *thalis*, but avoid Western. A/c. **Fast food** Shops on Ahmadabad Rd and Waghawadi Rd. Sell Indian sweets and snacks. *Baker's Basket*, Gogha Circle. For cakes and snacks. *Black Cat*, Gogha Circle. For vegetarian Indian and good cakes. *Laxmi*, near Pratap Garage, Waghawadi Rd. For homecooked delights, best *'kachoris, gulab jamuns* and *samosas* in Gujarat'. *Live-in*, Waghawadi Rd. Rooftop café, a young people's hangout. *Das*, near Nilambagh, *Ramkrishna*, near Piramal Chowk, and *Khatri*, on Waghawadi Rd, have melt-in-the mouth sweets (try *sangam*, a cashew nut candy, or the local *pedas* if you have a sweet tooth) and local savoury snacks like the famous Bhavnagar *ganthias*.

Shopping Textiles, locally embroidered cushion covers, shawls, *bandhni* and mock-silver jewellery are good buys. Try Vora Bazar, Radhanpuri Market, Amba Chowk, Darbargadh Lane and Talao fruit-and-veg market. Handlooms and handicrafts are best at *Khadi* stores in the Barton Museum building.

Transport **Local Auto-rickshaw**: Unmetered so fix rates. **Bike hire**: Near Amba Chowk. **Taxi**: Near Pill Gardens. **Long distance Air**: *Indian Airlines*, T439168, airport T493130, *Gujarat Airways*, T426100, and *Jet Airways*, T433371 fly to Mumbai. **Road Bus**: frequent rickety ST buses to other main towns; several to **Alang** (1¾ hrs); **Palitana** (1¾ hrs, Rs 10); **Una** for Diu (6 hrs); **Velavadhar** (1 hr). Private operators: *Tanna Travels*, Waghawadi Rd, has luxury coaches (reclining seats) to/from **Ahmadabad**, almost hourly from 0600, 4½ hrs plus short tea break, recommended and **Vadodara**, 5½ hrs, 3 daily. Others: *New Limda* and *Punjab*, Kalanala. **Train**: The station in the Old City is about 3 km north of the ST Bus station in the New Town. **Ahmadabad**: A slow journey as the line takes a circuitous route to skirt the marshes. *Bhavnagar Ahmadabad Exp 9935*, 1530, 5½ hrs; *Shetrunji Exp 9909*, 0540, 5½ hrs; *Link Exp, 9947*, 2300, 7 hrs.

Directory **Banks** *State Bank of Saurashtra*, Darbargadh, changes currency and TCs. Forest Office, near Nilambagh Palace, T428644. **Tour operators** *Parag* and *Tamboli*, on Waghawadi Rd, for air tickets. *Mafak*, Kalanala, for horse-drawn carriage!

Velavadhar National Park
N of Bhavnagar
(64 km by road)

The compact 36 sq km of flat grassland broken by dry open scrubland with some thorn forest was set up to protect the Indian blackbuck of which it has the largest population – about 1,000 within and another 1,000 which come in from the surrounding area. The Bhavnagar royal family came here for cheetah coursing, falconry and hunting, and also harvested grass for fodder for their cattle and horses.

The **blackbuck**, which is associated with ancient Indian legend, is the second largest of the antelopes and the fastest long distance runner of all animals. It can keep going at a steady 90 km per hour (easily outstripping the fastest Indian road traffic). The black and white dominant males sport spiral horns; the juvenile males are brown and white while the hornless females are brownish, with lighter parts. It is one of the most hunted animals in India, and so is an endangered species. The best time for viewing is October and November and during the main rutting season in February and March. Impressive males clash horns to establish territory and court females.

Wolves are the prime predator and although there are only two families, Velavadhar is one of the few places to see them. The park also contains a few sounders of wild boar in addition to 50 to 60 nilgai, usually seen near waterholes, jungle cat, which can be seen at dawn and dusk, and jackal. It has a rich birdlife with numerous birds of prey including the largest harrier roost in the world – some 1,500-2,000 of these light-bodied hawks gather here at sunset in November to January. During the monsoons the park is the best place in India for the Lesser florican. Roger Clark (Hawk & Owl Trust), New Hythe House, Reach, Cambridge, England, brings birding tours, specializing in birds of prey.

In addition to the two rivers that border the park, there are three waterholes and three small pools which attract animals at midday.

■ *US$ 5, still camera fee US$ 5; guide (some have no English), US$ 10 per trip, jeep US$ 25 per drive. Pay at Forest Range Office at park entrance. Best time to visit is Nov-May. The road approach is from Vallabhipur (32 km) from the park, which has a small interesting **museum** of finds excavated in the area. The park is 10 km off the Bhavnagar-Vadodara Highway. Buses leave from Bhavnagar, change at Vallabhipur.*

Sleeping and eating B *Kaliyar Bhuvan Forest Lodge*, simple but adequate, 5 small rooms, reasonably furnished, western toilets, hot water to 3 rooms, but now prohibitively priced at US$30 per room, meals US$5-10. Poor value. Reserve ahead at Forest Office in Bhavnagar, rear the bus stand, T426425.

Transport Few afternoon buses from Bhavnagar (2½ hrs); (others involve a change at Vallabhipur) Better to hire a car if you don't want to stay overnight. Alternatively hire a jeep/*chhakra* (motorbike trailer) from Vallabhipur. A new bridge being built near Bhavnagar port to Adhelai near the park will make access faster and easier.

Mid-way between Bhavnagar and Palitana, the former Gohil Rajput capital has the 17th-century hilltop Darbargadh Palace, now government offices. Though rather dilapidated, you can still see some intricate carved wooden balconies and pillars outside and fine 19th-century wall paintings inside. The galleries upstairs have splendid views. One of the sieges here, a re-creation of the Trojan horse story, is a popular theme in Kathiawadi bardic poetry. The Gautameshwar Dam, a scenic reservoir surrounded by hills, with the Sirohi Mata temple on a hilltop offers great views.

Sihor
27 km from Bhavnagar

The **Brahm Kund** (11th-12th century), 500 m to the south of the main road, about 2 km west of Sihor centre, is a deeply set stepped tank which is now dry. It has around 100 sculpted images of deities in small niches, a few of which are still actively worshipped. There are also pillared galleries with rich carvings of musicians. In the village nearby brass utensils are produced as a cottage industry by rolling scrap from the Alang ship breaking yard and beating it into attractive water pots. Villagers are only too happy to show you around their workshops. The Khodiyar temple on the Bhavnagar-Sihor road has a pretty situation among hills.

Saurashtra

Sleeping and eating E-F *Vijay Palace*, has simple rooms with baths, some a/c. *Gaylord*, opposite the Town Hall. North Indian and South Indian food. *Gokul* for Gujarati *thalis*. *Surbhi*, just before uphill path to Khodiyar temple, offers traditional Kathiawadi food in a garden setting.

★ Palitana

Phone code: 02848
Colour map 5, grid C5
Population: 42,000
Area: 13 sq km

Palitana is renowned for the extraordinary Jain temple complex on Shatrunjaya Hill which attracts domestic pilgrims as well as foreign visitors. No one is allowed to remain on the hill at night but even during the day there is a peaceful serenity as you listen to the temple bells and pilgrims chanting in the City of the Gods.

Ins & outs **Getting there** State buses come from Palitana from all major towns around and 7 seater taxis run the 56 km from Bhavnagar. There are trains from Ahmadabad and Bhavnagar. **Getting around** The town is itself is small enough to see on foot though taxis, rickshaws and tongas can be hired to go to nearby villages like Adpur. **Climate** Temperature in summer: maximum 46°C, minimum 24°C. In winter: maximum 38°C, minimum 17°C. Annual rainfall: 580 mm, mostly Jun-Sep. **Best season** Nov-Mar. Apr-Jun extremely hot.

The town Palitana was the capital of a small princely state founded by Shahji, a Gohel Rajput who belonged to the same clan as the Maharajah of Bhavnagar. The river bisects the town. The east bank has the hotels, eating places and shopping complexes and the bus and railway stations, while the west bank has the Willingdon Vegetable Market, vegetable vendors and some older Raj and royal buildings. The last ruler died leaving wives and sisters to fight over the royal palace and mansions which are now decaying but show signs of impressive architecture. The better houses are on Taleti Road. The busy little town is also known for diamond cutting and horse breeding. South African diamonds are imported from Belgium for cutting and polishing before being re-exported back to Belgium.

The site **Shatrunjaya Hill** is 3 km southwest. According to local tradition, Adinatha, the first Tirthankara, visited the hill several times and the first temple was erected by his son. Thereafter, the temple builders could not stop. Jains believe that Pundarika, the chief disciple of Adinatha, attained *nirvana* here.

Most of the temples are named after their founders and are mostly 16th century although the earliest may date from the 11th. It would appear that many others were destroyed by the Muslims in the 14th and 15th centuries, but later, when Jains obtained religious toleration they began rebuilding.

All the 863 temples are strung along the two ridges of the hill, with further temples in the hollow between, linking them. There are nine enclosures of fortifications (*tuks*) which provided defence. There are lovely views over the flat, cultivated black soils of the coastal plain, and on a clear day after the rains it is sometimes possible to see the Gulf of Khambat beyond Bhavnagar away to the east, and the Chamardi peak and the granite range of Sihor to the north.

If you wish to take the track down to Adpur turn left out of the complex entrance courtyard where you leave your shoes. Follow the sign to Gheti Pag gate

Routes There are two routes up the 600 m climb. The main route starts in the town of Palitana to the east of the hill, while a shorter and steeper route climbs up from the village of Adpur to the west. Both are excellently made stepped paths. Over 3500 steps (the dhooli bearers at the bottom may exaggerate!) lead up to the temples. There are two long flat stretches, but since some of the path is unshaded, even in winter it can get very hot.

Temples In the southern group they include one of **Ramaji Gandharia** (16th-century), and the **Bhulavani** (labyrinth, 18th-century) which is a series of crypt-like chambers each surmounted with a dome. The **Hathiapol** (Elephant Gate, 19th-century) faces southeast. The **Vimalavasi Tuk** occupies the west end of the south Ridge. In it is the **Adishvara Temple** (16th-century) which dominates the site. It has a double-storey *mandapa* inside which is a large image of Rishabhanatha with crystal eyes and a gold crown of jewels. The **Vallabhai Temple** (19th-century) with its finely clustered spires and the large **Motisah Temple** (1836) occupy the middle ground between the ridges. The **Khartaravasi Tuk** is the largest and highest temple complex, stretched out along the northern Ridge and includes the **Adinatha Temple** (16th-century). There are quadruple Tirthankara images inside the sanctuary over which rises a slender tower.

■ *0700-1900. Entry by a free permit at the entrance to the southern ridge. Camera Rs 40. Rules: Visitors should wear appropriate, clean clothes; leather articles (even watch straps) and food or drink may not be allowed in the temple area at the top of the hill. They can be left, along with shoes, at the entrance. Cloth and plastic footwear, and walking sticks, are available for hire at the bottom of the hill. Take lots of water and a sun hat or parasol. Very basic toilets are available at the entrance to the temple complex. Foreign visitors are required to sign a register before entering. Arrive by dawn to join the pilgrims, and allow 2 hr for the climb, and 4 to 5 hrs for the round trip. You can be carried up by a* dhooli *(string chair), Rs 500 return but the hassle from aggressive touts in the early stages of the climb can be considerable. Rates rise in summer, peaking during fairs and Mahavir Jayanti to Rs 1000.*

Stapitya Kala Sangrah and **Sri Vishal Jain Kala Sansthan**, Taleti Road, have **Museums** ivory carvings, miniatures, sculpture, narrative paintings, figures illustrating the life of Mahavir. Few English labels but no guide. ■ *1000-1200, 1500-2000. Rs 5, no photography.* Jambodit **Science Research Centre** is dedicated to proving the falseness of contemporary scientific views of the earth and its place in the universe including that the earth is a sphere and that it rotates around the sun. Based on a reading of early Jain scriptures it argues that the earth is flat and stationary and that one cannot land on the moon!

B *Vijay Vilas Palace* (Heritage Hotel), in Adpur, a colourful cattle herders' village ringed **Sleeping** by hills with a view of the temples. 3 rooms in 1906 royal lodge with the feel of an Italian country house. Gradually being restored. Delicious homecooked Indian meals, *Difficult to find cheap rooms but dormitory* local produce (non-residents Rs 250 with advance notice), 7 km from town (rickshaws *beds are Rs 20-50* Rs 50, shared motorbike-rickshaws Rs 3). The shorter but steeper route to the Palitana temple complex starts a few 100 m away at the temple in Adpur village (follow the milk maids carrying curd!). Recommended. Book ahead through *North West Safaris*, T079-6302019, F6300962, ssibal@ad1.vsnl.net.in **C-D** *Sumeru* (Gujarat Tourism), Station Rd, near Bus Stand, T2327. 7 comfortable rooms, 3 a/c, 5 dorms (Rs 50) with cold water only, limited menu restaurant (good English breakfast), tourist office, check-out 0900, mixed reports (like 'Fawlty Towers'). **E** *Shrinath*, Natraj Complex, ST Rd, T2542. 18 tiny rooms, dorm beds Rs 50, some rooms with western toilets Rs 400, extremely clean and comfortable, set on top of shopping complex (laundry, international phone nearby). **E** *Shravak*, opposite central bus station, T2428. 18 rooms with baths (western toilets, hot shower: Rs 300), Indian toilets (single Rs 100, double Rs 200), dorm beds (Rs 40) but not too clean. **F** *Patel House*, Station Rd, T42441. Run by a private farmer's trust, rather basic and impersonal but set around an open courtyard that shuts off some of the traffic noise, double rooms with or without bath (cold taps, hot water in buckets, Indian toilet), some 4 and 6-bedded, dorm beds Rs 20. There are over 150 *dharamshalas* with modern facilities catering primarily for Jain pilgrims, but enquire.

Saurashtra

Eating *Mansi Park*, Bhavnagar Rd. North Indian, Chinese. Pleasant open-air restaurant, tables on the lawn and in kiosks, hill views (main dishes Rs 35-50), also tea time treats (cheese toast, finger chips, idli, dosa) for about Rs 20 each, average quality. Many eateries in Taleti Rd offer Gujarati *thali* as well as pau-bhaji and ice cream. Along Station Rd, *thalis* are Rs 10-15.

Festivals *Teras Fair* at Gheti (Adpur-Palitana, 4 km from town) 3 days before Holi. Thousands of Jain pilgrims attend, joined by villagers who come for free lunches!

Shopping Local **handicrafts** include embroidery (saris, dresses, purses, bags, wall hangings etc) and metal engraving. You can watch the craftsmen making harmonium reeds. **Photography**: film shops in Main Rd. Nearest processing at Bhavnagar.

Transport **Local Taxi rickshaw** and **tonga**, rates are negotiable. **Long distance Air**: Bhavnagar (51 km northeast) is the nearest airport. **Road** ST**Bus** (0800-1200, 1400-1800) to Ahmadabad (often with a change at Dhandhuka), deluxe from Ahmadabad (0700, 0800, 0900) to **Bhavnagar**, **Jamnagar**, **Rajkot**, **Surat**, **Vadodara**. Private deluxe coaches to **Surat** and **Mumbai** via Vadodara. Surprisingly none to Ahmadabad. Operators: *Paras*, Owen Bridge, T2370. Opposite ST depot *P: Khodiar*, T2586 (to Surat) and *Shah*, T2396. **Taxi**: For up to 7, run between **Bhavnagar** (57 km by State Highway) and Palitana, Rs 15 each. **Train**: To Bhavnagar about every 3 hrs. From Ahmadabad, change at Sihor: from Sihor to Palitana dep 0722, 1525, 1924; to Sihor 0900, 1805, 2030.

Directory **Communications Post**: GPO on Main Rd with poste restante; PO, Bhairavnath Rd. **Medical services** Mansinhji Government Hospital, Main Rd; Shatrunjaya Hospital, Taleti Rd. **Tourist offices** At *Hotel Toran Sumeru*.

Alang
50 km S of Bhavnagar

The beach has turned into the world's largest scrapyard for dead ships, the industry yielding rich pickings from the sale of salvaged metal (steel, bronze and copper) and the complete range of ship's fittings from doors and portholes to diesel engines and lifeboats.

Alang village, has developed this surprising specialization because of the unusual nature of its tides. The twice monthly high tides are exceptional, reputedly the second highest tides in the world, lifting ships so that they can be beached well on shore, out of reach of the sea for the next two weeks. During this period the breakers can move in unhindered. Labourers' 'huts' line the coast road though many workers commute from Bhavnagar.

In early 2001, Alang Port was not open to visitors without special permission. Contact in advance, Port Officer, Gujarat Maritime Board, New Port, Bhavnagar, T293090 or the Gandhinagar office, Sector 10A, opposite Air Force Station, T0284235222. Foreigners are finding it difficult to get permission to enter the beach/port area. Hotels in Bhavnagar may be able to help individuals gain entry but permits for groups are virtually impossible. Photography is not allowed.

Although entry to Alang port is restricted and permission must be sought, the last few kilometres to the port are lined with the yards of dealers specialising in every item of ships' furniture. Valuable items are creamed off before the 'breaking' begins, but if you want 3-cm thick porthole glass, a spare fridge-freezer or a life jacket, this is the place to browse! However, customs officers always get first choice of valuables as they have to give permission for vessels to be beached, so don't expect too much.

Some described Alang as the most impressive 'sight' in India they had seen, while one visitor wrote: 'The place was like a war zone, I've never seen so much destruction'. Others have found the journey not worth the trouble since they couldn't enter the fenced off 'Lots'.

Saurashtra

■ *Getting there: From Bhavnagar buses from ST Bus Stand, through the day from 0600 (last return 1800), 1¾ hr, Rs 10. At Alang, tongas go up and down the beachfront past the shipyards for Rs 5. Taxis from Bhavnagar take 1½ hrs, Rs 400-500 return and auto-rickshaws Rs 300-400 (expect to bargain).*

The coastal town of Mahuva can be reached by two road. One way is via the **To Mahuva** hot springs at Tulshishyam in Sasan Gir National Park. They are 75 km south-west of Palitana and 60 km southeast of Mahuva. The road is very poor so expect a bumpy ride on the back of a bus. The alternative coastal route from Bhavnagar to Diu passes the Jain temples of Talaja and Jhanjmer Fort of the Kathi chieftain. Mahuva is a fairly picturesque town (pronounced Mow-va) known for its historic port. Beautiful handcrafted furniture with lacquerwork and intricate hand-painting is made here. A new port and ship-breaking yard is under construction at Pip-a-vav, 25 km to the west.

A few minutes offshore from Port Victor, near the new Pip-a-Vav coastal **Chanch Island** complex, Chanch has an imposing 1940s palatial summer mansion of the Maharajah of Bhavnagar. The island is so called because of its shape like a par-rot's beak (*chanch* in Gujarati), and has a nice beach (not safe for swimming) and a rocky shore with a natural swimming pool fed by the tide. You can get a boat for the two-minute ride to the island and then a rickshaw to the palace. Permission to visit is required from Nilambagh Palace in Bhavnagar.

About 30 km northeast of Mahuva, Gopnath is where the 16th-century mys- **Gopnath** tic poet, Narsinh Mehta is said to have attained enlightenment. Near the light-house, the 1940s mansion of late Maharajah Krishna Kumar Singhji of Bhavnagar was the summer home to which he would move with his entire office staff from April to September. A part of it is now a hotel. There are pleas-ant rocky, white-sand beaches (dangerous for swimming and wading but good for walking) near a 700-year-old temple, a kilometre away.

Sleeping and eating C *Gopnath Bungalow*, beautiful seaviews, 3 rooms in royal man-sion (Rs 1,200), 4 clean, well-renovated rooms in the 'English' bungalow (Rs 750) in a rambling complex, great views of sea and cliffs, meals on request, pool, understaffed so expect inconveniences. Contact *Nilambagh Palace*, Bhavnagar, T0278-424241. *Jai Chamunda*, opposite Gopnath Bungalow, is an outdoor eating place though fairly clean, gets rather overcrowded and noisy on Sun. Good Kathiawadi veg *thalis* with unlimited refills (Rs 40-45), Rs 10 for local desserts, sea food at night to order (catch of the day lob-ster Rs 350/400, shrimps Rs 200 per kg). Also *Bhojnalayas* near the temple offer cheap local food. Coconuts, mineral water, soft drinks and biscuits are available on the beach.

Western Saurashtra

Containing the only reserves of the Gir lion, much of Western Saurashtra's dry forest has now given way to farming. From Rajkot to Junagadh, between the edge of the Girnar and Datta Hills, and the coast, millets, sorghum, wheat and cotton dominate the cultivable land. To the south are large areas of brackish water and saline earth, but where the water is sweet, rich crops can be achieved on the allu-vial soils. Further west farming becomes progressively more marginal, and towards Dwarka, clay is occasionally interspersed with higher limestones. The old towns of Gondal and Junagadh retain a highly evocative atmosphere.

Gondal

Phone code: 02825
38 km S of Rajkot

The fascinating old town of Gondal was the capital of one of the most progressive, affluent and efficient princely states during the British period. The exemplary state ruled by Jadeja Rajputs had an excellent road network, free compulsory education for all children (including girls), sewage systems and accessible irrigation for farmers. The rulers rejected *purdah* (their palaces have no *zenanas*) and imposed no taxes on their subjects, instead earning revenue from rail connections between the port towns of Porbandar and Veraval with Rajkot and cities inland.

The **Naulakha Palace** (1748) with a sculpted façade, pretty *jharoka* windows and carved stone pillars, has an impressive Darbar Hall and a **museum** of paintings, brass and silver. Silver items include caskets, models of buildings and scales used for weighing the Maharajah, he was weighed against silver and gold on his 25th and 50th birthday; the precious metals were then distributed to the poor. A gallery has toys from the 1930s and '40s.

The Vintage and Classic **Car Museum** is one of the finest in the country (1910 New Engine, 1920s Delage and Daimler, 1935-55 models, horse-drawn carriages et cetera). Boating is possible on **Veri Lake** nearby, which attracts large numbers of rosy pelicans, flamingos, demoiselle and common eastern cranes and many others, particularly in January and February. You can visit the Bhuvaneshwari **Ayurvedic Pharmacy** founded in 1910 which still prepares herbal medicines according to ancient principles and runs a hospital which offers massages and treatment. There is also a horse and cattle **stud farm**. The early 20th-century **Swaminarayan Temple** has painted interiors on the upper floors.

Sleeping and eating The Heritage Hotels here are outstanding, with beautiful interiors and the ever helpful manager Mr Kanak Singh ('looks after guests like a father'), are worth the experience: **B** *Riverside Palace* (19th century) by River Gondali, T20002, F23332, www.gujarat.net/gondal With a glassed-in terrace, 11 large, attractive rooms, 4-posters etc, collection of textiles and crafts. **B** *Orchard Palace*, overlooking mango and lime groves, 7 rooms in a wing, attractive gardens, 35 vintage cars, pool (waiting to be filled), excellent dance performances, mosquito nuisance so burn rings, good food ('bland European dishes; order 'Indian' in advance every time'), good *kebabs* and Gujarati *thalis* but service can be slow (Rs 2,000 includes meals). **B** *Royal Saloon*, standing in garden near Orchard Palace. Beautifully renovated suite in Maharaja's old train, with drawing and dining rooms and sit-outs on the platform. There is also an antique kitchen with coal cooking but meals are catered for from the *Orchard Palace*. Sheer nostalgia. **D** *Bhuvaneswari Rest House*, a/c rooms with baths (Rs 350-700), simple but comfortable, *thali* meals. The Gondal family don't spend time with guests though 'the Maharani is delightful company'; request high tea in their fabulous private drawing room (French gilt furniture, crystals, Lalique etc). Reservations for all the above: *North West Safaris*, T079-6302019, F6300962, ssibal@ad1.vsnl.net.in

Jetpur

30 km from Gondal

Jetpur, on the Junagadh-Gondal highway, is a textile town known for its woodblock and screen printing and hand yarn-dyeing workshops. The craftspeople are friendly and helpful and will usually allow you to watch them in their workshops. *Jagdish Prints* has a retail outlet selling block printed textiles.

Dhoraji

Dhoraji was the second capital of the Gondal state and bears some reminders of the progressive rulers. The **Darbargadh** (Old Palace), now a government office, is an architectural masterpiece (similar to Jaisalmer), with fine sandstone carvings, *jarokha* balconies, *jali* windows and ornate doors. There is also a 100-year old water tower, an impressive railway station and the town gates.

Junagadh

The small town is surrounded by an old wall, large parts of which are now gone, but the narrow winding lanes and colourful bazars are evocative of earlier centuries. The old quarters are entered by imposing gateways. A large rock with 14 Asokan edicts, dating from 250 BC, stands on the way to the temple-studded Girnar Hill, believed to be a pre-Harappan site. Unfortunately the enchantment of the once picturesque town is marred by ugly new buildings and dirty slums.

Phone code: 0285
Colour map 5, grid C3
Population: 167,100

Getting there Trains and long distance buses arrive fairly close to the centre at Chittakhana Chowk with some hotels within easy reach. **Getting away** The town sites are possible to tackle on foot allowing plenty of time for Uparkot. It is best to get an early start on Girnar Hill with the help of a rickshaw, though.

Ins & outs
See page 324 for further details

Established by the Mauryans in the fourth century BC, from the second to fourth centuries Junagadh was the capital of Gujarat under the **Kshattrapa** rulers. It is also associated with the **Chudasama Rajputs** who ruled from Junagadh from 875 AD. The fort was expanded in 1472 by Mahmud Beghada, and again in 1683 and 1880. Sher Khan Babi, who took on the title of Nawab Bahadur Khan Babi, declared Junagadh an independent state in the 1700s. At the time of Partition the Nawab exercised his legal right to accede to Pakistan but his subjects were predominantly Hindu and after Indian intervention and an imposed plebiscite their will prevailed. The Nawab was exiled with his hundred dogs.

History

The **Uparkot citadel** on a small plateau is east of the town and was a stronghold in the Mauryan and Gupta Empires. It paled into insignificance in the sixth century AD when Vallabi rose to prominence. The present walls are said to date from the time of the Chudasama Rajputs (ninth-15th century). The Ottoman canons of Suleman Pasha, an ally of the Sultans, were moved here after the Muslim forces were unable to save Diu from Portuguese naval forces. The 16th-century Nilam canon is 5.7-m long. It was repeatedly attacked so there was a huge granary to withstand a long siege. The **Jama Masjid** here was built from the remains of a Hindu palace. The **Adi Chadi Vav** (11th century) is a *baoli* with 172 steps and an impressive spiral staircase. It is believed to commemorate the two slave girls who were bricked up as sacrifice to ensure the supply of water. The 52-m deep **Naghan Kuva** is a huge well (11th century) which has steps down to the water level through the rocks, with openings to ventilate the path.

The **Buddhist cave monastery** in this fort complex dates from Asoka's time. Two of the three levels are open to visitors. The drainage system was very advanced as seen in the rainwater reservoir. The ventilation cleverly achieved a balance of light and cool breezes. Other Buddhist caves are hewn into the hillsides near the fort.

In the town, the **Mausolea** of the Junagadh rulers (late 19th-century), not far from the railway station, are impressive. The **Maqbara** of Baha-ud-din Bhar with its silver doors and intricate, elaborate decoration, almost has a fairground flamboyance. The **Old Mausolea** at Chittakhana Chowk (opposite *Relief Hotel*, which has views of them from the roof), which were once impressive are now crumbling and overgrown.

The **Asokan rock edicts** carved in the Brahmi script on a large boulder is at the foot of the Girnar Hill, about 1 km east of the town. The emperor instructed his people to be gentle with women, to be kind to animals, to give alms freely and to plant medicinal herbs. See also page 376. ■ *0830-1100, 1400-1800, closed Wed and holidays.*

Sights
The deep moat inside the walls of the citadel is believe to have once had crocodiles

Saurashtra

The climb up this worn volcanic cone by 10,000 stone steps takes at least 2 hrs

Girnar Hill, rising 900 m above the surrounding plain, 3 km east of town, has been an important religious centre for the Jains from the third century BC. You start the climb just beyond Damodar Kund in teak forest, at the foot is the Asokan Edict while a group of 16 Jain temples surmounts the hill. The two near the top are the **Neminatha** (1128), one of the oldest, and **Mallinatha** temples (1231). There is also the **Samprati Raja Temple** (1453), a fine example of the later period, and the **Melak Vasahi** (15th-century). The climb can be trying in the heat so is best started very early in the morning. You will find tea stalls *en route* and brazen monkeys. *Dhoolis* are available but are expensive (charge depends on weight, Rs 1,500 for 60 kg!), to the first group of temples, which are the most interesting. There are good views from the top though the air is often hazy. ■ *Getting there: No 3 or 4 bus from the stand opposite the post office run to Girnar Taleti at the foot of the hill, but are often 'out of order'. Rickshaws, Rs 25 (Rs 40 return), require bargaining. There are plans for a ropeway which will make visiting the summit easier.*

Further reading *Junagadh* by KV Soundara Rajan, an ASI booklet, 1985, details the edicts and Buddhist caves on Uparkot. *Junagadh and Girnar* by SH Desai.

Museum **Durbar Hall Museum**, in the Nawab's Palace (circa 1870), Janta Chowk, houses royal memorabilia including portraits, palanquins, gem-studded carpets, costumes and weapons. Good labelling, particularly in the informative

Junagadh

Saurashtra

armoury section. ■ *0900-1215, 1500-1800, closed Wed, 2nd and 4th Sat of month. Rs 2 per photo. Small but recommended. Allow 30 mins.*

Sakkar Bagh Zoo, Rajkot Road, 3½ km north of town centre. Well kept, particularly with a good collection of birds and big cats. Attractive enclosures at the rear are for breeding Asiatic lions. Get permission to visit and photograph from the Superintendent. ■ *0800-1800, closed Mon, Rs 2*. The garden houses the fine **Junagadh Museum** with local paintings, Nawabi relics, textiles, manuscripts, archaeological finds and natural history. ■ *0900-1215, 1500-1800, closed Wed, 2nd and 4th Sat in the month, Rs 2. Getting there: Take bus No 1, 2 or 6.*

Parks & zoos

C-D *Lion Hill View Resort*, at the foot of Girnar Hill, is to open. **C-D** *President*, opposite Rly Workshop, T626773. 15 clean rooms, 6 a/c (comfortable but short beds), all with hot water (winter only) and TV, 'deluxe' front rooms on busy road, noisy, those at rear with view of hills better. **C-D** *Paramount*, Kalwa Chowk, T 622119, F650582. 31 rooms (some a/c) with TV and phone, attached baths, car rental and bus ticketing. **D** *Girnar* (Gujarat Tourism), Majwadi Darwaja, 2 km north, T621201. 24 decent rooms, some a/c with bath, best with balcony, unattractive building but in good location, poor management. **D-E** *National*, near Kalwa Chowk, T627891. 15 clean, comfortable rooms, 2 a/c dearer, some deluxe with TV, big discount for single, good value though several women visitors have complained of harassment on noisy road. **E-F** *Madhuwati*, Kalwa Chowk, T620087. 27 spacious rooms, some a/c, attached bath (hot showers in winter only), noisy location above a shopping complex, clean, comfortable, courteous, popular with budget groups. **E-F** *Relief*, Dhal Rd, T620280. 14 rooms (some share bath), hot water, 2 a/c, snacks available, untrained but friendly staff, courteous owner can help with excursions. **F** *Gautam*, Kalwa Chowk, T626432. Located on noisy intersection, small guest house with 12 simple rooms, most with shared bath, bucket hot water, cycle hire. **F** *Jayshree Guest House*, Jayshree Talkies, T621032 and **F** *Tourist Guest House*, around the Kalwa Chowk. **F** *Railway Retiring Rooms*, clean and well maintained.

Sleeping

Rates double during Diwali (Oct-Nov) when large number of Indians visit Girnar

Mid-range *Garden Café*, Girnar Rd, attractive outdoor restaurant with view of hills, among flowering plants and lawns, average food, good atmosphere and service; aquarium and small museum next door (10-1300, 1500-1800, entry Rs 5), handy for visitors to the hill. **Cheap** *Geeta* and *Sharda*, both near railway station, do good *thalis*. *Poonam*, Dhal Rd, Chittakhana Chowk, 1st floor. Unlimited Gujarati *thalis* (Rs 35-60). Excellent food and service. *Sagar*, Jayshree Talkies Rd, good Punjabi and Gujarati, vegetarian, Indian breakfast (Rs 50), a/c. *Santoor*, off MG Rd, near Kalwa Chowk, upstairs. Very good Indian and Chinese veg dishes, a/c, excellent value, 0945-1500, 1700-2300. *Swati*, Jayshree Talkies Rd. Mainly Punjabi, some South Indian and Chinese, all veg. Good food and lassi, courteous, young enthusiastic staff, clean and comfortable (though smell of spices pervades), a/c, one of town's most popular restaurants. *Sagar*, offers similar fare. A/c, great breakfasts (poori-aloo, idli, vada, lassi).

Eating

Near Kalwa Chowk, try Dal-Pakwana (a Sindhi brunch), stuffed parathas, fruit juices (Kesar mango from Apr-Jun). In Azad Chowk, try milk sweets, snacks & curds

Saurashtra

Feb-Mar: *Bhavnath Fair* at Sivaratri at Damodar Kund near the Girnar foothills is very spectacular. Attended by *Naga Bawas* (naked sages), who often arrive on decorated elephants to demonstrate strange powers (including the strength of their penis) and colourful tribal people who come to worship and perform *Bhavai* folk theatre (12-14 **Mar** 2002). **Nov-Dec**: A popular 10-day fair is held at the Jain temples starting at *Kartik Purnima* (1 **Nov** 2001; 20 Nov 2002).

Festivals

Shops sell good embroidery work.

Shopping

Transport **Local** **Cycle hire**: from shops on Dhal Rd, near *Relief Hotel*; Rs 2 per hr, may need to bargain. **Long distance** **Air**: No flights at present. **Road** **Bus**: Regular bus services to Ahmadabad, Rajkot (2 hrs), Veraval, Porbandar and Sasan Gir (2½ hrs). **Train**: Ahmadabad: *Somnath Mail 9923*, 1902, 9¼ hrs; *Girnar Exp 9845*, 2120, 9 hrs. **Rajkot**: *Veraval Rajkot Mail 9837*, 1318, 5¼ hrs; *Fast Pass 341*, 0530, 3¼ hrs; *347*, 1000, 3¾ hrs; *349*, 1550, 3¾ hrs. **Veraval**: *Girnar Exp 9846*, 0623, 1¾ hrs. For **Sasan Gir**: take *Fast Pass 352* to Delwada, 0605; a delightful journey. No steam trains run now.

Directory **Banks** *Bank of Baroda*, near the town post office is very efficient and changes TCs; *Bank of Saurashtra* changes currency.

★ Sasan Gir National Park

Phone code: 02877
Colour map 5, grid C4

The sanctuary covers a total area of 1,412 sq km in the Saurashtra Peninsula, of which 258 sq km at the core is the national park for which permits are required. As a result of over-grazing and agricultural colonization only about 10% of the park is forest. However, much of the natural vegetation in the region was scrub jungle. The area has rocky hills and deep valleys with numerous rivers and streams, and the vegetation is typically semi-deciduous with dry-forest teak dominating. There are also extensive clearings covered with savannah-like fodder grasses.

Ins & outs
See page 326 for further details

Getting there There are buses from Junagadh, Veraval and Ahmadabad. Sasan railway station (10-mins walk from the forest lodge) has convenient trains from Junagadh and Veraval. **Getting around** There are 6 routes in the park, between 22 and 50 km. Jeep (diesel, seats 4), from *Sinh Sadan*, bookings between 0700-1100 or 1500-1700 ('a scramble at 0630 as there are not enough jeeps. Eight officials filling forms with one pen between them!'). **When to go** From 15 Oct-15 Jun, best Mar-May, closed during monsoons. Temperature range, 42°C to 7°C. Rainfall, 1,000 mm.

Lions are more likely to be seen with the help of a tracker & guide (jeeps & guides available). Some visitors return frustrated & disappointed

The **Asiatic Lion** (*Panthera leo persica*) once had a wide range of natural territory running from North to West India through Persia to Arabia. It is now only found in the Gir forest; the last one seen outside India was in 1942, in Iran. Similar to its African cousin, the tawnier Asian is a little smaller and stockier in build with a skin fold on the belly, a thinner mane and a thicker tuft at the end of its tail. The 1913 census accounted for only 18 in the park. The lions' natural habitat was threatened by the gradual conversion of the forest into agricultural land and cattle herders grazing their livestock here. The conservation programme has been remarkably successful. In the mid-90s there were over 300 lions (some suggest too many for this sanctuary). These, and 294 panthers, make Gir India's best Big Cat sanctuary. There have been attacks on villagers by park lions, these were probably 'provoked' as there are few reported 'maneaters'. The Interpretation Zone's 'Safari Park' has a few lions.

A **watch tower** camouflaged in the tree canopy at Kamleshwar overlooks an artificial reservoir harbouring wild crocodiles but it is poorly located and overcrowded with bus loads of noisy visitors at weekends. Other towers are at Janwadla and Gola.

For **bird watching**, Adhodiya, Valadara, Ratnaghuna and Pataliyala, are good spots. A walk along Hiran River is also rewarding.

The **Tulsishyam hotsprings** in the heart of the forest (Tulsishyam is also a Krishna pilgrimage centre), and **Kankai Mata Temple** dedicated to Bhim, the *Mahabharata* hero, and his mother Kunti, add interest.

■ *Usually 0700-1200, 1500-1730 from mid-Oct to mid-Feb; 0630-1100, 1600 to sunset from mid-Feb to mid-Jun, depending on sunrise and sunset.*

Foreigners pay dollar rate, Rs 30, US$ 5. Still camera fee Rs 50, US$ 5; video Rs 2,500, US$ 200; guide (some have no English), Rs 50, US$ 10 per trip; vehicle entry Rs 100, US$ 10; Jeep US$ 25 per drive. Permits are only available from Sinh Sadan at Sasan, so do not try Tulsishyam entrance.

Gir Interpretation Zone, Devaliya, 12 km west of Sasan. Some 16 sq km of Gir habitat has been fenced in as a 'Safari Park' to show a cross-section of wildlife; the four or five lions here can be easily seen in open scrubland in the area. Photographers will find this a good place to shoot lion behaviour as these lions are less shy than those in the sanctuary. Other Gir wildlife include spotted deer, sambar, nilgai, peafowl. Permits are available at the Reception here. ■ *Same rates for entry as for the sanctuary. If you take the mini-bus tour you save US$20 (guide and vehicle fee). Open during park times except Wed. Getting there: local buses run along Sasan-Maliya Road. Jeeps from Sasan to Zone gate charge Rs 120.*

Orientation Centre, in *Sinh Sadan Complex*, offers an informative introduction to Sasan Gir and its wildlife. There is a film about lions at 1900. Souvenir shop sells good books.

Crocodile Rearing Centre, near the entrance to Sinh Sadan and road leading to *Lion Safari Lodge*, is full of marsh crocodiles varying in size from a few centimetres to 1 m for restocking the population in the sanctuary. Eggs are collected in the park and taken to Junagadh for hatching under controlled conditions. All the information is in Gujarati, but it is still worth a look. Unfortunately, keepers prod the crocodiles to make them move. ■ *0800-1200, 1500-1800. Free.*

Sleeping

AL-B *Gir Lodge* (Taj), Sasan, T85521, F85528. 27 comfortable refurbished rooms (better upstairs for views from balcony), 9 a/c (including Lion and Panther Suites), pleasant river-facing dining area but average meals at fixed times, slow service though friendly manager and chef, no pool, wildlife library and videos, jeep hire. **B** *Maneland Jungle Lodge*, 2 km before Sasan, T85555, on edge of sanctuary, well-appointed suites in bungalow (VIP faces jungle), and rooms in cottages resembling royal hunting lodges, restaurant with limited menu delightfully designed, jungle ambience, lions and panthers heard and occasionally spotted nearby, rich birdlife, wildlife videos, recommended, advance reservations: *North West Safaris*, T079-6302019, F6300962, ssibal@ad1.vsnl.net.in **B** *Sinh Sadan Forest Lodge* (Govt), overpriced and run down rooms (foreigners US$30), with Indian toilets, better a/c chalets (US$50), tents with shared bath (US$10), 30-bed dorm (Rs 60, US$5), comfortable 2-bed tents, with shared toilet and cold shower (Rs 100) – "fell asleep to the sound of a lion roaring nearby!", food must order in advance (mixed reports on quality). Book at least 1 week ahead, Dy CFS Superintendent, Wildlife Div, Sasan Gir, Dist Junagadh T362135. **D** *Umeng*, T85728, near Sasan bus stop. Backdrop of sanctuary but with crowded village on one side (calls from the mosque disturb the peace). 9 decent rooms with mediocre baths, rooftop dining room (order meal well ahead), jeep safaris, knowledgeable owner can help with visits to the sanctuary. **E** *Forest Dept Guest House*, small chalets with bath, spacious gardens, book direct 2 weeks in advance or through Gujarat Govt Office, Dhanraj Mahal, Apollo Bunder, Mumbai, T257039, or Information Centre, Baba Kharak Singh Marg, New Delhi, T343147. An **E** *Guest House*, has opened in the market with spartan rooms. **F** Gujarat Tourism *Toran Holiday Home*, Tulsishyam, 5 rooms, closed during monsoons, checkout 0900.

Saurashtra

Eating Order meals at one of the lodges. Nondescript shacks opposite *Sinh Sadan* sell biscuits, toothpaste, ice creams etc and also *chai*; roadside veg *dhabas* serve quite good *thalis*. *Gumalbar*, near Sinh Sadan.

Transport **Air** Nearest airport is **Keshod** (86 km). *Gujarat Airways*, T0287621918, daily to/from Mumbai via Porbandar. **Road Bus**: service to/from Junagadh (54 km), 2½ hrs, and Veraval (40 km), 2 hrs. Service to Una for Diu is unpredictable, morning dep 1100. Frequent buses from Ahmadabad. **Train** From **Junagadh** to Sasan Gir, *352*, 0650, 3 hrs, continues to **Delwada** near Diu; return to Junagadh, *351*, 1827, so possible to visit for the day. The route is very attractive. **Talala** is the last major station, 15 km before Sasan, so stock up with fruit, biscuits, liquids there. From **Veraval**, take *359* at 1039, or *353* at 1409, both bound for Khijadiya; return to **Veraval**, by *354* at 1138 or *360* at 1535.

Directory **Useful services** The post office in the village has an excellent 'frank' for postcards and letters. **Health centre**, **post office** and **bank** at Sasan. Market at Talala. **Forest office**, T8554.

Veraval Veraval is a noisy, extremely smelly, and not particularly attractive town, but it is a suitable base for visiting the Hindu pilgrimage centre of Somnath at Prabhas Patan. Before the rise of Surat, Veraval was the major seaport for pilgrims to Mecca. Its importance now is as a fishing port. The harbour is interesting and worth visiting. Sea-going *dhows* and fishing boats are still being built by the sea without the use of any instruments other than a tape-measure, traditional skills being passed down from father to son.

Sleeping **D** *Park*, Veraval-Junagadh Rd, T02876-22701. Refurbished, fairly well-appointed rooms, excellent location with spacious grounds, varied menu. **E** *Satkar*, opposite Bus Stand, T20120. Is well maintained and clean, 40 rooms, constant hot water, 8 a/c, dorm beds (Rs 50), but noisy, restaurant does good *thalis*. **D-E** *Madhuram*, Junagadh Rd, T02876-21938, F43676. Comfortable rooms, some a/c, taxis, travel desk, small cafeteria (limited menu). **D-E** *Rajdhani*, ST Rd, T23281, F41609. Some a/c rooms with modern amenities (hot showers, TV) in unimpressive building in noisy location but convenient for onward travel. **E** Gujarat Tourism *Toran Tourist Bungalow*, College Rd, T02876-20488. 6 rooms, hot showers, (Room 5 recommended), 5 dorms, run down. **F** *Railway Retiring Rooms*.

Eating *Ali Baba* near *Park Hotel*. Recommended for seafood. *Sagar*, Riddhi-Siddhi Complex, 1st flr, between bus stand and clocktower (a/c). Excellent service and food, reasonably priced veg Punjabi and South Indian. *Jill* (a/c) does mainly North Indian. *Foodlamp*, South Indian (*dosas*), *thalis* and Punjabi. Near the station: *La Bela*, *Swati* (a/c) and *New Apsara*, serve veg. *Supreme* also has non-veg.

Transport **Local** **Cycle hire**: from opposite bus station or rly station, but some are in poor condition, Rs 2 per hr, Rs 15 per day (road between Veraval and Somnath is appalling). **Taxi**: from Tower Rd and ST stands are cheaper than those at the railway station. *Deepak Ramchand Taxis*, PH 22591 has non-a/c Ambassador taxis. Transfer to Ahmedpur Mandvi via docks and Somnath Rs 500, Diu Rs 550-600, local tour of docks and Somnath Rs 200-250.

Long distance **Air**: Nearest airport is at Keshod (see above). *Somnath Travels*, Satta Bazar, will obtain tickets. **Bus**: To **Keshod** (1 hr), Diu via Kodinar, Porbandar via Chorwad and Mangrol (2 hrs), Rs 25, and to **Bhavnagar** (9 hrs). **Train**: Ahmadabad: *Somnath Mail 9923*, 1705, 11¼ hrs; *Girnar Exp 9845*, 1930, 10¾ hrs.

Saurashtra

Directory Banks *State Bank of India*, near railway station, only changes cash. No bank accepts TCs.

The **Somnath Temple**, a major Hindu pilgrimage centre, is said to have been built out of gold by Somraj, the Moon God (and subsequently in silver, wood and stone). In keeping with the legend the stone façade appears golden at sunset. Mahmud of Ghazni plundered it and removed the gates in 1024. Destroyed by successive Muslim invaders, it was rebuilt each time on the same spot.

Prabhas Patan (Somnath)
6 km E of Veraval

The final reconstruction did not take place until 1950 and is still going on. Unfortunately, it lacks character but it has been built to traditional patterns with a soaring 50-m high tower that rises in clusters. Dedicated to Siva, it has one of the 12 sacred *jyotirlingas*. ■ *Puja at 0700, 1200, 1900.*

Nearby is the ruined **Rudreshvara Temple** which dates from the same time as the Somnath Temple and was laid out in a similar fashion. The sculptures on the walls and doorways give an indication of what the original Somnath Temple was like.

Krishna was believed to have been hit by an arrow, shot by the Bhil, Jara, when he was mistaken for a deer at Bhalka Teerth nearby, and was cremated at Triveni Ghat, east of Somnath.

There is a small **Archaeological Museum** with pieces from the former temples. ■ *0900-1200, 1500-1800, closed Wed and holidays.*

Sleeping F *Mayuram*, Triveni Rd. Acceptable rooms, restaurant, good food, clean. **F** *Shri Somnath Guest House*, near temple has 20 very basic rooms, better accommodation at Veraval.

Transport Road: From Veraval, auto-rickshaw (bargain to Rs 25 return) or frequent bus (Rs 2).

★ Diu

The island of Diu has a fascinating history, some unspoilt beaches and a relaxed atmosphere with very little traffic. The north side of the island has salt pans and marshes which attract wading birds. The south coast has some fine limestone cliffs and pleasant, palm-fringed sandy beaches where government environment protection laws keep the immediate coastal strip clear of permanent structures. The branching Hoka palms, rarely seen on the mainland, were introduced from Africa by the Portuguese. Coconut palms are also very much in evidence. The island is still hardly visited by foreign travellers though its tavernas attract those deprived of alcohol from neighbouring Gujarat and the bars can get noisy especially at the weekend.

Phone code: 02875
Colour map 5, grid C4
Population: 40,000
13 km long, 3 km wide

Saurashtra

Getting there Daily flights from Mumbai arrive at the airport 6 km west of the town; auto-rickshaws charge around Rs 50 to transfer. Most visitors arrive by long distance buses either via Una or direct to the island. It is best to avoid the very poor coastal roads, and opt for rail travel to one of the towns nearby and get a bus from there. **Getting around** The small town of Diu is best seen on foot to soak in the atmosphere, while the island is ideal for exploring by cycle in the cooler season. State buses use the stand near the Ghogla bridge about 10 mins' walk from Bunder Chowk, the main square, with hotels and the market nearby. There are occasional buses from the local bus stand here to the beaches, and to Ghogla and Una.

Ins & outs
See page 331 for further details

The fishing village of Ghogla on the mainland is also part of Diu

Background Like Daman across the gulf, Diu was a Portuguese colony until 1961. In 1987 its administration was separated from Goa (some 1,600 km away), which then became a State – Diu remains a Union Territory. From the 14th to 16th centuries the Sultans of Oman held the reins of maritime power here. The Portuguese failed to take Diu at their first attempt in 1531 but succeeded three years later. Like Daman, it was once a port for the export of opium from Malwa (Madhya Pradesh) but with the decline of Portugal as a naval power it became little more than a backwater. About 5,000 of the elders here still speak fluent Portuguese. There are around 200 Catholic families and the local convent school teaches English, Gujarati, Portuguese and French. The Divechi people remain eligible for Portuguese passports and a few apply daily. Many families have a member working in Lisbon or former Portuguese Africa.

Diu town

Sights

The night market is a great place to have a drink & to wander round

The small town is squeezed between the fort on the east and a large city wall to the west. With its attractively ornamented buildings and its narrow streets and squares, it has more of a Portuguese flavour than Daman. While some visitors find it quite dirty and decaying, and are disappointed by the number of liquor shops, others find Diu delightful. Unlike Goa, there is little attempt to woo the Westerner with touristy 'ethnic' clothes and jewellery although the occasional moonlight beach party is organized.

St Paul's Church (1601-1610) has a fine baroque façade, impressive wood panelling and an attractive courtyard, and the Church of **St Francis of Assisi** (1593), part of which is a hospital (a doctor is available at 0930 for a free

Diu Town

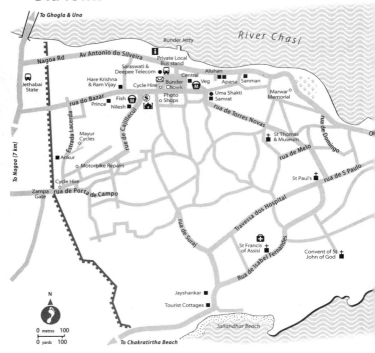

consultation). **St Thomas's Church** houses the **museum** with an interesting local collection (0800-2000). It has been renovated and now houses a collection including stone sculptures, wood carvings, and shadow clocks (as well as a café and pleasant rooms to let). These, and the fort, are floodlit at night.

Diu Fort (1535-41), considered one of the most important Portuguese forts in Asia, was built after the Mughal Emperor Humayun attacked the Sultan of Gujarat with the help of the Portuguese. It garrisoned 350 Portuguese soldiers until 1960. Skirted by the sea on three sides and a rock-cut canal on the fourth, it had two moats, one of which was tidal. Cannon and cannon balls litter the ramparts. The lighthouse stands at one end and parts of the central keep are still used as a jail but has few occupants. Some of the structures, gateways, arches, ramps, bastions, though damaged, still give us an idea of the formidable nature of the defences.It is well worth allowing an hour for a visit. ■ *0700-1800. Free.*

Makata Lane or Panchwati, near the Zampa gate, has some impressive old mansions of rich Portuguese and Indian merchants ranging from Venetian-Gothic style bungalows to typical carved wooden or stone havelis. The colourful three-storey **Nagar Sheth haveli** has porticoes, carved balconies, stone lions and intricate arches in the blend of European and Indian styles. There are plans to convert one of the mansions here into a heritage hotel. There are supposedly dozens of small underground shrines in private homes used for Hindu worship to avoid detection during periods of Muslim rule and subsequent Portuguese occupation.

Forte de Mar (Fortress of Panikot), built in 1535, was strategically important as an easily defended base for controlling the shipping lanes on the northeast part of the Arabian Sea. It has a lighthouse and a chapel to Our Lady of the Sea. It can be approa- ched from Diu jetty when canoes or motor boats are available although landing is not permitted at present.

The other fort at the eastern end of the island guarded the mint, while two others once guarded the west at Vanakbara and the bay to the south at Nagoa.

The creeks to the north of Diu island have been declared a **bird sanctuary**. There are watch towers to spot huge flocks of shore birds including oystercatchers, sanderlings, herons and plovers. Lots of ibises, flamingos, pelicans, ducks etc visit in winter (December-February). Jackals, foxes, jungle cat and porcupines are seen in the evening. Further afield, 80 km along the coast is **Somnath** via Kodinar. An alternative is to go inland to **Sasan Gir** (95 km) to visit the national park.

Excursions
Beaches nearby are listed below

Saurashtra

Sleeping

Most are fairly basic.
Some have a few a/c
rooms with TV &
charge double for the
luxury but offer good
discounts when
business is slow.
High season:
Christmas/New Year
& Apr-May, Diwali

C *Central*, Bunder Chowk, T52379, F53056. Some a/c rooms, some with seaview. **C** *Prince*, near Fish Market, T52265. 11 clean, well kept rooms (some deluxe), dorm (Rs 40), constant hot water, 1st floor rooms can be unbearably hot even at night, friendly staff. **C-D** *Ankur*, Estrada Lacerda, west of town, T52388. 13 basic rooms, 2 a/c (foreigners get good discount since they 'keep rooms cleaner than Indian guests!'), help-ful Portuguese owner. Recommended though overpriced. **C-D** *Apana Guest House*, Old Fort Rd, T52112, F52309. 29 clean rooms, 4 a/c, some with bath (best with TV, hot water, seaview and balcony) and dorm, can be noisy (mainly from Hindi films on TV) especially at weekends, roadside terrace with restaurant and bar. **C-D** *Alishan*, nearby, T52340, is similar. **C-D** *Samrat*, Collectorate Rd, T52354. 12 clean rooms, 3 a/c, balconies, good res-taurant, helpful manager. Recommended. (New hotel to open next door). **C-D** *Triveni*, opposite Sports Complex, T52045. 20 rooms with modern facilities, 4 a/c. **D-E** *Sanman*, Old Fort Rd, by the sea, T52252. 6 dark rooms, good seafood, friendly, staff, colonial house, attracts backpackers, changed management. **D** *Nilesh Guest House*, not far from fish market, T52319. 38 box-like rooms (some newer), some with bath, restaurant (average food, slow service) and lawfulî noisy bar, not best value though helpful man-ager. **D-E** *Hemal Garden*, opposite Sports Complex, T52227. 10 simple cottage like rooms, bar, restaurant, family run, pleasant garden, rather basic but pleasant. **F** *Hare Krishna*, opposite *Prince*, T52213. 9 rooms (Rs 100), basic (hard beds) but clean, some with balcony, friendly staff, popular restaurant, bar can be noisy.

Eating

Mid-range Near the museum some Catholic homes serve traditional 'Portuguese' food to Western travellers with an hour's notice (ask directions in the Christian locality near St Paul's Church): *Bom Appetite*, Mrs D'Souza's residence near St Paul's, T53137 to order 'Portuguese' lunches. *Martha's Place*, opposite the museum. Excellent home cooking, good views. **Cheap** *Apana*, Old Fort Rd. Large seafood platters (shark, lob-ster, kingfish, crab and veg), Rs 300, easily shared by 4-6. Highly recommended. Near the bus stand: *Saraswati* tea shop. Good for breakfast. Excellent *dosa* stall on opposite side of Bunder Chowk. *Ram Vijay*, near *State Bank of Saurashtra*. Excellent 'home-made' ice creams, milk shakes and sodas, friendly. Highly recommended. *St Thomas'*, great for a home-cooked evening meal and watch the sunset from the roof. *Uma Shakti*, near *Samrat*. Good food and service (try toasted cheese sandwiches).

Bars

The night market, near the post office, is very popular. King fisher beer, Turbo, London Pilsner, Rs 20-30 per bottle; tasty snacks from stalls too. Most bars close around 2130. *Nilesh* stays open until 2300.

Entertainment

Camels: On the dunes at Nagoa Rs 25. **Ponies** also available. **Watersports**: At Nagoa and Ahmedpur-Mandvi: 8-seater speed boat (10-15 mins)/parasailing/wind surfing, each Rs 500; waterskiing Rs 100 (jet skiing at Nagoa beach). A new pool/water slide com-plex is to open next to *Kohinoor* on the Diu-Nagoa road. **Evening cruises**: from Bunder Chowk jetty to Nagoa Beach, with music, Rs 100 per person; times from tourist office.

Shopping

The night market is very lively in the evenings. Government *Cottage Emporia* near the jetty sell local crafts of stone, metal and shell. *Jaysukh*, Sangaria Lane, has good shell crafts. Don't be tempted by beautiful star tortoise and turtle shell bangles and souve-nirs (originally imported from Mozambique); they are illegal under 'Wildlife Protection Act', severe penalties attached.

Local A road bridge connects Diu Town with Ghogla. **Auto-rickshaw**: Rs 30 to Nagoa. **Bus**: ST buses operate from the **Jethabai Bus Stand** near the bridge to Ghogla. **Local bus stand**: to Nagoa 3 daily; frequent service to Bucharwada-Vanakbara and Una, Rs 4 (minibus Rs 6). **Car hire**: Rs 900 per day, Rs 300 for Diu sightseeing; Rs 450 includes Nagoa beach. **Cycle hire**: *A to Z*, near Vegetable Market, Panchwati Rd, T54679; *Shilpa*, Bunder Chowk; *Mayur*, past *Ankur Hotel* (across rough ground, then 20m along alley to left), excellent bikes, unlimited use, Rs 20-30 per day, Rs 100 deposit; *Daud*, Zampa Gate, T418592, well maintained, new bikes; *Krishna Cycles* at Ghogla. **Motorbike** hire in the market area; about Rs 150 a day; *Kismet* has good new scooters Rs 100 per day, Rs 200 deposit; friendly service; repairs off Estrada Lacerda.

Transport
Buses often leave 15-20 mins early. For Bhavnagar ask for 'direct bus' (departs 1035), as some go through Mahuva & are packed

Long distance **Air**: *Gujarat Airways*, T52180; *Jet Airways*, at the airport, accepts credit card payment. Agents: *Oceanic Travels*, Bunder Chowk. **Mumbai**, daily (1050 and 1250 on alternate days), US$80.

Road **Bus**: most long distance buses operate from the Jethabai just south of the bridge; enquire beforehand. ST services to Ahmadabad via Bhavnagar, 0700 (10 hrs); Jamnagar via Junagadh, 0600; Porbandar, 1300; Rajkot, several 0445-1725 (7 hrs); Vadodara, 1730; Veraval, several 0400-1300 (2½ hrs). Private agents in the Main Sq offer buses from the private bus stand to Mumbai (deluxe) at 1000, and towns in Gujarat which are more reliable than ST buses. Ahmadabad, 1900; from Ahmadabad, a direct bus leaves from Paldi Chowrasta at 2100. *Goa Travels* runs buses to Bhavnagar, Junagadh (5 hrs), Palitana. A daily bus connects with **Mumbai** via Bhavnagar (20 hrs). **Una**, 30 mins from Diu (10 km), has more frequent buses to Ahmadabad, Bhavnagar, Junagadh, Rajkot, Veraval etc. *Shiv Shakti, Sahajanand* and *Gayatri Travels* run private buses from the main Bus Station to Ahmadabad, Bhavnagar, Mumbai, Vadodara etc. From Vanakbara, bus to Okha, 0700, 0800.

Train Delwada, 8 km north is the nearest railhead just south of Una; shared auto-rickshaws available from Diu to Una or Delwada, Rs 10 plus Rs 10 for rucksack! The station is a short walk from the centre of town – follow the locals! Slow train to **Junagadh** (stops at **Sasan Gir**) *351*, 1445; to **Veraval** *364*, 0615.

Banks *State Bank of Saurashtra*, near fish market opposite *Nilesh Hotel*, accepts TCs but not foreign currency immediately (only encashed after notes are verified by HQ); very slow. Authorised dealers next to *Reshma Travels* and *Alishan Hotel* are more efficient for exchange (sterling and US$ TCs and currency). **Communications** The main post office is on Bunder Chowk, the other is at Ghogla. **Internet** *Deepee* Telecom and cyber café, Bunder Chowk. **Medical services** *Manesh Medical Store* is a pharmacy with a doctor in the building. **Tour operators** *Oceanic*, Bunder Chowk, T521800; *Reshma*, T52241. **Tourist offices** At Tourist Complex, Ghogla. Mon-Fri, 0930-1315, 1400-1745. Information Asst, Diu jetty north of Bunder Chowk, T52212.

Directory

Saurashtra

Beaches near Diu

Several beaches on the south side of Diu Island are easy to get to from Diu town by cycle or auto-rickshaw. Beaches between Nagoa and Vanakbara are safe throughout the year except between May and July and are pleasantly empty, as is the beach along Ghogla. However, beware of the giant thorns which are hazardous to cycle tyres.

The beach to the south is lovely and the nearest to Diu. On the down side though there have been several reports of groups of teenage boys who not only come to watch and pester tourists but aggressively offer sex.

Jallandhar Beach

Sleeping and eating C *Pelican Resort*, T52654. 6 spacious rooms (2 a/c) in 3 cottages with sea views, clean but maintenance needed, reasonable restaurant. **E** *Jay Shankar Guest House*, next door, 1 min from beach, T52424. 15 rooms (Rs 200), some with bath, small dorm (Rs 50), excellent *Neelkant's Restaurant* serves delicious cheap *thalis*, new a/c for continental food, backpackers' meeting place, friendly, family run. Highly recommended.

Chakratirtha Beach Chakratirtha Beach just southwest, has a sunset view point, an open auditorium, and a small beach which is no longer the picture it was. This was a popular promenade for the townspeople until 'ruined by the cabins which are, in a way, the beginning of the end of beautiful beaches like Chakratirth' as an environment-conscious local person regrets.

Sleeping and eating D *Cabins*, 20 with bunks, a/c and non a/c. Colourful with Portuguese/Gujarati themes, attached baths, refrigerators, outstanding sea views. Reserve at *Pelican Resorts*, T52654. The nearest restaurant is in Jallandhar.

Fudam Just east of Diu Town, Fudam or Fofrara has the air of a Portuguese village with the crumbling Church of Our Lady of the Remedies. The **Malala Mines** are limestone quarries off the Nagoa road. The **Gangeshwar** temple nearby has an attractive Nandi and Sivalinga washed by the sea at high tide.

Sleeping and eating B-C *Kohinoor*, Fofrara, Diu-Nagoa Rd, T52209, F52613. 28 rooms in ritzy resort, most a/c, good restaurant serves Portuguese dishes, pool, gym-sauna, modern and pleasant rooms and amenities but no views, pastry shop and disco, gym, pool and water slide complex next door. **F** *Church hostel*, in the old Fudam church, simple rooms (Rs 100), use of kitchen, really quiet and pleasant. **F** *Estrella do Mar*, has basic rooms.

Nagoa Facing the Arabian Sea, 7 km from town, Nagoa offers the best location for a quiet stay away from Diu town. Its semi-circular palm-fringed beach suitable for swimming is popular with foreigners but also large numbers of Indian tourists who come to watch. There are quieter beaches nearby and the forests are pleasant for walks. A new **Sea Shell Museum** has opened near on the road from the airport to Nagoa. It displays a large number of mollusc and crustacean shells, corals, fish and marine life from the world over collected by a retired merchant navy captain. ■ *Rs 10*.

The entire stretch from Nagoa is being landscaped for development

Sleeping B *Radhika Beach Resort*, close to the beach, T52553, F52552. 24 comfortable a/c rooms in well designed 2-storey 'villas', excellent a/c restaurant, very good pool in beautifully tended garden, prompt service, small provisions store handy for beach. Recommended. **C-D** *Ganga Sagar*, right on the beach, T52249. 20 rather dirty cell-like rooms, some with bath (Rs 350). **D-F** *The Resort Hoka*, 100 m from the beach among *Hoka* palms and trees, T53036, F52298, resort_hoka@hot mail.com 10 decent rooms with bath (Rs 450), 3 with shared facilities (Rs 300-350), clean, pleasant garden restaurant (serves fresh fish), bar, laundry, travel, friendly management, good discounts for long stays, not very luxurious but pleasant and good value. Recommended. At **Kevdi** (2½ km away): **D** *Sea Gull*, 4 rooms.

Eating Mid-range: *Radhika Beach Resort*, wide choice of Indian, Chinese, some Continental. Well prepared meals from spotless kitchen, pleasant a/c surroundings and attentive service. **Cheap**: *Island Bar*, on Nagoa-Diu Rd, varied menu including Punjabi, Chinese, Continental. Food can be excellent or indifferent, service can be slow.

Transport Rickshaws from Diu bus stand, 20 mins, Rs 30, or hire a bicycle.

Ghogla's name changes to Ahmedpur Mandvi on crossing to the Gujarat side **Ghogla-** of the border. The beach is good for swimming and it has splendid views of **Ahmedpur** fishing villages and the fort and churches on Diu island. *Jyoti Watersports* and **Mandvi** *Magico Do Mar* offer a variety of watersports here including parasailing, speed boating and waterskiing. Beware of the **rip tide** just a few metres out to sea which has claimed several lives.

Sleeping and eating B-C *Magico do Mar*, T52116. Charming complex of 14 a/c huts with Saurashtrian décor, around a 1930s mansion of a Junagadh Nawab (best Nos 510-123), sea-facing lawns, *Hoka* palm groves, cheaper non a/c rooms in unimpressive bungalow next to the cottage resort needing renovation (with "more wildlife than Sasan Gir.. lizards in bed, and beefy cockroaches"), but fantastic views, eat in the mansion or the garden (excellent fish), some watersports, folk shows, staff friendly and helpful, charming setting, more expensive for foreigners. **B-C** *Suzlon Beach*, T52212. Cluster of attractive bungalows with good sized, well appointed a/c rooms, restaurant, bar, terrace opens onto beach and sea but lacks atmosphere. **B-C** *Sea View*, next to beach, T52371. 12 comfortable rooms, some a/c, most with sea views, modern facilities but rather garish décor, loud Hindi film music. **D** *Premalayai*, T52270. Simple rooms, serves Indian food.

Transport The bus between Una and Ghogla may stop if you request, otherwise take a rickshaw from Ghogla for 3 km, or take a shorter path on foot along the beach. The hotels are 3 km from Diu bridge off the Una Rd (right turn past the gate).

Bucharwada, to the north, lacks attractive beaches but has cheap spartan **Other beaches** rooms in *Viswas* hotel. **Gomtimata**, a secluded white-sand beach to the west, is where a *Tourist Hostel* is expected to open. **Vanakbara**, the fishing village on the western tip of the island, has the Church of Our Lady of Mercy. Get to the early morning fish market and watch the colourful trawlers unload catches of shark, octopus and every kind of fish imaginable. The drying fish on "washing lines" and waterside activities provide ample photo opportunities. You can also watch traditional dhow building. There is a ferry service across to Gomtimata. **C-D** *Hotel Maheshwari*, T51310, is on the road to Bucharwada. **Simbor Beach** is a pleasant and little known beach. It is 27 km from Diu town, off the Una road, and can be reached in 45 minutes from Diu by hiring a moped or scooter. Take something to eat and drink.

Saurashtra

Diu Island

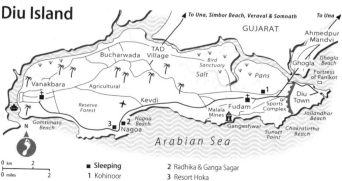

Porbandar

Phone code: 0286
Colour map 5, grid B2

The town is closely
associated with
Mahatma Gandhi

The port town on the coast of western Saurashtra has little to attract the visitor other than its close association with Mahatma Gandhi. The town beach is polluted and unsuitable for swimming though the tradition of dhow *building which continues on the seashore to the present day reflects Porbandar's maritime past when traded with North Africa and Arabia. Today, it produces gold and silver trinkets, manufactures fine quality silk and cotton and has chemical and cement factories.*

Sights Mahatma Gandhi was born in Porbandar in 1869. Next to the family home with its carved balconies is **Kirti Mandir**, a small museum that traces his life and contains memorabilia and a library. It is open from sunrise to sunset, but the guide takes a lunch break from 1300-1400. **Darbargadh**, a short walk from Kirti Mandir, the old palace of the Maharanas of Porbandar, built in the 1780s, is now deserted and has some intricate carvings and carved balconies. The rooms inside (if you can get in!) have interesting paintings. **Sartanji** (or Rana-no) **Choro** (1785), near the ST stand, is the beautiful pleasure pavilion of Maharajah Sartanji, a great poet, writer and music lover. The pavilion has domes, pillars and carved arches and its four sides represent the four seasons. The Maharana's deserted sprawling **Hazur Palace** is near the seafront. Ask for permission to visit the rooms inside at the office. **Daria Rajmahal**, the splendid turn-of-the-century palace of the Maharana of Porbandar, now a college, has intricate carvings, courtyards, fountains, carved arches and heavily embellished façades. The tower has excellent views of the seashore. **Chaya**, 2 km from Chowpatty sea face, is the old capital of the Jetwas. The Darbargadh Palace with a beautiful carved balcony, is believed to have secret tunnels and passages to temples and places of safety.

Porbandar

The **Bharat Mandir Hall** in Dayananda Vatika garden is across the Jubilee (Jyubeeli) Bridge. It has a large marble relief map of India on the floor and bas reliefs of heroes from Hindu legends on the pillars. Nearby **Arya Kanya Gurukul** is an experiment in education for girls based on ancient Indian tradition. The **Planetarium** has shows in Gujarati only. The architecture incorporates different religious styles illustrating Gandhi's open mind.

Jhavar Creek attracts scores of waterbirds. Flamingos, pelicans, storks and herons can be seen from the road gathering in the mangrove marshes. Fisheries have appeared around the creek where the fish put out to dry attract thousands of terns and gulls. The town beaches are polluted and unsuitable for swimming.

Bileshwar, 30 km away, is home to the early seventh-century Siva Temple with a multi-storey (*shikhara*) tower, one of the finest examples of early Hindu architecture in Gujarat, though the external decoration is somewhat covered by subsequent plastering. **Excursions**

Khambala Dam, 25 km away on the road to Ghumli, has created a scenic reservoir in the wooded Barda hills where the 1920s royal country lodge, Anant Niwas Palace, is decorated with classical sculptures, royal portraits and art deco furniture. It can be visited with permission from the Huzoor Palace in Porbandar. The hilltop site offers magnificent views.

The picturesque gorge at **Ghumli**, about 20 km north of Bileshwar, has ruins dating from the Solanki period (10th-13th centuries). The Vikia Vav (early 12th century), is one of the largest step-wells in Gujarat with decorated pavilions.

Khimeshwar, 15 km on Porbandar-Dwarka highway, has an ancient temple with a very pretty white sand beach with dunes and splendid seaviews. The scenic marshes near **Kuchri** village have plenty of birdlife, and **Madhavpur** beach has a historic temple where a fair in March to April is attended by Mer and Koli tribals. The Mer women in colourful costumes perform graceful dances of the Krishna legend.

C-D *Kuber*, Bhavsinhji Park, near ST station, T241025. The best in town, 19 rooms, most a/c, suites with fridge, restaurant (residents only), friendly and helpful manager, free airport transfer. Recommended. **C-D** *Indraprastha*, near ST Station, T242681. Modern hotel, comfortable non a/c rooms Rs 450, a/c Rs 900. **D** *New Oceanic*, Chowpatty, T20217. 17 rooms (10 new) some a/c, sea views, modern, good garden restaurant (Western, Indian) but rather expensive. **D-E** *Sheetal*, Arya Samaj Rd, opposite GPO, T247596, F241821. Some a/c rooms with shower, limited room service, "a 70s movie motel!". **D-E** *Host*, Blvd Bhavsinhji Park, T241901, F23888. 14 rooms, some a/c, Indian veg meals on the terrace garden, *Sanam* restaurant downstairs. **D-E** *Flamingo*, MG Rd, T23123. With some comfortable rooms (inspect), some larger dearer a/c, restaurant. **D-E** *Moon* ST Rd, near Bhavsinhji Park, ST Rd, T241172. Clean, cosy rooms with bath. **E** Gujarat Tourism *Toran Tourist Bungalow*, Chowpatty, 3 km centre, T22746. 20 rooms, 6 large a/c, 4 cheap dorms, quiet, sea views, neglected and run-down, no hot water, towels or soap, Gujarati meals on prior notice, some tourist information. **E** *Vaibhav*, MG Rd. Some a/c rooms. **F** *Rajkamal*, MG Rd. Basic rooms with toilets (Rs 80). **Sleeping**

Cheap *Adarsh*, MG Rd. A/c, Indian vegetarian and ice creams. *Khana Khazana*, MG Rd. Open sunset to past midnight, is recommended for cheese/chutney sandwiches, cheese toasts, burgers and coffee; South Indian snacks (hot *idlis*) on Sun; also takeaway. *Mehta*, Sudama Chowk. Snacks and ice creams. *Modern* near MG Rd. A/c, good non-veg meals, some seafood. *Raghuvanshi* near *Khadi Bhandar*. Good Gujarati *thalis*. *Swagath* MG Rd. Excellent *thalis*, pleasant. The bazar sells *khajli* (fried dough snack), *thabdi* and *peda* (milk sweets).

Eating
Sudama Chowk near the ST Stand is where locals gather for samosas, pakodas, bhel, kachori, pau bhaji etc in the evening

Saurashtra

Transport **Local** **Autorickshaws**: Fix price. **Bicycle hire**: From opposite Bus Stand. **Long distance** **Air**: Flights to **Mumbai, Road**: ST buses serve most centres of Gujarat. ***Bharat*** and ***Eagle Travels*** run regular private luxury buses to Ahmadabad, Jamnagar, Junagadh, Rajkot etc. **Train**: **Mumbai Central**: *Saurashtra Exp 9216*, 2000, 23½ hrs via Rajkot (8 hrs) and Ahmadabad (11 hrs).

Directory **Banks** *Bank of India*, Kedareshwar Rd, and ***State Bank of India***, MG Rd (and sometimes ***Bank of Baroda***) change TCs of reputed companies. After some frauds and fake notes, they are usually wary of currency.

★ Jamnagar

Phone code: 0288
Colour map 5, grid B3
Population: 381,600

Jamnagar, now an expanding town, was a 16th-century pearl fishing centre with one of the biggest pearl fisheries in the world until the beginning of the 20th century. The famous cricketer Ranjitsinghji was its ruler from 1907-33.

Ins & outs The bus stand is about 3 km west of the town centre – if arriving from Rajkot and planning to stay in Bedi Gate area, get off near the Gate (easily spotted) and walk 5-mins or take a rickshaw to the hotel.

Sights

The temple is in the 'Guinness Book of Records' for the continuous chanting (13,527 days over 37 years, 1 Sep 2001)

The **walled city** is famous for its embroidery, silverware and *bandhani* (tie-and-dye) fabrics which are produced in workshops in the narrow lanes. Pirotan Island in the middle of the Ranmal lake in the Old City, reached by a stone bridge, has the **Lakhota Fort** and **Kotha Bastion** with its arsenal. ■ *1030-1300, 1500-1730, closed Wed, 2nd and 4th Sun, no photography (unless tipped)*. The fort museum has a collection of sculpture and pottery found in ruined medieval villages nearby. It is also a pleasant, cool and quiet spot just to relax while listening to strains of '*Shri Ram, Jai Ram, Jai Jai Ram*' wafting across the lake from the **Bala Hanuman Temple**. The temple is worth a visit, especially early evening. The bastion has an old well from which water can be drawn by blowing into a small hole in the floor. The **Solarium** uses solar radiation to cure diseases. The **Jain temples** in the Old City are profusely decorated with glass, gilding and mirrors.

Excursions **Khijadia Lakes**, 10 km northeast of Jamnagar, are three freshwater lakes surrounded by salt pans and salt marshes. Popular with visitors interested in their rich birdlife, there is now also a 600 ha bird sanctuary. Entirely flooded in the wet season, the lakes remain fresh throughout the dry season, though they occasionally dry out completely. The lakes are an important staging post for migratory birds, including swallows, martins and wagtails, and many waterfowl.

Marine National Park, 30 km away, offshore from the southern coast of the Gulf of Kachchh, comprises an archipelago of 42 islands noted for their coral reefs and mangroves. It is possible to see dolphins, finless porpoise and sea turtles and a variety of colourful tropical fish. The area also attracts a host of waterbirds. The best island to visit is 1½ sq km **Pirotan**, which is uninhabited save for lighthouse staff. A permit is needed acquired the Director, Marine National Park, Jamnagar. ■ *Getting there: hire motor boats for 15-45 people from Jamnagar jetty (or from Okha); take a guide.*

Sleeping

Budget hotels are on Old Station Rd & in the New supermarket area

New **B** *Park Plaza* is best in town. **C-D** *Aram* (Heritage Hotel), Pandit Nehru Rd, 3 km northwest from centre, T551701, F554957. Good a/c rooms in 1940s character mansion (bit garish), Raj memorabilia, pleasant veg garden restaurant, friendly, good service. Recommended. **C-D** *Express*, Motikhavdi, out of town, towards the sea.

120 rooms, pool, gym, modern facilities. **C-D** *President*, Teen Batti, T557491, F558491.
27 clean rooms, some a/c, relaxing a/c restaurant (wide menu, efficient service). Recommended. **D-E** *Aashiana*, New Supermarket, Bedi Gate, 3rd Flr, T676525. 34 rooms,
14 clean a/c rooms with TV, simple restaurant serving inexpensive Indian veg, good
value. Recommended. **D-E** *Punit*, Pandit Nehru Marg, north of Teen Batti, T670560,
F670966. Reasonable, clean rooms, some a/c, better at rear, good value.

Kalpana, near Teen Batti. Cheap veg dishes, fruit ices from next door. *Ram*, Teen Batti.   **Eating**
Excellent dairy ice creams. *Rangoli*, near Anupam Talkies, near Bedi Gate. A/c, good but
more expensive veg Punjabi and South Indian, friendly, open lunch time and evening
(except Wed). Recommended. *Urvee*, Supermarket, Town Hall Rd, T671207. Good
Gujarati *thalis* at lunch time.

Air: Airport, 10 km west. *Indian Airlines*, T550211; to **Mumbai**. **Road Bus**: STC ser-   **Transport**
vices to Rajkot (frequent) and Ahmadabad; also Dwarka and Porbandar. **Train**: The rly
station is 6 km northwest of town. **Ahmadabad**: *Saurashtra Exp 9216*, 2243, 7¼ hrs;
Saurashtra Mail 9006, 1445, 7½ hrs. Both to **Mumbai Central**: 20¾ hrs and 17½ hrs via
Rajkot: 1¾ hrs and 2¼ hrs. **Vadodara (and Ahmadabad)**: *Okha-Puri Exp* 1115.

Communications *Head Post Office* at Chandni Chowk. Forestry Office, T552077.   **Directory**

★ Dwarka

A small coastal town on the tip of the Kathiawad Peninsula, Dwarka is one of the   Phone code: 02892
most sacred sites for Vaishnavite Hindus. It has the unique distinction of being one   Colour map 5, grid B1
of Hinduism's four 'Holy Abodes' as well as one of its seven 'Holy Places'. Heavily   Population: 27,800
geared up to receive pilgrims, the people are easy-going, friendly and welcoming,
even to the rarely seen tourist. The beach is good but without any palms for shade.

Archaeological excavations indicate that present day Dwarka is built on the   **Background**
sites of four former cities. Work in 1990 by the marine archaeologist SR Rao
discovered triangular anchors weighing 250 kg similar to those used in
Cyprus and Syria during the Bronze Age, suggesting that ships of up to
120 tonnes had used the port around the 14th century BC. Much of the town
was submerged by rising sea levels.

The present town is largely 19th century when the Gaekwad princes developed the town as a popular pilgrimage centre. Celebrated as Krishna's capital
after his flight from Mathura, thousands come to observe Krishna's birthday,
and also at Holi and Diwali.

Saurashtra

Sights The 12th-century **Rukmini Temple** has beautifully carved mandapa columns and a fine sanctuary doorway, but much else is badly weathered.

Dwarkadisha Temple, mainly 16th century, was supposedly built in one night, and some believe that the inner sanctum is 2,500 years old. The sanctuary walls probably date from the 12th century but it is suggested that the 50 m high tower which rises in a series of balconied layers is much later. The exterior is more interesting. The soaring five-storey tower is supported by 60 columns. The BJP started its '*Rath Yatra*' pilgrimage across India to the Babri Masjid in Ayodhya here in 1989, leading to widespread communal rioting. ■ *0600-1200, 1700-2100. Non-Hindus are presented with a form to complete by a temple 'Home Guard' and are allowed in after indicating some level of commitment to Hinduism and to Krishna (several choices given). No photography is allowed inside the temple. Cameras must be handed over at the entrance. Some visitors have been approached for a 'minimum donation' of Rs 100.*

The good humoured lighthouse keepers may treat you to a free private guided tour in exchange for any foreign coin (they all 'collect'). The views are beautiful – a very peaceful place to rest a while. ■ *1600-1800 or 1 hr before sunset, whichever is earlier, Re 1, no photography.*

Outside Dwarka, the **Nageshwar Mandir** contains one of the 12 *jyotirlingas* in an underground sanctum. Work is in progress. It helps to be fairly agile if you wish to catch a glimpse. **Gopi Talav Teerth** is associated with Krishna (and Arjun) and contains several shrines in the complex.

Tours Dwarka Darshan a tour of four local pilgrimage sites (Nageshwar Mandir, Gopi Talav Teerth, Beyt Dwarka, Rukmini Temple) by minibus, dep 0800, 1400, five hours (can take seven!). Tickets Rs 30. Book a day in advance for morning tour. Alternatively, visit only Beyt Dwarka for a worthwhile day spent with pilgrims.

Sleeping & eating
Most hotels are poorly maintained Poor choice of rather shoddy & dirty eating places

Off-season prices drop dramatically from Rs 150 to around Rs 70, on the appearance of a questioning frown. Best is **D-E** *Radhika*, opposite State Transport Bus Stand, T361754. Adequate rooms but dining not recommended. **E-F** *Toran Tourist Dormitories*, near Govt Guest House, T361313. 6 rooms with nets, dorm, checkout 0900. **F** *Meera* near rly station, T361335. Friendly, excellent *thalis*. **F** *Satnam Wadi*, near the beach. Rooms with bath and sea view. Recommended.

Festivals Aug/Sep: *Janmashtami* (see page 58). Special worship and fair (12 **Aug** 2001; 31 Aug 2002).

Transport **Road Bus**: To Jamnagar, Porbandar and Somnath. Private operators run to most major towns in Gujarat. **Train**: **Ahmadabad and Vadodara**: *Saurashtra Mail 9006*, 1215, 10 hrs, and **Mumbai Central**: 20 hrs. Also *Okha-Puri Exp* 0835.

Okha A small port at the head of the Gulf of Kachchh, Okha is 32 km north of Dwarka with a few **F** category hotels. You can visit the Marine National Park by hiring a motor boat from the jetty (see under Jamnagar). A pilgrimage to Dwarka is not complete until the island of **Beyt Dwarka** is visited off the coast from Okha. This is where Krishna is believed to have resided whilst Dwarka was his capital. The 19th-century temple complex contains several shrines and images of Krishna and his 56 consorts. Archaeological excavations have revealed Harappan artefacts dating from the second millennium BC. ■ *Getting there: From Ahmadabad by Saurashtra Mail 9006, 1120, 10¾ hrs. Local buses to Dwarka, 1 hr. Morning direct bus to Bhuj. From Okha, boats to Beyt Dwarka take 10-15 mins, each way.*

Kachchh

12

Kachchh

★ Kachchh (Kutch)

The scenic Maliya Miyana bridge, across salt marshes often filled with birds, gives a beguilingly attractive impression of the gateway to Kachchh. Yet perhaps this region is climatically the least appealing of Gujarat, and it is certainly the most sparsely populated. It is well and truly off the beaten tourist trail. The various communities such as Rabaris, Ahirs and Meghwals among others, each have a distinct dress and practise a particular craft. Kachchh was the region of Gujarat which suffered worst from the January 2001 earthquake, from which it is struggling to recover.

A deserted world

The region, the central peninsula, is surrounded by the seasonally flooded Great and Little Ranns. The Gulf of Kachchh to the south, a large inlet of the Arabian Sea, has a marine national park and sanctuary with 42 islands and a whole range of reefs, mudflats, coastal salt marsh and India's largest area of mangrove swamps.

The **Kachchh Peninsula** is relatively high, covered with sheets of volcanic lava but with often saline soil. Dry and rocky, there is little natural surface water though there are many artificial tanks and reservoirs. Intensive grazing has inhibited the development of the rich vegetation around the tanks characteristic of neighbouring Sindh in Pakistan, and there is only sparse woodland along the often dry river beds. The wetlands are severely over-exploited, but some of the lakes are important seasonal homes for migratory birds including pelicans and cormorants.

The Rann of Kachchh, the low lying Rann in the north, a part of the Thar desert, is a hard smooth bed of dried mud in the dry season. Some vegetation exists, concentrated on little grassy islands called bets, which remain above water level when the monsoons flood the mudflats. See Little Rann of Kachchh Wildlife Sanctuary below.

The monsoon

With the arrival of the southwest monsoon in June the saltwater of the Gulf of Kachchh invades the Rann and the Rajasthan rivers pour freshwater into it. It then becomes an inland sea and very dangerous for those who get trapped in it (in ancient times armies perished there). At this time Kachchh virtually becomes an island. From December to February, the **Great Rann** is the winter home of migratory flamingos when they arrive near **Khavda**. There are also sand-grouse, Imperial grouse, pelicans and avocets.

Kachchh

Handicrafts

Local traditional embroidery and weaving is particularly prized. When the monsoons flooded vast areas of Kachchh, farming had to be abandoned and handicrafts flourished which not only gave expression to artistic skills but also provided a means of earning a living. Mirrorwork, Kachchh appliqué and embroidery with beads, *bandhani* (tie-and-dye), embroidery on leather, gold and silver jewellery, gilding and enamelling and colourful wool-felt *namda* rugs are available.

Another important activity is **salt** production and railway lines back into the Rann to provide transport.

Festivals

Kutch Mahotsav, a desert festival, (10-12 March, 2002). Gujarat Tourism organizes tours of Bhuj and other towns and villages where craftsmen demonstrate their skills, and to pilgrimage centres and archaeological excavations.

The Kachchh earthquake

The area around Bhuj was devastated by the severe earthquake which hit Gujarat on the morning of 26th January 2001. With its epicentre near Bhuj, the massive quake reached 7.7 on the Richter scale and the tremors were felt as far away as Kolkata in the east, Chennai in the south and the Himalaya in the north. They virtually flattened the town of Bhuj and several nearby villages including Dhamanka and Bachau to the east, Zura to the north, and Anjar to the southeast. New tower blocks in Ahmadabad collapsed and people across the state were terrified by the two and a half minute tremors.

Within hours it was clear that thousands had been killed, the final count exceeding 30,000. Almost immediately volunteers began to pour into the region from elsewhere in India and abroad, setting up emergency medical and food centres. In May 2001 some areas were getting back to normal and the region was desperately keen to start welcoming visitors again. Some hotels had already reopened but some museums and monuments were severely damaged, and some, like the Chatedis, have crumbled. The surrounding villages and sites such as Dholavira and Mandvi are recovering and can now be visited again. Bhadreswar was badly hit but renovations are progressing at the Jain temples. Seek local advice from Gujarat Tourism before travelling to Kachchh.

Bhuj

Phone code: 02832
Colour map 5, grid A2
Population: 120,000

The old part of this walled town is a tightly packed maze of narrow winding streets where horse drawn tongas go about their business and the odd camel trundles past. It is a town with some character, where you breathe the air of the past, rub shoulders with tribal people turned out in colourful traditional costumes and where friendly shopkeepers in the bazar have not learnt the art of high pressure sales.

Ins & outs
See page 347 for further details

The whole of Bhuj closes from 1200-1500

Getting there Daily flights from Mumbai have made access easier but airlines are inclined to cancel their service when not many want to travel. The airport is 5 km north of town with taxis and auto-rickshaws (Rs 30) transfer. The metre gauge station is a km north of the city, while buses arrive at the stand to the south, not far from several, rather noisy, budget hotels. **Getting around** Auto-rickshaws run around town for about Rs 10, or you can hire a bike or scooter near the bus stand. Buses go to the principal villages around Bhuj, though a car with a driver is preferable.

History The town's 10.5-m high stone defensive wall, forming an irregular polygon studded with towers and five gates, is a reminder of Bhuj's medieval defences. The local raja, Rao Khengarji I, chose this to be his capital in 1548. The existing walls were built in 1723, though subsequently the town fell twice to attacking forces, on the latter occasion to the British in 1819. Far greater damage was caused in the same year by the great earthquake of Gujarat, which is reported to have destroyed 7,000 houses and killed over 1,000 people. The **Bhujia Fort** (1718-41) stands on a hill to the southeast, while it is bounded on the west by the Hamirsar Lake and the often dry Desalsar to the east. The Fort cannot be visited since it is occupied by the army.

The town Despite its rapid growth and the addition of new buildings since the eastern wall was knocked down after Independence to allow it to expand, Bhuj retains some of its picturesque medieval character. Some of the older buildings have

Kachchh

survived and can still be seen in the atmospheric bazar area. Take a walk down there at dawn (0400!), when shopkeepers begin to set up their stalls and merchandise – very surreal! However, visitors with high expectations will be disappointed by the usual dirt, noise and dust, and some report aggressive behaviour (stone throwing, pinching). **Further reading** *The Black hills – Kutch in History and legends*, by Rushbrook Williams, 1958. Rs 90, available locally.

Sights

Among the old buildings in the citadel is the palace of **Rao Lakha** (circa 1752), the fortunate patron of Ramsingh Malam, who after his European adventures became a master clockmaker, architect, glass-blower, tile-maker and much more. A large white mansion with carvings and fretwork, the palace contains a Darbar Hall, State Apartments and the noted **Aina Mahal** (Mirror Palace). It has exquisite ivory inlaid doors (circa 1708), china floor tiles and marble walls covered with mirrors and gilt decorations. In 1823, Colonel Tod described the English and Dutch chiming clocks, all playing at once! There are portraits, 18th-century lithographs, crystals and paintings. ■ *Rs 10*. The **Fuvara Mahal** (Music Room), next door, is a curiosity. Surrounded by a narrow walkway, the pleasure hall is a shallow tiled pool with a central platform where the Maharao sat in cool comfort to listen to music, watch dancers or recite his poetry. With its entrance shielded from the hot Kachchhi sun, the candlelit interior with embroidered wall hangings provided a welcome refuge. Ingenious pumps, designed by Ramsingh who was responsible for much of the palace's treasures, raised water to the tank above to feed the pool with sprinkling fountains. The small State Apartment has silk embroidery lining the floors and walls and the Art Gallery (Kala-Atari) contains some interesting items. ■ *Daily 0900-1200, 1500-1800, closed Sat, Rs 5. No photography, but the tourist office here sells good quality postcards and a booklet.*

The old palace

Rao Pragmalji's Palace (1865) in red brick is across the courtyard. The elaborate anachronism was designed by the British engineer Colonel Wilkins (though some guides will say by an Italian architect), to replace some stables and outhouses. It contained a vast Darbar Hall (12 m high), with verandahs, corner towers and *zenanas* all opulently decorated with carving, gilding, Minton tiles and marble. It is now used as government offices so only the Darbar Hall is open to visitors. ■ *0900-1200, 1500-1800, closed Wed, 2nd and 4th Sat in month, Rs 10, camera Rs 15, video Rs 50 (professionals must give 2 days' notice).*

Rao Pragmalji's Palace
Good views of the surrounding countryside from the tall clocktower connected to the palace by covered galleries

The colourful newer **Swaminarayan Temple** is behind the Palace and near the bazar. ■ *Closed 1200-1500.*

At Hathistan, Sarpat Gate, are the historic stables of the Maharao, where he kept his nine elephants. The gates are embellished with carvings of Ganesh and Hanuman. Some of the prettiest gates of the walled citadel and many colonial period buildings can be seen here.

Hathistan

Sarad Bagh Palace, west of Hamirsar, the last residence of the Maharao (died 1991) is set in very pleasant gardens where there is a plant nursery. Exhibits include hunting trophies, furniture, exotic ornaments. ■ *0900-1200, 1500-1800, closed Fri, camera Rs 10, video Rs 50.*

Sarad Bagh Palace

Kachchh

Maharaos'
chatedis
These memorial tombs, further south, built of red sandstone were severely damaged in the 1819 earthquake. Rao Lakha's polygonal chatedi (1770) contains beautiful statues of deities, Rao Lakha on horseback and *Sati stones* of 15 court musicians who committed *jauhar* after his death. The chatedi of Rao Pragmalji's father, Rao Desalji, has impressively carved wall panels, while Rao Pragmalji's own memorial has excellent modern carving. **Ramkund**, nearby, has a stone lined tank with carvings of Hindu deities.

Museums
For Aina Mahal
Museum, see above
The Italianate **Kachchh Museum** (1877), near Mahadev Gate, is the oldest in Gujarat. Exhibits include the largest collection of Kshatrap inscriptions (the earliest, of 89 AD), textiles, weaponry, paintings and an anthropological section ñ well maintained. Anyone interested in local traditional folk music and instruments may contact Mr UP Jadia here. ■ *Jul-Apr, 0900-1200, 1500-1800; May-Jun, 0830-1130, 1600-1900, closed Wed, 2nd and 4th Sat each month. Rs 2; Camera, Rs 2 per photo.*

Bharatiya Sanskriti Darshan, Mandvi Road, near Collector's Office. The small, delightful **Folk Museum** and Reference Library was developed by a

Bhuj

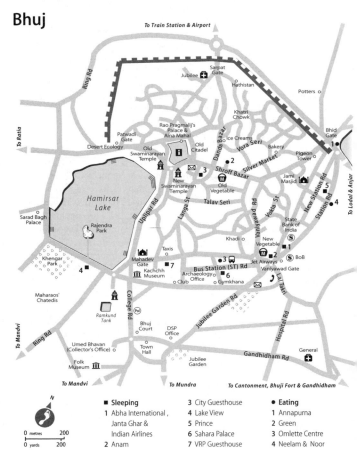

To Train Station & Airport

Kachchh

■ Sleeping	3 City Guesthouse	● Eating
1 Abha International ,	4 Lake View	1 Annapurna
Janta Ghar &	5 Prince	2 Green
Indian Airlines	6 Sahara Palace	3 Omlette Centre
2 Anam	7 VRP Guesthouse	4 Neelam & Noor

scholar of Kachchh culture, the late Mr Ram Sinh Rathore. The collection of 4,500 exhibits includes traditional handicrafts, textiles, weaponry, as well as artefacts of historic or artistic importance, and a recreated village of typical Kachchhi *bhungas* (huts) of different communities. *Kutch – People and their handicrafts* by PJ Jethi (Rs 100), and superb black/white postcards (Rs 6) for sale. ■ *Mon-Sat, 0900-1200, 1500-1800, Rs 5, camera Rs 50.*

Rudrani Dam, 14 km north, has the colourful Rudramata Temple (originally 17th century) nearby. Sati's 'rudra' (frightening) aspect is believed to have fallen on this spot and is hence a place of pilgrimage. You can stay at **B** *Garha Safari Lodge*, T079-6579672, F6575201, which has 14 white-washed *bhungas* (local style huts, tribal furniture), hot water, seven air-cooled (Rs 1,800), pricey soft drinks (even 'billed for welcome drink!'), exchange, pool, highly atmospheric, good views of lake, jeep tours (Rs 850 each), but mixed reports about food, cleanliness and service. ■ *Getting there: 30-mins drive from Bhuj on the Sumrasar Rd.* **Excursions**

The **Crafts villages** nearby are still worth visiting (see below), though some may be disappointed that quality has been sacrificed in order to satisfy increasing demand. You may not see crafts actually being produced and rumours suggest that much is being 'imported' from other areas. **Qasab** is an outlet for KMVS (Kutch Mahila Vikas Sangathan), a collective of 1,200 crafts-women from 130 local villages who are practising their traditional skills to produce high quality clothes (Indian and Western), home furnishings and some leather goods. The women market the products themselves, bypassing an intermediary, thus achieving a fairer deal for themselves and their pro-ducer group (see shopping).

Essentials

Sleeping
Prince & Lake View had reopened in April 2001; others were limping back

B-D *Prince*, Station Rd, T20370, F50373. 42 rooms with bath (non a/c from Rs 450), 30 a/c considerably better, good *Jesal* restaurant (varied menu), snacks in pleasant courtyard garden at rear, shops (books, clothes, tailoring, Qasab handicrafts), free air-port transfer, good guided tours of local villages Rs 1,500 per car, guides (Rs 350-800), good hotel but crowded area, street noise and loudspeakers during festivals, lacks character, no credit cards. **C-D** *Lake View* Rajendra Park, T53422, F50835. Non-a/c to deluxe a/c comfortable rooms, baths, fridges, garden restaurant, *thalis* indoors, gym, pool (open to non-residents, morning and afternoon), excellent views of Hamirsar, good birdlife at marshes after rains and at lake in Jan-Feb. **C-D** *Anam*, end of Station Rd, T21390, F53397. 27 clean rooms, (a/c over-priced; others good value), some 4-bedded, with bath (hot water), TV, phone, comfortable and modern, good a/c veg restaurant (try Kachchhi), inexpensive *thalis*, popular with business people. On noisy main road but recommended. **C-D** *Lake View*, T53422, T50835. attractive location fac-ing Hamirsar lake (birds in winter), outdoor dining, rather nondescript restaurant, pool, inefficient housekeeping. **D-E** *Abha International*, Siddharth Complex, Station Rd, T54451, F51424. 31 rooms, with bath (hot water), can be noisy, modern amenities, some a/c (non-a/c very good value); Gujarati/Punjabi/Chinese veg restaurant, cheaper sister hotel down the road is **F** *Janta Ghar*, dingy rooms (Rs 60-100), 'squeaky beds that hold on against the laws of nature', 'deluxe' have western toilets and excellent turbo shower, bucket hot water, steep staircases (no lift), Kachchhi meals, friendly, well maintained ('staff burst in at odd hours to clean'), budget choice if you have ear plugs. **D-E** *Sahara Palace*, on 2nd floor of a shopping complex opposite the noisy ST station, T20970. Ordinary non-a/c rooms, a/c better, overpriced **C** suites. **E-F** *Gangaram*,

Kachchh

A melting pot of tribes

Kachchh is a meeting point of Sindhi, Gujarati, Muslim and Rajasthani cultures; the local language is more Sindhi than Gujarati. The arid grasslands to the north, south and west of Bhuj are home to a number of pastoral tribes – the Bharwad shepherds and goat herds, the Rabari camel and cattle herders, Maldhars who keep buffaloes, Samra and Sindhi Muslim

cameleers and others. The communities have the Lohan merchants, Langa musicians of the Indian desert and Kanbi Patel agriculturalists among them. They came from near and far – some, like the Sodha Rajputs, originated from the area neighbouring Rajasthan now in Pakistan, the Jats from Baluchistan, while the Sidhis claim Abyssinian descent.

Darbargadh, T22948, F56474. Located at a busy intersection near Aina Mahal, extremely noisy area but good views of the old palace complex from the rooftop. 15 clean, comfortable rooms with TV and attached baths (tiled floors and walls, showers), new a/c rooms, no restaurant but tea, sandwiches, snacks served, pleasant courtyard and terrace, sights/shops nearby, good value for money. **F** *Annapurna*, Bhid Gate, T20831. Clean and well kept rooms but noisy, friendly owners, better known for its Kachchhi cuisine. **F** *City Guest House*, Langa St, near Bazar, 2 mins' walk from Aina Mahal, T21067. 32 clean, quiet rooms, some with own shower, new restaurant, attractive courtyard (and quiet garden for relaxing), cycle hire, helpful, well run, very good value, used by foreign backpackers. Recommended. **F** *Nityananda*, Station Rd, T20626: Small guest house next to Prince. Spartan rooms with balcony overlooking road, some 3 and 4-bedded, hot water in buckets, reasonably clean. **F** *VRP Guest House*, near Bus Station, T21388. Clean rooms (Rs 50-100) and *Green Rock* restaurant for unlimited tasty vegetarian *thalis*.

Eating

Strictly 'Dry' Foreigners may get a permit from the police, see page 348

Mid-range *Green*, Shroff Bazar, Punjabi. South Indian vegetarian. Well prepared food, friendly staff (one is a/c). *Neelam*, Station Rd opposite Prince. North Indian (best paneer curries in town), some Chinese and Continental. A/c, good variety and quality, friendly staff, popular. Recommended. *Toral*, at *Prince*, has good Gujarati, veg *thalis*; bit more expensive than elsewhere, but in a more comfortable setting. **Cheap** *Anando*, excellent for all sorts of Indian (including Gujarati) snacks. Friendly staff, up-market branch, a/c. *Jaldeep* near Vaniyawad market, and *Jethi* near Jubilee Garden, offer delicious Indian tea (spiced with ginger, cinnamon or cardamom) and biscuits. *Omlette Centre*, near bus station. Popular for breakfast and snacks, excellent omelettes fried in oil or butter ('Masala' is stuffed with coriander, onions etc), sandwiches and 'English tea'. *Tammu Fast Food*, between *Abha* and *Janataghar*, has good hot samosas, South Indian snacks and *batakawadas* (avoid bread). *Rasoi*, at *Abha International*, Indian vegetarian. Good Gujarati *thalis*, Kachchhi and Kathiawadi dishes, and a la carte. *Noor*, behind the bus station. Indian, popular for reasonably priced *biryani* and *chicken masala*. *Annapurna Guest House*, Bhid Gate. Kachchhi. Very cheap, authentic dishes, homely, allow you to sample each dish, 'refills never stopped coming', also few noisy rooms (Rs 100). **Snacks** Typical local *dhabelis* (spicy burger of peanuts and potatoes, in a roll), and *bhal* (nuts, gram, vegetables in a spicy sauce), can be sampled on Vaniyawad and Station Rd.

Festivals *Feb/Mar*: Four-day *Rann Utsav (Kachchh Festival)* organized by Gujarat Tourism during Sivaratri to coincide with the Dhrang fair at a temple near Bhuj – stalls sell tribal crafts, there are handicrafts demonstrations, performances of folk dances and music, and tours of nearby places of interest. Fairs in many villages in **Feb-Mar** (*Nag Panchami*), at March harvest, around *Janmashtami* in **Aug-Sep**, and *Sivaratri* in late **Feb-early Mar**. The *Ravechi Mela*, near Rapar, east of Bhuj, is vibrant and colourful.

Excellent folk embroidery, leather shoes, appliqué, mirrorwork, block-printed fabrics, painted pottery and local weaving are available. The market area stretches from station road to the Darbargadh Palace complex, a maze of alleys specialising in different handicrafts. **Crafts and textiles**: A number of NGOs have organised craft co-operatives for the benefit of artisans. *Qasab*, 11 Nootan Colony, T22124 and a small shop in *Prince Hotel*. See excursions above. Highly recommended. **Shroff Bazar** has craft shops for hassle-free browsing, and clothes: *Uday*, T24660, a talented designer (Rs 600 for trousers and top), interesting block-prints, excellent tailoring (made-to-measure in a few hours). In **Danda Bazar**: *Khatri Al Md Isha*, T23543, for outstanding tie-and-dye; *Khatri Daod* for block-prints, embroideries. In **Vaniyawad**: *Ratnadeep*, excellent block-printed table cloths. **Kansara bazar**, is famous for its silver jewellery. *Bandhini Ghar*, is known for its tie-and-dye. Block printed bedsheets are available on Station Rd and in alleys *near Jantaghar Guest House*. *Anand*, near the Aina Mahal offers reasonably priced embroideries and block printed textiles. *AA Wazir*, opp General Hospital, near High School, has a good selection of old pieces of embroideries and other handicrafts, interesting for textile students (an art and craft gallery is planned); some pieces are for sale. His son arranges tours of the handicraft villages of Kutch. **Photography**: *Pappu*, Rashtrabasha Shopping Centre, near bus station; *Pornal*, Darbargadh (near palaces), has an outstanding collection of slides of Kachchh.

Shopping
Bhuj is a shopper's paradise
Most shops are closed from 1200 to 1500

Local **Car hire**: From *Hotels Prince, Abha, Sahara Palace, Garha Safari Lodge* (and guides). **Cycle** and **scooter hire**: Near bus station. **Taxi**: About Rs 550 per day plus km charge.

Transport

Long distance Air: *Indian Airlines*, Station Rd, T50204, airport T22433, *Gujarat Airways*, T51185, and *Jet Airways*, *Prince Hotel*, T53671, airport T53674, fly to **Mumbai**. Security is tight: pack cameras away in your checked baggage, along with knives, scissors and batteries. **Road Bus**: frequent service to **Ahmadabad**, 411 km, most comfortable are the afternoon Bhuj-Ahmadabad-Surat luxury and the late-night Ahmadabad 'Super'. To **Mandvi, Rapar** from 0610; **Rajkot** from 0500, 5 hrs. Also to **Bhavnagar**, 0830, 2000; **Jaisalmer**, 1330, 8 hrs; **Jamnagar**, 0500, 2040, 2115; **Junagadh**, 0500, 2030, **Palitana**,1900; **Porbandar**, 0645, 2115, and **Veraval, Somnath**. Most long distance buses are scheduled to arrive at sunrise or sunset, so times are changed seasonally. 'Luxury buses' with reclining seats, more leg room, comfort stops etc are strongly recommended. Many private operators (eg *Sahajanand, Patel, Sitaram Travels*), cluster around the bus station, and run infrequent services to major towns in Gujarat. However, 'No bus' may simply mean 'No bus right now/today'! **Train**: The most convenient train from Mumbai is *Bombay-Gandhidham Kutch Exp 9031*, 1710, 14¾ hrs (from Ahmadabad 0155, 6 hrs); then 2 hrs by bus or train to Bhuj. Trains also to **Kandla Port**. For **Rajasthan**: go to **Palanpur** *JPJ Pass*, 2020, 11½ hrs; trains from there to **Abu Rd, Ajmer, Jaipur** etc or bus; from Abu Rd, bus to **Udaipur**, 5 hrs.

Banks *State Bank of India*, Station Rd changes Thomas Cook TCs, 1100-1500 weekdays, till 1300 Sat. *Bank of Baroda*, almost opposite changes Amex TCs (photocopy of passport needed). **Communications** Head post office: Lal Takri, 0700-1300, 1500-1800 (Mon-Sat). Sub post office in the chowk at entrance to Aina Mahal. **Tourist offices** *Gujarat Tourism*, 416 Bahumali Building, T24910. *Kachchh Explorer*, Aina Mahal, Bhuj. Mr Jethi there is very knowledgeable and enthusiastic, 0900-1200, 1500-1800, closed Sat. **Useful addresses** Fire: T21490. **Police**: T20892 (see permits below). Forestry Office: T50600.

Directory

Kachchh

Craft villages

Handicrafts are a living tradition of Kachchh and the girls of various communities make beautifully embroidered garments for their own trousseaus while women produce attractive fabrics for a second income. Some visitors to the villages are disappointed to find that the previously nomadic tribes are being housed in whitewashed urban housing in expanded older villages which are losing their traditional architecture. Cement and modern materials are replacing mud walls and cow dung. Now, requests for pens and chocolates from unruly village children can be heard even in the distant corners of Kachchh. However, the handicrafts of these villages are still of a high standard.

Noth of Bhuj **Banni** The vast grasslands meet the Great Rann in the Khavda region. They are home to numerous pastoral nomadic, semi-nomadic and resident people who keep sheep, goats, camels, buffaloes and other livestock. Various communities live in this region including Jats, Sodha Rajputs, Meghwal harijans, Ahirs and Rabaris. The 40 or so hamlets here are best known for the minute detail of their embroidery. More recently, these villages have started focusing on selling handicrafts as their main source of income and there are signs of modernisation and commercialisation. The traditional thatched huts (*bhungas*) are made from mud plastered with cow dung which are often decorated with hand-painted floral patterns and inlaid with mirrors during festivals. Traditional utensils are still used for cooking, eating and storage in the houses. The area is known for its raptors (eagles, vultures and other birds of prey).
■ *Getting there: Buses from Bhuj go to the main villages from the ST stand, around 0800 (check time), but may involve a 15-min walk. It is better to arrange a taxi.*

Permits may be needed by foreigners to visit nearby villages that lie north of an east-west 'line' drawn through Bhuj though this requirement was lifted in early 2001. If needed apply on a form from the DSP's Office (Police), south of town, and hand it in with your passport and photocopies of identification and visa pages. When these are returned, get your permit from *Umed Bhavan* (Collector's Office) nearby. Allow 2 hrs. Both offices are open 1100-1400, 1600-1800 (closed Sun, 2nd and 4th Sat of month). Dhorodo, Sumrasar and Loria are particularly rewarding. The same procedure applies for **liquor permits**.

Dhorodo The centre for Jat embroidery, using chain stitches inset with small mirrors, leather embroidery as well as silver jewellery, is 80 km north of Bhuj.

Sumrasar This village is famous for its Ahir embroidery and Soof embroidery of the Sodhas, done without a plan but by counting the warp and weft of the material. It is 25 km northeast of Bhuj. Daya Nathani, at Ami Baug, is an award-winning artisan and also an astute businesswoman (taxi-drivers are likely to know her house). *Kala Raksha*, Parkar Vas, Sumrasar Sheikh, near Collector's Office, T77238, is a grassroots organization which maintains a small museum of heirloom textiles. It works with and trains 180 artisans to create contemporary pieces inspired by their own traditions. Now run by Judy Frater, the American author of *Threads of Identity*.

Loria Some 60 km away, Loria, also called Ludia, has huts with painted and mirror inlaid walls, and is famed for its wood crafts.

Zura Embroidered footwear and other leather crafts are produced here some 30 km north of Bhuj. Copper bells are also made in the village.

Nirona This village has embroidery, lacquered wood crafts, wood carving and is the only home of highly skilful rogan-painting (fabrics painted using iron rods). It is 40 km northwest, buses take 1½ hours.

Nakhtarana Northwest in the heart of the craft village belt, Nakhtarana produces some tie-and-dye work. There is a Chinkara Sanctuary at **Narayan Sarovar**, 75 km away. At **Vithon** village, nearby you can stay at *Malir Garden Resort*, with 8 small, simple and rather dingy mud huts (very basic toilet/shower; no door!), Kachchhi meals and Rajput meat dishes, a village tank style pool, attractive orchard setting, friendly and enthusiastic owner Mohan Singh Sodha is a good host and acts as a guide to the Sodha Rajput village but "is not knowledgeable about handicrafts and textiles", packages Rs 1000. Reserve, well in advance, at *North West Safaris*, T079-6302019, F6300962, ssibal@ad1.vsnl.net.in The Malir fossil museum is an outdoor exhibition of wood and animal fossils (some several million years old) personally collected by Mohan Singh Sodha.

Charri Dund Lake A reservoir near Charri village offering splendid birdwatching opportunities. Flamingoes, pelicans, cranes, storks, ducks etc gather in large numbers, specially in winter, while nearby grasslands are filled with passerine and ground dwelling birds. The Banni grasslands are known for their huge eagle and vulture congregations. Bombay Natural History Society and other organisations monitor bird migrations in the Banni region, and bird banding camps are set up around Charri lake. The grasslands are home to wolf, hyena, jackal, Indian and desert foxes and lesser wild cats but are imperilled by the government's decision to convert Banni into pastureland.

Dholavira This is the site of excavation of a Harappan town (pre-2500BC) which some estimate to be larger than Moenjodaro, in Pakistan. It was only discovered in 1967 and excavation began in 1990. The drive to Khadir *beyt*, an oasis in the Great Rann, through dazzling salt flats is very scenic. Excavations show the complex to be on three levels (Citadel, Middle and Lower Towns) with pottery, stone cutting, coppersmithing, drainage systems and town planning at an advanced level. The fortifications with walls, bastions and double ramparts reflect danger from invasions or enemies. An inscribed tablet found here bears 10 letters in the Harappan script. Bus from Bhuj via Rapar takes seven hours.

There are numerous attractive villages and hamlets near **Rapar**, west of Bhuj, where commercial influences are still little known but it is not easy to find a guide to this region.

There are a number of interesting villages south of Bhuj *en route* to **South of Bhuj** Gandhidham. A few require no permit: Mandvi, Mundra on the coast and Bachau (84 km east). **Tunda Vandh** is a good place to see typical *bhungas* (huts) of Kachchh. Architecture students come to see, study and photograph the traditional architecture adapted to this hostile climate. The interiors have beautiful Rabari cupboards, chests, inlaid mirrors and paintings. ■ *Getting there: Buses to Rajkot or Ahmadabad can drop you off at most of the villages.*

Kachchh

Bhujodi Some 10 km southeast off the main road, this is the centre for pitloom weaving. The weavers have now been organized into a co-operative. They produce colourful *galichas* (carpets), *durries* (rugs), *dhablos* (blankets), and other items from wool, camel/goat hair, cotton, and even synthetic fibres. Some embroidery and tie-and-dye can be seen here as well. Mr Vanka Kana Rabari, T40005, has reasonably priced local embroidery et cetera, but not the most select quality. *Shrujan* sells upmarket embroideries and home furnishings. Bhujodi is a 10 minute walk from the bus stand.

Padhdhar *Ahir* embroidery using round mirrors with floral and geometrical patterns is produced here. The village is 22 km southeast of Bhujodi.

Dhaneti A centre for Ahir and Rabari embroidery. Meet Govindbhai (a local entrepreneur) and his friendly family who will show you the embroidered and mirror inlaid fabrics made for their own use. There are some intricate hero stones (*pallias*) by the village lake.

Dhamanka Famous for its block printed fabrics, table/bed linen, garments et cetera, using vegetable or chemical dyes. Used blocks can be bought here which make good decorative pieces. The village is 50 km east of Bhuj.

Anjar An early Jadeja Rajput capital of Kachchh, founded 450 years ago, 22 km southeast. The Jesal-Toral shrine has a romantic tale of the reform of an outlaw prince through the love of a village girl. Anjar is also known for its metalcrafts (especially betel nut crackers and ornaments), *bandhni* and block printing. The 1818 Bungalow of Captain McMurdoch (the first European to settle in Kachchh), now government offices, has some Kamangari paintings on the ground floor.

Mandvi
Population: 37,000

The creeks & wetlands of Mandvi are excellent for birdwatching

Mandvi is a pretty little seaside town, 54 km southwest of Bhuj, with a reservoir in the centre and a river beyond. During the 18th century the town outclassed Bhuj in importance, the sea-faring people dominating the sea trade, taking cotton, rice, spices et cetera to the Persian gulf, Arabia and Zanzibar. The skill of building *dhows* and boats using simple tools is being revived along the river; well worth watching.

The town is now a centre for handicrafts like *bandhni* tie-and-dyed fabrics, jewellery and shell toys. It is a desert town but important agricultural research for the Kachchh region is being carried out here in the Gujarat Agricultural University and the Vivekenand Research Institute, to improve farming in the often hostile environment.

There is an 18th-century **palace** with an *Aina Mahal* (Mirror Hall) and music rooms which have remains of intricate stone carvings of Dutchmen, tigers and dancing girls and woodcarvings in the courtyard. Out of town, you can visit a magnificent new Jain temple.

The beaches on the town side are good for swimming and even camel or horse riding. A wind farm next to the beach is working hard to produce an alternative energy source. The *Maharao*'s pleasant private beach with few onlookers is open to visitors. ■ *Rs 30 (worthwhile for women, to escape hassle from male onlookers)*.

The magnificent 1940s **Vijay Vilas** palace with huge domes, combines Indian and European styles. You can see the drawing room with royal memorabilia, and the attractive *jali* windows of the *zenana*. The terrace, reached by a spiral staircase, with excellent sea views, especially at sunset, is ideal for a picnic. ■ *Rs 5, Camera Rs 20, plus vehicle charge.*

Kachchh

Sleeping Beach: **D** *Vijay Vilas*, 4 km from town. Few poorly maintained rooms in the out-house, only *thalis* (for residents), contact *North West Safaris*, T079-6302019, F6300962, ssibal@ad1.vsnl.net.in **D-E** *Holiday cottages* (Gujarat Tourism), 5 small double bedroom cottages with bath (western toilets), some a/c, and tents (2 cots each, shared toilets), Indian-Continental restaurant planned. **Town**: **F** *Vinayak*, offers simple rooms (Rs 50).

Eating Town: *Rajneesh Osho*, near Azad Chowk, best value *thalis* in simple dining area, recommended. The bazar has fresh coconuts, biscuits, soft drinks and excellent local corn-on-the-cob; in the evening hand-carts emerge with popular snacks.

Transport Express bus from Bhuj, 1 hr; others very slow. From bus station, auto-rickshaws, Rs 50 for return trip to Palace after bargaining. Possible to visit Mundra from Mandvi on same day, which also has direct services to Bhuj.

Mundra

Mundra, a historic port of Bhuj, is visited for its old walls, intricate gates, woollen *namdas* (produced by an intricate process), *bandhni* saris and batik prints.

Bhuvad

On the Mundra Road, 19 km southwest of Anjar, Bhuvad has the ruined 13th-century temple of Bhuvaneshwar Mahadev. The mandapa (1289-90) is supported by 34 unusual pillars (square base, octagonal middle and circular upper section). A local legend describes how the headless body of the chieftain Bhuvad, who was killed in battle about 1320, fought its way to the village. The District Gazetteer records that a shrine with a red headless figure is dedicated to him, while the nearby tall shrines commemorate warriors killed in the same battle.

Bhadreshwar

Bhadreshwar (Vasai), 80 km from Mandvi, was important as an ancient seaport. The main **Jain Temple** (1248) is surrounded by small shrines which together reproduce the shape and form of the temple itself. The archway leading into the enclosure, added in the mid-12th century, shows Islamic influence. There are about 150 idols of the Tirthankars in the 52 cells; the main sanctuary now contains a Mahavir figure while the original Parasvanatha has been reinstalled in Cell No 19. The *rangamandap* and *poojamandap* have *patta* paintings of Jain temples and epics.

The more important of the two mosques here is the **Solah Khambi Masjid** which is the only known Islamic structure that existed before the Muslim conquests. All its original features are intact. There is also an ancient step well.
■ *Getting there: There are few direct buses to Bhuj; try going via Adipur for connecting buses. Easier by taxi.*

Kandla

Further east along the coast is the port of Kandla, built to replace declining Mandvi, with the help of British engineers. After independence, Kandla was further developed by the Government of India, to service the states in Northwest India. The airport here is an alternative for those who do not get reservations for Bhuj. ■ *Getting there: Gujarat Airways flies daily from Mumbai.*

Gandhidham
Population: 104,600
27 km N of Kandla

Gandhidham was founded by the Maharaos of Kachchh to accommodate refugees from Sindh in Pakistan after Partition in 1947. The enterprising community established made a promising start and now the town is a prosperous business centre though the old handloom and embroidery co-operatives for refugees still exist. The Institute of Sindhology here is researching on various aspects of Sindhi culture.

Kachchh

The establishment of the town was supported by the Government of India which wanted to develop Kandla as a port to cater to the needs of the massive hinterlands of northern India having lost Karachi sea port to Pakistan. There is little of interest in Gandhidham town for tourists except for the Adipur Gandhi Samadhi memorial where the Sindhis took the blessings of Mahatma Gandhi before setting up the new town, and the recently renovated Nat Mandir temple, one of the first buildings to be built here.

Sharma Resorts on the Gandhidham-Bhuj road is a complete health, sports and recreational resort with Ayurvedic massages and treatments, yoga and meditation lessons, a nature cure physician offering various therapies. The resort also has a swimming pool, gym, sauna, jacuzzi, tennis courts, riding and an artificial lake for fishing and boating.

Sleeping and eating C *Desert Palace (Sharma Resort)*, in Gandhidham-Anjar-Bhuj triangle. 26 a/c rooms, (35 more being added), in local style huts with modern bath, TV, fridge, comfortable though with rather garish decor, good choice of Indian/Chinese in outdoor restaurant (including fresh fish), avoid indoor restaurant (loud Hindi film music), travel, pool, sports, free transfer from nearby airports, a good alternative base to Bhuj, reserve ahead at *North West Safaris*, T079-6302019, F6300962, ssibal@ad1.vsnl.net.in **D** *Shiv*, 360 Ward 12-B (2 km from rly station), T02836-21297, F20985. 39 rooms, some **C** a/c, wide menu restaurant; **D** *Madhuban*, 22, Sector 9, T02836-22209, F23527, 38 rooms, most a/c, restaurant. **D** *Sayaji*, Sector 8, T21297. 40 rooms, central a/c, restaurant and usual facilities. Town eateries serve good Sindhi food: *pakwan dal* is a popular Sindhi breakfast.

Transport Bus: The station is a 3 min walk – turn right from the railway station. Frequent buses to **Bhuj**, but very crowded. **Train**: Gandhidham is the principal railhead of Kachchh. **Mumbai Cen**, *Kachchh Exp 9032* (excellent a/c sleeper and chair-car), 2045, 17 hrs. **Kandla Port**, *Fast Pass 177*, 0705; *173*, 0905; *175*, 1500: about 30 mins. **Vadodara**: *Gandhidham Vadodara Exp 9104*, 2305, 7¾ hrs; *Kachchh Exp 9032*, 2045, 8½ hrs. *Nagercoil-Gandhidham Exp 6336* via Thiruvananthapuram, Kochi etc.

Lakhpat   Lakhpat, at the northeast end of the Kori Creek, with a population of 40,000 at Independence in 1947, became India's westernmost town. However, the end to the trade between Sindh and Gujarat has resulted in a ghost town with no more than 250 people. There is a historic fort here.

★ Little Rann of Kachchh Sanctuary

Colour map 5 grid A4   *The 4,950 sq km Wild Ass Sanctuary of the Little Rann of Kachchh (created in 1973) and the 7,850 sq km desert wildlife sanctuary of the great Rann, together would comprise the largest contiguous tract of protected wildlife territory in India were it not divided by a road. The Little Rann is mostly a saline wilderness, broken by* beyts *(islands during the monsoon), covered with grass, bushes, acacia and thorn scrub that support wildlife. The area is under severe threat from the salt works, which clear the vegetation, release toxic effluents into the wetlands and pollute the air. Encroaching Prosopis juliflora, a fast growing thorn scrub, is destroying most other vegetation.*

Ins & outs   **Entry** The southern part of the sanctuary is accessible. Forest department fees, US$5
See page 354 for   (foreigners), still camera US$5, at Bajana and Dhrangadhra. **Climate** Temperature:
further details   maximum 42°C minimum 7°C. Annual rainfall: 1,000 mm. Best season is late-Oct to mid-Mar; very hot in Jun, inaccessible during rains.

This is the last home of the **Asiatic wild ass** (locally called *khacchar* or **Wildlife** *ghorker*), a handsome pale chestnut brown member of the wild horse family with a dark stripe down the back. Wild asses are usually seen as lone stallions, small groups of mares (occasionally bachelors) or harems of a male with mares. Large herds of 40 to 60 are sometimes seen but they are loosely knit. Males fight viciously, biting and kicking, for their females.

Nilgai, antelope and chinkara (Indian gazelle) are other mammals seen but the chinkara numbers have dwindled due to poaching. Blackbucks have become almost extinct in the Little Rann of Kachchh but are seen in villages nearby. Wolf is the primary predator though not common. You might spot jackal, desert fox, jungle and desert cat on a drive.

Birdlife is abundant. Houbara bustard, spotted and common Indian sand grouse, nine species of larks, desert warbler, desert wheatear, Indian and cream coloured courser, grey francolin and five species of quails are spotted at the *beyts*. The salt marshes teem with flamingos, pelicans, storks, ducks, herons and wading birds. Thousands of demoiselle and common eastern cranes spend the winter months here. See page 315 for bird watching tours.

The 13th-century **Jhinjwada Fort**, on the edge of Little Rann, west of Dasada, **Excursions** has majestic gateways. At the southeast corner of the Rann, **Kalaghoda**, southwest of Dasada on the way to Bajana Lake, is particularly interesting. The principal British salt trading post with an old village-pony express, it retains plenty of colonial architecture including Raj bungalows, a cricket pavilion and a bandstand!

Dasada is a convenient base for visits to the Little Rann. The interesting village has an old fort with wood carvings, 15th-century tombs, potters, block printers, a shepherd's colony (Bharwadvas) and nomadic settlements. The Malik Dynasty who received the 35 mile estate in return for military services to the sultan of Ahmadabad, now live in a 1940s mansion *Fatima Manzil*.

Dasada B *Camp Zainabad*, 9 km from Dasada. A cluster of 16 self-contained *kooba* **Sleeping** huts in a Eucalyptus grove (beds, hot shower, Western toilet). Rs 2000 each includes **& eating** meals and safaris. Recreating a local village, well located, atmospheric but small cots, hard mattresses and sometimes insipid food, owned and enthusiastically managed by former ruling family of Zainabad, well organised jeep safaris in the Little Rann, also camel/horse/village safaris, boating at nearby lake contact *Desert Coursers*, Camp Zainabad, via Dasada, Dt Surendranagar. **B** *Rann Riders*, comfortable air-cooled rooms in 15 Kachchhi *bhungas* and Kathiawadi *koobas* (huts) amid berry plantation and agricultural farms, "*bhungas* more spacious and attractive, but *koobas* recommended for those with hay fever!", comfortable cane furniture and tiled hot showers (some al fresco!), great atmosphere at night, home grown organic vegetables, fresh fish and poultry, hammocks in eucalyptus groves, dining area facing small lake, ethnic décor, delicious home cooked food (specially meat dishes), enthusiastic owner (Rs 1,650 each including meals and 2 safaris), good jeeps for tours, a little impersonal and lacking focus, contact *North West Safaris* T079-6302019, F6300962, ssibal@ad1.vsnl.net.in **C** *Fatima Manzil*, atmospheric English cottage-style outhouse of 1940s mansion, 2 simple rooms (could be cleaner), shared bath (bucket hot water), includes delicious generous Mughlai meals, Rs 1000-1,500 each, 'rather laid back', jeep safaris, Sarfraz Malik knows all about Rann wildlife, contact *North West Safaris*, T079-6302019, F6300962, ssibal@ad1.vsnl.net.in **E-F** Govt *Guest Houses* closer to the Rann, at Bajana and Dhrangadra where a jeep can be hired for visiting the Little Rann.

Kachchh

Transport State **buses** from main towns in Gujarat; frequent from Ahmadabad (93 km), 2½ hrs; some continue to Zainabad. From Dasada, Sarfraz Malik arranges transfer; local buses to Zainabad. To Bhuj it's short route by narrow road, 267 km; by NH8A, 400 km. Dasada is 33 km northwest of Viramgam station, which has **trains** from Mumbai and Ahmadabad. Hotels arrange transfer at extra cost on prior notice. Dhrangadra has trains from Mumbai.

Directory **Tours** Naturalist guide, Sarfraz Malik (see Fatima Manzil above), is full of information on history and insights into the area. Tours of Little Rann wildlife sanctuary and nearby areas known for birds and blackbuck (including white mutant bucks) by jeep, charges Rs 500 per person per day, plus jeep hire Rs 800 per day.

Kachchh

Mumbai

13

Mumbai

Mumbai

Mumbai is one of India's most remarkable cities. The commercial hub of the Indian economy for over 150 years, it remains uniquely open to the rest of the world and is yet a city shaped by India's diverse cultures. There is plenty to see in a short visit, including good museums, galleries and the Elephanta caves which, within an hour's boat ride across the harbour, illustrate the artistry of India's ancient craftsmen.

Phone code: 022
Population: 12.57 mn

Ins and outs

Sahar International air terminal is 30 km from Nariman Point, the business heart of the city. The domestic terminals at Santa Cruz are 5 km closer. Pre-paid taxis to the city centre are good value and take between 40 mins and 1½ hrs, depending on traffic but there are also cheaper but slower buses. If you arrive late at night without a hotel booking it is best to stay at one of the hotels near the domestic terminal before going into town early in the morning.

Getting there
See page 370 for further details

The sights are spread out and you need transport. Taxis are metered and generally good value. Autos are only allowed in the suburbs. There are frequent buses on major routes, and the two suburban railway lines are useful out of peak hours on some routes, but get extremely crowded.

Getting around

Mumbai, now India's largest city, is tightly packed into a long narrow peninsula. However, its remorseless growth has forced it to spill over, through informal townships and housing colonies up to 70 or 80 km north of the central core. The railway stations, Chhatrapati Sivaji Terminus (CST) – formerly the Victoria terminus or VT – and Churchgate, about 1 km apart, are close to the core of the commercial area, with the Stock market and a range of company head offices. The main area of cheap hotels and guest houses is about 1 km south in Colaba, around the Gateway of India. This area also has the world famous *Taj Hotel*, a range of shops and excellent restaurants, and the Prince of Wales Museum, the Jehangir Art Gallery and institutions like Bombay University and the Town Hall, built around the great maidans, or parks, which give Mumbai its breathing space. For Mumbaiites Mumbai has other important centres: Malabar Hill, a high class residential district but also home to the Hanging Gardens, the Parsi Towers of Silence and nearby the Gandhi Museum. Between Malabar Hill and the Airport at Sahar lies a series of suburban centres, including the centre of the Mumbai film industry at Bandra and Goregaon. Mumbai's 'beach resort' at Juhu, about 20 minutes by taxi from the airport, is now lined with middle and upper price range hotels which cater for the airport trade. There is also a cluster of hotels round the airport itself.

Orientation

Background

Hinduism had made its mark on Mumbai long before the Portuguese and then the British transformed it into one of India's great cities. The caves on the island of Elephanta were excavated under the Kalachuris (500-600 AD). From well before that until the arrival of the Portuguese, Arab *dhows* traded down the coast, but less than 350 years ago the area occupied by this great metropolis comprised seven islands inhabited by Koli fishermen (from whom we have the word 'coolie') and their families. The modern name of Mumbai is derived from the local Koli name for the goddess Parvati, Mumba devi.

Mumbai

To Airports

To Santa Cruz & Vile Parle Stations

DHARAVI

Mehboob Studio ○ Rangsharda

Mahim Bay

A

Mahim

WORLI

Matunga Road

Matunga

Arabian Sea

B

Dadar

10

3

Wadala

Elphinstone Road

Parel

Sewri

Lower Parel

Curry Rd

Chinchpoli

Cotton Green

Stadium

C

Mahalaxmi Race Course

Maha-lakshmi

Reay Road

Haji Ali's Tomb

Victoria Gardens

Mahalakshmi Temple

Bombay Central

4

Byculla

A/C M

7

Catholic Cathedral

Tata Garden

1

J B Behram Marg

Dockyard Rd

Kemp's Corner

Christ Church

12

Grant Road

1

Sandhurst Road

D

4

3

2

5

2

Chor Bazar

Grant Rd (M Shaukat Ali Rd)

Mani Bhavan

S Patel Rd

Falkland Rd

Towers of Silence

All Saints'

8

Masjid

11

Charni Road

Walkeshwar Temple

Chowpatty Beach

London Pub

Marine Lines

○ Raj Bhavan

Back Bay

E

Churchgate

Vir Nariman Rd

CST

Madam Cama Rd

Tata Institute of Fundamental Research

World Trade Centre

Gateway of India

F

St John's

Shahid Bhagat Singh Rd

A

Homi Bhabha Auditorium

Sassoon Dock

Catholic Church

N

Observatory

0 km   1

0 miles   1

1   2   3

Related map
A Central Mumbai,
page 361

■ **Sleeping**
1 Anukool *D2*
2 Kalpana Palace & Café Heaven *D2*
3 Red Rose *B3*
4 YMCA International *C2*

● **Eating**
1 Biscotti *D1*
2 Bombay A1 *D2*
3 China Garden *D1*
4 Chinatown *D1*
5 Chopsticks *D2*
6 Goa Portuguesa *A3*
7 Kamat *C2*
8 New Yorker *D1*
9 Only Fish *A3*
10 Rashtriya *B3*
11 Revival *D1*
12 Under the Over *D1*

The big screen

Mumbai is the centre of the hugely successful film industry they call 'Bollywood'. Nearly 200 films per year are produced making Bollywood the world's second largest film maker after Hong Kong. The Hindi film industry comes mainly out of the tradition of larger-than-life productions with familiar story lines performed as escapist entertainment for the community. The stars lead fantasy lives as they enjoy cult status with a following of millions. It is not surprising that should they choose to turn their hand to politics, they find instant support in an unquestioning, adoring electorate. The experience of a Bollywood film is not to be missed – at least once in your life. Television has made a visit to a cinema redundant though it's always easy to find one in any sizeable town; the gaudy posters dominate every street scene. Be prepared for a long sitting with a standard story line, set characters and lots of action as the typical multi-million rupee blockbusters attempt to provide something to please everybody. Marathon melodramas consist of slapstick comedy contrasted with tear-jerking tragedy, a liberal sprinkling of moralizing with a tortuous disentangling of the knots tied by the heroes, heroines, villains and their extended families.

The usual ingredients are the same: shrill Hindi "film music", unoriginal songs mouthed to the voice of playback artistes, hip-jerking dancing by suggestively clad figures which lack all subtlety when it comes to sexual innuendo, honeymooning couples before a backdrop of snowy mountains, car chases and violent disasters – these will keep you enthralled for hours. On a serious note, there are ample examples of truly brilliant works by world-class Indian film makers (Satyajit Ray, Rithwik Ghatak, Shyam Benegal, Aparna Roy to name a few) but they are not usually box office successes or made for popular consumption so they have to be sought out.

The stars live in sumptuous dwellings, many of which are on Malabar Hill, Mumbai's Beverley Hills. It is difficult to get permission to visit a studio during filming but you might try **Film City**, Goregaon East, T8401533 or **Mehboob Studios**, Hill Rd, Bandra West, T6428045.

The British acquired these marshy and malarial islands as part of the marriage dowry paid by the Portuguese when Catherine of Braganza married Charles II in 1661. Some suggest that Bombay took its English name from the Portuguese Bom Bahia, or 'good harbour'. Four years later, the British took possession of the remaining islands and neighbouring mainland and in 1668 the East India Company leased the whole area from the crown for £10 sterling per year, which was paid for nearly 50 years.

Today Mumbai has become the hub of India's commercial activity. It is the home of India's main stock exchange and headquarters for many national and international companies. It is also a major industrial centre.

Mumbai is still growing fast. One third of the population live in its desperately squalid *chawls* of cramped, makeshift and miserable hovels. There are also many thousands of pavement dwellers, yet despite the extreme poverty Mumbai remains a city of hope for millions.

Mumbai

Sights

Gateway of India The Indo-Saracenic-style Gateway of India (1927), designed by George Wittet to commemorate the visit of George V and Queen Mary in 1911, is modelled in honey-coloured basalt on 16th-century Gujarati work. The arch was the point from which the last British regiment serving in India signalled the end of the empire when it left on 28 February 1948. The whole area has a huge buzz at weekends. Scores of boats depart from here for Elephanta Island.

The original red-domed **Taj Mahal Hotel** has been adjoined by a modern skyscraper (the *Taj Mahal Inter-Continental*). Jamshedji Tata, a Mumbai Parsi, was behind the enterprise; designed by West Chambers.

The **Bombay Natural History Society** (BNHS), Hornbill House on SB Singh Marg, opposite Regal Cinema, founded over 100 years ago, is dedicated to the conservation of India's flora and fauna. It has an informative PR officer, a shop, wildlife collection and library.

Colaba South of the Gateway of India is the crowded southern section of Shahid (literally 'martyr') Bhagat Singh Marg (Colaba Causeway). The Afghan Memorial **Church of St John the Baptist** (1847-58) is at the northern edge of Colaba itself. Fishermen still unload their catch early in the morning at **Sassoon Dock**, the first wet dock in India; photography is prohibited.

Central Mumbai

The area stretching north from Colaba Causeway to Victoria Terminus dates from after 1862, when Sir Bartle Frere became Governor (1862-7).

Pope Paul (Oval) Maidan
The old buildings of the centre are floodlit after 1900

The Oval garden has been restored to a pleasant public garden. On the east side of the Pope Paul (Oval) Maidan is the Venetian Gothic style old **Secretariat** (1874), with a façade of arcaded verandahs and porticos faced in buff-coloured Porbander stone from Gujarat. The **University Convocation Hall** (1874) to its north was designed by Sir George Gilbert Scott in a 15th-century French decorated style.

The **High Court** (1871-79), in early English Gothic style, has a central tower flanked by lower octagonal towers topped by the figures of Justice and Mercy. Opposite, is the former General Post Office (1869-72).

Horniman Circle From the imposing Horniman Circle, Vir Nariman Road leads to Flora (or Frere) Fountain (1869), now known as **Hutatma Chowk** On the west edge are the Venetian Gothic **Elphinstone Buildings** (1870) in brown sandstone. The **Cathedral Church of St Thomas**, begun in 1672, has a number of monuments inside forming a heroic 'Who's Who of India'. The **Custom House** is believed to incorporate a Portuguese barrack block of 1665. Over the entrance is the crest of the East India Company. Parts of the old Portuguese fort's walls can be seen.

The Mint (1824-29), built on the fort rubbish dump, has Ionic columns and a water tank in front of it. The **Town Hall** (1820-3) has been widely admired as one of the best neo-classical buildings in India. The Corinthian interior houses the Assembly Rooms and the Bombay Asiatic Society.

Behind Horniman Circle on the water's edge lies the **Old Castle**. Entry is not permitted. Going north to CST (VT) station you pass the **Port Trust Office** on your right, while a little farther on, to your right by the station is the **General Post Office** (1909).

Central Mumbai

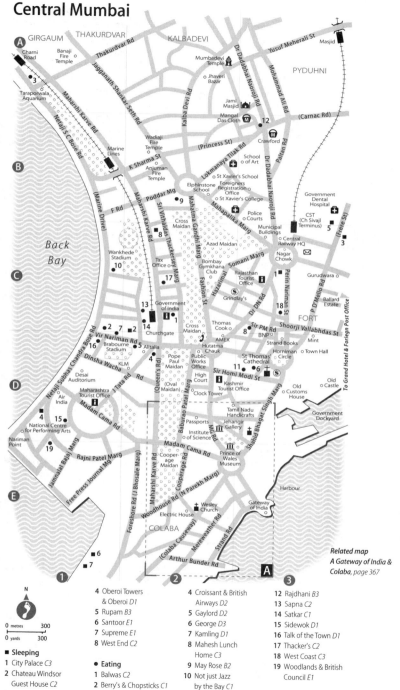

GIRGAUM · THAKURDVAR · KALBADEVI · PYDUHNI

Charni Road · Banaji Fire Temple · Taraporwala Aquarium · Thakurdvar Rd · Jagganath Shankar Seth Rd · Mumbadevi Temple · Jhaveri Bazar · Yusuf Meherali St · Masjid

Marine Lines · Wadiaji Fire Temple · (Princess St) · Jami Masjid · Mangal Das Cloth · Crawford · (Carnac Rd) · Mohammad Ali Rd · Dr Dadabhai Naoroji Rd · Patani Rd

K Sharma St · Anjuman Fire Temple · Lakhmanya Tilak Rd · School of Art · St Xavier's School · Foreigners Registration Office · St Xavier's College · Government Dental Hospital

Poddar Mg · Elphinstone School · Mahatma Gandhi Marg · Police Courts · Municipal Buildings · Central Railway HQ · CST (Ch Sivaji Terminus) · (Frere St)

Back Bay · Cross Maidan · Azad Maidan · Bombay Gymkhana Club · Nagar Chowk · Gurudwara · Ballard Estate

Wankhede Stadium · Tax Office · Fashion St · Rajasthan Tourist Office · Grindlay's · D'Mello Rd · Perin Nariman St

Government of India · Churchgate · Cross Maidan · Thomas Cook · Sir PM Rd · BNP · Shoorji Vallabhdas St · FORT · Town Hall · Mint

Vir Nariman Rd · Brabourne Stadium · Alitalia · AMEX · Strand Books · Horniman Circle · St Thomas' Cathedral · Old Custom House

Dinsha Wacha · KLM · Pope Paul Maidan · Public Works Office · Sir Homi Modi St · Old Castle

Desai Auditorium · (Queen's Rd) · High Court · Kashmir Tourist Office · Clock Tower · Government Dockyard

Air India · Maharashtra Tourist Office · Madam Cama Rd · Passports · Tamil Nadu Handicrafts · Jehangir Gallery · Institute of Science

National Centre for Performing Arts · Rajni Patel Marg · Cooper-age Maidan · Prince of Wales Museum · Harbour

Nariman Point · Jamnalal Bajaj Marg · Free Press Journal Mg · Madam Cama Rd · Woodhouse Rd (N Parekh Marg) · Wesley Church · Electric House · Gateway of India

COLABA · (Colaba Causeway) · Arthur Bunder Rd · Mereweather Rd · Strand Rd

Related map
A Gateway of India &
Colaba, page 367

Mumbai

N

0 metres 300
0 yards 300

■ **Sleeping**
1 City Palace *C3*
2 Chateau Windsor Guest House *C2*
3 Manama *C3*
4 Oberoi Towers & Oberoi *D1*
5 Rupam *B3*
6 Santoor *E1*
7 Supreme *E1*
8 West End *C2*

● **Eating**
1 Balwas *C2*
2 Berry's & Chopsticks *C1*
3 Copa Cabana *A1*
4 Croissant & British Airways *D2*
5 Gaylord *D2*
6 George *D3*
7 Kamling *D1*
8 Mahesh Lunch Home *C3*
9 May Rose *B2*
10 Not just Jazz by the Bay *C1*
11 Piccolo Café *D3*
12 Rajdhani *B3*
13 Sapna *C2*
14 Satkar *C1*
15 Sidewok *D1*
16 Talk of the Town *D1*
17 Thacker's *C2*
18 West Coast *C3*
19 Woodlands & British Council *E1*

CST or 'VT'
(Victoria
Terminus)
Station area

The **Chhatrapati Sivaji Terminus** (formerly Victoria Terminus or VT) (1878-87), the most remarkable example of Victorian Gothic architecture in India, was opened during Queen Victoria's Golden Jubilee year. The first train in India had left from this terminus for Thane in April 1853. Known today as 'CST' over half a million commuters use the station every day. The booking hall with its arcades, stained glass and glazed tiles was inspired by London's St Pancras station. As Tillotson argues, the introduction of Gothic allowed a blending of western traditions with Indian (often Islamic Indian) motifs, which became known as the Indo-Saracenic style. The new giant caterpillar-like walkway with perspex awnings looks incongruous against the gothic structure of 'VT'. Opposite the CST station are the grand Municipal Buildings (1893).

Crawford Market (1865-71), now Jyotiba Phule Market, was designed by Emerson in the 12th-century French Gothic style. Over the entrance is more of Lockwood Kipling's work; the paving stones are from Caithness! The market is divided into sections for fruit, vegetables, fish, mutton and poultry.

Marine Drive &
Malabar Hill

You can do an interesting half-day trip from Churchgate Station, along Marine Drive to the Taraporewala Aquarium, Mani Bhavan (Gandhi Museum), the Babulnath Temple, past the Parsi Towers of Silence to Kamla Nehru Park, the Hanging Gardens and the Jain Temple. If you wish you can go further towards Malabar Point to get a glimpse of Raj Bhavan and the Walkeshwar Temple.

At Marine Drive and Chowpatty Beach the long stretch of white sand beach looks attractive from a distance, but is polluted. Swimming here is not recommended but there is a lot of interesting beach activity.

The **Hanging Gardens** (Pherozeshah Mehta Gardens) immediately south of the Towers of Silence, in the centre of a low hill, are so named since they are located on top of a series of tanks that supply water to Mumbai. The gardens themselves have little of interest but there are good views over the city from the children's park across the road. Snake charmers operate from the roadside.

Museums

Mahatma Gandhi Museum (**Mani Bhavan**) This private house, at 19 Laburnum Road, where Mahatma Gandhi used to stay on visits to Mumbai, is now a memorial museum and research library with 20,000 volumes. It is well worth a visit. The display of photos and letters on the first floor is interesting and includes letters Gandhi wrote to Hitler (1939) asking him not to go to war. Cards, pamphlets et cetera at the door. ■ *0930-1800. Rs 3. West of Grant Rd, allow 1 hr.*

Victoria and Albert Museum (Bhav Daji Laud Museum) Inspired by the V&A in London and financed by public subscription, it was built in 1872 in a Palladian style. Sir George Birdwood, a noted physician and authority on Indian crafts, became its first curator. The collection covers the history of Mumbai and contains prints, maps and models. ■ *Mon, Tue, Thu, Fri, Sat 1030-1700, Sun 0830-1645, closed Wed. North of Byculla station.*

In front of the museum is a Clocktower (1865) with four faces (morning, noon, evening and night) and a stone statue of an elephant found by the Portuguese in the harbour. Elephanta Island was named after it. The **Victoria Gardens** are very attractive. A list at the entrance shows which trees are in blossom.

Prince of Wales Museum (Soon to be the Chhatrapati Shivaji Museum if the trend continues) This was designed by George Wittet to commemorate the visit of the Prince of Wales to India in 1905. The archaeological section has three main groups: Brahminical, Buddhist and Jain; Prehistoric and Foreign. The Indus Valley section is well displayed. The art section includes an excellent collection of Indian miniatures and well displayed *tankhas*. There are also works by Gainsborough, Poussin and Titian as well as Indian silver, jade, tapestries and a collection of arms. The Natural History section is based on the collection of the Bombay Natural History Society founded in 1833, and includes dioramas. ■ *Closed Mon. 1015-1730 (Oct-Feb), 1015-1800 (Jul-Sep), 1015-1830 (Mar-Jun). Entry (foreigners) Rs 150. Camera fee Rs 15 (no flash or tripods). Good guide books and reproductions on sale. South end of MG Road.*

Jehangir Art Gallery (in the Prince of Wales Museum complex). Mumbai's modern art gallery which hosts short term exhibitions. The '*Samovar*' café is good for a snack and a drink including chilled beer; pleasant garden-side setting. ■ *1030-1900, closed Mon.* **National Gallery of Modern Art**, Sir Cowasji Jehangir Hall, MG Rd opposite Prince of Wales Museum.

The heavily forested Elephanta Island, often barely visible in the mist from Mumbai only 10 km away, rises out of the bay like a giant whale. The setting is symbolically significant: the sea is the ocean of life, a world of change (Samsara) in which is set an island of spiritual and physical refuge. The temple caves dedicated to Siva were excavated in the volcanic lava high up the slope of the hill. They saw Hindu craftsmen over 1,000 years ago express their view of spiritual truths in massive carvings of extraordinary grace. Sadly a large proportion have been severely damaged, but enough remains to illustrate something of their skill.

Elephanta Caves

Ins and outs Maharashtra Tourism launches with good guides from the Gateway of India every 30 mins from 0900 (last one leaves Elephanta at 1730) except during the monsoon from Jun-Sep. The very pleasant journey takes 1½ hrs (Rs 65-85 return). Reservations, T2026364. Small private boats without guides continue during the monsoon when the seas can be very rough. From the landing place, a 300 m path along the quayside and then about 110 rough steps lead to the caves at a height of 75 m. The walk along the quay can be avoided when the small train functions (Rs 6). The climb can be trying for some, especially if it is hot, though *doolies* (chairs carried by porters) are available for Rs 300+ (unnecessary for the reasonably fit). The monkeys can be aggressive. Elephanta is very popular with local day-trippers so avoid the weekend rush. Entrance US$10 for foreigners, Rs 10 Indians. MTDC, T2848323, has 2 rooms for resting during the day (Rs 400).

Early morning is the best time for light & also for avoiding large groups with guides which arrive from around 1000. The caves tend to be quite dark so carry a powerful torch

Pick up *Mumbai This Fortnight*, an informative free booklet on everything that is hot in the city. Free from larger bookshops and stores. **Just Dial 888 8888** for free telephonic Yellow Pages service.

Essentials

Most hotels are concentrated in the central area (Marine Drive, Nariman Pt, Apollo Bunder and Colaba). Juhu and Vile Parle (pronounced 'Veelay Parlay') are convenient for late arrivals and early morning departures from the airport. Prices are much higher than elsewhere in India but there are some moderately priced hotels immediately behind the *Taj Mahal Hotel*. It is difficult to find even dormitory beds under Rs 200. **Hotlink**, India's 1st on-line reservation system, links 300 medium to top class hotels, T6152394.

Accommodation in Mumbai is usually very heavily booked. Whenever possible make reservations in advance. If you have not, arrive as early in the day as possible

Sleeping:
Airport,
Bandra &
Juhu Beach

Juhu Beach (20 km from the centre) used to be quite an attractive and relaxed seaside area but the sea is now polluted. On Sun evenings the beach takes on a fairground atmosphere. Most airport hotels offer free transfer. The Tourist Information Counter at the airport will help to book.

Airport LL-L *Leela Palace*, Sahar (near International Terminal), T86363636, F86360606. 460 modern rooms, excellent restaurants, pricey but excellent, no bar to non-residents after 2300. **L-AL** *Orchid*, 70C Nehru Rd, Vile Parle (east), T6100707, F6105974, 5 mins' walk from domestic terminal. Totally refurbished, attractive rooms, 'eco-friendly' (energy saving, recycling etc), *Boulevard* boasts a '15 minute lightening menu' and good midnight buffet, handy coffee shop. **B-C** *Airport International*, 5/6, Nehru Rd, Vile Parle (east), F6141773, near domestic terminal. 27 rooms, modern business hotel, clean, comfortable. **B-C** *Atithi*, 77A Nehru Rd, Vile Parle (east) 7 mins' walk from domestic terminal, T6116124, F6111998. 47 rooms, functional, clean, popular. **B** *Host Inn*, opposite Marol Fire Brigade, Andheri-Kurla Rd, Andheri (east), near International airport, T8360105, F8391080. Decent, clean rooms, friendly. **B-C** *Kumaria Presidency*, Andheri-Kurla Rd, facing Leela Palace, Andheri (east), T8352601, F8373850. 32 a/c rooms, 24-hr exchange, friendly, 24 hr room-service. **B-C** *Transit*, off Nehru Rd, Vile Parle (east), T6105812, F6105785. 54 rooms, modern, reasonable "overnight halt" for airport, excellent restaurant (good food and service, draught beer), airport transfer.

Bandra LL *Regent*, Land's End, Bandra Bandstand, T6551234, F6512471, buscent.regent@lokhandwalahotels.com City's newest luxury hotel, very spacious and chic, top facilities. **B** *Metro Palace*, Hill Rd, near Bandra station (W), T6427311, F6431932. Close to domestic airport, good restaurant (excellent buffet lunches, Rs 150).

Most are under 10 km
from the airport

Juhu Beach L-AL *Holiday Inn*, Balraj Sahani Marg, T6204444, F6204452. 190 rooms, 2 pools, courtesy coach to town, reliable. **AL** *Sun-n-Sand*, 39 Juhu Beach, T6201811, F6202170. 118 rooms, best refurbished, comfortable, though cramped poolside, good restaurant. **A** *Citizen*, 960 Juhu Tara Rd, T6117273, F6227270, citizen@bom2.Vsnl.net.in 45 smallish but very well appointed rooms, suites, efficient airport transfer. **B** *Juhu Hotel*, Juhu Tara Rd, T6184014. Spacious comfortable cottage-style rooms, sea-facing lawns, good restaurant (try seafood and Mughlai), soundproofed disco. **B** *Sands*, 39/2 Juhu Beach, T6204511, F6205268. 40 rooms, excellent restaurant.

Mumbai airport & Juhu Beach

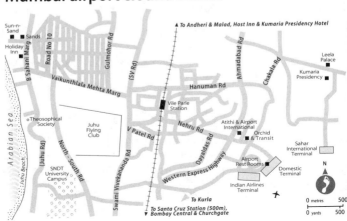

Mumbai

Mid-range *Gazalee*, Kadambari Complex, Hanuman Rd, Vile Parle (E), T8388093. Finest coastal cuisine. *Just around the Corner*, 24th-30th road junction, TPS III, Bandra (W). Bright casual American style diner. Extensive breakfast menu (0800-1100), excellent salads. *Out of the Blue*, at Pali Hills. Steak and fondue, great sizzlers, flavoured ice teas, flambéed desserts. *Trim with Taste*, 500 Sant Kutir, Linking Rd, Bandra (lane behind KBN department store). Small, spotless, serving unusual health food. **Cheap** *China Town*, Marol-Maroshi Rd, Andheri (E), excellent Indian, Chinese, wide choice, very friendly. *Crunchy Munchy*, Agarwal Market, next to Vile Parle (E) station. Open-air café serving veg Indian and Mexican mini-meals. *Kanchi*, Mittal Industrial Estate, Andheri-Kurla Road, Marol, Andheri (E). Excellent South Indian vegetarian. *Lucky*, 9 SV Rd (Hill Rd junction), Bandra (W). Good Mughlai and tandoori. *Potpourri*, Carlton Court, Turner/Pali Rd junction, opposite HSBC. Streetside café serving great Italian food and desserts.

**Eating:
Airport,
Juhu Beach &
Bandra**
*Bandra has some
exciting options*

C *Sagar*, Nagpada Junction (Bellasin Rd/JB Behram Marg corner), Byculla, T3092727, F3072408. Very clean rooms, good restaurant, friendly. **C-D** *Red Rose*, Gokuldas Pasta Rd, (behind Chitra Cinema) Dadar East, T4137843. 31 rooms, some a/c, mostly shared but clean baths, flexible checkout, friendly – "welcoming at 0530 with no booking". **D** *Anukool*, 292-8 Maulana Saukat Ali Rd, T3081401, F3078187, hotelanukool@ hotmail.com 23 rooms, some a/c, friendly, helpful, good value. **D** *Kalpana Palace*, 181 P Bapurao Marg, opposite Daulat Cinema, Grant Rd, T3000846. 30 decent rooms, some a/c. **D-E** *YMCA International House*, 18 YMCA Rd, near Mumbai Central, T3091191. Decent rooms, shared bath, meals included, temp membership Rs 60, deposit Rs 1,300, good value, book 3 months ahead with deposit.

**Sleeping:
Dadar, Mumbai
Central &
Grant Rd area**
■ *on map, page 358
Dadar can be a
good option to stay –
plenty of restaurants
& good trains to
Churchgate & CST*

Expensive *Biscotti*, Crossroads, Haji Ali, T4955055. Excellent Italian. Wholesome, leisurely dining, bistro-style complete with fiddler. *Goa Portuguesa*, THK Rd, Mahim. Goan. Authentic dishes, taverna-style with guitarist. *Only Fish*, Hotel Rosewood, J Dadaji Rd, Tulsiwadi, Tardeo, T4940320. Indian regional recipes (including Bengali). Seafood too, small but stylish. *Revival*, Chowpatty Sea Face (near footbridge). Classy, good Indian/continental buffets and desserts, ices. **Mid-range** *Bombay A1*, 7 Vadilal A Patel Marg (Grant Rd Junc). Parsi. Cheerful, varied menu, try *Patrani machli*. *Chinatown*, 99 August Kranti Marg. Szechwan, Cantonese, Mandarin. Varied menu (27 soups), upstairs more comfortable. *Copper Chimney*, Dr AB Rd, Worli, T4924488. Indian. Window into kitchen, excellent food from extensive menu, undiscovered by tourists. *Rajdhani*, Mangaldas Rd, opposite Crawford Market. Indian. An a/c oasis, excellent lunch *thali*, very friendly welcome. *Rashtriya*, Rd leading to Dadar (East) stairway. South Indian vegetarian. Good food and excellent coffee. *Under the Over*, 36 Altamount Rd (by flyover). Bistro like, for Mexican, Creole dishes, sizzlers and rich desserts, no alcohol. **Cheap** *Heaven*, corner of Grant Rd/P Bapurao Marg. Very cheap, friendly (eg *aloo matar* Rs 10). *Kamat*, Navrose Mansion, Tardeo Rd. Indian. Very inexpensive *thalis* and veg snacks. **Fast food** *Kobe*, Hughes Rd, 12 Sukh Sagar. For Japanese sizzlers. *New Yorker*, 25 Chowpatty Sea Face. Pizzas, sandwiches and Mexican fast food, ice cream. *Swaati,* Tardeo Rd for clean *bhelpuri* and *chaats*.

**Eating:
Dadar, Mumbai
Central & Grant
Rd area**

LL-AL *The Oberoi*, Nariman Pt, T2325757, F2041505. 350 large rooms, the newer Oberoi combining modern technology with period furniture, excellent restaurants. **LL-AL** *Oberoi Towers*, Nariman Pt, T2324343, F2043282. 650 rooms, superb views from higher floors, good buffets, garden pool, excellent shopping complex. **A-B** *West End*, 45 New Marine Lines, T2039121, F2057506. 80 small, pleasant suites but need refurbishing, good restaurant, excellent service, well located. **B-C** *Chateau Windsor Guest House*, 86 Vir Nariman Rd, T2043376, F2851415. 36 rooms (some a/c) vary, some very small and dark, room service for light snacks and drinks, friendly, clean. Cash only. **C-D** *Supreme*, 4 Pandey Rd, T2185623. Clean rooms with bath, good service but a little noisy.

**Sleeping:
Central
Mumbai**
■ *on map, page 361
Price codes:
see inside front cover*

Mumbai

Eating:
Central
Mumbai

Expensive *Indian Summer*, 80 Vir Nariman Rd, T2835445. Indian. Excellent food, tasty *kebabs*, interesting modern glass décor, smart dress, reserve. *Gaylord*, Vir Nariman Rd, T2821231. Indian. Good food (huge portions) and service, tables inside and out, barbecue, pleasant, good bar, tempting pastry counter. *Santoor*, Maker Arcade, Cuffe Parade, T2182262. North Indian. Small place, Mughlai and Kashmiri specialities. *Sidewok*, next to NCPA theatre, T2818132. Interesting southeast Asian/fusion cuisine. Innovative menu, imaginative cocktails (try non-alcoholic too), surprise entertainment by staff, a special, fun dining experience. Reserve. **Mid-range** *Berry's*, Vir Nariman Rd, near Churchgate Station, T2875691. North Indian. Tandoori specialities, good *kulfi*. *Chopsticks*, 90A Vir Nariman Rd, Churchgate, T2832308. Chinese, good, hot and spicy Schezwan. Offering unusual dishes (taro nest, date pancakes, toffee bananas). *Kamling*, 82 Vir Nariman Rd, T2042618. Genuine Cantonese. Simple surroundings, but excellent preparations, try seafood, often busy. *May Rose*, Cinema Rd (next to 'Metro'), T2081104. Chinese. Clean a/c, very good food. *Sapna*, Vir Nariman Rd. Indian, very traditional Mughlai delicacies, bar, some tables outside, attentive service. *Satkar*, Indian Express Building, opposite Churchgate station, T2043259. Indian. Delicious vegetarian, fruit juices and shakes; a/c section more expensive. **Cheap** *Balwas*, Maker Bhavan, 3 Sir V Thackersey Marg. Inexpensive, well-prepared food. *Piccolo Café*, 11A Sir Homi Mody St. Parsi. 0900-1800, closed Sat afternoon and Sun, profits to charity, homely, clean, good *dhansak*. **Cafés and fast food** *Croissants*, Vir Nariman Rd, opposite Eros Cinema. Burgers, sandwiches, hot croissants with fillings, ice cream, lively atmosphere. *Fountain*, MG Rd. For sizzlers and apple pie in a café atmosphere.

Sleeping:
CST (VT) & Fort
■ *on map, page 361*
Price codes:
see inside front cover

B *Grand*, 17 Sprott Rd, Ballard Estate, T2618211, F2626581. 73 a/c rooms, exchange, bookstand, old-fashioned, built around a simple, central courtyard, helpful service, very relaxing. **C-D** *City Palace*, 121 City Terrace (Nagar Chowk), opposite CST Main Gate, T2615515, F2676897. Tiny though spotless rooms (some without window), with bath (Indian WC), some a/c, renovated, modern, room service, good value. **D-E** *Manama*, 221 P D'Mello Rd, T2613412. Reasonable rooms, few with bath and a/c, popular. **D-E** *Rupam*, 239 P D'Mello Rd, T2618298. 37 rooms, some a/c with phone, clean, friendly, comfortable beds.

Eating:
CST (VT) & Fort

Mid-range *Bharat*, 317 SB Singh Marg, opposite Fort Market, T2618991. Excellent seafood and crab as well as *naans* and *rotis*. *George*, 20 Apollo St (near Horniman Circle). Pleasant quiet atmosphere, faded colonial feel, good service, lunchtime *biriyanis* and *thalis* unique charm may disappear after 2001 renovation). *Mahesh Lunch Home*, Sir PM Rd, Fort. Excellent for Mangalorean, Goan and *tandoori* seafood, a/c, bar, very popular. *West Coast*, Rustom Sidhwa Rd, off Sir Perin Nariman Rd. Very good meals.

Sleeping:
Gateway of
India & Colaba
■ *on map*
Price codes:
see inside front cover

Rooms with seaview
are more expensive

AL *Taj Mahal*, the original, with great style and character, 294 rooms, and *Taj Mahal Intercontinental*, Apollo Bunder, T2023366, F2872711. 306 rooms, excellent restaurants (no shorts). *Tanjore* (good *thalis*), Indian dance performance (evenings), open to non-residents (Rs 100, 1 hr). **L-AL** *Fariyas*, 25 off Arthur Bunder Rd, Colaba, T2042911, F2834992. 80 upgraded rooms, good restaurants, 'pub', roof garden, pool (open to non-residents), obliging service. **A** *Strand*, 25 PJ Ramchandani Marg, T2882222. Friendly, clean, decent rooms, some with bath and seaview. **B** *Apollo*, 22 Lansdowne Rd, Colaba, behind *Taj*, T2020223, F2871592. 39 rooms, some a/c, not all with sea view, excellent, helpful, friendly service. **B** *Diplomat*, 24-26 BK Boman Behram Marg (behind *Taj*), T2021661, F2830000, diplomat@vsnl.com 52 a/c rooms, restaurant, quiet, friendly, relaxed atmosphere, good value. **B** *Regent*, 8 Ormiston Rd (Best Marg), T2871854. Well furnished a/c rooms, no restaurant but good room service. **B** *Suba Palace*, Apollo Bunder, T2020636, F2020812, just behind *Taj*. Clean, modern, well run.

Mumbai

B-C *Godwin*, 41 Garden Rd, T2841226, F2871592. 48 large, clean, renovated, a/c rooms (upper floors have better views), good restaurant, rooftop garden, very helpful management. **B-C** *Shelley's*, 30 PJ Ramchandani Marg, Colaba, T2840229, F2840385. Large comfortable, bright airy a/c rooms, some sea-facing with TV and fridge (more expensive), a 'heritage' building with character, breakfasts only, helpful and friendly owners. **C** *Bentley's*, 17 Oliver Rd, off Garden Rd, T2841474, F2871846, bentleyshotel@ hotmail.com 37 rooms (some large with bath better value), 4 a/c, breakfast included, avoid annexe ("dirty, with rats"), young owner, very helpful. **C-D** *YWCA International*

Gateway of India and Colaba

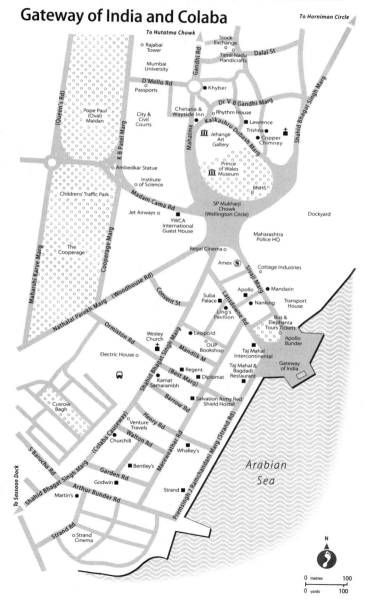

To Horniman Circle

To Hutatma Chowk

Stock Exchange
Dalal St
Tamil Nadu Handicrafts

o Rajabai Tower

Mumbai University

Gandhi Rd

D'Mello Rd
Passports

● Khyber

Dr V B Gandhi Marg

Chetana & Wayside Inn
o Rhythm House

Pope Paul (Oval) Maidan
City & Civil Courts
Kaikashru Dubash Marg
■ Lawrence
Trishna ●
Copper Chimney

Jehangir Art Gallery

K B Patel Marg
Mahatma

o Ambedkar Statue

Prince of Wales Museum

Institute of Science

BNHS

Childrens' Traffic Park

Madam Cama Rd

SP Mukharji Chowk (Wellington Circle)

Dockyard

Jet Airways o

YWCA International Guest House

Maharashtra Police HQ

Cooperage Marg

The Cooperage

Regal Cinema ■

Amex $

Cottage Industries

Sivaji Marg

Apollo ● ● Mandarin

Suba Palace ■
Nanking ●
Transport House

Ling's Pavilion

Bus & Elephanta Tours Tickets

Nathalal Parekh Marg (Woodhouse Rd)

Ormiston Rd

Convent St

Lansdowne Rd

Wesley Church
● Leopold
OUP Bookshop

Apollo Bunder

Taj Mahal Intercontinental

Electric House o

Mandlik M

Maharshi Karve Marg

Regent ■
(Best Marg)
Kamat Samarambh ■
■ Diplomat
Taj Mahal & Bagdadi Restaurant
Gateway of India

Shahid Bhagat Singh Marg

Barrow Rd
■ Salvation Army Red Shield Hostel

Cusrow Bagh

Henry Rd
o Venture Travels
● Churchill

Walton Rd

Mereweather Rd

Whalley's ■

Arabian Sea

S Barucha Rd

Garden Rd
■ Bentley's
Godwin ■

Premsingh J Ramchandani Marg (Strand Rd)

Strand ■

Martin's ●

Arthur Bunder Rd

Shahid Bhagat Singh Marg

o Strand Cinema

Strand Rd

To Sassoon Dock

(Queen's Rd)

Shahid Bhagat Singh Marg

 Ambedkar

Colaba Causeway

N

0 metres 100
0 yards 100

Mumbai

Centre, 2nd Flr, 18 Madam Cama Rd (entrance on side), fort, T2020122, F2020445. For both sexes, 34 clean, pleasant rooms with bath (mostly Rs 600 per person), breakfast and dinner included, temp membership Rs 60 – essential to write in advance with Rs 1,300 deposit. **C-D** *Whalley's*, 41 Mereweather Rd, T2834206. 25 rooms (inspect first), some good a/c with balcony and bath, includes breakfast, accepts TCs, old-fashioned.

Few budget hotels are left in the area charging under Rs 400 though you may get a dormitory bed for Rs 250

D *Lawrence*, Rope Walk Lane, behind Prince of Wales Museum, T2843618. 9 rooms, usually full, very good value. **D** *Sea Shore*, 4th Flr, 1/49 Kamal Mansion, Arthur Bunder Rd, T2874237, F2874238. Has good rooms facing sea (avoid others), clean. Some **E-F** category hotels are clustered around the *Taj Mahal Hotel*: **Salvation Army Red Shield Hostel**, 30 Mereweather Rd, T2841824. Mostly dorm (about Rs 150 including breakfast, Rs 200 including meals), some double rooms (Rs 450, all meals), lockers Rs 30 per item 0800-2200, showers Rs 30, check out 0900, book in advance or arrive early, friendly, but could be cleaner.

Eating: Gateway of India & Colaba
● *on map*

Expensive *Apoorva*, near Horniman Circle, Fort, T2881457. Very good seafood, especially crabs and prawns. *Excellent Sea*, Ballard Estate, T2668195. Excellent crab, prawn and lobster. *Khyber*, 145 MG Rd, Kala Ghoda, Fort, T2632174. North Indian. For an enjoyable evening in beautiful surroundings , excellent food, especially lobster and *reshmi* chicken kebabs, try *paya* soup, outstanding restaurant, reserve. *Ling's Pavilion*, 19/21 KC College Hostel Building, off Colaba Causeway (behind *Taj* and Regal Cinema), T2850023. Stylish décor, good atmosphere and delightful service, colourful menu, seafood specials, generous helpings. *Nanking*, Apollo Bunder, T2881638. Chinese. Good choice of very good Cantonese dishes. *Trishna*, 7 Rope Walk Lane, behind Kala Ghoda, by Old Synagogue, T2672176. Indian. Good coastline cuisine, seafood, excellent crab. "Swinging, crowded and fun", close after lunch at 1600.

Mid-range *Bagdadi*, Tullock Rd (behind *Taj Hotel*), T2028027. Mughlai. One of the cheapest, first class food, fragrant biryani, delicious chicken (Rs 40), crowded but clean. *Chetana*, 34 K Dubash Marg, opposite Jahangir Gallery, T2844968. Gujarati, Rajasthani vegetarian. Excellent *thalis*, unique dining experience (also small religious bookshop), "memorable". *Mandarin*, T2023186. Chinese. Excellent food and service (also cold beer). *Ming Place*, Apsara Building, Colaba Causeway, T2872820. Chinese.

Cheap *Bade Miyan*, behind Ling's Pavilion. Street side kebab corner but very clean. *Kamat Samarambh*, opposite Electric House, SB Singh Marg. Indian vegetarian. Very good *thalis* and snacks, try *chola battura*. *Martin's*, near Strand Cinema. Goan. Simple, authentic Goan food, excellent seafood and pork *sorpotel*. *Paradise*, Sindh Chambers, Colaba Causeway. Parsi and others. Spotless, excellent *dhansak*; closed Mon (not a/c).

Cafés and fast food Many serve chilled beer: *Churchill*, opposite Cusrow Baug, Colaba Causeway, T2844689. Good late breakfasts, continental and steaks served in small a/c café, choice of desserts, ices, shakes. *Leopold's*, Colaba, T2830585. Still full of young backpackers for good Western food friendly but getting expensive. *Wayside Inn*, 38 K Dubash Marg, T2844324. Quaint country inn-style good breakfast menu, average continental, breezy, laid back and leisurely.

Bars & discos Many pubs expect couples Fri-Sun. Most pubs charge Rs 175-250 for a 'pitcher' (bottle); cocktails Rs 75-150.

Expensive Gateway area *Taj Mahal*, on top floor of the newer building, has excellent all-round views. *Oberoi* too, but all at a price. Taj's *Beyond 1900s*. Exclusive disco, expensive drinks (Rs 330 entry). **Central Mumbai** Ambassador's (Churchgate) *Flavors*.

Bright 24-hr coffee shop-resto-bar. Chic, interesting cocktails and starters (PSP prawns, Corn and spinach toast), barbecue buffet lunch (Rs 300-800). Fun at a price. Casual. *Not Just Jazz by the Bay*, 143 Marine Drive, T2851876. Modern chrome and glass, live music (varied), good food, generous portions, very lively.

Mid-range Central Mumbai *Café Olé*, ground floor, Cross Roads, Haji Ali, T4955123. Classic sports bar, chrome and glass, interesting menu (some Indianized), try Cactus Passion or Red Ginger (non-alcoholic), mini dance floor, DJ at weekends, fun place, affordable drinks. *Copa Cabana*, Dariya Vihar, 39/D Girgaum, Chowpatty, T3680274. Small, playing 70s hits and Latino music, packed at weekends so little space for dancing. *Ghetto*, B Desai Rd (100 m from Mahalakshmi Temple). Western pop from 60s, 70s, 80s, free entry (couples only), neon graffiti. *Geoffreys*, *Hotel Marine Plaza*, Marine Drive, T2851212. Soft music, relaxing for a drink and a bite, no dancing. **Juhu** *Paparazzi*, opposite Juhu Bus Depot, Juhu Beach Rd, T6602199. Small, cosy disco bar, packed after 2300, drinks and snacks. Closed Mon. *Razzberry Rhinoceros* Juhu Tara Rd, T6184012. Disco, night club. Lots of space for dancing, pool tables, check for live acts.

Cheap Popular bars behind *Taj Mahal Hotel* include *Gokul*.

Most shops are open 1000-1900 (closed Sun), the bazars sometimes staying open as **Shopping** late as 2100. Mumbai prices are often higher than in other Indian cities and hotel arcades tend to be very pricey but carry good quality select items. *Crossroads & Pyramid*, Haji Ali, are modern shopping centres.

Bazars *Crawford Market*, MR Ambedkar Rd (fun for bargain hunting) and *Mangaldas Market*. Other shopping streets are South Bhagat Singh Marg, M Karve Rd and Linking Rd, Bandra. For a different experience try *Chor (Thieves') Bazaar*, on Maulana Shaukat Ali Rd in central Mumbai, full of finds – from Raj left-overs to precious jewellery. On Fri, 'junk' carts sell less expensive 'antiques' and fakes. **'Antiques'**: (it is illegal to take anything over 100 years old out of the country) *Natesan* in Jehangir Gallery basement and in *Taj Hotel* for fine antiques and copies; *Phillips*, Madame Cama Rd opposite Regal Cinema is an Aladdin's cave of bric-a-brac and curios.

Books *Crossword*, 22 B Desai Rd (near Mahalakshmi Temple), smart, spacious, good selection; *Danai*, 14th Khar Danda Rd, is good for books and music; *Nalanda*, *Taj Mahal Hotel*, excellent art books. *Strand Books*, off Sir PM Rd near HMV, T2061994, excellent selection, shipping (reliable). **Antiquarian** books and prints: *Jimmy Ollia*, Cumballa Chambers (1st Flr), Cumballa Hill Rd. **Second-hand**: lines of stalls along Churchgate St and near the University. *Dial-a-book*, T6495618, for quick delivery. **Fashion St** opposite Mumbai Gymkhana, South Bhagat Singh Marg, but check quality (often export surplus) and bargain vigorously.

Crafts and textiles Govt emporia from many states sell good handicrafts and textiles; several at *World Trade Centre,* Cuffe Parade. *Cottage Industries Emporium*, Apollo Bunder. Represents a nationwide selection, especially Kashmiri embroidery, South Indian handicrafts and Rajasthani textiles. New shop at Colaba Causeway, next to BEST, with additional fabrics, ethnic ware, handicrafts. *Khadi and Village Industries*, 286 Dr DN Rd. *Anokhi*, 4B August Kranti Marg, opposite Kumbala Hill Hospital. Good gifts. *Bombay Store*, PM Rd, Fort. Spacious, ethnic lifestyle, gifts (open Sun). *Contemporary Arts & Crafts*, 19 Napeansea Rd, classy collection (moderate prices). *Good Earth*, 104 Kemp's Corner. Smart, trendy, pottery, glass, handmade paper stationery. In Colaba, a street *Craft Market* is held on Sun (Nov-Jan) in K Dubash Marg. *Yamini* President House, Wodehouse Rd, Colaba, especially for vibrant textiles.

Mumbai

Getting to and from the airport

Buses *Red* BEST *buses connect both terminals with the city (Rs 38-45 plus baggage). Drop-off and pick-up points in town are* Air India *and* Indian Airlines *offices,* Taj Mahal Hotel *and* Prince of Wales Museum. *From the airports every two hours (odd hours);* **from the city,** *the bus starts from* Air India, Nariman Pt.

Pre-paid taxis *From the counter at the International terminal, recommended.*

Retain your receipt as the driver requires this at the end of the journey. Small additional charge for luggage. To Nariman Pt or Gateway, about Rs 260, one hour. During the rush hour it can take two hours.

Train *Outside the 'rush hour' and if travelling light, between Churchgate/ Dadar and Santa Cruz (Domestic)/Andheri (International), the train is a good option.*

Music *Groove*, West Wing, 1st Flr, Eros Cinema, Churchgate. Has café. *Hiro*, SP Mehta St. Good Indian classical CDs. *Planet M*, opposite CST station. Also has book/poetry readings, gigs. *Rhythm House*, north of Jehangir Gallery. Excellent selection of jazz and classical CDs at good prices.

Transport   **Local Auto-rickshaw** Not available in central Mumbai (south of Mahim). Metered; about Rs 8 per km, revised tariff card held by the driver (x8, in suburbs) 25% extra at night (1200-0500). **Taxi** Metered yellow-top and a/c blue: easily available. Rs 12 for first km and Rs 12 for each Re 1 on metre. Revised tariff card held by drivers. Always get a prepaid taxi at the airport. **Train** Suburban electric trains are economical. They start from Churchgate for the west suburbs and CST (VT) for the east suburbs but are often desperately crowded. Avoid peak hours (southbound 0700-1100, northbound 1700-2000), and keep a tight hold on valuables. **Bus** BEST (Bombay Electrical Supply Co) buses are available in most parts of Greater Mumbai, T4128725. Within the Central Business Dist, buses are marked 'CBD'.

There can be long **Long distance Air** Sahar International airport, T6329090, 8366700. Left Luggage
queues at counter, across the drive from end of Departure terminal, Rs 35 per item. International
immigration Departure Tax, Rs 500 (Rs 250 within South Asia). Departure tax is now often included in the price of your ticket. Look for 'FT' in the tax column.

Domestic terminals (Santa Cruz) The domestic terminal (1A), exclusively for *Indian Airlines*, is about 400 m from the **old** terminal (1B), used by others. Enquiries: T140, 143; *Indian Airlines*, T6156633. Mumbai has daily flights to Ahmadabad US$75, Bhuj US$100, Delhi US$175, Jaipur US$155, and non-daily to Jodhpur US$150.

Transport to and from the airport Pre-paid taxis into town, from counter at the exit at the **Sahar** International terminal (ignore taxi touts near the baggage hall). Give the exact area or hotel, and the number of pieces of luggage. Hand the receipt to the driver at the end of the journey. There is no need to tip. To Nariman Pt or Gateway, about Rs 260, 1 hr. During 'rush hour' it can take 2 hrs. To Juhu Beach Rs 150. From **Santa Cruz**: metered taxis should charge around the same. **Buses** The red BEST buses connect both terminals with the city.

Indian Airlines: Air India Building, Nariman Pt, T2876161, F2830832, flies to all major cities. *Jet Airways*: B1 Amarchand Mansions, Madam Cama Rd, T2855788, airport, T6156666, www.jetairways.com to 23 destinations. *Sahara*: T2882718, airport T6134159: **Delhi, Jaipur** and others.

Mumbai

It is often difficult to get reasonable **accommodation** in Mumbai, particularly late in the evening. Touts are very pushy at both terminals but the hotels they recommend are often appalling. It is worth making your own telephone call to hotels of your choice from the airport. The rest rooms in the old domestic terminal are clean, comfortable (rooms Rs 500, dorm Rs 200); available for those flying within 24 hrs, but are often full; apply to the Airport Manager.

Bus Maharashtra RTC operates bus services to all the major centres including Ahmadabad. Information on services from MSRTC, Central Bus Stand, Mumbai Central, T3076622, or Parel Depot, T4374399. Private buses also travel long distance routes. Some long distance buses also leave from Dadar where there are many travel agents. Information and tickets from Dadar Tourist Centre, just outside Dadar station, T4113398.

Car hire For 8 hrs or 80 km: luxury cars, a/c Rs 1,500; Maruti/Ambassador: a/c Rs 1,000, non a/c Rs 800. *Auto Hirers*, 7 Commerce Centre, Tardeo, T4942006; *Blaze*, Colaba, T2020073; *Budget*, T4942644, and *Sai*, Phoenix Mill Compound, Senapati Bapat Marg, Lower Parel, T4942644, F4937524. *Wheels*, T2822874.

Train Central Railway, enquiries, T134/135. Reservations, T2659512, 0800-1230, 1300-1630 (Foreigners' Counter opens 0900; best time to go); **Western Railway**, Churchgate, and Mumbai Central, 0800-1345, 1445-2000. All for 1st Class bookings and Indrail Passes. **Foreign tourists**: Tourist Quota counter on mezzanine floor above tourist office opposite Churchgate Station. Otherwise, queue downstairs at reservations. At CST, tourist counter on ground floor (towards the left), credit cards upstairs. Railway Tourist Guides at CST and Churchgate (Bus 138 goes between the two). *Times for trains & planes are published each Sat in the Indian Express newspaper. To book trains foreign tourists must have either foreign currency or an encashment certificate & passport*

The following depart from **Mumbai Central**: Ahmadabad: *Shatabdi Exp, 2009*, 0625, except Fri, 7 hrs; *Karnavati Exp, 2933*, 1340, except Wed, 7¾ hrs; *Saurashtra Mail, 9005*, 2025, 9 hrs; *Gujarat Mail, 2901*, 2150, 9 hrs; *Gujarat Exp, 9011*, 0545, 9¾ hrs; *Lokshakti Exp, 9143*, 1935, 9¾ hrs. New Delhi: *Rajdhani Exp, 2951*, 1655 (C), 17 hrs; *Golden Temple Mail, 2903*, 2130 (C), 21½ hrs; *Paschim Exp, 2925*, 1135 (C), 23 hrs; *Punjab Mail, 2137*, 1910, 25¼ hrs; *August Kranti Rajdhani Exp, 2953*, 1740 (C), 17¼ hrs (to Hazrat Nizamuddin).

Banks Most are open 1000-1400, Mon-Fri, 1000-1200, Sat. Closed on Sun, holidays, 30 Jun, 31 Dec. Best to change money at the airport, at Bureau de Change (upstairs) in Air India Building, Nariman Pt or at *Thomas Cook*, 324 Dr DN Rd, T2048556; also at 102B Maker Tower, 10th Flr, F Block, Cuffe Parade; TCI, Chander Mukhi, Nariman Pt and at International Airport. *American Express*, Regal Cinema Building, Colaba. *ATMs* for VISA card holders using their usual PIN have opened at *British Bank of the Middle East* BBME (16 Vir Nariman Rd); *Citibank* (Air India Building, Nariman Pt, 293 Dr DN Rd); *Hongkong Bank* (52/60 MG Rd, Fort); *Standard Chartered* (81 Ismaili Building, Dr DN Rd, 264 Annie Besant Rd). Also available at other branches across the city. *State Bank of India*, Bombay Samachar Marg (at *Centaur Airport Hotel* until 2200) and Churchgate, behind India Tourist Office, among others. **Credit Cards:** *American Express*, Lawrence & Mayo Bldg, Dr DN Rd; *Diners Club*, Raheja Chambers, 213 Nariman Pt; *Mastercard*, C Wing, Mittal Tower, Nariman Pt; *VISA*, Standard Chartered Grindlays Bank, 90 MG Rd.

Directory

Communications Usually open 1000-1700. Sahar Airport 24 hrs. Post offices all over the city and most 5 star hotels. GPO: Nagar Chowk. Mon-Sat, 0900-2000 (*Poste Restante* facilities 0900-1800) and Sun 1000-1730; parcels from 1st Flr, rear of building, 1000-1700 (Mon-Sat). **Internet:** Among many are *British Council*, 'A Wing' 1st Flr, Mittal Tower, Nariman Pt, T2823560, 1000-1745, Tue-Sat. Excellent library. *Cybercafé*, Waterfield, Bandra. *Infotek*, Express Towers, ground floor, Nariman Pt. *Shyam*

Mumbai

Communication, near *Grand Hotel*, WH Marg, Ballard Estate, T2614720. Very helpful service, Rs 40 per hr.

Hospitals and medical services Most hotels have a doctor on call. The telephone directory lists hospitals and General Practitioners. Admission to private hospitals may require a large cash advance (eg Rs 50,000). Guarantees from insurers may not be sufficient. *Prince Aly Khan Hospital*, Nesbit Rd near the harbour, T3754343, has been recommended. **Chemists:** several open day/night especially opposite Bombay Hospital. *Wordell*, Stadium House, Churchgate; *New Royal Chemist*, New Marine Lines; *Karnik's*, opposite RN Cooper Hospital, Gulmohar Rd.

Tour companies and travel agents Among many: *American Express*, Regal Cinema Building, Colaba, T2046361. *Cox and Kings*, 270-271 Dr DN Rd, T2070314. *Mercury*, 70VB Gandhi Rd, T2024785. *Sita*, 18 Atlanta, Nariman Pt, T2840666, F2044927. *Thomas Cook*, Cooks Building, Dr DN Rd, T2813454. *Space Travels*, 4th Flr, Sir PM Rd, T2864773, for discounted flights and special student offers, Mon-Fri, 1000-1700, Sat 1030-1500. *TCI*, Chandermukhi, Nariman Pt, T2021881. *Venture*, Ground Floor, Abubakar Mansion, South Bhagat Singh Marg, T2021304, F2822803, efficient, helpful and friendly.

Tourist offices Govt of India, 123 M Karve Rd, opposite Churchgate, T2093229, F2014496, Mon-Sat 0830-1730 (closed 2nd Sat of month from 1230). Counters open 24 hrs at both airports, and at *Taj Mahal Hotel*, Mon-Sat 0830-1530 (closed 2nd Sat from 1230). Helpful staff who can also issue Liquor Permits (essential for Gujarat). **Maharashtra**: www.mtdcindia.com CDO Hutments, opposite LIC Building, Madam Cama Rd, T2024627; Express Towers, 9th Flr, Nariman Pt, T2024482, F2024521; counters at international and domestic terminals. Also at Koh-i-Noor Rd, near *Pritam Hotel*, Dadar T4143200; CST Rly Station, T2622859 and Gateway of India, T2841877. **Gujarat**, Dhanraj Mahal, Apollo Bunder, T2024925; **Rajasthan**, 230 Dr DN Rd, T2075603.

Useful numbers Police Emergency: T100. **Fire:** T101. **Ambulance:** T102.

14

374

Background

History

Settlement and early history

Rajasthan and Gujarat were among the first regions of South Asia to be settled. Lower Palaeolithic – Old Stone Age – sites have been discovered in the Mahi, Sabarmati, Karjan and Orsang valleys in Gujarat, dating from between half a million and 50,000 years ago. Similarities between hand axes and cleavers discovered in the Chittaurgarh region of southeastern Rajasthan and northern Gujarat and those found in the Olduvai gorge in Africa have led archaeologists to suggest a slow diffusion from Africa to India, the Indian tools being much more recent.

Rajasthan and Gujarat are particularly rich in Middle Palaeolithic artefacts, dating from between 17,000 and 40,000 years before the present, probably during a considerably wetter period than at present. The settlers made use of even apparently inhospitable environments. In Gujarat and the Marwar region of Rajasthan, sand dunes often encloses shallow lakes which were the source of aquatic food for the inhabitants, while the dunes themselves were covered in thick scrub which supported a rich fauna, a source of food for hunters.

The first settlers

By 3500 BC agriculture had spread throughout the Indus Plains and had reached north-western India. Between 3000 BC and 2500 BC many new settlements sprang up in the heartland of what from 2500 BC became the Harappan or Indus Valley civilization, including cities such as Kalibangan in Rajasthan. Numerous townships of this Harappan period (2500-1500 BC) have been excavated in Rajasthan and Gujarat, most of them along rivers, near the sea coast, or in hills suitable for stone quarrying. In north-western Rajasthan Kalibangan was a major town and there are many other sites in the now dried up river beds of the Ghaggar and Sarasvati rivers. In Gujarat Surkotada in Kachchh has both a citadel and a lower town and the fortifications still rise to over 4 m. The 120-acre walled township of Dholavira is perhaps the most imposing of the many Indus sites excavated in India because smoothed blocks, columns, gateways and engraved stone have been found within the town's fortifications. Lothal offers an insight into the mature phase of the Indus civilization, with its great dry dock and bead factory. Like Lothal, Kuntasi was a port and had a 'factory' associated with it. Its importance as a trading port is suggested by the discovery of a copper ring with a spiral motif very similar to that found in Crete.

The Indus Valley Civilization was entirely home grown. What stimulated its origins however remains unclear, but its emergence as a distinct culture seems to have been sudden. Speculation continues to surround the nature of its language, which is still untranslated. It may well have been an early form of the Dravidian languages which today are found largely in South India, though as even the most basic characteristics such as whether the script should be read from left to right or right to left have not been conclusively demonstrated the questions far outnumber the reliable answers.

India from 2000 BC to the Mauryas

By 1700 BC the entire Indus Valley civilization had disintegrated. The causes remain uncertain. Sir Mortimer Wheeler's early explanation that the violent arrival of new waves of Aryan immigrants was responsible has now been discarded. Increasing desertification of the already semi-arid landscape, a shift in the course of the Indus as the result of an earthquake such as that which created the so-called "Allah's Bund" in Kachchh in 1819, and internal political decay have each been suggested as instrumental in its downfall. Whatever the causes in Rajasthan and Gujarat some features of Indus Valley culture were carried on by succeeding generations.

Possibly a little before 1500 BC northern India entered the Vedic period. Aryan settlers moved southeast towards the Ganga valley. Classes of rulers (rajas) and priests (brahmins) began to emerge. Conflict was common. In one battle of this period a confederacy of tribes known as the Bharatas defeated another grouping of 10 tribes. They gave their name to the region to the east of the Indus which is the official name for India today – Bharat.

The centre of population shifted east from the banks of the Indus to the land between the rivers Yamuna and Ganga, the doab (pronounced doe-ahb, literally 'two waters'). This region became the heart of emerging Aryan culture, which, from 1500 BC onwards, laid the literary and religious foundations of what ultimately became Hinduism. Little is known of developments in Rajasthan and Gujarat at this time, but the centre of gravity of the emerging Hindu culture was clearly to the north and east.

The first fruit of this development was the **Rig Veda**, the first of four Vedas (literally knowledge', composed, collected and passed on orally by Brahmin priests from 1300 BC to about 1000 BC. The later Vedas show that the Indo-Aryans developed a clear sense of the Ganga-Yamuna doab as 'their' territory. Later texts extended the core region from the Himalaya to the Vindhyans and to the Bay of Bengal in the east. Beyond lay the land of mixed peoples and then of barbarians, outside the pale of Aryan society.

The Mauryas

Chandragupta Maurya Within a year of the retreat of Alexander the Great from the Indus in 326 BC, Chandragupta Maurya established the first indigenous empire to exercise control over much of the subcontinent. Under his successors that control was extended to all but the extreme south of peninsular India.

Asoka The greatest of the Mauryan emperors, Asoka took power in 272 BC. He inherited a full blown empire, but extended it from Afghanistan to Assam and from the Himalaya to Mysore.

Asoka (described on the edicts as 'the Beloved of the Gods, of Gracious Countenance') left a series of inscriptions on pillars and rocks were written in Prakrit, using the Brahmi script, although in the northwest they were in Greek using the Kharoshti script. They were unintelligible for over 2,000 years after the decline of the Mauryan empire until James Prinsep deciphered the Brahmi script in 1837. Although Buddhist influence was never as strong in Gujarat and Rajasthan as in some parts of India, Asoka left an engraved rock at Girnar near Junagadh in modern Gujarat with fourteen of his edicts, indicating that Kathiawad was an important Mauryan stronghold on the west coast of the Indian peninsula.

Through the edicts Asoka urged all people to follow the code of dhamma or dharma – translated by the Indian historian Romila Thapar as 'morality, piety, virtue and social order'.

Sakas The Sakas or Scythians, and other Central Asian tribes, entered from the northwest. They set up rule in Gujarat and Rajasthan before the Christian era. Colonel Tod, in his 'Annals of Mewar', suggests that the Kathi royal families of Kathiawadi states like Jasdan, Jetpur, Bhilkha are direct descendants of the Sakas. Rudraman, one of their major rulers, left edicts which can be seen in suburban Junagadh, Gujarat.

The Classical Period – the Gupta Empire AD 319-467

Although the political power of Chandra Gupta and his successors never approached that of his unrelated namesake, nearly 650 years before him, the Gupta Empire produced developments in every field of Indian culture. Their influence has been felt profoundly across South Asia to the present.

Geographically the Guptas originated in the same Magadhan region that had given rise to the Mauryan Empire. Extending their power by strategic marriage alliances, Chandra Gupta's empire of Magadh was extended by his son, Samudra Gupta, who took power in AD 335, across North India. He also marched as far south as Kanchipuram in modern Tamil Nadu, but the heartland of the Gupta Empire remained the plains of the Ganga. Chandra Gupta II reigned for 39 years from AD 376 and was a great patron of the arts. Trade with Southeast Asia, Arabia and China all added to royal wealth.

Many Gupta period terracottas and artefacts have been found in Rajasthan (which are displayed in the state's museums). Kathiawad was an important part of the Gupta empire and many Gupta period Buddhist caves and rock inscriptions have been found in and around Junagadh's Uparkot fortress.

Throughout the Gupta period, the Brahmins, Hinduism's priestly caste, were in the key position to mediate change. They refocused earlier literature to give shape to the emerging religious philosophy. In their hands the Mahabharata and the Ramayana were transformed from secular epics to religious stories. The excellence of contemporary sculpture both reflected and contributed to an increase in image worship and the growing role of temples as centres of devotion.

Eventually the Gupta Empire crumbled in the face of repeated attacks from the northwest, this time by the Huns. By the end of the sixth century Punjab and Kashmir had been prised from Gupta control and the last great Hindu empire to embrace the whole of North India and part of the Peninsula was at an end.

Regional kingdoms and cultures

The collapse of Gupta power opened the way for successive smaller kingdoms to assert themselves. After the comparatively brief reign of **Harsha** in the mid-seventh century, which recaptured something both of the territory and the glory of the Guptas, the Gangetic plains were constantly fought over by rival groups. In Gujarat the Maitrekas came to power and set up capital at Vallabhi (probably present day Vallabhipur near Bhavnagar) which became an important centre for Buddhist studies and also had a Jain council. The Gurjaras ruled Gujarat from Bharuch in the sixth or seven century and gave the state its name.

The political instability and rivalry that resulted from the ending of Gupta power opened the way for new waves of immigrants from the northwest and for new groups and clans to seize power. The most significant of these were the Rajputs (meaning 'sons of kings').

Rajput clans trace their origins to one of three mythical sources. The *Suryavanshi* Sisodias (Guhilot) dynasties claim direct descent from the Sun God. They had their capital at Vallabhi in Kathiawad before moving to Nagda and Chittaurgarh in the seventh century, and ultimately to Udaipur after the Mughal conquest of Chittaurgarh. Further north the Kachhawahas, who also claim descent from the sun, took over the Amber region in 967 AD.

The *Krishnavanshi* Bhatti Rajputs, like the Jadeja Rajputs of Kachchh-Kathiawad, claim descent from the Moon God and Lord Krishna. They migrated to the western desert in the early eleventh century and established Jaisalmer in 1156.

The Rajputs
Although the Rajputs are primarily associated with Rajasthan, Rajput clans exercised a major influence in Gujarat & western Madhya Pradesh

Background

According to the legend recorded by Chanda Bardai in his epic *Prithviraja Raso*, written for the Rajput King Prithviraj III of Delhi between 1178-92, a third myth suggests that the four original Rajput warriors were created out of the sacrificial fire-pit – the *agni kula* – of sage Vashista on Mount Abu. The *rishis* – ascetic sages – called them into being to oppose the *rishis'* enemies. By the sixth century the four clans which claim descent from the sacrificial fire, the Paramaras (Pawar), Parihar (Pratihara), Chauhan (Chahamma) and Chalukya (Solanki or Vaghela) clans, came to control large areas of the Deccan and Malwa.

While the myths of the origins of the Rajput clans are clear, their history has always been rather less certain. According to some historians, the Rajput clans are descendants of ancient Indian dynasties, Gurjaras, Scythians, Indo-Greeks, Huns and other warriors. BD Chattopadhyaya has argued that the myths of Rajput origin have clouded the essential processes by which Rajput identity evolved. From the seventh century AD the evidence suggests that a wide range of chieftains and clans expanded their settlement into modern Rajasthan. Such chieftains came from a wide variety of social groups, and early medieval references to the *rajputaras* made it clear that they were of mixed castes.

The chief criterion for inclusion in the lists of Rajput clans was the scale of their estates. New colonisation in the medieval period previously tribal, and "untamed", territory into the domain of agriculture, trade and the Hindu mainstream. But alongside the colonisation process ran an equally important strand of widening social inclusion into the "Kshatriya" ranks. Chattophadhyaya illustrates the point by reference to the according of Kshatriya status to formerly tribal groups such as the Medas and Hunas.

Each of the major dynasties established control over specific territories. The Chalukyans (Solankis) took Anhilwara (present day Patan) in 961 AD and became sovereign in the Gujarat region stretching from Mount Abu to Malwa. This period saw the rise of western India's finest Hindu and Jain temples, including those of Modhera, Dilwara, Girnar, Taranga, Kumbhariyaji, Somnath, Osian, Menal, Jhalawar and Bardoli. The Solankis introduced important water harvesting systems while the Chauhans built impressive defence structures such as the hill forts at Ranthambhore and Nagaur in Rajasthan and Pawagadh fort in Gujarat. There were two Chauhan lines, the Sambhar dynasty from Ajmer, which became a national power under Raja Prithviraj, and the Kheechi line which ultimately set up a kingdom at Pawagadh.

Rajput chivalry Through their myths of an essential Rajput identity the Rajputs fostered a reputation for chivalry, valour and honour in battle and their attitude to women. In the commonly presented idealised view of Rajputs they strove against all odds to preserve the civilization of their ancestors, although they were successively forced to accept the suzerainty of first the Mughals and then the British. Death was preferable to dishonour, and before their greatest battles, when certain defeat was anticipated, their queens and princesses committed mass suicide (*jauhar*) to save themselves from being touched by enemy hands, the men then marching naked to the battlefield. See page 197.

The spread of Islamic power

The Delhi Sultanate From about 1000 AD the external attacks which inflicted most damage on Rajput wealth and power came increasingly from the Arabs and Turks. Mahmud of Ghazni raided the Punjab, Rajasthan and ultimately Gujarat virtually every year between 1000 and 1026, attracted both by the agricultural surpluses and the wealth of India's temples. By launching annual raids during the harvest season, Mahmud financed his struggles in Central Asia and his attacks on the profitable trade conducted along the Silk road between China and the Mediterranean. The enormous wealth in cash, golden images and jewellery of North India's temples drew him back every year and his hunger for gold, used to re-monetise the economy of the remarkable Ghaznavid Sultanate of Afghanistan, was insatiable. He sacked many wealthy centres in the northwest until his death in 1030.

Muslim political power was heralded by the raids of Mu'izzu'd Din and his defeat of massive Rajput forces at the Second Battle of Tarain in 1192. He made further successful raids inflicting crushing defeats on Hindu opponents from Gwalior to Varanasi. The foundations were then laid for the first extended period of Muslim power, which came under the Delhi sultans.

Qutb u'd Din Aibak took Lahore in 1206, although it was his lieutenant **Iltutmish** who really established control from Delhi in 1211. Qutb ud din Aibak converted the old Hindu stronghold of Qila Rai Pithora in Delhi into his capital and began several magnificent building projects, including the Quwwat-ul-Islam mosque and the Qutb Minar, a victory tower. Iltutmish was a Turkish slave – a *Mamluk* – and the Sultanate continued to look west for its leadership and inspiration. However, the possibility of continuing control from outside India was destroyed by the crushing raids of **Genghis Khan** through Central Asia and from 1222 Iltutmish ruled from Delhi completely independently of outside authority.

In 1290 the first dynasty was succeeded by the Khaljis, which in turn gave way to the Tughluqs in 1320. Despite its periodic brutality, this period marked a turning point in Muslim government in India, as Turkish Mamluks gave way to government by Indian Muslims and their Hindu allies. The Delhi sultans were open to local influences and employed Hindus in their administration. In the mid-14th century their capital, Delhi, was one of the leading cities of the contemporary world but in 1398 their control came to an abrupt end with the arrival of the Mongol Timur.

Timur's limp caused him to be called Timur-i-leng (Timur the Lame, known to the west as Tamburlaine). This self-styled 'Scourge of God' was illiterate, a devout Muslim, an outstanding chess player and a patron of the arts. He cut a bloody swathe through to Delhi. He is believed to have been responsible for five million deaths. Famine followed the destruction caused by his troops and plague resulted from the corpses left behind. It was a carnage which however offered temporary political opportunity to opponents of Sultanate rule to the south. In 1398 the Tomar Rajput Bir Singh Deo recaptured Gwalior from the Muslims and became Raja of Gwalior, establishing a dynasty which was to leave a profound impression on the development of Rajput architecture.

The Gujarat Sultanate

The Delhi Sultanate never achieved the dominating power of earlier empires or of its successor, the Mughal Empire. It exercised political control through crushing military raids and the exaction of tribute from defeated kings, but there was no real attempt to impose central administration. Power depended on maintaining vital lines of communication and trade routes, keeping fortified strongholds and making regional alliances. Gujarat's early history illustrates the failure of the Delhi Sultanate to maintain central control. Ala-ud-din Khilji conquered Gujarat in the late-13th century and ended the reign of the Solankis. He appointed regional governors and one of them, Zafar Khan, formally assumed independence in 1401 AD, starting the Gujarat sultanate and renaming himself Sultan Muzaffar Shah.

The Gujarat sultanate spanned an area from southwestern Rajasthan to Daman along Gujarat's southern coast, and from Malwa in the east to Kachchh in the west. Ahmad Shah, the grandson of Muzaffar Shah, moved the capital of Gujarat from Anhilwara Patan to Ahmadabad, which he developed into a magnificent architectural city in 1414 AD. His grandson took the Sultanate to its zenith capturing the impregnable hill forts of Uparkot (Junagadh) and Pawagadh (Champaner), following long sieges, and became known as Mahmud Bhegara (Mahmud of two forts).

Background

First impressions of India

Babur, used to the delights of Persian gardens and the cool of the Afghan hills, was unimpressed by what he saw of India. In his autobiography he wrote: "Hindustan is a country that has few pleasures to recommend it. The people are not handsome. They have no idea of the charms of friendly society, of frankly mixing together, or of familiar intercourse. They have no genius, no comprehension of mind, no politeness of manner, no kindness or fellow-feeling, no ingenuity or mechanical invention in planning or executing their handicraft works, no skill or knowledge in design or architecture; they have no horses, no good flesh, no grapes or musk melons, no good fruits, no ice or cold water, no good food or bread in their bazars, no baths or colleges, no candles, no torches, not a candlestick".

Muzaffar Shah's was not the only independent sultanate to be established in Gujarat. The **Lohani** dynasty, descendants of Afghans who came to Marwar in search of employment, declared themselves independent after serving for some-time as the ministers of the Mandore rulers. They set up capital at Jalore in the 14th century and moved to Palanpur in north Gujarat after the Mughals handed over the rule of Jalore to the Maharajahs of Marwar. They ruled Palanpur up to the accession in 1948 and are considered the longest ruling Islamic dynasty in India.

The period of Empire

The Mughal Empire

The descendants of conquerors, with the blood of both Tamburlaine (Timur) and Genghis Khan in their veins, the Mughals came to dominate Indian politics from Babur's victory near Delhi in 1526 to Aurangzeb's death in 1707. Their legacy was not only some of the most magnificent architecture in the world, but a profound impact on the culture, society and future politics of South Asia.

Babur Founder of the Mughal Dynasty, Babur was born in Russian Turkestan on 15 February
(the tiger) 1483, the fifth direct descendant on the male side of Timur and 13th on the female side from Genghis Khan. He established the Mughal Empire by leading his cavalry and artillery forces to a stupendous victory over the combined armies of Ibrahim Lodi, last ruler of the Delhi Sultanate and the Rajput Raja of Gwalior, at **Panipat**, 80 km north of Delhi, in 1526. When he died four years later, the Empire was still far from secured, but not only had he laid the foundations of political and military power but he'd also begun to establish courtly traditions of poetry, literature and art which became the hallmark of subsequent Mughal rulers. Babur was charismatic. He ruled by keeping the loyalty of his military chiefs, giving them control of large areas of territory.

Humayun The strength of Babur's military commanders proved a mixed blessing for Humayun, his successor. Almost immediately after Babur's death Humayun was forced to retreat from Delhi by two of his brothers and one of his father's lieutenants, the Afghan **Sher Shah Suri**. Humayun's son Akbar, who was to become the greatest of the Mughal emperors, was born at Umarkot in Sindh, modern Pakistan, during this period of exile, on 23 November 1542.

Humayun found the artistic skills of the Iranian court stunningly beautiful and he surrounded himself with his own group of Iranian artists and scholars. Planning his move back into India proper, Humayun urged his group of artists to join him and between 1548 and his return to power in Delhi in 1555, he was surrounded by this highly influential entourage.

One year after his final return to Delhi, Humayun died from the effects of a fall on the stairs of his library in the Purana Qila in Delhi. Akbar was therefore only 13 when he took the throne in 1556. The next 44 years were one of the most remarkable periods of South Asian history, paralleled by the Elizabethan period in England, where Queen Elizabeth I ruled from 1558 to 1603. Although Akbar inherited the throne, it was he who really created the empire. At the age of 15 he had conquered Ajmer and large areas of Central India. Chittaurgarh and Ranthambhore fell to him in 1567-68, bringing most of what is now Rajasthan under his control.

Akbar Builder of Empire

This opened the door south to Gujarat, which he took in 1573 in an astonishing military feat. He marched the 800 km from his new capital city, Fatehpur Sikri, to Ahmadabad, with 3,000 horsemen in nine days. On the 11th day after his departure he defeated the massed armies of Gujarat and 32 days later was back in Fatehpur Sikri. He celebrated his victory by building the massive Buland Darwaza (gate) in his new capital city.

Through his marriage to a Hindu princess he ensured that Hindus were given honoured positions in government, as well as respect for their religious beliefs and practices. He sustained a passionate interest in art and literature, matched by a determination to create monuments to his empire's political power and he laid the foundations for an artistic and architectural tradition which developed a totally distinctive Indian style. This emerged from the separate elements of Iranian and Indian traditions by a constant process of blending and originality of which he was the chief patron.

Akbar deliberately widened his power base by incorporating Rajput princes into the administrative structure and giving them extensive rights in the revenue from land. He abolished the hated tax on non-Muslims (*jizya*) – ultimately reinstated by his strictly orthodox great grandson Aurangzeb – ceased levying taxes on Hindus who went on pilgrimage and ended the practice of forcible conversion to Islam.

Artistic treasures abound from Akbar's court – paintings, jewellery, weapons – often bringing together material and skills from across the known world. Emeralds were particularly popular, with the religious significance which attaches to the colour green in mystic Islam adding to their attraction. Some came from as far afield as Colombia. Akbar's intellectual interests were extraordinarily catholic. He met the Portuguese Jesuits in 1572 and welcomed them to his court in Fatehpur Sikri, along with Buddhists, Hindus and Zoroastrians, every year between 1575 and 1582.

The art of the Mughal court

Despite their artistic achievements, Mughal politics could also be cruel & violent. Akbar himself ordered that the beautiful Anarkali, a member of his harem, should be buried alive when he suspected that she was having an affair with his son Jahangir

Akbar's eclecticism had a political purpose, for he was trying to build a focus of loyalty beyond that of caste, social group, region or religion. Like Roman emperors before him, he deliberately cultivated a new religion in which the emperor himself attained divinity, hoping thereby to give the empire a legitimacy which would last. While his religion disappeared with his death, the legitimacy of the Mughals survived another 200 years, long after their real power had almost disappeared.

Akbar died of a stomach illness in 1605. He was succeeded by his son, Prince Salim, who inherited the throne as Emperor Jahangir ('*world seizer*'). He commissioned works of art and literature, many of which directly recorded life in the Mughal court. Hunting scenes were not just romanticized accounts of rural life, but conveyed the real dangers of hunting lions or tigers; implements, furniture, tools and weapons were made with lavish care and often exquisite design.

Jahangir

Background

Nur Jahan   Jahangir's favourite wife, Nur Jahan, brought her own artistic gifts. Born the daughter of an Iranian nobleman, she had been brought to the Mughal court along with her family as a child and moved to Bengal as the wife of Sher Afghan. She made rapid progress after her first husband's accidental death in 1607, which caused her to move from Bengal to be a lady in waiting for one of Akbar's widows.

At the Mughal court in 1611 she met Jahangir. Mutually enraptured, they were married in May. Jahangir gave her the title Nur Mahal (Light of the Palace), soon increased to Nur Jahan (Light of the World).

By 1622 Nur Jahan effectively controlled the empire. She commissioned and supervised the building in Agra of one of the Mughal world's most beautiful buildings, the **I'timad ud-Daula** ('Pillar of government'), as a tomb for her father and mother. Her father, **Ghiyas Beg**, had risen to become one of Jahangir's most trusted advisers and Nur Jahan was determined to ensure that their memory was adequately honoured. She was less successful in her wish to deny the succession after Jahangir's death at the age of 58 to Prince Khurram. Acceding to the throne in 1628, he took the title of Shah Jahan (*Ruler of the World*) and in the following 30 years his reign represented the height of Mughal power.

Shah Jahan   The Mughal Empire was under attack in the Deccan and the northwest when Shah Jahan became Emperor. He tried to re-establish and extend Mughal authority in both regions by a combination of military campaigns and skilled diplomacy and most of the Deccan was brought firmly under Mughal control.

He also commissioned art, literature and, above all, architectural monuments, on an unparalleled scale. The Taj Mahal may be the most famous of these, but a succession of brilliant achievements can be attributed to his reign. From miniature paintings and manuscripts, which had been central features of Mughal artistic development from Babur onwards, to massive fortifications such as the Red Fort in Delhi, Shah Jahan added to the already great body of outstanding Mughal art.

Throughout this period Rajput rulers adjusted in varying degrees to the dominance of the Mughal emperors. Seeking to maximise their own remaining authority without risking punitive raids which would have destroyed what control they had, many of the clan leaders made direct arrangements with successive emperors which gave them continued effective control over their own territories. Sometimes clan leaders took sides in the internal feuding within the Mughal court. Udai Singh of Udaipur for example gave the young Prince Khurram, the future Emperor Shah Jahan, shelter in his Jag Mandir palace in Lake Pichola when he was fleeing his father Jahangir's wrath, and it is striking that both Jahangir and Shah Jahan had Rajput mothers.

Aurangzeb   All this changed with the ascension of Aurangzeb ('The jewel in the throne') to the throne. He needed all his political and military skills to hold on to an unwieldy empire that was in permanent danger of collapse from its own size.

Aurangzeb realized that the resources of the territory he inherited from Shah Jahan were not enough to sustain the empire's power. One response was to push south, while maintaining his hold on the east and north. Initially he maintained his alliances with the Rajputs in the west, which had been a crucial element in Mughal strategy. However, in 1678 he claimed absolute rights over Jodhpur and went to war with the Rajput clans, at the same time embarking on a policy of outright Islamisation. For the remaining 29 years of his reign he was forced to struggle continuously to sustain his power.

Background

New powers in the Peninsula

Even before the Mughal Empire had finally lost its grip Rajasthan and Gujarat had begun to feel the force of new external influences. Immediately to their south the rising power of Sivaji and the Marathas posed a new threat, while European colonial powers showed an increasing interest in the wealth of India.

The first power to make their presence felt were the Portuguese. For the first Portuguese, their encounter with Islam on the coast of India was simply an extension of the contest for power between Catholicism and Islam in the Iberian Peninsula. They had come, not only to rescue the early Syrian Christians who had been converted by the Nestorians in the fourth century from the threat of Muslim dominance, but also to bring them under the influence of Rome. The Portuguese were also intent on setting up a string of coastal stations to the Far East in order to control the lucrative spice trade.

The Portuguese

Vasco da Gama landed in India in 1498 and Goa became the first Portuguese possession in Asia when it was taken by **Afonso de Albuquerque** in 1510.

During the 16th century, the Portuguese established themselves as a superior maritime power along the western peninsular coast, building forts in small enclaves close to Bombay (as at Bassein) and further north at Daman and Diu, encapsulated by modern Gujarat. They captured Diu from the Sultan of Oman in 1534, three years after they had established their fort at Daman. They terrorized Indian ships and those of the other colonizing countries to protect their monopoly in spices and the trade of cotton goods from the sub-continent to Southeast Asia, and under their control Diu and Daman became centres for the trade in opium from the Malwa region of modern southeastern Rajasthan and Madhya Pradesh.

While Portuguese Goa grew, Portugal's other Asian interests shrank. Struggles in continental Europe, notably between Britain and Napoleonic France, had an impact on alliances in India, and Goa itself was occupied by the British between 1799 and 1813.

By the end of the Second World War when the rest of India was on the point of achieving Independence there were less than 30 Portuguese officials based in Goa and a handful in Daman and Diu. The Portuguese came under increasing pressure in 1948 and 1949 to cede Goa, Daman and Diu to India, and in response despatched over 4000 troops to hold on to the territory. The problem festered until 19 December 1961 when the Indian Army, supported by a naval blockade, marched in and brought to an end 450 years of Portuguese rule. However, in Diu there was a far more bitter struggle, and Portuguese resistance in the fort was ended by an air strike. Originally Goa became a Union Territory together with Daman and Diu.

The decline of Portuguese power

The Maratha challenge

Of far greater significance for Mughal and Rajput control of Rajasthan and Gujarat through the eighteenth century than that of Portuguese colonialism was the development of the power of the **Maratha confederacy**. The Marathas were unique in India in uniting different castes and classes in a nationalist fervour for the region of Maharashtra. When the Mughals ceded the central district of Malwa, the Marathas were able to pour through the gap created between the Nizam of Hyderabad's territories in the south and the area remaining under Mughal control in the north.

By 1750 they had reached the gates of Delhi. When Delhi collapsed to Afghan invaders in 1756-57 the Mughal minister called on the Marathas for help. Yet again Panipat proved to be a decisive battlefield, the Marathas being heavily defeated by the Afghan forces of Ahmad Shah on 13 January 1761. However Ahmad Shah was forced to retreat to Afghanistan by his own rebellious troops demanding two years arrears of pay, leaving a power vacuum. The Maratha confederacy dissolved into five independent powers, with whom the incoming British were able to deal separately. For them, the door to the north was open.

The decline of Muslim power

Aurangzeb never fully came to terms with the rising power of the Marathas, though he did end their ambitions to form an empire of their own. Nor was Aurangzeb able to create any wide sense of identity with the Mughals as a legitimate popular power. Instead, under the influence of Sunni Muslim theologians, he retreated into insistence on Islamic purity. He imposed Islamic law, the *Sharia*, promoted only Muslims to positions of power and authority, tried to replace Hindu administrators and revenue collectors with Muslims and reimposed the *jizya* tax on all non-Muslims. By the time of his death in 1707 the empire no longer had either the broadness of spirit or the physical means to survive.

The East India Company and the rise of British power

The British were unique among the foreign rulers of India in coming by sea rather than through the northwest and in coming first for trade rather than for military conquest. The ports that they established – Madras (Chennai), Bombay (Mumbai) and Calcutta (Kolkata) – became completely new centres of political, economic and social activity. Before them Indian empires had controlled their territories from the land. The British dictated the emerging shape of the economy by controlling sea-borne trade.

In its first 90 years of contact with South Asia after the Company set up its first trading post at Masulipatnam, on the east coast of India, it had depended almost entirely on trade for its profits. In 1608 it established its warehouse on the west coast at Surat, already an important port, and it remained their headquarters until it moved to Bombay in 1674. The Company was accepted and sometimes welcomed, partly because it offered to bolster the inadequate revenues of the Mughals by exchanging silver bullion for the cloth it bought.

Alliances In the century and a half that followed the death of Aurangzeb, the British East India Company extended its economic and political influence into the heart of India. As the Mughal Empire lost its power India fell into many smaller states. The Company undertook to protect the rulers of several of these states from external attack by stationing British troops in their territory. In exchange for this service the rulers paid subsidies to the Company. As the British historian Christopher Bayly has pointed out, the cure was usually worse than the disease and the cost of the payments to the Company crippled the local ruler. The British extended their territory through the 18th century as successive regional powers were annexed and brought under direct Company rule.

Progress to direct British control was uneven and often opposed. The Sikhs in Punjab, the Marathas in the west and the Mysore sultans in the south, fiercely contested British advances. The Marathas were not defeated until the war of 1816-18, a defeat which had to wait until Napoleon was defeated in Europe and the British could turn their wholehearted attention once again to the Indian scene. Even then the defeat owed as much to internal faction fighting as to the power of the British-led army.

In 1818 India's economy was in ruins and its political structures destroyed. Irrigation works and road systems had fallen into decay and gangs terrorized the countryside. Thugs and dacoits controlled much of the open countryside in Central India and often robbed and murdered even on the outskirts of towns. The peace and stability of the Mughal period had long since passed. Between 1818 and 1857 there was a succession of local and uncoordinated revolts in different parts of India. Some were bought off, some put down by military force.

Gujarat came under the control of the East India Company in 1818 and after the 1857 Mutiny (Rebellion), government authority was assumed by the Crown. The state was then divided into Gujarat province (25,900 sq km), with the rest comprising numerous princely states. Until Independence Kathiawad was one of the most highly fragmented regions of India, having 86 distinct political units. The largest, Junagadh, had an area of less than 9,000 sq km and a population of under 750,000 in 1947.

A period of reforms

While existing political systems were collapsing, the first half of the 19th century was also a period of radical social change in the territories governed by the East India Company. **Lord William Bentinck** became Governor-General at a time when England itself was entering a period of major reform. In 1828 he banned the burning of widows on the funeral pyres of their husbands (*sati*) and then moved to suppress the ritual murder and robbery carried out in the name of the goddess Kali (*thuggee*). But his most far reaching change was to introduce education in English.

From the late 1830s massive new engineering projects began to be taken up; first canals, then railways. However, it was in eastern India that British control was most directly imposed and the consequent changes were most sharply felt. Although much of modern Gujarat was also brought under direct British control, under the governance of Bombay, most Rajput areas remained under their subordinate authority as Rajputana.

British-led innovations stimulated change and change contributed to the growing unease with the British presence, particularly under the Governor-Generalship of the Marquess of Dalhousie (1848-56). The development of the telegraph, railways and new roads, three universities and the extension of massive new canal irrigation projects in North India seemed to threaten traditional society, a risk increased by the annexation of Indian states to bring them under direct British rule. The most important of these was Oudh.

The Rebellion

Out of the growing discontent and widespread economic difficulties came the Rebellion or 'Mutiny' of 1857 (now widely known as the First War of Independence). Although it had little support among the Rajput rulers and Rajputana remained seemingly uninvolved, no part of India was unaffected. The 1857 rebellion marked the end not only of the Mughal Empire but also of the East India Company, for the British Government in London took overall control in 1858. After the establishment of the British Indian Empire, the Rajput Princely States gained in the appearance and show of power just as they lost its reality.

Pomp & circumstance

The British awarded gun salutes on the basis of importance. Rajasthan had 19 'gun salute' states, 17 of them ruled by various Rajput clans, Bharatpur by a Jat dynasty and Tonk by a Muslim Nawab, with countless non salute chieftains. The three regions of Gujarat – Kachchh, Kathiawad and mainland Gujarat – had more than 20 salute states and over 200 non salute states, ruled by Rajputs, Marathas, Kathi durbars, Muslim nawabs and Patels. The princes maintained huge fleets of European and American cars, stables of elephants and horses, chariots and horse drawn

Background

Mahatma Gandhi

Gandhi was asked by a journalist when he was on a visit to Europe what he thought of Western civilization. He paused and then replied: "It would be very nice, wouldn't it". The answer illustrated just one facet of his extraordinarily complex character. A westernized, English educated lawyer, who had lived outside India from his youth to middle age, he preached the general acceptance of some of the doctrines he had grown to respect in his childhood, which stemmed from deep Indian traditions – notably ahimsa, or non-violence. From 1921 he gave up his Western style of dress and adopted the hand spun dhoti worn by poor Indian villagers, giving rise to Churchill's jibe that he was a 'naked fakir' (holy man). Yet if he was a thorn in the British flesh, he was also fiercely critical of many aspects of traditional Hindu society. He preached against the discrimination of the caste system which still dominated life for the overwhelming majority of Hindus. Through the 1920s much of his work was based on writing for the weekly newspaper Young India, which became The Harijan in 1932. The change in name symbolized his commitment to improving the status of the outcastes, Harijan (person of God) being coined to replace the term outcaste. Often despised by the British in India he succeeded in gaining the reluctant respect and ultimately outright admiration of many. His death at the hands of an extreme Hindu chauvinist in January 1948 was a final testimony to the ambiguity of his achievements: successful in contributing so much to achieving India's Independence, yet failing to resolve some of the bitter communal legacies which he gave his life to overcome.

carriages, and travelled in their own royal rail saloon carriages which could be attached to regular trains for their journeys across the subcontinent. Some even had private aircraft. This was a period of grand darbars, parties, banquets, weddings, processions, polo and cricket matches and royal hunting camps. A strict order of precedence was maintained according to gun salutes awarded to each state. The Maharajah of Baroda was entitled to 21 gun salutes, the Maharana of Udaipur to 19 gun salutes, the Maharajahs of Jaipur, Jodhpur, Bundi, Bikaner, Kachchh, Kota, Karauli and Bharatpur to 17 gun salutes and so on.

While the show of power was far from reality, for these Maharajahs came under the British Raj, the princes were given considerable freedom of rule and many of them proved to be capable rulers. Their highnesses Ganga Singh of Bikaner, Sayajirao Geakwad of Baroda, Bhagwat Singhji of Gondal and other rulers introduced wide ranging reforms that are landmarks in administration in India. British political agents, collectors and other residents were appointed to look into affairs of state, and when a crown prince inherited the throne as a minor a British representative was selected to handle the state of his behalf. Ahmadabad, Kheda, Rajkot and Ajmer were seats of British administrators, and during the summer months Mount Abu was a popular retreat for British and royal residents of Gujarat-Rajasthan to escape the heat of the plains.

Yet within 30 years a movement for self-government had begun and there were the first signs of a demand that political rights be awarded to match the sense of Indian national identity. This took varied forms. In Udaipur the Maharishi Dayanand wrote the Satyarath Prakash which was a call to restore Hinduism to its "pure" form, and the founding in 1875 of the Arya Samaj on the basis of these principles placed the emphasis on a return to Vedic Hinduism at the core of its view of Indian national identity, a view which is still a powerful influence through the current BJP government.

Background

The movement for independence went through a series of steps. The creation of the Indian National Congress in 1885 was the first all-India political institution and was to become the key vehicle of demands for independence. However, the educated Muslim élite of what is now Uttar Pradesh saw a threat to Muslim rights, power and identity in the emergence of democratic institutions which gave Hindus, with their built-in natural majority, significant advantages. Sir Sayyid Ahmad Khan, who had founded a Muslim University at Aligarh in 1877, advised Muslims against joining the Congress, seeing it as a vehicle for Hindu and especially Bengali, nationalism.

The Indian National Congress

The educated Muslim community of North India remained deeply suspicious of the Congress, making up less than eight percent of those attending its conferences between 1900-1920. Muslims from Uttar Pradesh created the All-India Muslim League in 1906. However, the demands of the Muslim League were not always opposed to those of the Congress. In 1916 it concluded the Lucknow Pact with the Congress, in which the Congress won Muslim support for self-government, in exchange for the recognition that there would be separate constituencies for Muslims. The nature of the future Independent India was still far from clear, however. The British conceded the principle of self-government in 1918, but however radical the reforms would have seemed five years earlier they already fell far short of heightened Indian expectations.

The Muslim League

Into a tense atmosphere Mohandas Karamchand Gandhi returned to India in 1915 after 20 years practising as a lawyer in South Africa. On his return the Bengali Nobel Laureate poet, Rabindranath Tagore, had dubbed him 'Mahatma' – Great Soul. The name became his. He arrived as the government of India was being given new powers by the British parliament to try political cases without a jury and to give provincial governments the right to imprison politicians without trial. In opposition to this legislation Gandhi proposed to call a *hartal*, when all activity would cease for a day, a form of protest still in widespread use. Such protests took place across India, often accompanied by riots.

Mahatma Gandhi

Through the 1920s Gandhi developed concepts and political programmes that were to become the hallmark of India's Independence struggle, and Gujarat, Gandhi's birthplace, was to play a significant part in Gandhi's campaigns for independence. Rejecting the 1919 reforms Gandhi preached the doctrine of *swaraj*, or self rule, developing an idea he first published in a leaflet in 1909. He saw *swaraj* not just as political independence from a foreign ruler but, in Judith Brown's words, as made up of three elements: "It was a state of being that had to be created from the roots upwards, by the regeneration of individuals and their realization of their true spiritual being... unity among all religions; the eradication of Untouchability; and the practice of *swadeshi*." Swadeshi was not simply dependence on Indian products rather than foreign imports, but a deliberate move to a simple life style, hence his emphasis on hand spinning as a daily routine.

The thrust for Independence

Ultimately political Independence was to be achieved not by violent rebellion but by *satyagraha* – a "truth force" which implied a willingness to suffer through non-violent resistance to injustice. This gave birth to Gandhi's advocacy of "non-cooperation" as a key political weapon and brought together Gandhi's commitment to matching political goals and moral means. Although the political achievements of Gandhi's programme continues to be strongly debated the struggles of the 1920s established his position as a key figure in the Independence movement.

As the American historian Stanley Wolpert has pointed out it is a remarkable coincidence that Mahatma Gandhi's Hindu merchant *bania* family should have settled barely 30 miles from the home of the grandparents of Mohammad Ali Jinnah,

Background

The Indian flag

In 1921, the All Indian Congress considered a red and green flag to represent the two dominant religious groups (Hindu and Muslim); Gandhi suggested white be added to represent the other communities, as well as the charka (spinning wheel) symbolizing the Swadeshi movement, now centred in the party flag.

In 1931, the Indian National Congress adopted the tricolor as the national flag. This was intended to have no communal significance. The deep saffron denoted 'Courage and Sacrifice', the white 'Truth and Peace' and dark green 'Faith and Chivalry'. On the white stripe, the Dharma chakra represented the Buddhist Wheel of Law from Asoka's Lion capital at Sarnath.

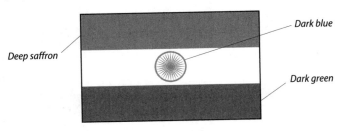

Deep saffron

Dark blue

Dark green

and that therefore "the parents of the Founding fathers of both India and Pakistan should have shared a single mother tongue, Gujarati" – though as he acerbically notes, "that never helped their brilliant offspring communicate." A third key figure of the Independence movement, Independent India's first Home Minister Sardar Vallabhai Patel, who was responsible for persuading the Princely States to accept integration with India, was also a Gujarati.

By the end of the Second World War the positions of the Muslim League, now under the leadership of **Mohammad Ali Jinnah** and the Congress led by Jawaharlal Nehru, were irreconcilable. While major questions of the definition of separate territories for a Muslim and non-Muslim state remained to be answered, it was clear to General Wavell, the British Viceroy through the last years of the War, that there was no alternative but to accept that independence would have to be given on the basis of separate states.

The transition to Independence and Partition

On 20 February 1947, the British Labour Government announced its decision to replace Lord Wavell as Viceroy with Lord Mountbatten, who was to oversee the transfer of power to new independent governments. It set a deadline of June 1948 for British withdrawal. The announcement of a firm date made the Indian politicians even less willing to compromise and the resulting division satisfied no one.

When Independence arrived – on 15 August for India and the 14 August for Pakistan because Indian astrologers deemed the 15th to be the most auspicious moment – many questions remained unanswered. Several key Princely States had still not decided firmly to which country they would accede. The Muslim Nawab of Junagadh exercised his right to accede to Pakistan, but the Indian Government, arguing that Junagadh had a predominantly Hindu population and lay surrounded by Hindus, insisted on organising a plebiscite under Indian government supervision, and the Nawab was forced to flee into exile. Equally the future accession of Kashmir remained unclear with results that have lasted to the present day.

At Independence the 216 smallest states were abolished and merged into neigh-bouring provinces. Some 275 Princely states across India, including Rajasthan, had either acceded to the Indian union or signed standstill agreements with the new government while permanent arrangements were agreed. They were integrated ini-tially into five new unions, each with its provincial governor or *Rajpramukh*. A further 61 states were brought under direct central government control. These arrange-ments, intended as temporary, were shortlived. The first stage of transition was com-pleted in 1950 when they all became part of the Indian Union under an agreement in which the Princes retained their titles and government subsidies, known as their privy purses. The region's 18 princely states were ultimately absorbed into the new state of Rajasthan on 1 November 1956. In 1971 Mrs Gandhi abolished the remaining rights of the Maharajahs and took away their privy purses.

The successors of royal families have lost power but still retain wide respect and considerable political influence. The palaces, many of them converted to hotels with varying degrees of success, maintain the memory of princely India.

Rajasthan and Gujarat's place in modern India

Rajasthan and Gujarat are among India's least densely populated states, though pop-ulation growth rates continue to be relatively high at over 1.5% a year. India, with over 1 billion people in 2001, is the second most populated country in the world after China. That population size reflects the long history of human occupation and the fact that an astonishingly high proportion of India's land is relatively fertile. Some 60% of India's surface area is cultivated today, compared with about 10% in China and 20% in the United States.

Although the birth rate has fallen steadily over the last 40 years, initially death rates fell faster and the rate of population increase has continued to be about two percent – or 18 million – a year. Today nearly 30% of the population lives in towns and cities have grown dramatically. In 1971, 109 million people lived in towns and cities. The figure grew to over 300 million in 2001.

At Independence in 1947, Gujarat proper was incorporated into Bombay state. In 1956 Saurashtra and Kachchh were added. On 1 May 1960 Bombay state was split into present day Maharashtra and Gujarat states and in 1961 India forcibly annexed Daman and Diu. After Partition the possession of the Rann of Kachchh was disputed by India and Pakistan. In 1965 they fought over it, and following the ceasefire on 1 July, division of the area was referred to an international tribunal. In 1968 the tribunal recommended that 90% should remain with India and 10% pass to Pakistan.

India's constitution and political institutions

In the years since independence, India has recorded some striking political achieve-ments. With the two year exception of 1975-77, when Mrs Gandhi imposed a state of emergency in which all political activity was banned, India has sustained a demo-cratic system in the face of tremendous pressures. The general elections of Septem-ber 1999, which involved an electorate of over 400 million, were the country's thirteenth.

Background

The constitution Establishing itself as a sovereign democratic republic, the Indian parliament accepted Nehru's advocacy of a secular constitution. The President is formally vested with all executive powers exercised under the authority of the Prime Minister. Effective power lies with the Prime Minister and Cabinet, following the British model. In practice there have been long periods when the Prime Minister has been completely dominant. In principle parliament chooses the Prime Minister. The Parliament has a lower house (the *Lok Sabha*, or 'house of the people') and an upper house (the *Rajya Sabha* – Council of States). The former is made up of directly elected representatives from the 543 parliamentary constituencies (plus two nominated members from the Anglo-Indian community), the latter of a mixture of members elected by an electoral college and of nominated members. Constitutional amendments require a two-thirds majority in both houses.

India's federal constitution devolves certain powers to elected state assemblies. Each state has a Governor who acts as its official head. Many states also have two chambers, the upper generally called the Rajya Sabha and the lower (often called the Vidhan Sabha) being of directly elected representatives. In practice many of the state assemblies have had a totally different political complexion from that of the Lok Sabha. Regional parties have played a far more prominent role, though in many states central government has effectively dictated both the leadership and policy of state assemblies.

States & union territories Union territories such as Diu, Daman, or the Capital territory of Delhi, are administered by the President "acting to such an extent as he thinks fit". In practice Union territories have varying forms of self-government. The 69th Amendment to the Constitution in 1991 provided for a legislative assembly and council of Ministers for Delhi, elections for which were held in December 1993. The Assemblies of Union Territories have more restricted powers of legislation than full states. Some Union Territories – Dadra and Nagar Haveli, Daman and Diu, all of which separated from Goa in 1987 when Goa achieved full statehood – have elected bodies known as Pradesh Councils. These councils have the right to discuss and make recommendations on matters relating to their territories.

The Union Territories of Daman and Diu are governed by collectors appointed by the Central government. Tourism is one of the main sources of revenue for these UTs, with their fine beaches and monuments. As these UTs are free from liqour prohibition regulations imposed by the state of Gujarat, which surrounds them on three sides, they attract local tourists wanting a drink and bars and liquor shops have mushroomed in both the townships. As taxes are lower in UTs than in the states, many visitors visit them for shopping (something that may stop soon as the centre plans to have uniform taxation on many commodities).

Secularism One of the key features of India's constitution is its secular principle. This is not based on the absence of religious belief, but on the commitment to guarantee freedom of religious belief and practice to all groups in Indian society. Some see the commitment to a secular constitution as under increasing challenge, especially from the Hindu nationalism of the Bharatiya Janata Party, the BJP. The BJP persuaded a number of minor regional parties to join it in government after the 1998 elections, appearing to move away from its narrowly defined conception of a Hindu state. In the 1999 elections the BJP achieved a compromise between the narrowly defined Hindu beliefs of its core support and the electoral demands of an enormously varied population, and in 2001 seemed likely to run its full electoral term of five years in government.

India's Supreme Court has similar but somewhat weaker powers to those of the United States. The judiciary has remained effectively independent of the government except under the Emergency between 1975-77. In recent years it has played an increasingly prominent role in public interest cases, defining legal principles in matters such as environmental protection and human rights which have often been both independent and well ahead of the political parties.

The judiciary

India's police service is divided into a series of groups, numbering nearly one million. While the top ranks of the Indian Police Service are comparable to the Indian Administration Service (IAS), lower levels are extremely poorly trained and very low paid. In addition to the domestic police force there are special groups: the Border Security Force, Central Reserve Police and others. They may be armed with modern weapons and are called in for special duties.

The police

Unlike its immediate neighbours India has never had military rule. It has approximately one million men in the army – one of the largest armed forces in the world. Although they have remained out of politics the armed services have been used increasingly frequently to put down civil unrest especially in Kashmir, where there are currently around 400,000 troops.

The armed forces

For over 40 years Indian national politics was dominated by the **Congress Party**. Its strength in the Lok Sabha often overstated the volume of its support in the country, however and state governments have frequently been formed by parties – and interests – only weakly represented at the centre. The Congress built its broad based support partly by championing the causes of the poor, the backward castes and the minorities. Yet in 1998 its popular support completely disappeared in some regions and fell below 30% nationally. Currently under the leadership of Sonia Gandhi, Rajiv Gandhi's Italian born widow, it returned to power in the last Rajasthan state elections, but has failed to make an impression nationally.

Party politics

Political activity outside the Congress can seem bewilderingly complex. There are no genuinely national parties. The only alternative governments to the Congress have been formed by coalitions of regional and ideologically based parties. Parties of the left – Communist and Socialist – have never broken out of their narrow regional bases in West Bengal and Kerala.

The Non-Congress Parties

The most organized political force outside the Congress, the Jan Sangh, merged with the **Janata Party** for the elections of 1977. After the collapse of that government it re-formed itself as the **Bharatiya Janata Party (BJP)**. In 1990-91 it developed a powerful campaign focusing on reviving Hindu identity against the minorities. In the decade that followed it became the most powerful opponent of the Congress across northern India and established a series of footholds and alliances in the South, enabling it to become the most important national alternative to the Congress.

The 1999 national elections in India saw the BJP return as the largest single party, though without an overall majority. This time however they were able to forge some previously impossible alliances with regional parties and they formed the new government under the Prime Ministership of Atal Behari Vajpayee. The emergence of Sonia Gandhi as an effective campaigner for the Congress in the Assembly elections and her subsequent election as Congress Party President, suggested that the Nehru-Gandhi dynasty may not yet be dead in Indian political life. However, the election results confirmed the BJP government in power at the head of a broad coalition, the National Democratic Alliance (NDA) under the Prime Ministership of Atal Behari Vajpayee, and appeared to offer the prospect of a more extended period of political stability.

Recent developments

Background

With the sole exception of 1977, Gujarat remained one of the Congress Party's chief strongholds throughout the period after Independence until 1989. It produced a number of national leaders after Mahatma Gandhi, including the first Prime Minister of the Janata Government in 1977, Morarji Desai. However, since the State Assembly elections of March 1995 the BJP has held control. In October 1999 the BJP led the national trend by winning 19 of the 26 Lok Sabha seats while the Congress (I) suffered further setbacks. The Lok Sabha results gave the Gujarat Chief Minister a breathing space in the internal strife within the state's BJP, where about 50 of the party's 117 Legislative Members had threatened to stage a revolt. In the summer of 2000 the government faced a challenge of a wholly different sort as it struggled to cope with the worst water shortage in the state for many years. It blamed the shortage on poor monsoons in the previous year, though the World Bank put the blame on inadequate water policy measures taken by both the State and Central Governments. Today Gujarat has the only BJP majority state assembly in India, although the Congress has surged ahead in local self government polls held in Aug/Sept 2000.

In the 1998 Lok Sabha elections in Rajasthan the BJP retained only five of the 25 seats, 18 of the remainder going to the Congress, and the BJP also lost power in the state assembly elections at the end of 1998.

Economy

Rajasthan and Gujarat have always been known for their mercantile achievers, from the days when Surat, Cambay (Khambhat) and the ports of Saurashtra were landing points for overseas traders, and the desert cities of Jaisalmer, Jodhpur and Bikaner were on important overland trade routes of merchant caravans travelling between the near east and the Far East. Several families of Gujarat and Rajasthan have attained international fame as industrialists, and a large percentage of India's richest people are from these two states. The Patels of Gujarat have prospered as landowners, generating great wealth from agriculture in central and north Gujarat, and as the division of land has made personal land holding too small to sustain a family many have migrated overseas and become successful in business and the professions.

Although the people of Marwar and Shekhawati are well known for their business acumen, Rajasthan does not have a strong commercial or industrial base and remains one of India's poorer states. Tourism, gems and jewellery, handicrafts and mineral mining make the major contribution to the regional economy in a state that has always been primarily agricultural and pastoral with most of the Rajasthani business houses preferring to set up industry at Mumbai, Ahmadabad, Delhi, Kolkata, Coimbatore, Chennai, Bangalore and Hyderabad. In contrast, Gujarat has extensive areas of highly productive agriculture with some remarkably successful agricultural developments, notably in the field of dairy products, associated with the co-operative movement. It also has a rapidly growing industrial base, capitalising on its long history in textiles, but now broadening to a range of industries. The most dramatic example of Gujarat's push to industrialisation is the huge petro-chemical refinery now operating at Jamnagar, one of the largest in the world.

Rajasthan's economy **Agriculture** Rajasthan's low and erratic rainfall puts irrigation at a premium, but most of the crops are rainfed: wheat, hardy *bajra* (pearl millet) in the more arid areas; *jowar* (sorghum), maize and pulses (peas, beans and lentils) elsewhere. Cotton is important in the north and south of the state. Rajasthan shares waters from the Bhakra Dam project with Punjab, and the Chambal Valley project with Madhya Pradesh. With improved management techniques over 30% of the sown area could be brought under irrigation. The enormously ambitious Rajasthan canal is working much less efficiently than had originally been planned. Rajasthan has a very large livestock population and is the largest wool producing state. It also breeds camels.

Minerals Rajasthan accounts for India's entire output of zinc concentrates, emeralds and garnets, 94% of its gypsum, 76% of silver ore, 84% of asbestos, 68% of feldspar and 12% of mica. It has rich salt deposits at Sambhar and elsewhere, and copper mines at Khetri and Dariba. The white marble favoured by the Mughal builders is mined at Makrana north of Ajmer. The famous Makrana white marble is mined near Ajmer. The Aravalli hills north of Udaipur are the mining zone for dolomite based marble in white and other colours. Kesriyaji (Rishabdeo) to the south of Udaipur is known for its serpentine based green marble, popular for cladding, Mount Abu for its black and panther spotted marble. The hills of Jalor, Barmer and Sirohi districts are have extensive granite, while Jaisalmer, Barmer, Bikaner and Jodhpur districts have sandstone, gypsum, lignite, silica sand and China clay. Other important minerals are limestone in the Kota-Jhalawar-Baran triangle (the famous Kota stone slabs are used as bathroom and kitchen counters in many houses, and for flooring), copper, lead, zinc, silver, limestone, mica and soap-stone in Ajmer, Alwar, Dungarpur, Chittaurgarh and Banswara districts. Gypsum, quartz and other stones are exploited in Bharatpur, and slate at Dhaulpur.

Industries The main large scale industries are textiles, the manufacture of rugs and woollen goods, vegetable oil and dyes. Heavy industry includes the construction of railway rolling stock, copper and zinc smelting. The chemical industry also produces caustic soda, calcium carbides and sulphuric acid, fertilizer, pesticides and insecticides. There is a rapidly expanding light industry which includes precision instrument manufacture at Kota and television assembly. The principal industrial complexes are at Jaipur, Kota, Udaipur and Bhilwara. Traditional handicrafts such as pottery, jewellery, marble work, embossed brass, block printing, embroidery and decorative painting are now very good foreign exchange earners.

Gujarat has been an economic force in India for centuries with important ports and some of the country's earliest modern textile mills. From the late-19th century Ahmadabad emerged with its cotton industry as the `Manchester of India'. Kandla was set up on the northern coast of the Gulf of Kachchh as a major port to feed the hinterlands of north Gujarat, Rajasthan, Delhi, Uttar Pradesh and Haryana. There is now a private port at Mundara on the Kachchh shores, coastal projects at Pip-a-Vav near Bhavnagar, and Surat in south Gujarat, as well as one of the world's largest ship scrapping zones at Alang.

Gujarat's economy

In the late-1970s and early-80s there was a decline in the textile industry and most of Ahmadabad's textile mills were closed by the recession and `piracy' of brand names by smaller units. Ahmadabad, Surat and Jetpur have a number of textile factories. Gujarat is a national leader in many industries. Refineries and natural gas pipelines have made the state a major producer of petroleum, oil and LPG. Some of India's largest petrochemical, dyes and chemicals, pharmacy and fertilizer manufacturing units are in Gujarat. On the agricultural front, Gujarat is known for its cotton, ground nut (commonly used for cooking oil), tobacco, chillies and food grains grown in Kathiawad and north Gujarat. Central Gujarat, specially Kheda district, fed by the Mahi canal, and the Narmada river area near Baruch, are known for wheat and millets.

Tourism has not been an important source of revenue for Gujarat but in recent years the state government has started taking an interest in promoting the state's resources by way of monuments and beaches. The '*Royal Orient*' is Gujarat's answer to the famous 'Palace on Wheels'. The *Heritage Hotels* in atmospheric old palace and fort conversions offer the traveller the unique opportunity to stay in off-the-

Background

beaten-track locations. Some tour operators specialize in visiting these unusual properties, wildlife parks and even royal garages!

Religion

It is impossible to write briefly about religion in India without greatly oversimplifying. Over 80% of Indians are Hindu, but there are significant minorities. Muslims number about 120 million and there are over 20 million Christians, 18 million Sikhs, six million Buddhists, two million Jains and a number of other religious groups. Although nearly all these groups are represented in Rajasthan and Gujarat the balance varies. Buddhism is barely represented, and there are only small communities of Sikhs and Christians. While Hinduism is dominant, there is a significant Muslim minority, especially in Gujarat, and the greatest concentration of Jains in India.

One of the most persistent features of Indian religious and social life is the caste system. This has undergone substantial changes since Independence, especially in towns and cities, but most people in India are still clearly identified as a member of a particular caste group. The government has introduced measures to help the backward, or 'scheduled' castes – the *dalits*, meaning 'oppressed'- though in recent years this has produced a major political backlash.

Hinduism

It has always been easier to define Hinduism by what it is not than by what it is. Indeed, the name 'Hindu' was given by foreigners to the peoples of the subcontinent who did not profess the other major faiths, such as Muslims or Christians. The beliefs and practices of modern Hinduism began to take shape in the centuries on either side of the birth of Christ. But while some aspects of modern Hinduism can be traced back more than 2,000 years before that, other features are recent.

Key ideas

Some Hindu scholars and philosophers talk of Hinduism as one religious and cultural tradition. Yet there is no Hindu organization, like a church, with the authority to define belief or establish official practice. There are spiritual leaders who are widely revered and there is an enormous range of literature that is treated as sacred. In view of these characteristics, many authorities argue that it is misleading to think of Hinduism as a religion at all. Be that as it may, the evidence of the living importance of Hinduism is visible across India. Hindu philosophy and practice has also touched many of those who belong to other religious traditions, particularly in terms of social institutions such as caste.

Darshan One of Hinduism's recurring themes is 'vision', 'sight' or 'view' – *darshan*. Applied to the different philosophical systems themselves, such as *yoga* or *vedanta*, 'darshan' is also used to describe the sight of the deity that worshippers hope to gain when they visit a temple or shrine hoping for the sight of a 'guru' (teacher). Equally it may apply to the religious insight gained through meditation or prayer.

The four human goals Many Hindus also accept that there are four major human goals; material prosperity (*artha*), the satisfaction of desires (*kama*) and performing the duties laid down according to your position in life (*dharma*). Beyond those is the goal of achieving

Karma – an eye to the future

According to the doctrine of karma, every person, animal or god has a being or 'self' which has existed without beginning. Every action, except those that are done without any consideration of the results, leaves an indelible mark on that 'self', carried forward into the next life.

The overall character of the imprint on each person's 'self' determines three features of the next life: the nature of his next birth (animal, human or god), the kind of family he will be born into if human and the length of the next life. Finally, it controls the good or bad experiences that the self will experience. However, it does not imply a fatalistic belief that the nature of action in this life is unimportant. Rather, it suggests that the path followed by the individual in the present life is vital to the nature of its next life and ultimately to the chance of gaining release from this world.

liberation from the endless cycle of rebirths into which everyone is locked (*moksha*). It is to the search for liberation that the major schools of Indian philosophy have devoted most attention. Together with dharma, it is basic to Hindu thought.

The Mahabharata lists 10 embodiments of **dharma**: good name, truth, self-control, cleanness of mind and body, simplicity, endurance, resoluteness of character, giving and sharing, austerities and continence. In *dharmic* thinking these are inseparable from five patterns of behaviour: non-violence, an attitude of equality, peace and tranquillity, lack of aggression and cruelty and absence of envy. Dharma, an essentially secular concept, represents the order inherent in human life.

Karma

The idea of *karma*, 'the effect of former actions', is central to achieving liberation. As C Rajagopalachari put it: "Every act has its appointed effect, whether the act be thought, word or deed. The cause holds the effect, so to say, in its womb. If we reflect deeply and objectively, the entire world will be found to obey unalterable laws. That is the doctrine of karma".

Rebirth

The belief in the transmigration of souls (*samsara*) in a never-ending cycle of rebirth has been Hinduism's most distinctive and important contribution to Indian culture. The earliest reference to the belief is found in one of the Upanishads, around the seventh century BC, at about the same time as the doctrine of karma made its first appearance. By the late Upanishads it was universally accepted and in Buddhism and Jainism it is never questioned.

Ahimsa

AL Basham pointed out that belief in transmigration must have encouraged a further distinctive doctrine, that of non-violence or non-injury – *ahimsa*. The belief in rebirth meant that all living things and creatures of the spirit – people, devils, gods, animals, even worms – possessed the same essential soul. It was an idea that became particularly important for the Jains.

Schools of philosophy

It is common now to talk of six major schools of Hindu philosophy. *Nyaya, Vaisheshika, Sankhya, Yoga, Purvamimansa* and *Vedanta*.

Yoga

Yoga, can be traced back to at least the third century AD. It seeks a synthesis of the spirit, the soul and the flesh and is concerned with systems of meditation and self denial that lead to the realization of the Divine within oneself and can ultimately release one from the cycle of rebirth.

Background

The four stages of life

Popular Hindu belief holds that an ideal life has four stages: that of the student, the householder, the forest dweller and the wandering dependent or beggar (sannyasi). These stages represent the phases through which an individual learns of life's goals and of the means of achieving them.

One of the most striking sights today is that of the saffron clad sannyasi (sadhu) seeking gifts of food and money to support himself in the final stage of his life. There may have been sadhus even before the Aryans arrived. Today, most of these have given up material possessions, carrying only a strip of cloth, a danda (staff), a crutch to support the chin during achal (meditation), prayer beads, a fan to ward off evil spirits, a water pot, a drinking vessel, which may be a human skull and a begging bowl. You may well see one, almost naked, covered only in ashes, on a city street.

Vedanta These are literally the final parts of the Vedic literature, the Upanishads. The basic texts also include the Brahmasutra of Badrayana, written about the first century AD and the most important of all, the Bhagavad-Gita, which is a part of the epic the Mahabharata. There are many interpretations of these basic texts.

Worship

Puja
The great majority of Hindu homes will have a shrine to one of the gods of the Hindu pantheon
For most Hindus today worship ('performing puja') is an integral part of their faith. Acts of devotion are often aimed at the granting of favours and the meeting of urgent needs for this life – good health, finding a suitable wife or husband, the birth of a son, prosperity and good fortune. Puja involves making an offering to God and *darshan* (having a view of the deity). Hindu worship is generally, though not always, an act performed by individuals. Thus Hindu temples may be little more than a shrine in the middle of the street, tended by a priest and visited at special times when a *darshan* of the resident God can be obtained. When it has been consecrated, the **image**, if exactly made, becomes the channel for the godhead to work.

Rituals & festivals The temple rituals often follow through the cycle of day and night, as well as yearly lifecycles. The priests may wake the deity from sleep, bathe, clothe and feed it. Worshippers will be invited to share in this process by bringing offerings of clothes and food. Gifts of money will usually be made and in some temples there is a charge levied for taking up positions in front of the deity in order to obtain a *darshan* at the appropriate times.

Holy places Certain rivers and towns are particularly sacred to Hindus. There are seven holy rivers, seven holy places, and four holy abodes, Dwarka in modern Gujarat associated with Lord Krishna having the unique distinction of being both a holy abode and a holy place. The lakes of Pushkar in Rajasthan and Narayan Sarovar in Kachchh are among the five holiest in India. The shore temple of Somnath is among the 12 *jyotirlingas* where Siva is said to be specially present according to the Siva Poornima.

Hindu deities

Today three Gods are widely seen as all-powerful: Brahma, Vishnu and Siva. While Brahma is regarded as the ultimate source of creation, Siva also has a creative role alongside his function as destroyer. Vishnu in contrast is seen as the preserver or protector of the universe. Vishnu and Siva are widely represented in sculpture and art (where Brahma is not) and have come to be seen as the most powerful and important. Their followers are referred to as Vaishnavites and Shaivites respectively and numerically they form the two largest sects in India.

Brahma

In the literal sense the name Brahma is the masculine and personalized form of the neuter word Brahman. Popularly Brahma is recognised as the Creator. In the early Vedic writing, Brahman represented the universal and impersonal principle which governed the Universe. Gradually, as Vedic philosophy moved towards a monotheistic interpretation of the universe and its origins, this impersonal power was increasingly personalized. In the Upanishads, Brahman was seen as a universal and elemental creative spirit.

By the fourth and fifth centuries AD, the height of the classical period of Hinduism, Brahma was seen as one of the trinity of Gods – *Trimurti* – in which Vishnu, Siva and Brahma represented three forms of the unmanifested supreme being. It is from Brahma that Hindu cosmology takes its structure. The basic cycle through which the whole cosmos passes is described as one day in the life of Brahma – the *kalpa*. It equals 4,320 million years, with an equally long night. One year of Brahma's life – a cosmic year – lasts 360 days and nights. The universe is expected to last for 100 years of Brahma's life, who is currently believed to be 51 years old.

By the sixth century AD Brahma worship had effectively ceased (before the great period of temple building), which accounts for the fact that there are remarkably few temples dedicated to Brahma. Nonetheless images of Brahma are found in most temples. Characteristically he is shown with four faces, a fifth having been destroyed by the fire from Siva's third eye. In his four arms he usually holds a copy of the Vedas, a sceptre and a water jug or a bow. He is accompanied by the goose, symbolizing knowledge.

Sarasvati

Seen by some Hindus as the 'active power' of Brahma, popularly thought of as his consort, Sarasvati , the goddess of education and learning, is worshipped in schools and colleges with gifts of fruit, flowers and incense. The development of her identity represented the rebirth of the concept of a mother goddess, which had been strong in the Indus Valley Civilization over 1,000 years before and which may have been continued in popular ideas through the worship of female spirits.

In addition to her role as Brahma's wife, Sarasvati is also variously seen as the wife of Vishnu and Manu or as Daksha's daughter, among other interpretations. Normally white coloured, riding on a swan and carrying a book, she is often shown playing a *vina*. She may have many arms and heads, representing her role as patron of all the sciences and arts.

Vishnu

Vishnu is seen as the God with the human face. From the second century a new and passionate devotional worship of Vishnu's incarnation as Krishna developed in the South. By 1,000 AD Vaishnavism had spread across South India and it became closely associated with the devotional form of Hinduism preached by **Ramanuja**, whose followers spread the worship of Vishnu and his 10 successive incarnations in animal and human form. For Vaishnavites, God took these different forms in order to save the world from impending disaster. AL Basham has summarized the 10 incarnations (see Table).

Rama and Krishna By far the most influential incarnations of Vishnu are those in which he was believed to take recognizable human form, especially as Rama (twice) and Krishna. As the Prince of Ayodhya, history and myth blend, for Rama was probably a chief who lived in the eighth or seventh century BC.

Background

Although Rama (or Ram – pronounced to rhyme with *calm*) is now seen as an earlier incarnation of Vishnu than Krishna, he came to be regarded as divine very late, probably after the Muslim invasions of the 12th century AD. The story has become part of the cultures of Southeast Asia.

Krishna is worshipped extremely widely as perhaps the most human of the gods. Often shown in pictures as blue in colour and playing the flute, he is the playful child stealing butter or the amorous young man teasing the young women looking after the cattle. His advice on the battlefield of the Mahabharata is one of the major sources of guidance for the rules of daily living for many Hindus today.

Lakshmi Commonly represented as Vishnu's wife, Lakshmi is widely worshipped as the goddess of wealth. Earlier representations of Vishnu's consorts portrayed her as Sridevi, often shown in statues on Vishnu's right, while Bhudevi, also known as Prithvi, who represented the earth, was on his left. Lakshmi is popularly shown in her own right as standing on a lotus flower, although eight forms of Lakshmi are recognized.

Hanuman The Ramayana tells how Hanuman, Rama's faithful monkey servant, went across India and finally into the demon Ravana's forest home of Lanka at the head of his monkey army in search of the abducted Sita. He used his powers to jump the sea channel separating India from Sri Lanka and managed after a series of heroic and magical feats to find and rescue his master's wife. Whatever form he is shown in, he remains almost instantly recognizable.

Siva Siva is interpreted as both creator and destroyer, the power through whom the universe evolves. He lives on Mount Kailasa with his wife **Parvati** (also known as **Uma**, **Sati**, **Kali** and **Durga**) and two sons, the elephant-headed Ganesh and the six-headed Karttikeya. To many contemporary Hindus they form a model of sorts for family life. In sculptural representations Siva is normally accompanied by his 'vehicle', the bull (*nandi* or *nandin*).

Siva is also represented in Shaivite temples throughout India by the linga, literally meaning 'sign' or 'mark', but referring in this context to the sign of gender or phallus and *yoni*. On the one hand a symbol of energy, fertility and potency, as Siva's symbol it also represents the yogic power of sexual abstinence and penance. The linga has become the most important symbol of the cult of Siva.

A wide variety of myths appeared to explain the origin of linga worship. The myths surrounding the 12 *jyotirlinga* (linga of light) found at centres like Somnath in Gujarat go back to the second century BC and were developed in order to explain and justify linga worship.

Siva's alternative names Although Siva is not seen as having a series of rebirths, like Vishnu, he nonetheless appears in very many forms representing different aspects of his varied powers. Some of the more common are:

Chandrasekhara The moon (*chandra*) symbolizes the powers of creation and destruction.

Mahadeva The representation of Siva as the god of supreme power, which came relatively late into Hindu thought, shown as the linga in combination with the *yoni*, or female genitalia.

Nataraja, the Lord of the Cosmic Dance The story is based on a legend in which Siva and Vishnu went to the forest to overcome 10,000 heretics. In their anger the heretics attacked Siva first by sending a tiger, then a snake and thirdly a fierce black dwarf with a club. Siva killed the tiger, tamed the snake and wore it like a garland and then put his foot on the dwarf and performed a dance of such power that the dwarf and the heretics acknowledged Siva as the Lord.

Rudra Siva's early prototype, who may date back to the Indus Valley Civilization.

Virabhadra Siva created Virabhadra to avenge himself on his wife Sati's father, Daksha, who had insulted Siva by not inviting him to a special sacrifice. Sati attended the ceremony against Siva's wishes and when she heard her father grossly abusing Siva she committed suicide by jumping into the sacrificial fire. This act gave rise to the term *sati* (*suttee*, a word which simply means a good or virtuous woman). Recorded in the *Vedas*, the self immolation of a woman on her husband's funeral pyre probably did not become accepted practice until the early centuries BC. Even then it was mainly restricted to those of the Kshatriya caste.

Nandi

Siva's vehicle, the bull, one of the most widespread of sacred symbols of the ancient world, may represent a link with Rudra who was sometimes represented as a bull in pre-Hindu India. Strength and virility are key attributes and pilgrims to Siva temples will often touch the Nandi's testicles on their way into the shrine.

Ganesh

Ganesh, one of Hinduism's most popular gods, is seen as the great clearer of obstacles. Shown at gateways and on door lintels with his elephant head and pot belly, his image is revered across India. Meetings, functions and special family gatherings will often start with prayers to Ganesh and any new venture, from the opening of a building to inaugurating a company, will not be deemed complete without a Ganesh puja.

Shakti, The Mother Goddess

Shakti is a female divinity often worshipped in the form of Siva's wife Durga or Kali. As Durga she agreed to do battle with Mahish, an *asura* (demon) who threatened to dethrone the gods. Many sculptures and paintings illustrate the story in which, during the terrifying struggle which ensued, the demon changed into a buffalo, an elephant and a giant with 1,000 arms. Durga, clutching weapons in each of her ten hands, eventually emerges victorious. As Kali ('black') the mother goddess takes on her most fearsome form and character. Fighting with the chief of the demons, she was forced to use every weapon in her armoury, but every drop of blood that she drew became 1,000 new giants just as strong as he. The only way she could win was by drinking the blood of all her enemies. Having succeeded she was so elated that her dance of triumph threatened the earth. Ignoring the pleas of the gods to stop, she even threw her husband Siva to the ground and trampled over him, until she realized to her shame what she had done. She is always shown with a sword in one hand, the severed head of the giant in another, two corpses for earrings and a necklace of human skulls. She is often shown standing with one foot on the body and the other on the leg of Siva.

Gods of the warrior caste

Modern Hinduism has brought into its pantheon over many generations gods who were worshipped by the earlier pre-Hindu Aryan civilizations. The most important is **Indra**, often shown as the god of rain, thunder and lightning. To the early Aryans, Indra destroyed demons in battle, the most important being his victory over Vritra, 'the Obstructor'. By this victory Indra released waters from the clouds, allowing the earth to become fertile. To the early Vedic writers the clouds of the southwest monsoon were seen as hostile, determined to keep their precious treasure of water to themselves and only releasing it when forced to by a greater power. Indra, carrying a bow in one hand, a thunderbolt in another and lances in the others and riding on his vehicle Airavata, the elephant, is thus the Lord of Heaven.

Mitra and **Varuna** have the power both of gods and demons. Their role is to sustain order, Mitra taking responsibility for friendship and Varuna for oaths and as they have to keep watch for 24 hours a day Mitra has become the god of the day or the sun, Varuna the god of the moon.

Background

Soma The juice of the soma plant, the nectar of the gods guaranteeing eternal life, Soma is also a deity taking many forms. Born from the churning of the ocean of milk in later stories Soma was identified with the moon. The golden haired and golden skinned god **Savitri** is an intermediary with the great power to forgive sin and as king of heaven he gives the gods their immortality. **Surya**, the god of the sun, fittingly of overpowering splendour, is often described as being dark red, sitting on a red lotus or riding a chariot pulled by the seven horses of the dawn (representing the days of the week). **Usha**, sometimes referred to as Surya's wife, is the goddess of the dawn, daughter of Heaven and sister of the night. She rides in a chariot drawn by cows or horses.

Devas & Asuras In Hindu popular mythology the world is also populated by innumerable gods and demons, with a somewhat uncertain dividing line between them. Both have great power and moral character and there are frequent conflicts and battles between them.

The **Nagas** and **Naginis** The multiple-hooded cobra head often seen in sculptures represents the fabulous snake gods the Nagas, though they may often be shown in other forms, even human. Worshipped throughout India, in Rajasthan the *naga* – or *sesa* – is widely revered. The thousand-headed cosmic serpent is seen as the God Vishnu in the form of the snake. **Sesa** has the power to destroy the world at the end of every age by his fiery breath.

Hindu society

Dharma is seen as the most important of the objectives of individual and social life. Hindu law givers laid down rules of family conduct and social obligations related to the institutions of caste and *jati* which were beginning to take shape at the same time.

Caste Although the word caste was given by the Portuguese in the 15th century AD, the main feature of the system emerged at the end of the Vedic period. Two terms – *varna* and *jati* – are used in India itself and have come to be used interchangeably and confusingly with the word caste.

Varna, which literally means colour, had a fourfold division. By 600 BC this had become a standard means of classifying the population. The fair-skinned Aryans distinguished themselves from the darker skinned earlier inhabitants. The priestly *varna*, the Brahmins, were seen as coming from the mouth of Brahma; the Kshatriyas (or Rajputs as they are commonly called in Northwest India) were warriors, coming from Brahma's arms; the Vaishyas, a trading community, came from Brahma's thighs and the Sudras, classified as agriculturalists, from his feet. Relegated beyond the pale of civilized Hindu society were the untouchables or outcastes, who were left with the jobs which were regarded as impure.

Jati Many Brahmins and Rajputs are conscious of their *varna* status, but the great majority of Indians do not put themselves into one of the four *varna* categories, but into a *jati* group. There are thousands of different *jatis* across the country. While individuals found it impossible to change caste or to move up the social scale, groups would sometimes try to gain recognition as higher caste by adopting practices of the Brahmins such as becoming vegetarians. Many used to be identified with particular activities and occupations used to be hereditary. Caste membership is decided simply by birth. Although you can be evicted from your caste by your fellow members you cannot join another caste and technically you become an outcaste. Right up until Independence in 1947 such punishment was a drastic penalty for disobeying one's dharmic duty. In many areas all avenues into normal life could be blocked, families would disregard outcaste members and it could even be impossible for the outcaste to continue to work within the locality.

The sacred thread

The highest three varnas *were classified as "twice born" and could wear the sacred thread symbolizing their status. The age at which the initiation ceremony* (upanayana) *for the upper caste child was carried out, varied according to class – 8 for a Brahmin, 11 for a Kshatriya and 12 for a Vaishya.*

The boy, dressed like an ascetic and holding a staff in his hand, would have the sacred thread (yajnopavita) *placed over his right shoulder and under his left arm. A cord of three threads, each of nine*

twisted strands, it was made of cotton for Brahmans, hemp for Kshatriyas or wool for Vaishyas. It was, and is, regarded as a great sin to remove it.

The Brahmin who officiated would whisper a verse from the Rig Veda in the boy's ear, the Gayatri mantra. Addressed to the old solar god Savitr, the holiest of holy passages, the Gayatri can only be spoken by the three higher classes. AL Basham translated it as: "Let us think on the lovely splendour of the god Savitr, that he may inspire our minds".

The Dalits Gandhi spearheaded his campaign for independence from British colonial rule with a powerful campaign to abolish the disabilities imposed by the caste system. Coining the term *harijan* (meaning 'person of God') Gandhi demanded that discrimination be outlawed. Lists – or 'schedules' – of backward castes were drawn up during the early part of this century in order to provide positive help to such groups. The term *harijan* has been rejected by many former outcastes as paternalistic and as implying an adherence to Hindu beliefs which some explicitly reject. Many argue passionately for the use of the secular term 'dalits' – the 'oppressed'.

Affirmative action Since 1947 the Indian government has extended its positive discrimination (a form of affirmative action) to scheduled castes and scheduled tribes, particularly through reserving up to 50% of jobs in government-run institutions and in further education, leading to professional qualifications for these groups. Members of the scheduled castes are now found in important positions throughout the economy. Most of the obvious forms of social discrimination have disappeared. Yet caste remains an explosive political issue. Attempts to improve the social and economic position of dalits and what are termed 'other backward castes' (OBCs) continues to cause sometimes violent conflict.

Marriage Even in cities, where traditional means of arranging marriages have often broken down and where many people resort to advertising for marriage partners in the columns of the Sunday newspapers, caste is frequently stated as a requirement. Marriage is generally seen as an alliance between two families. Great efforts are made to match caste, social status and economic position, although the rules which govern eligibility vary from region to region. In some groups marriage between even first cousins is common, while among others marriage between any branch of the same clan is strictly prohibited.

Hindu reform movements

Hinduism today is a more self-conscious religious and political force than it was even at Independence in 1947. Reform movements of modern Hinduism can be traced back at least to the early years of the 19th century. These movements were unique in Hinduism's history in putting the importance of political ideas on the same level as strictly religious thinking and in interrelating them.

The **Arya Samaj**, founded in 1875 at Ajmer by Dayanand Sarasvati, was established to restore India to its Vedic Aryan religious roots. Particularly strong in Rajasthan and northwestern India, the Arya Samaj held that the Vedas contain all knowledge and truth. In its extreme form this has led to claims that references to everything ever invented can be found in the Vedas, including space travel and nuclear weapons, but the Arya Samaj also had a significant social reforming dimension.

The Hindu calendar While for its secular life India follows the Gregorian calendar, for Hindus, much of religious and personal life follows the Hindu calendar (see also page 58). This is based on the lunar cycle of 29½ days, but the clever bit comes in the way it is synchronized with the 365 day Gregorian solar calendar of the west by the addition of an 'extra month' (*adhik maas*), every 2½ to three years.

Hindus follow two distinct eras. The *Vikrama Samvat* which began in 57 BC and the *Salivahan Saka* which dates from 78 AD and has been the official Indian calendar since 1957. The *Saka* new year starts on 22 March and has the same length as the Gregorian calendar. In North India the New Year is celebrated in the second month of *Vaisakh*.

The year itself is divided into two, the first six solar months being when the sun 'moves' north, known as the *Makar Sankranti* (which is marked by special festivals), and the second half when it moves south, the *Karka Sankranti*. The first begins in January and the second in June. The 29 ½ day lunar month with its 'dark' (*Krishna*) and 'bright' (*Shukla*) halves based on the new (*Amavasya*) and full moons (*Purnima*), are named after the 12 constellations, and total a 354 day year. The day itself is divided into eight *praharas* of three hours each and the year into six seasons: *Vasant* (spring), *Grishha* (summer), *Varsha* (rains), *Sharat* (early autumn), *Hemanta* (late autumn), *Shishir* (winter).

Hindu, and corresponding Gregorian, calendar months

Chaitra	March-April	*Ashwin*	September-October
Vaishakh	April-May	*Kartik*	October-November
Jyeshtha	May-June	*Margashirsha*	November-December
Aashadh	June-July	*Poush*	December-January
Shravan	July -August	*Magh*	January-February
Bhadra	August-September	*Phalgun*	February-March

Islam

Islam is a highly visible presence in India today. Even after partition in 1947 over 40 million Muslims remained in India and today there are just over 120 million. It is the most recent of imported religions. From the creation of the Delhi Sultanate in 1206, by Turkish rather than Arab power, Islam became a permanent living religion in India.

The victory of the Turkish ruler of Ghazni over the Rajputs in AD 1192 established a 500-year period of Muslim power in India. The contact between the courts of the new rulers and the indigenous Hindu populations produced innovative developments in art and architecture, language and literature. Hindus and Hindu culture were profoundly affected by the spread and exercise of Muslim political power, but Islam too underwent major modifications in response to the new social and religious context in which the Muslim rulers found themselves.

From the middle of the 13th century, when the Mongols crushed the Arab caliphate, the Delhi sultans were left on their own to exercise Islamic authority in India. From then onwards the main external influences were from Persia. Small numbers of migrants, mainly the skilled and the educated, continued to flow into the Indian courts.

Muslims only became a majority of the South Asian population in the plains of the Indus and west Punjab and in parts of Bengal. Elsewhere they formed important minorities, notably in the towns of the central heartland such as Lucknow. In the central plains there was already a densely populated, Hindu region, where little attempt was made to achieve converts.

Muslim populations

The **Mughals** wanted to expand their territory and their economic base. To pursue this they made enormous grants of land to those who had served the empire, and new land was brought into cultivation. At the same time, shrines were established to Sufi saints who attracted peasant farmers. By the 18th century many Muslims had joined the **Sunni** sect of Islam.

In some areas Muslim society shared many of the characteristic features of the Hindu society from which the majority of them came. Many of the Muslim migrants from Iran or Turkey, the élite **Ashraf** communities, continued to identify with the Islamic élites from which they traced their descent. They held high military and civil posts in imperial service. In sharp contrast, many of the non-Ashraf Muslim communities in the towns and cities were organized in social groups very much like the *jatis* of their neighbouring Hindu communities. While the élites followed Islamic practices close to those based on the Qur'an as interpreted by scholars, the poorer, less literate communities followed devotional and pietistic forms of Islam. The distinction is still very clear today and the importance of veneration of the saints can be seen at tombs and shrines in Rajasthan and Gujarat.

The beliefs of Islam (which means 'submission to God') could apparently scarcely be more different from those of Hinduism. Islam, often described as having "five pillars" of faith (see box) has a fundamental creed; 'There is no God but God; and Mohammad is the Prophet of God' (*La Illaha illa 'Ilah Mohammad Rasulu 'Ilah*). One book, the Qur'an, is the supreme authority on Islamic teaching and faith. Islam preaches the belief in bodily resurrection after death and in the reality of heaven and hell.

Muslim beliefs

The idea of heaven as paradise is pre-Islamic. Alexander the Great is believed to have brought the word into Greek from Persia, where he used it to describe the walled Persian gardens that were found even three centuries before the birth of Christ. For Muslims, Paradise is believed to be filled with sensuous delights and pleasures, while hell is a place of eternal terror and torture, which is the certain fate of all who deny the unity of God.

Islam has no priesthood. The authority of Imams derives from social custom and from their authority to interpret the scriptures, rather than from a defined status within the Islamic community. Islam also prohibits any distinction on the basis of race or colour and most Muslims believe it is wrong to represent the human figure. It is often thought, inaccurately, that this ban stems from the Qur'an itself. In fact it probably has its origins in the belief of Mohammad that images were likely to be turned into idols.

During the first century after Mohammad's death Islam split in to two sects which were divided on political and religious grounds, the Shi'is and Sunni's.

Muslim sects

The **Sunnis** – always the majority in South Asia – believe that Mohammad did not appoint a successor and that Abu Bak'r, Omar and Othman were the first three caliphs (or vice-regents) after Mohammad's death. Ali, whom the Sunni's count as the fourth caliph, is regarded as the first legitimate caliph by the Shi'is, who consider Abu Bak'r and Omar to be usurpers. While the Sunni's believe in the principle of election of caliphs, Shi'is believe that although Mohammad is the last prophet there is a continuing need for intermediaries between God and man. Such intermediaries are termed *Imams* and they base both their law and religious practice on the teaching of the *Imams*.

Background

The five pillars of Islam

In addition to the belief that there is one God and that Mohammed is his prophet, there are four further obligatory requirements imposed on Muslims. Daily prayers are prescribed at daybreak, noon, afternoon, sunset and nightfall. Muslims must give alms to the poor. They must observe a strict fast during the month of Ramadan. They must not eat or drink between sunrise and sunset. Lastly, they should attempt the pilgrimage to the Ka'aba in Mecca, known as the Hajj. Those who have done so are entitled to the prefix Hajji before their name.

Islamic rules differ from Hindu practice in several other aspects of daily life. Muslims are strictly forbidden to drink alcohol (though some suggest that this prohibition is restricted to the use of fermented grape juice, that is wine, it is commonly accepted to apply to all alcohol). Pork and any meat from an animal not killed by draining its blood is regarded as unclean and so eating them is prohibited. Meat prepared in the appropriate way is called Halal. Finally, usury (charging interest on loans) and games of chance are forbidden.

The Islamic Calendar The calendar begins on 16 July 622 AD, the date of the Prophet's migration from Mecca to Medina, the Hijra, hence AH (Anno Hejirae). The Muslim year is divided into 12 lunar months, totalling 354 or 355 days, hence Islamic festivals usually move 11 days earlier each year according to the solar (Gregorian) calendar. The first month of the year is *Moharram,* followed by *Safar, Rabi-ul-Awwal, Rabi-ul-Sani, Jumada-ul-Awwal, Jumada-ul-Sani, Rajab, Shaban, Ramadan, Shawwal, Ziquad* and *Zilhaj.*

Jainism

Like Buddhism, Jainism started as a reform movement of the Brahmanic religious beliefs of the sixth century BC. Its founder was a widely revered saint and ascetic, Vardhamma, who became known as **Mahavir** – 'great hero'. Mahavir was born in the same border region of India and Nepal as the Buddha, just 50 km north of modern Patna, probably in 599 BC. Thus he was about 35 years older than the Buddha. His family, also royal, were followers of an ascetic saint, Parsvanatha, who according to Jain tradition had lived 200 years previously.

Mahavir's life story is embellished with legends, but there is no doubt that he left his royal home for a life of the strict ascetic. He is believed to have received enlightenment after 12 years of rigorous hardship, penance and meditation. Afterwards he travelled and preached for 30 years, stopping only in the rainy season. He died aged 72 in 527 BC. His death was commemorated by a special lamp festival in the region of Bihar, which Jains claim is the basis of the now-common Hindu festival of lights, Diwali.

Some Jain ideas, such as vegetarianism and reverence for all life, are widely recognized by Hindus as highly commendable, even by those who do not share other Jain beliefs. The value Jains place on non-violence has contributed to their importance in business and commerce, as they regard nearly all occupations except banking and commerce as violent.

Jain beliefs Jains (from the word Jina, literally meaning 'descendants of conquerors') believe that there are two fundamental principles, the living (*jiva*) and the non-living (*ajiva*). The essence of Jain belief is that all life is sacred and that every living entity, even the smallest insect, has within it an indestructible and immortal soul. Jains developed the view of *ahimsa* – often translated as 'non-violence', but better perhaps as

The Jain spiritual journey

The two Jain sects differ chiefly on the nature of proper ascetic practices. The Svetambara monks wear white robes and carry a staff, some wooden pots and a woollen mop for sweeping the path in front of them, wool being the softest material available and the least likely to hurt any living thing swept away. The highest level of Digambara monks will go completely naked, although the lower levels will wear a covering over their genitalia. They carry a waterpot made of a gourd and peacock feathers to sweep

the ground before they sit.

Jains believe that the spiritual journey of the soul is divided into 14 stages, moving from bondage and ignorance to the final destruction of all karma and the complete fulfilment of the soul. The object throughout is to prevent the addition of new karma to the soul, which comes mainly through passion and attachment to the world. Bearing the pains of the world cheerfully contributes to the destruction of karma.

'non-harming'. *Ahimsa* was the basis for the entire scheme of Jain values and ethics and alternative codes of practice were defined for householders and for ascetics.

The five vows may be taken both by monks and by lay people. A Jain must not to kill any living being for food, sport or pleasure but the use of force is permissible in defending one's country, society, family or property. Jains practise strict vegetarianism – and even some vegetables, such as potatoes and onions, are believed to have microscopic souls. Where injury to life is unavoidable, a Jain is required to reduce this to a minimum by taking all precautions. The other vows require a Jain to speak the truth, not to steal (or cheat or use dishonest means in acquiring material wealth), to abstain from sexual relations (except with one's spouse for the lay people) and to set a limit on acquiring possessions and to use any surplus for the common good. The essence of all the rules is to avoid intentional injury, which is the worst of all sins.

Like Hindus, the Jains believe in *karma*, by which the evil effects of earlier deeds leave an indelible impurity on the soul. This impurity will remain through endless rebirths unless burned off by extreme penances.

Jains also regard the manner of dying as extremely important. Although suicide is deeply opposed, vows of fasting to death voluntarily may be regarded as earning merit in the proper context. Mahavir himself is believed to have died of self-starvation, near Rajgir in modern Bihar.

Jains have two main sects, whose origins can be traced back to the fourth century BC. The more numerous **Svetambaras** – the 'white clad' – concentrated more in eastern and western India, wear only two or three unsewn white garments. The **Digambaras** – or 'sky-clad'– among whom the male monks go naked.

Jain sects

Unlike Buddhists, Jains accept the idea of God, but not as a creator of the universe. They see him in the lives of the 24 **Tirthankaras** (prophets, or literally 'makers of fords' – a reference to their role in building crossing points for the spiritual journey over the river of life), the 24 leaders of Jainism, whose lives are recounted in the Kalpsutra – the third century BC book of ritual for the Svetambaras. **Vardhamana Mahavir** (599-527 BC) who followed **Parsvanatha** (877-777 BC), is regarded as the last of these great spiritual leaders. The first and most revered of the Tirthankaras, **Adinatha Rishabdeva**, who lived in pre-historic times, is widely represented in Jain temples.

Gujarat is one of the modern strongholds of Jainism. Jains devote great attention to the care of sick animals and birds and run a number of special animal hospitals. Note the '*parabdis*', special feeding places for birds, in the town.

Background

Buddhism

India was the home of Buddhism, which had its roots in the early Hinduism, or Brahmanism, of its time. Siddharta Gautama, who came to be given the title of the Buddha – or *enlightened one* – was born a prince into the kshatriya caste about 563 BC. By the time he died the Buddha had established a small band of monks and nuns known as the *sangha* , and had followers across northern India. During the early centuries BC and AD Buddhist caves mushroomed across Saurashtra. Buddhist relics can be seen at Talaja near Bhavnagar, Junagadh and surrounds, and at Khambilida near Gondal. Today however Buddhism is practised only on the margins of the subcontinent, from Ladakh, Nepal and Bhutan in the north to Sri Lanka in the south, where it is the religion of the majority Sinhalese community. Most are very recent converts, the last adherents of the early schools of Buddhism having been killed or converted by the Muslim invaders of the 13th century.

Sikhism

Guru Nanak, the founder of the religion, was born just west of Lahore and grew up in what is now the Pakistani town of Sultanpur. His followers, the Sikhs, (derived from the Sanskrit word for 'disciples') form perhaps one of India's most recognizable groups. Beards and turbans give them a very distinctive presence and although they represent less than two percent of the total population of India – and a far smaller proportion in Rajasthan and Gujarat – they are both politically and economically significant.

Sikh beliefs The first Guru, accepted the ideas of *samsara* – the cycle of rebirths – and *karma* (see page 395) from Hinduism. However, Sikhism is unequivocal in its belief in the oneness of God, rejecting idolatry and any worship of objects or images. Guru Nanak believed that God is One, formless, eternal and beyond description.

Guru Nanak also fiercely opposed discrimination on the grounds of caste. He saw God as present everywhere, visible to anyone who cared to look and as essentially full of grace and compassion. One of the many stories about his travels tells of how he was rebuked on his visit to Mecca for sleeping with his feet pointing towards the Qa'aba, an act Muslims would consider sacrilegious. Apologizing profusely, he had replied "If you can show me in which direction I may lie so that my feet do not point towards God, I will do so". His contact with Muslim families when still young prompted him to organize community hymn singing when both Hindus and Muslims were welcomed. Along with a Muslim servant, he also organized a common kitchen where Hindus of all castes and Muslims could eat together, thereby deliberately breaking one of the strictest of caste rules.

Guru Nanak preached that salvation depended on accepting the nature of God. If man recognized the true harmony of the divine order (*hookam*) and brought himself into line with that harmony he would be saved. Rejecting the prevailing Hindu belief that such harmony could be achieved by ascetic practices, he emphasized three actions; meditating on and repeating God's name (*naam*), 'giving', or charity (*daan*) and bathing (*isnaan*).

Many of the features now associated with Sikhism can be attributed to **Guru Gobind Singh**, who on 15 April 1699, started the new brotherhood called the *Khalsa* (meaning 'the pure', from the Persian word *khales*), an inner core of the faithful, accepted by baptism (*amrit*). The 'five ks' date from this period: *kesh* (uncut hair), the most important, followed by *kangha* (comb, usually of wood), *kirpan* (dagger or short sword), *kara* (steel bangle) and *kachh* (similar to 'boxer' shorts). The dagger and the shorts reflect military influence.

In addition to the compulsory 'five ks', the new code prohibited smoking, eating *halal* meat and sexual intercourse with Muslim women. These date from the 18th century, when the Sikhs were often in conflict with the Muslims. Other strict prohibitions include: idolatry, caste discrimination, hypocrisy and pilgrimage to Hindu sacred places. The *Khalsa* also explicitly forbade the seclusion of women, one of the common practices of Islam. It was only under the warrior king Ranjit Singh (1799-1838) that the idea of the Guru's presence in meetings of the Sikh community (the *Panth*) gave way to the now universally held belief in the total authority of the **Guru Granth**, the recorded words of the Guru in the scripture.

Christianity

There are about 23 million Christians in India. Christianity ranks third in terms of religious affiliation after Hinduism and Islam and there are Christian congregations in all the major towns of India.

The great majority of the Protestant Christians in India are now members of the Church of South India, formed from the major Protestant denominations in 1947, or the Church of North India, which followed suit in 1970. Together they account for approximately half the total number of Christians. Roman Catholics make up the majority of the rest. Many of the church congregations, both in towns and villages, are active centres of Christian worship.

Origins Some of the churches owe their origin either to the modern missionary movement of the late 18th century onwards, or to the colonial presence of the European powers. However, Christians probably arrived in India during the first century after the birth of Christ. There is evidence that one of Christ's Apostles, **Thomas**, reached India in 52 AD, only 20 years after Christ was crucified. He settled in Malabar and then expanded his missionary work to China. It is widely believed that he was martyred in Tamil Nadu on his return to India in 72 AD and is buried in Mylapore, in the suburbs of modern Chennai. St Thomas' Mount, a small rocky hill just north of Madras airport, takes its name from him. Today there is still a church of Thomas Christians in Kerala. In north India the influence of Christian missions in education and medical work was greater than as a proselytizing force. Education in Christian schools stimulated reform movements in Hinduism itself and mission hospitals supplemented government-run hospitals, particularly in remote rural areas.

Zoroastrianism

Zoroastrians trace their beliefs to the prophet **Zarathustra**, who lived in northeast Iran around the seventh or sixth century BC. The first Zoroastrians arrived on the west coast of India in the mid-eighth century AD, forced out from their native Iran by persecution of the invading Islamic Arabs. Until 1477 they lost all contact with Iran and then for nearly 300 years maintained contact with Persian Zoroastrians through a continuous exchange of letters. They became known by their now much more familiar name, the **Parsis** (or Persians).

Although they are a tiny minority (approximately 100,000), even in the cities where they are concentrated, they have been a prominent economic and social influence, especially in West India. Zoroastrians originally made landfall at Diu and then travelled to Sanjan on the east coast of the Gulf of Cambay. They finally settled at Udwada near

Daman where the most sacred fire temple is sited with the original fire. Other temples lit from the fire are at Surat and Navsari in south Gujarat and four at Mumbai.

Parsis adopted westernized customs and dress and took to the new economic opportunities that came with colonial industrialization. After Mumbai, which has more than 50% of the Parsi population, Gujarat has a sizeable proportion of the 100000 Zoroastrian population. Families in West India such as the Tatas continue to be among India's leading industrialists, just part of a community that in recent generations has spread to Europe and north America.

Parsi beliefs The early development of Zoroastrianism marked a movement towards belief in a single God. Ahura Mazda, the Good Religion of God, was shown in rejecting evil and in purifying thought, word and action. Fire plays a central and symbolic part in Zoroastrian worship, representing the presence of God. There are eight Atash Bahram – major fire temples – in India; four are in Mumbai, two in Surat and one each in Navsari and Udwada. There are many more minor temples, where the rituals are far less complex – perhaps 40 in Mumbai alone.

Earth, fire and air are all regarded as sacred, while death is the result of evil. Dead matter pollutes all it touches. Where there is a suitable space therefore, dead bodies are simply placed in the open to be consumed by vultures, as at the 'Towers of Silence' in Mumbai. However, burial and cremation are also common.

Culture

Language

Rajasthan and Gujarat each has its own distinct though related language, Rajasthani and Gujarati. They are Indo-Aryan languages – the easternmost group of the Indo-European family – among which Hindi is predominant. Sir William Jones, the great 19th-century scholar, discovered the close links between Sanskrit (the basis of nearly all North Indian languages) German and Greek. He showed that they all must have originated in the common heartland of Central Asia, being carried west, south and east by the nomadic tribes who shaped so much of the subsequent history of both Europe and Asia.

Sanskrit As the pastoralists from Central Asia moved into South Asia from 2000 BC onwards, the Indo-Aryan languages they spoke were gradually modified. **Sanskrit** developed from this process, emerging as the dominant classical language of India by the sixth century BC, when it was classified in the grammar of **Panini**. It remained the language of the educated until about AD 1000. The Muslims brought Persian into South Asia as the language of the rulers.

Hindi & Urdu The most striking example of Muslim influence on the earlier Indo-European languages is that of the two most important languages of India and Pakistan, Hindi and Urdu respectively. Most of the modern North Indian languages were not written until the 16th century or after. Hindi developed into the language of the heartland of Hindu culture, stretching from Punjab to Bihar and from the foothills of the Himalaya to the marchlands of central India, while Urdu became as the language of urban Muslims.

Rajasthani & Gujarati In Rajasthan, the principal language is **Rajasthani**, while the four most important dialects are *Marwari* in the west, *Jaipuri* in the east, *Malwi* in the southeast and *Mewati* in the northeast. Hindi is rapidly replacing Rajasthani as the lingua franca.

Gujarati is derived from Sanskrit but it was heavily influenced by *Apabrahmsa*, widely spoken in northwest India from the 10th to the 14th centuries. Maritime contacts with Persia, Arabia, Portugal and England led to the introduction of many words from these languages. Persian influence was particularly strong in Ahmadabad. Gujarati is spoken in mainland Gujarat, but dialects are common. Kathiawadi is spoken in Saurashtra and Kachchhi which is a blend of Gujarati and Sindhi being near the Sindh border. The Parsis speak Gujarati with a different accent. Near the Maharashtra border some of the tribes have a dialect/language influenced by the Konkan languages.

Scripts

The earliest ancestor of scripts used in India today was **Brahmi**, in which Asoka's famous inscriptions were written in the third century BC. Written from left to right, a separate symbol represented each different sound. For about a thousand years the major script of northern India has been the Nagari or Devanagari, which means literally the script of the 'city of the gods', though Gujarati has its own running script which developed as part of Gujarat's mercantile tradition.

Numerals

Many of the Indian alphabets have their own notation for numerals. This is not without irony, for what in the western world are called 'Arabic' numerals are in fact of Indian origin. Local numerical symbols are still in use, but by and large you will find that the Arabic number symbols familiar in Europe and the West are common.

The role of English

English now plays an important role across India. It is widely spoken in towns and cities and even in quite remote villages it is usually not difficult to find someone who speaks at least a little English. Other European languages are almost completely unknown. The accent in which English is spoken is often affected strongly by the mother tongue of the speaker and there have been changes in common grammar which sometimes make it sound unusual. Many of these changes have become standard Indian English usage, as valid as any other varieties of English used around the world.

Literature

Both Gujarat and Rajasthan have a long tradition of vernacular poetry in local dialects. Mystic poets like princess Meera of Mewar and Narsinh Mehta of Gujarat influenced vernacular literature in-between the 15th and 17th centuries. However, the literature of both states has been profoundly influenced by the wider traditions of literature in India.

Sanskrit was the first all-India language. Its early literature was memorized and recited. The hymns of the Rig Veda probably did not reach their final form until about the sixth century BC, but the earliest may go back as far as 1300 BC.

The Vedas

The Rig Veda is a collection of 1,028 hymns, not all directly religious. Its main function was to provide orders of worship for priests responsible for the sacrifices which were central to the religion of the Indo-Aryans. Two later texts, the Yajurveda and the Samaveda, served the same purpose. A fourth, the Atharvaveda, is largely a collection of magic spells.

At some time after 1000 BC a second category of Vedic literature, **the Brahmanas**, began to take shape. Story telling developed as a means to interpret the significance of sacrifice. The most famous and the most important of these were the Upanishads, probably written at some time between the seventh and fifth centuries BC. The Brahmanas gave their name to the religion emerging between the eighth and sixth centuries BC, Brahmanism, the ancestor of Hinduism. Two of it's

Background

The story of Rama

*Under Brahmin influence, **Rama** was transformed from the human prince of the early versions into the divine figure of the final story. Rama, the 'jewel of the solar kings', became deified as an incarnation of Vishnu. The story tells how Rama was banished from his father's kingdom. In a journey that took him as far as Sri Lanka, accompanied by his wife Sita and helper and friend Hanuman (the monkey-faced God depicted in many Indian temples, shrines and posters), Rama finally fought the king **Ravana**, again changed in late versions into a demon. Rama's rescue of Sita was interpreted as the Aryan triumph over the barbarians. The epic is widely seen as*

South Asia's first literary poem and is known and recited in all Hindu communities.

texts remain the best known and most widely revered epic compositions in South Asia, the Mahabharata and the Ramayana.

The details of the great battle recounted in **the Mahabharata** are unclear. Tradition puts its date at precisely 3102 BC, the start of the present era and names the author of the poem as a sage, Vyasa. Evidence suggests however that the battle was fought around 800 BC, at **Kurukshetra**. It was another 400 years before priests began to write the stories down, a process which was not complete until 400 AD. The original version was about 3,000 stanzas long, but it now contains over 100,000 – eight times as long as Homer's Iliad and the Odyssey put together. The battle was seen as a war of the forces of good and evil, the **Pandavas** being interpreted as gods and the **Kauravas** as devils. The arguments were elaborated and expanded until about the fourth century AD. A comparatively late addition to the Mahabharata, the Bhagavad-Gita is the most widely read and revered text among Hindus in South Asia today.

Valmiki is thought of in India as the author of the second great Indian epic, **the Ramayana**, though no more is known of his identity than is known of Homer's. Like the Mahabharata, it underwent several stages of development before it reached its final version of 48,000 lines.

Sanskrit literature Sanskrit was always the language of the court and the élite. Other languages replaced it in common speech by the third century BC, but it remained in restricted use for over 1,000 years after that period. The remarkable Sanskrit grammar of Panini helped to establish grammar as one of the six disciplines essential to understanding the Vedas properly and to conducting Vedic rituals. The other five were phonetics, etymology, meter, ritual practice and astronomy. Sanskrit literature continued to be written in the courts until the Muslims replaced it with Persian, long after it had ceased to be a language of spoken communication. One of India's greatest poets, **Kalidasa**, contributed to the development of Sanskrit as the language of learning and the arts.

Literally 'stories of ancient times', the Puranas are about Brahma, Vishnu and Siva. Although some of the stories may relate to real events that occurred as early as 1500 BC, they were not compiled until the fifth century AD. Margaret and James Stutley record the belief that "during the destruction of the world at the end of the age, Hayagriva is said to have saved the Puranas. A summary of the original work is now preserved in Heaven!"

The stories are often the only source of information about the period immediately following the early Vedas. Each Purana was intended to deal with five themes: "the creation of the world (*sarga*); its destruction and recreation (*pratisarga*); the genealogy of gods and patriarchs (*vamsa*); the reigns and periods of the Manus (*manvantaras*); and the history of the solar and lunar dynasties".

For considerable periods between the 13th and 18th century, **Persian** became the language of the courts. Classical Persian was the dominant influence, with Iran as its country of origin and Shiraz its main cultural centre, but India developed its own Persian-based style. Two poets stood out at the end of the 13th century AD, when Muslim rulers had established a sultanate in Delhi, Amir Khusrau, who lived from 1253 to 1325 and the mystic Amir Hasan, who died about AD 1328.

Muslim influence

The Mughal emperor Babur left one of the most remarkable political autobiographies of any generation, the Babur-nama (History of Babur), written in **Turki** and translated into Persian. His grandson Akbar commissioned a biography, the 'Akbar-nama', which reflected his interest in all the world's religions. His son Jahangir left his memoirs, the Tuzuk-i Jahangiri, in Persian. They have been described as intimate and spontaneous and showing an insatiable interest in things, events and people.

The use of Persian was already in decline during the reign of the last great Muslim Emperor, **Aurangzeb** and as the British extended their political power so the role of English grew. There is now a very wide range of Indian literature accessible in English, which has thus become the latest of the languages to be used across the whole of South Asia.

Colonial period

In the 19th century English became a vehicle for developing nationalist ideals. However, notably in the work of **Rabindranath Tagore**, it became a medium for religious and philosophical prose and for a developing poetry. Tagore himself won the Nobel Prize for Literature in 1913 for his translation into English of his own work, Gitanjali.

Science: early India

By about 500 BC Indian texts illustrated the calculation of the calendar, although the system itself almost certainly goes back to the eighth or ninth century BC. The year was divided into 27 *nakshatras*, or fortnights, years being calculated on a mixture of lunar and solar counting. See page 402.

Calendar

Early Indian views of the universe were based on the square and the cube. The earth was seen as a square, one corner pointing south, rising like a pyramid in a series of square terraces with its peak, the mythical Mount Meru. The sun moved round the top of Mount Meru in a square orbit and the square orbits of the planets were at successive planes above the orbit of the sun. These were seen therefore as forming a second pyramid of planetary movement. Mount Meru was central to all early Indian schools of thought, Hindu, Buddhist and Jain.

Views of the universe
A 'science museum' has been set up in Palitana which attempts to demonstrate the continuing validity of Jain ideas, including the belief that the earth is flat and that space flight is impossible

However, about 200 BC the Jains transformed the view of the universe based on squares by replacing the idea of square orbits with that of the circle. The earth was shown as a circular disc, with Mount Meru rising from its centre and the Pole Star directly above it. These views have not completely lost their currency among some Jains today.

Conceptions of the universe and the mathematical and geometrical ideas that accompanied them were comparatively advanced in South Asia by the time of the

Mathematics

Mauryan Empire and were put to use in the rules developed for building temple altars. Indians were using the concept of zero and decimal points in the Gupta period. Furthermore in AD 499, just after the demise of the Gupta Empire, the astronomer Aryabhatta calculated Pi as 3.1416 and the length of the solar year as 365.358 days. He also postulated that the earth was a sphere rotating on its own axis and revolving around the sun and that the shadow of the earth falling on the moon caused lunar eclipses.

Art and architecture

Both have developed with a remarkable continuity through successive regional and religious influences and styles. Rajasthan and Gujarat, while sharing many features common to wider Indian traditions, have their own distinctive regional styles of both religious and secular building which have continued to evolve right up to the present day.

The Buddhist stylistic influence on early Hindu architecture was profound. The first Hindu religious buildings to have survived into the modern period were constructed in south and east India from the sixth century AD.

The early Muslims destroyed much that was in their path. Yet the flowering of Islamic architecture which followed was not simply a transplant from another country or region, but grew out of India's own traditions. That continuity reflected many forces, not least the use made by the great Mughal emperors of local skilled craftsmen and builders. The first Emperor, Babur, expressed his admiration for the magnificence of the Rajput palace at Gwalior, and successive emperors tried to emulate and exceed the sumptuousness of Rajput forts and palaces while incorporating key elements from Muslim traditions.

Painting, sculpture, inlay work, all blended skills from a variety of sources and craftsmen – even occasionally from Europe. What emerged was another stepping stone in a tradition of Indian architecture, which wove the threads of Hindu tradition into new forms. The Taj Mahal was the ultimate product of this extraordinary process. Yet regional styles developed their own special feature and the main thrust of Hindu and Muslim religious buildings remains fundamentally different.

Architecture

Hindu temple buildings The principles of religious building were laid down by priests in the *sastras*. Every aspect of Hindu, Jain and Buddhist religious building is identified with conceptions of the structure of the universe. This applies as much to the process of building – the timing of which must be undertaken at astrologically propitious times – as to the formal layout of the buildings. The cardinal directions of north, south, east and west are the basic fix on which buildings are planned. In addition to the cardinal directions, number is also critical to the design, the ultimate scale of the building is being derived from the measurements of the sanctuary at its heart.

Indian temples were nearly always built to a design based on philosophical understandings of the universe. This cosmology of an infinite number of universes, isolated from each other in space, proceeds by imagining various possibilities as to its nature. Its centre is seen as dominated by **Mount Meru** which keeps earth and heaven apart. The concept of separation is crucial to Hindu thought and social practice. Continents, rivers and oceans occupy concentric rings around the mountain, while the stars encircle the mountain in another plane. Humans live on the continent of **Jambudvipa** characterized by the rose apple tree (*jambu*).

The *sastras* show plans of this continent, organized in concentric rings and entered at the cardinal points. This type of diagram was known as a **mandala**. The centre of the *mandala* would be the seat of the major god. *Mandalas* provided the ground rules for the building of stupas and temples across India and gave the key to the symbolic meaning attached to every aspect of religious buildings.

Temple design The focal point of the temple, its sanctuary, was the home of the presiding deity, the 'womb-chamber' (*garbhagriha*). A series of doorways, in large temples leading through a succession of buildings, allowed the worshipper to move towards the final encounter with the deity to obtain *darshan* – a sight of the god. Both Buddhist and Hindu worship encourage the worshipper to walk clockwise around the shrine, performing *pradakshina*.

The elevations are symbolic representations of the home of the gods. Mountain peaks such as Kailasa are common names for the most prominent of the towers. In North and East Indian temples the tallest of these towers rises above the *garbagriha* itself, symbolizing the meeting of earth and heaven in the person of the enshrined deity. The basic structure is usually richly embellished with sculpture. When first built this would usually have been plastered and painted and often covered in gems. In contrast to the extraordinary profusion of colour and life on the outside, the interior is dark and cramped but here it is believed, lies the true centre of divine power.

The Rajputs expressed their power in a variety of architectural forms. Although they were great patrons of Hindu religious art and worship, their most significant architectural legacy has been secular, paying particular attention to the construction of massive forts and lavish palaces. Merchants under Rajput protection also developed superb domestic architecture in their *havelis*. The main period of Rajput building dates from the mid-fifteenth to the mid-eighteenth centuries. It is no accident that this coincides with the period of Mughal dominance in north India, for it was a period during which the Rajputs had a relatively secure hold on power within their own territories, guaranteed in many cases by the superior force of the Mughals with whom for long periods they had close, protected relationships. The Rajput city capitals became the sites of the most extravagant palace building extravaganza in India.

In his book *The Rajput Palaces* Tillotson observed that "A Rajput palace was a symbol of dynasty, and each raja sought to outdo his neighbours and his predecessors in the splendour of his building projects". Palaces were sometimes doubled up as fortresses, others were designed and occupied for periods of peace. The standard features included a division into men's and women's quarters (*mardana* and *zenana*), the creation of large open courtyards as public space and much more confined rooms for private residence. The function of the palace was to demonstrate power, wealth and status, and thus the halls of public audience (*diwan-i*-am) played a prominent role and were often richly decorated. The hall of private audience (*diwan-i-khas*) was contained within the private quarters and was on a much smaller scale. Many Rajput palaces include a picture gallery – the *chitra shali* – and a bedroom with inlay mirror work, the *sheesh mahal*, while there would also be armouries and treasuries. The zenana, always less prolifically decorated, nonetheless would often have wonderfully constructed *jali* screens of pierced or latticed stone work, through which the women could watch proceedings outside without being seen.

The similarity of some of these features to those of Islamic building in India tempted early scholars to infer that Rajput architecture was simply derivative of Islamic, and in particular Mughal, traditions. Tillotson has argued that this view is mistaken, and points to the clear existence of a distinct Rajput palace complex style in the earliest remaining Rajput capital site of Chittaurgarh which existed well before the Mughals became supreme. A wealth of detail from later palaces, Tillotson argues, can

Rajput architecture

Background

be attributed to earlier Hindu temple models: the use of "square based columns, the *jarokha*, or cradle balcony; the *chajja* or deep eave; the *jali* or pieced stone screen; coloured tile decoration; the lotus rosette, and the first tentative use of the cusped arch."

It is clear that Rajput secular architecture borrowed from the tradition of religious architecture, a tradition of great antiquity. The Solanki, Parmara, Chauhan, Jetwa and Parihar rulers of eighth-13th century AD followed an architectural lay-out which is better known as the Chalukyan style. The Hindu and Jain temples of this period had a multi-columned portico entered through *torana* archways, an assembly hall called a *Sabha mandapam* and a shrine room. The outer walls and inside pillars were decorated with exquisite panels of sculpture depicting gods, goddesses, human and animal figures. Some of them portrayed voluptuous women and erotic friezes. The interior domes were corbelled and carved in detail, some of them had panels of carvings in concentric circles leading to the apex of the dome, superimposed by carved brackets. The interiors of the sanctum were usually plain and rarely had any carvings, certainly no erotica. Some temples like the Sun temple at Modhera had a `kund' where devotees could have a bath before entering the portico of the temple for their worship. Temples such as those at Dilwara and Osian follow this layout and made extensive use of marble and other stones.

This period also saw the building of one of the region's most distinctive features, the highly decorated step-well (*baoli* or *vav*). The early works were simple but later in Gujarat more elaborate structures came into existence like the seven storeyed Rani-ki-Vav stepwell of Patan believed to date from 1052 AD, the Vikia Vav at Ghumli near Porbandar probably dating to the 12th century and the five storeyed *vav* at Adalaj near Gandhinagar dating from the late 15th century. These stepwells had landings between flights of steps, exquisite carvings along the walls and pavilions/galleries/chambers cooled by air wafting off the water surface. It is believed these galleries may have doubled as caravanserais or as royal chambers for the ruling family to retreat from the heat of the summer sun.

Gujarati provincial architecture flowered between 1300 and 1550. The mosques and tombs that resulted reflect the new combination of Muslim political power and Hindu and Jain traditions. Thus, although the mosques obey strict Islamic principles they contain important features that are derived directly from Hindu and Jain precedents.

Haveli architecture Both Rajasthan and Gujarat have a style of domestic residential architecture which reflected the needs and aspirations of the rich and powerful merchant class, the haveli, built around a courtyard and ornately decorated. Gujarat was known for its wooden architecture. The medieval royal fort palaces, called Darbargadhs, had wooden brackets, balconies, pillared galleries. The merchants and other wealthy communities dwelt in wooden havelis, often as extended families. These havelis had exquisite wood carvings and pierced wooden *jali* screens. Wooden havelis can be seen in the *pols* of Ahmadabad and the older areas of towns like Bhavnagar and Patan. In Rajasthan these havelis were built from local stone. The sandstone havelis of Jaisalmer, Bikaner, Jodhpur here are masterpieces of stone carving. The Shekhawati mansions had their courtyards decorated with wall paintings which has been referred to an open-air art gallery. See also box, page 137.

Minor architectural features Both Rajasthan and Gujarat have a number of other distinctive architectural features. The Solankis for example endowed their kingdom with ponds (*kunds*), and tanks or reservoirs (*talaos*), which were sanctified by rows of shrines. Good examples are Sahasralinga Talao at Patan, the Munsar Tank at Viramgam and the Brahma Kund at Sihor. Rajput princes also characteristically built commemorative pavilions (*chattris* or *devals*), to mark royal cremation sites. The style of such *chattris* is often replicated in external features on both Rajput and Mughal buildings, including on the Taj Mahal.

Although the Muslims adapted many Hindu features, they also brought totally new forms. Dominating the architecture of many North Indian cities are the mosques and tomb complexes (*dargah*). The use of brickwork was widespread and they brought with them from Persia the principle of constructing the true arch and succeeded in producing a variety of domed structures, often incorporating distinctively Hindu features such as the surmounting finial. By the end of the great period of Muslim building in 1707, the Muslims had added magnificent forts and palaces to their religious structures, a statement of power as well as of aesthetic taste.

Muslim religious architecture

Nearly two centuries of architectural stagnation and decline followed the demise of Mughal power. The Portuguese built a series of remarkable churches in their territories, including Daman and Diu, that owed nothing to local traditions and everything to Baroque developments in Europe. Not until the end of the Victorian period, when British imperial ambitions were at their height, did the British colonial impact on public rather than domestic architecture begin to be felt. Fierce arguments divided British architects as to the merits of indigenous design. The ultimate plan for New Delhi was carried out by men who had little time for Hindu architecture and believed themselves to be on a civilizing mission. Others at the end of the 19th century wanted to recapture and enhance a tradition for which they had great respect. They have left a series of buildings, both in formerly British ruled territory and in the Princely States, notably in Rajasthan, which illustrate this concern through the development of what became known as the Indo-Saracenic style. The princes themselves often demonstrated highly eclectic tastes, importing such contrasting styles as Venetian-Gothic, Greek Doric and other Europeans styles for their new palaces and mansions. British architects like Sir Samuel Swinton Jacob, William Emerson, and Charles Mant, as well as local state architects and Parsi architects/builders, blended European and Indian features. Victorian, art deco and other European furnishings appointed the palaces, besides traditional arts, crafts, furniture and utensils of the region.

European buildings

In the immediate aftermath of the colonial period, Independent India set about trying to establish a break from the immediately imperial past, but was uncertain how to achieve it. In the event foreign architects were commissioned for major developments, such as Le Corbusier's and Louis Kahn's buildings in Ahmadabad. The latter, a centre for training and experiment, contains a number of new buildings such as those of the Indian architect Charles Correa.

Art

Painting

Rajasthan is well known for its wall paintings. Murals were painted on forts, temples, palaces and other historic buildings for centuries, but the fresco technique of Italy (painting on wet plaster) arrived with the Muslims to India. Mudwall painting is popular in Rajasthan and Kachchh, most of these paintings being done on hut walls by women during festivals and family celebrations. In the villages of Kachchh these are often set with mirrors and other decorations. *Pithoras* are the wall paintings of the tribal communities. The subjects are generally animistic, and pithoras on the wall are said to keep the houses free from evil spirits. The Rathwa villages around Chotta Udepur in eastern Gujarat are well known for their pithoras. These tribes now make pithoras on paper and cloth for tourists to decorate their homes. High quality *pichhwais* (temple paintings) are produced in Nathdwara, Udaipur and Bhilwara.

Miniature paintings The early miniature paintings in Western India are believed to originate from the classical murals of the Buddhist caves and ancient Jain art. In the 11th century, miniature paintings adorned palm leaf and cloth bound manuscripts, principally those of the Jains of Rajasthan and Gujarat. In the 16th century, the Mughals in India introduced Persian and West Asian techniques which strongly influenced the Rajasthani schools.

The Rajasthan princely states were important patrons of medieval miniature painting and various schools developed in different areas, drawing from local traditions and combining them with Mughal art. While Indian paintings had specialised in full frontal and three-quarter portraits, the Islamic painters introduced profiles. The Rajasthani painters depicted nature with bold colors and emphasized human forms while the Mughals introduced royal, courtly painting. Soon, flamboyant Rajput court culture began to appear as a popular theme but this was tempered by Hindu and Jain elements, local traditions and folk lore. Popular tales portrayed by the miniaturists were those from epics like the Ramayana and Mahabharata, Sanskrit writings like the Puranas and Shringara, iconography of the seasons (*Barah masa* or 12 months), and music (the Ragamala). Rajasthani ballads (love stories of Dhola-Maru, Sohni-Mahival, Nala-Damyanti etc), festivals, historical events, battles and hunts, sports like polo and pig sticking, all found a place, while the painters looked at dunes, hills, forests, orchards and historic buildings for their backdrops.

Miniature paintings were usually done on paper, sheets being bound together to make a firm surface. Mineral and organic colours were applied using squirrel hair and featherquill brushes and adhesives like gum arabic were used for fixing. Terracotta was sometimes brushed over the subject to give the raised effect, enhanced by gold leaf or powder work. Rare and expensive ivory lent itself as a suitable base for prized miniaturist art which were done with transparent colours so that the base of ivory was visible. This was favoured by affluent Jains and royalty who commissioned paintings of religious subjects, portraits and courtly scenes.

Handicrafts

Weaving Kota in eastern Rajasthan is known for its Doria saris with hundreds of weavers in the village of Khaitoon working to produce fine silk and cotton textiles with embroidered zari borders. Often the warp and weft threads are dyed in different colours to create a shot effect in Kota. Weavers of Kachchh, Barmer, Jaisalmer, Jodhpur and other districts work on pit-looms to produce *durrie* rugs, carpets, woollen cloth and other fabrics. Weaving of traditional woollen *durries* also became associated with Bikaner, Jaipur and Ahmadabad jails but today attractive *durries* in pastel colours cater to the modern taste. Floor coverings called *jajams* are produced in Chittaurgarh.

Handloom weaving on cradle looms is practised throughout Gujarat and Rajasthan. Gandhiji's policy of promoting *khadi* (handloom fabric) as part of the Swadeshi movement has resulted in a number of ashrams developing handloom weaving as a source of employment in rural Gujarat.

Printing Hand-held wood blocks are carefully cut to enable patterns in different colours to be printed; up to five blocks may be used for an elaborate design. Children apprenticed to block makers and printers, master the craft by the age of 14 or 15. Traditionally colours were based on vegetable pigments though now many use chemical dyes. Printing is done in a long shed and after the block printing is complete, the fabric is boiled to make the dye fast. Good examples can be seen in the City Museum in Jaipur. Sanganer, just south of the city, is still well known for block-printing. Delightfully unspoilt, a trip there is worthwhile (see page 132). Herbal and mineral colours are still used by some artisans in Kachchh (before the 2001 earthquake Dhamanka village near Bhuj was known for its vegetable dye printed fabrics, and efforts are being made to help the villagers back into production), Barmer, Sanganer and Bagru, though now many use chemical dyes. Kachchh also has Rogan painters who hand paint fabrics using iron rods. Traditional hand-dyed fabrics are used as temple curtains by the Waghris, including those who dwell in cities like Ahmadabad. Pethapur, a suburb of Gandhinagar, capital of Gujarat, has wood carvers who pierce wood to create printing blocks.

Tie-and-dye

Bandhani tie-dye is another intricate process and ancient technique common throughout Rajasthan and Gujarat. The fabric is pinched together in selected places, tied round with twine or thread and then dyed. Afterwards, the threads are removed to reveal a pattern in the original or preceding colour. The process is often repeated, the dyeing sequence going from light to dark colours. Jaipur, Jodhpur, Udaipur, Kachchh and Jamnagar districts are well known for their *bandhani*. Wadhwan in Surendranagar district too has a number of bandhini artisans who use a tie-dye process which creates a dotted pattern. Another form of dyeing is the *lehariya* of eastern Rajasthan which leaves long lines or bands running diagonally on the fabric surface.

Jewellery

Uncut gemstones are strung or set in typical Rajasthani jewellery, Jaipur being particularly famous for its gems and jewellery. Typical items are nose rings, ear ornaments, bangles and necklaces. *Kundan* work specializes in setting stones in gold; sometimes *meenakari* (enamelling) complements the setting on the reverse side of the pendant, locket or earring. Khambat, on the Gulf of Cambay in Gujarat, is known for its semi-precious stone cutting workshops. Surat, Palanpur and Bhavnagar have diamond polishing factories and cottage industries.

Pottery

The best known pottery in Rajasthan is the 'Jaipur Blue'. This uses a coarse grey clay that is quite brittle even when fired. It is then decorated with floral and geometric patterns along Persian lines utilizing rich ultramarines, turquoise and lapis colours on a plain off-white/grey background. In the villages, the common pot is made from a combination of earth, water and dung. The coarse pots are thrown on a simple stone wheel, partially dried, then finished with a hammer before being simply decorated, glazed and fired.

Terracotta is one of the world's oldest media of artistic expression. Tribes still pray at shrines of terracotta horses and other animistic figures, made in villages like Bhenswara in the Jalor Bhil belt, Poshina in the Sabarkanta Garasia area, and Chotta Udepur in eastern Rajasthan, among others. Pottery for water storage, ornamental plants and other utilities are made by Kumhars in most cities, towns and villages. Clay plaques for wall décor are available at Molela near Nathdwara. Pokharan produces attractive red pottery, while Merta near Ajmer is known for its delicate Kagazi pottery.

Embroidery

The historic living craft of Kachchh, the vibrant colours and designs of the artisans of the Kachchh district adding vivid colour to the arid landscape around their villages. Each community has a distinct style of embroidery, using different stitches, colours and motifs, and sometimes setting them with beads or mirrors. The Ahirs, the Rabaris, the Jats, the Mutwas, the Lohanas and the people of the Banni region have their own embroidery techniques, and within each community there are sub-groups who have evolved their own combinations and patterns. For centuries pastoral women have embroidered their own trousseau and embellished their dowry packages with exquisite handiwork, and today the rich embroideries of Kachchh are an important source of income for many of the craft villages that run the length and breath of the district. Besides textiles, embroidery is done on leather for footwear, bags and other products. Appliqué or patch-work is another popular article of production in the craft villages of Kachchh. Beadwork is practised in Kachchh and Kathiawad.

Background

Barmer, Jaisalmer and other districts of the western desert in Rajasthan are well known for their embroidered fabrics set with mirrors and other ornamentation. Leather embroidery is a well known craft of Kachchh, north Gujarat, Jalor, Barmer and Jodhpur districts. The most popular article of production is footwear called *mojdi*, with bold embroidery patterns, with Bhinmal in Jalor district being specially well known for its embroidered shoes. Camel leather work is done by the Ustas of Bikaner though this is losing popularity because of the high prices of each product.

Wood carving   Barmer is known for its woodwork – surprising given the town's location in the desert – perhaps because of its tradition of wood block printing and the camel saddle market. Fancy wood crafts and furnishings are produced for domestic and export markets, sometimes with brass and other metal inlaid patterns. Udaipur is well known for its wooden toys and lacquered wood, Bassi near Chittaurgarh for wooden figures, Jaipur in recent times for wooden furniture. Sankheda in Gujarat is famous for its lacquered furniture, with vermilion patterns. Mahuva near Bhavnagar, Billimoria near Surat and Kachchh district are known for their wood crafts. Jodhpur and Sawai Madhopur districts are also well known for their attractive furniture.

Metalware   Kachchh and Rajkot district of Gujarat, Jaipur city, and various districts of Rajasthan, are famous for their silver ornaments, utensils and artefacts. Jaipur is particularly well known for its engraved brassware with floral motifs or lacquered effect patterns. Zinc water bags/bottles are made in the desert cities and towns of Rajasthan. Gaduliya Lohars are nomadic smiths in Rajasthan, while Kachchh has a tradition of making metal utensils and copper bells. There is a brass industry in Jamnagar and utensils of brass, copper and other metals are made at Sihore. Artisans at Wadhwan make silver and brass utensils and ornaments. Silver furniture is made in Surendranagar district of Gujarat. The swordsmiths of Sirohi, Udaipur and Alwar specialise in metal inlays.

Stone carving   The Silavats and other artisans of Rajasthan excel in carving marble, sandstone and other material into beautiful *jali*-work (lattice), utensils and ornamental pieces. Surendranagar district of Gujarat has a number of stone carving artisans. Ambaji, well known for its marble, has a large cottage industry of marble carving in north Gujarat. Outdoor furniture made from carved marble and other stones are made in Sirohi, Kishangarh and other districts of Rajasthan.

Other crafts   Other crafts practised in Rajasthan include *khari* (embossed printing using gold and silver), engraving and lacquering brassware and embroidering camel skin. Papermaking is important in the Jaipur- Bagru-Sanganer triangle, mudwall painting in Kachchh, zari embroidery at Surat, Jamnagar and Jaipur, and the making of marble bangles or grass tribal jewellery.

Music and dance

Music   Indian music can trace its origins to the metrical hymns and chants of the Vedas, in which the production of sound according to strict rules was understood to be vital to the continuing order of the Universe. Through more than 3,000 years of development and a range of regional schools, India's musical tradition has been handed on almost entirely by ear. The chants of the **Rig Veda** developed into songs in the **Sama Veda** and music found expression in every sphere of life, reflecting the cycle of seasons and the rhythm of work.

Over the centuries the original three notes, which were sung strictly in descending order, were extended to five and then seven and developed to allow freedom to move up and down the scale. The scale increased to 12 with the addition of flats and sharps and finally to 22 with the further subdivision of semitones. Books of musical rules go back at least as far as the third century AD. Classical music was totally intertwined with dance and drama, an interweaving reflected in the term *sangita*.

At some point after the Muslim influence made itself felt in the north, north and south Indian styles diverged, to become Carnatic (Karnatak) music in the south and Hindustani music in the north. However, they still share important common features: *svara* (pitch), *raga* (the melodic structure) and *tala* (rhythm).

Hindustani music probably originated in the Delhi Sultanate during the 13th century, when the most widely known of North Indian musical instruments, the *sitar*, was believed to have been invented. **Amir Khusrau** is also believed to have invented the small drums, the *tabla*. Hindustani music is held to have reached its peak under *Tansen*, a court musician of Akbar. The other important northern instruments are the stringed *sarod*, the reed instrument *shahnai* and the wooden flute. Most Hindustani compositions have devotional texts, though they encompass a great emotional and thematic range. A common classical form of vocal performance is the *dhrupad*, a four-part composition.

The essential structure of a melody is known as a *raga* which usually has five to seven notes and can have as many as nine (or even 12 in mixed ragas). The music is improvised by the performer within certain governing rules and although theoretically thousands of *ragas* are possible, only around a hundred are commonly performed. *Ragas* have become associated with particular moods and specific times of the day. Music festivals often include all night sessions to allow performers a wider choice of repertoire.

The rules for classical dance were laid down in the Natya shastra in the second century BC, which is still one of the bases for modern dance forms. The most common sources for Indian dance are the epics, but there are three essential aspects of the dance itself, *Nritta* (pure dance), *Nrittya* (emotional expression) and *Natya* (drama). The religious influence in dance was exemplified by the tradition of temple dancers, *devadasis*, girls and women who were dedicated to the deity in major temples. India is also rich in folk dance traditions which are widely performed during festivals.

Dance

Folk dance Typical community folk dances of the Rajasthan-Gujarat region are based on the *Rasa* tradition of dancing in circles, clapping hands or striking sticks in unison to set the rhythm. The *Ghoomer* of Rajasthan and the *Garba* of Gujarat are generally for women, who clap their hands or strike small sticks to the simple rhythm. The *Ger* of Rajasthan and *Dandia-Ras* of Gujarat are similar dances for men using larger sticks. Combination dances, for both men and women, are also performed. Some intricate dances for women in Gujarat involve balancing pots and even tossing them to one another (*Heench*) according to the rhythm. The best period to witness these dances is Navratri in Gujarat, Holi, Gangaur, Navratri and other festivals of Rajasthan.

Kachchhi Ghodi is a dance performed by men riding hobby-horses and sporting swords. The dances are accompanied by songs that recite tales of the Bavaria outlaws of Shekhawati, the Robin Hoods of Rajasthan. Similar horse dances can be seen at Chotta Udepur in eastern Gujarat.

Sidh Naths of Bikaner are deservedly famous for their fire dances. The performers dance on the fire as if it did not exist, and even put burning coals in their mouths, to the beat and rhythm of pipes and drums. The Dholis of Jalore district are known for their drum dance which is a sword, stick and scarf dance performed to powerful beats of five or more drums, as well as cymbals and other percussion instruments.

One of the most colourful dancing communities is the Kalbelia (generally snake charmers and nomadic workers by profession). The women wear embroidered veils called *odhnis*, skirts called *gaghras*, blouses called *cholis* and artistic jewellery, while men wear red turbans.

A vigorous dance is the *Terah Tal* of Ramdeora near Pokaran, which has now become a popular dance throughout Rajasthan.

Bhavai is a dance drama, the folk theatre of Gujarat. In Rajasthan tribal dancers recite the tale of the mystic Pabhuji, unravelling a long narrative painting of the hero's life. Langas and Manganiars of western Rajasthan (the former are also in Kachchh) are professional singers whose haunting melodies recall the feel of the desert. Mirasis are professional musicians, usually employed for weddings and celebrations, sometimes accompanied by dancers, while the Naths of Rajasthan are acrobats who perform spell-binding acts to the tune of singing and music.

Tribal dance The tribal people have their own dances. The Dangs region is well known for its vigorous and often spectacular tribal dances. The Rathwa dances and pyramid acrobatics of Chotta Udepur are interesting, as much for the rhythm and vigour as for their colourful make up and costumes.

The pastoral communities of Gujarat and Rajasthan have dances based on the Dandia, Garba, Ger and Ghoomer formations. The dances of the Bharwad shepherds of Kathiawad can be experienced during the Tarnetar fair. The fishing communities like the Padhars and the Kolis of Gujarat have dances that recall the motions and activities of the seas and lakes. During Holi in Rajasthan, Bhils perform the Ger-Ghoomar which begins with men in an outer circle and women in the inner circle, but as the dance progresses both sexes get together.

The people

The population of Rajasthan and Gujarat is almost wholly of Indo-Aryan stock. However, they have a much higher percentage of scheduled tribes than the national average.

Tribal peoples

The tribal population of Rajasthan and Gujarat constitute about 12% of the states' population, nearly double the national average. The Bhils and Minas are the largest groups, but the less well known Sahariyas, Damariyas, Garasias and Gaduliya Lohars are all important. The tribes share many common traits but differences in their costumes and jewellery, their gods, fairs and festivals also set them apart from one another.

Bhils The Bhils comprise nearly 40% of Rajasthan's tribal population with their stronghold in Baneshwar. *Bil* (bow) describes their original talent and strength. Today, the accepted head of all the Rajput clans of Rajasthan – the Maharana of Udaipur – is crowned by anointing his forehead with blood drawn from the palm of a Bhil chieftain, affirming the alliance and the loyalty of his tribe. Rajput rulers came to value the guerrilla tactics of the Bhils, and Muslim and Maratha attacks could not have been repelled without their active support. Furthermore, they always remained a minority and offered no real threat to the city-dwelling princes and their armies. Physically, the Bhils are short, stocky and dark with broad noses and thick lips. They once lived off roots, leaves and fruits of the forest and the increasingly scarce game. Most now farm land and keep cattle, goats and sheep, while those who live near towns often work on daily wages. Thousands congregate near the confluence of the Mahi and Som rivers in Dungarpur district for the Baneshwar fair in January and February.

Elopement marriages

The **Garasias** (under 3% of Rajasthan's tribals), have an interesting custom of marriage through elopement, which usually takes place at the annual Gaur fair in March. After the elopement, which can be spontaneous or pre-arranged, a bride price is paid to the bride's father. Once the couple have 'disappeared' they have to remain hidden in the jungle for three days while the rest of the tribe hunts for them. If caught during that period they are severely beaten and forcibly separated. However, if they have proved their skills in survival and in remaining hidden, their marriage is recognized and they return to live with the rest of the tribe. Should the arrangement not work out, the woman returns home. Widows are obliged to remarry, since their children – and not they – are given a share in the husband's property.

Minas

The Minas are Rajasthan's most widely spread tribal group. They may have been the original inhabitants of the Indus Valley civilization, mentioned in the *Vedas* and the *Mahabharata*, who were finally dispersed into the Aravallis by the Kachhawaha Rajputs. The Minas are tall, with an athletic build, light brown complexion and sharp features. The men wear a loincloth round the waist, a waistcoat and a brightly coloured turban while the women wear a long gathered skirt (*ghaghra*), a small blouse (*kurti-kanchali*) and a large scarf. Most Minas are cultivators who measure their wealth in cattle and other livestock. They worship Siva in temples decorated with stone carvings, and also Sheeta Mata (Shitala), the goddess of smallpox. Like other tribal groups they have a tradition of giving grain, clothes, animals and jewellery to the needy. The forest dwellings, *Mewas*, comprise a cluster of huts or *pals*. Though their marriage ceremony, performed round a fire, is similar to a Hindu one, divorce is not uncommon or particularly difficult. A man wanting a divorce tears a piece of his clothes and gives this to his wife, who then leaves the home carrying two pitchers of water. Whoever helps her unload the pitchers becomes her new husband! Of the tribes of Rajasthan the Minas have progressed the most and only in a few pockets do they follow traditional practices.

Gaduliya Lohars

The Gaduliya Lohars, named after their beautiful bullock carts (*gadis*), are nomadic blacksmiths, said to have wandered from their homeland of Mewar because of their promise to their 'lord' Maharana Pratap who was ousted from Chittaurgarh by Akbar. This clan of warring Rajputs vowed to re-enter the city only with a victorious Maharana Pratap. Unfortunately the Maharana was killed on the battlefield, so even today many of them prefer a nomadic life.

Sahariyas

The Sahariyas are jungle dwellers, their name possibly deriving from the Persian *sehr* (jungle). They are regarded as the most backward tribe in Rajasthan and eke out a living as shifting cultivators and by hunting and fishing. More recently they have also undertaken menial and manual work on daily wages. In most respects their rituals are those of Hindus. One difference is that polygamy and widow marriage (*nata*) are permitted, though only to a widower or divorcee.

Bishnois

With the growing recent interest in environmental conservation the Bishnois of Rajasthan's desert districts have come into prominence. For centuries, they have protected wildlife and vegetation with a religious passion inspired by their medieval leader Jamboji. Jalore, Barmer, Nagaur, Jodhpur and Bikaner district have large groups of Bishnois. Their hamlets, called *dhannis*, comprise picturesque huts with thatch roofing and mud walls. Each *dhanni* is surrounded by vegetation. Antelope and gazelle feel safe in Bishnoi areas and are less shy than anywhere else.

Background

Garasias One of the most colourful tribal communities is the Garasia adivasi, inhabitants of the Aravalli foothills of Sabarkanta and Banaskanta districts in north Gujarat, and Udaipur, Sirohi and Pali districts of Rajasthan. Garasia adivasis claim descent from Rajput men who married Bhil women (*Garasia* = landowner, *adivasi* = original inhabitant) and consider themselves superior to other tribes of the Aravalli foothills. They still own cultivable land and work on fields, the reason for the importance of the spring harvest in the life of this tribal community. Garasia homes are typically made from mud and bamboo decorated during festivals with line art and wall paintings. The women dress in colourful clothes, sport facial tattoos and wear artistic silver and grass jewellery. The men wear turbans of different colours, *kurtas* and ear ornaments, and pride themselves on being skilful archers. Potters make terracotta horses and other figurines for the animistic worship. The community can be seen at their colourful best during tribal fairs in March and April like the Gaur fair near Mount Abu and Chitra Vichitra fair near Poshina. These fairs feature ancestor mourning, music, dancing, revelry and match-making (elopement is not uncommon!).

Rathwas Like the Garasia Adivasis of northern Gujarat, the Rathwa of eastern Gujarat love music, dancing, colourful clothes and attractive ornaments, and are skilled archers. The Rathwas usually live in picturesque village houses, made of mud and roofed with intricately thatched straw, leaves, timber or locally made clay tiles. The interiors of these houses are embellished with a profusion of faunal figures called *pithoras*. The tribes worship at shrines comprising terracotta horses and other animistic clay figures and are strong believers in ghosts, spirits, ancestor worship and the Hindu pantheon. The *pithora* paintings are believed to be magical and ward away evil spirits.

The beautiful villages are often surrounded by agricultural fields, and may be set next to palm groves that the tribes tap for toddy, or in the heart of wooded hill country. Today, many of these tribal people have taken employment as mine workers, farm labourers and watchmen, but traditional handicrafts like wood carving, basket weaving and arrow crafting continue in this tribal belt, and the men still carry bows, arrows and guns when they travel. Ephemeral village markets (*haats*) are a daily event in the Rathwa tribal belt, with one of the largest being the Saturday bazaar at Chotta Udepur. The area comes alive with music, dancing, acrobatics and a showcase of colourful tribal dress during the fairs of Dasara and Holi. The Kawant fair offers an interesting insight into the tribes of this region, their clothing, ornaments, music and dancing.

Dangs tribals Compared to the Garasias and Rathwas, the tribes of the 300 odd villages of the Dangs district of south Gujarat are less colourful and wear simpler ornaments, but are equally interesting. Music and dancing are a significant cultural aspect of tribal life in the Dangs. The array of musical instruments and the rhythmic yet vigorous tribal dances of the Dangs are awe-inspiring. The main groups of the area are Kunbis, Bhils, Gamits and Warlis. They are strong believers in rituals, superstitions, animistic spirits, magic and sorcery. One of the main deities of this region is the Waghdeva or Tiger God. The usual houses are made from mud and bamboo. Hunting is usually by bow, arrow and catapult, fishing by bamboo traps. The Dangs Durbar in March-April is an assembly of tribal chieftains, who are still entitled to their privy purses.

Rabaris The Rabari (also called **Raika** in Rajasthan), the best known of the semi-nomadic herders, are widespread with many distinct subgroups. They have attractive houses in their villages, but travel with camels and cattle in search of pasture seasonally.

Bharwads The Bharwad shepherds of Saurashtra are known for their very colourful clothing, and the men wear just as attractive ornaments as the women. During the Tarnetar fair in August-September, pastoral tribes of Saurashtra gather for religious rituals, revelry and match-making.

The Barda and Gir hills of Saurashtra are home to the Maldharis, a pastoral group comprising various cattle owning communities. The Maldharis surround their hutment settlements with hedges called *nesses*, and during the day men lead their buffaloes and other livestock to pasture while women churn butter. They are bardic poets and sing jungle lore of the Gir forests.

Maldharis

The Siddis live either side of the Rajasthan-Gujarat border, and are believed to have originally come from Africa in the 13th century. Employed by the Gujarat sultanate as mercenary warriors or slaves, some rose to become generals, working to protect important ports like Daman and Diu from Portuguese naval invasions. The Siddis of Gir live in hamlets that would not be out of place in the African bush, and retain many of their traditions and beliefs handed down through generations. Among their many Africans inheritances is the natural sense of rhythm reflected in their drumming and dance performances. They also retain some elements of African dress and custom such as breaking coconuts with their heads and fire-walking.

Siddis

Along the Gujarat coastline and in the Rann of Kachchh are villages and settlements of the **Kolis** who are traditionally fishing people, and have taken to salt gathering in the Little Rann of Kachchh. The **Padhars** are the fishing people of the Surendranagar reservoirs, seen at their most colourful around the massive Nalsarovar lake.

Others

The **Jats** inhabit Kachchh and the northwestern arid zone from Gujarat and Rajasthan to the North Western Frontier Province of Pakistan. Their turbans and dress are reminiscent of the days when camel caravans plied from the Near East to the Far East across the desert areas of western India. The **Ahirs** are an agricultural community of Kachchh. Their women are known for their colourful embroidery

Land and environment

Geography

Rajasthan and Gujarat lie on the northwestern edge of the Indian Peninsula, the southernmost of India's three major geological regions. To its north are the alluvial plains of the Ganges and Indus rivers, and to their north again the great mountain chain of the Himalaya.

Only 100 million years ago the Indian Peninsula was still attached to the great land mass of what geologists call 'Pangaea' alongside South Africa, Australia and Antarctica. Then as the great plates on which the earth's southern continents stood broke up, the Indian Plate started its dramatic shift northwards. About 55 million years ago the northernmost tip of the peninsula collided with the Asian plate, in the next 20 million years bringing the first Himalayan uplift in what are now the western Himalaya. From 36 to five million years ago the peninsula continued its northward movement under the Asian plate but also rotated in an anticlockwise direction, pushing up a succession of parallel mountain ranges from Himachal Pradesh eastwards through Nepal to the eastern Himalaya. The Indian Plate is still moving north under the Tibetan Plateau at a rate of up to 2½ cms a year. This movement

The origins of India's landscapes

continues to have major effects on the landscapes of the entire region. The Himalaya are still rising, in places by several millimetres a year, and along the faulted junctions of the Indian and the Asian plates are some of the world's most active earthquake zones. The western borders of Gujarat and Rajasthan are particularly affected by this seismic activity. In 1819 the whole drainage of the Rann of Kachchh was dramatically altered by an earthquake which raised the 50 mile long Allah's Bund, a vertical cliff about 6 m high. On 26 January 2001 the Bhuj region of Gujarat experienced another devastating earthquake which caused up to 30,000 deaths and massive destruction of buildings in the town and surrounding villages.

The ancient rocks of the peninsula have also been disturbed by its continuing thrust under the Asian plate, the ancient sandstones of the Vindhyan ranges in southeastern Rajasthan and the Aravallis showing evidence of the buckling power of the impact.

The crystalline rocks of the Peninsula are some of the oldest in the world, some being over 3,100 million years old. Over 60 million years ago a mass of volcanic lava welled up through cracks in the earth's surface and covered some 500,000 sq km of southern Gujarat, Rajasthan, and Madhya Pradesh, while stretching south to Maharashtra and northern Karnataka.

The fault line which severed India from Africa was marked by a north-south ridge of mountains, known today as the Western Ghats, set back from the sea by a coastal plain which is never more than 80 km wide. Southeastern Gujarat occupies this coastal plain, backed by the northernmost scarps of the Western Ghats, penetrated by the Narmada and the Tapti flowing from the east.

Rajasthani landscape Running like a spine through Rajasthan the **Aravalli Hills** are one of the oldest mountain systems in the world. They form a series of jagged, heavily folded ranges, stretching from **Mount** Abu in the southwest (1,720 m) to Kota and Bundi in the east. Mount Abu is granite but the range has a mixture of ancient sedimentary and metamorphic rocks, and Rajasthan is the source of the glittering white **Makrana marble** used in the Taj Mahal. The ancient sandstones of the Vindhyan mountain system of Madhya Pradesh extend northwards into southeastern Rajasthan, eroded in places to form great cliff-topped scarps overlooking the often fertile alluvial plains below, as at Ranthambhore and Bundi.

The watershed between the eastward draining Chambal river system, which ultimately flows into the Bay of Bengal, and the Luni which flows into the Arabian Sea, runs along the crest line of the Aravallis from Udaipur in the southeast to Jaipur in the northwest.

To the west of this line is the arid and forbidding **Thar Desert**, with its shifting sand dunes and crushingly high summer temperatures. Carol Henderson has written that James Tod, the first British emissary to the region, was constantly reminded that the names for the region – *Marwar, Maroosthali,* or *Maru-desh,* mean 'the land of death'. Before Partition from Pakistan Jaisalmer and Bikaner dominated the overland routes to the west. However, the Great Indian desert is not completely barren but covered with shrubs and trees, interspersed with farmland, and fed by rivers like the Luni. Sand dunes rise over 70 m in Jaisalmer, Jodhpur, Bikaner and Barmer districts. The Indira Canal and other projects have greened vast stretches of the desert, making them suitable for cultivation and plantation, though they have not entirely achieved what was envisaged. Salt lakes like Sambhar and Tal Chapper, and dry beds of rivers like the Luni, are frequently seen in the desert and arid stretches of the Aravallis.

Jodhpur lies on the edge of this arid tract, the link between the true desert and the semi arid but cultivable regions to the east. To the southeast of the Aravalli divide are the wetter and more fertile river basins of the Chambal and its tributaries, though even here there are some outstandingly barren rocky hills and plateaus.

Around Jaipur and Bharatpur, cultivated land is interspersed with rocky outcrops such as those at Amber. In the south the average elevation is higher (330-1,150 m). Around Bharatpur the landscape forms part of the nearly flat Yamuna drainage basin. Mewar, the southeast region of modern Rajasthan, with Udaipur and Chittaurgarh as two of the region's former capitals, is hilly, and drains northeastwards into the only perennial river of southern Rajasthan, the Chambal. The surface geology of the southeast has been modified greatly by the great volcanic lava flows which have weathered to give rich black soils, especially fertile when irrigated and well drained.

Both the geology and the landscapes of Gujarat contrast sharply with those of Rajasthan. Unlike landlocked Rajasthan, Gujarat has nearly 1,600 km of coastline, and no part of the state is more than 160 km from the sea.

Gujarat's landscape

Kachchh (Kutch), on the northwest border of the peninsula, rises to heights of around 300 m, and like the plains of the Indus into which it drops almost imperceptibly, it is almost desert. It has a central ridge of Jurassic sandstones, with underlying basalts breaking through from place to place. To the north is the Great Rann of Kachchh, a 20,700 sq km salt marsh. To the southeast is the Little Rann. During the monsoon the Rann floods, virtually making Kachchh an island, while during the hot dry summer months it is a dusty plain. The Gulf of Kachchh has 42 islands fringed by coral reefs and mangrove swamps, and separates the Kathiawad Peninsula along its southern coast district.

Earthquakes have had dramatic effects on the landscape. A particularly large quake in 1819 formed a new scarp up to 6 m high and 80 km long, diverting the old channels of the Indus. It has become known as Allah's Bund – *God's embankment*.

Saurashtra is to the southeast of the Gulf of Kachchh also known as the **Kathiawad Peninsula**. Rarely rising to more than 180 m, it is flanked by sandstones in the north. Over most of Kathiawad are great sheets of Deccan lavas, cut across by lava dykes. Around the ancient and holy city of Dwarka in the west and Bhavnagar in the east are limestones and clays, separated by a 50 km belt of alluvium, whose creamy-coloured soft stone is widely used as 'Porbandar stone'.

Northeast Gujarat is a continuation of central Kachchh and is characterized by small plains and low hills.

Climate

The Tropic of Cancer runs through northern Gujarat and the southernmost tip of Rajasthan, and the climate of the region reflects this tropical position at the northwestern corner of the Indian subcontinent.

In common with the rest of India, the climate of Rajasthan and Gujarat is dominated by the monsoon. The term monsoon refers to the wind reversal which replaces the dry northeasterlies, characteristic of winter and spring, with the very warm and wet southwesterlies of the summer. What makes the Indian monsoon quite exceptional is not its regularity but the depth of moist air which passes over the subcontinent. Over India, for example, the highly unstable moist airflow is over 6,000 m thick compared with only 2,000 m over Japan, giving rise to the bursts of torrential rain which mark out the wet season. However, most of Gujarat and Rajasthan are to the north of the main rainbearing southwesterlies, and rainfall decreases sharply from the southeast to the northwest, which is true desert. Rajasthan's location on the margins of pure desert has made much of it particularly susceptible to climatic change throughout settlement history, and fossil sand dunes found as far east as Delhi testify to the advance and retreat of the desert over the last 5,000 years.

The monsoon
An Arabic word meaning 'season'

Background

The wet season The monsoon season in Rajasthan and Gujarat lasts approximately three months. It brings an enveloping dampness which makes it very difficult to keep things dry. However, nowhere except the hills of southern Gujarat receives more than 1,000 mm a year, and the rain comes mainly in the form of heavy isolated showers. Rainfall generally decreases towards the northwest, Rajasthan and northern Gujarat merging imperceptibly into genuine desert.

Humidity The coastal regions have high humidity levels during the rainy season which can be very uncomfortable. However, sea breezes often bring some relief on the coast itself. Moving north and inland, between December to May humidity drops sharply, often falling as low as 10% during the daytime. In Ahmadabad the maximum winter temperature is 27°C, although nights are cold and sub-zero cold spells have been recorded. In summer it is extremely hot and maximum temperatures can reach 48°C. Further south the winter temperatures never fall as far, and the summer temperatures are slightly more moderate.

In the far south around Daman rainfall is still strongly affected by the southwest monsoon and totals often exceed 1,500 mm, nearly all between June and October. However, because Gujarat is marginal to the main rain-bearing winds the total amounts are highly variable, decreasing rapidly northwards. Ahmadabad normally receives about 900 mm a year while Kachchh, on the borders of the true desert, has recorded under 25 mm.

Winter In winter high pressure builds up over Central Asia. Most of India is protected from the cold northeast monsoon winds that result by the massive bulk of the Himalaya and daytime temperatures rise sharply in the sun. In winter the daily maximum in most low lying areas is 22°C-28°C and the minimum 8°C-14°C, but the air is often almost bitingly dry. The sharp drop in temperature on winter nights makes warm clothing essential between late November and mid February. To the south the winter temperatures increase having minima of around 20°C. Despite the night-time cold, Rajasthan and Gujarat often have beautiful weather from November through to March.

Summer From April onwards northwestern India becomes almost unbearably hot. Except in the hills the summer maxima exceed 46°C and the average from May to August is 38°C. In winter the daily maximum in most low lying areas is 22°C-28°C and the minimum 8°C-14°C. The Aravallis, notably Mount Abu, offer welcome relief in the hot season and are noticeably colder in winter.

At the end of May the upper air westerly jet stream, which controls the atmospheric system over the Indo-Gangetic plains through the winter, suddenly breaks down. It re-forms to the north of Tibet, thus allowing very moist southwesterlies to sweep across South India and the Bay of Bengal. They then double back northwestwards, bringing rain across the Indo-Gangetic Plains to northwest India.

Vegetation

The dry tropical monsoon climate gives Rajasthan and Gujarat a quite distinctive natural vegetation. Dry deciduous woodland being the most common cover in the wetter areas, shading to desert vegetation in the arid west. Today forest cover has been greatly reduced as elsewhere in India, mainly as a result of the need for agricultural land.

Deciduous forest Neither of the two types of deciduous tree dominant elsewhere in India, Sal (*Shorea robusta*) and teak (*Tectona grandis*), are common in Rajasthan and Gujarat, teak only being found in the Aravallis or the hill areas of Gujarat, and sal absent altogether.

Western Rajasthan has distinct desert vegetation like the Sewan grasslands near Jaisalmer, Phog which grows on sand dunes, capparis, a cactus-like *euphorbia*, aak or *calotropis*, all three of which are fairly succulent and sustain life in the desert. Kharjal (*Salvadora persica*) and the thorny khejra (*Prosopis cineraria*) are trees of the desert. The second is often used for a dish called Ker-Sangri that is part of the Marwar diet, while rohira, a truly desert tree, is used by wood carvers of Barmer and other desert towns.

Many Indian trees are planted along roadsides to provide shade and they often also produce beautiful flowers. The **silk cotton tree** (*Bombax ceiba*), up to 25 m in height, is one of the most dramatic. The pale greyish bark of this buttressed tree usually bears conical spines. It has wide spreading branches and keeps its leaves for most of the year. The flowers, which appear when the tree is leafless, are cup-shaped, with curling, rather fleshy red petals up to 12 cm long while the fruit produce the fine, silky cotton which gives it its name.

Flowering trees

Other common trees with red or orange flowers include the dhak, the gulmohur and the Indian coral tree. The smallish (6 m) deciduous **dhak** (*Butea monosperma*) has light grey bark and a gnarled, twisted trunk and thick, leathery leaves. The large, bright orange and sweet pea-shaped flowers appear on leafless branches from late March to May. The 8-9 m high umbrella-shaped **gulmohur** (*Delonix regia*), a native of Madagascar, is grown as a shade tree in towns. The fiery coloured flowers make a magnificent display after the tree has shed its feathery leaves. The scarlet flowers of the **Indian coral tree** (*Erythrina indica*) also appear when its branches with thorny bark are leafless.

Often seen along roadsides the **jacaranda** (*Jacaranda mimosaefolia*) has attractive feathery foliage and purple-blue thimble-shaped flowers up to 40 mm long. When not in flower it resembles a gulmohur, but differs in its general shape. The valuable **tamarind** (*Tamarindus indica*) has a short straight trunk and a spreading crown. An evergreen with feathery leaves, it bears small clusters of yellow and red flowers. The noticeable fruit pods are long, curved and swollen at intervals. In parts of India, the rights to the fruit are auctioned off annually for up to Rs 4,000 (US$100) per tree.

The large, spreading **mango** (*Mangifera indica*) bears the delicious, distinctively shaped fruit that comes in hundreds of varieties. The **banana** plant (*Musa*), actually a gigantic herb (up to 5 m high) arising from an underground stem has very large leaves which grow directly off the trunk. Each large purplish flower produces bunches of up to 100 bananas. The **papaya** (*Carica papaya*) grows to about 4 m with the large hand-shaped leaves clustered near the top. Only the female tree bears the fruit, which hang down close to the trunk just below the leaves.

Fruit trees

Coconut palms (*Cocos nucifera*) are only found in coastal Gujarat. They have tall (15-25 m), slender, unbranched trunks, feathery leaves and large green or golden fruit with soft white flesh filled with milky water.

Palm trees

Of all Indian trees the **banyan** (*Ficus benghalensis*) is probably the best known. It is planted by temples, in villages and along roads. The seeds often germinate in the cracks of old walls, the growing roots splitting the wall apart. If it grows in the bark of another tree, it sends down roots towards the ground. As it grows, more roots appear from the branches, until the original host tree is surrounded by a 'cage' which eventually strangles it.

Other trees

The Gujarat coast has mangrove tree cover along the southern shores of the Gulf of Kachchh near Jamnagar & Kori creek

Related to the banyan, the **pipal** or **peepul** (*Ficus religiosa*), also cracks open walls and strangles other trees with its roots. With a smooth grey bark, it too is commonly found near temples and shrines. You can distinguish it from the banyan by the absence of aerial roots and its large, heart shaped leaf with a point tapering into a

Background

pronounced 'tail'. It bears abundant 'figs' of a purplish tinge which are about a centimetre across.

Acacia trees with their feathery leaves are fairly common in the drier parts of India. The best known is the **babul** (*Acacia arabica*) with a rough, dark bark. The leaves have long silvery white thorns at the base and consist of many leaflets while the flowers grow in golden balls about 1 cm across.

The **eucalyptus** or **gum tree** (*Eucalyptus grandis*), introduced from Australia in the 19th century, is now widespread and is planted near villages to provide both shade and firewood. There are various forms but all may be readily recognized by their height, their characteristic long, thin leaves which have a pleasant fresh smell and the colourful peeling bark.

The wispy **casuarina** (*Casuarina*) grows in poor sandy soil, especially on the coast and on village waste land. It has the typical leaves of a pine tree and the cones are small and prickly to walk on. It is said to attract lightning during a thunder storm.

Bamboo (*Bambusa*) strictly speaking is a grass which can vary in size from small ornamental clumps to the enormous wild plant whose stems are so strong and thick that they are used for construction and for scaffolding and as pipes in rural irrigation schemes.

Flowering plants

Many other flowering plants are cultivated in parks, gardens and roadside verges. The attractive **frangipani** (*Plumeria acutifolia*) has a rather crooked trunk and stubby branches, which if broken give out a white milky juice which can be irritating to the skin. The big, leathery leaves taper to a point at each end and have noticeable parallel veins. The sweetly scented waxy flowers are white, pale yellow or pink. The **Bougainvillea** grows as a dense bush or climber with small oval leaves and rather long thorns. The brightly coloured part which appears like a flower, is formed by large papery bracts, not by the petals, which are quite magnificent.

The **hibiscus** has an unusual trumpet shaped flower as much as 7 or 8 cm across, has a very long 'tongue' growing out from the centre and varies in colour from scarlet to yellow or white. The leaves are somewhat oval or heart-shaped with jagged edges.

On many ponds and tanks the floating plants of the **lotus** (*Nelumbo nucifera*) and the **water hyacinth** (*Eichornia crassipes*) are seen. Lotus flowers which rise on stalks above the water can be white, pink or a deep red and up to 25 cm across. The very large leaves either float on the surface or rise above the water. The rather fleshy leaves and lilac flowers of the water hyacinth float to form a dense carpet, often clogging the waterways.

Crops

Rajasthan and Gujarat may have been the original home of millet cultivation in South Asia. The semi-arid climate means that millets, wheat and barley remain the staple cereal crops, though rice is grown on some irrigated land. There are many different sorts of **millet**, but the ones most often seen are finger millet, pearl millet (*bajra*) and sorghum (*jowar*). **Sugar cane** (*Saccharum*) is another commercially important crop. This looks like a large grass which stands up to 3 m tall. The crude brown sugar is sold as jaggery and has a flavour of molasses. **Cotton** (*Gossypium*) is important especially in Gujarat. The cotton bush is a small knee-high bush and the cotton boll appears after the flower has withered. This splits when ripe to show the white cotton lint inside. The Malwa region of southeastern Rajasthan and the neighbouring districts of Madhya Pradesh have been centres of cultivation of the **opium poppy** (*Papaver somniferum*) for at least 500 years. It is grown on tiny plots under strict government supervision, but provides a highly distinctive white patchwork character to the landscape. See page 178.

Wildlife

India has an extremely rich and varied wildlife, though many species only survive in very restricted environments.

Alarmed by diminishing numbers of wild animals and the rapid loss of wildlife habitat the Indian Government established the first conservation measures in 1972, followed by the setting up of national parks and reserves. Some 25,000 sq km were set aside in 1973 for Project Tiger. Tigers have been reported to be increasing steadily in several of the game reserves, but threats to their survival continue, notably through poaching. The same is true of other, less well known species. Their natural habitat has been destroyed both by people and by domesticated animals (there are some 250 million cattle and 50 million sheep and goats). Gujarat and Rajasthan have some of India's best known parks, including Ranthambhore, Bharatpur and Gir. The Indian Government has defined national parks as areas in which no human activity is allowed, whereas in wildlife parks some grazing and minor forest produce collection can be permitted. The entry fee for foreigners and vehicle charges at some parks have been raised dramatically in recent years.

Conservation

The **asiatic lion** (*Panthera leo*) is now found only in the Gir National Park. Compared to the African lion, the Asiatic lion has a fuller coat, longer tail tassel and visible tuft of hair on the elbow and belly but a scantier mane. The Asian lion is nine feet long on an average. Lions once roamed a vast area of Eurasia but now are restricted to the teak forests of Gir. The lion hunts at dawn and dusk but they are more diurnal than the tiger or the panther and their roaring is frequently heard at daybreak and dusk. The lions have come into conflict with the Maldharis who graze their buffaloes and other livestock in the grassy patches of Gir. Buffaloes have become a major prey species of the lion and many fear that they may have lost their ability to hunt game, which could be a problem after the entire Maldhari population is relocated. The Gir lion is gregarious and often hunts in pairs or even prides.

The cat family

The **tiger** (*Panthera tigris*), which prefers to live in fairly dense cover, is most likely to be glimpsed as it lies in long grass or in dappled shadow. Unlike the lion, it leads a quite solitary life. It is more nocturnal and depends on cover for hunting, the reason it is more difficult to spot. Rajasthan has two tiger reserves. Ranthambhore offers better chances of spotting a tiger over a two or three day visit than Sariska, the other tiger reserve. The tiger is a magnificent animal, richly coloured with bold stripes, up to 10 ft long and weighing about 200 kg. Females are smaller and weigh 20% less than the males. You will often hear of tiger sightings in the hills of Rajasthan and south Gujarat but you are unlikely to see one outside the two tiger reserves.

The **leopard** or **panther** as it is often called in India (*Panthera pardus*), is far more numerous and widespread than the tiger, but is even more elusive. The hills of Gujarat and Rajasthan have a sizeable panther population but they are not often seen, being nocturnal and shy. Panthers average 7 ft in length, females being shorter. The typical colour is dull yellow with black rosette markings that become solid black spots on the head, neck, limbs and belly, and a whitish underside. Gir is one of the best places to spot a panther during game drives. Panther sightings are not uncommon in the Kachida valley of Ranthambhore National Park and they are also seen in the arid hills of Pali and Jalore district as the cats here have turned on livestock following the decimation of their natural prey like the gazelle. They often visit villages and waterholes. The panthers in these arid areas, close to the desert, are paler in colour than those of the hilly forest tracts, and sometimes also smaller.

Background

Project Tiger

At one time the tiger roamed freely throughout the sub-continent and at the beginning of this century the estimated population was 40,000 animals. Gradually, due mainly to increased pressure on its habitat by human encroachment and resulting destruction of the habitat, the numbers of this beautiful animal dwindled to fewer than 2,000 in 1972. This was the low point and *alarmed at the approaching extinction of the tiger, concerned individuals with the backing of the Government and the World Wildlife Fund, set up Project Tiger in 1973. Initially nine parks were set up to protect the tiger and this was expanded over the years. However, despite encouraging signs in the first decade the latest tiger census suggests that there are still fewer than 2,500.*

The colour and markings of the **leopard cat** make it look like a miniature panther. They are seen in forest areas. The jungle cat is more common, having adapted to a variety of habitats from grasslands, thorn scrub, forests, agricultural areas, surrounds of wetlands and even proximity to towns and villages. Its longer legs and shorter tail distinguish the jungle cat from the domestic and other lesser wild cats. The jungle cat varies in colour from sandy grey in the arid areas to a brighter yellowish grey in greener areas. The **fishing cat** hunts at the marshes of the Keoladeo Ghana Sanctuary of Bharatpur, Rajasthan. Besides being adept at fishing with a blow of its paw and feeding on molluscs, it also hunts mammals and birds. Fishing cats do not enter the water but grab fish or mollusc from rocks and other vantage points on the shores of the marshlands. The desert zone is home to the **desert cat**, which has greyish yellow fur marked with black spots, striped cheek and a black ring on its tail.

The **caracal** is an agile, medium sized cat with pointed, tufted ears, and a short tail. They are rarely seen though present in many scrub jungles of the Gujarat-Rajasthan belt. The **rusty spotted cat** has been seen in the Dangs and Gir.

The dog family The **Indian wolf** has become an endangered species, not least because it tends to turn on livestock, making it a target for pastoral communities. The grasslands of Kachchh have a sizeable wolf population, and among wildlife reserves the savannas of Velavadar National Park and the scrublands of Kumbhalgarh Sanctuary have shown a proliferating population of wolves. Wolves have different methods of hunting depending on the habitat. In the desert the wolf hunts by chasing its prey at a steady pace waiting for it's quarry to get tired, while in areas that are more vegetated the strategy is to hunt by surprise. Wolves grow to about 75 cm at shoulder, and 95 cm in length. Holes in rocks and ground are their favoured homes in drylands. In the desert they may dig burrows on the dunes, while in the forests they will find shelter in bushes.

The **jackal** (*Canis aureus*), a lone scavenger in towns and villages, looks like a cross between a dog and a fox and varies in colour from shades of brown through to black. They feed on carcasses and the prey of larger carnivores but they will hunt smaller game and when in large packs even bring down deer, antelope and gazelle. The bushy tail has a dark tip. It is a common sight while driving through Gujarat and Rajasthan after dark. Their howling is often heard at dawn, dusk and sometimes at night.

There are two kinds of **fox** found in this region. The Indian fox is common in the plains and is grey in colour. The white footed desert fox is distinguished from the Indian fox by its white tipped tail as opposed to the black tipped tail of the latter and black markings on its ears. The habitats of the desert and Indian fox overlap in the Rann of Kachchh and western Rajasthani desert.

The dreaded **wild dog** or **dhole** has been sighted at Sariska and Ranthambhore national parks as recently as January 2001, though they had previously been thought to have become extinct in Rajasthan.

The **sloth bear** (*Melursus ursinus*), about 75 cm at the shoulder, lives in broken forest, but may be seen on a lead accompanying a street entertainer who makes it 'dance' to music as a part of an act. They have a long snout, a pendulous lower lip and a shaggy black coat with a yellowish V-shaped mark on the chest. The sloth bear is present in many wildlife parks of the Aravallis including Ranthambhore and Kumbhalgarh in Rajasthan, and Jessore, Ratanmahal and Shollpaneshwar in Gujarat, but are not easily seen as they are active after dusk and shy of human presence. Being short sighted they are known to be nervous and attack human visitors to their habitat. Bears are omnivores. They will hunt other animals, feed on termites and other invertebrate, and climb trees for fruits, berries and flowers.

Other carnivores

The **common mongoose** (*Herpestes edwardsi*) lives in scrub and open jungle. It kills snakes, but will also take rats, mice and chicken. Tawny coloured with a grey grizzled tinge, it is about 90 cm in length, of which half is pale-tipped tail. The **ratel or honey badger** is seen at Sariska.

Deer, antelope, oxen and their relatives

Once widespread, these animals are now largely confined to the reserves. The deer, unlike the antelopes who inhabit the grass and scrub, are animals of the forests and are rarely seen outside the wildlife sanctuaries.

The largest deer and one of the most widespread, is the magnificent **sambhar** (*Cervus unicolor*) which can be up to 150 cm at the shoulder. It has a noticeably shaggy coat, which varies in colour from brown with a yellowish or grey tinge through to dark, almost black, in the older stags. The sambhar is often found on wooded hillsides and lives in groups of up to 10 or so, though solitary individuals are also seen. The sambhar is common in Ranthambhore, Sariska, Gir and Bharatpur national parks. The small **chital** or **spotted deer** (*Axis axis*), only about 90 cm tall, are seen in herds of 20 or so, in grassy areas. The bright rufous coat spotted with white is unmistakable; the stags carry antlers with three tines. It is seen in good numbers at Ranthambhore, Sariska, Gir and Bharatpur.

Deer

These animals live in open grasslands, never too far from water. The beautiful **blackbuck** or **Indian antelope** (*Antilope cervicapra*), up to 80 cm at the shoulder, occurs in large herds. The distinctive colouring and the long spiralling horns make the stag easy to identify.

Antelope

The larger and heavier **nilgai** or **blue bull** (*Boselaphus tragocamelus*), like the blackbuck and chowsingha, is one of a kind in its genus. The largest antelope in India, the Nilgai has a very small cone shaped horn in ratio to its height of 130 cm. The mature bull is iron grey in colour, the juveniles are tawny. The females are tawny and hornless. They are often seen in sparsely wooded hills and fields in batches of four to ten.

The very graceful **chinkara** or Indian Gazelle (*Gazella gazella*) is only 65 cm at the shoulder. The light russet colour of the body has a distinct line along the side where the paler underparts start. Both sexes carry slightly S-shaped horns. Chinkara live in the desert and can thrive on minimal vegetation and obtain water from succulent leaves. Fleet footed and graceful, the chinkaras can be seen widely and in good numbers in the Desert National Park of Jaisalmer district, Kachchh district in Gujarat and in the surrounds of Bishnoi villages of Jodhpur, Nagaur, Jalore, Barmer and Bikaner districts.

Background

Bishnois and blackbucks

The blackbuck is one of the handsomest antelopes with its elegant carriage and striking colour combination. Fleet footed, it often resorts to a bounding run across the countryside – the preferred habitat is grassland. The mature bucks are a deep brownish black with contrasting white underparts, and have spiralling horns, while juvenile males are brown and white. Does are fawn brown with white underparts, and are completely hornless. During the rutting season the bucks attain a remarkable sheen and they strut with heads raised and horns swept along their backs in a challenging stance. The rutting season varies locally but is generally around October and February-March. Velavadhar National Park has one of the largest blackbuck populations among Indian sanctuaries. Gajner near Bikaner, the Sambhar Salt Lake, Tal Chappar in Shekhawati and Keoladeo Ghana National Park at Bharatpur are other good reserves for sightings. Blackbucks are held sacred by the Bishnois, the reason for their good numbers near Guda Bishnoi village of Jodhpur district. The Patels have protected them at Visadpura in north Gujarat and Visavadar in Kathiawad Peninsula, and the Aiyars of Mahuva, near Bhavnagar. The Jain Panjrapole Trust of Botad provides support fodder for several hundred blackbucks in the dry months. Mutant white animals are sometimes seen, specially at Visadpura.

The **chowsingha** or four horned antelope is the only animal in the world with two pairs of horns. Unlike the blackbuck they prefer forests to grasslands. Being diminutive in size and favouring the woodlands they are difficult to spot though they are present in good numbers at Gir, Sariska and Ranthambhore national parks, sanctuaries like Kumbhalgarh and Sitamata.

Oxen   The commonest member of the oxen group is the **Asiatic wild buffalo** or water buffalo (*Bubalus bubalis*). About 170 cm at the shoulder, the wild buffalo, which can be aggressive, occurs in herds on grassy plains and swamps near rivers and lakes. The black coat and wide-spreading curved horns, carried by both sexes, are distinctive.

The **Indian bison** or **gaur** (*Bos gaurus*) can be up to 200 cm at the shoulder with a heavy muscular ridge across it. Both sexes carry curved horns. The young gaur is a light sandy colour, which darkens with age, the old bulls being nearly black with pale sandy coloured 'socks' and a pale forehead.

Others   The rare **Asiatic wild ass** (*Equus hemionus*) roams the Rann of Kachchh in numbers exceeding 1000. This is the last habitat of the wild ass in the Indian lowlands, the other being the high desert of Ladakh. The wild ass is pale chestnut brown and white in colour with a deep brown mane. It is a fast runner and makes an attractive sight against the monochrome desert backdrop. Wild asses are usually seen in small herds, larger herds are not very tightly knit and often scatter when disturbed. Stallions fight viciously for the best mares, biting and kicking one another.

The **wild boar** (*Sus scrofa*) has mainly black body and a pig-like head, the hairs thicken down the spine to form a sort of mane. A mature male stands 90 cm at the shoulder and, unlike the female, bears tusks. The young are striped. Quite widespread, they often cause great destruction among crops.

One of the most important scavengers of the open countryside, the **striped hyena** (*Hyena hyena*) usually comes out at night. It is about 90 cm at the shoulder with a large head with a noticeable crest of hairs along its sloping back.

Background

The **common giant flying squirrel** (*Petaurista petaurista*) are common in the larger forests of India. The body can be 45 cm long and the tail another 50 cm. They glide from tree to tree using a membrane stretching from front leg to back leg which acts like a parachute.

The **common langur** (*Presbytis entellus*), 75 cm, is a long-tailed monkey with a distinctive black face, hands and feet. It is the main primate of the Gujarat-Rajasthan region and is common at Sariska National Park, Sitamata sanctuary and other wildlife reserves. They are adaptable and are frequently seen in gardens of large cities like Ahmadabad and around Hanuman temples where they are fed. The **rhesus macaque** (*Macaca mulatta*), 60 cm, is more solid looking with shorter limbs and a shorter tail. It can be distinguished by the orange-red fur on its rump and flanks.

Monkeys

Palm squirrels are very common. The five-striped (*Funambulus pennanti*) and the three-striped palm squirrel (*Funambulus palmarum*) are 30 cm long (about half of which is tail). The five-striped is usually seen in towns. **Flying squirrel** is reported from Sitamata sanctuary and Giant squirrel in the Dangs but are rarely seen.

Squirrels

The two bats most commonly seen in towns differ enormously in size. The larger so-called **flying fox** (*Pteropus giganteus*) has a wing span of 120 cm. These fruit-eating bats roost in large noisy colonies where they look like folded umbrellas hanging from the trees. In the evening they can be seen leaving the roost with slow measured wing beats. The much smaller **Indian pipistrelle** (*Pipistrellus coromandra*), with a wing span of about 15 cm, is an insect eater. It comes into the house at dusk to roost under eaves and has a fast, erratic flight.

Bats

Three subspecies of **Indian hare** are present – the *blacknaped* is usually seen in the more wooded area, the *desert* in western Rajasthan and other arid areas, and the *Kachchhensis* in Kachchh. The **pale hedgehog** is common, the longeared species being seen in the desert, while **gerbils** are typical rodents of the desert, their bounding movement reminiscent of a miniature kangaroo. The **Indian elephant** (*Elephas maximus*) has been domesticated for centuries and today it is still used as a beast of burden. There are no wild elephants in Rajasthan and Gujarat.

Others

Birds

Gujarat and Rajasthan comprise one of the most prolific birding areas in India. During the winter birds gather in large assemblages at lakes and parks, including those in towns, cities and villages, and while travelling between destinations a birder will find a fabulous variety of birds.

The endangered **great Indian bustard** is often sighted in the Desert National Park of Jaisalmer district and in the scrub and grass of Bikaner and Kachchh districts. The **lesser florican**, another rapidly declining species, visits the grasslands of Kathiawad and Kachchh during the southwest monsoon to nest. Both these members of the bustard family have spectacular breeding displays. The **houbara bustard** is a winter visitor to western Rajasthan, Kachchh and Kathiawad.

Dry land & desert birds

The **blackbellied** or **imperial sandgrouse** is another winter visitor, flocking in large numbers at Gajner lake and waterholes in the Desert national park for their daily drink. **Spotted sandgrouse** is frequently seen during the winter months in the drylands. The **common Indian sandgrouse** breeds in the arid belt of Kachchh and western Rajasthan. **Painted sandgrouse** frequent the wooded areas and taller grasses.

The **grey francolin** or partridge is a common sight in the countryside of both states, and their challenging cries can be heard almost everywhere. The **black francolin** is seen in good numbers in Kachchh. Painted francolin frequents forested areas like Gir, Kumbalgarh and Ranthambhore.

Water & waterside birds The *jheels* (marshes or swamps) of Rajasthan and Gujarat form one of the richest bird habitats in India. The magnificent **sarus crane** (*Grus antigone*, 150 cm) is one of India's tallest birds. The bare red head and long red legs and grey plumage make it easy to identify. The migrant **common crane** (*Grus grus*, 120 cm), present only in winter, flocks to the Little Rann of Kachchh, Kachchh district, Bhal plains of Kathiawad, Nalsarovar bird sanctuary and elsewhere numbering tens of thousand making a wonderful sight. It has mainly grey plumage with a black head and neck. There is a white streak running down the side of the neck and above the eye is a tuft of red feathers. **Demoiselle cranes** are seen in good numbers near Jodhpur, specially at Khichan where they are fed by the villagers. **Siberian cranes** visit Bharatpur but are becoming very rare as they are often lured to traps on their way south each winter. There are also large stork heronries at Bharatpur.

The **openbill stork** (*Anastomus oscitans*, 80 cm) and the **painted stork** (*Ibis leucocephalus*, 100 cm) are common too and are spotted breeding in large colonies. The former is white with black wing feathers and a curiously shaped bill. The latter mainly white, has a pinkish tinge on the back and dark marks on the wings and a broken black band on the lower chest. The bare yellow face and yellow down-curved bill are conspicuous.

Rosy, spotbilled and other **pelicans** are frequent visitors to many lakes including Sardar Sammand, Keoladeo Ghana National Park, Jawai dam, Nalsarovar and Thol bird sanctuaries near Ahmadabad and the reservoirs of Jamnagar, Bhavnagar and Porbandar, the Rann of Kachchh and the Mahi river estuary near Cambay.

White, black and glossy ibises, spoonbill and various **herons** including the Little and cattle egrets and grey heron are frequently seen at wetlands of both states. Reef herons nest along the Gujarat coastline in spectacular numbers specially near Bhavnagar and at the islands offshore from Jamnagar. Purple heron is also seen at lakes.

Greater and Lesser **flamingos** are frequently seen at lakes, rivers, marshes and reservoirs of Gujarat and occasionally in Rajasthan. These long necked rosy white birds, with heavy bills, are graceful and attractive. When seen in flight, lesser flamingos can be distinguished by their shorter trailing legs. During the monsoon, flamingos nest in the Rann of Kachchh but their breeding grounds are usually inaccessible except by camel. Nalsarovar bird sanctuary, the creeks of Porbandar, Kachchh and the salt marshes of Bhavnagar and Jamnagar port areas, are some good places to view flamingos. Alaniya dam near Kota, and the river Luni in western Rajasthan also attract flamingos in good numbers.

By almost every swamp, ditch or rice paddy up to about 1,200 m you will see the **paddy bird** (*Ardeola grayii*, 45 cm). An inconspicuous, buff-coloured bird, it is easily overlooked as it stands hunched up by the waterside.

The commonest and most widespread of the Indian kingfishers is the jewel-like **common kingfisher** (*Alcedo atthis*, 18 cm). With its brilliant blue upper parts and orange breast it is usually seen perched on a twig or a reed beside the water.

Birds of open grassland, light woodland & cultivated land The **cattle egret** (*Bubulcus ibis*, 50 cm), a small white heron, is usually seen near herds of cattle, frequently perched on the backs of the animals.

The **rose-ringed parakeet** (*Psittacula krameri*, 40 cm) is found throughout India up to about 1,500 m while the **pied myna** (*Sturnus contra*, 23 cm) is restricted to northern and central India. The rose-ringed parakeet often forms huge flocks, an impressive sight coming in to roost. They can be very destructive to crops, but are attractive birds which are frequently kept as pets. The pied myna, with its smart black and white plumage is conspicuous, usually in small flocks in grazing land or cultivation. The all black **drongo** (*Dicrurus adsimilis*, 30 cm) is almost invariably seen perched on telegraph wires or bare branches. Its distinctively forked tail makes it easy to identify.

Weaver birds are a family of mainly yellow birds, all remarkable for the intricate nests they build. The most widespread is the **baya weaver** (*Ploceus philippinus*, 15cm) which nest in large colonies, often near villages. The male in the breeding season combines a black face and throat with a contrasting yellow top of the head and the yellow breast band. In the non-breeding season both sexes are brownish sparrow-like birds.

India's national bird, the magnificent **peafowl** (*Pavo cristatus*, male 210 cm, female 100 cm), is more commonly known as the peacock. Semi-domesticated birds are commonly seen and heard around towns and villages. In the wild it favours hilly jungles and dense scrub.

Reptiles and amphibians

India is famous for its reptiles, especially its snakes which feature in many stories and legends. In reality, snakes keep out of the way of people.

Snakes

Four main species of venomous snakes are seen in Rajasthan and Gujarat, the Indian **cobra**, both spectacled black, is the best known. The **common krait** has the most toxic venom but is less aggressive than the cobra and also more nocturnal and shy. **Saw scaled viper** is common in the plains, rocks and desert areas of Kachchh, Kathiawad and Rajasthan. The saw scaled viper uses a locomotion called side winding to negotiate the hot sands of the desert dunes. **Russel's viper**, with its chain like markings, inhabits forests like Gir, the Dangs and Ranthambhore.

A large snake favoured by street entertainers is the cobras. The various species all have a hood which is spread when the snake draws itself up to strike. They are all highly venomous and the snake charmers prudently de-fang them to render them harmless. The best known is probably the **spectacled cobra** (*Naja naja*), which has a mark like a pair of spectacles on the back of its hood. The largest venomous snake in the world is the **king cobra** (*Ophiophagus hannah*) which is 5 m in length. It is usually brown, but can vary from cream to black and lacks the spectacle marks of the other. In their natural state cobras are generally inhabitants of forest regions.

Equally venomous, but much smaller, the **common krait** (*Bungarus caeruleus*) is just over 1 m in length. The slender, shiny, blue-black snake has thin white bands which can sometimes be almost indiscernible.

The **bamboo pit viper**, much less potent than the big four, inhabits the bamboo forests of south Gujarat. The **Indian rock python** (*Python molurus*), about 4 m in length, is a 'constrictor' which kills it's prey by suffocation. The python point at Bharatpur is a good place to see them.

In houses everywhere you cannot fail to see the **gecko** (*Hemidactylus*). This small harmless, primitive lizard is active after dark. It lives in houses behind pictures and curtain rails and at night emerges to run across the walls and ceilings to hunt the night flying insects which form its main prey. It is not usually more than about 14 cm long, with a curiously transparent, pale yellowish brown body. At the other end of the scale is the **monitor lizard** (*Varanus*), which can grow to 2 m in length. They can vary from a colourful black and yellow, to plain or speckled brown. They live in different habitats from cultivation and scrub to waterside places and desert.

Lizards

The desert areas of western Rajasthan and Kachchh are home to **spiny tailed lizard**, an omnivore that feeds on desert succulent vegetation, as well as termites and

Background

other insects, but their numbers are declining as they are sought after by `medicine men' for their so-called aphrodisiac qualities. **Chameleons** inhabit forests of south Gujarat and Gir.

Crocodiles The most widespread crocodile is the freshwater **mugger** or **marsh crocodile** (*Crocodilus palustrus*) which grows to 3-4 min length. Muggers are often seen at reservoirs like Kamleshwar dam in Gir, Jawai dam near Pali, Sitamata and Kumbalgarh sanctuary lakes, Jaisammand Lake, and Ranthambhore National Park. The only similar fresh water species is the **gharial** (*Gavialis gangeticus*) which lives in large, fast flowing rivers. Up to twice the length of the mugger, it is a fish-eating crocodile with a long thin snout and, in the case of the male, an extraordinary bulbous growth on the end of the snout. They are found along the River Chambal in eastern Rajasthan.

Marine life Marine mammals seen along the Gujarat coastline, especially in the Gulf of Kachchh Marine National Park, are the **dolphin** and **porpoise**. Marine reptiles include the **green sea turtle**, **olive ridley turtle** and **sea snakes**. The marine nature reserve has 42 islands, fringed by coral reefs and mangrove swamps which are rich in invertebrate. There are many species of **molluscs**, including octopus and sea hare, feather star, sea cucumber etc, sea anemone, sea fans, sea pens, reef forming coral, sponge etc. The variety of **fish** include puffer, parrot and butterfly typical of coral habitats.

Footnotes

15

Footnotes

Language

Hindi words and phrases

a as in ah	i as in bee	**Pronunciation**
o as in oh	u as oo in book	
nasalized vowels are shown as an un etc		

Hello, good morning, goodbye	namaste	**Basics**
Thank you/no thank you	dhanyavad or shukriya/nahin shukriya	
Excuse me, sorry	maf kijiye	
Yes/no	ji han/ji nahin	
nevermind/that's all right	koi bat nahin	

What is your name?	apka nam kya hai?	**Questions**
My name is...	mera nam... hai	
Pardon?	phir bataiye?	
How are you?	kya hal hai?	
I am well, thanks, and you?	main thik hun, aur ap?	
Not very well	main thik nahin hun	
Where is the?	kahan hai?	
Who is?	kaun hai?	
What is this?	yeh kya hai?	

How much?	Kitna?	**Shopping**
That makes (20) rupees	(bis) rupaye	
That is very expensive!	bahut mahanga hai!	
Make it a bit cheaper!	thora kam kijiye!	

What is the room charge?	kiraya kitna hai?	**The hotel**
Please show the room	kamra dikhaiye	
Is there an airconditioned room?	kya a/c kamra hai?	
Is there hot water?	garam pani hai?	
... a bathroom/fan/mosquito net	... bathroom/pankha/machhar dani	
Is there a large room?	bara kamra hai?	
It's not clean	saf nahin hai	
Please clean it	saf karwa dijiye	
Are there clean sheets/blanket?	saf chadaren/kambal hain?	
This is OK	yah thik hai	
Bill please	bill dijiye	

Where's the railway station?	railway station kahan hai?	**Travel**
How much is the ticket to Agra?	Agra ka ticket kitne ka hai?	
When does the Agra bus leave?	Agra bus kab jaegi?	
How much?	kitna?	
left/right	baien/dahina	
go straight on	sidha chaliye	
nearby	nazdik	
Please wait here	yahan thahariye	
Please come at 8	ath bajai ana	
quickly	jaldi	
stop	rukiye	

Restaurants	Please show the menu		menu dikhaiye
See further Food &	No chillis please		mirch nahin dalna
drink on page 443	…sugar/milk/ice		…chini/doodh/baraf
	A bottle of water please		ek botal pani dijiye
	sweet/savoury		mitha/namkin
	spoon, fork, knife		chamach, kanta, chhuri

Time & days	right now	abhi	month	mahina
	morning	suba	year	sal
	afternoon	dopahar	Sunday	ravivar
	evening	sham	Monday	somvar
	night	rat	Tuesday	mangalvar
	today	aj	Wednesday	budhvar
	tomorrow/yesterday	kal/kal	Thursday	virvar
	day	din	Friday	shukravar
	week	hafta	Saturday	shanivar

Numbers	1	ek	13	terah
	2	do	14	chaudah
	3	tin	15	pandrah
	4	char	16	solah
	5	panch	17	satrah
	6	chhai	18	atharah
	7	sat	19	unnis
	8	ath	20	bis
	9	nau	100/200	sau/do sau
	10	das	1000/2000	hazar/do hazar
	11	gyara	100,000	lakh
	12	barah		

Basic vocabulary Words such as airport, bank, bathroom, bus, doctor, embassy, ferry, hotel, hospital, juice, police, restaurant, station, stamp, taxi, ticket, train are used locally though often pronounced differently eg daktar, haspatal.

and	aur	open	khula
big	bara	police station	thana
café/food stall	dhaba/hotel	road	rasta
chemist	dawai ki dukan	room	kamra
clean	saf	shop	dukan
closed	band	sick (ill)	bimar
cold	thanda	silk	reshmi/silk
day	din	small	chhota
dirty	ganda	that	woh
English	angrezi	this	yeh
excellent	bahut achha	town	shahar
food/ to eat	khana	water	pani
hot (spicy)	jhal, masaledar	what	kya
hot (temp)	garam	when	kab
luggage	saman	where	kahan/kidhar
medicine	dawai	which/who	kaun
newspaper	akhbar	why	kiun
of course, sure	zaroor	with	ke sathh

Gujarati words and phrases

hello, how are you?	kem chho?	
thank you	abhar	
excuse me/sorry	maf karjo/meharbani karjo	
yes/no	ji han/na	
never mind/that's all right	chal se	
What is your name?	tamaroo shubh naam?	
My name is	maroo naam chhe	
Pardon?	fari vaar kehejo?	
What is this?	aa shoo chhe?	
Who is this?	aa kaun chhe?	
goodbye	aavjo	
come with me	chalo	
How much is this?	aa ketla no che?	**Shopping**
How much does that make?	ketla thya?	
That is very expensive!	bahu mahungoo che	
Make it cheaper!	thik bhaav aapon	
What is the room tariff?	ketla no room che?	**The hotel**
May I see the room?	room dekharo?	
Is there an airconditioned room?	a/c room joiye?	
Is there hot water?	room maa garam pani che?	
... bathroom/fan/mosquito net	...bathroom/pankha/machhar dani	
I want to see a larger room	moto room dekharo	
I want a clean room	saaf room joiye	
Please clean the room	room saaf karine rakho	
Clean bedsheet/blankets	saaf chadareb/kambal	
This is OK	aa chalse	
Make the bill	banavine aapo	
Which is the way to the railway station?	Station no raasto batavjo?	**Travel**
How much is the ticket to Jaipur?	Jaipur soodhi ticket no bhaav shoo che?	
When does the bus leave?	bus ketla vaage upadshe	
left/right	dabhi/jamni	
go straight on	sidha jaon/aagar che	
nearby	paase che	
Please wait here	aiyaraha juo	
Please come at 8.00	aath vaage aavjo	
quickly	jaldi karo	
hurry	utaval	
stop	ubha raho	
Show me the menu	menu aapjo/menu dekharo	**Restaurant**
no chillis please	marcha nahin	
sugar/milk/ice	chini/doodh/baraf	
A bottle of water please	ek batli pani apjo	
Do not open the bottle	kholso nahin	
sweet/savoury	mitha/namkin	
spoon, fork, knife	chamach, kanta, chhuri	

Time & days			
right now	hamra	Sunday	ravivar
morning	savare	Monday	somvar
afternoon	bapore	Tuesday	mangalvar
evening	sanjhe	Wednesday	budhvar
night	raatre	Thursday	guruvar
year	varas	Friday	shukravar
month	mahino	Saturday	sanivar
week	atvadiyo		

Numbers			
1	ek	13	ter
2	be	14	chaud
3	tran	15	pandar
4	char	16	sol
5	panch	17	satar
6	chha	18	athar
7	saat	19	ognees
8	aath	20	bis
9	nau	100	sau
10	das	1000	hazar
11	agiyar	100,000	lakh
12	bar		

Food and drink

Eating out is normally cheap and safe. Rajasthani food includes desert-based specialities such as *ker sangri*, made with desert fruit and beans. A typical Gujarati *thali* consists of one variety of *daal kadhi* (yogurt curry), two to three vegetables, pulses, salad,
snacks, sweets, local breads, rice, chutnies, pickles and papad. Gujarati food is generally
sweetened with jaggery. Here are some Hindi and Gujarati words to help you with the
often dauntingly long and unfamiliar menus.

gosht, mas	meat, usually mutton (sheep)	**Meat**
jhinga	prawns	
macchli	fish	
murgh	chicken	
aloo	potato	**Vegetables**
bain gan	aubergine	**(sabzi)**
band go bi	cabbage	
bhindi	okra, ladies' fingers	
gajar	carrots	
khumbhi	mushroom	
matar	peas	
piaz	onion	
phool gobi	cauliflower	
sag	spinach	
amb	mango	**Fruit (phal)**
ananas	pineapple	
dab	green coconut	
kela	banana	
lichi	lychee	
nariyal	coconut	
nimbu	lemon	
santra	orange	
seb	apple	
masoor dal	pink, round split lentils	**Pulses**
chana dal	chick pea	
rajma	red kidney beans	
urhad dal	small black beans	
adrak (ada)	ginger	**Spices & herbs**
dal chini	cinnamon	
dhaniya	coriander	
elaichi	cardamom	
garam masala	aromatic mixture of 'hot' spices, whole or ground (cardamom, cinnamon, cloves, cumin, black peppercorn etc)	
haldi	turmeric	
imli	tamarind	
jira (zeera)	cumin	
kari patta	'curry' leaf	
kalonji	onion seed	

444

laung	clove
mirch	chilli
pudina	mint
sarson	(rai) mustard
saunf	fennel
tej patta	bay leaf
til	sesame
zafran/kesar	saffron

Styles of cooking Many items on restaurant menus are named according to methods of preparation, roughly equivalent to terms such as 'Provençal' or 'sauté'.

bhoona in a thick, fairly spicy sauce
chops minced meat, fish or vegetables, covered with mashed potato, crumbed and fried
cutlet minced meat, fish, vegetables formed into flat rounds or ovals, crumbed and fried (eg prawn cutlet, flattened king prawn)
do piaza with onions (added twice during cooking)
dumphuk steam baked
jhal frazi spicy, hot sauce with tomatoes and chillies
Kashmiri cooked with mild spices, ground almonds and yoghurt, often with fruit
kebab skewered (or minced and shaped) meat or fish; a dry spicy dish cooked on a fire
kima minced meat (usually 'mutton')
kofta minced meat or vegetable balls
korma in fairly mild rich sauce using cream /yoghurt
masala marinated in spices (fairly hot)
Madras hot
makhani in butter rich sauce
moli South Indian dishes cooked in coconut milk and green chilli sauce
Mughlai rich North Indian style
Nargisi dish using boiled eggs
navratan curry ('9 jewels') colourful mixed vegetables and fruit in mild sauce
Peshwari rich with dried fruit and nuts (Northwest Indian)
tandoori baked in a tandoor (special clay oven) or one imitating it
tikka marinated meat pieces, baked quite dry
vindaloo hot and sour Goan meat dish using vinegar

Typical dishes **aloo gosht** potato and mutton stew
aloo gobi dry potato and cauliflower with cumin
aloo, matar, kumbhi potato, peas, mushrooms in a dryish mildly spicy sauce
bataka no shak a Gujarati potato curry
bharela baigan aubergine stuffed with herbs and spices
bharela bhindi okra stuffed with herbs and spices
bhindi bhaji lady's fingers fried with onions and mild spices
boti kebab marinated pieces of meat, skewered and cooked over a fire
chakki ki sabji gram flour shaped into rectangles and cooked in a spicy gravy
dahi bat ete nu Shak potatoes marinated in a curd mixture and cooked in ghee
dal makhani lentils cooked with butter
dum aloo potato curry with a spicy yoghurt, tomato and onion sauce
ganthia nu shaak fried dough dumplings cooked in spicy gravy
gatte ki sabj gram flour dumplings in a spicy gravy
jungli maas/murg sheep/goat meat or chicken cooked in spices

445

ker sangri locally grown ker and sangri pods popular in the arid Marwar region of Rajasthan

kima mattar mince meat with peas

lal maas sheep and goat meat in a spicy gravy flavoured with tomatoes and onion

matar panir curd cheese cubes with peas and spices (and often tomatoes)

murgh massallam chicken in rich creamy marinade of yoghurt, spices and herbs with nuts

nargisi kofta boiled eggs covered in minced lamb, cooked in a thick sauce

pasinda/tikka/suley Rajasthani kebabs

ringana nu shak aubergine curry

rogan josh rich, mutton/beef pieces in creamy, red sauce

sag gosht mutton and spinach

sag panir drained curd (panir) sautéd with chopped spinach in mild spices

sev tameta tomato curry with gram flour vermicelli

undhiya seasonal winter vegetables made into a spicy stew

valore shak bean curry

Rice & millets

bhat/sada chawal plain boiled rice

biriyani partially cooked rice layered over meat and baked with saffron

daal baati wheat dumplings in the shape of rounds (*baati*) served with lentil soup (*daal*) often with a powdery dessert (*churma*)

Kheechada/bajra ki khichdi millet porridge flavoured with daal and salt served hot with ghee or milk or cold with yogurt

khichdi rice and lentils cooked with turmeric and other spices

masala baati wheat dumplings in the shape of rounds (*baati*) stuffed with peas spices and vegetables

masala puris puris friend with spices

missi raati gram flour dumplings

pulao/pilau fried (and then boiled) rice cooked with spices (cloves, cardamom, cinnamon) with dried fruit, nuts or vegetables. Sometimes cooked with meat, like a biriyani

wagharela bhaat rice seasoned with spices and mustard

Roti – breads

Bakhri stiffer version of chapati

besan parathas made from gram flour

chapati (roti) thin, plain, wholemeal unleavened bread cooked on a tawa (griddle), usually made from ata (wheat flour). Makkaikiroti is with maize flour. Soft, thicker version of poori, made with white flour

nan oven baked (traditionally in a tandoor) white flour leavened bread often large and triangular; sometimes stuffed with almonds and dried fruit

paratha fried bread layered with ghi (sometimes cooked with egg or stuffed with potatoes)

thepla spicy roti

poori thin deepfried, puffed rounds of flour

Accom-paniments

achar pickles (usually spicy and preserved in oil)

chutni often fruit or tomato, freshly prepared, sweet and mildly spiced

dahi plain yoghurt

namak salt

papad, pappadom deep fried, pulse flour wafer rounds

raita yoghurt with shredded cucumber, pinapple or other fruit, or bundi tiny batter balls

Sweets These are often made with reduced/thickened milk, drained curd cheese or powdered lentils and nuts. They are sometimes covered with a flimsy sheet of decorative, edible silver leaf.

barfi fudgelike rectangles/diamonds
gajar halwa dry sweet made with thickened milk, carrots and spice
gor paapdi jaggery candi
gulab jamun dark fried spongy balls, soaked in syrup
gulabpak cashew and rose petal based dessert
halwa rich sweet made from cereal, fruit, vegetable, nuts and sugar
khir, payasam, paesh thickened milk rice/vermicelli pudding
kopra pak coconut flavoured dessert
kulfi coneshaped Indian ice cream with pistachhios/almonds, uneven in texture
jalebi spirals of fried batter soaked in syrup
laddoo lentil based batter 'grains' shaped into rounds
malpooda/malpuva pancakes fried in a sweet syrup
mohantal a gram flour fudge like dessert cut into squares or rectangles
rabdi/rabari a thickened and extremely sweet kheer
rasgulla (roshgulla) balls of curd in clear syrup
rasmalai spongy curd rounds, soaked in sweetened cream and garnished with pistachio nuts
sandesh dry sweet made of curd cheese
seera wheat flour roasted in ghee with sugar and cardamom
shahi tukra pieces of fried bread soaked in syrup and creamy thickened milk then sprinkled with nuts
srikhand West Indian sweet made with curds, sometimes eaten with fried puris
suji ladoo semolina-based batter grains shaped into rounds
thabdi milk-based *halwa*

Snacks **batata vaada** batter fried potato dumplings
bhaji, pakora vegetable fritters (onions, potatoes, cauliflower, aubergine etc) deep-fried in batter
chat sweet and sour cubed fruit and vegetables flavoured with tama rind paste and chillis
chana choor, chioora ('Bombay mix') lentil and flattened rice snacks mixed with nuts and dried fruit
daal dhokli *dhokla* in lentil sauce
dosai South Indian pancake made with rice and lentil flour; served with a mild potato and onion filling (masala dosai) or without (ravai or plain dosai)
ganthia crunchy snack made of gram flour seasoned with chilli and turmeric powder
haandva a savoury cake made from different grain flour and baked with vegetables and spices
idli steamed South Indian rice cakes, a bland breakfast food given flavour by its spiced accompaniments
kachori fried pastry rounds stuffed with spiced lentil/ peas/potato filling
khandvi chick peas served as rolls with mustard seeds and spices
methi vaada/methi gota batter fried fenugreek dumplings
muthia a papad like wheat snack
namkin savoury pastry bits
pakoda/bhajia deep batter fried fritters
samosa cooked vegetable or meat wrapped in pastry circle into 'triangles' and deep fried
sabudana vaada made from semolina dough

utthappam thick South Indian rice and lentil flour pancake cooked with spices/onions/tomatoes

vadai deep fried, small savoury lentil 'doughnut' rings. **Dahi vada** are similar rounds in yoghurt

aam ras rich mango juice/milkshake served as an accompaniment with rice/khichdi **Drinks**

chai tea boiled with milk and sugar

doodh milk

kafi ground fresh coffee boiled with milk and sugar

kairi pani raw mango juice

lassi cool drink made with yoghurt and water, salted or sweetened

nimboo pani refreshing drink made with fresh lime and water, chilled bottled water, added salt or sugar syrup but avoid ice. Also, fresh lime soda

pani water

Glossary

Words in *italics* are common elements of words, often making up part of a place name

A

aarti (arati) Hindu worship with lamps

abacus square or rectangular table resting on top of a pillar

abad peopled

acanthus thick-leaved plant, common decoration on pillars, esp Greek

acharya religious teacher

Adi Granth Guru Granth Sahib, holy book of the Sikhs

Adinatha first of the 24 Tirthankaras, distinguished by his bull mount

agarbathi incense

Agastya legendary sage who brought the Vedas to South India

Agni Vedic fire divinity, intermediary between gods and men; guardian of the Southeast

ahimsa non-harming, non-violence

akhand path unbroken reading of the Guru Granth Sahib

alinda verandah

ambulatory processional path

amla/amalaka circular ribbed pattern (based on a gourd) at the top of a temple tower

amrita ambrosia; drink of immortality

ananda joy

Ananda the Buddha's chief disciple

Ananta a huge snake on whose coils Vishnu rests

anda literally 'egg', spherical part of the stupa

Andhaka demon killed by Siva

anna (ana) one sixteenth of a rupee (still occasionally referred to)

Annapurna Goddess of abundance; one aspect of Devi

antarala vestibule, chamber in front of shrine or cella

antechamber chamber in front of the sanctuary

apsara celestial nymph

apse semi-circular plan, as in apse of a church

arabesque ornamental decoration with intertwining lines

aram pleasure garden

architrave horizontal beam across posts or gateways

ardha mandapam chamber in front of main hall of temple

Ardhanarisvara Siva represented as half-male and half-female

Arjuna hero of the Mahabharata, to whom Krishna delivered the Bhagavad Gita

arrack alcoholic spirit fermented from potatoes or grain

Aruna charioteer of Surya, the Sun God; Red

Aryans literally 'noble' (Sanskrit); prehistoric peoples who settled in Persia and North India

asana a seat or throne (Buddha's) pose

ashram hermitage or retreat

Ashta Matrikas The eight mother goddesses who attended on Siva or Skanda

astanah threshold

atman philosophical concept of universal soul or spirit

atrium court open to the sky in the centre In modern architecture, enclosed in glass

aus summer rice crop (Apr-Aug) Bengal

Avalokiteshwara Lord who looks down; Bodhisattva, the Compassionate

avatara 'descent'; incarnation of a divinity

ayah nursemaid, especially for children

B

baba old man

babu clerk

bada cubical portion of a temple up to the roof or spire

badgir rooftop structure to channel cool breeze into the house (mainly North and West India)

badlands eroded landscape

bagh garden

bahadur title, meaning 'the brave'

baksheesh tip 'bribe'

Balabhadra Balarama, elder brother of Krishna

baluster (balustrade) a small column supporting a handrail

bandh a strike

bandhani tie dyeing (West India)

bania merchant caste

banian vest

baoli or vav rectangular well surrounded by steps

baradari literally 'twelve pillared', a pavilion with columns

barrel-vault semi-cylindrical shaped roof or ceiling

bas-relief carving of low projection

basement lower part of walls, usually with decorated mouldings

basti Jain temple

batter slope of a wall, especially in a fort

bazar market

bedi (vedi) altar/platform for reading holy texts

begum Muslim princess/woman's courtesy title

beki circular stone below the amla in the finial of a roof

belvedere summer house; small room on a house roof

bhabar coarse alluvium at foot of Himalayas

bhadra flat face of the sikhara (tower)

Bhadrakali Tantric goddess and consort of Bhairav

Bhagavad-Gita Song of the Lord; section of the Mahabharata

Bhagiratha the king who prayed to Ganga to descend to earth

bhai brother

Bhairava Siva, the Fearful

bhakti adoration of a deity

bhang Indian hemp

Bharata half-brother of Rama

bhavan building or house

bhikku Buddhist monk

Bhima Pandava hero of the Mahabharata, famous for his strength

Bhimsen Deity worshipped for his strength and courage

bhisti a water-carrier

bhogamandapa the refectory hall of a temple

bhumi literally earth; a horizontal moulding of a sikhara

bidi (beedi) tobacco leaf cigarette

bigha measure of land – normally about one-third of an acre

bo-tree (or Bodhi) *Ficus religiosa*, pipal tree associated with the Buddha

Bodhisattva Enlightened One, destined to become Buddha

bodi tuft of hair on back of the shaven head (also *tikki*)

Brahma Universal self-existing power; Creator in the Hindu Triad

Brahmachari religious student, accepting rigorous discipline (eg chastity)

Brahman (Brahmin) highest Hindu (and Jain) caste of priests

Brahmanism ancient Indian religion, precursor of modern Hinduism

Buddha The Enlightened One; founder of Buddhism

bund an embankment

bundh (literally closed) a strike

burj tower or bastion

burqa (burkha) over-dress worn by Muslim women observing purdah

bustee slum

C

cantonment planned military or civil area in town

capital upper part of a column

caryatid sculptured human female figure used as a support for columns

catamaran log raft, logs (*maram*) tied (*kattu*) together (Tamil)

cave temple rock-cut shrine or monastery

cella small chamber, compartment for the image of a deity

cenotaph commemorative monument, usually an open domed pavilion

chaam Himalayan Buddhist masked dance

chadar sheet worn as clothing

chai tea

chaitya large arched opening in the façade of a hall or Buddhist temple

chajja overhanging cornice or eaves

chakra sacred Buddhist wheel of the law; also Vishnu's discus

chala Bengali curved roof

Chamunda terrifying form of the goddess Durga

Chandra Moon; a planetary deity

Chandrasila step before a shrine, moonstone

chankramana place of the promenade of the Buddha at Bodh Gaya

chapatti unleavened Indian bread cooked on a griddle

chaprassi messenger or orderly usually wearing a badge

char sand-bank or island in a river

char bagh formal Mughal garden, divided into quarters

char bangla (char-chala) 'four temples' in Bengal, built like huts

charka spinning wheel

charpai 'four legs' – wooden frame string bed

chatt(r)a ceremonial umbrella on stupa (Buddhist)

chauki recessed space between pillars: entrance

chaukidar (chowkidar) night-watchman; guard

chaultri (choultry) travellers' rest house (Telugu)

chaumukha Jain sanctuary with a quadruple image, approached through four doorways

chauri fly-whisk, symbol for royalty

chauth 25% tax raised for revenue by Marathas

chhang strong mountain beer of fermented barley maize rye or millet or rice

chhatri umbrella shaped dome or pavilion

chhetri (kshatriya) Hindu warrior caste

chikan shadow embroidery on fine cotton (especially in Lucknow)

chikki nut crunch, a speciality of Lonavla

chitrakar picture maker

chlorite soft greenish stone that hardens on exposure

choli blouse

chowk (chauk) a block; open place in a city where the market is held

chunam lime plaster or stucco made from burnt seashells

circumambulation clockwise movement around a shrine

clerestory upper section of the walls of a building which allows light in

cloister passage usually around an open square

coir fibre from coconut husk

corbel horizontal block supporting a vertical structure or covering an opening

cornice horizontal band at the top of a wall

crenellated having battlements

crewel work chain stitching

crore 10 million

cupola small dome

curvilinear gently curving shape, generally of a tower

cusp, cusped projecting point between small sections of an arch

D

daal lentils, pulses

dacoit bandit

dada (dadu) grandfather; elder brother

dado part of a pedestal between its base and cornice

dahi yoghurt

dais raised platform

dak bungalow rest house for officials

dak post

dakini sorceress

Dakshineshvara Lord of the South; name of Siva

dan gift

dandi wooden 'seat' carried by bearers

darbar (durbar) a royal gathering

dargah a Muslim tomb complex

darshan (darshana) viewing of a deity

darwaza gateway, door

Dasara (dassara/dussehra/d assehra) 10 day festival (Sep-Oct)

Dasaratha King of Ayodhya and father of Rama

Dattatraya syncretistic deity; an incarnation of Vishnu, a teacher of Siva, or a cousin of the Buddha

daulat khana treasury

dentil small block used as part of a cornice

deodar Himalayan cedar; from *deva-daru*, the 'wood of the gods'

dervish member of Muslim brotherhood, committed to poverty

deval memorial pavilion to mark royal funeral pyre

devala temple or shrine (Buddhist or Hindu)

devasthanam temple trust

Devi Goddess; later, the Supreme Goddess

dhaba roadside restaurant (mainly North India) truck drivers' stop

dhansak Parsi dish made with lentils

dharamshala (dharamsala) pilgrims' rest-house

dharma moral and religious duty

dharmachakra wheel of 'moral' law (Buddhist)

dhobi washerman

dhol drums

dholi (dhooli) swinging chair on a pole, carried by bearers

dhoti loose loincloth worn by Indian men

dhyana meditation

digambara literally 'sky-clad' Jain sect in which the monks go naked

dikka raised platform around ablution tank

dikpala guardian of one of the cardinal directions mostly appearing in a group of eight

dikshitar person who makes oblations or offerings

dipdan lamp pillar

distributary river that flows away from main channel

divan (diwan) smoking-room; also a chief minister

Diwali festival of lights (Oct-Nov)

diwan-i-am hall of public audience

diwan-i-khas hall of private audience

diwan chief financial minister

doab interfluve, land between two rivers

dokra tribal name for lost wax metal casting (cire perdu)

dosai (dosa) thin pancake

double dome composed of an inner and outer shell of masonry

Draupadi wife-in-common of the five Pandava brothers in the Mahabharata

dry masonry stones laid without mortar

duar (dwar) door, gateway

dun valley

dupatta long scarf worn by Punjabi women

durg fort

Durga principal goddess of the Shakti cult

durrie (dhurrie) thick handloom rug

durwan watchman

dvarpala doorkeeper

dvipa lamp-column, generally of stone or brass-covered wood

eave overhang that shelters a porch or verandah

ek the number 1, a symbol of unity

ekka one horse carriage

epigraph carved inscription

F

faience coloured tilework, earthenware or porcelain

fakir Muslim religious mendicant

fan-light fan-shaped window over door

fenestration with windows or openings

filigree ornamental work or delicate tracery

finial emblem at the summit of a stupa, tower, dome, or at the end of a parapet

firman edict or grant issued by a sovereign

foliation ornamental design derived from foliage

frieze horizontal band of figures or decorative designs

gable end of an angled roof

gadba woollen blanket (Kashmir)

Footnotes

gaddi throne

gadi/gari car, cart, train

gali (galli) lane; an alley

gana child figures in art

Gandharva semi-divine flying figure; celestial musician

Ganesh (Ganapati) elephant-headed son of Siva and Parvati

Ganga goddess personifying the Ganga river

ganj market

ganja Indian hemp

gaon village

garbhagriha literally 'womb-chamber'; a temple sanctuary

garh fort

Garuda Mythical eagle, half-human Vishnu's vehicle

Gauri 'Fair One'; Parvati

Gaurishankara Siva with Parvati

ghagra (ghongra) long flared skirt

ghanta bell

ghat hill range, hill road; landing place; steps on the river bank

ghazal Urdu lyric poetry/love songs, often erotic

ghee clarified butter for cooking

gherao industrial action, surrounding home or office of politician or industrial manager

giri hill

Gita Govinda Jayadeva's poem of the Krishnalila

godown warehouse

gola conical-shaped storehouse

gompa Tibetan Buddhist monastery

Gopala (Govinda) cowherd; a name of Krishna

Gopis cowherd girls; milk maids who played with Krishna

gopuram towered gateway in South Indian temples

Gorakhnath historically, an 11th-century yogi who founded a Saivite cult; an incarnation of Siva

gosain monk or devotee (Hindi)

gram chick pea, pulse

gram village; gramadan, gift of village

gudi temple (Karnataka)

gumbaz (gumbad) dome

gumpha monastery, cave temple

gur palm sugar

guru teacher; spiritual leader, Sikh religious leader

gurudwara (literally 'entrance to the house of God'); Sikh religious complex

H

Haj (Hajj) annual Muslim pilgrimage to Mecca

hakim judge; a physician (usually Muslim)

halwa a special sweet meat

hammam Turkish bath

handi Punjabi dish cooked in a pot

Hanuman Monkey devotee of Rama; bringer of success to armies

Hara (Hara Siddhi) Siva

harem women's quarters (Muslim), from 'haram', Arabic for 'forbidden by law'

Hari Vishnu Harihara, Vishnu- Siva as a single divinity

Hariti goddess of prosperity and patroness of children, consort of Kubera

harmika the finial of a stupa in the form of a pedestal where the shaft of the honorific umbrella was set

hartal general strike

Hasan the murdered eldest son of Ali, commemorated at Muharram

hat (haat) market

hathi pol elephant gate

hathi (hati) elephant

hauz tank or reservoir

haveli a merchant's house usually in Rajasthan

havildar army sergeant

hawa mahal palace of the winds

Hidimba Devi Durga worshipped at Manali

hindola swing

hippogryph fabulous griffin-like creature with body of a horse

Hiranyakashipu Demon king killed by Narasimha

hiti a water channel; a bath or tank with water spouts

Holi spring festival (Feb-Mar)

hookah 'hubble bubble' or smoking pipe

howdah seat on elephant's back, sometimes canopied

hundi temple offering

Hussain the second murdered son of Ali, commemorated at Muharram

huzra a Muslim tomb chamber

hypostyle hall with pillars

I

lat pillar, column

icon statue or image of worship

Id principal Muslim festivals

Idgah open space for the Id prayers

ikat 'resist-dyed' woven fabric

imam Muslim religious leader

imambara tomb of a Shiite Muslim holy man; focus of Muharram procession

Indra King of the gods; God of rain; guardian of the East

Ishana Guardian of the North East

Ishvara Lord; Siva

iwan main arch in mosque

J

jadu magic

Jagadambi literally Mother of the World; Parvati

Jagannath literally Lord of the World; particularly, Krishna worshipped at Puri

jagati railed parapet

jaggery brown sugar, made from palm sap

jahaz building in form of ship

jala durga water fort

jali literally 'net'; any lattice or perforated pattern

jamb vertical side slab of doorway

Jambudvipa Continent of the Rose-Apple Tree; the earth

Jami masjid (Jama, Jumma) Friday mosque

Jamuna Hindu goddess who rides a tortoise; river

Janaka Father of Sita

jangha broad band of sculpture on the outside of the temple wall

jarokha balcony

jataka stories accounts of the previous lives of the Buddha

jauhar mass suicide by fire of women, particularly in Rajasthan, to avoid capture

jawab literally 'answer,' a building which duplicates another to provide symmetry

jawan army recruit, soldier

jaya stambha victory tower

jheel (jhil) lake; a marsh; a swamp

jhilmil projecting canopy over a window or door opening

-ji (jee) honorific suffix added to names out of reverence and/or politeness; also abbreviated 'yes' (Hindi/Urdu)

jihad striving in the way of god; holy war by Muslims against non-believers

Jina literally 'victor'; spiritual conqueror or Tirthankara, after whom Jainism is named

Jogini mystical goddess

Jyotirlinga luminous energy of Siva manifested at 12 holy places, miraculously formed lingams

K

kabigan folk debate in verse

kachcha man's 'under-shorts' (one of five Sikh symbols)

kacheri (kutchery) a court; an office for public business

Kailasa mountain home of Siva

kalamkari special painted cotton hanging from Andhra

kalasha pot-like finial of a tower

Kali literally 'black'; terrifying form of the goddess Durga, wearing a necklace of skulls/heads

Kalki future incarnation of Vishnu on horseback

kalyanamandapa marriage hall

kameez women's shirt

kanga comb (one of five Sikh symbols)

kankar limestone pieces, used for road making

kantha Bengali quilting

kapok the silk cotton tree

kara steel bracelet (one of five Sikh symbols)

karma impurity resulting from past misdeeds

Kartikkeya (Kartik) Son of Siva, God of war

kashi-work special kind of glazed tiling, probably derived from Kashan in Persia

kati-roll Muslim snack of meat rolled in a `paratha` bread

kattakat mixed brain, liver and kidney (Gujarat)

keep tower of a fort, stronghold

keystone central wedge-shaped block in a masonry arch

khadi woven cotton cloth made from home-spun cotton (or silk) yarn

khal creek; a canal

khana suffix for room/office/place; also food or meal

khanqah Muslim (Sufi) hospice

kharif monsoon season crop

khave khana tea shop

kheda enclosure in which wild elephants are caught; elephant depot

khet field

khondalite crudely grained basalt

khukri traditional curved Gurkha weapon

kirpan sabre, dagger (one of five Sikh symbols)

kirti-stambha `pillar of fame,' free standing pillar in front of temple

kohl antimony, used as eye shadow

konda hill (Telugu)

kos minars Mughal `mile` stones

kot (kota/kottai/kotte) fort

kothi house

kotla citadel

kovil (koil) temple (Tamil)

Krishna Eighth incarnation of Vishnu

kritis South Indian devotional music

Kubera Chief yaksha; keeper of the treasures of the earth, Guardian of the North

kumar a young man

Kumari Virgin; Durga

kumbha a vase-like motif, pot

Kumbhayog auspicious time for bathing to wash away sins

kumhar (kumar) potter

kund lake, well or pool

kundan jewellery setting of uncut gems (Rajasthan)

kurta Punjabi shirt

kurti-kanchali small blouse

kutcha (cutcha/kacha) raw; crude; unpaved; built with sun-dried bricks

kwabgah bedroom; literally `palace of dreams`

L

lakh 100,000

Lakshmana younger brother of Rama

Lakshmi Goddess of wealth and good fortune, consort of Vishnu

Lakulisha founder of the Pashupata sect, believed to be an incarnation of Siva

lama Buddhist priest in Tibet

lassi iced yoghurt drink

lath monolithic pillar

lathi bamboo stick with metal bindings, used by police

lena cave, usually a rock-cut sanctuary

lingam (linga) Siva as the phallic emblem

Lingaraja Siva worshipped at Bhubaneswar

lintel horizontal beam over doorway

liwan cloisters of a mosque

Lokeshwar `Lord of the World`, Avalokiteshwara to Buddhists and form of Siva to Hindus

lunette semicircular window opening

lungi wrapped-around loin cloth, normally checked

M

madrassa Islamic theological school or college

mahamandapam large enclosed hall in front of main shrine

maha great

Mahabharata Sanskrit epic about the battle between the Pandavas and Kauravas

Mahabodhi Great Enlightenment of Buddha

Mahadeva literally `Great Lord'; Siva

mahal palace, grand building

mahalla (mohulla) division of a town; a quarter; a ward

mahant head of a monastery

maharaja great king

maharana Rajput clan head

maharani great queen

maharishi (Maharshi) literally `great teacher`

Mahavira literally `Great Hero'; last of the 24 Tirthankaras, founder of Jainism

Mahayana The Greater Vehicle; form of Buddhism practised in East Asia, Tibet and Nepal

Mahesha (Maheshvara) Great Lord; Siva

Mahisha Buffalo demon killed by Durga

mahout elephant driver/keeper

mahseer large freshwater fish found especially in Himalayan rivers

maidan large open grassy area in a town

Maitreya the future Buddha

makara crocodile-shaped mythical creature symbolizing the river Ganga

makhan butter

malai hill (Tamil)

mali gardener

Manasa Snake goddess; Sakti

manastambha free-standing pillar in front of temple

mandala geometric diagram symbolizing the structure of the Universe

mandapa columned hall preceding the temple sanctuary

mandi market

mandir temple

mani (mani wall) stones with sacred inscriptions at Buddhist sites

mantra chant for meditation by Hindus and Buddhists

maqbara chamber of a Muslim tomb

Mara Tempter, who sent his daughters (and soldiers) to disturb the Buddha's meditation

marg wide roadway

masjid literally `place of prostration'; mosque

mata mother

math Hindu or Jain monastery

maulana scholar (Muslim)

maulvi religious teacher (Muslim)

maund measure of weight about 20 kilos

mausoleum large tomb building

maya illusion

medallion circle or part-circle framing a figure or decorative motif

meena enamel work

mela festival or fair, usually Hindu

memsahib married European woman, term used mainly before Independence

Meru mountain supporting the heavens

mihrab niche in the western wall of a mosque

mimbar pulpit in mosque

Minakshi literally `fish-eyed'; Parvati

minar (minaret) slender tower of a mosque

mitthai Indian sweets

mithuna couple in sexual embrace

mofussil the country as distinct from the town

Mohammad `the praised`; The Prophet; founder of Islam

moksha salvation, enlightenment; literally `release`

monolith single block of stone shaped into a pillar

moonstone the semi circular stone step before a shrine (also chandrasila)

mouza (mowza) village; a parcel of land having a separate name in the revenue records

mridangam barrel-shaped drum (musical)

muballigh second prayer leader

mudra symbolic hand gesture

muezzin mosque official who calls the faithful to prayer

Muharram period of mourning in remembrance of Hasan and Hussain, two murdered sons of Ali

mukha mandapa, hall for shrine

mullah religious teacher (Muslim)

mund Toda village

muqarna Muslim stalactite design

mural wall decoration

musalla prayer mat

muta limited duration marriage (Leh)

muthi measure equal to `a handful`

N

nadi river

Naga (nagi/nagini) Snake deity; associated with fertility and protection

nagara city, sometimes capital

nakkar khana (naggar or naubat khana) drum house; arched structure or gateway for musicians

nal staircase

nal mandapa porch over a staircase

nallah (nullah) ditch, channel

namaaz Muslim prayers, worship

namaste common Hindu greeting (with joined palms) translated as: `I salute all divine qualities in you'

namda rug

Nandi a bull, Siva's vehicle and a symbol of fertility

nara durg large fort built on a flat plain

Narayana Vishnu as the creator of life

nata mandapa (nat-mandir; nritya sala) dancing hall in a temple

Nataraja Siva, Lord of the cosmic dance

nath literally `place' eg Amarnath

natya the art of dance

nautch display by dancing girls

navagraha nine planets, represented usually on the lintel or architrave of the front door of a temple

navaranga central hall of temple

navaratri literally '9 nights'; name of the Dasara festival

nawab prince, wealthy Muslim, sometimes used as a title

niche wall recess containing a sculpted image or emblem, mostly framed by a pair of pilasters

Nihang literally `crocodile': followers of Guru Gobind Singh (Sikh)

nirvana enlightenment; literally `extinguished'

niwas small palace

nritya pure dance

O

obelisk tapering and usually monolithic stone shaft

ogee form of moulding or arch comprising a double curved line made up of a concave and convex part

oriel projecting window

P

pada foot or base

padam dance which tells a story

padma lotus flower, Padmasana, lotus seat; posture of meditating figures

paga projecting pilaster-like surface of an Orissan temple

pagoda tall structure in several stories

pahar hill

paisa (poisa) one hundredth of a rupee

palanquin covered carrier on poles for one

pali language of Buddhist scriptures

palli village

pan leaf of the betel vine; sliced areca nut, lime and other ingredients wrapped in leaf for chewing

panchayat a `council of five'; a government system of elected councils

pandal marquee made of bamboo and cloth

pandas temple priests

pandit teacher or wise man; a Sanskrit scholar

pankah (punkha) fan, formerly pulled by a cord

parabdis special feeding place for birds (Jain)

parapet wall extending above the roof

pargana sub-division of a district usually comprising many villages; a fiscal unit

Parinirvana the Buddha's state prior to nirvana, shown usually as a reclining figure

parishads political division of group of villages

Parsi (Parsee) Zoroastrians who fled from Iran to West India in the eighth century to avoid persecution

parterre level space in a garden occupied by flowerbeds

Parvati daughter of the Mountain; Siva's consort

pashmina fine wool from a mountain goat

Pashupati literally Lord of the Beasts; Siva

pata painted hanging scroll

patan town or city (Sanskrit)

patel village headman

patina green film that covers materials exposed to the air

pattachitra specially painted cloth (especially Orissan)

pau measure for vegetables and fruit equal to 250 grams

paya soup

pediment mouldings, often in a triangular formation above an opening or niche

pendant hanging, a motif depicted upside down

peon servant, messenger (from Portuguese *peao*)

peristyle range of columns surrounding a court or temple

Persian wheel well irrigation system using bucket lift

pettah suburbs, outskirts of town (Tamil: *pettai*)

pice (old form) 1/100th of a rupee

pida deul hall with a pyramidal roof in an Orissan temple

pida (pitha) basement

pietra dura inlaid mosaic of hard, semi-precious stones

pilaster ornamental small column, with capital and bracket

pinjra lattice work

pinjrapol animal hospital (Jain)

pipal Ficus religiosa, the Bodhi tree

pir Muslim holy man

pitha base, pedestal

pithasthana place of pilgrimage

podium stone bench; low pedestal wall

pol fortified gateway

porch covered entrance to a shrine or hall, generally open and with columns

portico space enclosed between columns

Pradakshina patha processional passage

prakaram open courtyard

pralaya the end of the world

prasadam consecrated temple food

prayag confluence considered sacred by Hindus

puja ritual offerings to the gods; worship (Hindu)

pujari worshipper; one who performs puja (Hindu)

pukka literally 'ripe' or 'finished'; reliable; solidly built

punya merit earned through actions and religious devotion (Buddhist)

Puranas literally `the old' Sanskrit sacred poems

purdah seclusion of Muslim women from public view (literally curtains)

pushkarani sacred pool or tank

Q

qabr Muslim grave

qibla direction for Muslim prayer

qila fort

Quran holy Muslim scriptures

qutb axis or pivot

R

rabi winter/spring season crop

Radha Krishna's favourite consort

raj rule or government

raja king, ruler (variations include rao, rawal)

rajbari palaces of a small kingdom

Rajput dynasties of western and central India

Rakshakas Earth spirits

Rama Seventh incarnation of Vishnu

Ramayana Sanskrit epic – the story of Rama

Ramazan (Ramadan) Muslim month of fasting

rangamandapa painted hall or theatre

rani queen

rath chariot or temple car

Ravana Demon king of Lanka; kidnapper of Sita

rawal head priest

rekha curvilinear portion of a spire or sikhara (rekha deul, sanctuary, curved tower of an Orissan temple)

reredos screen behind an altar

rickshaw 3-wheeled bicycle-powered (or 2-wheeled hand-powered) vehicle

Rig (Rg) Veda oldest and most sacred of the Vedas
Rimpoche blessed incarnation; abbot of a Tibetan Buddhist monastery (gompa)
rishi 'seer'; inspired poet, philosopher
rupee unit of currency in India
ryot (rayat/raiyat) a subject; a cultivator; a farmer

S

sabha columned hall (sabha mandapa, assembly hall)
sabzi vegetables, vegetable curry
sadar (sadr/saddar) chief, main especially Sikh
sadhu ascetic; religious mendicant, holy man
safa turban (Rajasthan)
sagar lake; reservoir
sahib title of address, like 'sir'
sahn open courtyard of a mosque
Saiva (Shaiva) the cult of Siva
sal a hall
sal hardwood tree of the lower slopes of Himalayan foothills
salaam literally 'peace'; greeting (Muslim)
salwar (shalwar) loose trousers (Punjab)
samadh(i) literally concentrated thought, meditation; a funerary memorial
samsara transmigration of the soul
samudra large tank or inland sea
sangam junction of rivers
sangarama monastery
sangha ascetic order founded by Buddha
sangrahalaya rest-house for Jain pilgrims
sankha (shankha) the conch shell (symbolically held by Vishnu); the shell bangle worn by Bengali women
sanyasi wandering ascetic; final stage in the ideal life of a man
sarai caravansarai, halting place
saranghi small four-stringed viola shaped from a single piece of wood

Saraswati wife of Brahma and goddess of knowledge
sarkar the government; the state; a writer; an accountant
sarod Indian stringed musical instrument
sarvodaya uplift, improvement of all
sati (suttee) a virtuous woman; act of self-immolation on a husband's funeral pyre
Sati wife of Siva who destroyed herself by fire
satyagraha 'truth force'; passive resistance
sayid title (Muslim)
schist grey or green finely grained stone
seer (ser) weight (about 1 kg)
sepoy (sepai) Indian soldier, private
seth merchant, businessman
seva voluntary service
shahtush very fine wool from the Tibetan antelope
Shakti Energy; female divinity often associated with Siva
shala barrel-vaulted roof
shalagrama stone containing fossils worshipped as a form of Vishnu
shaman doctor/priest, using magic, exorcist
shamiana cloth canopy
Shankara Siva
sharia corpus of Muslim theological law
shastras ancient texts defining temple architecture
shastri religious title (Hindu)
sheesh mahal palace apartment with mirror work
shehnai (shahnai) Indian wind instrument like an oboe
sherwani knee-length coat for men
Shesha (Sesha) serpent who supports Vishnu
shikar hunting
shisham a valuable building timber
sikhara (shikhara) curved temple tower or spire
shloka (sloka) Sanskrit sacred verse
sileh khana armoury
sindur vermilion powder used in temple ritual; married women mark their hair parting with it (East India)

singh (sinha) lion; Rajput caste name adopted by Sikhs
sinha stambha lion pillar
sirdar a guide who leads trekking groups
Sita Rama's wife, heroine of the Ramayana epic
sitar classical stringed musical instrument with a gourd for soundbox
Siva (Shiva) The Destroyer in the Hindu triad of Gods
Sivaratri literally 'Siva's night'; a festival (Feb-Mar)
Skanda the Hindu god of war; Kartikkeya
soma sacred drink mentioned in the Vedas
spandrel triangular space between the curve of an arch and the square enclosing it
squinch arch across an interior angle
sri (shri) honorific title, often used for 'Mr'; repeated as sign of great respect
sridhara pillar with octagonal shaft and square base
stalactite system of vaulting, remotely resembling stalactite formations in a cave
stambha free-standing column or pillar, often for a lamp or figure
steatite finely grained grey mineral
stele upright, inscribed slab used as a gravestone
sthan place (suffix)
stucco plasterwork
stupa hemispheric Buddhist funerary mound
stylobate base on which a colonnade is placed
subahdar (subedar) the governor of a province; viceroy under the Mughals
Subrahmanya Skanda, one of Siva's sons; Kartikkeya in South India
sudra lowest of the Hindu castes
sufi Muslim mystic; sufism, Muslim mystic worship
sultan Muslim prince (sultana, wife of sultan)
Surya Sun; Sun God
svami (swami) holy man; a suffix for temple deities
svastika (swastika) auspicious Hindu/ Buddhist cross-like sign
swadeshi home made goods
swaraj home rule

swatantra freedom
syce groom, attendant who follows a horseman

T

tabla a pair of drums
tahr wild goat
tahsildar revenue collector
taikhana underground apartments
takht throne
talao (tal, talar) water tank
taluk administrative subdivision of a district
tamasha spectacle; festive celebration
tandava (dance) of Siva
tank lake dug for irrigation; a masonry-lined temple pool with stepped sides
tapas (tapasya) ascetic meditative self-denial
Tara literally 'star'; a goddess
tarkashi Orissan silver filigree
tatties cane or grass screens used for shade
Teej Hindu festival
tehsil subdivision of a district (North India)
tempera distemper; method of mural painting by means of a 'body,' such as white pigment
tempo three-wheeler vehicle
terai narrow strip of land along Himalayan foothills
terracotta burnt clay used as building material
thali South and West Indian vegetarian meal
thana a police jurisdiction; police station
thangka (thankha) cloth (often silk) painted with a Tibetan Mahayana deity
thug professional robber/murderer (Central India)
tiffin snack, light meal
tika (tilak) vermilion powder, auspicious mark on the forehead; often decorative
tikka tender pieces of meat, marinated and barbecued
tillana abstract dance
tirtha ford, bathing place, holy spot (Sanskrit)
Tirthankara literally 'ford-maker'; title given to 24 religious 'teachers', worshipped by Jains

454

Footnotes

tonga two-wheeled horse carriage

topi (topee) pith helmet

torana gateway; two posts with an architrave

tribhanga triple-bended pose for standing figures

Trimurti the Hindu Triad, Brahma, Vishnu and Siva

tripolia triple gateway

trisul the trident chief symbol of the god Siva

triveni triple-braided

tuk fortified enclosure containing Jain shrines

tulsi sacred basil plant

tykhana underground room for use in hot weather (North India)

tympanum triangular space within cornices

Uma Siva's consort in one of her many forms

untouchable 'outcastes', with whom contact of any kind was believed by high caste Hindus to be defiling

Upanishads ancient Sanskrit philosophical texts, part of the Vedas

usta painted camel leather goods

ustad master

uttarayana northwards

vahana 'vehicle' of the deity

vaisya the 'middle-class' caste of merchants and farmers

Valmiki sage, author of the Ramayana epic

Vamana dwarf incarnation of Vishnu

vana grove, forest

Varaha boar incarnation of Vishnu

varna 'colour'; social division of Hindus into Brahmin, Kshatriya, Vaishya and Sudra

varnam South Indian musical etude, conforming to a raga

Varuna Guardian of the West, accompanied by Makara (see above)

Vayu Wind god; Guardian of the northwest

Veda (Vedic) oldest known Hindu religious texts

vedi (bedi) altar, also a wall or screen

verandah enlarged porch in front of a hall

vihara Buddhist or Jain monastery with cells around a courtyard

vilas house or pleasure palace

vimana towered sanctuary containing the cell in which the deity is enshrined

vina plucked stringed instrument, relative of sitar

Vishnu a principal Hindu deity; the Preserver (and Creator)

vyala (yali) leogryph, mythical lion-like sculpture

-wallah suffix often used with a occupational name, eg rickshaw-wallah

wav (vav) step-well, particularly in Gujarat and western India (baoli)

wazir chief minister of a raja (from Turkish `vizier')

yagya (yajna) major ceremonial sacrifice

Yaksha (Yakshi) a demi-god, associated with nature

yali see vyala

Yama God of death, judge of the living

yantra magical diagram used in meditation; instrument

yatra pilgrimage

Yellow Hat Gelugpa Sect of Tibetan Buddhism – monks wear yellow headdress

yeti mythical Himalayan animal often referred to as `the abominable snowman'

yoga school of philosophy stressing mental and physical disciplines; yogi

yoni a hole symbolising female sexuality; vagina

zamindar a landlord granted income under the Mughals

zari silver and gold thread used in weaving or embroidery

zarih cenotaph in a Muslim tomb

zenana segregated women's apartments

ziarat holy Muslim tomb

zilla (zillah) district

Index

Shorts

Maps

Footnotes

Advertisers

www.footprintbooks.com

A new place to visit

Sales & distribution

Footprint Handbooks
6 Riverside Court
Lower Bristol Road
Bath BA2 3DZ England
T 01225 469141
F 01225 469461
discover
@footprintbooks.com

Australia
Peribo Pty
58 Beaumont Road
Mt Kuring-Gai
NSW 2080
T 02 9457 0011
F 02 9457 0022

Austria
Freytag-Berndt Artaria
Kohlmarkt 9
A-1010 Wien
T 01533 2094
F 01533 8685

Freytag-Berndt
Sporgasse 29
A-8010 Graz
T 0316 818230
F 3016 818230-30

Belgium
Craenen BVBA
Mechelsesteenweg 633
B-3020 Herent
T 016 23 90 90
F 016 23 97 11

Waterstones
The English Bookshop
Blvd Adolphe Max 71-75
B-1000 Brussels
T 02 219 5034

Canada
Ulysses Travel Publications
4176 rue Saint-Denis
Montréal
Québec H2W 2M5
T 514 843 9882
F 514 843 9448

Europe
Bill Bailey
16 Devon Square
Newton Abbott
Devon TQ12 2HR. UK
T 01626 331079
F 01626 331080

Denmark
Nordisk Korthandel
Studiestraede 26-30 B
DK-1455 Copenhagen K
T 3338 2638
F 3338 2648

Scanvik Books
Esplanaden 8B
DK-1263 Copenhagen K
T 3312 7766
F 3391 2882

Finland
Akateeminen Kirjakauppa
Keskuskatu 1
FIN-00100 Helsinki
T 09 121 4151
F 09 121 4441

Suomalainen Kirjakauppa
Koivuvaarankuja 2
01640 Vantaa 64
F 09 852751

France
FNAC – major branches

L'Astrolabe
46 rue de Provence
F-75009 Paris 9e
T 01 42 85 42 95
F 01 45 75 92 51

VILO Diffusion
25 rue Ginoux
F-75015 Paris
T 01 45 77 08 05
F 01 45 79 97 15

Germany
GeoCenter ILH
Schockenriedstrasse 44
D-70565 Stuttgart
T 0711 781 94610
F 0711 781 94654

Brettschneider
Feldkirchnerstrasse 2
D-85551 Heimstetten
T 089 990 20330
F 089 990 20331

Geobuch
Rosental 6
D-80331 München
T 089 265030
F 089 263713

Gleumes
Hohenstaufenring 47-51
D-50674 Köln
T 0221 215650

Globetrotter Ausrustungen
Wiesendamm 1
D-22305 Hamburg
T040 679 66190
F 040 679 66183

Dr Götze
Bleichenbrücke 9
D-2000 Hamburg 1
T 040 3031 1009-0

Hugendubel Buchhandlung
Nymphenburgerstrasse 25
D-80335 München
T 089 238 9412
F 089 550 1853

Kiepert Buchhandlung
Hardenbergstrasse 4-5
D-10623 Berlin 12
T 030 311 880
F 030 311 88120

Greece
GC Eleftheroudakis
17 Panepistemiou
Athens 105 64
T 01 331 4180-83
F 01 323 9821

India
India Book Distributors
1007/1008 Arcadia
195 Nariman Point
Mumbai 400 021
T 91 22 282 5220
F 91 22 287 2531

Israel
Eco Trips
8 Tverya Street
Tel Aviv 63144
T 03 528 4113
F 03 528 8269

For a fuller list, see www.footprintbooks.com

Italy
Librimport
Via Biondelli 9
I-20141 Milano
T 02 8950 1422
F 02 8950 2811

Libreria del Viaggiatore
Via dell Pelegrino 78
I-00186 Roma
T/F 06 688 01048

Netherlands
Nilsson & Lamm bv
Postbus 195
Pampuslaan 212
N-1380 AD Weesp
T 0294 494949
F 0294 494455

Waterstones
Kalverstraat 152
1012 XE Amsterdam
T 020 638 3821

New Zealand
Auckland Map Centre
Dymocks

Norway
Schibsteds Forlag A/S
Akersgata 32 - 5th Floor
Postboks 1178 Sentrum
N-0107 Oslo
T 22 86 30 00
F 22 42 54 92

Tanum
Karl Johansgate 37-41
PO Box 1177 Sentrum
N-0107 Oslo 1
T 22 41 11 00
F 22 33 32 75

Olaf Norlis
Universitetsgt 24
N-1062 Oslo
T 22 00 43 00

Pakistan
Pak-American Commercial
Hamid Chambers
Zaib-un Nisa Street
Saddar, PO Box 7359
Karachi
T 21 566 0418
F 21 568 3611

South Africa
Faradawn CC
PO Box 1903
Saxonwold 2132
T 011 885 1787
F 011 885 1829

South America
Humphrys Roberts
Associates
Caixa Postal 801-0
Ag. Jardim da Gloria
06700-970 Cotia SP
Brazil
T 011 492 4496
F 011 492 6896

Southeast Asia
APA Publications
38 Joo Koon Road
Singapore 628990
T 865 1600
F 861 6438

In Hong Kong, Malaysia,
Singapore and Thailand:
MPH, Kinokuniya, Times

Spain
Altaïr
C/Balmes 69
08007 Barcelona
T 933 233062
F 934 512559

Altaïr
Gaztambide 31
28015 Madrid
T 0915 435300
F 0915 443498

Libros de Viaje
C/Serrano no 41
28001 Madrid
T 01 91 577 9899
F 01 91 577 5756

Il Corte Inglés – major
branches

Sweden
Hedengrens Bokhandel
PO Box 5509
S-11485 Stockholm
T 08 611 5132

Kart Centrum
Vasagatan 16
S-11120 Stockholm
T 08 411 1697

Kartforlaget
Skolgangen 10
S-80183 Gavle
T 026 633000
F 026 124204

Lantmateriet Kartbutiken
Kungsgatan 74
S-11122 Stockholm
T 08 202 303
F 08 202 711

Switzerland
Office du Livre OLF
ZI3, Corminboeuf
CH-1701 Fribourg
T 026 467 5111
F 026 467 5666

Schweizer Buchzentrum
Postfach
CH-4601 Olten
T 062 209 2525
F 062 209 2627

Travel Bookshop
Rindermarkt 20
Postfach 216
CH-8001 Zürich
T 01 252 3883
F 01 252 3832

Tanzania
A Novel Idea
The Slipway
PO Box 76513
Dar es Salaam
T/F 051 601088

USA
Publishers Group West
1700 Fourth Street
Berkeley
CA 94710
T 510 528 1444
F 510 528 9555

Barnes & Noble, Borders,
specialist travel bookstores

Will you help us?

We try as hard as we can to make each Footprint Handbook as up-to-date and accurate as possible but, of course, things always change. Many people email or write to us – with corrections, new information, or simply comments. If you want to let us know about your experiences and adventures – be they good, bad or ugly – then don't delay; we're dying to hear from you. And please try to include all the relevant details and juicy bits. Your help will be greatly appreciated, especially by other travellers. In return we will send you details about our special guidebook offer.

email Footprint at:
raj1_online@footprintbooks.com

or write to:

Elizabeth Taylor
Footprint Handbooks
6 Riverside Court
Lower Bristol Road
Bath
BA2 3DZ
UK

Footprint travel list

Footprint publish travel guides to over 120 countries worldwide. Each guide is packed with practical, concise and colourful information for everybody from first-time travellers to travel aficionados . The list is growing fast and current titles are noted below. For further information check out the website
www.footprintbooks.com

Andalucía Handbook
Argentina Handbook
Bali & the Eastern Isles Hbk
Bangkok & the Beaches Hbk
Bolivia Handbook
Brazil Handbook
Cambodia Handbook
Caribbean Islands Handbook
Chile Handbook
Colombia Handbook
Cuba Handbook
Dominican Republic Handbook
East Africa Handbook
Ecuador & Galápagos Handbook
Edinburgh Handbook
Egypt Handbook
Goa Handbook
India Handbook
Indian Himalaya Handbook
Indonesia Handbook
Ireland Handbook
Israel Handbook
Jordan Handbook
Jordan, Syria & Lebanon Hbk
Laos Handbook
Libya Handbook
London Handbook
Malaysia Handbook
Myanmar Handbook
Mexico Handbook
Mexico & Central America Hbk
Morocco Handbook
Namibia Handbook
Nepal Handbook
Pakistan Handbook
Peru Handbook

Rajasthan Handbook
Rio de Janeiro Handbook
Scotland Handbook
Scotland Highlands & Islands Hbk
Singapore Handbook
South Africa Handbook
South American Handbook
South India Handbook
Sri Lanka Handbook
Sumatra Handbook
Syria & Lebanon Handbook
Thailand Handbook
Tibet Handbook
Tunisia Handbook
Turkey
Venezuela Handbook
Vietnam Handbook

In the pipeline – Costa Rica, Guatemala, Nicaragua, Barcelona & New Zealand

Also available from Footprint
Traveller's Handbook
Traveller's Healthbook

Available at all good bookshops

466

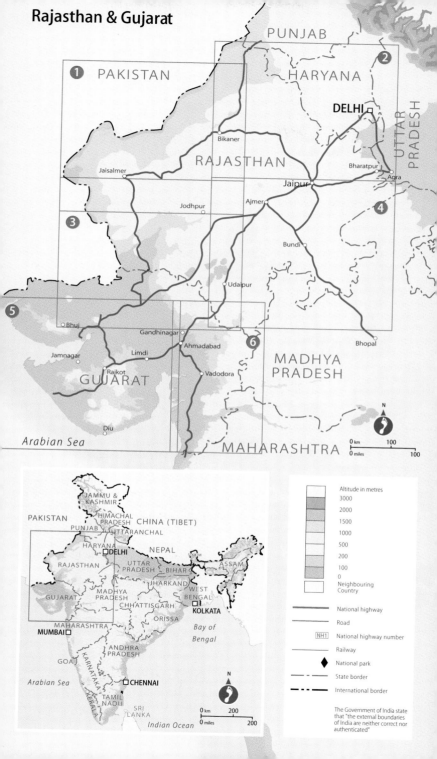

Rajasthan & Gujarat

Map 1

A

N

0 km 20
0 miles 20

The Government of India state that
"the external boundaries of India
are neither correct nor authenticated"

B

PAKISTAN

Kishangarh

Bhuttewal

Ghotaru

Ramgarh

NH15

Jaisalmer

Sam

Map 3

C

◆ *Desert NP*

Khuri

Shiv

1

2

3

Map 2

P U N J A B

Mansa

Ganganagar

Hanumangarh

Sirsa

A

Suratgarh

Rawatsar

Sarupsar

upgarh

Kalibangan

Nohar

Bhadra

NH15

Map 1

Mahajan

Rajgarh

B

Sardarshahr

Churu

Bissau

Jhunjhunun

Bikaner

Dungargarh

Ratangarh

Mandawa

Fatehpur

Nawalgarh

Deshnoke

Sujangarh

NH11

Nokha

Ladnun

Sikar

R A J A S T H A N

Didwana

Danta

Ringa

Ramgarh

C

Nagaur

Kuchaman

Khimsar

Makrana

Sambhar Salt
Lake

Map 4

Phulera

Merta Rd

1

2

3

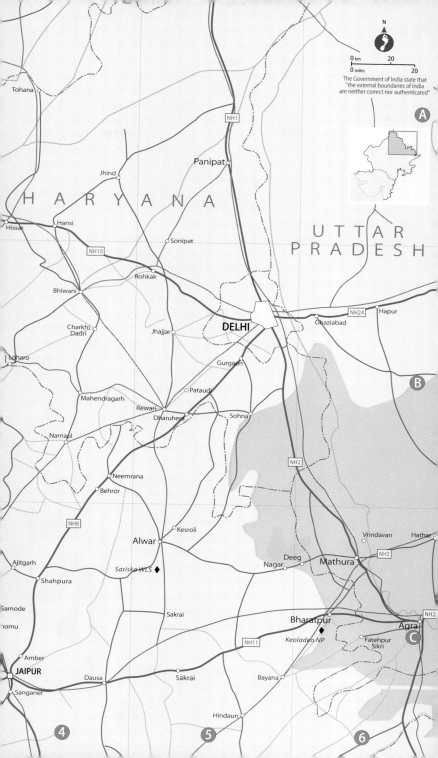

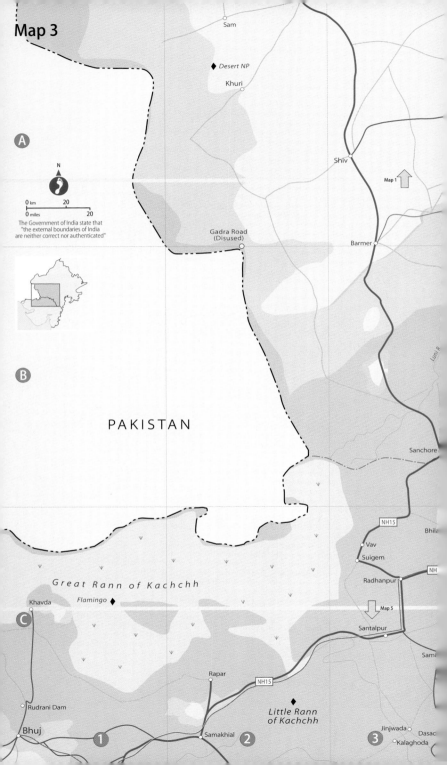

JAIPUR

Bagru

Sanganer

Dausa

Bayana

Hindaun

Nawai

Gangapur

Karauli

A

NH12

Tonk

Sawai
Madhopur

Ranthambore NP

Uniara

Lakheri

Sheopur

Bundi

Shivpuri

B

Kota

Baran

Chambal

M A D H Y A

P R A D E S H

Darrah
WLS

rdoli

Jhalawar

Jhalarapatan

N

0 km   20
0 miles   20

The Government of India state that
"the external boundaries of India
are neither correct nor authenticated"

C

Biora

Agra

Sarangpur

4

5

6

Map 5

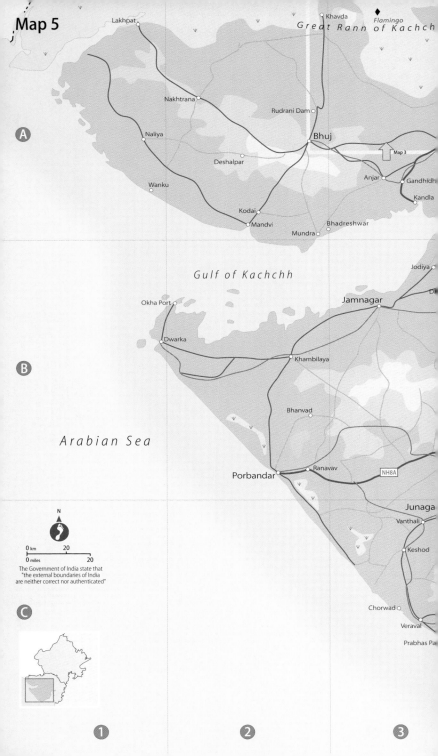

Lakhpat

Khavda

Flamingo

Great Rann of Kachch

Nakhtrana

Rudrani Dam

A

Naliya

Bhuj

Map 3

Deshalpar

Anjar Gandhidh

Wanku

Kandla

Kodai

Mandvi

Bhadreshwar

Mundra

Gulf of Kachchh

Jodiya

Di

Okha Port

Jamnagar

Dwarka

B

Khambilaya

Arabian Sea

Bhanvad

Porbandar Ranavav

NH8A

Junaga

Vanthali

N

Keshod

0 km   20

0 miles   20

The Government of India state that
"the external boundaries of India
are neither correct nor authenticated"

Chorwad

C

Veraval

Prabhas Pa

1   **2**   **3**

Main Railways

Note: Indications about
gauges are approximate

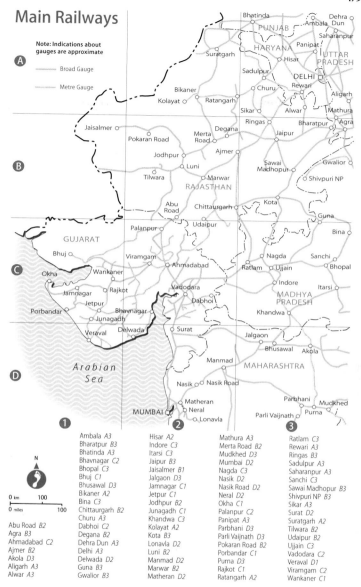

Broad Gauge

Metre Gauge

What the papers say

"Seriously well-researched, the best of the lot."
The Observer

"Footprint can be depended on for accurate travel information and for imparting a deep sense of respect for the lands and people they cover."
World News

"This is the best guidebook on the sub-continent yet published, it has everything...super Michelin."
Royal Society for Asian Affairs

"Packed with in-depth information"
The Express

Mail order
Available worldwide in bookshops and on-line. Footprint travel guides can also be ordered directly from us in Bath, via our website **www.footprintbooks.com** or from the address on the imprint page of this book.

Acknowledgements

We are greatly indebted to Anil Mulchandani who has given invaluable assistance in the preparation of this book by his extensive and detailed comment on the area and for providing additional background material.

We are most grateful to Mr Gajendra Singh and the Forts and Palaces Tours team who very carefully checked through the Rajasthan section, and helped us to keep pace with constantly changing telephone numbers.

We would also like to warmly thank the following travellers who have written to us during the last few months, in particular, Michael Pears of Durham, UK, and BL Underwood of Nayland, UK who wrote at great length.

Peter M Baker, UK; Jade Bell, Australia; Mike and Sue Bomford, UK; Harly Bonilla; Rob Clarke, UK; Nicole Collins, UK; Caroline Cooper, UK; Rod Daldry, UK and India; Stefan Farey; Elizabeth Fehnrich; Birgitta Johansen; Alan Johnstone, Australia; Sanjay Joshi; Raphael Kessler; Isabelle Willemart Khan; Silke Klappich, Germany; Arun Kundu, Haryana, India; Bernard Lazarevitch, France; Hana Lee, New Delhi, India; Angela McNair; Petter Mejilaender, Norway; David Milliot, Thailand; C and A Mueller, Canada; Priscilla Nuttall, UK; Valerie Parkinson; Solvej Pawelczuk, Belgium; Donella Perkins; Arie Rijkaart, Netherlands; Neil Salt, Conwy, UK; Richard Sant, UK; Alice Simper, UK; Yvette Slaughter, Victoria, Australia; Nicole Slaven, Switzerland; Pia Stadt, Germany; André C Stort, Brazil; Philippe Studer, Switzerland; Brian and Ingrid Surkan; Severn Taylor, Switzerland; TJF Tucker; Ana Maria Uribe, Argentina; Anne Vilsboel, Strynoe, Denmark; Florian Weissroth, Germany; Dominic Wright.

Robert and Roma Bradnock

Robert went to India overland as a research student at Cambridge to spend a year in South Asia. That journey was the first of many visits, living and working throughout the sub-continent. A member of the Department of Geography at the School of Oriental and African Studies in London University, he is currently researching into geopolitics and environmental change in the sub-continent. An international authority on India and its neighbours, Robert broadcasts frequently about the region on networks across the world, and lectures extensively in Britain and Europe.

A Bengali by birth, Roma was brought up in Kolkata (Calcutta) where, after graduating, she worked as a librarian. Her travels across the subcontinent had started early but to widen her horizons she went to Europe, and England subsequently became her home. In addition to the India Handbook, she and her husband now write regional handbooks for visitors to Goa, the Indian Himalaya, South India and also Sri Lanka. They return to the subcontinent each year to research and seek out yet unexplored corners.

Anil Mulchandani

Anil was born in Mumbai but has spent most his life in Ahmadabad. As a travel consultant he has travelled extensively in Gujarat and Rajasthan and as an expert in the field he has written and lectured widely on the region for government and other tourism organisations.